Rediscovering History

CULTURAL SITINGS

Elazar Barkan, Editor

Rediscovering History

Culture, Politics, and the Psyche

EDITED BY

Michael S. Roth

STANFORD
UNIVERSITY
PRESS

Stanford,
California
1994

Stanford University Press
Stanford, California
© 1994 by the Board of Trustees of the
Leland Stanford Junior University
Printed in the United States of America

CIP data appear at the end of the book

Stanford University Press publications are distributed
exclusively by Stanford University Press within the United
States, Canada, and Mexico; they are distributed exclusively by Cambridge University Press throughout the rest
of the world.

Published with the assistance of the Getty Grant Program

Essays in honor of Carl E. Schorske

Cultural Sitings

A series edited by Elazar Barkan

CULTURAL SITINGS will present focused discussions of major contemporary and historical cultural issues by prominent and promising scholars, with a special emphasis on multidisciplinary and transnational perspectives. By bridging historical and theoretical concerns, CULTURAL SITINGS will develop and examine narratives which probe the spectrum of experiences that continuously reconfigure contemporary cultures. By rethinking chronology, agency, and especially the siting of historical transformation, the books in this series will go beyond disciplinary boundaries and notions of what is marginal and what is central to knowledge. By juxtaposing the analytical, the historical, and the visual, this challenging new series will provide a venue for the development of cultural studies and for the rewriting of the canon.

Acknowledgments

I am very grateful for the cooperation of all the authors in this collection. They have helped me in every step of the preparation of the book. I would also like to thank Thomas Bender, Arno Mayer, Hayden White, and especially Norman O. Brown for their thoughtful advice on how to put this volume together. Joanna Hitchcock was very helpful in the early stages of this project. Nancy Burson was indefatigable in making sure the right pages went to the right places at the right times. I would like to thank Scripps College for its consistent support in helping me to prepare this volume for publication, and Muriel Bell and John Feneron of Stanford University Press for their thoughtful and effective efforts. I am especially grateful to Elazar Barkan for opening the Cultural Sitings series with this book.

I also wish to acknowledge the prior publication of three of the essays in this volume. Martin Jay's essay first appeared in *Leviathan* 13 (Athens, 1993). Portions of Peter Jelavich's essay appeared in his *Berlin Cabaret* (Cambridge: Harvard University Press, 1993). Louis Rose's essay appeared in *The Psychoanalytic Quarterly* 61 (1992): 590–623.

My thanks to Jeremy and Max for keeping the secret in the last stretch and for wondering what Carl taught their Dad. And thanks to Kari for helping me rediscover many things that we can continue to acknowledge together.

M.S.R.

Contents

Contents

Contributors

PIERRE BOURDIEU holds a Chair in Sociology at the Collège de France. Among his recent works are *Language and Symbolic Power* (Harvard University Press, 1991), *The Political Ontology of Martin Heidegger* (Stanford University Press, 1991), and *Field of Cultural Production: Essays on Art and Literature* (Columbia University Press, 1993).

T. J. CLARK teaches the history of art at the University of California, Berkeley, and is working on a book, *A Completely New Set of Objects: Essays After Modernism,* as well as a study of French art in 1891.

GARY B. COHEN is Associate Professor of History at the University of Oklahoma, Norman. He is the author of *The Politics of Ethnic Survival: Germans in Prague, 1861–1914* (Princeton University Press, 1981), and is currently writing a book on education and society in late nineteenth-century Austria.

THOMAS CROW is Professor of the History of Art at the University of Sussex. He is the author of *Painters and Public Life in Eighteenth Century Paris* (Yale University Press, 1985). His *Brothers in Arms: Making Artists for Revolutionary France* and *The Simple Life: Essays Around Fine Art and Vernacular Culture* are forthcoming.

CARLO GINZBURG is Franklin D. Murphy Professor of History at the University of California, Los Angeles. Among his recent books are *Clues, Myths and the Historical Method* (Johns Hopkins University Press, 1989), and *Ecstasies: Deciphering the Witchs' Sabbath* (Pantheon, 1991).

JAN GOLDSTEIN is Professor of History at the University of Chicago and author of *Console and Classify: The French Psychiatric Profession in the Nineteenth Century* (Cambridge University Press, 1987) and editor of *Foucault and the Writing of History* (Blackwell, 1994). Her new book in progress examines competing conceptions of the self in France during the half-century following the Revolution.

LIONEL GOSSMAN, M. Taylor Pyne Professor of French and Chairman of the Department of Romance Languages at Princeton University, has written on seventeenth- and eighteenth-century French literature, Enlightenment and Romantic historians and historiography, and Basle culture in the nineteenth century. His most recent book is *Between History and Literature* (Harvard University Press, 1990).

MARTIN JAY teaches European intellectual history at the University of California, Berkeley. Among his recent works are *Fin-de-siècle Socialism and Other Essays* (Routledge, 1988), *Force Fields: Between Intellectual History and Cultural Critique* (Routledge, 1993), and *Downcast Eyes: The Denigration of Vision in Twentieth-Century French Thought* (University of California Press, 1993).

PETER JELAVICH teaches modern European intellectual and cultural history at the University of Texas at Austin. He is the author of *Munich and Theatrical Modernism: Politics, Playwriting and Performance, 1890–1914* (1985), and *Berlin Cabaret* (1993), both published by Harvard University Press.

HARRY LIEBERSOHN teaches intellectual history at the University of Illinois, Urbana-Champaign. He is the author of *Fate and Utopia in German Sociology, 1870–1923* (MIT Press, 1988), and is currently working on the history of ethnography in early nineteenth-century Europe.

PATRIZIA LOMBARDO teaches French and Cultural Studies at the University of Pittsburgh. She is the author of *Edgar Poe et la Modernité* (Summa Publications, 1985) and *The Three Paradoxes of Roland Barthes* (University of Georgia Press, 1989). She is currently working on a book about Hippolyte Taine and the discipline of history.

PETER LOEWENBERG is Professor of History at the University of California, Los Angeles. He is the author of over one hundred research publications and of *Decoding the Past: The Psychohistorical Approach* (Knopf, 1983, 1985). He is also a Board-certified practicing psychoanalyst and Chair of the Research Clinical Training Committee of the Southern California Psychoanalytic Institute.

WILLIAM J. MCGRATH is Professor of History at the University of Rochester, and is the author of *Dionysian Art and Populist Politics in Austria* (Yale University Press, 1974) and *Freud's Discovery of Psychoanalysis: The Politics of Hysteria* (Cornell University Press, 1986).

LOUIS ROSE is Assistant Professor of Modern European History at Otterbein College. His work has appeared in *The Psychoanalytic Quarterly*.

MICHAEL S. ROTH is the Hartley Burr Alexander Professor of Humanities at Scripps College and Director of the European Studies Program at the Claremont Graduate School. He is the author of *Psycho-

Analysis as History: Negation and Freedom in Freud (1987) and *Knowing and History: Appropriations of Hegel in Twentieth Century France* (1988), both published by Cornell University Press.

J E R R O L D   S E I G E L teaches European history at New York University. He has written *Marx's Fate: The Shape of a Life* (Princeton University Press, 1978), *Bohemian Paris: Culture, Politics and the Boundaries of Bourgeois Life, 1830–1930* (Viking, 1986), and essays on recent French thinkers.

J A M E S   J.   S H E E H A N is Dickason Professor of the Humanities and Professor of History at Stanford University. His most recent book is *German History, 1770–1866* (Oxford, 1989). He is now working on a history of German art museums in the nineteenth century.

D E B O R A   S I L V E R M A N is Professor of History at the University of California, Los Angeles. She is the author of *Selling Culture: Bloomingdale's Diana Vreeland, and the New Aristocracy of Taste in Reagan's America* (Pantheon, 1986) and *Art Nouveau in Fin-de-Siècle France: Politics, Psychology, and Style* (University of California Press, 1989).

M I C H A E L   P.   S T E I N B E R G, Associate Professor of History at Cornell University, is the author of *The Meaning of the Salzburg Festival: Austria as Theater and Ideology, 1890–1938* (Cornell University Press, 1990). He has written recently on Brahms, Richard Strauss, Mendelssohn, and Theodor Adorno, and is currently working on a project on critical and aesthetic discourses of modernity, from the Mendelssohn family to Aby Warburg and Walter Benjamin.

J O H N   T O E W S is Professor of History and Director of the Program in the Comparative History of Ideas at the University of Washington. He is completing a book on cultural politics in Prussia in the 1840s.

A N T H O N Y   V I D L E R is Professor and Chair of Art History at the University of California, Los Angeles. Among his recent books are *The Architectural Uncanny: Essays in the Modern Unhomely* (MIT Press, 1992), and *Claude-Nicolas Ledoux: Architecture and Social Reform at the end of the Ancien Régime* (MIT Press, 1990).

Rediscovering History

MICHAEL S. ROTH

Introduction

This collection of essays examines some of the major problems and themes critical to the historical study of European culture, problems and themes which the contributors have come to understand in important ways through the work of Carl E. Schorske. In his teaching at Wesleyan University, at the University of California, Berkeley, and at Princeton University, in his books and essays, and in his active participation in an historical approach to the humanities, Schorske has developed a reflexive approach to understanding ideas and cultures, texts and contexts. During a time when the status of historical understanding has changed greatly, he has deepened our awareness of the limits and capacities of historical consciousness in modernity. The essays in this book explore these limits and capacities and share a concern with how cultural productions are connected to self and society, and with how these connections are affected by change over time. The authors severally try to comprehend cultural artifacts in relation to continuity and change. They investigate not only how ideas, art, and institutions hang together in complex networks of synchronic significance, but also how their powers and dangers can be reconstructed under the ordinance of time.

The volume is divided into four parts: "Ideas, Institutions, Professions," "Aesthetic Politics and Aesthetic Religion," "Constructing the Self," and "Narrative, History, Temporality." The essays together share the theme, so central to Schorske's work, of the interactions between culture and politics. In Part I, "Ideas, Institutions, Professions," the authors trace the interaction of ideas and socio-political conditions. How do new conceptions of the individual and of society emerge in specific national, generational, professional, and gendered contexts? What are the pressures which give birth to these ideas, and how in turn do the new conceptualizations reshape their historical contexts? Part II, "Aesthetic Politics and Aesthetic Religion," focusses on the ways in which specific culture makers respond to the political and religious issues around them through the creation of new artistic forms. We see here not so much the displacement of politics by art, but a response to political and moral issues through the power of the aesthetic. The aesthetic is not seen against a social "background" but in dynamic relation to the contextual elements woven together by the historian. "Constructing the Self" shifts the focus toward the psychological, but not as a field divorced from either politics or aesthetics. This part explores specific notions of the self which are created in the face of historical crises, and conceptions of the self which are constituted on models of crisis and loss. The development of the self can be grasped within a context of social, political, and aesthetic pressures, as these factors are given new significance by the creative self. Finally, "Narrative, History, Temporality" turns back to historical understanding itself, asking how certain constructions of history and of time are related to forms of narrative structure and performance. What are the contexts that historical texts require or attempt to generate in order to be effective?

The role of historical understanding in the humanities has taken various forms over the last fifty years. Between the two world wars, history was seen as a key to the sophisticated understanding of art, literature, and the social sciences. In many ways, the value of historical understanding was linked with the value of progress, and as faith in the latter declined so did the prominence of the former. As the comprehension of where we had been came to seem irrelevant to where we were going (in science, in art, in politics), historical understanding took a back seat to conceptually well-tooled synchronic analysis. Even within the discipline of history, new modes of systematic investigation displaced efforts to weave continuity and change into narrative forms.

When Carl Schorske began work on *German Social Democracy, 1905–1917* (1955), he was pursuing a question about the failure of historical progress. Why had democracy and socialism come together in the form that they did, and "Why had that unity failed to hold together? What was the historical dynamic that made of democracy and socialism incompatibles in Germany?"[1] Possibilities for creative, significant political change had been missed in Germany. Why? An historical account of the strengths and weaknesses of social democracy in the German context would reveal possibilities that remained unfulfilled but possibilities which had nonetheless been real.

By the mid 1950s, the very notion of unfulfilled historical possibilities had come under attack from a variety of sources. The criticism suggested that in constructing or projecting historical possibilities the historian was not confronting the structures and functions of societies and cultures. At least since Nietzsche, historical understanding had come under heavy fire as privileging continuity, progress, and conservatism. In the 1950s and 1960s, Nietzschean suspicions about the burdens of historical consciousness were linked to new social scientific accusations about the superficiality and fuzziness of historical thinking. With the decline of the idea of progress and concomitant rise of modernism's emphasis on the autonomy of particular practices, faith in a general account of the meaning and direction of change over time all but disappeared. The notion that understanding was achieved through an account of how things were and how they changed suffered in a culture that no longer assumed that changes were moving in the same direction.[2] Indeed, what was the point of understanding how things had changed if this bore no relation to how we might alter our own lives?

Schorske has described his project on fin-de-siècle Vienna as the product of his resolve "to explore the historical genesis of modern cultural consciousness, with its deliberate rejection of history."[3] Vienna offered the combination of a circumscribed historical context with a multitude of diverse and powerful cultural currents. "The modern mind has been growing indifferent to history because history," Schorske wrote, "conceived as a continuous nourishing tradition, has become useless to it."[4] This is the central theme of *Fin-de-siècle Vienna: Politics and Culture.* Schorske is the historian of de-historicization. He describes how the moderns in Vienna cut themselves free from history, but he describes this historically. On the one hand, he shows tremendous respect for some of the products that result from this struggle to be free from history; but on the other, he also remains committed to showing that this struggle is dangerous, and perhaps futile. By weaving a history around the modern retreat from the historical, Schorske has been able to fashion meaning anew from the modernist movements while simultaneously vindicating the resources of historical consciousness.

Fin-de-siècle Vienna: Politics and Culture did not try to present the city as a tightly interwoven, unified whole. Only facile readers believed that Schorske thought he had found the real or essential Vienna. Each essay established particular connections through time. Schorske proposed no meta-narrative to provide neat closure. The form of the book owes much to the aesthetic sensibility of the moderns Schorske reinscribes in history. Indeed, the book's design and the collage effect of its essays owes much to the modernist's formal innovations. As Schorske wrote of Hofmannsthal: "Thus the poet, rather like the historian, accepts the multiplicity of things in their uniqueness and reveals the unity in their dynamic interrelationship. He brings the discordant into harmony through form."[5] Using psychological explanations to understand politics and art, Schorske employs the methods he is historicizing. Even as he explains the move to the psychological depths as a retreat from the political, he applies the insights gained in the course of this retreat to significant political and cultural figures in turn-of-the-century Vienna.

But this is not unique to one project. Through his essays, books, and teaching, Carl Schorske has been showing that history thrives on making connections, on relativizing claims for autonomy made by various intellectual and cultural movements. For historians, the search for disciplinary autonomy can risk being a form of willed sterility. That is exactly why the modernist gesture to seek out the autonomous bases of all disciplines can be fatal to historical consciousness. History is an *essentially* combinatory activity; and intellectual history can only exist by bringing together cultural productions within a perspective which privileges temporal connectedness.[6] Intellectual or cultural history can never be a tightly coherent discipline, since it thrives on and demands crossing borders into diverse fields of intellection. There is no one method of contextualization; there are styles of making historical interconnections. Schorske has remarked that his own work reveals "a kind of basic archetypical mental disposition to synthesize or unify forces whose dynamics resist integration."[7] The essays in this volume also express this disposition, or place it under historical scrutiny. They explore or perform what is at stake in creating or disclosing "temporal connectedness." There is no single conceptual thread which ties them all together, but they are united by a common aspiration to "connected inclusiveness." That is, the essays create or discover connections through time which make sense of our relations to our pasts in order to enliven us to the possibilities and the constraints in our own time. And they do so by weaving texts and contexts together in diverse patterns that are dynamic, multilayered, and often surprising.

In the process of weaving these histories, the essays also change the way we think about a text or object of study in intellectual or cultural history. Thus, this volume does not present a choice between an emphasis on text and an emphasis on context, but a rethinking of both terms. Neither the arrogance of formalist methodology nor the naiveté of common sense realism will allow one to see cultural artifacts in an active dialogue with the persistence of traditions, possibilities for innovation, and desires in the present. The essays in "Ideas, Institutions, Professions" examine how writers or teachers struggled to define their concepts and ideals under the pressure of events and traditions. We are introduced to the connections between science and subjectivity, morality and psychological health, pedagogic goals and economic and social constraints. The composition of poetry, the development of political theory, and the conceptualization of national identity are all made clearer by showing their connections to changing psychological, political, and aesthetic conditions.

In "Aesthetic Politics and Aesthetic Religion," some of the crucial themes of intellectual and cultural history are revisited. How does artistic creativity arise out of and fit into ongoing developments in a culture? How do political or religious crises reconfigure the ways in which culture is produced and consumed? The essays in this part not only explore how a historical approach can change the ways we understand and take pleasure from painting, music, and dance; they also allow us to rethink important trends in history through interpretations of these cultural productions. Throughout this section, the *value* of the aesthetic in relation to the past and to our own concerns is raised as a problem for historical and theoretical consideration.

As "Aesthetic Politics and Aesthetic Religion" traced the creation and display of art in relation to politics and society, "Constructing the Self" connects the creation and display of the self to general historical trends and theoretical problems. The representation of the self is a central dilemma for the intellectual and cultural historian, whether that representation appears in a psychological theory, or on a canvas or a couch. The display of the self in a portrait, or the analysis of the self in a theory, takes place within a fabric of political, moral, and aesthetic concerns. The display and the analysis must obscure even as they represent the self, as the historical understanding of the fabric will ignore some of its strands as it highlights others. How artists and theorists acknowledge and contend with the necessary "failure" to portray the self fully should be understood in relation to how historians acknowledge and contend with the "failure" to capture the past as it really was in contextualizing it. The history of the self and its constructions confronts historians with the ways in which their own work obscures as it reveals. As self portraits can never make visible the unconscious (although they can acknowledge it, perhaps point to it), historical portraits, too, always leave some part of the past inaccessible to us. The necessary loss in any historical representation can also be acknowledged. [8]

"Narrative, History, Temporality" brings historical representation into focus as a problem. It does so by asking us to consider conventions of historical and fictional representation. How do narrative codes condition our expectations about time, change, continuity? What can fictional representations of change over time tell us about historical accounts, and how have historical accounts changed our approach to fiction? In all of the essays in this part we are confronted with both the fictional elements in historical construction and the historical elements in fictional construction. Moreover, we are shown how the strategies of historical representation at work in film can disclose both the potential and the limitation of particular approaches to the past. Of course, the problems of historical representation are not only formal. Historical work of the most compelling sort has often been a response to crisis, and has always taken place within a multilayered and dynamic context. Understanding the conditions of and possibilities for cultural history in contexts of crisis is a specific goal of the concluding essay and a general goal of the volume as a whole.

The essays in this volume manifest a commitment to the historical study of culture, but they also recognize that neither "history" nor "culture" is an unproblematic concept. Culture cannot be reduced to "popular" practices and beliefs; nor can history be taken merely as the context to be discovered in the archives. To say that history and culture are problematic, however, is neither a call to theorize, nor an inhibition on the attempt to comprehend continuity and change. On the contrary, the recognition that the changing meanings of history and culture, and of text and context, are to be constructed in the very *practice* of historical writing has been an important component of the recent revitalization of intellectual and cultural history. More than most forms of historiography, intellectual and cultural history have been given to much self-examination. Indeed, intellectual history has long been the (marginal) field in which the historical profession permits reflexive questions to be asked.[9] The continuing relevance and power of cultural and intellectual history, however, have not stemmed from their capacities for metahistorical reflection, important though they may be. Instead, the ability of this field to raise reflexive questions about contemporary practices and methodologies while making connections with cultural artifacts from the past has been essential to its development. Carl Schorske's work has raised such questions as it has created historical contexts with which we can make meaning from the past.

Although most of the authors of the essays in this volume are friends, colleagues, and students of Carl Schorske (who had no role, however, in the planning of this book), some of them have no such personal connection. For all the participants in this collection, however, there is a deep and vital link to the themes, methodologies, and goals of this historian who has through his practice of intellectual history changed the past with which we continue to work today, and enriched our understanding of what it means to work and live with (and sometimes against) the past. Intellectual and cultural history continues to have important effects on a variety of disciplines in large part because of the reflexive, self-critical dimension that writers like Schorske put at the heart of their enterprise. For him, history continues to be "the ground on which the problems of our destiny must be debated." The essays in this collection extend and deepen the debates and acknowledge the resources that Carl Schorske's ongoing work continues to provide as we struggle to understand the past and our connections with it.

PART I

Ideas, Institutions, Professions

Psychopathologies of Modern Space: Metropolitan Fear from Agoraphobia to Estrangement

If one were to search for a common and often explicit theme that underlay the different responses of writers and social critics to the big cities of the nineteenth century, it would perhaps be found in the general concept of "estrangement": the estrangement of the inhabitant of a city too rapidly changing and enlarging to comprehend in traditional terms; the estrangement of classes from each other, of individual from individual, of individual from self, of workers from work. These refrains were constant from Rousseau to Marx, Baudelaire to Benjamin. The theme, a commonplace of Romantic irony and self-enquiry and the *leitmotif* of the Marxist critique of capital, was perceived as both a psychological and a spatial condition. From Baudelaire's laments over the disappearance of old Paris ("the form of a city changes, alas, more rapidly than a man's heart"), to Engels's wholesale critique of what he called "Haussmannization," the physical fabric of the city was identified as the instrument of a systematized and enforced alienation. The political critique of urban redevelopment forced by the growth of cities came together with the nostalgia of cultural conservatives lamenting the loss of their familiar quarters to create a generalized sense of distantiation, of individual isolation, from the mechanical, mass-oriented, rapidly moving, and crowded metropolis.

This "spatial pathology" of the city, already fully present in the organicist metaphors of romantic, realist, and naturalist novelists from Balzac through Hugo to Zola, gained new and apparently scientific support in the last quarter of the nineteenth century with the gradual emergence of the disciplines of sociology, psychology, political geography, and psychoanalysis. The space of the new city was now subjected to scrutiny as a possible cause of an increasingly common psychological alienation—the Vienna Circle was to call it "de-realization"—of the metropolitan individual, and further, as an instrument favoring the potentially dangerous behavior of the crowd.[1] By the late 1880s the diagnoses of George Miller Beard, who had, in 1880, identified neurasthenia as the principle mental disease of modern life, were commonplaces of urban criticism. Max Nordau's "degeneration" joined with Jean-Martin Charcot's interpretation of *la neurasthénie* to construct a climate of interpretation in which the metropolis figured as the principle agent of the *"surmenage mental"* of modern civilization, as Charles Richet termed it.[2] In this process what had been a generalized sense of estrangement was given all the dimensions of a psychological complex, constructed out of a gamut of newly identified mental diseases, from neuroses to phobias, that seemed undeniably tied to their urban context.

The extension of individual psychological disorders to embrace the social conditions of an entire metropolis, was on one level perhaps no more than a simple exercise in metaphorical hyperbole. On another level, however, the discovery of these new phobias seems to have been a part of a wider process of re-mapping the space of the city according to its changing social and political characteristics. Whether identifying illnesses like agoraphobia or claustrophobia as predominately bourgeois, or investigating the more threatening illnesses of the working classes, from vagabondage to ambulatory automatisms, doctors were at once reflecting and countering an emerging and generalized fear of metropolis.

Agoraphobia

Recently a unique nervous disorder has been diagnosed—"agoraphobia" [*platzscheu*]. Numerous people are said to suffer from it, always experiencing a certain anxiety or discomfort, whenever they have to walk across a vast empty place.
Camillo Sitte.[3]

Juxtaposed in a spatial complicity that joined the fear of distance to the horror of proximity, agoraphobia and claustrophobia captured the imagination of those who attempted to characterize the special kind of anxiety engendered by the modern metropolis: on the one hand, the fear of open space, exacerbated by the scale of the squares and boulevards of the late nineteenth-century city; on the other, the fear of being closed in, heightened by the increasing interiority of private life in mass society. These "topophobias," as George Miller Beard termed them, at once medical diagnoses and metaphoric descriptions of the alienation and estrangement of individuals, seemed especially at home in the modern metropolis.

It was in these terms that the Viennese architect Camillo Sitte attacked what he saw as the spatial emptiness of the new Ringstrasse, contrasting its apparently limitless and infinite expanses to the compositional qualities and smaller scale of traditional squares and streets. Supporting his nostalgic evocation of the past by the new psychology, Sitte extended his argument by associating the causes of this new sickness of agoraphobia with the new space of urbanism. In traditional cities, with their small, intimate, and human-scaled spaces, the illness was unknown.

Agoraphobia is a very new and modern ailment. One naturally feels very cozy in small, old plazas and only in our memory do they loom gigantic, because in our imagination the magnitude of the artistic effect takes the place of actual size. On our modern gigantic plazas, with their yawning emptiness and oppressive ennui, the inhabitants of snug old towns suffer attacks of this fashionable agoraphobia.[4]

The "universal trend of the time," concluded Sitte, was the fear of open spaces.[5] Underlining his point by couching it in the form of an aesthetic principle of monumental scale, Sitte proposed wittily that even statues might suffer from this disease:

We might supplement this observation on psychology with an artistic one: that also people formed out of stone and metal, on their monumental pedestals, are attacked by this malady and thus always prefer (as already mentioned) to choose a little old plaza rather than a large empty one for their permanent location. What dimensions should statues on such colossal plazas have? They should be at least double or triple life size, or even more. Certain artistic refinements are, in such a case, utterly impossible.[6]

Sitte was, of course, ironically using the new psychology to "prove" an observation that had become a commonplace of the aesthetic criticism of urbanism since the brothers Goncourt had complained of the "American deserts" created by the cutting of the modern boulevards. Such a merging of aesthetic and psychological criteria was readily adopted by counter-modernists and latter-day Ruskinians searching for psychological grounds on which to combat modernist planning, as well as by modernists who argued that such primitive psychological regressions should be overcome.

Indeed, agoraphobia was also adopted as an instrument for the aesthetic criticism of modernity by Wolfgang Worringer in his thesis *Abstraktion und Einfühlung*, published in 1908. For Worringer, agoraphobia was no more nor less than the root cause of abstraction in art, a "life-denying inorganic" force literally born out of the spatial fear of early peoples:

Now what are the psychic presuppositions for the urge to abstraction? We must seek them in these peoples' feeling about the world, in their psychic attitude toward the cosmos. Whereas the precondition for the urge to empathy is a happy pantheistic relationship of confidence between man and the phenomena of the external world, the urge to abstraction is the outcome of a great inner unrest inspired in man by the phenomena of the outside world. . . . We might describe this state as an immense spiritual dread of space [*geistiger Raumscheu*].[7]

Worringer compared this original fear to the pathological condition of the "physical dread of open places [*platzangst*]"; he noted the fear of space [*raumscheu*] demonstrated in Egyptian architecture, where any impression of "free space" was destroyed by the multiplicity of columns.[8] This "spiritual dread of space" was in the end, he concluded, something like a "kind of spiritual agoraphobia in the face of the motley disorder and caprice of the phenomenal world."[9]

Sitte's fashionable disease had been first diagnosed in the late 1860s by a number of doctors in Berlin and Vienna who were struck by the common responses of a number of their patients to public spaces. The first comprehensive memoir was published by the Berlin psychologist Carl Otto Westphal in 1871. The symptoms of what he called "agoraphobia" included palpitations, sensations of heat, blushing, trembling, fear of dying, and petrifying shyness, that occurred, Westphal noted, when his patients were walking across open spaces or through empty streets or when they anticipated such an experience with a dread of the ensuing anxiety.[10] Their fears were to a certain extent alleviated by companionship, but were seriously exacerbated by the dimensions of the space, especially when there seemed to be no boundary to the visual field. A variety of terms existed to categorize this disease—the year before the publication of Westphal's article, another doctor, Benedikt, had dubbed it "*platzschwindel*" or dizziness in public places; and it had been variously called "*platzangst*," "*platzfurcht*," "*platzscheu*," "*angoisse des places*," "*crainte des places*," "*peur d'espace*," "*horreur de vide*," "*topophobia*," and "street fear." The term "agoraphobia" had been already defined in Littré and Robin's *Dictionnaire de médecine* of 1865 as a "form of alienation consisting in an acute anxiety, with palpitation and fears of all kinds"; and with the support of Westphal it would emerge, despite the objections of a few French psychologists, as the generally accepted term.[11]

Westphal recounted three major cases that would be repeated in the literature for decades: a commercial traveller who experienced rapid heart beats on entering a public square, or when passing by long walls or through a street with closed shops; at the theater or in church; a shopkeeper who found it impossible to cross squares or streets when the shops were closed, could not travel on the omnibus, or attend the theater, concert, or any gathering of people without feeling a strange anxiety, accompanied by rapid heart palpitation; and an engineer who felt anxiety the moment he had to cross a square, especially if deserted, having the sense that the pavement was rushing as if in a torrent beneath his feet. A certain relief was found by these patients in physical aids: a walking-stick, or the presence of a friend for example. Westphal cited the case reported by a Dr. Brück of Driburg of a priest who was terrified if he was not covered by the vaulted ceiling of his church, and who was forced when in the open to walk beneath an umbrella.[12]

If agoraphobia by definition was an essentially spatial disease, many psychologists insisted that it was an equally urban disease, the effect of life in the modern city. Westphal's engineer, indeed, stated that he felt less anxiety in a large space not surrounded by houses than in a space of the same size in a city: open nature was refreshing, the city was terrifying. Indeed, writing in 1880, the doctor E. Gélineau argued for the term *"kénophobie"* as better characterizing this fear of the void that "strikes only the inhabitant of cities . . . developing under the influence of that debilitating atmosphere of the big towns that has been called *malaria urbana.*"[13] Two years earlier, Legrand du Saulle had refused the word agoraphobia precisely because, in his terms, it limited the disturbance to one specific kind of public space. He preferred the vaguer term *"peur des espaces"* as comprising all spatial fears: "the patients suffer from fear of space, of the void, not only in the street but also in the theater, in church, on an upper floor, at a window giving onto a large courtyard or looking over the countryside, in an omnibus, a ferry or on a bridge."[14]

Legrand's synthetic description of the disease was as dramatic as it was unambiguous in characterizing its setting:

The fear of spaces, ordinarily compatible with the most robust health, is frequently produced at the very moment when the neuropath leaves a street and arrives at a square, and it is marked by a sudden anxiety, a instantaneous beating of the heart. The patient, then prey to an indefinable emotion finds himself isolated from the entire world at the sight of the void that is presented to him and frightens him immeasurably . . . he feels as if he is destroyed, does not dare to descend from the sidewalk to the roadway, makes no step either forward or backward, neither advances nor retreats, trembles in all his limbs, grows pale, shivers, blushes, is covered with sweat, grows more and more alarmed, can hardly stand up on his tottering legs and remains unhappily convinced that he could never face this void, this deserted place, or cross the space that is before him. If one's gaze was suddenly to be plunged into a deep gulf, if one were to imagine being suspended above a fiery crater, to be crossing the Niagara on a rigid cord or feel that one was rolling into a precipice, the resulting impression could be no more painful, more terrifying, than that provoked by the fear of spaces.[15]

He concluded: "no fear without the void, no calm without the appearance of a semblance of protection."[16] The symptoms were similar for all patients:

This anxious state . . . is ordinarily accompanied by a sudden feebleness of the legs, an overactivity of the circulation, by waves of tingling, by a sensation of numbness starting with chills, by hot flushes, cold sweats, trembling, a desire to burst into tears, ridiculous apprehensions, hypochondriac preoccupations, half-spoken lamentations and by a general disturbance that is truly painful with different alternations of facial coloration and physiognomical expression.[17]

Legrand's own observations confirmed Westphal's in every detail. A "Madame B . . .," the vivacious and sociable mother of three children, experienced the symptoms on returning from vacation and finding herself unable to cross the Champs-Elysées, the boulevards, or large squares unaccompanied.[18] Fearful of empty churches without benches or chairs, of eating alone in spacious hotel dining rooms, and of being in carriages when there were no passers-by in the street, she even needed help in mounting the wide stair to her apartment. Once indoors she was never able to look out of the window onto the courtyard; she filled her rooms with furniture, pictures, statuettes and old tapestries to reduce their spaciousness. She lived, noted Legrand, "in a veritable bazaar": "the void alone frightened her."[19] Legrand's second case was a "M. Albert G.," an infantry officer, interested in literature, poetry, music, and archaeology, who was unable to cross deserted public squares out of uniform. Again his fear was evoked by the void, whether on terraces or in a large gothic church.[20] Legrand concluded, agreeing with most other students of agoraphobia, that "it was the space that caused him anxiety."[21]

To the fear of empty and open space was added that of crowded and populated places. Legrand noted: "It has been remarked that the fear of spaces is produced among certain patients in a very frequented place, or among crowds," a form of anxiety that was quickly assimilated to the more general study of crowd behavior as sketched by Gustave Le Bon. The supplement to Emile Littré's dictionary published in 1883 had already defined agoraphobia in this way, as a "sort of madness in which the patient fears the presence of crowds, and, for example, cannot decide to cross a busy street."[22]

In these ways, the notion of agoraphobia was quickly extended in popular parlance to embrace all urban fears that were seemingly connected to spatial conditions. Entire urban populations, it was thought, might become susceptible to the disease as a result of specific events. Thus Legrand remarked on the change in the behavior of Parisians following the siege of Paris by the Germans in 1871. Describing a patient whose agoraphobia seemed to be precipitated or at least aggravated by over-indulgence in strong stimulants such as coffee,[23] he found an increase in the abuse of coffee among women workers to be directly linked to the famine of the population during the Commune, leading to the dangerous abuse of all kinds of stimulants. This habit had been continued after the withdrawal of German troops. In Legrand's terms, the successive closing and sudden opening of the city had the effect of fostering the veritable cause of spatial fear.[24]

By 1879 agoraphobia had been joined by its apparent opposite, "claustrophobia," popularized in France by Benjamin Ball in a communication to the Société Médico-psychologique.[25] He cited the case of a young soldier with a fear of contact, a *"délire de propreté"* accompanied by a panic fear of being alone in a closed space, a sensation of being in a passage getting narrower and narrower, to the point of being able to go neither forward nor back, an intolerable terror that was generally followed by a flight into the fields.[26] A second patient panicked while climbing the stairs of the Tour Saint Jacques.[27] Neither could remain in an apartment when the doors were closed. Ball, disagreeing with Beard, who had proposed to categorize all morbid fears of space under the general heading "topophobia," asserted the special characteristics of claustrophobia and of agoraphobia, to be treated as linked but nevertheless distinct and different psychoses.

Whether the etiology of these spatial disorders was traced to visual causes or ascribed to heredity, both agora- and claustrophobia were inevitably ranked among the most characteristic of anxieties produced by life in the modern city—exaggerated but typical forms of the all-pervasive neurasthenia. Gilles de la Tourette, concerned to modify the over-encompassing category of Beard, identified agoraphobia with a special state of "neurasthenic vertigo," (*une vertige neurasthénique*) accompanied by "a sensation of cerebral emptiness accompanied by a weakness of the lower limbs. . . . A veil spreads before the eyes, everything is grey and leaden; the visual field is full of black spots, flying patches, close or distant objects are confused on the same plane."[28] Such vertigo was increased, he observed, by the daily commute to and from the job; sufferers were "pushed to creep along walls, follow houses, and flee the crossing of wide squares."[29]

For Gilles de la Tourette, neurasthenia proper had to be distinguished from agoraphobia on the grounds that the latter was an inherited disease, and largely incurable. He described a case falsely diagnosed as *neurasthénie constitutionelle*, or hereditary neurasthenia, but which he claimed was rather a vertigo, or agoraphobia, that confined the patient to his room, and which was inherited directly from his mother, whose "life had been tormented by the fear of spaces, by an agoraphobia that had poisoned her entire existence."[30] Such hereditary disorders were most evident, according to Gilles, in large cities, among clerks, laborers, and accident victims, who "once touched by hysterical neurasthenia . . . become part of those marginalized by the large towns, vagabonds" suffering from incurable mental stigmatisms.[31]

Gilles de la Tourette was here following his teacher Charcot, whose celebrated "Tuesday Lessons" featured many cases of vagabondage associated, according to the doctor, with agoraphobia. For Charcot, as he explained in his lesson 27 March 1888, these "hysterical-epileptic attacks, these vertigos, this anxiety erupting at the moment when a public square has to be crossed, all this is very interesting as an example of the combination of different neuropathic states that, in reality, constitute distinct and autonomous morbid species," that were, of course, hereditary.[32] He presented the case of a young man who suffered from such attacks of epilepsy, agoraphobia, and vertigo, who described his inability to cross the Place du Carrousel or the Place de la Concorde without fear of their emptiness and a corresponding sensation of paralysis. Charcot easily identified the malady as "what one would call agoraphobia, a special nervous state the knowledge of which we owe to Professor Westphall [sic] of Berlin (in German: *Platzangst, Platzfurcht*)." But the patient went on to describe other symptoms that occurred at night in an enclosed railway carriage: "I was frightened, because I had the sense of being closed in. I don't like to stay in a narrow space, I feel ill." For Charcot this added another dimension: "It is not only agoraphobia, you see, it is as well claustrophobia, as Dr. Ball says." To conclude this synthetic case, Charcot diagnosed a profound vertigo, that resulted in a sense of falling, whether in trains or when climbing towers.[33]

Neither Charcot's belief in heredity, nor his student Sigmund Freud's opposing view that, as he noted in his German translation of the *Leçons du mardi*, "the more frequent cause of agoraphobia as well as of most other phobias lies not in heredity but in abnormalities of sexual life,"[34] would remove the urban and spatial associations from the illness. It was as if, no matter what the particular circumstances of individual patients or the arguments of doctors, the cultural significance of agoraphobia was greater than its medical etiology. The resonance of a sickness associated with open or closed spaces, of symptoms that whatever their cause seemed to be triggered by the new configurations of urban space introduced by modernization, was irresistible to critics and sociologists alike. Summarizing and extending the geographical range of Beard's "American" neurasthenia, Charcot's former student Fernand Levillain claimed all cities as the privileged sites of "*surmenage intellectuel et des sens*" and neurasthenia: "It is in effect in the great centers of agglomeration that all the types of *surmenage* we have reviewed are collected and developed to their maximum."[35] Despite his belief in Charcot's theory of heredity and his criticism of Beard for having included the phobias within simple neurasthenia, Levillain nevertheless admitted that the neurasthenic inhabitant of the big city might well experience otherwise hereditary maladies in a less acute form—agoraphobia, claustrophobia, monophobia (fear of solitude and isolation), fear of touching (*délire de toucher*), and all other instances of spatial fear.

Estrangement

Objects remain spellbound in the unmerciful
separation of space, no material part can commonly share its space with another, a real unity
of diverse elements does not exist in space.
>   Georg Simmel, "Brücke und Tür."

As both medical ailment and cultural metaphor, agoraphobia thus emerged by the end of the century as a specific instance of that generalized "estrangement" identified by social critics as the principal effect of life in metropolis. It was, indeed, a central metaphor for the more generalized psychological interpretation of modern space undertaken by sociologists who, starting with Georg Simmel, sought to establish a science of social form and structure that treated space as a central category for modeling social relations, a point of reference for the study of individuals and groups.

In the face of the crowded disorder of the modern metropolis, argued Simmel, the "sensitive and nervous modern person" required a degree of spatial isolation as a kind of prophylactic against psychological intrusion.[36] If such a personal boundary were to be transgressed, a "pathological deformation" might be observed in the individual, who would present all the symptoms of what Simmel called "fear of touching," or *Berührungsangst*. This fear of coming into too close a contact with objects, was, he argued, "a consequence of hyperaesthesia, for which every direct and energetic contact causes pain."[37] Simmel's diagnosis was at once spatial and mental: the real cause of the neurosis was not, as Westphal and Sitte had implied, solely spatial. Rather, he argued, it was a product of the rapid oscillation between two characteristic moods of urban life: the over-close identification with things, and alternatively, too great a distance from them. In both cases, as with the symptoms of agoraphobia, the mental oscillation had spatial roots, being the result of the open spaces of the city, those very large expanses in which the crowds of metropolis found their "impulsiveness and enthusiasm."[38]

Out of this understanding of the spatial dimensions of social order, Simmel went on to construct a theory of estrangement that was once and for all tied to the space of metropolis.[39] To the place and role of individuals in society as defined by their spatial relations of proximity and distance, he added the psychological dimension, asserting, "what creates the characteristic phenomena of neighborliness or strangeness, is not spatial proximity or spatial distance, but *a specific psychological content*."[40] Space as the *expression* of social conditions would then be open to the sociological gaze: "Spatial relations are only the condition, on the one hand, and the symbol, on the other, of human relations." As effects of human activities, spaces were important indications of social processes, of the interaction between human beings conceived of and experienced as *space-filling*. The "empty space" between individuals, filled and animated by their reciprocal relations, was, in these terms, both a spatial and a functional concept.[41] Viewed in this way, space might allow for the study of the social boundaries that defined the limits of territorial groupings; spatial unities might be identified, within borders coincident with the locations of particular social groups. Such borders, the spatial expression of sociological and functional unity alike, intersected social space like a network of imaginary lines, articulating the activity of society as a frame isolates a picture from its background.

The metropolis presented the most exacerbated condition of these psychological boundaries. In his essay "Metropolis and Mental Life," of 1903, Simmel characterized the "psychological foundation, upon which the metropolitan individuality is erected . . . the intensification of emotional life due to the swift and continuous shift of external and internal stimuli," as spatial by definition: "To the extent that the metropolis creates these psychological conditions—with every crossing of the street, with the tempo and multiplicity of economic, occupational and social life—it creates in the sensory foundations of mental life, and in the degree of awareness necessitated by our organization as creatures dependent on differences, a deep contrast with the slower, more habitual, more smoothly flowing rhythm of the sensory-mental phase of small town and rural existence."[42]

The social relations of the metropolitan inhabitant would then be intellectual rather than oral and emotional; the conscious would dominate the unconscious; habits would be adaptable and shifting, rather than rooted and apparently eternal; the impersonal would overcome the personal; objective distance would replace subjective empathy. The fundamental cause of these differences was the nature of metropolitan temporality, the speeded-up tempo of life itself and its regulation according to the standards of "punctuality, calculability, and exactness." For Simmel,

The metropolis is the proper arena for this type of culture which has outgrown every personal element. Here in buildings and educational institutions, in the wonders and comforts of space-conquering technique, in the formations of social life and in the concrete institutions of the State is to be found such a tremendous richness of crystallizing, depersonalized cultural accomplishments that the personality can, so to speak, scarcely maintain itself in the face of it.[43]

It was the very nature of social relations in the big city that forced distance and thus alienation, for self-defense and for functional reasons. And distance was first and foremost a product of the omnipotence of sight; as opposed to the knowledge of individuals based on intimacy and oral communication in a small community, metropolitan connections were rapid, glancing, and ocular:

Social life in the large city as compared with the towns shows a great preponderance of occasions to *see* rather than to *hear* people. . . . Before the appearance of omnibuses, railroads and street cars in the nineteenth century, men were not in a situation where for periods of minutes or hours they could or must look at each other without talking to one another. The greater perplexity which characterizes the person who only sees, as contrasted with the one who only hears brings us to problems of the emotions of modern life; the lack of orientation in the collective life, the sense of utter lonesomeness, and the feeling that the individual is surrounded on all sides by closed doors.[44]

This distance was necessarily reinforced by the very character of daily life itself. In *The Philosophy of Money*, Simmel wrote,

For the jostling crowdedness and the motley disorder of metropolitan communication would simply be unbearable without such psychological distance. Since contemporary urban culture, with its commercial, professional and social intercourse, forces us to be physically close to an enormous number of people, sensitive and nervous modern people would sink completely into despair if the objectification of social relationships did not bring with it an inner boundary and reserve. The pecuniary character of relationships, either openly or concealed in a thousand forms, places an invisible functional distance between people that is an interior protection and neutralization against the overcrowded proximity and friction of our cultural life.[45]

In a series of excursuses to his essay on social space, Simmel treated of a number of characteristic types—the poor, the adventurer, the stranger—as indicative of the power of space to determine role. Of these, the last, the stranger, was most exemplary.[46] If, Simmel stated, wandering equalled the *liberation* from every given point in space and was the conceptual opposite to *fixation* at such a point, then the sociological form of the stranger combined these two characteristics in one. That is, the stranger was not the "wanderer who comes today and goes tomorrow but the person who comes today and stays tomorrow." Fixed within a particular spatial group, the stranger was one who has not belonged from the beginning. "In the stranger," Simmel concluded, "are organized the unity of nearness and remoteness of every human relation," in such a way that in relationship to the stranger "distance means that he, who is close by, is far, and strangeness means that he, who also is far, is actually near." Here Simmel anticipated Freud's reflections on that form of estrangement known as the uncanny, where relations of the familiar and the unfamiliar—*heimlich* and *unheimlich*—become ambiguous and merge with one another. Simmel, himself the epitome of the stranger, cultivated, urban, Jewish, and excluded from the normal academic career of his contemporaries Max Weber and Wilhelm Dilthey, thus defined the role of a being at once strange and estranged in the money economy of capitalism.

Of all Simmel's students and followers, it was Siegfried Kracauer who, trained as an architect, most profoundly absorbed these lessons of spatial sociology and, especially, of the analysis of spatial formations applied to the understanding of estrangement. From his student experience in Berlin in 1907, when he had taken detailed notes at Simmel's lecture on "The Problem of Style in Art," to the completion of his still unpublished monograph on Simmel in 1917, Kracauer found in Simmel a methodological guide to the present. And while his early architectural designs between 1916 and 1918 were by no means infused with a direct sociological "distance," when redescribed in his later autobiographical novel *Ginster* they took on the character of moments in a slow development towards what Ernst Bloch would recognize as the personality of "the detached hero concerned about nothing and entirely without pathos."[47]

Thus, his project for the Military Memorial Cemetery, designed in Frankfurt in 1916, was, in Kracauer's recollection, a moment of transition between a reliance on mysterious and picturesque traditional models—the cemetery of Genoa and the cathedral of Milan—and an ironic and distanced modern model deeply implicated in the forms of war:

to hide the tombs like Easter eggs, this project seemed too soft for these times of general war. Such times called for a cemetery where their horror would be reflected. In place of using the sketches he had developed until then, Ginster . . . elaborated a system of a cemetery that was similar to a project of military organization.[48]

Thence the "scientifically lined up," rectilinear tombs set at right angles along *allées* lined by geometrically-cut foliage, surrounding a funery monument that took the form of an elevated cube with a stepped-back quasi-pyramidal top that served to display the names of the dead: "During these years of war the key word for the ruling-classes," Kracauer observed, "was simplicity."[49]

Even the "prettiness" of his design for a *siedlung* at Osnabrück, drawn up in November 1918, with its "little detached houses and gardens with pitched roofs," seemed to "Ginster-Kracauer" to be premature at the very least: in the present conditions of war, "they would," he observed, "inevitably be destroyed," and if not, these pretty houses would become the objects of destruction in a new war, attaching the workers to their defense. "Certainly," concluded Kracauer, "one could not house workers in holes, but it would be perhaps more suitable to place tomb-stones in the gardens."[50] Similar transformations from symbolism to rationalism were to be traced in the projects of the Swiss architect Hannes Meyer for *siedlungen* and cemeteries between 1919 and 1923: the Freidorf Housing estate near Basle, 1919–21, with its "Palladian," almost neoclassical layout, but with pitched roofs, and the central cemetery in Basle, 1923, which seems to echo the contemporary interest in the "Revolutionary" architecture of the late eighteenth century. These seem to mirror the projects of Kracauer, even though Meyer's later move towards the "new objectivity" would doubtless have been condemned by Kracauer.

Kracauer's account of his self-distancing from architectural practice seems to have been accompanied by a growing awareness of the distancing powers of architectural space itself, or, rather, the potential of space to act as a powerful emblem of social estrangement. Kracauer characterized his 1919 essay on Simmel as an "existential topography," comparing it to those developed by Simmel himself. In his subsequent writings the concept of an inhabited topography was extended literally with the aid of Simmel's sociology to the spaces of modern life: the hotel lobby, that became the focus of an unpublished essay on the detective novel in 1922–25; the "pleasure barracks" of the cafes and music halls, together with their despondent counterparts, the unemployment exchanges, described in his study of the white collar workers in 1930; the boulevards or "homes for the homeless" that form the setting of his life of Offenbach published in 1936.[51]

Of these, the hotel lobby (*hotelhalle*), seen by Kracauer as the paradigmatic space of the modern detective novel, and thus as epitomizing the conditions of modern life in their anonymity and fragmentation, was perhaps the most Simmelian in its formulation.[52] Kracauer compared the modern hotel lobby to the traditional church; the one a shelter for the transient and disconnected, the other for the community of the faithful. Using Simmel's categories of spatial description, Kracauer elaborated the distinction between what he termed *erfülter Raum*, or the "inhabited space" of *Verknüpfung*, or "communion," and the void or empty space of physics and the abstract sciences—what he characterized as the *ratio* of modern life. Shut out of the religiously bonded community, the modern urban dweller could rely only on spaces, like that of the hotel lobby, "which bear witness to his non-existence." Detached from everyday life, individual atoms with no connection save their absolute anonymity, the hotel guests were scattered like atoms in a void, confronted with "nothing" (*vis-à-vis de rien*); stranded in their armchairs, the guests could do little more than find a "disinterested pleasure in contemplating the world."[53] In this way, "the civilization which tends towards rationalization loses itself in the elegant club chair," in the ultimate space of indifference. Even the conventional silence of the setting parodied that of the church. Kracauer quoted Thomas Mann in *Death in Venice*: "In this room there reigned a religious silence which is one of the distinctive marks of grand hotels. The waiters serve with muffled steps. One hardly hears the noise of a cup or tea-pot, or a whispered word."[54] In Kracauer's vision of spatial alienation,

Rudiments of individuals slide in the nirvana of relaxation, faces are lost behind the newspaper, and the uninterrupted artificial light illumines only mannequins. It is a coming and going of unknowns who are changed into empty forms by forgetting their passwords, and who parade, imperceptible, like chinese shadows. If they had an interiority, it would have no windows.[55]

The mystery of the lobby, proper site of the detective novel, was no longer religious, but base, a mystery among the masks. Kracauer cited the detective novel *Death Enters the Hotel,* by Sven Elvestad: "One sees thus once again that a grand hotel is a world apart, and this world resembles the rest of the big world. The clients wander here in their light and carefree summer life, without suspecting what strange mysteries evolve among them."[56] Here, the "pseudo-individuals," or guests, spread themselves like molecules in "a spatial desert without limits," never destined to come together, even when compressed within the *grossstadt.* Their only link, Kracauer concluded, was indifferent enough: what he called, suggestively, the strategic grand routes of convention.[57]

Vagabondage

> Would it be the case that vagabondage leads to
> hysterical neurasthenia, or rather the reverse,
> that neurasthenia leads to vagabondage? This is a
> delicate question, that is in the first instance in-
> teresting from the social point of view and that
> will some day merit deeper study.
> Jean-Martin Charcot, *Leçons du mardi*

It was the analysis of Kracauer's "boulevards for the homeless" that formed the basis of Walter Benjamin's study of the big city, research that under the title of *Das Passagen-Werk*—work on the "passages" or covered shopping arcades of Paris—took up the last ten years of his life. Evoking the urban *flâneur,* Benjamin extolled the art of "slow walking" as the instrument of modern urban mapping. Franz Hessel, whose *Promenades in Berlin* he reviewed with special interest, seemed, for Benjamin, to take this art to its highest form. At once recording the streets and spaces of modern Berlin with an irony that exposed the shallow propositions of architect-planners, and searching to record the rapidly vanishing old city with minute observations, Hessel bore witness to a moment of transition that would, for Benjamin, never be repeated:

> The *flâneur* is the priest of the *genius loci.* This discreet passer-by with his priesthood and his detective's flair, there surrounds his erudition something like that which surrounds the Father Brown of Chesterton, that master of criminalistics.[58]

But the dandified figure of the stroller was complemented in Benjamin by another, more subversive image: that of the vagabond, who alone, criminal and exiled, possessed the marginal vision that transgressed boundaries and turned them into thresholds, a way of looking that engendered what Benjamin called the "peddling [*colportage*] of space." [59] Writing of the Place du Maroc in Belleville, Benjamin noted this strange power of names and spaces to construct, as if with hashish, a complex and shifting image beyond that of their material existence. Entering the deserted square on a Sunday afternoon, Benjamin found himself not only in the Morrocan desert but also in a colonial monument: "the topographic vision intersected in it with an allegorical signification, and it did not for all that lose its place at the heart of Belleville. But it is ordinarily reserved for drugs to be able to arouse such a vision. In fact, the names of streets, in these cases, are inebriating substances that render our perception richer in strata and in spheres. One could call the force with which they plunge us into this state an 'evocative virtue.'" [60]

Referring to the many cases of "ambulatory automatism" examined by Charcot and his followers, Benjamin compared this perception to that of the vagabond amnesiac: "it is not the association of images that is here decisive, but their compenetration. This fact should also be remembered in order to understand certain pathological phenomena: the sick man who wanders the city during the hours of night and forgets the way back has perhaps felt the hold of this power." [61]

In using the metaphor of the amnesiac, Benjamin was evoking a tradition of medical cases that from the 1880s had attempted to link the incidence of certain neurasthenias to social class and even race. For, if agoraphobia and claustrophobia were, at least in the majority of cases studied, spatial afflictions of the middle class, another variety of urban disorder, named by Charcot "ambulatory automatism," seemed more prevalent among the working classes and especially the out-of-work. For Charcot and his followers ambulatory diseases were inevitably associated with the criminal activity of vagabondage, seeming differentiated only in terms of degree. They were most evident, as Charcot wrote, among those "without avowed profession, without fixed domicile, in a word vagabonds, those who often sleep under bridges, in quarries or lime kilns and who are exposed at any instant to the blows of the police." [62]

Charcot presented two kinds of cases to the audience of his Tuesday lessons. The first were those of vagabonds properly speaking, the second those of workers who were evidently suffering attacks of hysterical or epileptic amnesia. In the first category, the case of a Hungarian Jew who suffered from a "*manie des voyages,*" was of especial interest, as perhaps indicating the hereditary nature of this "Israelite" disease: "He is Israelite, you see it well, and the sole fact of his bizarre peregrinations presents itself to us as

mentally submitted to the regimen of instincts."[63] In the second classification, Charcot concentrated on the case of a young delivery man whose
periodic loss of memory led to his wandering through and outside Paris for
days on end.

Here is a man walking the streets of Paris for 14 hours. It goes without saying that
he must have looked appropriate; if not, he would have been stopped by the police.
He must have had his eyes open, or else he would have brought attention to
himself. . . . So he must have acted as you or I would on the street, but he was
unconscious.[64]

In the light of the repeated nature of these excursions, Charcot diagnosed
ambulatory automatism caused by epilepsy. The doctor was fascinated by
the apparent coincidence between his patient's amnesia or somnambulism,
and that depicted by Shakespeare in *Macbeth*: "if I wanted to define this
patient's mental state, I would, like both the poet and physician, say that
here is a patient who appears asleep but who behaves like you and me, and
we, of course, are awake."[65]

In transposing what for Charcot was an attempt to demonstrate the heredity or racial aspects of vagabondage into a poetic metaphor for pathological vision, Benjamin was privileging a particular point of view: not that of
the doctor-observer, but that of the patient. Such a pathological reading of
the city now took on a critical aspect, to be emulated by the writer/*flâneur*
as he sought to recapture the primal resonances of natural paths in the urban
labyrinth. Only a state of dream-like suspension might enable the wanderer
to cross between physical surroundings and their mental contents.

Viewed through these lenses, the urban street regained something of the
original terror of the nomadic route. Where the original road carried with
it the "terrors of wandering," embedded in the mythical unconscious of the
wandering tribes, the street engenders a new form of terror, that of the bore-
dom inspired by "the monotonous ribbon of asphalt." Drawing these two
terrors together, and still to be found buried in the subterranean routes of
the modern city, was the figure of the labyrinth, site of endless and monotonous wandering.[66]

This underground, which was for Benjamin in some way an equivalent
to the unconscious of the city, was to be explored with all the techniques of
a geographer. Reading the city "topographically," Benjamin tried to recapture its strange, landscape character. He cited Hofmannsthal's characterization of Paris—"a landscape composed of pure life"—and added that if so,
it was "a volcanic landscape": "Paris is, in the social order, the pendant to
Vesuvius in the geographical order." In his imagination Paris was trans-

formed into the semblance of an antique site, with its ruins, its sacred places, and even its entrances to the underworld. In this sense, it was also like a dream; hence his fascination with "the passages, architectures where we live once again oneirically the life of our parents and our grand-parents, like the embryo in the womb of its mother repeats phylogenesis. Existence flows in these places without particular accentuation, as in the episodes of dreams. Flânerie gives its rhythm to this somnolence."[67]

Adding rhythm to sleepwalking, the art of the slow walker, the *flâneur*, was only to be matched by the technique of the film, that alone might succeed through montage in representing the true "depth" of the plan of Paris. "Could one not shoot a passionate film of the plan of Paris? Of the development of its different figures in temporal succession? Of the condensation of a secular movement embracing streets, boulevards, passages, squares, in the space of a half-hour? And what else does the flâneur do?"[68]

Like the troglodyte inhabitants of Gabriel Tarde's future underground society, however, Benjamin's *flâneurs* were tracing the final paths through the traditional city. The development of the boulevards represented only the first stage in the process of the eventual dissolution of the urban fabric. In Benjamin's history of modern urban vision, the rise of deeper and more public perspective in the public, commercial realm was accomplished at the expense of individual interiority. From the Biedermeier interiors of the 1830s, with their windows shaded by layers of drapery ("It is thus something like a perspective which opens from the interior towards the window"), to the "suffocating perspective" of the panoramas and arcades, to the broad open vistas opened up by Haussmann, the development depicted by Benjamin moved with all the inexorable logic of modern spatialization: from claustrophobia to agoraphobia.

And this opening up was brought to its inevitable conclusion in modernism. Hessel, the modern wanderer was, Benjamin claimed, celebrating "the last monuments of an ancient art of dwelling."

The last: because in the imprint of this turning-point of the epoch, it is written that the knell has sounded for the dwelling in its old sense, dwelling in which security prevailed. Giedion, Mendelssohn, Le Corbusier have made the place of abode of men above all the transitory space of all the imaginable forces and waves of air and light. What is being prepared is found under the sign of transparency.[69]

The ideology of transparency, the battle cry of modernism, was, as Benjamin recognized, the agent of a spatial dissolution to which only the *flâneur* was privy: "The sensation of the entirely new, of the absolutely modern, is a form of becoming as oneiric as the eternal return itself. The perception of space that corresponds to this perception of time, is the transparency of the world of the flâneur."[70]

What for Le Corbusier represented a liberation from the closed and infected Balzacian quarters of the nineteenth-century city, was, in the historically nuanced terms of Benjamin, the substitution of the void for the home. Without comment Benjamin copied a passage from Sigfried Giedion's *Bauen in Frankreich* of 1928:

The houses of Le Corbusier define themselves neither by space nor by forms: the air passes right through them! The air becomes a constitutive factor! For this, one should count neither on space nor forms, but uniquely on relation and compenetration! There is only a single, indivisible space. The separations between interior and exterior fall.[71]

These "new spatial conditions of modernity" were as present in the city as in the house:

The "ville contemporaine" of Le Corbusier is an old village on a major road. Except for the fact that it is now taken over by cars and airplanes that land in the middle of this village, nothing has changed.[72]

The ironic assertion of timeless space here gave force to Benjamin's belief that, finally, space had been destroyed by time. That this process had begun in the late eighteenth century only made the nineteenth the more hallucinatory in retrospect, suspended as it were between a past of walls and doors and a future of voids.

HARRY LIEBERSOHN

Selective Affinities:
Three Generations of
German Intellectuals

The recent remaking of Germany has contributed to the twentieth century's awakening to its own unsettled fin de siècle. Until 1989 the postwar division of Central Europe seemed solidly in place, but the opening of the Berlin Wall on November ninth of that year gave the world a symbol of boundaries in disarray. Like many others, Germans responded with a mixture of jubilation and unease. Phrases of familial intimacy, which expressed a genuine sense of separation in the 1950s, turned ironic on either side of the former border as "brothers from the East" lined up for Western housing and jobs while siblings from the West made claims on long-lost property. Though historical allegiance and economic interest drove the two partners together, they had some second thoughts about the outcome of their sudden merger. No one quite knew if it was a union or a reunion. To be "German" at that moment meant, among other things, to confront the strangeness of one's next of kin.

The dissolving of Cold War boundaries returned German identity from a state of deep freeze to the flow of history. Before 1945 the discourse of German identity never demarcated a clear entity; many factions competed to name the obscure object of desire. One critical contender was the Protestant *Bildungsbürgertum*, or educated elite, of the nineteenth century. More than anyone else, its members formulated the ideology of nationalism for the Prussian victors in the struggle for Central European hegemony. A language of kinship—of origins, genealogies, foreignness, and affinities—aided these educated Protestants in their generations of German identity. Their notions of affine and alien were no less peculiar than the Balinese systems of family relationship studied by a James Boon or Clifford Geertz. In its seemingly less exotic setting, Germany's *Bildungsbürgertum* did not uncover natural connections any more than any other kinship system does, but created an essential Germanness where none had been before.[1]

Three thinkers will suggest some of the changes in educated definitions of German nationhood in the nineteenth and early twentieth centuries. At the beginning of the Romantic era Friedrich Schlegel explored linguistic affinities linking German and Brahmin lettered elites; in the years of national unification Heinrich von Treitschke defined an inbred Teutonic nationality for the Prussian-German state; in the age of Imperial expansion Max Weber defined German identity through world-historical comparisons. Each of them pondered the relationship of Protestant to Catholic and Jew, and of the educated to other classes, in the making of German identity. Each aspired to the role of leading spokesman of his age and class in response to the politics of revolution, nation-building, and empire—and with the special fervor kindled by membership in a tiny, at times missionary, milieu. Related by class and culture yet different in their specific methods and ideals, they illustrate how conceptions of national identity could shift from generation to generation while retaining a family likeness within the *Bildungsbürgertum*.[2]

We begin with Schlegel as an exponent of linguistic affinity. Language is of course a defining feature of collective identity in the ideology of nationalism. Observers have frequently pointed out that in the absence of political boundaries, Central European intellectuals stressed language as a mark of cultural and ethnic cohesion. To the extent that this is so, Schlegel takes on special interest as a founder of the nineteenth-century method of establishing linguistic affinities. It was almost an incidental achievement at the end of his great creative period. By 1800 he stood out, at age twenty-eight, as the critical genius of the newly emerging Romantic School in Germany.

National character engaged his attention early on. His correspondence to his brother from the early 1790s, when he was barely out of his teens, registers his awareness of, and passionate wish to further, Germany's awakening sense of national destiny. Yet—*contra* the cliché that German nationalism always defines itself against an external or internal enemy—he resisted the temptation to make invidious comparisons to France.[3] His very definition of Romanticism involved appreciation of foreign cultures as a validation of modern, "Romance" literatures against the tyranny of classical models. German *Bildung* as he imagined it in his famous critical fragments and early essays was to be an education to humanity, reaching around the world and reflecting on the possibilities of comprehending (and miscomprehending) cultural differences. Like other thinkers and artists of his generation (notably the brothers Humboldt), Schlegel received first lessons in cosmopolitanism in the celebrated Jewish salons of Berlin, where divisions of rank, religion, and sex dissolved and gave way to shared cultural pursuits. The example of George Forster, who accompanied Cook's second voyage and wrote a famous account of it, also stimulated him to think of *Bildung* as expanding beyond classical education and European boundaries to include a knowledge of the most diverse peoples and places.[4]

Schlegel's own scholarship dramatically expanded beyond European boundaries after 1802, the year he went to Paris in order to do research at the Bibliothèque Nationale. While learning Persian there he met a British officer and scholar returning from India (and temporarily stranded in Paris), Sir Alexander Hamilton, who could teach him Sanscrit. The outcome of his studies, published in 1808, was his famous book *On the Language and Wisdom of the Indians*. Just a few years before, Sir William Jones, the celebrated English Indologist, had briefly noted the similarities between Sanscrit and Western languages; Schlegel took up the hint and expanded it into a suggestive analysis of their structural affinities. The opening lines of the first chapter proclaim: "Ancient Indian Sanscrit . . . has the greatest affinity [*Verwandtschaft*] to Latin and Greek, as well as to German and Persian. The similarity lies not just in a large number of roots . . . but extends to the innermost structure and grammar. The correspondence is not accidental, to be explained by intermingling, but an essential one that signifies a common descent [*Abstammung*]. Comparison reveals further that the Indian language is the elder, the others younger and derived from it."[5] Schlegel thus unfurled the organizing image of the book, the family tree. Sanscrit was the trunk from which all the languages of the West had grown, the original classical language, deserving of study as a source of wisdom older and more perfect than Latin or Greek. Grammatical inflection distinguished this linguistic family from all others, according to Schlegel, and gave it superior powers of creation and organic form. Schlegel hesitated over this judgment; at times he warned his readers that other, non-Indo-European languages had their distinctive and equally valuable qualities.[6] The book invites more than one plausible reading, establishing a hierarchy of language and seeming superiority of Western language and culture, but simultaneously subverting any exclusive cultural canon by locating Western culture's origin outside itself.

Comparative philology was often used later as a means to document racial difference. Not yet in Schlegel, who separated his linguistic inquiry from, and belittled the importance of, physical descent.[7] Nor was he an ideologue of German cultural purity or political unity. Rather, by 1808 he had turned into a conservative man of letters interested in legitimating the established social order. In the historical part of his book Schlegel argued that the Brahmins were the receivers of a pure and ancient wisdom, embodied in both their language and their scriptures. He pleaded for a continuation of the lineage of learning that had come from India (by way of refugee intellectuals fleeing civil war, he conjectured—a theory that recent European experience may have made appealing).[8] German identity for Schlegel resided not in race or popular will, but ultimately in language, the spiritual medium that joined it to a larger cultural family. In this scheme of things the learned elite took on a priestly function as the guardian of language. Schlegel could feel at home with such a restoration of intellectual order as a "Brahmin" son of a Protestant pastor from a family of *Gebildete*. His youthful literary circle, tied together by romantic liaisons, perpetuated a cultural aristocracy across the incipient historical transition from society of orders to class society.

Schlegel's book contains inner paradoxes that reveal the educated elite's difficulties in maintaining hegemonic status at a moment of political and cultural turbulence. While writing the book Schlegel lost his enthusiasm for India as the fount of wisdom and just after its completion converted to Catholicism (making him one of the first nineteenth-century Protestant converts; even his reactionary impulses were avant-garde). The move was an integrative one on Schlegel's part, an attempt to restore spiritual order after the disruptions of the Revolutionary era. After his wanderings among exotic literatures it looked like a retreat to the security of Judaeo-Christian tradition. But his imminent conversion created a problem for the linguistic and cultural argument of the book: what was the place of Hebrew? The concluding chapter puzzled unsatisfactorily over the question of how the sacred language could fall outside the family he called inflected. On the one hand Schlegel treated Hebrew as an Oriental language, radically distinct from European thinking and culture; on the other hand he argued that the inhabitants of Asia and Europe should be considered members of one family.[9] Perhaps he had already solved the problem in a different way by marrying Dorothea Veit, daughter of the famous Jewish philosopher Moses Mendelssohn. Since Schlegel seems to have had serious prophetic ambitions of founding a new religion for a while, one wonders if this was a strategic alliance, unifying Indo-European and Semitic wisdom in his own household. At any rate, Schlegel's attitude toward Hebrew in 1808 (later he ranked it above the Indo-European languages) and toward Dorothea Veit were quite removed from the narrow nationalism that admirers and detractors alike have sometimes deemed Romantic and "naturally" German.

At first sight, Treitschke looks like a convenient contrast to Schlegel—and to some extent, he is. If Schlegel embodies romance with the exotic, joining India to the West and Protestant to Jew, Treitschke seems to stand for the *Bildungsbürgertum's* alliance with blood-and-iron politics after mid-century. Born in 1834, he came to prominence in the 1860s as one of a generation of liberal historians (among his allies were Theodor Mommsen, Hermann Baumgarten, Johann Gustav Droysen, and Heinrich von Sybel) who advocated unification under Prussian leadership. His uncompromising devotion to the idea of German unification earned him fame and left him at odds with many of his former compatriots. The persistence of class, confessional, and regional differences after 1871 embittered him, and he abandoned his constitutional scruples to become one of Bismarck's most uncritical admirers.

Treitschke was primarily an advocate of the state, an admirer of strong political leadership who felt ambivalent at best toward the middling and lower social orders. Yet by the end of the decade this *political* historian, who tried to teach his contemporaries to confront the constraints of statecraft, was ready to take up populist and racial definitions of German national identity. This incipient populism overlapped with another agenda that contrasts with Schlegel: his religious intolerance. To him and his fellow historians of the *kleindeutsch* school, Prussian unification signified the triumph of Protestant Prussia over Catholic Austria in the struggle for Central European hegemony. After unification he stood in the forefront of the so-called *Kulturkampf*, the "struggle for culture" which Protestant bureaucrats and publicists waged against Catholics. The will to level cultural difference was such second nature that the prophet of *Realpolitik* failed to anticipate its real effects of disgracing liberalism and degrading public discourse.[10]

An essay of November 1879, "Our Prospects," set off a memorable public controversy, the so-called "Berlin Antisemitism Controversy" (*Berliner Antisemitismusstreit*).[11] Treitschke accused Germany's Jews of financial manipulations, press sensationalism, social pushiness, and, altogether, un-Germanness. His reasoning was ambivalent. As an advocate of reason of state, and one still not altogether insensitive to liberal constitutional principles, he called for radical assimilation of Jews: "What we must demand of our Israelite fellow citizens is simple: they should become Germans, should simply and completely feel themselves to be Germans."[12] But the other side of his story was that they could never altogether do so. Assimilation could not erase the "chasm between Western and Semitic natures."[13] A significant anti-Semitic political campaign had begun earlier the same year, led by the Court Preacher, Adolf Stoecker. His essay excused its excesses as a consequence of the inevitable difference between Semites and Teutons: "The noisy agitation of the moment," he wrote, "comes as a brutal and hateful but natural reaction of Germanic folk feeling to a foreign element that is taking up all too large a space in our life."[14] Neither *Verwandtschaft* nor any comparable vocabulary of exogamy entered Treitschke's essay; it pursued a logic of separation and purity. The racial grounding of national identity had potentially revolutionary implications, for if the German nation-state had a prehistoric right to unify all "Germans," it might shatter historically established political boundaries, including those of the Bismarckian state. His Berlin colleague Theodor Mommsen pointed this out to him, warning of the dangers of questioning the citizenship of a minority and ridiculing his invention of a lineal Germanic purity. To no avail; Treitschke refused to make the slightest concession to Mommsen or any of his other critics.

A similar tension between political and ethnic categories occurs in Treitschke's *German History in the Nineteenth Century*, which had appeared earlier in 1879 and sold widely among the educated public. On the one hand it analyzed how Prussia's rational statecraft had overcome Germany's inherited historical differences. On the other hand it praised comparative philology for rediscovering the nation's hitherto lost genealogy. Introducing the brothers Grimm, he wrote: "And now Friedrich Schlegel's proud credo that the historian is a prophet turned backwards was confirmed. Suddenly the distant youth of the Indo-Germanic peoples, until then beyond the reach of investigation, was illuminated by research which shed a clarifying light on the foundations of present-day European culture."[15] Philology had freed the nineteenth century, according to Treitschke, from what he called the mad faith in natural right, individual freedom, and reason, by showing in the history of language "that the individual can only live in and with his *Volk*." He commented on Schlegel's successor, Bopp: "Now the limits of the Indo-Germanic language group could be firmly fixed. Each one of these languages could take its place nearer or farther from its older sister and thus the historical family tree of the various peoples could be determined."[16]

Equally revealing is his allergic reaction to Schlegel. He hated both the youthful author of *Lucinde* and the mature convert to Catholicism, and dismissed his book on India as a dilettante's work.[17] What a sad descent from Schlegel's to Treitschke's use of linguistic affinities: whereas Schlegel reminded readers of far-flung cultural kin, Treitschke removed Germany as far as he could from the rest of the human family; the free play of cultural partners (how Treitschke disliked the undercurrent of erotic merriment in Schlegel!) was rejected for the incestuous purity of race.

And yet one may observe a certain continuity from Schlegel to Treitschke. For all the differences between the cosmopolitan and the Prussophile nationalist, they shared a mood of the nineteenth-century *Bildungsbürgertum* which may be called the pathos of cultural grandeur. By this I mean a *bourgeois* aspiration to a *noble* condition transcending the commercial, egoistic ethos of nineteenth-century European society.[18] This paradoxical mood corresponded to the paradoxical situation of the *Bildungsbürgertum*, perched between its privileged status in the society of orders and its class interests in capitalist society. Treitschke came from a bourgeois family, with successful businessmen and artists among his forebears; his father was a socially mobile army officer who was ennobled by the Saxon king and married into an old noble family. The young Treitschke admired the energy and the economic achievements that could only come from the bourgeoisie, and he furthered its dream of national unity with religious fervor; but he accused it of being too cautious and too bound by self-interest ever to overturn the rule of kings and create a new order in German politics. For that task he looked to the Prussian nobility.

Within his vocation, too, Treitschke embodied class ambiguity. To be a university professor was to exercise a bourgeois calling; but he interpreted it in an aristocratic spirit, regarding himself as one of the privileged few with the gift of political vision and the right to educate the nation. Torn in his early years between his talent for scholarship and that for literature, he remained distant from the mere fact-mongers of the historical profession and wrote to recreate the pageant of German history. A sense of cultural mission, secular in its end but religious in origins and fervor, inspired him no less than Schlegel. Both dreamed of a nobler Germany than anything that could or did materialize; and they oscillated between bourgeois and aristocratic values, sometimes defending the new class of the nineteenth century, sometimes seeking to infuse it with a heroism worthy of the new nation in the making. Memories of German Protestant destiny looking back to the Reformation, a lingering *esprit de corps* inherited from the society of orders, a network of family traditions and intermarriages, education in elite secondary schools and universities, and an ethos of state service: all persisted in the nineteenth century and nurtured both thinkers' sense of prophetic calling. Treitschke gave belligerent expression to it, leading the Protestant *Bildungsbürgertum*'s drive to cultural hegemony in the German Empire by fabricating an inbred national identity against supposed internal aliens and external enemies.

Max Weber was born in 1864, the same year in which Prussia won its first war of national expansion. Like Schlegel and Treitschke, he came from the upper reaches of the educated elite, with ties through his maternal grandmother to a distinguished Huguenot family. Even though the young Weber never wrote poetry as did Schlegel and Treitschke, he shared a pathos of cultural grandeur. His, however, was self-consciously bourgeois. He was eager to tear down aristocratic power and prestige in German society and strained—for himself, for the public life of his time—toward a heroic ethos distinct from Anglo-American utilitarianism and from the kind of petit bourgeois existence ridiculed by Wilhelm Busch. The German culture Weber had in mind was virtually synonymous with the culture of the Protestant *Bildungsbürgertum*. Not that he put it that way explicitly; it was simply his working assumption against the pretensions of other confessions and classes. Like Treitschke, to whom he had a highly ambivalent relationship, he acted as guardian of the educated elite's class interests and tried to school it in political realism.[19] And he had a new fear, the successor generation's worry that it could not equal the achievements of the founding fathers who had unified the Empire. The educated—university students in particular— might grow soft, lose their fighting edge, and choose a life of comfort in a greater Switzerland; against this temptation he summoned them to the harsh historical calling of defending German interests and prestige. But here the affinity to Treitschke ended. Weber moved from a rather involuted involvement with family and Protestant *Gebildete* to ever-widening reaches of friendship and scholarship. On his visit to North America he absorbed impressions of the new continent with great gusto and came back an admirer of Yankee voluntarism. At home he attracted to his acerbic scholarly asceticism such antipodes as the mystical, later revolutionary Georg Lukács, and the poet-aesthete-cult leader Stefan George. A genuine liberality, a delight in diversity even while holding to his own convictions with intemperate insistence, distinguished him from Treitschke.

Weber's relationship to German national identity was a typical mixture of engagement and icy distance. The irrepressible imperialist did not isolate it as Treitschke did, but situated it in a constellation of cultural types. Consider the first important work of his mature years, *The Protestant Ethic and the Spirit of Capitalism*. The original essay of 1904–5 included a concerted comparison between Lutheranism and other Christian confessions, and the revised version of 1920 added observations on many of the other literate religions of the world as well. How did Weber determine Germany's cultural affinities? In the first edition the vocabulary was already one of kinship: think for example of the famous image of the *Wahlverwandtschaft*, or elective affinity, between capitalism and decaying Calvinism. Weber's use of the concept "elective affinity" denoted the relationship between two historically independent institutions, one economic and one cultural, which converged in a fateful and irreversible union, forming the iron cage of modern capitalism and its culture of goal-oriented activity.

But there was more going on, too, in Weber's many-layered text; his discussion of affinities redrew lines within the Western family tree. He used notions of *Verwandtschaft* to disrupt historical genealogies, fracturing the spiritual and chronological lines of descent from Catholicism to Lutheranism to Calvinism.[20] Catholicism figured as a repository of superstition and magic, inculcating only a low grade of innerworldly rational activity compared to Protestantism (writing in confessionally divided Baden, Weber was not about to miss a chance to continue the *Kulturkampf* by other means). Lutheranism figured as a more interesting case of *superficial* resemblance to Calvinism and other forms of ascetic Protestantism. In an ingenious piece of philological detective work, Weber traced the modern concept of "calling" to Luther but argued that Lutheranism's concept of calling remained traditional and inimical to capitalism. Despite their historical proximity, Lutheranism and Calvinism turned out almost to be foreign to one another. Their common origins indicated little about their cultural affinities.

As for Judaism, that problematic affine for Schlegel and outcast extreme for Treitschke—the first edition of *The Protestant Ethic* played down its affinity to Calvinism; while admitting some resemblance, it concluded that Judaism was a variety of "Oriental traditionalism" in contrast to Calvinist asceticism. By the time of his revisions for the second edition, however, Weber had made a closer examination of ancient Judaism and viewed the prophetic tradition as the first great manifestation of the morality that created an instrumental work ethic. Though still emphasizing the ultimate limitations on Jewish asceticism compared to Calvinist, he also now discovered their inner affinity. Historically disparate, they were cultural cousins, nearer in spirit than Calvinism and its Christian fellows.[21]

This affinity stands out even more clearly if we turn to the contrasting case of Lutheranism. Weber writes in his conclusion: "For Luther, as we saw, the integration of human beings into the given estates and callings (which followed from the objective historical order) flowed directly from God's will, and thus the *perseverence* of the individual in the position and the limits God had allotted him became religious duty." The footnote to this passage compared Lutheran practice to Hinduism, the extreme example of occupational traditionalism linked to salvation, and contrasted Hinduism with Judaism and Puritanism.[22] The affinities game had gotten very odd indeed: the Jewish Semites, whom Treitschke demoted to the status of Orientals, turned out to be the first instance of Western rationality and anticipated its mature Calvinist form, while German Protestants, formerly the vanguard of the modern West, had some affinity to the passive and mystical East! Once again the boundaries of German identity were redrawn, as had occurred throughout the nineteenth century.

National identity is a human construction. Germany today has repudiated the grandiose mentality of the years before 1945, and despite the anxiety of some Western European and American observers, there has been no revival of German imperial ambitions since the fall of the Wall.[23] Educated Germans in particular strive anxiously to be good Europeans and resist any policy that might lead to a revival of militarism. As for Germany's political leaders, they have turned into stalwart guardians of European stability and have no intention of retreating from the role that has brought them political possession of former East Germany and continental economic hegemony. The heartfelt contemporary German abhorrence of war suggests the transience of so-called national character traits. But though a construction, national identity is not a fiction. Shared language, collective memories, economic interests, and shared political experiences are among the *faits socials* that permitted the speedy merging of the former East German state with the West. The very fact of common language alone promises to ease the initially painful process of economic and cultural integration.

The enlarged German state inherits burdens as well as boons from the common past. The myth of affinity persists: Germany continues to view itself as a homogeneous, ethnic nation defined by common descent. This inherited definition contradicts the contemporary reality of a country peopled by "Ossies" and "Wessies" from the two sides of the Cold War, repatriated ethnic Germans from Eastern Europe, guest workers' children born and raised in Germany, Western Europeans who cross state borders to marry and work there, and economic and political refugees from Africa and Asia. Will Germany's educated elite rethink the national identity to make room for newcomers? In a country where thinkers and poets still enjoy great prestige, where political founders are scarce but cultural glories abundant, can intellectuals redefine national identity to embrace a diversity of citizens within German boundaries? Their passage to a contemporary cosmopolitanism will be one condition of peace in the newly united Germany.

The Moral Journey of the First
Viennese Psychoanalysts

I

The first organization for the study of psychoanalysis and diffusion of Sigmund Freud's ideas emerged from a small group of followers who in 1902 began to meet with Freud once a week at his home. In 1908 this group adopted the name, Vienna Psychoanalytic Society. The society met continuously until the *Anschluss*, even during the years of World War One, refusing to relinquish its commitment to what by 1914 was an international movement. Its members always remained conscious of themselves as a vanguard, not only within the psychoanalytic world, but within European intellectual life.

Viennese psychoanalysts frequently looked back to thinkers who they believed had helped prepare their way. Of particular interest was Friedrich Nietzsche. Members of the Vienna Society found remarkable similarities between Nietzsche's psychological theories and those of Freud. On April 1, 1908, during the society's first meeting devoted to Nietzsche's life and thought, Paul Federn commented that "Nietzsche has come so close to our views that we can ask only, 'Where has he not come close?'" Federn pointed out that the philosopher had grasped "the significance of abreaction, of repression, of flight into illness, of the instincts—the normal sexual ones as well as the sadistic instincts."[1] At the second meeting on Nietzsche, however, Freud drew attention to a distinction between his own work and that of the philosopher. "And thus he begins with great perspicacity—in endopsychic perception, as it were—to recognize strata of his self. He makes a number of brilliant discoveries in himself. But now illness takes hold. Nietzsche is not satisfied with correctly fathoming these connections, but projects the insight gained about himself outward as a general imperative [*Lebensforderung*]. To his psychological insight is added the teaching, the pastoral element that derives from his Christ ideal. . . . The degree of introspection achieved by Nietzsche had never been achieved by anyone, nor is it likely ever to be reached again. What disturbs us is that Nietzsche transformed 'is' into 'ought,' which is alien to science. In this he has remained, after all, the moralist; he could not free himself of the theologian."[2]

To free oneself of the moralist—the step which Nietzsche could not achieve, Freud demanded of his own followers. He chose his words carefully. He knew that the core of his recruits had joined the movement out of a sense of moral outrage with the world. He expected, even counted on, this alienation, righteous anger, and earnest sense of calling. Freud set himself the task of molding his moralists into psychoanalysts. In accomplishing this task, he opened a new phase in the history of Viennese psychoanalysis. Moralists-turned-psychologists would play an indispensable role in organizing and defending Vienna's Freudian movement.

This essay will identify the coordinates of the moral journey completed by these disciples. Like their spiritual ally, the critic Karl Kraus, the moral *enragés* within Freud's early circle had perceived within Viennese society a crisis of responsibility, what the writer Hermann Broch would describe in his study of Vienna on the eve of World War One as a "value vacuum."[3] In response, they, like Kraus, had sought to destroy intellectual illusions which masked the extent and depth of the crisis. Authentic heirs of the Enlightenment, they firmly believed that ethical responsibility must follow from intellectual clarity. The demand for clarity, however, also fostered the search for scientific truths. Thus, the origins of the Freudian movement in Vienna lay in the contribution of moral estrangement and anger to the demand for scientific understanding.

The anger of future psychoanalysts can be traced to the impact on them of political and social changes in late nineteenth-century Austria. The Austrian Constitution of 1867 had provided support and protection to the middle class, especially the Jewish middle class, and furthered the Liberal agenda for political and cultural reform. Constitutional guarantees of individual rights, together with steps toward greater secularization of education and the appointment of a Liberal ministry, held the promise of conditions for complete freedom of conscience, an opportunity of unusual significance in clerical and aristocratic Austria. Forces of reaction, however, suppressed that promise, and in the aftermath members of the middle class quietly abandoned faith in it. Instead, they pursued cultural assimilation with the Catholic aristocracy.

Toward the turn of the century there came into being a group of university students and young Viennese writers for whom the preservation of moral responsibility in a hostile world now seemed especially urgent. Victims not only of political reaction, but of moral betrayal, these righteous individuals found themselves not only under siege, but spiritually alone. This sense of urgency and alienation led the young philosopher Otto Weininger inward to a stringent analysis of the nature of individual ethical obligation. Others pressed outward, along the path followed by Karl Kraus. In Kraus's journal, *Die Fackel*, bourgeois *enragés* attacked corruption throughout society. The core of Freud's recruits belonged to this Viennese intellectual cohort. Moral outrage at the world provided them with a dissenting consciousness and sense of mission. It did not, however, give them a critical method or positive commitment. The psychoanalytic movement channeled their personal sense of calling into a professional vocation, and their moral rage into intellectual radicalism. At the furthest reaches of moral criticism, their explorations and questioning led to Freud's circle, and the science of psychoanalysis.

Who formed the psychoanalytic vanguard in Vienna? In the years before World War One the Vienna Society had a fluid structure and shifting base of membership. It drew on lay and medical professions and incorporated diverse cultural and clinical interests. Furthermore, a greater number of members occupied the fringes of the organization than toiled at its center.[4] The society did not represent an official school with a consistent number of instructors and students until after the war. Yet, a small number of active members emerged as an intellectual and professional vanguard of Viennese psychoanalysis. These members fulfilled essential functions as advocates of a new intellectual movement, either by their attendance at meetings from the days of the informal gatherings at Freud's home, publication of psychoanalytic articles, or application of Freudian theory and method in their own occupations as doctors or writers.[5] From the pre-psychoanalytic writings of this inner circle the world-view of the moral critics emerged strongly. It could be found in a physician, such as Eduard Hitschmann, or a layman, such as Theodor Reik; in a critic, such as Max Graf, or a publicist, such as Fritz Wittels. Most importantly, it could be seen in Otto Rank and Hanns Sachs, who in 1913 founded *Imago: Journal for the Application of Psychoanalysis to the Cultural Sciences*. This essay will explore the vanguard's moral reaction to the world of late nineteenth-century Vienna, concentrating on the attitudes of those members who continued to defend the cause beyond the schism with Alfred Adler.[6] As we shall see, those who would become Freudian activists turned from the examination of conscience to the scientific exploration of the psyche, and so finally to the meetings of the Vienna Psychoanalytic Society.

II

With the insurrections of 1848, Austrian Liberals launched a battle for political change within both the Habsburg monarchy and the city of Vienna. After nearly twenty years of political bargaining and disastrous Habsburg military adventures, the Constitution of 1867 finally created a Liberal ministry, expanded the powers of Parliament, and formally recognized equality before the law and freedom of conscience. The Liberal party, however, retained its share of power through a narrow franchise and debilitating concessions to the aristocracy and imperial officials. The year 1879 saw its permanent defeat in national politics and, with the conservative ministry of Count Taafe, a successful reaction against its reforms. In the city of Vienna, the party managed to hang on to the reins of power until 1897, when Karl Lueger, at the head of the populist and anti-Semitic Christian Social movement, ousted it from office.

Throughout this period, elites of the liberal middle classes and intelligentsia sought political and cultural partnership with the aristocracy. They hoped that humanist instruction and self-cultivation—*Bildung*—would create a unified educated class both to lead a reformed state and to nourish cultural life. As Carl Schorske has explained, with the defeat of political reform, the middle class fostered with ever greater energy the pursuit of cultural integration. Consequently, appropriation of the traditional aesthetic culture of the Catholic aristocracy became the most vital component of assimilation. To cement their alliance with the lower nobility and imperial administrators, Viennese industrialists, bankers, lawyers, and professors promoted this aesthetic culture through instruction and patronage in the fine arts, theater, and music. An "amoral *Gefühlskultur*" united these social strata within Vienna's "Second Society." As Schorske wrote, "Elsewhere in Europe, art for art's sake implied the withdrawal of its devotees from a social class; in Vienna alone it claimed the allegiance of virtually a whole class, of which the artists were a part."[7] Throughout the middle classes and intelligentsia the ideology of "art for art's sake" served as an ideology of assimilation.

In their background and education, the Viennese psychoanalysts received fully the liberal inheritance, and its dilemmas. The occupations of their fathers offered a cross section of the economic and professional groups providing the chief support of Austrian liberalism.[8] More than half of these occupations belonged to the liberal professions or civil service. Friedrich von Winterstein fit the model of Vienna's "Second Society" in wealth and prestige. A privy councillor and vice-governor of the Austro-Hungarian Bank, he handed down the title of *Freiherr* to his son Alfred. Hanns Sachs's father and uncles became successful lawyers, and expected Sachs to continue in their vocation.[9] The physician Salomon Federn counted patients among the "Second Society," but found his friends and associates among reformist, middle-class supporters of Social Democracy. The elder Federn provided a link with the revolutionary tradition of 1848, for he fought at the side of fellow medical students in the streets of Vienna.[10] Eduard Hitschmann's grandfather was a physician, his father an accountant, one of his brothers a bank director, and another brother a lawyer.[11] Marcellin Reitler held a directorship in the *Nordwestbahn*; Max Reik, Theodor Reik's father, supported a large household as a railway inspector.[12] Otto Rank recorded the occupation of his father, Simon Rosenfeld, as civil servant.[13] Hermann Tausk, a firm believer in the Habsburg monarchy as the guardian of a liberal empire, accepted a post in the government press office in Sarajevo after working both as a schoolteacher and as editor of his own literary journal.[14] The psychoanalysts' fathers covered the spectrum of liberal vocations and state service.

With the exception of Rank's household, each family provided its son with the education of a classical *Gymnasium*.[15] The parents ensured that their sons received educations in practical professions, but also provided them with opportunities to acquire the aesthetic culture so highly prized by the Austrian bourgeoisie. They expected that art would give way to law or science at the university, but their sons refused to relinquish their creative aspirations. At the time he started his career in general practice, Wilhelm Stekel also began work on a novel.[16] Soon after graduating from Vienna's school of law, Victor Tausk and Alfred von Winterstein attempted careers as writers. Another law graduate, Hanns Sachs, published a translation of Rudyard Kipling's poetry. Upon leaving the university, Max Graf and David Bach immediately took up their vocations as music critics. These psychoanalysts knew well the world of literary ambition and devotion gripping the younger generation of Viennese liberals.

All but two of the psychoanalysts under discussion were Jewish.[17] In nineteenth-century Vienna, the German-speaking, Western Jews of the Habsburg lands trusted that constitutional reform would secure equality before the law, careers open to talent, and freedom of conscience and education. The political program of the Liberal party conformed to their intellectual and social aims: in Hanns Sachs's words, "full assimilation without apostasy."[18] Some of the psychoanalysts' families could point to significant successes. During the first round of liberalization following suppression of the rebellion of 1848, Salomon Federn became one of the first Jewish general practitioners in Vienna.[19] In the final decades before World War One, however, the triumphs of Lueger and the Christian Socials exerted ever greater pressure on middle-class Jews to seek cultural assimilation and religious conversion. The Jewish bourgeoisie experienced viscerally the historical conflict in Viennese liberalism between the ideology of gradual progress through political and educational reform, and the drive toward cultural and religious integration with the aristocracy.

Although themselves apostates from tradition, the future psychoanalysts stood against full religious assimilation.[20] Nor did they share in much of the striving after cultural integration with the upper orders. Their families had preserved a commitment to liberalism's reformist tradition and a faith in Jewish upward mobility through education and professional advancement. As the turn of the century approached, however, the sons nurtured few hopes for the realization of these expectations. Amidst middle-class desertion and defeat, personal moral commitment seemed to them essential as a last defense against the assimilationist options. Without an institutional mooring for the liberal cause and faced with the expanding tendency to assimilation, they hammered out a highly individualistic and moralistic response. The disappointment of a young, liberal intelligentsia grew finally into a profound sense of moral alienation.

III

In their social position, professional and cultural education, and religious training, Freud's future disciples maintained the legacy of Austrian liberalism. Radical moral dissent, however, drove a deep wedge between them and that tradition. This break with the past initiated the journey which would bring them to the psychoanalytic movement. The moral discontent of their youth not only expressed itself in their writing at the time, but left its imprint in their later memoirs. In both types of writing, psychoanalysts concerned themselves chiefly with the values of the Viennese bourgeoisie in a time of reaction, sharply emphasizing that the drive to integrate with the aristocracy corrupted their social class.

The origins of the striving toward assimilation, Max Graf wrote, could be traced to the rise of a "new society of finance nobility, industrial and business *arrivés*, and their allies, the old aristocracy: a society with riches, cosmopolitan attitude, love of pleasure, and like every upwardly mobile caste, energy for making newly gained ground its property."[21] It masked its humble origins in the "monstrosity of the Roman, Greek, Gothic and Renaissance building decoration" along the Ring.[22] Bourgeois elites adopted the behavior of the aristocracy and aspired to its privileges and honors: "The new industrial and Stock Exchange men, streaming with wealth, crowded themselves into the court society to receive orders and titles from the Emperor. When they gave parties in their new houses, they invited aristocrats as window dressing. The young sons of Viennese manufacturers dressed themselves like aristocrats and aped their accent and manner."[23] To solidify their inward identification with the aristocracy, "new plutocrats" joined with the old nobility in building and patronizing the Viennese palaces of art.[24]

In his memoirs, Hanns Sachs recalled with bitterness how the nobility, like a silent, corrosive force, emptied the parliamentary process and the rule of law of meaning: "Austria was a constitutional monarchy with all the usual trappings: a charter of liberties, two houses of parliament, responsible ministers, independent law courts, the usual machinery of government. Yet, it was an open secret that none of all these institutions possessed a scrap of real power, not even the bureaucracy. This power was in the hands of the Austrian 'eighty families'. . . . Closely knit together as they were, yet without any trace of organization or leadership, this amorphous, anonymous, irresponsible power could only work in one way: to inhibit any innovation, to exclude all new forces from cooperation."[25] Those in power, and those who wanted power, kept constitutional forms and the ideal of law as covers for favoritism, patronage, and political extortion: "Political parties and elections, heated parliamentary debates, the voting of laws and the creation of public offices to execute them, all this went on just as in a grade A democracy. But all this was a false front made for outsiders and those afflicted with congenital blindness. To get anywhere it was necessary to have backing from 'above' either directly or, if that was not possible, through one of the henchmen to whom the ruling class had delegated the execution of power. Without that no move, however strictly within the bounds of the constitution, could prosper; with it any law could be infringed or somehow circumvented."[26] In the process of carrying out its strategy of assimilation, the middle class sacrificed its cultural identity and ethical responsibility: "The style of life of the privileged class became, as a matter of course, the pattern after which the middle class tried to model its conduct, imitating it down to the slightest mannerisms. (The rich Jews, after they had surmounted the religious barrier, were easily in the forefront.) The result oscillated between simple and downright snobbism, and high, exalted aestheticism; one variant of this attitude, called *fin de siècle*, boasted that it preferred 'beauty'—but beauty in inverted commas—to morals, and proudly called itself 'decadent'."[27]

No psychoanalyst had felt a greater sense of rage against this moral de-
featism than Fritz Wittels. In 1904, the year of his graduation from Vienna's
school of medicine, Wittels published his first polemic, *The Baptized Jew*.
For the young pamphleteer, religious conversion embodied the crisis con-
suming liberalism. Virtually every baptism, Wittels wrote, had at bottom
the overriding motive of "social ambition" [*Strebertum*].[28] The docent desired to become a professor, the lawyer set his sights on a judgeship or ministerial post, and the parvenu ached to attend the hunts and feasts of the
high nobility. The Constitution of 1867, Wittels reminded the reader, guaranteed equality before the law, established freedom of religion, and declared
public offices open to every citizen. Yet Jews had often been excluded from
positions in the ministry, the bureaucracy, the judiciary, the officer corps,
and the university; had regularly found their promotions blocked in these
institutions; and faced continuing exclusion from local administrations and
private enterprises.[29] Too many Jews made peace with the new politics and
society. In Parliament, in local assemblies and in the press, they relinquished
the "battle for *Recht*."[30]

In Wittels's world-view, the most severe consequence of the drive toward
assimilation consisted in the crime against oneself. Official baptism marked
the last victory over conscience: "Just as one can commit an injustice because he tolerates it, so the state has become far less of a guilty party than
those Jews who allowed it all to take place, and so sacrifice their personality."[31] To the young Wittels, the most disturbing aspect of assimilation
within the Jewish middle class lay in the act of self-betrayal. This breach of
faith governed Wittels's view of society. Social life depended on a moral
covenant: "Each individual citizen has the right to demand that his trust,
his belief in honesty, not be injured, at least not through a falsely *solemn*
assertion, and therefore the perjury through which an individual man is
deceived is as culpable as the one through which generations are over-
thrown."[32] Disappointment, mistrust, and "disharmony with society" now
dominated the consciousness of Western Jewish youth. Within their spiritual life, absolute negation continuously undermined the impulse toward
moral affirmation: "It [Western Jewish consciousness] is, on one side, the
method of analytical reason, the spirit of relentless criticism, undermining
everything, a Mephistophelian orgy of the destruction of all that which has
become obsolete, worn out, traditional: 'for all things from the void called
forth deserve to be destroyed.' On the other side, it throws itself with blind
passion on everything new, seizes it, works it through, spreads it over the
globe, for since he [the young, Western Jew] has destroyed the old, he must
seek happiness and satisfaction in what is still unexplored, what is hardly

understood, until such time that, furiously disappointed, with his harlequin's sword he plays catch with the stars that a short while ago he himself fastened onto the heavens."[33] In Wittels, blank rage and the longing for virtue combined to produce a sense of desperation and estrangement. Feeling betrayed by his class and his co-religionists, he committed his judgements to print as a warning to individual conscience and a public indictment for the day of reckoning.

Wittels expressed most ardently and darkly the disillusionment and embitterment shared by the moral *enragés* among Freud's eventual recruits. Their trust betrayed, these future disciples viewed Viennese society and politics as an elaborate game of mirrors. Glittering words and polished moral surfaces endlessly reflected and distorted each other. Disoriented and perplexed, they searched for a core of integrity and authenticity in the world around them. Although aware of the social purposes and political strategies of the ruling class and their assimilationist, middle-class allies, they initially identified individual ethical obligation as the antidote to the system of corruption. Their moral disappointment and anger marked the first important turn from the path laid down for them by the liberal tradition.

IV

Psychoanalysts did not find themselves alone in their puritanical intensity. In equal measure and for similar reasons, Otto Weininger and Karl Kraus were fired with righteous indignation. Yet, despite their common anger at the political destruction of their moral hopes and their fury at the turpitude of the middle class, these moral *enragés* did not steer in the same direction. Weininger turned inward for solace and reflection, while Kraus and allies on *Die Fackel* pushed outward for the activity of the public arena. The reactions of future psychoanalysts also divided between inwardness and engagement. Freudians, however, later differentiated themselves from both Weininger and Kraus by leaving the moral forum for the fields of science.

Throughout his university education, Otto Weininger lived in intellectual self-exile. Emerging at the age of 21 from extremes of withdrawal and estrangement, he claimed to have found the key to the ego's salvation from moral corruption. At the same time, he also claimed to have discovered the path from moral philosophy to scientific psychology, and thus became for future psychoanalysts a figure with which to reckon.

Within Viennese intellectual circles, Weininger incarnated the penitent who, in isolation from society and its corrupting influences, hoped to guarantee his own salvation. In his Manichaean vision, the forces of morality and antimorality warred continually for mastery of the soul. His book *Sex and Character*, published in 1903, defined these contending forces in sexual terms. Men embodied the principles of character, self-knowledge, and moral independence. The principle of sexuality governed women, rendering them incapable of intellectual consciousness and moral pride. Weininger arrived at this conclusion having first established his "psychology of individual differences," founded on an analysis of the balance between male and female psychic forces within the individual.[34] In the chapter "Talent and Memory," he explained that this new science of characterology, or "theoretical biography," would "deal with the investigation of the permanent laws that rule the mental development of an individual. . . . The new knowledge will seek general points of view and the establishment of types."[35]

The central concern of characterology, however, became not the "psychology of individual differences," or developmental laws, which Weininger thought solved in any case, but the study of character as "the ruling force of the Ego."[36] The ego, Weininger wrote in "Talent and Memory," had to be understood as the "will to value." To express this will, the artist or philosopher chose to live apart from the world, lay aside anger, and "acquiesce in his loneliness."[37] The chapter "Talent and Genius" explained that the genius could endure such isolation because his personality contained the complete range of human psychological types.

Weininger's own thought showed no such complexity, but degenerated into Manichaeanism and misogyny. His moral independence became a denial of life, and his intellectual iconoclasm yielded to pious introspection. In woman, who, dominated by the principle of sexuality, lived without moral consciousness, he found a destructive force against which to do battle. According to Weininger, the Jews, his former co-religionists, also lacked moral enlightenment, with the exception that they retained the possibility of self-renunciation and a return to the ascetic ideal. "The birth of the Kantian ethics, the noblest event in the history of the world," he exalted, "was the moment when for the first time the dazzling awful conception came to him, 'I am responsible only to myself; I must follow none other; I must not forget myself even in my work; I am alone; I am free; I am lord of myself.'"[38] Weininger held in contempt those for whom "the earth can only mean the turmoil and press of those on it."[39] The torment barely concealed in his ideal ended in suicide.

On February 24, 1904, two years before joining Freud's Wednesday meetings, Otto Rank wrote in his diary, "I am now reading Otto Weininger,

Sex and Character. What happened to me while reading the sections 'Talent and Genius' and 'Talent and Memory' stands forth uniquely as an event in my reading of literature. Everything which is expressed as special in these two chapters, I myself had already experienced earlier in me, and at many points I thought Weininger could have added there still one thing or another that belongs within the domain of this complex of thoughts. And hardly had I thought that and formulated the supplement, when indeed I came upon it also in the book; it stood there almost in my own words."[40] What most appealed to Rank in Weininger's philosophy was the modern conception of an invisible moral elect, and the possibility of confirming one's membership in this new moral vanguard through introspection.

Rank grew up within a struggling lower-middle-class, Jewish family in Leopoldstadt. His father, suffering from alcoholism, frequently became violent towards his wife and two sons. Rank's older brother attended *Gymnasium* and eventually studied law. When Rank finished his early schooling, however, his father started him on a program of technical instruction, which concluded with three years in the machine section of an advanced technical school.[41]

Rank's journals, kept after 1903 while he worked as an apprentice and finally a clerk in a machine factory, expressed despondency and confusion. He began several literary endeavors in 1903 and 1904: a notebook of poems, one act of a play, and a short story. Echoing Weininger, Rank described the artist as the embodiment of the ideal of intellectual and moral self-reliance: "Highly gifted spirits are always fine observers of mankind, deep psychologists, because they concentrate in themselves the whole concept of humanity; they have the tendencies of all possibilities of mankind in themselves and can develop them in ideas."[42] In the realm of philosophy, Weininger's "will to value" had succeeded Schopenhauer's "will to life" and Nietzsche's "will to power."[43] It provided a sense of consolation, as well as independence: "Kant's ethic: There are only duties toward oneself. I have only to answer for me to myself. I stand *alone*, am *free*, am my own *master*. Weininger."[44] Like Weininger, Rank welcomed isolation from society as the condition of moral freedom.

Gradually, Rank drifted from Weininger's program. Under the influence of Freud's work, he slowly relinquished his goal of spiritual transcendence, endeavoring instead to fathom the inner world of psychic conflict. After his family physician, Alfred Adler, introduced him to *The Interpretation of Dreams*, Rank abandoned his moral investigations of genius. His journals turned into drafts of a book on the libidinal sources of creativity, published

finally as *The Artist* in 1907. According to Rank, the human conflict between unsatisfied libido and the forces of resistance raged most intensely
within artists, who, in the creative process, never ceased renewing their
efforts to allay in themselves the feeling of want.

Wilhelm Stekel employed a similar conception of psychic struggle to
explain Otto Weininger's life and work. Weininger's inner battles, however,
led not to temporary repose, but frenzied disequilibrium. His rage against
sexuality and women, Stekel wrote, finally resulted in a "pathological illusion of grandeur."[45] Meanwhile, another physician, Eduard Hitschmann,
sought to separate the psychological wheat from the moral chaff in Weininger's philosophy. In Hitschmann's view, Weininger's psychological method
needed to be preserved from the philosopher's all-consuming redemptive
mission. In his review of P. J. Möbius's pathography of Arthur Schopenhauer, Hitschmann stated that Otto Weininger's characterology, in contrast
to psychopathography, constituted "a genuine and practical psychology,"
doing justice both to the personality of the individual and the demands of
science: "psychology set out to become theoretical biography, whose task
consisted in the research of constant laws of the mental development of the
individual [*Individuum*], in the determination of types."[46] What caused the
collapse of this scientific project? Schopenhauer's division of the world into
will and idea provided the key: "Hypersexuality with idealistic struggle, powerful instinctual drive at war with asceticism, longing for mental peace,
clarity and intensive, undisturbed capacity for work, gradually led to the
accumulation in him of hatred and contempt for—the essential female."[47]
Schopenhauer's own life and work became dominated by the same striving
after redemption, the same struggle to transform sensual urges into spiritual
powers, the psychological phenomenon "characteristic in this 'Schopenhauer type.'"[48]

Viennese psychoanalysts differentiated their work from the endeavors of
thinkers, past and present, who searched the psyche for a road to salvation.
Psychologists, such as Weininger, who presumed to offer a route to personal
redemption opened dangerous moral paths. For Freud's disciples, to explore
and make intelligible, not transcend, inner conflict defined the true vocation of psychology.

V

Although notoriety came quickly and overwhelmingly to Weininger, he
never purposefully sought access to the public stage. Led by Karl Kraus,

however, others from the camp of moral critics sought assiduously to expose to scrutiny the veins of corruption buried throughout society. If psychoanalysts defined themselves in opposition to seekers after redemption, such as Weininger, many of them saw in Kraus a potential brother-in-arms. Among Freud's most loyal adherents were those who had taken their moral criticism and intensity into a campaign against the corruption of culture. Like Kraus, they extended their offensive to an attack on the prevailing sexual ethic, and its social and psychological consequences. In this fight, one of their number, Fritz Wittels, formally joined forces with *Die Fackel*. Not only Wittels, but Sachs, Reik, and Graf started on the road to psychoanalysis, to use Wittels's description of his mentor Kraus, as "anticorruptionists." Although they soon parted ways with Kraus, they traveled furthest with him in the years before they joined the movement.

As a satirist and polemicist, Karl Kraus concentrated and channeled the moral fury of Viennese youth, giving it method and identifying its targets. His satire did not rely on exaggeration or invention to expose its objects. Rather, he used his opponents' own words against them. In the cold light of Kraus's essays the true intentions behind distended and contorted expressions of venal writers, politicians, and propagandists stood revealed. Throughout his lifetime Kraus tirelessly purged Viennese prose so as to restore words to their authentic meanings. As on the printed page, so too in drama and the arts. Kraus became the leader of what have been called the "last puritans," those critics "who rejected the use of art as a cultural cosmetic to screen the nature of reality."[49] A zealous muckraker and austere guardian of the word, Kraus sought above all else to preserve the sanctity and immediacy of language. His bitterness reflected disappointment and estrangement far less than it expressed complete absorption in the fight. Walter Benjamin summarized in but a few words the origins of Kraus's method: "Here we find confirmation that all the martial energies of this man are innate civic virtues; only in the *mêlée* did they take on their combative aspect. But already no one recognizes them any more; no one can grasp the necessity that compelled this great bourgeois character to become a comedian, this guardian of Goethean linguistic values a polemicist, or why this irreproachably honorable man went berserk. This, however, was bound to happen, since he thought fit to begin changing the world with his own class, in his own home, Vienna. And when, recognizing the futility of his enterprise, he abruptly broke it off, he placed the matter back in the hands of nature—this time destructive, not creative nature."[50]

Kraus began his own moral odyssey with a condemnation of the withdrawal and introversion of the new bourgeois aesthetic culture. Kraus's first pamphlet, *Literature Demolished*, attacked the Viennese literary representatives of "art for art's sake"—Hugo von Hofmannsthal, the young Arthur Schnitzler, and the artists, critics, and hangers-on of *Jung Wien*—for their moral detachment and psychological resignation. Their work, Kraus maintained, exalted the virtue of personality without understanding its ethical significance. Nor did it comprehend the individual's confrontation with the world. Naturalism had no influence among them: "'Secret nerves' the phrase now went; one set about observing 'mental states,' and wanted to flee the ordinary clarity of things."[51] Kraus's wrath focussed on the "shallow impressionism" of their spokesman, Hermann Bahr, whose critical judgements contained "vague potshots" without "purposeful aggression."[52]

With an aim not unlike Kraus's, Hanns Sachs published a translation of Rudyard Kipling's barrack-room ballads to make available poetry which "refused to bow to the principle of 'art for art's sake.'"[53] From Kipling's work one learned that the foundation of the British empire came from criminals, youths dissatisfied with "cramped bourgeois life," and the poor, all outcasts who served the government, but were in turn abused by it. In the barrack-room ballads, according to Sachs, "artistic form is only the expression of a striving for the factual."[54]

Similarly, Theodor Reik's first publication, a study of his Viennese contemporary, the writer Richard Beer-Hofmann, warned against the introversion and amorality of Vienna's "culture of aesthetes." In subject matter, Beer-Hofmann's first stories centered on reflections and memories of the "favorite of the salon," "men of the world" without commitments or attachments. Like Arthur Schnitzler's Anatol, Beer-Hofmann's hero remained the "cool observer of his own ego" and "refined dissector of his own moods." In that early stage of his literary career, Beer-Hofmann "ran the risk that his fertile, but chaste inwardness would evaporate into the elegant, tasteful, 'merely beautiful;' that he would see art as a refuge for persons unsuited for the confusing rush of life, as a place of asylum for psychological drifters."[55]

From similar moral starting points the paths of Kraus and the psychoanalysts ultimately diverged sharply. Thus, Theodor Reik concluded that Beer-Hofmann had rescued himself by turning to psychology. Works such as *Miriams Schlaflied* depicted the survival through the generations of Jewish spiritual identity. In this way, Beer-Hofmann's introspection finally led to recognition of the silent bonds between individuals and generations. His inwardness thus produced "insight into the lawfulness [*Gesetzlichkeit*] of our life, the physical and spiritual."[56]

Hanns Sachs' own "striving for the factual," his endeavor to see the psyche as one would, in Kraus's words, see the "ordinary clarity of things," ultimately led him away from the work of moral criticism. Literature guided Sachs in an unforeseen direction, ending at Freud's evening lectures at the University of Vienna. "The connecting link," he wrote, "was formed by my boundless admiration for Dostoevsky. I wanted to find, led by the hand of science, the secrets of the soul in their nakedness; I hoped to tread in broad daylight the obscure and labyrinthine paths of passion he had traced." [57]

To strip reality of all artifice, Karl Kraus, however, delved even further into the corruption of society. Although fighting his own battles, Kraus again found common ground with psychoanalysts. In his eyes, society revealed the depth of its corruption and the insatiability of its appetite by simultaneously attacking moral freedom and natural drives. Thus, the moralist preached sexual freedom, for in the domain of sexuality, intervention by the authorities "always produced the most wicked antimorality." [58]

Crimes perpetrated in the courtroom, the arena in which society sought to complete its victory over individual freedom, became the targets of Kraus's anger and despair. In 1906, prosecution of the madam of a brothel, Regine Riehl, drew Kraus's fire in part as an example of the diversion of moral scrutiny from issues of genuine public importance: "society despises [the prostitute] more deeply than the corrupt public functionary, than the most venal bureaucrat, and the journalist most easily bribed, rages against the prostitution of women as if it endangered the most important social interests, and considers the corruption of men a matter of individual ethics." [59] The Riehl case, however, demonstrated to Kraus more than the existence of a persistent confusion between civic concerns and matters of private morality. Interference by the state in sexual life opened sexual desire to criminal exploitation.

Although Riehl had been accused and finally convicted of the economic exploitation and physical mistreatment of her employees, her establishment, Kraus pointed out, had existed for years with the protection and patronage of the authorities. Riehl's trial unmasked a system of social control. Wardens existed for exploited segments of the population, in this case, prostitutes: "The usurious landlady of the bordello is an assistant to the authorities, an executive organ of morality." To keep watch, the state also appointed "guardians of morality," and a "moral police": judges, prosecutors, and magistrates. [60] The procuress occupied the anomalous and dangerous position of go-between for members of society and the state. At any time, the state could choose to make an example of her. The abused and alienated had no recourse to justice. In reality, social mores were the rules with which society kept a banished population confined: "The invaluable possession of humanity in graciousness and elementary naturalness is outlawed. Around it, a barbed wire fence; behind this begins the order of society. From the latter, when it becomes dark, hordes of scornful men scurry into the unholy district. For those, however, who live within, no path leads into the order of society. Often, the blood of those who cannot feel pride in being ostracized sticks to the barbed wire. But always those from the order of society spring across; they have contempt for those expelled by day, because these must submit to their love at night. So those on the other side have for centuries preserved a heroic passivity toward the order of society, which daily devises new, malicious sport against them."[61] Morality and sexuality fell prey to the same corrupt forces.

Die Fackel's cause won over young Viennese writers who shared Kraus's fire and indignation. Victor Tausk explained to his fellow psychoanalysts that Kraus's "greatest merit" lay in his struggle against the "vulgarization of thinking and feeling."[62] From 1907 to 1909 Fritz Wittels contributed to *Die Fackel* a series of articles arguing for the legalization of abortion, open treatment of venereal disease, enlightened sexual education, and unrestricted sexual freedom for married and unmarried alike. Through association with *Die Fackel* and his membership in the Vienna Psychoanalytic Society, Wittels intended to be the first to unite the work of Kraus and Freud. In the introduction to the publication of his essays in book form, Wittels explained that sexual misery created by the "artificial quieting of passion" constituted the invisible suffering of "bourgeois society." Psychoanalysis confronted sexual suppression with "individual struggle." Nevertheless, Freud's teaching confirmed Kraus's indictment of society and had to be brought before the public: Freud "must put up with others carrying into life the truths he discovered. Men must live out their sexuality, otherwise they become cripples. One will surely not suppress this blessed truth out of the consideration that it is unpopular. Freud has pointed out new paths to psychology. Perhaps it belongs to the better part of virtue to travel early these newly opened paths."[63]

Kraus's recent biographer, Edward Timms, has shown that Wittels departed from the views of both Kraus and Freud on this point.[64] For Kraus, the naturalness of sexuality stood in stark contrast to the public's—and Wittels's—unholy hunger for sensationalism, as Kraus wrote, "Whoever places on the title page of a book this motto: 'Men must live out their sexuality, otherwise they become cripples' is an honest fellow who is serious about sexual enlightenment and for whom nothing is more important than sexuality, with the possible exception of success."[65] Similarly, as Wittels expected, Freud took exception to his follower's advocacy of unlimited sexual license. At a meeting of the Vienna Society devoted to Wittels's proposals, Freud explained that the book "stems from two different sources—from, so to say, a paternal and maternal source. The first one, represented by the *Fackel*, goes part of the way with us in its assertion that suppression of sexuality is the root of all evil. But we go further, and say: we liberate sexuality through our treatment, but not in order that man may from now on be dominated by sexuality, but in order to make a suppression possible—a rejection of the instincts under the guidance of a higher agency. The *Fackel* stands for living out one's instinctual desires to the point of satiating them [*ausleben*]; we distinguish, however, between a pathological process of repression and one that is to be regarded as normal."[66]

Freud later informed Wittels and the society that his own "personal relation to Kraus was such that, even before Wittels became one of our collaborators, he had the idea that the cause [of psychoanalysis] could obtain an effective helper in Kraus."[67] In October 1904, at the time when Freud actively began to seek recruits from outside the medical profession, he initiated communication with Kraus.[68] After an occasional exchange of letters and information stretching over two years, Kraus sent Freud a copy of "The Riehl Trial." Freud took the opportunity to raise the possibility of the two joining forces. In a letter dated November 11, 1906, he wrote, "My heartfelt thanks for the reprint. I have, of course, read the 'Riehl' case in the *Fackel*. Some of it is indescribably beautiful. Once again, people will praise you for your style and admire you for your wit; but they will not be ashamed of themselves which is what you really try to achieve. For this, they are too numerous and too secure in their solidarity. The few of us should therefore stick together."[69] The project for an alliance, however, came into the world of Viennese cultural life stillborn. In ethics and science, unity between Freud and Kraus had been temporarily forced upon them by their common antagonists.[70]

VI

The process of education within the Vienna Psychoanalytic Society can be interpreted in part as an endeavor to transform awareness gained from moral indignation into scientific consciousness. As Freud wrote to Carl Jung, with reference to prospective allies in Switzerland, he hoped "to be able to draw the moralists to ΨA rather than let the Ψ-analysts be turned into moralists."[71] Although the alliance between Freud and Kraus never transpired, Freud continued in these first years of the Vienna Society's existence to search for recruits among cultural critics. When Max Graf joined the society in 1905 Freud pressed him to bring to the cause his associates from the literary professions.[72] Graf himself embodied the critic-turned-psychologist that Freud valued so greatly among his followers. His personal odyssey epitomized the moral journey of the early disciples of Viennese psychoanalysis.

Psychology completed Graf's journey through the Wagnerian subculture of his Viennese youth. Renouncing the quest for prophetic powers or personal salvation so ardently pursued by Viennese Wagnerians, Graf turned to psychological investigation. Wagner no longer appeared to him as a visionary or private messiah, but rather as a historical and psychological problem. The historical problem consisted in the composer's attempt to assume the role of prophet and restore the supposedly lost connection between art and society. The psychological problem lay in the internal conflicts which produced Wagner's need for personal redemption.

In the 1870s, Wagner's aim to regenerate German cultural life with a new art found enthusiastic followers among university students in Vienna. Disappointed with the inadequacy of liberalism's political reforms and dissatisfied with its rationalist view of man, they looked forward to a society in which the populace would enjoy full political participation, economic equality, and social unity. Bonds of community would draw sustenance from the emotions, which art would bring to the center of social life. Their movement was short-lived. After leaving the university, those students genuinely committed to the rights of humanity helped found Austrian Social Democracy. Malcontents descended with Wagner into right-wing German nationalism and anti-Semitism.[73]

Graf described this first generation's "idealism" as the source of a distorted picture of the composer: "According to their own images, the fighters of German battles sketched the image of Wagner: the image of the German epic poet, the herald of heroic emotions, the master of every strong and triumphant art."[74] The culturally regenerative force within Wagner's art proved artificial: "[His] artwork did not, like Greek tragedy, stand at the beginning of an age, a civilization, a people, but at the end, as a grandiose resumé. . . . [It] rests on the fragments of an old culture and attempts to resolve its highest conscious forces once more into unconscious ones."[75]

The university generation of the 1890s, Graf's cohort, lost interest in the composer's vision of cultural transformation. Instead, they adopted the message of personal salvation proclaimed in *Parsifal*: "No music in the world spoke so to our passions, our longing, our torments. . . . Thus we saw in Wagner not, like that old generation, the bard of heroic emotions, but the great musical sorcerer of all wounds and mental suffering."[76] The new Romantics, like the first Wagnerians, clung to a belief in the power of art to transcend conflict, whether that conflict be societal or psychic.

According to Graf, psychology finally dissolved Wagnerian illusions. The science of the mind uncovered the meaning of art in the inner foundations of creativity.[77] Subjected to psychological analysis, artworks revealed their creator's "psychic type." In the case of Wagner, musical creation expressed longing for release from inner struggle. The source of his creativity from the conception of *The Flying Dutchman* to the completion of *Parsifal* came from his ceaseless effort to escape the psychological conflict between forces of sensuality, power, and health, and those of denial, disgust, and sickness. In *Parsifal*, Wagner finally embraced the Schopenhauerian prescription for inner freedom: extinguishing desire.

Behind Graf's analysis of Wagner, art, and psychology stood the figure of Friedrich Nietzsche. In *The Birth of Tragedy*, the young Nietzsche exalted Wagner's aim to regenerate society through art and to revive the force of instinct within music. Wagner's Viennese followers, however, observed the philosopher's estrangement from the composer and his renunciation of Wagnerian idealism. Graf, together with other Viennese of his generation, incorporated Nietzsche's new teachings: "A great guide, our instructor in the battles of spiritual life plunged with violent force into the chasm of eternal night. Honor to the memory of Friedrich Nietzsche!"[78]

Nietzsche, according to Graf, had suffered internal struggles similar to those of Wagner. *The Birth of Tragedy* presented Greek tragic drama as the constructive interplay of forces furiously battling each other within the philosopher: "Dionysus is the moving principle—the struggle, the tumult of instincts, the swirl of passion; Apollo gives order and binds. . . . A passionate, Dionysian underworld, over which the eyes of Apollo look out with blessed clarity: so the image of the Greek world appeared to him, a grand likeness of his inner being."[79] Aeschylus, the "Dionysian dramatist," gave voice to the philosopher's suffering. To the young Nietzsche, Wagner seemed to be the tragic poet's modern incarnation. As his inner conflict became more severe, however, Nietzsche's view of the world, and of the composer, became more trenchant. Bayreuth did not sublimate unconscious desire, but served up stimulants and dangerous illusions. In the end,

Nietzsche renounced completely the goal of cultural transformation: "He had seen the world as a Dionysian Romantic: now it appeared disenchanted to him, the fantastic cloud appeared to tear and with hard, clear vision he saw the forces which moved the world at work."[80]

"The degree of introspection achieved by Nietzsche had never been achieved by anyone, nor is it likely ever to be reached again. What disturbs us is that Nietzsche transformed 'is' into 'ought,' which is alien to science. In this he has remained, after all, the moralist." With this comment, Freud not only distinguished the ideas of Nietzsche from those of psychoanalysis. He also reminded his followers of the radical step they had taken by joining the Vienna Society, and the inner vigilance required to protect the intellectual independence of the movement. Those who stayed the course permanently left their earlier, sacred vocation for a scientific one. Moral righteousness and protest marked these psychoanalysts' initial break with their society and their past, while their commitment to the movement marked the second, and decisive, one.

The first Viennese recruits to psychoanalysis undertook a journey of a great distance, during which they discarded their moral absolutism for a framework with which to interpret scientifically the dualism of the psyche. Yet, awareness of the dynamics between repression and desire, and of the duality of ego and id never constituted a matter of science alone. With the unique exception of Karl Kraus, Viennese moralists sought desperately to discount this psychic dualism, either by exalting the dictates of conscience, or glorifying the demands of instinct. Nietzsche became for them a cipher in which they read either message as the spirit moved them. Within the psychoanalytic movement, however, Freud slowly brought his recruits not only to intellectual understanding, but to inward acceptance of the ineradicable dualism of the human soul. In the process, their moral perception and scientific awareness became imbued ever more deeply with tragic consciousness. Thus, those psychoanalysts who finally completed their journey followed a path leading not only to the discoveries of *The Interpretation of Dreams*, but to the final conceptualization in *Civilization and Its Discontents* of the eternal struggle between Eros and death.

It was, perhaps, ironic that conscience originally led these individuals to the movement. Yet, righteous anger certainly provided impetus and confidence to support Freud's intellectual revolution. Nor can one overlook the importance of their fervent sense of commitment. Even the schisms which consistently plagued the movement in Vienna reflected the uncompromising character of its members. More significantly, however, the movement in its turn utilized and affirmed their sense of calling, giving it new content and direction. Among the members of the Vienna Society, moral intensity preserved itself in the dedication of their lives to the movement. For the Viennese, psychoanalysis meant "the cause," an odyssey which became a life's work.

A Viennese journey: dissatisfied youths became moralists, moralists became psychoanalysts. Thus, the movement in Vienna came into being as a transformation of its opposite.

PETER LOEWENBERG

Psychoanalysis, Sexual Morality, and the Clinical Situation

> In my view, your *Analysis* suffers from the heredi-
> tary vice of—Virtue; it is the work of an overly de-
> cent man who feels himself committed to
> discretion. . . . Discretion is incompatible with a
> good presentation of psychoanalysis. One must be-
> come a bad character, disregard the rules, sacrifice
> oneself, betray, behave like an artist who buys
> paints with his wife's household money or burns
> the furniture to heat the studio for his model.
> Without such a bit of criminality there is no real
> achievement.
>
> Sigmund Freud to Oskar Pfister (1910)[1]

Institutionalized psychoanalysis is currently often charged with having become "too cautious," "too civilized," too adapted to the dominant values of
the acquisitive material culture, even of having "forfeited its critical soul."[2]
Herbert Marcuse, ever an appreciative critic of psychoanalysis, charged that:
"Therapy is faced with a situation in which it seems to help the Establishment rather than the individual."[3]

Clinical work is where theory engages daily and urgently with the exigen-
cies of life. Decisions must be made. Here the mandates of society exert
their pressure on the life of the analysand and analyst. Here, in the tension
and *agon* of the clinical consulting room, where commitment to the ongoing therapeutic work and the welfare of the patient meets the counter-
pressures of each of their ideals and standards, their personal values and the
dicta of social norms and legal sanctions, existential decisions are made and
accommodations to reality are shaped or avoided. The clinical couch and
consulting room are where moral and legal theory meets *praxis*.

This paper argues that psychoanalysts are, at their best, in a classic nineteenth-century liberal position of championing the individual against the coercive social-legal sanctions of the state. The clinical encounter is a deep experience between two people in which the intrusion of legal imperatives is anti-therapeutic. I conclude that psychoanalysts would do well to reaffirm Freud's liberal stance of defying social norms in the service of individual autonomy.

My strategy of presentation is guided by the cardinal rule of psychoanalytic technique—free association—filtered by the structures of intellectual history, the histories of western sexuality and of psychoanalysis, the anxieties and tensions of clinical practice and of being a parent and a citizen, and the ethnographic observations of non-Western cultures and pre-modern societies. These disparate data from different levels of immediacy, fluctuating from experience near to experience distant, interweave to make a fabric of ambiguous texture and conflicting values, as is a psychoanalysis, and life itself.

Nietzsche and the Relativity of Morality

The late nineteenth-century counter-Enlightenment,[4] which includes both Sigmund Freud (1856–1939) and Friedrich Nietzsche (1844–1900), postulated that modern man, in his biological body and with his tormented subjective sensibility, confronts a coercive social order. Freud and Nietzsche both admired those men and women who were able to create their own morality rather than live by the received moral codes of social institutions, religions, family, or the state.

Nietzsche's was the voice of a skepticism that is both psychologically and historically situated in the counter-Enlightenment. He made it hard to take at their face value the claims of positivism, progress, moral strictures and ethical theory. He converted tradition into mythology, suggesting that morals have a genealogy and are based on power relations. He unfolded a relativistic concept of truth and a conception of reality which include the possibility of multiple realities and meanings. Nietzsche posed the power of self-reflection against the force of reason. In so doing he focussed on the intimate relation between knowledge and interests and thus psychologized morality:

Deeply mistrustful of epistemological dogmas, I loved to look first out of one window and then out of another, keeping myself from fixating myself in them, for I considered this harmful—and finally, is it likely that a tool *can* criticize its own fitness??—What I paid attention to, rather, was that no epistemological skepticism or dogmatism ever came into being without ulterior motives,—and that they have a second rate value as soon as one considers *what* really *forced* them into this position. Fundamental insight: Kant as well as Hegel and Schopenhauer—the skeptical-epochistic as well as historicizing and pessimistic—are of *moral* origin.[5]

For Nietzsche the basis of knowledge in personal motives affected the basis of morality as such. The central principle of psychoanalytic technique—free association—is a moral one implying a non-censorial, non-judgmental freedom to fantasy. Said Nietzsche:

As long as the word "knowledge" has any meaning at all, the world is knowable. But it can be *interpreted* differently; it does not have a meaning behind it, but innumerable meanings—"Perspectivism." Our needs *interpret the world*; our instincts and their pro and con. Every instinct is a form of the search for power, each has its perspective which it would like to force on all other instincts as the norm.[6]

Nietzsche glorified those who defied conventional morality and instead defined their own ethics, who created values, who did not humble themselves to live by the values of others. He postulated that morality was a social creation, had a genealogy, and was imposed by the weak upon the strong.

The noble type of man experiences *himself* as determining values; this type does not need approval; it judges, "what is harmful to me is harmful in itself"; it knows itself to be that which first accords honor to things; it is *value-creating*.[7]

There are substantial differences between Nietzsche and the other "liberals" whom I will invoke, such as Mill and Freud, Holmes and Brandeis. Nietzsche's was the final and most extreme statement of a century of development of radical asocial individualism. The great difference between Nietzsche and Mill is that Nietzsche lacked, indeed he had contempt for, any compassion in his system of values. He accepted no limitation on freedom for the sake of the social good. Were he philosopher-king, Nietzsche would not hesitate to trample afoot individual rights in the furtherance of the creativity of his "Overman." He believed that freedom to create took primacy over protecting people from cruelty. Psychoanalyst and analysand together "create" an explanatory life narrative.[8] According to Nietzsche, we are all motivated by a will to create, a "will to power." His value for us is his radical perspectivism concerning the conflicting realities which arise in a clinical situation. Needless to say, Nietzsche, who died in 1900, was not responsible for National Socialism and would have held its "herdmen" in contempt.

Freud, Psychoanalysis, and the Individual

While treasuring the achievements of civilization, Freud also appreciated personal self-development, autonomy, and value-creation as cherished cultural goals. The Nietzschean narcissistic strand of indifference to others, which also frequently emerges in psychoanalytic treatment, conflicts with the psychoanalytic healing ethos that we do what we can to alleviate both individual and social human suffering. This paradox can be fruitful when it forces analysts to face their assumptions about themselves as helpers and rescuers. Here we confront the counter-transference: In what way do we perceive ourselves as freed from traditional morality? Do we truly know, and can we tolerate, our own antisociality? Can we achieve some Nietzschean irony regarding our own judgments, especially our "value free," "non-directive," and "helping" role?

Freud shared Nietzsche's respect for those who do not bend the knee to convention, who are not "conciliatory and resigned" (*konziliant und resigniert*) to the imperatives of culture.[9] Indeed, using Nietzsche's categories of strong and weak, Freud predicted in 1908:

The number of strong natures who openly oppose the demands of civilization will increase enormously, and so will the number of weaker ones who, faced with the conflict between the pressure of cultural influences and the resistance of their constitution, take flight into neurotic illness.[10]

As late as 1929, Freud invoked Nietzschean values and idioms of the strong who defy convention and the weak who submit:

Only the weaklings have submitted to such an extensive encroachment upon their sexual freedom, and stronger natures have only done so subject to a compensatory condition, which will be mentioned later.[11]

The compensation Freud referred to is the attainment of some measure of security.

Early psychoanalysts quickly perceived the affinity between the structure and content of Nietzsche's insights and their own discoveries. In a 1908 meeting Alfred Adler stressed "that among all great philosophers who have left something for posterity, Nietzsche is closest to our way of thinking." Paul Federn stated:

Nietzsche has come so close to our views that we can ask only, "Where has he not come close?" He intuitively knew a number of Freud's discoveries; he was the first to discover the significance of abreaction, of repression, of flight into illness, of the instincts—the normal sexual ones as well as the sadistic instincts.

In the same discussion Freud, while emphasizing that he did not know Nietzsche's work, said that "occasional attempts at reading it were smothered by an excess of interest."[12] Half a year later Freud commented that Nietzsche made "a number of brilliant discoveries in himself. . . . The degree of introspection achieved by Nietzsche had never been achieved by anyone, nor is it likely ever to be reached again." After this grandiloquent praise Freud reaffirmed that he had

never been able to study Nietzsche, partly because of the resemblance of Nietzsche's intuitive insights to our laborious investigations, and partly because of the wealth of ideas, which has always prevented [him] from getting beyond the first half page whenever he has tried to read him.[13]

Freud saw the erotic needs of individual sexuality as being in tension with the claims of society and the state. He viewed sexual love as having no place among the social emotions, explicitly presenting the self-sufficient dyad of two people in love as an anti-group constellation:

The direct sexual drives are unfavorable to the formation of groups . . . the more important sexual love became for the Ego, the more it developed being in love, the more forcefully it demanded the limitation to two persons—*una cum uno*—as is prescribed by the genital aim. . . . The two persons dependent on each other for sexual gratification, to the extent that they seek to be alone, are demonstrating against the herd instinct, the group feeling [*demonstrieren gegen den Herdentrieb, das Massengefühl, indem sie die Einsamkeit aufsuchen*].[14]

Freud's position on homosexuality was that it is the result of an unsatisfactory resolution of oedipal conflicts. He was consistently outspoken throughout his career in insisting that it is neither a crime, nor an illness, but a deviation in development which was expressed in the choice of the sexual object. Freud's position on sexual morality is most eloquently stated when he invokes the Greeks as a superior and more tolerant sexual and cultural ideal. For example, in the "Dora" case, Freud admonishes:

We must learn to speak without indignation of what we call the sexual perversions—instances in which the sexual function has extended its limits in respect either to the part of the body concerned or to the sexual object chosen. The uncertainty in regard to the boundaries of what is to be called normal sexual life, when we take different races and different epochs into account, should in itself be enough to cool the zealot's ardour. We surely ought not to forget that the perversion which is the most repellent to us, the sensual love of a man for a man, was not only tolerated by a people so far our superiors in cultivation [*einem uns so sehr kultur-überlegenen Volke wie den Griechen*] as were the Greeks, but was actually entrusted by them with important social functions. The sexual life of each one of us extends to a slight degree—now in this direction, now in that—beyond the narrow lines imposed as the standard of normality. The perversions are neither bestial nor degenerate in the emotional sense of the word. [15]

In Freud's parallel text of psychodynamic theory, which was published the same year as the "Dora" case, he stresses the distinction between inverts and degenerates and argues:

Account must be taken of the fact that inversion was a frequent phenomenon—one might almost say an institution charged with important functions—among the peoples of antiquity at the height of their civilization. [16]

Freud notes with approval the turn from social marginalization of homosexuals to an historical and ethnographic relativism: "The pathological approach to the study of inversion has been displaced by the anthropological." [17]

A third of a century later, when writing an American mother, Freud wrote:

I gather from your letter that your son is a homosexual. I am most impressed by the fact that you do not mention this term yourself in your information about him. May I question you why you avoid it? Homosexuality is assuredly no advantage, but it is nothing to be ashamed of, no vice, no degradation; it cannot be classified as an illness; we consider it to be a variation of the sexual function, produced by a certain arrest of sexual development. Many highly respectable individuals of ancient and modern times have been homosexuals, several of the greatest men among them. (Plato, Michelangelo, Leonardo da Vinci, etc.) It is a great injustice to persecute homosexuality as a crime—and a cruelty, too. [18]

Contemporary psychoanalysis recognizes, in the words of Jacob Arlow, "there is no naturally inherent morality. A moral code is a social acquisition, the product of centuries of communal living." [19] Modern psychoanalysis goes further to recognize what John Kafka terms the "relativity of realities." With sensitivity to the nuances of perception, Kafka demands of the therapist the tolerance of the ambiguity of inner and outer realities to promote "just enough familiarity with estrangement to avoid alienation." [20] As he puts it:

Psychological reality for a person at any one time is a pattern of organization of stimuli and can be described in terms of a pattern of subjective equivalences. [21]

Kafka calls on the psychoanalyst to explore and affirm the analysand's multiple, paradoxical, and individual realities:

To the extent that the analyst is responsive to his patient's own multiple ways of gaining experiences of time, he is responsive to his patient's multiple—and perhaps paradoxical—realities. As the analysand awakens—or reawakens—to the possibilities of shared rhythms of organizing experiences, he is better able to explore and develop his own individual variations of those rhythms and those realities.[22]

Analyst and analysand join in a moral contract to use free association. The analysand agrees to honor and try to carry out the fundamental rule of psychoanalysis: "Whatever comes into one's perception must be shared without criticizing it."[23] The course of the psychoanalysis is the study by the two parties to the contract of how observance of the rule weakens and is eventually breached: "There comes a time in every analysis when the patient under the dominance of resistances disregards it."[24] This failure we label "resistance." Psychoanalysis is a study of self-deceptions—the defenses we use to protect ourselves from unpalatable and unpleasant realities.

The moral contract of free association into which analyst and analysand enter is premised on the psychoanalyst's commitment to absolute, unconditional confidentiality which must be inviolable and sacred for free association to work. Any implication that confidentiality is partial or conditional is, on the part of the psychoanalyst, a "window" or loophole equivalent to a mental reservation against free association by the analysand. It is license permitted the analysand not to talk about certain, usually aggressive or sexual, subjects which will defeat the therapy. As Freud put it in a striking allegory:

It is very remarkable how the whole task becomes impossible if a reservation is allowed at any single place. But we have only to reflect what would happen if the right of asylum existed at any one point in a town; how long would it be before all the riff-raff of the town had collected there?[25]

The contract of psychotherapy depends on confidentiality. When the sanctity of the therapeutic session is breached, the freedom of fantasy and discovered meanings is sacrificed, and therewith the most important of curative agents of psychotherapy—the trust in intimacy of one human being to another.

The State, Its Laws, and the Psychotherapist's Dilemmas

Anti-social conduct such as the destruction of property and stealing is punished by society. Attempted suicide is punished by some jurisdictions; sometimes the punishment is the confiscation of property. The extra clinical burden for the psychoanalyst with a suicidal patient is possible civil litigation by the family of the suicide for negligence and malpractice for not having done enough to prevent a suicide or not having treated the patient correctly or competently. Some categories of patient conduct are protected by the psychotherapist-patient privilege.[26] But the privilege is not absolute. In some areas it is severely restricted. One of these is when the patient threatens "serious danger of violence" to self or others or the property of others.

In a clinical situation where a patient has communicated a serious threat of physical violence against a reasonably identifiable victim, under California case law and statute, which has been extended to twelve states and federal jurisdictions, there is a duty by the psychotherapist to communicate the threat to the victim and to a law enforcement agency.[27] In *Tarasoff v. Regents of University of California*, Prosenjit Poddar, a patient at the Cowell Memorial Hospital on the Berkeley campus of the University of California, told a psychotherapist of his intention to kill Tatiana Tarasoff. The police were informed and briefly detained the patient at the request of the therapist but released him when he appeared to be rational. Tatiana and her parents were not warned of the threat. Two months later Prosenjit killed Tatiana. The court held that

Once a therapist does in fact determine, or under applicable professional standards reasonably should have determined, that a patient poses a serious danger of violence to others, he bears a duty to exercise reasonable care to protect the foreseeable victim of that danger.[28]

Further, "The protective privilege ends where the public peril begins."[29] *Tarasoff* has had a chilling effect on therapeutic confidentiality. As Oppenheimer and Swanson recently counselled therapists:

In view of *Tarasoff* and its extensions, one might assume that it is best to err in the direction of breaking confidentiality and warn persons that they are potential victims of a patient's threats.[30]

The judicial dissents in Tarasoff are in the tradition of Justice Brandeis in being more sensitive to the individual liberties of privacy implicit in the realities of clinical practice than the majority who posited a "duty to warn." Justice Mosk questioned the court's invocation of the "standards of the profession" in holding a therapist liable for failing to predict the patient's tendency to violence if other practitioners pursuant to the "standards of the profession" would have done so. Appropriately Justice Mosk asked: "What standards?" He went on to say:

I would restructure the rule designed by the majority to eliminate all reference to conformity to standards of the profession in predicting violence. If a psychiatrist does in fact predict violence, then a duty to warn arises. The majority's expansion of that rule will take us from the world of reality into the wonderland of clairvoyance.[31]

Justice Clark held with the legislative recognition that effective treatment and society's safety are necessarily intertwined and that effective and confidential treatment is preferred over imposition of a duty to warn. He pointed out that by establishing a duty to warn, the court has imposed a "Draconian dilemma on therapists—either violate confidentiality and sacrifice treatment or incur potential civil liability." The therapist is left to decide the subtle questions as to when each of the opposing interests applies. This, said Justice Clark, "is manifestly unfair."[32] The duty to warn, he said, will not benefit society; it frustrates treatment, invades fundamental patient rights, and increases violence because those requiring treatment will be deterred from seeking assistance. The guarantee of confidentiality is essential in eliciting the full disclosure necessary for effective treatment. Trust in the therapist is "the very means by which treatment is effected." The duty to warn cripples the use and effectiveness of psychotherapy. "Forcing a therapist to violate the patient's trust will destroy the interpersonal relationship by which the treatment is effected."[33] Further, whereas only a few people in treatment present a risk of violence, the number making threats is huge—and their treatment would be impaired and their risk of deprivation of liberty by unnecessary commitment increased. Now the therapist "must instantaneously calculate potential violence from each patient on each visit." Justice Clark vividly captured both the impossibility of the demand for accurate prediction and the moral dilemma of the therapist whose instrument is the patient's trust and confidence.

In positing the behavior of the therapist in this situation, Justice Clark took a cynical but realistic view of the expected choice in favor of the therapist's self-interest at the sacrifice of the patient's trust and effective treatment:

One can expect most doubts will be resolved in favor of the psychiatrist protecting himself. However compassionate, the psychiatrist hearing the threat remains faced with potential crushing civil liability for a mistaken evaluation of his patient and will be forced to resolve even the slightest doubt in favor of disclosure or commitment.[34]

In my view the major benefit of professional malpractice liability insurance is to ease the psychotherapist's anxiety so he may work in the best interest of the patient without concern over a suit. The psychoanalyst is in a fiduciary relationship with his patient, but not with the patient's presumed victim. A focus of attention outside the primary fiduciary relationship in order to protect against litigation by a third party is at the expense of the patient. An analyst will find it impossible to place the interest of his patient first when he must constantly exercise defensive care against outside liability.

In the real world, as is usually the case, practitioners find ways to create options for treatment that allow compliance with the *Tarasoff* decision. An example is that when a wish to do violence has been expressed by a patient, the therapist poses the question: "Is this an actual serious threat? If so, I will have to report you to the authorities and inform the potential victim. However, if this is just a fantasy, an expression of feeling, with no serious intent to do violence, we can treat this as clinical material." This gives the patient a graceful and comfortable way of avoiding being reported and is an expression by the therapist of confidence in the patient's ego strength and ability to decide the level of danger. It keeps the therapy going and builds the essential trust of the working alliance between therapist and patient.

The dissent's fears that a result of the *Tarasoff* decision would be to deter treatment for those who need it most has been validated by current research. A 1989 Arizona study on a diverse patient population of 427 individuals stressed the importance of information and psychological privacy to patients as a precondition to successful treatment. The authors conclude:

Privacy, as has been increasingly demonstrated by research these past several years, is a concept so vital to human beings that they are willing to fight for it across organizational and political boundaries. Within the medical context, the issue of privacy encompasses not only publicly discussed assaults on individuals' privacy, such as information collection and dissemination, but also personal concerns. What must be regarded as part of patients' privacy is not only how physicians handle patients' private files but how physicians facilitate patients' perceptions of physical, interactional, and psychological privacy.[35]

A controlled 1990 Philadelphia study of 42 individual psychotherapy outpatients from two centers demonstrated that patients would be unwilling to admit to "sensitive" thoughts and behaviors concerning substance abuse, harm to self or others, homosexuality or "socially controversial sexual practices," child abuse, or criminal behavior if there were limits to clinical confidentiality. The research confirms the anticipation by Justice Clark that a breach in confidentiality will keep out of treatment precisely those individuals who could most benefit from mental health care. Thus Taube and Elwork:

The findings suggest that laws that limit the privacy of particular types of "confessions" may discourage certain patients from being candid in the first place. As a result, such laws may fail to achieve their intended aim of protecting society, and they may hinder treatment.[36]

A recently Wisconsin Supreme Court decision expanded *Tarasoff* by deeming the harm to be foreseeable even before any intent to harm is verbalized or otherwise suggested by the patient's behavior.[37] The court was also quite confident of the psychotherapist's ability to assess the dangerousness of a patient. This position defies the overwhelming weight of research findings on psychotherapists' inability successfully to predict violence,[38] leading one critic to

hope that the evaporating buffer zone of *Tarasoff* will not be replaced by dogmatic lawyers and judges assuming too quickly their own competence in a discipline subject to significant controversy and ambiguity. . . . It remains to be seen if *Altenberg* represents a prototype of emerging legal logic, a mere aberration, or the arrival at a brief pinnacle in a reactionary trend of expansive liability.[39]

Current legal pressures on the mental health community cause us to draw upon an older, saner, individualistic liberal tradition—that of John Stuart Mill and Friedrich Nietzsche, who understood the moral constraints on lawmaking and who would have kept the law out of the bedrooms and sexual lives of citizens. Mill had one very simple principle—that no one's liberty may be restrained, except to prevent harm to others. As he put it in his classic tract *On Liberty*:

As soon as any part of a person's conduct affects prejudicially the interests of others, society has jurisdiction over it, and the question whether the general welfare will or will not be promoted by interfering with it becomes open to discussion.[40]

Mill clearly presents the tension between the integrity of individual autonomy and the social good. This is the conflict to which psychotherapists are subject by reporting laws. Realistic public policy must allow for a multitude of interests, often exerting competing claims on the psychotherapist, which each of us has to live with and reconcile with our obligations to patients and commitments to effective therapeutic technique. Harm to others is the only reason for the criminalization of behavior.[41] However, the issue of "harm" is not an open and shut matter. Variables such as parental supportiveness or anger and punishment, the use of coercion, force or violence, and penetration, are all significant. The law and most researchers treat sexual abuse *en bloc*, as critiqued by Richard Green: "It either happened or it did not. Thus, one experience at fourteen of fondling by a nineteen-year-old is treated in the same way as repeated acts of intercourse by a father with a prepubescent child."[42] Damage to virtue or community tradition or moral offense, is a cost that must be borne for the preservation of liberty, personal autonomy, and the values of relationship therapy. There are countries where those seeking psychoanalysis have had to do so secretly. Unless we would follow such a course and make psychotherapy a secret interaction, we should press for at least the same privilege of communication among patient and therapist as those enjoyed by our fellow professionals, attorneys and clergymen, who have a greater range of privileged communication with their clients, parishioners, or congregants. The attorney-client privilege draws a distinction between the past and the future. The privilege extends to past, not future, acts. There is no privilege to plan a crime, or to continue the commission of a crime, with one's lawyer. The clerical privilege of confidentiality is absolute. The law provides no exceptions to the clergyman's and penitent's rights of privacy in communication.[43]

Child Abuse and Molestation

There is a class of cases about which psychoanalysts behave as Clemenceau enjoined the French to feel toward Alsace-Lorraine—"Always think about it, never speak of it." These are cases affected by the mandated reporting laws for child abuse and child molestation which have existed in all states since 1967.

Sexual molestation may be a trauma with serious sequelae of fears, disturbed sexual life, and an inability to trust and relate.[44] I shall forgo presenting clinical cases of child molestation in order to protect the confidentiality of those involved. There is, however, a vivid and intimate description of her experience of childhood sexual abuse by a genius of literary sensibility. Virginia Woolf was sexually abused as a little girl and as an adolescent by her two half-brothers, Gerald and George Duckworth.[45] Sexual frigidity, feelings of guilt, and emotional numbing and distancing marked her work as well as her life. She describes herself as "feeling ecstacies and raptures spontaneously and intensely and without any shame or at least sense of guilt, *so long as they were disconnected with my own body*" (italics mine). She reasoned: "I must have been ashamed or afraid of my own body." She recalled a memory which "may help to explain this":

There was a slab outside the dining room door for standing dishes upon. Once when I was very small Gerald Duckworth lifted me onto this, and as I sat there he began to explore my body. I can remember the feel of his hand going under my clothes; going firmly and steadily lower and lower. I remember how I hoped that he would stop; how I stiffened and wriggled as his hand approached my private parts. But it did not stop. His hand explored my private parts too. I remember resenting, disliking it—what is the word for so dumb and mixed a feeling? It must have been strong, since I still recall it. This seems to show that a feeling about certain parts of the body; how they must not be touched; how it is wrong to allow them to be touched; must be instinctive.[46]

Woolf's nephew and biographer, Quentin Bell, sums up the effects of the molestation on her person and literary style:

She regarded sex, not so much with horror, as with incomprehension; there was, both in her personality and in her art, a disconcertingly aetherial quality and, when the necessities of literature compel her to consider lust, she either turns away or presents us with something as remote from the gropings and grapplings of the bed as is the flame of a candle from its tallow.[47]

The California statute, and other jurisdictions are similar, requires a psychotherapist to report to law enforcement agencies within 36 hours of clinical knowledge of child abuse or sexual child molestation. The reporting statute is very broad on who is ordered to report (among those included are dental hygienists, optometrists, medical technicians, and paramedics),[48] and on what constitutes abuse ("mental suffering," "emotional well-being endangered in any other way),"[49] and is stringent regarding timing:

Any child care custodian, health practitioner, or employee of a child protective agency who has knowledge of or observes a child in his or her professional capacity or within the scope of his or her employment whom he or she knows or reasonably suspects has been the victim of child abuse shall report the known or suspected instance of child abuse to a child protective agency immediately or as soon as practically possible by telephone and shall prepare and send a written report thereof within 36 hours of receiving the information concerning the incident.[50]

For many mental health practitioners this reporting statute presents no clinical or ethical problem. They unquestioningly comply with its provisions because it is the law.[51] For others, these provisions, for clinical and instrumental reasons, conflict with the best interests of the patient and of society.[52]

The law is supplemented by courses on sexual abuse required for relicensure by psychologists and social workers and by marriage, family, and child counselors. Many of these courses convey an attitude of hysteria, moral zealousness, and self-righteousness, which is far removed from an attempt at clinical detachment, empathy, or understanding. The atmosphere is of fanatical crusading, testimonial "witnessing," and punitive anger.[53]

Herzberger focusses on the elaborate social process behind labeling an act "child abuse," singling out such variables as definition, ambiguity of evidence, gender of parent, gender of child, race, ethnicity, and socioeconomic status, ages of perpetrator and victim, and the child's provocation.[54] A recent research finding on a representative sample of 1874 child sexual, physical abuse and neglect reports from New York state is that the number of reports has more than doubled, but the percentage of reports that were substantiated following investigation has decreased. Whereas in 1974 over half of all reports were substantiated, in 1984 only 35 percent were substantiated.[55] False allegations of sexual molestation are not unusual and may be a weapon in child custody disputes. This may be due to persuasion of the child, misinterpretation, confused thought processes, or projective identification of a dominant caregiver.[56] Kaplan's 1986 Philadelphia study of misdiagnosed child abuse reports points out that such zealous reporting is not without serious risk to the patient and the treatment:

Inappropriate reporting may . . . do irreparable harm to the patient-physician relationship, once the possibility of abuse is raised. Regaining a parent's confidence may be impossible even when an organic cause can later be found. . . . In some instances, the misdiagnosis of abuse will allow treatable diseases to go unrecognized.[57]

This is a field where public pressure for stringent state regulation is creating rapid legal changes in an increasingly intrusive direction. A 1989 modification in Maryland law made mandatory the reporting of all disclosures suggesting sexual abuse of children by adult patients seeking treatment or already in treatment. The famed Johns Hopkins Sexual Disorders Clinic treats from 180 to 220 patients at a time, of whom about 55 percent are diagnosed as pedophiles. A total of 73 self-referred patients, who had previously engaged in some type of sexual activity involving children, entered treatment at the clinic in the decade between 1979 and 1989. None of these self-disclosures in treatment subsequently came to the attention of the criminal authorities. What is distressing to those concerned with preventive treatment is that, in the year after the law changed, not a single self-referred patient not facing criminal charges, who had a previously undetected history of sexual activity with children, entered treatment. The patient's disclosures of child abuse during treatment also dropped to zero. Berlin, Malin, and Dean tragically note in their recent most important evaluation:

Because patients made no disclosures of relapse during treatment after the law changed, no children at risk could be identified. . . . The availability of this type of clinical information allowed early intervention—intervention that is no longer possible in the absence of such disclosure. . . . One cannot intervene clinically if individuals who need help refrain from identifying themselves in the first place. . . . Mandatory reporting . . . appears to have deterred honest disclosure by patients in treatment and to have deterred unidentified potential patients from entering treatment. This deprives clinicians of the opportunity to try to intercede constructively, and some children may therefore remain unnecessarily at risk.[58]

The Psychoanalyst's Countertransference

Very few cases in the clinical literature deal with the intense conflicts in the psychoanalyst generated by the tension between the ethic of individual clinical integrity and conformity with social norms and the broader civic interest. Countertransference reactions of the psychoanalyst include anxiety about personal criminal and civil jeopardy; omnipotent rescue fantasies along the lines of: "I can make this person well and change his or her life"; indignation as a parent with the ever-present question: "What if this were my son or daughter at risk?" Not least, they also include the social obligations of wishing to be a law-abiding citizen and professional in conflict with the humane considerations which raise questions regarding the value of public shaming rituals and penal incarceration for sexual deviants.

The therapists' tension between their social conscience and the clinical imperatives compounded with countertransference and rescue fantasies often make the crucial variable for reporting: Who is the patient they are treating and empathizing with, perpetrator or victim? The difficulties in predicting violent and acting out behavior create an existential crisis for the therapist with each decision to report or not to report. Pollak and Levy found that

Reactions of guilt and shame, often accompanied by feelings of helplessness and depression, are likely to occur in cases where mandated reporting is experienced in one or more of the following terms: (1) as an unacceptable violation of confidentiality and betrayal of trust; (2) as a punitive act perpetrated against the needy and disempowered; (3) as treatment impasse or failure; and (4) as representing a "test" of professional or personal adequacy.[59]

The compassionate work on child abuse of Leonard Shengold, for example, presents numerous cases of past and present child abuse, but does not discuss the problems of the law or reporting. The reader is left to assume that none of the cases were reported to legal authorities.

Weinstock and Weinstock stress the serious threat to therapeutic confidentiality presented by child abuse statutes. They present cases in which therapists, complying with legal advice but against the wishes of the patient, reported abuse which occurred long ago and when no child was currently at risk. They also recount cases where therapists decided to maintain clinical confidentiality and not to report, stating:

> Therapists are placed into the disquieting position of masquerading as emphatic clinicians who become undercover police agents by betraying patient confidences. . . . Punishment is not a function of therapists and should not be a reason to violate confidentiality.[60]

A further eloquent exception to the general silence on treating child abusers is provided by Harold P. Blum, who is treating an abuser and did not report her to legal authorities. A critical consideration was that his patient was "filled with conscious shame, guilt, and remorse."[61] Although the patient was motivated toward understanding and had capacities for observation, reflection, and verbalization, when she lost control she would scream, curse, express hatred, and engage in physical abuse including slapping the child in the face and head and going "for the throat."[62] Treatment continues with the outcome "still unpredictable."[63] Blum writes of

> the tormenting burdens upon the analyst in the analytic treatment of abusive parents. Distrust, traumatic anxiety, and fear of recurrence or retaliation fuel massive resistance. The analyst may be conflicted about responsibility for the welfare of the patient and his or her child and possibly complicity in abuse. Analytic regression and acting out may endanger the child. . . . The analyst may lose objectivity, becoming judgmental and critical or compassionate and conciliatory; or he may have rescue fantasies concerning the parent, child, and analyst being rescued from rage, revenge, and violence. Indignation, shock, horror, outrage may pervade the transference-countertransference field. . . . The analyst may defend against his own violent fantasies with disbelief or underestimation of the disorder, and such patients may be mistakenly appraised as unlikely to maltreat their child again. . . . Countertransference pressures may be intense, complicated by familial, social, legal, and ethical issues.[64]

Many of the finest and most ethical psychoanalysts respond to these multiple pressures by taking an absolute non-reporting stance. If the law is antitherapeutic, they will not comply. In my presence and in front of his wife, an internationally distinguished psychoanalyst said on this subject: "I tell all of my patients that I will not talk to anyone about them even at their own request. You have to be willing to break the law. I am willing to go to prison. I am clear about that." This psychoanalyst is in the Nietzschean position of being a maker of values and, I think without risking hyperbole, one may say his is a heroic, Ibsenian, stance in defiance of social and political convention.

The governing pragmatic factor is often a judgment of what will, in fact, happen to whom if the law intervenes. Too often the legal process is a crude instrument like a jackhammer when a scalpel would be appropriate.

Reflections on Social Policy

The mental health community and the legal system are essentially two cultures whose approaches to child abuse are in decisive conflict.[65] The venerable sanctity of patients' confidences is enshrined in the Oath of Hippocrates: "All that may come to my knowledge in the exercise of my profession . . . which ought not to be spread abroad I will keep secret and will never reveal." Whereas the psychotherapist is committed to minimizing and repairing the trauma of abuse on the victim, the criminal justice system is interested in determining and assigning fault, in answering the questions: Who did what to whom, when; and who saw it happen?[66] The ironies of enforcement, such as the trauma-producing effect of reporting for the patient, or that the most treatable offenders, those who admit to being abusers and have taken steps to assume responsibility for it, are removed from their home, while those who vociferously deny the abuse are allowed to remain, are anathema to the mental health community.[67] As professor of psychiatry and attorney Virginia Weisz said on this point:

If the psychiatrist reports abuse to the authorities, then the authorities should look on the fact that the abuser is in therapy as very positive. But sometimes the authorities intervene in a punitive way where they would mandate that the abuser leave the home or remove the child from the home. We need to work at services so there won't be such a negative impact and so [abusers seeking treatment] are supported and get the therapy they need.[68]

The privacy concerns in a psychotherapist-patient relationship are grave, since the patients may well wish to disclose thoughts and feelings, fantasies and wishes, which they are unwilling to disclose to family or close friends, let alone to the public. A Texas study of 79 patients found that for as many as "fifty-four percent of patients confidentiality was a concern when they first considered therapy," and "twenty-eight percent of patients had asked their psychotherapists about confidentiality"; also "ninety-six percent of these individuals relied more heavily on the therapist's ethics for confidentiality than on a privilege statute."[69] To these overwhelming figures, I would say that were the existence of therapeutic confidentiality of consequence to only a few patients in a few cases, it would accord with the policy interests of society to protect these few patients' privacy, just as we deem it vital to protect the singular religious deviant or that sole person who avails herself of the right of free speech. The number of utilizations of interest ought not be our criterion for the value of individual rights.

The privacy of the therapeutic relationship is essentially the privacy of individual emotions, which Warren and Brandeis, over a century ago, in a classic statement of Anglo-Saxon liberalism, termed

the more general right of the individual to be let alone. It is like the right not to be assaulted or beaten, the right not to be maliciously prosecuted, the right not to be defamed. . . . The principle which protects . . . an inviolate personality. . . . the decisions indicate a general right to privacy for thoughts, emotions, and sensations, these should receive the same protection, whether expressed in writing, or in conduct, in conversation, in attitudes, or in facial expression. . . . as a part of the more general right to the immunity of the person—the right to one's personality.[70]

Compliance with the mandated reporting statute by mental health professionals is selective and discretionary. A 1987 RAND study of mental health professionals in 15 states reported that of 1,196 respondents, one third, by their own account, chose not to report some incidents of suspected child abuse. The researchers conclude:

What is striking about the profile of discretionary reporters is that they are the professionals most involved with child abuse. . . . Our data . . . indicate that the most informed and expert reporters are characterized by discretionary reporting. . . . But such discretionary reporting violates the reporting laws, which are clear in prohibiting the use of professional judgment in making reports. Perhaps we need to reexamine the assumptions inherent in these laws that professional judgment is never acceptable and that all suspected maltreatment should be reported.[71]

One prominent attorney who counsels psychoanalysts says to his clients: "Keep no records. If something is in writing, someone is going to want to see it."

The law has loose, spongy language similar to the "reasonable man" tort standard for civil negligence:

For the purpose of this article, "reasonable suspicion" means that it is objectively reasonable for a person to entertain such a suspicion, based upon facts that could cause a reasonable person in a like position, drawing when appropriate on his or her training and experience, to suspect child abuse.[72]

Most appropriately Justice Mosk in his *Tarasoff* dissent challenged such a "reasonable person" standard by posing the question: "What standards" of the profession? [73]

In cases of child abuse we do not utilize to the fullest the potential of our Anglo-Saxon common law to adjust to the intricate shadings of real life situations. The common law has the potential for a fine-tuning of the nuances of a life situation which are not utilized under the current legal mandates governing clinical practice. Justice is best served when it refracts reality into the nuanced, textured ambiguities of the moral choices of life and of our historical and cultural traditions, rather than the total "black" or "white" of moral absolutes. Justice and the law, at their best, should be calibrated on a moral continuum which may include the various shades of gray that exist in every case if we know it in depth. Any consideration of public policy should weigh the factors of precision and clarity in law and the negative effect of having laws violated on principle by a substantial sector of the community. It is not in the public interest to have laws flaunted or subverted by indirection.

The kinds of changes in child abuse legislation I call for would draw the lines of the law to recognize the differences among past, present, and future offenses; the factors of ongoing abuse and imminence of danger to the child; and the differences in treating and reporting victims or abusers. They also would acknowledge therapeutic judgement by actively-involved treating psychotherapists.

There is no evidence that criminalization has either a deterrent or a rehabilitative effect on sexual abusers. Incarceration is unlikely to provide effective therapy for the prisoner and may make him a victim of other inmates' prejudices. It is socially disruptive, taking the abuser out of any therapeutic efforts to alter the family dynamics to reconstitute nurturing, non-abusive parenting. A therapist who is addressing the patient's problems is more likely to be effective in meliorating an abusive family situation than would be an overworked, understaffed government agency which is new to the case. We should admit that the state has not provided better treatment for troubled families than can a motivated psychotherapist. Punishment should be the function of the judicial system, not of psychotherapy. Personal clinical data should be protected by law unless, in the Millian mode, an overriding danger to another exists, which means where there is ongoing abuse. [74] There should be an option to report only the suspected victim if the suspected abuser is in ongoing therapy.

Reporting should not be mandated when the victim is no longer a child, or no child is currently at risk, or the circumstances under which abuse occurred have substantially changed, or the victim and the family are opposed to a report, or there is ongoing therapy which has the potential to prevent a recurrence of the abuse. A victim's request for privileged communication should be protected by law. Criminal penalties should be removed for treating psychotherapists who have good clinical reasons for preferring to pursue alternatives to reporting. This means an exemption from mandated reporting for well trained, competent psychotherapists, who should be allowed the flexibility to choose appropriate alternatives to reporting in treatment. Psychotherapists need more than 36 hours to prepare a victim they are treating, particularly if he or she is a minor, for the excruciatingly stressful reporting process, which may include a trial in open court and attendant media publicity.[75]

There are two basic ways to change an unsatisfactory or unlivable law:

1. *Judicial modification.* This course would be an effort to gain judicial revision of overbroad, imprecise, or unconstitutional statutory language. It involves finding a "hero" or a group of "heroes" who believe so strongly in the inequity and irrationality of the law, or its moral offensiveness, that they are willing to defy it by publicly breaking the law and being prosecuted at the risk of criminal incarceration and civil damages.

2. *Change the law.* This means gaining wide popular, organizational, and media support. It then involves getting a sponsor in each house of a bicameral legislature, careful legal drafting to declare exactly what one wants and to steer clear of conflicting interests of other groups, advance staff work, briefings, lobbying pivotal legislators, and testimony before several legislative committees (Business and Professions, Public Health, Ways and Means). If the committee recommendations are favorable and they report the bill to the floor, support must be garnered from individual legislators. If the bill passes both houses, any discordances between the versions must be compromised in committee, and the Governor's signature secured. This exercise in applied politics introduces the bill's advocates to the vagaries of local pressure groups. They will receive cold questions from legislators such as: "What does this bill do for Latinos, Asians, or Blacks?" or "Where does the Gay community stand on your bill?"[76]

The Nietzschean existential predicament of the practicing psychotherapist is that he or she must define the patient's and his or her own reality, personal and social morality, and must live in a world of ambiguity where the fixed moorings of certainty do not exist. The public's expectation of mental health professionals is a clear-cut prediction of future behavior with a "Yes" and "No" answer and with no room for the ambiguity and uncertainty which is an integral and necessary part of a therapeutic encounter.

The Autonomy of the Therapeutic Encounter and the Liberal Tradition

As a humane science, psychoanalysis stands in opposition to categories of "right" and "wrong" as postulated in law and natural science. The legal categories "guilt" and "innocence" are not appropriate to a binary human encounter of interpretation. That this is so has decisive implications for the psychoanalyst's stance toward reporting laws, child abuse, sexual molestation, perversions, marital life, and infractions of the law encountered clinically. The clinical setting is an arena of the individual definition of morality with neither penalties nor consequences for fantasies and wishes. Actions in the "outside" world do have consequences which may be calculated. By contrast, the clinical forum invites a value-free quest for understanding, not judgment. The psychoanalyst is not the agent of the state nor of the received morality. His/her task is to ally with the observing ego of the analysand to comprehend the past and the present predicament, and to achieve the freedom to act in the future. Together analyst and analysand construct a narrative historical explanation of a life in a culture. Psychoanalysis is a mode of developmental, longitudinal, yet synoptic, understanding that is a unique encounter of two human beings determined to promote a dialogue on what each views as essential to a realized life.

There is an absolute difference between the social world and a relationship with the unconscious of another person. In a psychoanalysis or a psychotherapy it must be safe to relate without inhibition the intimate fusion of fantasy and reality. The analyst and the analysand are in the position of postulating pragmatic guidelines of what will happen to whom, of the integration of Id, Ego, and Super-ego, and of what is in the best interest of, in the first instance, the analysand, and secondarily, of society.

For psychoanalysis morality becomes central when the analysand feels guilt or moral impulses and wishes to reflect on them. The psychoanalyst is not concerned with objective truth. He or she is concerned with the reality of the analysand. A psychoanalysis is not a court to determine what really took place. The reality the analysand brings is the "truth" which becomes the focus of clinical attention.[77] The analysand may communicate freely on his or her subjective inner life. This implies what D. W. Winnicott terms "a secure holding area" in which anything that may come up is welcomed and worked with, including anti-social feelings and actions. Winnicott put it clearly when he said that the word "therapeutic"

has to do with putting oneself in a position in which one can be communicated with from a deep level. . . . In the therapeutic session . . . there is no question of morality except that which may turn up in the child. The therapeutic session is not a fact-finding commission and whoever is doing this therapeutic work is not concerned with objective truth, but is very definitely concerned with what feels real to the patient.[78]

Psychoanalysis is a hermeneutic discipline designed to confer meanings, not a science of truth and falsehood. As such, it takes account of, and draws from, the historical, humanistic, and ethnographic knowledge of the cultural relativity and situational contingency of sexual morality. The psychoanalyst is daily on the Nietzschean ground of being responsive as the analysand becomes the creator of his or her own morality. The psychoanalyst breaks new ethical ground with each individual and situation. This view places psychoanalysis in the position of the nineteenth-century ideology of liberal individualism whose prophet was Nietzsche, the psychologizer and relativizer of morality; and whose instrumentalizer was Mill, the champion of personal autonomy and socially responsible liberty.

In these anomic times clinical psychoanalysis, which claims as its own the realm of fantasy, sexual behavior, and personal trust integral to the deep encounter between two human beings, should reaffirm the high personal ethics of value-creating which is the best heritage of nineteenth-century liberalism, of Nietzsche, and of Freud.

GARY B. COHEN

Ideals and Reality in the Austrian Universities, 1850–1914

In 1810 Wilhelm von Humboldt, Johann Gottlieb Fichte, and their colleagues established a new university in Berlin based on the dual freedoms of
teaching and learning. Both the professors and the students were expected
to pursue scholarship and to give primacy to theoretical and conceptual
understanding before engaging in any practically-oriented specialization.
Ostensibly not reserved for any one estate or social class, the Humboldtian
model of university education was still directed at an elite element who could
appreciate learning for its own sake and not at those youth who wanted
merely the prerequisites for employment.[1] In the late nineteenth century
professors throughout Central Europe honored the Berlin reformers' humanist values as the basis for university education. So widely revered were
those ideals that they even influenced Central European technical colleges,
which at the end of the century increasingly tried to model themselves after
the universities.

The enormous growth in the numbers of Central European universities
and technical colleges and in their enrollments during the late nineteenth
century, however, gave rise to conditions that confounded many of the Berlin reformers' ideals. The legal and medical faculties were clearly the largest
of all the faculties in many universities, and their students seemed primarily
concerned with passing examinations and moving into successful careers.
Professors and students in the technical colleges insisted on equal status with
their university counterparts notwithstanding the applied, professional orientation of their studies. Around the turn of the century, university professors as well as conservative politicians lamented that the huge increase in
enrollments was bringing unworthy elements into higher education and creating a dangerous excess of ill-prepared graduates. In May 1910, for instance, Rector Philipp Zorn of the Bonn University commented that while
the growth of his university pleased him, he feared for the students' futures:
"What shall become of the thousands upon thousands who irresistibly crowd
into the universities and liberal professions? . . . The fear that an academic

proletariat could arise which would have to fight its way through life even harder than an unskilled worker haunts me time and again."[2]

Writing in a letter in 1882, the Swiss historian Jakob Burckhardt decried the consequences of the unprecedented growth of secondary and higher education in Switzerland: "dissatisfaction of everyone with everything . . . pressure to attain higher positions, which are available only in limited numbers, not to mention the utterly crazy learning in the girls' schools. A city nowadays is a place to which poor parents move because children are educated there for all possible pretensions."[3] Burckhardt in fact raised this complaint at a time when the enrollment of the Basel University reached barely two hundred.

In Austria as well, academic figures and politicians expressed serious reservations about the growth of secondary and higher education during the late nineteenth century. In a series of controversial writings beginning in 1876, Theodor Billroth, the famous professor of surgery at the Vienna University, attacked the filling of the Austrian medical schools with many youth who lacked both adequate preparation and genuine intellectual interest, particularly poorer Jewish students from Galicia, Bukovina, and Hungary. Billroth went on to call for restrictions on admissions.[4] In 1880 the Austrian Ministry for Religion and Instruction tried to reduce enrollments in the *Gymnasien* and *Realschulen* by issuing new directives to their directors to encourage parents of new students, particularly those from farming, craft, and petty commercial backgrounds, to pursue the alternatives of vocational and craft schools. The minister's directive argued that, despite the welcome growth of educational opportunities, many of the students from lower-class origins lacked the abilities and financial means needed to realize the benefits of academic education. In this case the educational authorities had "the obligation to counteract the tendency of the population to deprive agriculture and the crafts of some of the best talents and to create an unproductive and dissatisfied proletariat of unemployed educated people."[5] Emperor Francis Joseph's speech from the throne at the opening of the Austrian parliament session in September 1885 repeated the government's commitment to divert some of the flow of students from academic secondary schools to vocational education.[6]

Neither the professors nor the bureaucrats, however, could overcome the strong pressures in Austrian society which worked to increase the demand for academic secondary and higher education. The depressed economic conditions of the late 1870s and the 1880s caused declines in the growth rates for enrollments in secondary schools and universities and absolute declines in the technical colleges, but growth increased again in the 1890s and particularly after 1900. An obvious tension persisted, indeed increased, between the ideals that underlay Austrian *Gymnasium* and university education and the everyday realities of teaching ever larger numbers of students who came from diverse social origins and desired mainly professional training. Professors like Billroth who wanted university education to be committed to broad intellectual inquiry and theorization had much to worry about.

The modernization of higher education in Austria began later than in Germany, but many of the principal Austrian reforms in the nineteenth century followed German models. In 1848–49 liberal reformers began the work of remaking the Austrian universities along the lines of the Prussian universities, and the neo-absolutist regime of the 1850s continued and institutionalized many of those initiatives. Professor Franz Exner and Count Leo Thun-Hohenstein, who directed the efforts, wanted to make the Austrian universities equal to the German in quality. They accepted the Berlin reformers' principles of *Lehr-und Lernfreiheit* (freedom of teaching and study) and of the unity of teaching and research. The Austrian government abandoned its former tight control over course content, and, as in Germany, the full professors gained broad powers over the institutions' internal governance. The Austrian *Gymnasien* took over the preparatory "philosophical studies" that were previously the major concern of the philosophical faculties, and the latter were now put on the same plane with law, medicine, and theology. The Austrian universities also followed the German model for the preparation of professors by instituting in 1848–49 the process of *Habilitation* and the position of the *Privatdozent*. In the early 1870s, the Austrian educational authorities adopted higher standards for the comprehensive examinations (*Rigorosen*) for doctoral degrees and introduced scholarly dissertations in place of the old shorter treatises for the doctorates of philosophy and theology.[7] Through the 1870s the Austrian government also strengthened the ties with German higher education by encouraging the appointment of scholars from Germany. The conversion of the universities in Hungary and Austrian Galicia after 1860 to Magyar and Polish institutions, respectively, forced German-speaking professors in the western provinces of the Monarchy to look even more to the community of scholars in Germany and Switzerland.

The Berlin reformers' model of university education presumed a secondary school curriculum which accorded central importance to the classical languages and to literature, philosophy, and logic. To provide an adequate basis for Austria's reformed universities, secondary education also had to be transformed and strengthened. Here, too, the Habsburg authorities followed Prussian models, although with some important exceptions. In 1849 Franz Exner and Hermann Bonitz, a former Prussian *Gymnasium* teacher, drafted measures to extend the curriculum of Austria's classical *Gymnasien* to an eight-year course, somewhat different from Prussia's nine-year program.[8] They also established a final examination, the *Maturitätsprüfung* or *Matura* to certify mastery of the classical secondary curriculum and to grant admission to any Austrian university, paralleling the function of the *Abitur* codified in Prussia in 1834.

Once the classical curriculum was adopted, it became orthodoxy. The Austrian authorities proved even more hesitant than their German counterparts to grant equal status with the *Gymnasien* to more modern secondary schools for preparing university students. After 1868 Austria's *Realschulen* were expanded to seven-year institutions emphasizing mathematics, natural sciences, and modern languages; and from 1872 they were able to grant their own *Matura* leading to study in the *technische Hochschulen*. Efforts during the 1860s and 1870s to develop a *Realgymnasium* curriculum with less emphasis on the classical languages than in the *Gymnasien* failed to win ministerial approval. Only as late as 1908 did the Austrian Ministry of Religion and Instruction provisionally authorize an eight-year *Realgymnasium* based on the Prussian model with their own *Matura* for admission to universities. Until the last decade before World War One then, graduates of other types of secondary schools were at a serious disadvantage compared to those of the classical *Gymnasien*; they had to make up deficiencies in their course work and pass the *Gymnasium Matura* before they could matriculate in any Austrian university faculty.

Neither the Berlin reformers nor Exner and Thun in Austria had envisioned the formal admission of women to university studies, and the growth in numbers of Austrian students after the mid-nineteenth century benefitted women only belatedly. Women first gained admission to Austrian universities as regular students around 1900—the same period as in Germany. The Austrian philosophical faculties permitted women to audit lectures after the early 1880s but first accepted them as matriculated students in 1897–98. The medical faculties followed at the end of 1900, but the faculties of law and public administration did not admit female students until after World War One. The Austrian ministerial authorities and most of the university professoriate were clearly reluctant to make the changes in the established modes of *Gymnasium* education and in the administration of the *Matura* needed to accommodate women. Austrian women had to have the *Matura* to be admitted to a university; but it only became possible for them to complete a full secondary education in their own schools and to take the *Matura* examination there after 1910, when the existing six-year *Mädchenlyzeen* began to be converted into eight-year women's secondary schools modeled after the *Realgymnasium*.[9]

The expansion of enrollments in the Austrian and German university systems during the second half of the nineteenth century brought into the institutions a larger portion of the total population than ever before, including elements from social strata that were formerly ill-represented and had little apparent interest in broad education or scholarly inquiry. After a period of stagnation in the late 1830s and 1840s, the German universities grew enormously, from around 12,200 matriculated students in 1850 to 55,600 in the summer of 1911. Relative to Germany's total population, enrollment increased from around 0.34 per 1,000 to 0.85 per 1,000.[10] Between 1851 and 1909–10, the total number of matriculated university students in Austria quadrupled, from 5,646 to 23,068—an increase, relative to Austria's total population, from 0.32 per 1,000 to 0.82 per 1,000 (See Table 1).[11]

TABLE 1
Enrollments in Austrian and German Universities
Relative to Population, 1880–1910/11

Year/country	No. of matric. students per 1,000 in total population	No. of matric. students per 1,000 inhabitants in age group[a]
1880		
Austria	0.37	5.2
Germany	0.47	6.8
1890		
Austria	0.53	7.6
Germany	0.59	8.4
1900		
Austria	0.56	7.8
Germany	0.60	8.2
1910/11		
Austria (1910)	0.82	12.1
Germany (1911)	0.85	12.4

SOURCES: German statistics cited in Fritz K. Ringer, *Education and Society in Modern Europe* (Bloomington, IN, 1979), and Austrian age and enrollment statistics published in *Österreichische Statistik*, vol. 2, 1. Heft; vol. 3, 2. & 4. Heft; vol. 28, 4. Heft; vol. 32, 1. Heft; vol. 68, 3. Heft; N.F., vol. 1, 3. Heft; and N.F., vol. 7, 3. Heft.

[a]The Austrian enrollments are measured against the 19-to-22-year-old age group in the total population; the German enrollments against the 20-to-23-year-old cohort.

Relative to the school-aged population, there was roughly a doubling in the rate of university attendance in both Germany and Austria between 1880 and 1910, the period for which there are reliable time-series data on age-stratification. By this measure, Austria lagged significantly behind Germany at the beginning of the 1880s but closed the gap thereafter (See Table 1). In effect, Austria's university enrollments grew more rapidly than Germany's relative to the school-aged population; by 1910–11 there was virtually no difference in the overall enrollment rate between Germany and the western half of the Habsburg Monarchy.[12]

With the growth in university enrollments, Austria's Slavic nationalities and the religious minorities were able to increase their representation among the students. The German-speaking element saw its advantage decline over the period: in the winter semester 1881–82 individuals with German mother tongue made up nearly 49 percent of all matriculated and non-matriculated university students, but in 1909–10 only 40 percent, compared to the German-speakers' 36 percent share of the total citizen population (see Table 2). Czechs and Poles made particularly strong gains: the Czechs accounted for 16.4 percent of all university students in winter 1909–10, compared to their 23 percent of the total Austrian population; the Poles, 24.4 percent, compared to their 18 percent.[13] Austria's formerly disadvantaged Protestant and Jewish religious minorities benefitted particularly from the general expansion in university enrollments. Between 1880 and 1910, Protestants regu-

TABLE 2

Religion and Mother Tongue of Austrian University Students,
Matriculated and Non-matriculated, 1869–1910

Category	Winter semester					Pop., 1910 census
	1869–70	1881–82	1889–90	1899–1900	1909–10	
Total enroll-ment	8,992	10,594	15,121	17,209	27,531	—
Religion						
Catholic	79.6%	76.3%	71.8%	76.7%	75.0%	90.8%
Jewish	12.6	16.6	20.1	16.7	17.5	4.6
Protestant	3.7	3.7	4.0	3.3	3.4	2.1
E. Orthodox	1.8	2.9	3.3	2.9	3.1	2.3
Mother tongue						
German	45.6%	48.9%	45.4%	46.5%	40.5%	35.6%
Czech	20.2	15.5	21.4	20.5	16.4	23.2
Polish	14.6	15.7	15.4	17.3	24.4	17.8
Ukrainian	5.7	4.8	3.8	3.8	5.4	12.6
Slovene	—	1.8	1.0	2.2	2.0	4.5

SOURCES: *Österreichische Statistik*, vols. 3, 28, 68; N.F., *Statistisches Jahrbuch für das Jahr 1869.*

larly accounted for between 3 and 4 percent of all university students, compared to only 2.1 percent of the population in the latter year. As in many parts of Germany, the enrollment of Jews in Austria's universities greatly exceeded their share of the population by the beginning of the twentieth century: in 1909–10, 14.7 percent of the matriculated and non-matriculated Austrian university students declared themselves Jews compared to 4.6 percent of the total population.[14] In Prussia, by comparison, Jews made up 5.6 percent of the university students in 1911–12, although only 1.0 percent of the population.[15]

The Berlin reforms and the subsequent parallel changes in the Austrian universities put special emphasis on enhancing the philosophical faculties to support increased study of the liberal arts and sciences. Nonetheless, until around 1890 in most Austrian universities the faculties of law and medicine each typically drew far more students than did either the philosophical or theological faculties. In Austria, as in Germany, there was commonly an inverse relationship between changes in legal and medical enrollments, suggesting that these faculties competed for many of the same students. Prospects of a future in a profession of high status and relatively secure income, whether law, state employment, or medicine, apparently motivated many of these youth in the choice of faculty. The Catholic theological faculties' share of all university students declined significantly over the period in all the Austrian universities but Innsbruck; Catholic theological students accounted for 14 percent of all the matriculated in 1861, but only 5.9 percent in the winter semester of 1909–10.[16]

The Austrian philosophical faculties had relatively small enrollments until the last decade or two of the century. When enrollments in the humanities and natural sciences began to grow significantly after 1890 in both Austria and Germany, social and economic considerations were more obvious causal factors than were intellectual concerns. In that era the humanities and natural sciences drew increasing numbers of the lower-middle-class male students and eventually middle- and lower-middle-class women, who were attracted by the growing academic prestige of these fields and by employment opportunities in the now much expanded secondary schools.[17]

The economic motivations and career goals of many students were also apparent in the relationship between university and technical college enrollments in much of Central Europe. In both Germany and Austria, the two tracks of *Gymnasium*/university and *Realschule*/*technische Hochschule* competed to some extent for the same pool of potential students. The universities, though, enjoyed the considerable advantages of tradition and high prestige, and the higher status and security of the professions to which they led. The polytechnical institutes of Lower Austria and Bohemia languished during the first half of the century, and only in 1872 did the Austrian Ministry of Religion and Instruction recognize such institutions as *Hochschulen* on a par with the universities. Germany's *technische Hochschulen* granted their first doctoral degrees in 1899, Austria's in 1902.[18] In periods of economic boom, both the universities and the technical colleges saw increases in enrollments; but the Austrian universities grew much more strongly than did the polytechnical institutes during the boom era of the 1860s and early 1870s. During the late 1870s and 1880s, when the *technische Hochschulen* in both countries lost students, the universities showed particularly strong gains.[19]

While universities in both Austria and Germany enrolled an increasing fraction of the total school-aged population between the 1850s–60s and World War One, they also tended to recruit a sizable percentage of their students from the lower-middle class. There is a long tradition of statistical studies of the German educational system, but no Austrian governmental body ever published comprehensive statistics on the socio-economic origins of students in secondary or higher education during the nineteenth century. One must rely on samples of the individual student registration records for various universities in selected semesters in order to analyze the Austrian students' occupational and class backgrounds.

The student bodies of the Vienna and Prague universities are particularly revealing of the recruitment patterns for Austrian university education. These two institutions, actually three after the Czech-German division in Prague in 1882, were the oldest and largest of the universities in the western provinces of the Monarchy; and they offered the broadest array of academic programs. Despite the growth of other institutions, the Vienna and Prague universities together continued to enroll the majority of all university students in the Austrian half of the Monarchy throughout the second half of the nineteenth century: two-thirds or more of all matriculated students in the 1850s, 1860s, and 1870s, and still 54 percent of the total as late as winter 1909–10.[20] Based on the occupations of the students' fathers or guardians, Tables 3–4 and Figures 1–6 present socio-economic analyses of matriculated students, broken down by mother tongue and religion, for the Vienna and Prague universities in the winter semesters of 1859–60, 1879–80, 1899–1900, and 1909–10.[21]

Already in 1860 more than half the matriculated students in the Vienna and Prague universities came from the lower-middle and laboring classes,

TABLE 3
Social Origins of Matriculated University Students in Vienna, 1860–1910

Students/winter sem.	Propertied (%)	Educated (%)	Lower middle class				Laborers (%)
			Old +	New =		Sum (%)	
Matriculated students							
1859–60 (n = 456)	13.8	34.4	30.9	11.6 =	42.5	9.0
1879–80 (n = 559)	18.6	30.7	32.7	13.0 =	45.7	4.8
1899–1900 (n = 564)	16.1	29.8	28.7	18.4 =	47.1	6.6
1909–10 (n = 908)	17.7	32.6	26.9	18.3 =	45.2	4.4
German Christians (and without relig.)							
1879–80 (n = 249)	18.9	42.6	20.5	14.5 =	35.0	3.6
1899–1900 (n = 299)	14.7	37.1	20.1	19.7 =	39.8	8.4
1909–10 (n = 362)	17.0	39.1	18.0	20.2 =	38.2	5.8
Jews							
1879–80 (n = 160)	16.2	11.2	55.0	12.5 =	67.5	5.0
1899–1900 (n = 150)	17.3	15.3	49.3	15.3 =	64.6	1.3
1909–10 (n = 228)	14.5	19.7	46.5	18.0 =	64.5	0.9

SOURCES: Author's samples of the manuscript registration records in the Archiv der Universität Wien, Vienna.

NOTE: "n" equals the sample size in each case. The 1859–60 registration records of the Vienna University do not include information about the students' mother tongue.

and during the following half century the representation of those social strata kept pace with the total expansion. The actual tuition for Austrian *Gymnasien* and most university programs was relatively low and exemptions were frequent, but the total real costs in time and money of eight years in a secondary school and of four, five, or more years of university study represented a major hurdle for the children of peasants, small businessmen, craftsmen, clerks, and wage-earners.[22] In Austria, as in Germany, university education continued to carry high social prestige; and the popular image persisted of well-heeled students pursuing gentlemanly studies by day—at least when examinations approached—and the entertainments of drinking, dueling, and occasionally radical politics by night and on weekends. In fact, the professors of the Vienna University faced a student body which throughout the era was no less than around 40 percent lower-middle class with another 4 to 9 percent the offspring of laboring elements. Even more of the Prague university students came from the lower-middle class: after 1900 over 50 percent of the German University's matriculated students and more than 60 percent of the Czech University's students were from the lower-middle classes.

Few sons of Germany's nobility attended universities in the late nineteenth century, and even fewer Austrian noblemen could be found in the

TABLE 4
Social Origins of Matriculated University Students in Prague, 1860–1910

University/winter sem.	Propertied (%)	Educated (%)	Lower middle class			Sum (%)	Laborers (%)
			Old	+ New	=		
Czech Christians (and without relig.)							
Prague Univ./1859–60	8.8	17.4	58.2	9.8	=	68.0	4.9
(n = 328)							
Prague Univ./1879–80	7.5	19.8	53.0	9.8	=	62.8	9.6
(n = 479)							
Czech Univ./1899–1900	7.5	20.2	42.3	20.0	=	62.3	9.4
(n = 456)							
Czech Univ./1909–10	7.0	20.7	38.9	24.0	=	62.9	9.2
(n = 458)							
German Christians (and without relig.)							
Prague Univ./1859–60	5.9	37.7	34.3	15.5	=	49.8	4.6
(n = 239)							
Prague Univ./1879–80	15.4	40.4	26.6	11.7	=	38.3	5.3
(n = 188)							
German Univ./1899–1900	16.5	29.9	29.5	19.2	=	48.7	4.6
(n = 613)							
German Univ./1909–10	9.1	27.7	27.7	27.0	=	54.7	7.6
(n = 541)							
Jews							
Prague Univ./1859–60	7.4	9.3	72.2	9.3	=	81.5	0
(n = 54)							
Prague Univ./1879–80	10.9	16.3	55.4	14.1	=	69.5	3.3
(n = 92)							
German Univ./1899–1900	14.6	18.0	54.9	11.5	=	66.4	0.34
(n = 295)							
German Univ./1909–10	15.1	23.7	43.4	17.1	=	60.5	0.66
(n = 152)							

SOURCES: Author's samples of the manuscript registration records in the Archiv Univerzity Karlovy, Prague.

NOTE: "n" equals the sample size in each case. The Jewish students are analyzed for the German University after 1882 but not for the Czech University because of the low Jewish enrollments in the Czech faculties.

Vienna and Prague universities. The tendency of Austria's great aristocrats to hold themselves aloof from bourgeois society extended to university education: even in the Vienna University, typically less than 1 percent of the matriculated students in any semester had aristocratic titles. Students with petty titles were more numerous in the Vienna and Prague universities than were the aristocrats, but they still remained few, generally making up only 3 or 4 percent of the matriculated students in Vienna, 2 percent or less in Prague.[23]

During the late nineteenth century then, the Vienna and Prague universities, like many of the institutions in Germany, enrolled substantial

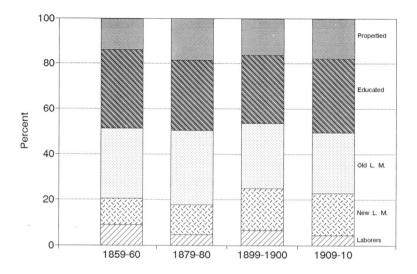

F I G. 1. Social origins of matriculated university students in Vienna, 1860–1910

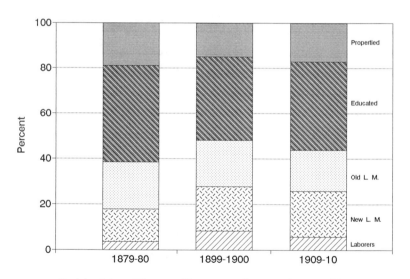

F I G. 2. Social origins of German Christian students in Vienna, 1880–1910

GARY B. COHEN

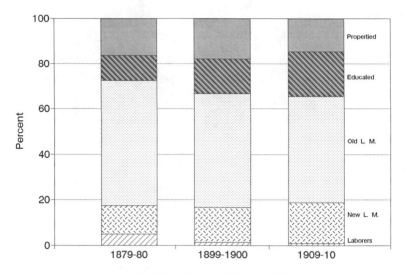

FIG. 3. Social origins of Jewish students in Vienna, 1880–1910

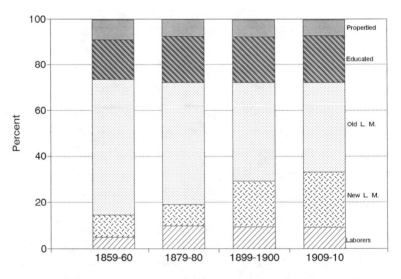

FIG. 4. Social origins of Czech Christian students in Prague (Czech University), 1860–1910

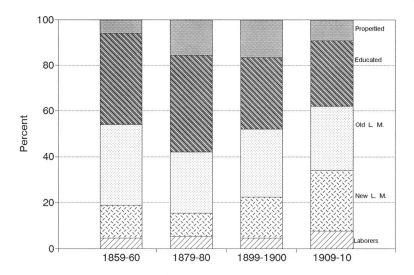

F I G. 5. Social origins of German Christian students in Prague (German University), 1860–1910

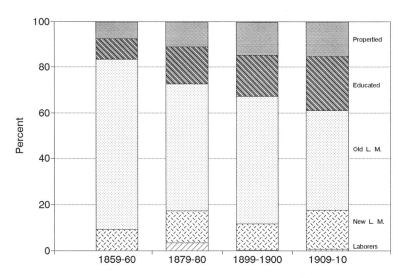

F I G. 6. Social origins of Jewish students in Prague (German University), 1860–1910

numbers of students from relatively modest origins. While professors who followed the Humboldtian values expected students to join them in the pursuit of new learning, most of the students from poorer economic backgrounds attended the universities with the goal of going on to more secure, more prestigious, and, they hoped, better paid careers than their fathers'. An outspoken defender of the broad humanistic model of university education like Theodor Billroth found many of these students lacking in the necessary intellectual curiosity, preparation, and ability. He frankly preferred students from the families of lesser officials, teachers, clergy, and others who already had some higher education, hoping that their offspring would show more interest in science and scholarship than in mere professional training.[24]

Of course, children of better educated parents might be just as professionally motivated as the less advantaged; and, in any case, after 1860 typically only around one-third of the fathers (or guardians) of the Vienna students had academic higher education themselves. This share approximately equaled that reported by Konrad Jarausch for Berlin, Bonn, Leipzig, and Tübingen from the 1870s to 1910. The recruitment of students for all Prussian universities after 1900 was somewhat less elitist, and the share whose fathers were educated stood at only around 20 percent.[25] In Prague after 1880 generally no more than one-fifth of the Czech Christian university students were offspring of persons with higher education (See Fig. 4). After 1870 Germany's propertied elites provided between 20 and 40 percent of the students in the various universities of the *Reich*, but in economically less well developed Austria, propertied elements accounted for only 10 to 18 percent of the Vienna University's or of Prague's German Christian university students and less than 10 percent of Prague's Czech Christian university students. While the numbers of workers' and other wage-earners' children were low among the Vienna or Prague university students at all times between 1860 and 1910, their share of the total here clearly exceeded the corresponding 1 or 2 percent of the students in most *Reich* universities.[26]

Of course, growth in the total numbers of petty officials and of public and private white-collar employees in Central Europe was probably the primary cause for any increase in the lower-middle-class contingents among the university students during the late nineteenth century. Nonetheless, throughout the era a significant fraction of the German and Austrian students came from families in such "old" lower-middle-class pursuits as peasant farming, estate management, medium and small commerce, and craft production. Students from the new lower-middle class first overtook the old lower-middle-class elements in the Prussian universities around 1911–12, when the former outnumbered the latter, 29.9 percent to 27.9 percent.[27] In Austria, even in the Vienna University as late as winter 1909–10, the students from the old lower-middle class still exceeded those from the new lower-middle class, 26.9 percent to 18.3 percent (see Fig. 1). The recruitment of Prague's Czech Christian university students from old lower-middle-class strata remained remarkably strong and greatly exceeded the numbers of Czech students from new lower-middle-class origins throughout the whole era after 1860 (see Fig. 4). In 1910, the children of Czech independent farmers and peasants still accounted for 20 percent of the matriculated students in the Czech University, those of independent small and medium businessmen 11 percent, and those of independent craftsmen 8 percent.[28] Many of these lower-middle-class students faced economic and social pressures which made the pursuit of broad education and scholarship for its own sake a luxury indeed.

Throughout the late nineteenth century, the Jewish university students in Vienna and Prague were even more likely to be the offspring of people in old lower-middle-class occupations than were the Czech Christian students in Prague. Indeed, until after 1900 over half the Jewish students in the Vienna and Prague universities came from old lower-middle-class strata. It should be remembered that despite the Austrian Jews' increasing occupational diversity in the late nineteenth century, 44 percent of all those resident in the Austrian half of the Monarchy in 1900 still derived their livelihoods from commerce. In that same year 29 percent were involved in manufacture and only 16 percent depended on public employment, free professions, and rents.[29] The Vienna University in winter 1899–1900 had 55 percent of the Jewish students enrolled in all Austrian universities; in that semester around eight out of ten of all matriculated Jewish old lower-middle-class students in the Vienna University were the offspring of intermediate and small businessmen.[30] In contrast, the Czech Christian lower-middle-class students in both Prague and Vienna included significant peasant and handicraft elements.

The Jewish students' choice of faculties within the Austrian universities reflected the importance of economic and social motivations in their pursuit of higher education. Like the Catholic and Protestant students in Vienna and Prague, the great majority of the Jews enrolled in the legal and medical faculties; but even smaller fractions of the Jewish than of the Catholic and Protestant university students enrolled in the philosophical faculties. Teaching in Austrian secondary schools was the primary occupational destination of students in the humanities and natural sciences. While legally Jews could be employed as teachers in state schools after the liberal constitutional reforms of the 1860s, they still saw fewer career opportunities in secondary teaching than in medicine, independent law practice, or private administration and management. During the winter semester 1899–1900, for example, only 44 of the total 413 matriculated and non-matriculated Jewish students in Prague's German University studied in the philosophical faculty, compared to 202 in the medical faculty and 167 in faculty of law and public administration. At the Vienna University, Jewish enrollment in the medical faculty reached a peak of around 55 percent of all the students in that faculty in the early 1880s. In winter 1899–1900 around one half of the Vienna University's Jewish students were enrolled in law and public administration, a little more than a third in medicine (39 percent of the students in that faculty), and only one-sixth in philosophy.[31]

Through the last decades before World War I, officials of the Austrian Ministry of Religion and Instruction and leading professors continued to invoke as their ideal the Berlin reformers' vision of a broad but scholarly university education that would develop each student's intellect and personality. Nonetheless, the Austrian educators, like their colleagues elsewhere in Central Europe, worked in institutions that had to serve a wide range of intellectual and social purposes. In Austria, as in Germany and Switzerland, the humanist ideals were challenged, if not flatly contradicted, by the everyday realities of providing professional education for an increasing range of pursuits, of conducting intensive empirical research and offering instruction in a myriad of narrow specialties, and of responding to the aspirations of lower-middle-class youth for economic security and upward mobility. Indeed, throughout Central Europe in the nineteenth century, universities had to serve utilitarian, specialized, and professionally-oriented functions from the beginnings of reform onward.[32]

The Austrian educational authorities did succeed in raising the level of scholarship in their universities. The reforms of the 1850s and 1870s elevated the status of the philosophical faculties and expanded their role. In all faculties the quality and quantity of professors' publications increased, and candidates for the doctorates of philosophy and theology had to produce scholarly dissertations. Nonetheless, enrollments in the latter faculties remained small compared to medicine and law until philosophy began to grow in the 1890s. Moreover, the great majority of the students in the philosophical faculties both before and after 1890 were headed into secondary school teaching and completed their studies merely with state examinations and diplomas.[33]

Ironically, the policy of insisting on higher standards of professorial research, which the reformers of the 1850s initiated and their successors in the government continued, led away from the concept of a broad, humanistic, and theoretically oriented scholarship championed by Humboldt and Fichte. Austria's master researchers generally followed the model of their German colleagues in the pursuit of increasingly narrow disciplinary specialties. The proliferation of separate institutes in the Austrian universities began in the 1850s and 1860s and continued unabated to the end of the Monarchy.

The evolution of Theodor Billroth's own thinking about medical education was indicative of the conflicts between ideals and reality in the Austrian universities. He wrote in 1876:[34]

Teaching will become more truly academic, and different from the mere passing on of traditions, which was the sole method in the past, only when the students are not merely taught the subject matter, but are forced to think about these subjects together with their teachers, as today's scientific methods of academic teaching require. These differences in teaching methods form part of the distinction between academic teaching in a medical faculty and teaching in a simple vocational school.

Billroth remained true to this vision of the academic and scientific character of medical education during the balance of his career, but he and his colleagues found it impossible to escape the growing contradictions. Billroth, for instance, supported the proliferation of specialized institutes. Faced with the continuing overcrowding of the Vienna faculty's courses, institutes, and clinics and the growth of many new specialties, he, like most of his professorial colleagues, proved willing to compromise some of the old principle of *Lernfreiheit*. By the late 1880s Billroth was advocating compulsory measures to insure appropriate balances in students' selection of courses and clinics along with ceilings on enrollments and restrictions on the admission of students who did not have an Austrian *Matura*.[35] In response to the medical students' needs for practical professional training, Billroth agreed in 1894 to support the introduction of a year of required hospital service at the end of the medical curriculum to make up for the insufficiency of clinical hours during the normal course of studies.[36]

Whatever the Austrian professors thought and recommended about university curricula, however, the officials of the Ministry of Religion and Instruction ultimately decided all major questions. In secondary and higher education, as in many areas of policy, Austria remained a bureaucratic authoritarian state (*Obrigkeitsstaat*), even in the era of rising mass politics. In issuing regulations, the ministerial officials were caught in the same web of contradictions between humanistic ideals and utilitarian reality as were the professors. In December 1895, for instance, when convening a commission of ministerial officials and representatives of the faculties to review the medical curriculum and examinations, the minister, Paul Gautsch Freiherr von Frankenthurn, assured the group, "I shall speak out against all efforts which aim to turn our faculties into technical schools or training institutions for physicians."[37] In practice, of course, all who held Gautsch's post had to balance the claims of the humanistic ideals with a range of often wildly conflicting political, social, and fiscal considerations. Indeed, Exner, Thun, and the other reformers of the 1850s were themselves as much concerned with improving the training of officials and secondary school teachers in the interests of a stronger, more modern Austrian state as with raising the intellectual quality of the universities. It was no accident that they took steps as early as 1849–50 to introduce new state examinations for future bureaucrats and secondary teachers.[38]

Despite the conflicts, the Austrian ministerial officials managed to preserve down to 1918 much of the secondary and higher educational system first devised by Exner, Thun, and Bonitz. Doubtless, this was partly out of conviction and partly out of bureaucratic conservatism and the fear of protests against change. Through the last decades of the Monarchy, the bureaucrats displayed their continuing loyalty to at least some of the original ideals in their defense of the classical *Gymnasium* curriculum, in their mostly good record in respecting the university professors' *Lehrfreiheit*, and in their commitment to at least some *Lernfreiheit* for the students. Of course, the ministerial officials had obvious utilitarian goals in designing, for example, the state examinations for secondary school teachers and the legally-trained state bureaucrats. The Ministry always sought advice from the university professoriate in revising the state examinations and doctoral *Rigorosen* for the various faculties and generally followed it. Nonetheless, that advice often reflected the professors' own awareness of the increasingly sophisticated requirements of professional certification and their own deepening engagement in narrow research specialties.

The fears of conservative political interests and some educators that enrollments were growing too quickly and that ill-qualified students were flooding secondary and higher education elicited only cautious responses from the Austrian Ministry of Religion and Instruction. In 1870, 1880, and 1895, the Ministry tried to stiffen admissions requirements for the *Gymnasien* and *Realschulen* and to divert some students to vocational education.[39] Apparently these efforts had little long-term effect, but the Ministry never dared break tradition by increasing the requirements for admission to the universities beyond the *Matura*. Within the university faculties the educational authorities responded to ballooning enrollments by trying to force students to take the state examinations and *Rigorosen* on tighter schedules and to reduce their years of study. In this respect the Ministry and the professors were willing to restrict somewhat the students' *Lernfreiheit*, but they would not formally invoke a *numerus clausus* in the universities of the Alpine and Bohemian lands during the periods of greatest pressure.[40] Similarly, with regard to tuition the Ministry showed its respect for tradition as well as popular pressures by continuing liberal policies on exemptions.

The Berlin reformers' goal of the broadly, humanistically educated person, interested in theorization and continuing inquiry, had such compelling appeal that it was hard for Central European educators to abandon it or even to admit how far the reality of university education diverged in the late nineteenth century. In practice, the demands of the learned professions and the state bureaucracy, of ambitious students and their parents, and of the pursuit of knowledge in a growing array of esoteric specialties were leading the universities down other paths. Austrian educators were conscious of the conflicts, but they proved to be no more able to resolve the contradictions between their old humanist ideals and the practical realities of their universities than were their colleagues elsewhere in Central Europe. Indeed, university education has continued to face many of the same conflicts in all modern societies.

WILLIAM J. MCGRATH

Freedom and Death:
Goethe's *Faust* and the
Greek War of Independence

Having experienced the upheavals of the French Revolution and the Napoleonic wars, the German poet J. W. Goethe had developed a horror of revolution by the time the Greeks began their struggle to throw off Turkish domination in 1821. In the Greek case, however, Goethe found his fear of violent disorder at odds with his deep love of classical Greek culture, and eventually he became so deeply engrossed in the Greek cause that he decided to weave it into the continuation of his Faust story. In 1825, after Byron died fighting for the Greeks at Missolonghi, Goethe was inspired to resume work on *Faust Two* after an interruption of many years. This new impetus eventually brought the work to completion, and it also produced significant changes in the original conception. Goethe observed, "Earlier I had in mind a quite different conclusion; I had conceptualized it in various ways and once quite well. . . . Then the times brought me this with Lord Byron and Missolonghi, and I gladly let all the rest go."[1]

The importance of Byron to Goethe's description of Euphorion in *Faust Two* has long been recognized, but its significance has not been fully appreciated. Goethe's allusions to the recently deceased poet expressed much more than just admiration for him or his work; Byron served as a focal point for Goethe's broader interest in the issues underlying the Greek struggle. Alluding to him through Euphorion allowed Goethe to take a position on a matter of great political importance to his time by advancing his own peculiarly German idea of freedom in opposition to the more radical views of such thinkers as Jeremy Bentham.

I

Although Goethe's initial response to the Greek revolution was hostile, his skepticism gradually gave way to sympathy. Wilhelm Mommsen fails to grasp the complexity of Goethe's views on the Greek cause in saying that he "was in no way friendly toward it and calls Philhellenism a 'disguise for another political party.'" Nor is Mommsen correct in saying that the loss of the Turkish fleet at Navarino, the key to the eventual Greek victory, was "regretted as much by Goethe as by Metternich."[2] In fact, Goethe had by then become a friend of the Greek cause, even though he remained ambivalent about its politics.

Goethe's conversations with Friedrich von Müller, who supported the Greeks, reveal that over a period of several years Goethe's initial opposition gave way to increasing interest, and by mid 1825 Müller noted that Goethe had "much greater sympathy for the Greeks than before."[3] By that time, Goethe was deeply engaged in realizing the new conception of *Faust Two* inspired by Byron's death, and over the next year he completed Act III, the "Helena" section. Goethe's diaries show that he resumed work on *Faust Two* on February 26, and one of his conversations from that time shows the importance of Byron to the final development of the "Helena" section, the birth and early death of Euphorion. Goethe remarked that Byron's "disposition always to strive for the unbounded . . . nonetheless stands in a good relationship to the restriction which he imposed on himself through observation of the three unities. If he had only known how to limit himself similarly in the moral sphere!" Goethe believed Byron's failure to do so "was his ruin, and it can very probably be said that he was destroyed by his lack of restraint."[4] Goethe contrasted Byron's belief in freedom as an ideal with the lack of freedom in his personal life, a paradox which paralleled Euphorion's loss of freedom in his reckless striving for freedom.

Having re-embarked on his Faust story under the impact of the events in Greece, Goethe threw himself into reading about the Greek cause. His diary entries and conversations from the Spring and Summer of 1825 contain repeated references to various books on Greece, particularly Colonel Leicester Stanhope's *Greece in 1823 and 1824*[5] and William Parry's *The Last Days of Lord Byron*.[6] Parry's account of the English poet was sharply at odds with that of Stanhope, and Goethe's comments leave no doubt that he favored Parry's point of view. On June 6, he wrote to Karl Zelter: "If you encounter William Parry's *The Last Days of Lord Byron* in translation, quickly seize it; one is not easily raised to so high and clear a standpoint. Everything previously said about him sinks and disappears like fog in a valley."[7]

Goethe's enthusiasm for Parry's book helps to explain the apparent contradiction suggested by his later statement that "he was no Philhellene."[8] While Philhellenes from all parts of Europe aided the Greeks with money, men, and supplies, by far the most important help came from England, where the London Greek Committee provided the focal point for much of that aid. Colonel Stanhope was the Committee's primary agent in Greece, and he had sharply criticized Byron in his book. Parry was determined to counter those criticisms. There were fundamental differences between the Committee, which was strongly influenced by the theories of Jeremy Bentham, and Byron, whose efforts often had a more practical thrust. Goethe's sympathy for Byron and Parry was in accord with his deeply ingrained dislike of Bentham's ideas; and in *Faust Two* he was able to use the model of Byron's experience in Greece to advance a conception of freedom diametrically opposed to that of the English prophet of utility.

Parry's criticism of Stanhope and the Greek Committee focussed on their overly theoretical approach to helping the Greeks. Instead of concentrating on military victory, the Committee seemed more intent on implementing Bentham's political and educational schemes. Parry described a series of projects aimed at "making Mr. Bentham the apostle of the Greeks,"[9] and Stanhope's letters to the Committee confirm this intention. In sending a copy of "our Chronicle," the new Greek newspaper on which he placed much hope, Stanhope noted that "The last article in the Chronicle is on Mr. Bentham. Its object is to dispose the people to read and contemplate his works. Conviction follows."[10] This blind faith in Bentham's ideas irritated Byron, and Parry used it effectively as a source of ridicule.

In the dispute between Byron and the Benthamites it was the political shape of the emerging Greek nation and the basic meaning of freedom that were most at issue. The Benthamites hoped that Greece would become a republic which would enjoy the wide range of freedoms found in England. Above all, Stanhope and the Benthamites had an almost fanatical faith in freedom of the press, a faith which led them to rush printing presses to Greece at a time when the lack of arms and supplies threatened to extinguish the hopes of the Greeks at any minute. In Byron's view, what the Greeks most needed was "the energy and the unity derived from an organized system of government, taming some of the passions and directing others to the public good."[11] Where Stanhope's fear was that Greek freedom might be extinguished by a tyrannical executive overpowering a weak legislature,[12] Byron emphasized that freedom without plan could lead to disintegration. Where the Benthamites worked to establish a Greek republic, Byron believed that the form of government should be decided by the Greeks on the basis of their particular needs.

There can be no doubt about where Goethe stood on these different programs for Greek independence and on the underlying differences in principle on which these programs rested. The records of his conversations show that he repeatedly referred to Bentham as a fool.[13] Friedrich Soret's report of a May 12, 1830 conversation is typical: "Goethe was not edified by the enthusiasm . . . shown for the writings of Bentham whom he always holds for a fool—read by fools."[14] In contrast to the liberal faith in freedom and the republican individualism of the Benthamites, the more controlled conception of freedom expressed by Byron and Parry was much more congenial to Goethe.

The issue of freedom was particularly important to Goethe and to the changes in *Faust Two* inspired by Byron's death in the Greek cause. The Greek battle cry was "freedom or death," but Goethe held a cynical view of this love of freedom. In 1813, he had observed, "The Greeks were indeed friends of freedom, but each only of his own; therefore in every Greek there was a tyrant which only needed an opportunity to develop."[15] Goethe believed in a very different kind of freedom, which he explained to his friend Johann Eckermann in a conversation of January 18, 1827, after he had finished the "Helena" section of Faust. The topic emerged from a discussion of Schiller's idealism, which led Goethe to compare Schiller with Lord Byron. He speculated about what a meeting between the two would have been like and what Schiller "would have said to so similar a spirit." Byron was as celebrated a freedom poet as Schiller, and Goethe recalled the evolution which the "idea of freedom" underwent over the course of Schiller's life. "In his youth it was physical freedom which concerned him and which passed over into his poetry; in later life it was ideal freedom."[16] Goethe even suggested that "this idea killed" Schiller, because it led him to make demands on himself which he wasn't strong enough to sustain.[17]

The idea of freedom advanced by Goethe had a distinctly conservative cast. As he observed, "There is a wonderful thing about freedom; everyone easily has enough if he only knows how to be satisfied and how to find himself."[18] In exploring the origins of the German idea of freedom, Leonard Krieger shows how it was rooted in the immunities, liberties, and rights enjoyed by German aristocrats under feudal law and custom. This tradition was still alive in the Germany of Goethe's youth, and Krieger discusses the way Frederick the Great utilized it in his 1784 plan for a League of German Princes, a project which "embodied the identification of sovereign interests with aristocratic freedom. He called for a revival of the anti-Imperialist tradition, appealing to the Golden Bull for authority. . . . He summarized the particularistic tradition as 'the rights and immunities of the German princes.'"[19] As Krieger observes, even though this League of Princes had an openly reactionary quality, it "was a vital expression of the German nation for the sixteen princes who adhered to it and for the whole section of the politically interested German public to which Goethe later gave voice in his memoirs."[20]

The influence of this tradition, which tied freedom to the observation of customary obligations within a hierarchical social order, can be seen in Goethe's January 1827 discussion of freedom as recorded by Eckermann. He observed that "we are all free only under certain circumstances which we must fulfill. The burgher is as free as the noble so long as he holds himself within the bounds appointed to him by God through the class [*Stand*] into which he was born. The noble is as free as the prince, for if he only observes a small ceremonial at court he can feel himself his equal."[21] Goethe then went on to extend this idea to a general cultural principle of great importance in his own work and in that of such later thinkers as Nietzsche and Freud. He says that "We are not made free by the desire to acknowledge nothing as being above us, but rather by honoring something that is above us. For when we honor it we raise ourselves up to it and manifest through our recognition that we ourselves bear the higher within us and are worthy of being equal to it."[22] This idea, which anticipates Nietzsche's doctrine of self-overcoming and Freud's theory of the ego-ideal, plays a vital role in the final version of *Faust Two*. An examination of the way Goethe used this concept to shape the central themes of that work reveals one of the paths by which this idea achieved broad dissemination.

II

The interrelated issues of freedom and authority are prominently announced in Act II of *Faust Two*, in the "Laboratory" scene, where the prospect of Faust's journey back in time to ancient Greece is first broached. Reading Faust's dream thoughts, Homunculus bids Mephisto to take him to the land of his dreams—specifically to the plains of Thessaly near Pharsalus. Pharsalus was the site of the battle in 48 B.C. between Caesar and Pompey, a battle sometimes taken to mark the end of the ancient tradition of freedom (with the defeat of the forces backing the Roman Senate); and while Mephisto clearly recognizes the political significance of the destination, he rejects this "Republican" interpretation of the battle in favor of a more cynical view:[23]

> No more! That privilege I gladly waive,
> Of hearing about tyrant versus slave. . . .
> They fight, they say, dear freedom's cause to save;
> But seen more clearly, slave is fighting slave.

This view is elaborated in the subsequent scene when the travelers—Homunculus, Mephisto, and Faust—arrive on the fields of Pharsalus. Before they arrive, Erichto, a local witch, ponders the political significance of the battle scene:[24]

> The theme returns, how often now! And will return
> For evermore repeated . . . None will empire yield
> To other; none to him who won it with strong arm
> And strongly rules. For every man who has not wit
> To rule his inner self will be most apt to rule
> His neighbor's will, according to his own proud whim . . .
> Yet here a great example in the fight was proved,
> How force against a force more puissant makes a stand
> How freedom's fair and thousand-flowered wreath is rent
> And the stiff laurel coiled to bind the victor's brow.

Goethe establishes the importance of the theme of freedom at the outset of the Greek journey in which Faust will seek and find Helen of Troy. Since Faust eventually takes on the role of sovereign ruler in this quest, the relevance of Erichto's words to his situation is clear, particularly since he has heretofore found it so difficult to learn how "to rule his inner self."

The meeting between Faust and Helen occurs in Act III, the "Helena" section which Goethe published separately in 1827. Of this act's three scenes, the first depicts the return of Helen from Troy, the second focusses on the union of Faust and Helen, and the third describes the birth and death of their son Euphorion. In terms of freedom and authority, the movement is from the presentation of Helen as the representative of authority under challenge, to the synthesis of freedom and authority symbolized by the marriage of Faust and Helen, to the loss of balance and restraint expressed by the wild freedom of Euphorion.

In the first scene, before the palace of Menelaus at Sparta, Helen approaches her earlier home in a state of uncertainty; but having been sent ahead by Menelaus, she cites his words as the warrant for her action in taking control of the household:[25]

> Seeking that high and princely mansion, enter in
> And summon all my maids whom I departing left,

> Together with my old sagacious stewardess, . . .
> Then all things will you find preserved in order; for
> This is a prince's privilege, that when he comes
> Again to his home he finds, in trusty keeping, all
> Possessions ranged in his house, as when he went away;
> For in the slave there lives no power to bring in change.

The authority to take control is contrasted with the slave's lack of freedom to introduce change. However, when Helen attempts to assert her authority she is challenged by the "sagacious stewardess," who is actually Mephisto in disguise. Helen tells her retinue of captive Trojan women: "With the voice of firm command I bade her to her work," [26] but Mephisto-Phorkyas bars Helen's way and forces her to retreat. When Phorkyas criticizes these women, Helen again attempts to assert her authority: [27]

> Who chides the waiting maids before their lady's face
> Lays an audacious hand upon her household right;
> For hers alone it is to give the praise deserved.

Phorkyas persists in the criticism, and when a quarrel develops Helen intervenes to restore order: [28]

> With naught of wrath, nay sorrowful I intervene,
> Forbidding to and fro of quarrelling hubbub here,
> For no harm greater can assail the sovereign's state
> Than trusted servants' strife, in secret pledge of feud.

Although further sparring with Phorkyas so disturbs Helen that she faints, she soon recovers, declaring, "Still it befits a Queen, as it does all mankind/ to be self controlled." [29] With this Phorkyas is willing to accept her authority: "Now you rise up in your greatness, in your beauty stand you there,/With commanding eyes most regal: what your will is tell us now." [30] The scene strongly emphasizes the idea expressed by Erichto in Act II, that true authority begins with self-control.

In the scene which follows, the meeting of Helen and Faust becomes a vehicle for exploring the relationship between this legitimate authority and true freedom. The meeting occurs after Phorkyas, playing on Helen's fears of Menelaus, persuades her to seek the protection of a powerful warlord who has settled near by in Menelaus's absence. Helen and her retinue are then conducted to the medieval fortress of this lord, who is actually Faust. When Faust appears he is dressed in the court costume of a medieval knight, and the language of this scene reflects the elaborate conventions associated with the tradition of courtly love. Faust approaches Helen with a man in chains

at his side. This man, the castle's watchman, has been deprived of his freedom as punishment for failing to see the approach of Helen—thereby pre-
venting her from being welcomed appropriately. Helen is told to decide
whether he will be put to death or shown mercy for this offense. As a fair
judge she first gives the accused a chance to plead his case, and when he
offers a plausible explanation she renders her decision: "Remove this innocent man and set him free."[31] In this situation Helen's just use of authority
confers freedom.

Helen rightly sees this act of judgment as a test, and when she passes it
Faust acknowledges her as his liege lady. Using the appropriate medieval
language he declares: "at your feet allow me, freely and truly [*frei und treu*]
to acknowledge you as mistress [*Herrin*]" (9270–71). The words recall the
feudal origins of the German idea of freedom as well as those remarks of
Goethe to Eckermann linking freedom to the acknowledgment of something
superior to which one aspires. Helen is the inspiring ideal or form for Faust's
restless energy, and by acknowledging her authority he gains freedom and
mastery over himself.

On a psychological level Faust's allegiance to Helen symbolizes the taming of wild emotion through the classical ideals of balance, form, and order.
This idea is reinforced by the words of the castle watchman, Lynceus, when
he describes the activities of the warriors who are Faust's followers:[32]

> We wandered from the Rising Sun,
> And soon the West was over-run. . . .
> We forged [*drängten*] along, we stormed [*stürmten*] along
> In every place victorious, strong;
> And where I lorded it today
> The morrow's thief would rob and prey.

Like their leader, they are full of energy and drive which often prove destructive without the proper restraining influence.

When Faust and his followers recognize Helen's authority she responds
by making Faust co-regent of her realm. Here the action of the play echoes
a favorite theme of nineteenth-century German historiography. This was
the idea that when the invasions of the Roman empire by the German tribes
shattered the despotic authority of the late classical world it allowed the
rejuvenating force of German freedom to produce a fruitful combination of
freedom and authority within the feudal system. The co-regency and the
marriage of Helen and Faust represent this union just as they also represent
the final phase of Goethe's own poetic evolution from *Sturm und Drang* to
classical to a synthesis of both styles. Lynceus's words, "Wir drängten fort,

wir stürmten fort" (We forged along, we stormed along) [9289] literally recall the *Sturm and Drang* movement, and when Faust and his followers
come under Helen's sway it signifies the synthesis of this literary style with
the classical. This is apparent in the scene where Faust teaches Helen
(whose speech had heretofore been metered but not rhymed) how to add to
her words the feeling conveyed by rhyme.[33]

The poetic and psychological meanings of Faust's union with Helen are
closely related to the political symbolism conveyed by their marriage. The
political form produced by this coming together of the Germanic with the
classical is suggested by the actions which follow the lessons in poetry.
Phorkyas enters to warn the loving couple that Menelaus is about to attack,
and Faust responds by organizing his forces. Each of his tribes—Goths,
Saxons, Franks and so on—is given a different province of the Peloponese
on the understanding that it is to be defended in behalf of Helen. In essence,
he constructs a feudal hierarchy:[34]

> I hail you with the ducal title
> Thus bids the Queen from Sparta's throne
> Valleys and hills in glad requital
> Lay at her feet, her wealth your own.

Faust's instructions reveal that the German dukes receive the land for their
use in return for their military service: "There each in settled habitation/
Fire, strength to outward foes make known."[35] But he also leaves no doubt
that Helen of Sparta retains the supreme authority: "Still Sparta will rule
over you [*euch überthronen*]" [9476]. The relationship is one of reciprocal
obligations within a hierarchy headed by Helen's Sparta.[36]

> There in your single powers residing,
> Rejoice in wealth as in her sight;
> And, at her feet, seek faith-abiding
> Authority and law and light.

Faust's words suggest a balance between the individual prerogatives of the
feudal lords and the central authority of Sparta, which parallels his earlier
"free and true" acknowledgment of Helen as his liege lady. Within this ideal
feudal order the authority of the monarch and the various rights or freedoms
of the vassals were to coexist in balanced harmony.

The third scene of the Helena reveals the dangers inherent in the loss of
this balance. The couple are blessed with a son, Euphorion, who resembles
Faust much more than Helen. He possesses boundless energy, which he
absolutely refuses to restrain.[37]

> Let me be springing
> Let me be leaping
> Pressing on, mounting
> Through the clouds sweeping.

Faust and Helen urge caution, but Euphorion ignores them.[38]

> Still will I leap ever higher,
> Still a wider world survey.
> Now perceive I where I stand,
> In the midst of Pelops' land.

Here Goethe's poetry reveals Euphorion most clearly as the representative of Byron and the Greek cause. Standing in the middle of the Peloponnese, the center of Greek resistance to the Turks, Euphorion declares,[39]

> All whom this land has bred,
> Ever on peril fed,
> Free their own blood to spend
> In courage without end . . .
> May these from toils of war
> Have noble gain.

Despite the warnings of Helen, Faust, and the Chorus that he is risking death, Euphorion, like Byron, renounces the role of the spectator in favor of action and engagement:[40]

> Shall I view from far disaster?
> Nay, their bitter woes I'll share.

The actions and the fate of Euphorion convey the complexity of Goethe's views on Byron and the cause of Greek freedom. Despite his sympathy for the Greeks, Goethe believed that a wild, uncontrolled, and selfish freedom was dangerously destructive. In his tragic climb to the mountain heights Euphorion declares, "*Keine Wälle, Keine Mauern,/Jeder nur sich selbst bewusst.*" "No walls, no restraints,/Each aware only of himself" (9855–56). His lack of self control and his disregard for social integration were inimical to what Goethe regarded as true freedom. The direct contrast between this sort of wild freedom and genuine freedom of the will is explicitly pointed out by the chorus following the death of Euphorion. They lament, "*Doch du ranntest unaufhaltsam/Frei ins willenlose Netz,/So entzweitest du gewaltsam/Dich mit Sitte, mit Gesetz*"; "Thus you ran headlong/Free into a will-less net,/Thus did you forcefully separate/Yourself from morality and law" (9923–26). His fate mirrors what Goethe observed of Byron, that with "the most unbounded personal freedom . . . the world was still a prison to him. His going to Greece was not a decision of his own free will [*freiwilliger Entschluss*]; his troubled relationship with the world drove him there."[41] Goethe saw his pursuit of boundless personal freedom as a destructive enslavement to passion.

Even so, since Goethe saw Byron as able in his poetry if not in his life to accept restraints (as shown by his adherence to the classical unities of time, space, and action), it was not incongruous to associate him with Euphorion as a symbol of modern poetry. Eckermann notes that in a discussion of Byron's poetic genius he stated his opinion that Goethe had been "completely right in establishing for him [Byron] in the Helena an undying monument of his love." To which Goethe replied, "I could use no one, as the representative of the modern poetic era, other than him, who is without question the greatest talent of the century. Moreover, Byron is neither antique nor romantic, but is like the present day itself."[42] Euphorion and Byron could exemplify the poetic spirit with its uplifting and liberating quality. As Euphorion pursues his dangerous climb up the mountain heights the chorus declares, "Mounting to heaven, see/Blest soul of Poesie!"[43] Since honoring something above us makes us free, poetry could foster such an attitude. With Euphorion's death near the end of Act III, the allusions to Byron become quite open when the stage directions observe, "We believe we recognize in the dead boy a well known figure" (9902–3), thus emphasizing how Byron's poetry represents human striving for high ideals.

So far as the ideal of freedom is concerned, however, the impulsive actions of Euphorion and Byron serve primarily as negative examples which prepare the way for the positive treatment of this issue presented in Act V. The example of balance and moderation provided by Faust's experience with Helen increasingly shapes his development as he becomes more involved in productive social activity. At the beginning of Act IV he formulates his last great project as he looks out from a mountain top toward the Dutch coast and envisions a land reclamation plan that clearly symbolizes the hoped-for resolution of his long inner conflict between reason and passion. Observing the destructive force of the waves, he declares:[44]

> There wave on wave, by hidden power heaved,
> Reigns and recedes, and nothing is achieved.
> This thing can sadden me to desperation,
> Wild elements in aimless perturbation!
> To soar beyond itself aspired my soul:
> Here would I strive and this would I control.

In the final act, this project is realized when Faust gains control of this territory and sets about building dikes and draining the land. But this so-cially constructive task leads to the tragic death of Baucis and Philemon when Faust, out of impatience, invokes Mephisto's aid to deprive them of their land.

Seen as a moral crisis, the death of Baucis and Philemon resulted from Faust's egotistical desire to have an unobstructed view of his accomplish-ments. When he understands the consequences of his immoral action, how-ever, he is able to achieve a new level of self-mastery. Alone in his palace he observes, "I have not yet fought my way to freedom" (11403), and he realizes he must renounce the devil's aid to achieve true autonomy. In the following scene, when he is confronted by Care, he refuses to rely on magic to avoid being harmed, and this results in his being blinded. Even so, his personal loss is associated with inner enlightenment. He declares, "Deep falls the night, in gloom precipitate;/What then? Clear light within my mind shines still."[45] Faust's blindness is at once an appropriate punishment for the moral weakness that caused the Baucis and Philemon tragedy (his vain desire "To look on all that I've achieved"),[46] and more positively a sign that his inner reason will henceforth prevail over the temptations of the external world. Following both Rousseau and Kant, Goethe presents Faust as achieving true freedom by learning to curb his selfish impulses in favor of the common good of society. Having been blinded to the outer world, Faust relies on the inner light of moral reason in enunciating his last great vision of the future:[47]

> I work that millions may possess this space,
> If not secure, a free and active race. . . .
> A paradise our closed-in land provides,
> Though to its margin rage the blustering tides; . . .
> Here wisdom speaks its final word and true,
> None is of freedom or of life deserving
> Unless he daily conquers it anew. . . .
> Such busy, teeming throngs I long to see,
> Standing on freedom's soil, a people free.

Freedom results from a self-imposed order which channels and controls self-ish emotional energies just as the dikes control and utilize the aimless power of the sea.

The concept of freedom that emerges in Act V is related not only to the moral freedom found in the philosophies of Kant and Rousseau but also to the aristocratic tradition described by Leonard Krieger in *The German Idea of Freedom*. For Kant and Rousseau ethical conduct rested on a recognition that the moral law of the general will or the categorical imperative was superior to the desire for individual advantage; one gained autonomy and freedom from the slavery of these desires by a rational decision to subject oneself to this higher moral law. This has an exact analogue in the tradition of aristocratic freedom, which also rested on the individual's recognition of a higher order. In the feudal hierarchy a lord's freedoms or liberties were restricted to his own domain or fief where he was autonomous, and ideally he could only exercise those liberties after acknowledging loyalty to his over-lord. Goethe illustrates this ideal medieval social model in his description of Helen's relationships with her vassals in Act III, and he also gives a contrasting instance showing the dangers of unlimited freedom at the end of Act IV. There the Emperor allows all real authority to slip away when he parcels out his domain to his five great vassals, saying "Indeed as lords you have possession completely free" (*Zwar habt ihr den Besitz als Herren völlig frei*) (10967).

The more modern world of Act V has its roots in this feudal tradition, for Faust is only able to realize his great project after the Emperor grants him the coastal territory as a fief in return for the valuable military service he has rendered.[48] But in contrast to the weak Emperor, Faust becomes a powerful and dynamic ruler.[49] After his confrontation with Care, when he finally achieves autonomy and is blinded, he immediately gives orders to complete his project: "What I conceived I hasten to complete;/The lord's word alone gives weight" (11501–2). For Goethe, true freedom was always associated with authority.

III

To demonstrate the importance of the political events of the 1820s to the idea of freedom developed in *Faust Two* it is necessary to consider when those passages dealing with the issue of freedom took shape. With respect to the various sections of Act V, controversy has been fueled in part by Goethe's August 1815 comment that the end of the Faust poem was "already finished, and is very well turned out and imposing, out of the best time."[50] The "best time" refers to the period around 1800 when Goethe was closely associated with Schiller, but scholars disagree about what Goethe later added to Act V and how much of this early "finished" version he retained. Certain aspects of the puzzle, however, have been resolved by Alexander Hohlfeld, who focusses particular attention on the "Midnight,"

"Great Outer-court of the Palace" and "Burial" scenes of Act V, the scenes which contain the key statements of Goethe's concept of freedom.

Hohlfeld notes that in the 1826 manuscript version of Faust's last speech, which describes his great land reclamation project, there is an unresolved conflict between the idea of simply draining water from a swampy area and the much grander project of pushing back the sea with dikes and break-waters. He shows that the former concept, which probably dated back to the "best time," was overtaken in 1825–26 by the idea of Faust as a fighter against the destructive power of the sea, a theme underlying key parts of Acts IV and V in the final version. Since Faust sees the sea as analogous to his own wild feelings, this idea reflects the psychological theme of gaining freedom through the imposition of self control, and this suggests that these two themes came together in the 1825–26 period when Goethe resumed work on *Faust Two* in the wake of Byron's death. [51]

Although parts of the "Midnight," "Great Outer-court," and "Burial" scenes may go back to the period before the 1820s, Hohlfeld shows that only a few lines of Faust's final speech could possibly have originated then, and in the preserved manuscript fragments relevant to this passage the references to freedom are all later additions. For example, lines 11579–80 of the fin-ished poem read: "Such busy, teeming throngs I long to see,/Standing on freedom's soil, a people free," [*Auf freiem Grund mit freiem Volke stehn,*] but in the early version they read: "There I will live among you,/Standing truly on my own soil and land." [*Auf warhaft eigenem Grund und Boden stehn.*][52] The other freedom references in this speech (lines 11564 and 11575) are also missing in the earlier version. Similarly, in the earlier manu-script fragments of the "Midnight" scene, Faust's line (11403): "I have not yet fought my way to freedom" [*Noch hab' ich mich ins Freie nicht ge-kämpft*], does not appear. [53]

While there is general agreement that most of Act III was written after 1825, the first half of the opening scene (lines 8489–802) was largely com-pleted some 25 years earlier, [54] and the idea of Faust's encounter with Helen is one of the oldest parts of the poem's original design. It has been argued that this early material decisively shaped the subsequent continuation of Act III and that the later parts of the Helena reflect the basic plan which devel-oped at the time of Goethe's friendship with Schiller around 1800. Karl Meissinger argues that "the decisive idea of the Helena act was already at hand in a fully developed form in 1800. It lay in . . . bringing together the medieval-modern man Faust with Helen, the essence of antique beauty . . . [thereby conveying] the idea of an *aesthetic education* of the hero through the purity and discipline of the antique."[55] Meissinger rightly emphasizes the influence of Goethe's earlier association with Schiller in the development of this idea, but he fails to appreciate the complex historical relationship which tied this idea to the issue of freedom.

Summarizing the ideas on the beautiful which Schiller developed out of Kant's philosophy, Meissinger observes that "Through an aesthetic education one could prepare people for the good. . . . The beautiful is the light rainbow bridge over the chasm which for the first time makes believable to the sensualist, to the cowardly slave of the desires, the possibility of a passage into the realm of freedom."[56] This concept underlies the role of Helen in *Faust Two* where she, the essence of beauty, points the way to Faust's eventual passage (in Act V) into the realm of morality and freedom. While this basic element of the Helena may well go back to the time of Goethe's friendship with Schiller, Meissinger underrates the importance of Goethe's further development of the Helena in the wake of Byron's death. He concedes that "Byron's death gave the impetus to the completion of the third act and also of Part Two. The figure of Euphorion absorbs into itself the great mass of experiences with which Goethe's great practical wisdom had been enriched by a quarter century of romanticism." But he then maintains that "for the over-all movement of the action in *Faust* . . . this enrichment of the third act is without significance."[57] This view neglects the fact that Goethe's outlook and the figure of Euphorion were also enriched by a quarter century of dramatic historical events.

While the turmoil of the Napoleonic period had made Goethe skeptical of any unbridled advocacy of political freedom, the events of the 1820s produced a subtle but important shift in his views. Goethe's love of ancient Greek culture gradually brought him to support the Greek War of Independence despite the fact that its success involved a breach in the conservative system he had previously seen as a bulwark against revolutionary disorder. This qualified support of the Greek cause nonetheless left him at odds with such Philhellenes as Bentham and Stanhope, whose revolutionary freedom he regarded as dangerously destabilizing. The death of Byron gave him an opportunity to put forth in *Faust Two* an alternative to this revolutionary position, an alternative drawing on the aristocratic, particularist tradition of freedom, with its acceptance of hierarchical limits, as well as on Schiller's idea of the beautiful as freedom in the world of phenomena, an idea which also rests on the acceptance of limits. Absorbing Byron into the figure of Euphorion, he used Act III to contrast the negative example of a life destroyed by unrestrained freedom with the positive model of beauty provided by Byron's poetry, which united passion with discipline.

Faust's further activities in the final two acts draw out the political implications of this conception of freedom. Having learned the important lessons of balance and restraint from Helen and Euphorion, Faust then goes on in Act IV to participate in the political struggle between the Emperor and Anti-Emperor, an allusion to the central historical events of Goethe's life: the overthrow of the *ancien régime*, the Napoleonic wars, and the restoration. Faust's morally questionable (magical) support helps the Emperor, but this ruler's own weakness nonetheless undermines the unity of his state. Only in Act V, after becoming lord of his own domain, can Faust express his final vision of freedom synthesizing striving with self control. This last stage of Faust's development reveals the political ideal of Goethe's final years. Having gained personal freedom through self mastery, Faust represents the effective enlightened ruler who can bring both technological progress and disciplined freedom to his people.

The conception of freedom which Goethe opposed to that of the Benthamites both reflected and helped to perpetuate the profound political and cultural differences between Western and Central Europe. For Bentham and his enthusiastic followers among the London Greek Committee, freedom was, as much as anything else, a political slogan which could be used as a weapon against the conservative system established by the Holy Alliance. On his first trip to Greece in 1823, Stanhope had occasion to explain the aims of the Committee to various sympathetic groups he contacted along the way, and his accounts of these meetings reveal the ideological character of his efforts. When he met with the Zurich Greek Committee, he told them that "the grand object of the Committee was to give freedom and knowledge to Greece." He explained that "To communicate knowledge to the Greeks was an object the Committee had near at heart. From this source spring order, morality, freedom, and power. The venerable Bentham . . . had employed his days and his nights in contemplating and writing on the constitution of Greece, and in framing for her a body of rational laws, the most useful of human offerings."[58] Stanhope next traveled to Bern where he met with Count Capo d'Istria, who later became the leader of the new Greek state. Their discussion concerned the complex international context of the struggle: "The Count thought our end should be to enlighten Greece and to act upon utilitarian principles. Yes, said I, Count, but do you think that the *Sainte Alliance* will allow Greece to establish a virtuous republic. His Excellency . . . then said that it was not in the nature of things that monarchs should encourage republics." [59] The Benthamite plan for bringing freedom to the Greeks was revolutionary above all in its insistence that Greece should become a republic rather than a monarchy, and this goal represented a profound threat to the established order.

Bentham himself forcefully expressed this view in one of his letters to the Greeks. On November 24, 1823, he wrote, "Grecians!—Some there are among you who say—Give yourselves to a king! Give yourselves to a king? Know that, if you do so, you give yourselves to an enemy." Advising them to look to the "Anglo-American republic" for their model, he declared: "So sure as you have a king, so sure has the Holy Alliance another member. And what is the Holy Alliance, but an alliance of all kings, against all those who are not kings." The strength of this international conservative system drove Bentham to the alternative of international revolution: "When there was no Holy Alliance, in each State, oppression . . . might, for a time, be more or less mitigated by a revolution in that State. It was so in England in 1688. But now, under the Holy Alliance, there can be no . . . revolution in any one State, without a revolution in every other." [60] During the 1820s, when liberal revolutionary movements developed in Spain, Portugal, Italy, and South America, as well as Greece, Bentham tried to persuade the leaders of these movements to adopt a standardized legal code based on his own philosophical and political principles. [61] So the London Greek Committee was in fact part of an international revolutionary movement.

From Goethe's Central European perspective the activities of the Benthamites were as foolish as they were dangerous, and he saw his ideas as diametrically opposed to theirs. In March 1830, just two years before he and Bentham were to die, Goethe compared himself to Bentham in a conversation with Friedrich Soret. Noting the courage required to live a long life, he pointed to Bentham, "this grand fool of a radical; he is holding out well, although he is several weeks my senior." When Soret observed that they also shared a youthful vitality, Goethe responded, "It is true, but we are at the two ends of the chain. He wants to tear down; for myself I would like to preserve everything. To be so radical at his age is the height of extravagance." Soret then suggested that there were two kinds of radicalism, "One which at the risk of turning everything upside down wishes to tear down in order to reconstruct" and a second which "recognizes the weak parts of a government, points out its vices, indicates the means to remedy them, and wishes to produce the good without using violent means. Your Excellency, transported to the soil of England, would not be able to avoid this second type of radicalism."[62] Although Goethe was not convinced, the contrast between the critical descriptions of the old order in Acts I and IV of *Faust Two* and the progressive world of Act V supports Soret's point.

For Goethe political freedom could not be detached from the concept of free will, an idea which had no place in Bentham's mechanistic philosophy; and following Kant and Schiller, Goethe associated free will with self-imposed authority. Where Bentham and his followers feared that the newly liberated Greeks might succumb to authoritarian rule, Goethe felt the greater danger was a chaotic disintegration of authority such as he described in the medieval German context of *Faust Two*, Acts I and IV. After Capo d'Istria became president of the Greek republic in 1828, Goethe predicted that he would not last long because "he is no soldier. We have no example in which a cabinet man has been able to organize a revolutionary state and subordinate the military and the generals to himself. With a sabre in the fist, at the head of an army one may command and give orders, and one can be sure of being obeyed." Goethe assured Eckermann that he would see his prediction fulfilled because "it lies in the nature of things."[63] In fact Capo d'Istria was murdered three years later, and Greece was eventually forced to accept a monarchy.

Goethe's conviction that a revolutionary republic would fail was based on the close relationship he saw between freedom and authority. The German idea of freedom required the acceptance of some higher authority which imposed limits on the expression of individual interests and inclinations, and for Goethe the disorder of revolution made acknowledging such limits impossible. Holding to the ideal of enlightened reform from above, he advanced in *Faust Two* a concept of freedom which established the achievement of individual moral autonomy as a fundamental element of a just political order. Such a conception of freedom, nourished in the more conservative cultural and political context of central Europe, necessarily turned the attention of the individual seeking reform in an inward direction, thus reinforcing the "*innerlichkeit*" which is so prominent a feature of the German cultural landscape. While western European radicals such as Bentham had little patience for the metaphysical refinements of this inwardness, it contributed to that second kind of radicalism to which Soret referred.

The debate between Goethe and the Benthamites concerning the Greek War of Independence and the nature of freedom testifies to the increasingly transnational character of politics and culture in nineteenth-century Europe, and both points of view in the debate proved important to the emerging liberal tradition. John Stuart Mill, having been rigorously educated within the framework of Bentham's philosophy, eventually found its neglect of the inner emotional realm unsatisfying and turned to what he called the Germanic school of Kant and Goethe to redress the balance.[64] Sigmund Freud, who drew on the English empiricists in developing his psychological theories and was no less indebted to the German tradition of Kant, Schopenhauer, and Goethe, alluded specifically to Faust's great project to contain and channel the force of the sea in illustrating the interplay between the rational ego and the emotional forces of the id.[65] Faust's vision of a free people on freedom's soil rested on a psychological conception of freedom which saw the individual as an active, autonomous force capable of improving the world by using reason to channel and control the otherwise destructive forces of human passion. For Mill and Freud as well as many other representatives of nineteenth-century liberal culture, this vision provided an essential counterpoint to the mechanistic explanation of physical nature which they also accepted. For all the opposition between the ideas of Bentham and Goethe, the nineteenth century seems to have needed them both.

Experience Without a Subject:
Walter Benjamin and the Novel

"However paradoxical it may seem," Hans-Georg Gadamer writes in *Truth and Method*, "the concept of experience seems to me one of the most obscure that we have."[1] "Of all the words in the philosophical vocabulary," Michael Oakeshott agrees in *Experience and its Modes*, "it is the most difficult to manage."[2] Derived from the Latin *experientia*, which meant trial, proof, and experiment (an acceptation still current in French), it has come to mean a welter of different things. Accordingly, the term has generated enormous controversy. Literary critics like Philip Rahv have denounced the "cult of experience" in American literature, while historians like Joan Scott have bemoaned its privileged role as evidentiary foundation in the work of figures as diverse as R. G. Collingwood and E. P. Thompson.[3] And for all those who resist so-called "identity politics," in which legitimation comes from who you are—your "subject position," in the current jargon—and not from the force of what you say, the appeal to something called experience has also become a prime target.

And yet, obscurity and unmanageability notwithstanding, "experience" remains a key term in both everyday language and the lexicons of esoteric philosophies. Indeed, Gadamer, Oakeshott, and a host of other twentieth-century thinkers, from Martin Buber to Georges Bataille, from Edmund Husserl to John Dewey, from Ernst Jünger to Jean-François Lyotard, have felt compelled to mull over its multiple meanings and contradictory implications. But perhaps no one has had as profound an effect on our appreciation of its varieties as Walter Benjamin; nor has anyone else made us as sensitive to the crisis of at least one of those varieties. Indeed, experience has rightly been called "Benjamin's great theme . . . the true focal point of his analysis of modernity, philosophy of history, and theory of the artwork."[4]

As a result, a formidable exegetical literature has developed around Benjamin's discussion of the concept, a literature whose central contributors would include among others, Richard Wolin, Marleen Stoessel, Thorsten

Meiffert, Michael Jennings, Miriam Hansen, and Michael Makropolous.[5] It is not my goal to rehearse their complicated arguments, or provide a way to adjudicate their differences. Instead, I want to suggest that we might find an important confirmation of Benjamin's theory of experience in a place where he himself never thought to find it: in that modern literary genre towards which he felt so ambivalent, the novel. I want to argue that it was in a vital linguistic aspect of the novel, which Benjamin for all his fascination with language failed to explore, that this confirmation can be found.

Before making this case, however, it will be necessary to present in very general terms Benjamin's theory of experience. Most of the attention paid to it has been to his mature reflections, in particular the crucial distinction between *Erlebnis* and *Erfahrung* he developed in such works as *One-way Street*, "Experience and Poverty," "The Storyteller," and "On Some Motifs in Baudelaire."[6] Benjamin's juxtaposition of these terms was not, to be sure, his own invention. Following the lead of Rousseau and Goethe, Wilhelm Dilthey had contrasted *Erlebnis* (or sometimes *das Erleben*), which he identified with "inner lived experience," to *aüssere Erfahrung*, by which he meant "outer sensory experience."[7] Whereas the latter was grounded in the discrete stimuli of mere sensation, the former involved the internal integration of sensations into a meaningful whole available to hermeneutic interpretation. Edmund Husserl had likewise disdained the scientific and neo-Kantian notion of *Erfahrung*, based on conceptual reflection, as inferior to the richer, intuitively meaningful *Erlebnis* of the pre-reflexive *Lebenswelt*.[8] And Ernst Jünger had celebrated war as the arena of an authentic *Erlebnis* absent from the desiccated *Erfahrung* of bourgeois, civilian existence.[9] In all these cases, *Erlebnis* was an honorific term for subjective, concrete, intuitive responses to the world that were prior to the constructed abstractions of science or the intellect.

What set Benjamin apart from his predecessors was his disdain for both the alleged immediacy and meaningfulness of *Erlebnis* and the overly rational, disinterested version of *Erfahrung* defended by the positivists and neo-Kantians. Instead, he favored an alternative closer to what Gadamer has called a dialectical concept of experience, a learning process over time, combining negations through unpleasant episodes with affirmations through positive ones to produce something akin to a wisdom that can be passed down via tradition through the generations.[10] Unlike Dilthey, he did not give the name *Erlebnis* to such a dialectical process. The immediate, passive, fragmented, isolated, and unintegrated inner experience of *Erlebnis* was, Benjamin argued, very different from the cumulative, totalizing accretion of transmittable wisdom, of epic truth, that was *Erfahrung*. Here the echoes of the German word for taking a journey (*fahren*), a narratable exploration of parts hitherto unknown, could be heard.

Such an historically grounded notion of experience, moreover, was necessarily more than individual, for cumulative wisdom could occur only within a community, which could transmit the tales of the tribe through oral traditions such as storytelling. Thus, it was the Haggadic quality of truth, its ability to be handed down from generation to generation, like the Passover story, through collective memory rather than official historical records, that marked genuine experience. The contrast between the Jewish notion of *Zakhor*, group memory, and historical science, to which Yosef Yerushalmi has recently drawn attention, was thus implicitly active in Benjamin's antithetical concepts of experience.[11]

Benjamin, as we know, was deeply skeptical about the possibility of restoring genuine *Erfahrung* in the modern, capitalist world.[12] Although he resisted claiming it had been completely extirpated, he spoke movingly about its "atrophy" (*Verkümmerung*),[13] in particular after World War One. The continuum of *Erfahrung* had already been broken by the unassimilable shocks of urban life and the replacement of artisanal production by the dull, non-cumulative repetition of the assembly line. Meaningful narrative had been supplanted by haphazard information and raw sensation in the mass media. Only the Revolution, he contended in his more Marxist moods, might create a new community in which the lost "integrity of the contents"[14] of transmitted dialectical truth would be regained.

But even when Benjamin's theory of experience can be called most materialist,[15] his doubts about the restoration of the fabric of genuine *Erfahrung* remained strong. A primary reason for those doubts was the stubbornly theological dimension of his work, which was never fully disentangled from its Marxist counterpart. For it was here that a powerful component of his theory of experience can also be found, a component Gershom Scholem called his quest for "absolute experience."[16] In one of his first considerations of this theme, his 1917–18 essay "On the Program of the Coming Philosophy," Benjamin explicitly faulted the neo-Kantian concept of experience, exemplified in Hermann Cohen's *Kants Theorie der Erfahrung*, for being too narrowly empirical and scientific, and thus excluding metaphysical and religious experiences.[17] Although unwilling to make the latter the *only* source of genuine experience, which he pluralistically called "the uniform and continuous multiplicity of knowledge,"[18] Benjamin clearly thought that without a religious component, experience would remain woefully impoverished. For "there is a unity of experience that can by no means be understood as a sum of experiences, to which the concept of knowledge as theory is *immediately* related in its continuous development. The object and the content of this theory, this concrete totality of experience, is religion." [19]

Religious experience is particularly important, Benjamin suggested, because it transcends the problematic dichotomy of subject and object, which underlay both the scientific notion of empirical *Erfahrung* and the non-rationalist notion of *Erlebnis*. It is a "true experience, in which neither god nor man is object or subject of experience but in which this experience is based on pure knowledge. . . . The task of future epistemology is to find for knowledge the sphere of total neutrality in regard to the concepts of both subject and object, in other words, it is to discover the autonomous, innate sphere of knowledge in which this concept in no way continues to designate the relation between two metaphysical entities." [20] Later, in his more Marxist phase, Benjamin contrasted a collective subjective experience, that of the community to be created after the Revolution, to the isolated individual *Erlebnis* of modern, capitalist life; but here he was arguing for an experience that paradoxically went beyond that of any subject, collective or individual, an experience that might justly be called noumenal or ontological. As such, it was far less a synonym for active human making than his later concept of *Erfahrung* has seemed to Benjamin's commentators. [21]

Rather than musing on the "varieties of religious experience," in the manner of William James, Benjamin focussed on only one. The locus of that experience, he argued in "On the Program of the Coming Philosophy," was to be found not in sensation or perception, but rather in language, that region of human endeavor Johann Georg Hamann had been the first to challenge Kant in stressing. "A concept of knowledge gained from reflection on the linguistic nature of knowledge will create a corresponding concept of experience," Benjamin insisted, "which will also encompass regions that Kant failed to integrate into his system. The realm of religion should be mentioned as the foremost of these." [22] Here language reveals itself as more than a mere tool of communication in which the feelings, observations, or thoughts of a subjective interiority reveal themselves to another subject. Here the divine word manifests itself ontologically, prior to the subjective conventionalism of human name-giving.

A religiously inflected notion of language in which the dichotomy of subject and object is transcended and ontological truth revealed—the early Benjamin is clearly invoking a concept of experience unlike any we have previously mentioned. Kantian *Erfahrung* is the empirical experience of the transcendental, scientific, cognitive subject; Diltheyan *Erlebnis* is the inner experience of the contingent subject prior to rational reflection or scientific cognition; even the Haggadic, epic truth transmitted through narrative continuity can be understood as that of a collective subject, a communal meta-subject beyond the isolated, damaged subjects of modern life. But religious (or "absolute") experience, as Benjamin describes it, implies a point of indifference between subject and object, an equiprimordiality prior to their differentiation. As Winfried Menninghaus has put it, "his emphatic concept of experience" is "an ultimately messianic category of unrestricted synthesis," which is linked to forms of meaning that might even be called mythical.[23] It was for this reason that even his close friend Theodor Adorno could grow uneasy:

His target is not an allegedly over-inflated subjectivism but rather the notion of a subjective dimension itself. Between myth and reconciliation, the poles of his philosophy, the subject evaporates. Before his Medusan glance, man turns into the stage on which an objective process unfolds. For this reason Benjamin's philosophy is no less a source of terror than a promise of happiness.[24]

As a consequence, suggestive comparisons might be drawn to a similar notion of ontological experience in the work of Martin Heidegger, who was also skeptical of the overly subjective bias of individual *Erlebnis* and scientific *Erfahrung*, and had no use for collective meta-subjects either.[25] Or perhaps the poetry of Hölderlin, important for both Benjamin and Heidegger, might be adduced to demonstrate what they were after.[26] It might also be fruitful to situate Benjamin's search for an experience that transcends the subject/object opposition in the context of many other such attempts by twentieth-century artists. The Surrealists, whose writings Benjamin himself claimed were concerned primarily with experiences, come immediately to mind.[27] And we might focus on the heterodox means, such as hashish, Benjamin explored to provide nonreligious glimpses of absolute experience, those profane illuminations that broke down the barrier between subject and object.

But, rather than follow these well-trodden paths, I want to go down instead the one that Benjamin himself suggested was the locus of nonsubjective experience, that of language. And I want to suggest that even if we jettison the religious and magical underpinnings of Benjamin's own complicated theory of language, with its hope for the recovery of divinely inspired names and nonsensuous, mimetic similarities, we can still discover in the highly secular language of the modern novel unexpected warrant for his argument. We can, I want to claim, identify an intriguing example of experience without a subject that is independent of a redemptive, quasi-mythical notion of metaphysical or religious truth, or a magical notion of analogical correspondences, which are bound to make many of us uncomfortable in this age of cynical reason.

Benjamin's own mixed feelings about the novel are, to be sure, widely appreciated. Following Georg Lukács's lead in *The Theory of the Novel*, he saw it as the genre for an age of "transcendental homelessness" in which the community underpinning the oral transmission of tales was shattered.[28] The printed book undermined the need for collective group memory through public narration; epic meaning survived only in the endangered form of the tale. "The birthplace of the novel," Benjamin charged, "is the solitary individual, who is no longer able to express himself by giving examples of his most important concerns, is himself uncounseled, and cannot counsel others. To write a novel means to carry the incommensurable to extremes in the representation of human life."[29]

Although novels center on "the meaning of life," they never get beyond demonstrating that life in the age of information is inherently meaningless; the experience they depict is thus that of *Erlebnis* at its emptiest. The fate of the characters, indeed their very deaths, can only provide a simulacrum of meaning for readers, whose lives are deprived of it. Novels rely on psychological explanations instead of depicting the inherent meaning of the world of the epic, a meaning which is self-evident and in need of no external explanatory scaffolding. Even when novels like Proust's *À la recherche du temps perdu* attempt to restore coherent retrospective meaning, they can only do so through the subjective gloss of memory rather than through a presentation of objectively intelligible experience.[30] Although "involuntary memory," the technique Proust appropriated from Bergson, was closer than its voluntary counterpart to the anamnestic moment in true *Erfahrung*, it was only artificially generated through the novelist's fiat.

How then, we might ask, can the novel provide any confirmation of Benjamin's belief in the possibility of experience without a subject? How can it serve as the placeholder of an "absolute experience" beyond mere *Erlebnis* or even the lost *Erfahrung* of the storyteller? The answer resides in an aspect of the novel, which Benjamin, to my knowledge, never acknowledged: its frequent adoption of a stylistic mode that was absent from virtually all previous genres, a mode which is known in French as the "*style indirect libre*," in German as "*erlebte Rede*," and in English as "represented speech." It is further connected to the grammatical variant known as "the middle voice," which differs from active and passive voices and has been identified by critics like Roland Barthes as characteristic of "the intransitive" writing of modernism.[31] Although the presence of these linguistic phenomena does not suggest that the novel taken as a coherent, generic whole represents a prefiguration of "absolute experience," it allows us to believe that within certain novels, there exist moments that do. Such moments, to be sure, may not prefigure the fully redemptive version of that experience hoped for by Benjamin at his most utopian, but perhaps they are instances of what he liked to call the "*weak* Messianic power"[32] permitted to us even in the darkest of times.

The "*style indirect libre*" was first singled out for serious analysis by the Swiss linguist and student of Saussure, Charles Bally, in 1912,[33] and then given special significance by Proust in his celebrated essay of 1920 on Flaubert's style.[34] A year later, Étienne Lorck coined the term "*erlebte Rede*" for its German counterpart; and in 1924 Otto Jespersen introduced the less widely adopted "represented speech" for the English variant.[35] In the years since, a host of linguists and literary critics, among them V. N. Vološinov, Stephen Ullmann, Dorrit Cohn, Roy Pascal, Hans Robert Jauss, and Ann Banfield, have explored every aspect of its usage.[36] Even intellectual historians like Dominick LaCapra have evoked it to argue that Flaubert's prose style, rather than his apparently salacious content, led to the trial of *Madame Bovary* in 1857.[37]

Its significance for the issue of experience is suggested, if in somewhat misleading ways, by the fact that the German variant was called "*erlebte Rede*" by Lorck, who was a student of Karl Vossler, the Romantic linguist of individualist subjectivism. Vossler, an opponent of Saussure, stressed the psychological content of linguistic performance, psychology understood not in positivist/empiricist terms, but in those of *Lebensphilosophie*.[38] That is, language expressed the internal, subjective state of mind of the speaker, rather than an impersonal sign system, and the linguist studied stylistics and *Spracheseele* (the soul expressed through style) rather than grammar. Accordingly, as one commentator has noted, "the chief reason Lorck invented the term '*erlebte Rede*' was to stress the irrational and rapturous in contrast to the informational function of language. It was thus related to philosophies of 'life' and immediate 'experience.'"[39]

How then can we claim that the indirect free style instantiates Benjamin's notion of "absolute experience" prior to the split between subject and object, if it seems to be an example of *Erlebnis* at its most objectionable? Let us examine more closely its implications for the answer. Lorck contrasted "*erlebte Rede*" to the direct discourse he called "*gesprochene Rede*" (repeated speech) and the indirect discourse he dubbed *"berichtete Rede"* (communicated speech). Direct discourse or repeated speech is uttered by a speaker, say a hero in a play, as his own thoughts—for example, Faust saying "Habe nun, ach! Philosophie, Juristerei." Indirect discourse or communicated speech occurs when a second person cites the speech of a first to a third.' "Faust hat gesagt: 'Habe nun, ach! Philosophie, Juristerei.'" But *"erlebte Rede"* takes place when a second person wants to recreate in his own mind Faust's thoughts: "Faust hat nun, ach! Philosophie, Juristerei," or insofar as they are past thoughts, "Faust hatte nun, ach!"

Another, much discussed example comes from *Madame Bovary*, where Emma, looking in a mirror after her first act of adultery, is described in the following way:

Elle se répétait: J'ai un amant! un amant! se délectant à cette idée comme à celle d'une autre puberté qui lui serait survenue. Elle allait donc enfin posséder ces plaisirs de l'amour, cette fièvre de bonheur dont elle avait désespéré. Elle entrait dans quelque chose de merveilleux, où tout serait passion, extase, délire.

She repeated: "I have a lover! a lover!" delighting at the idea as if a second puberty had come to her. So at last she was to know those joys of love, that fever of happiness of which she had despaired! She was entering upon a marvelous world where all would be passion, ecstacy, delirium.[40]

What made this passage so scandalous and confusing to Flaubert's critics was their inability to attribute with certainty the shocking sentiments in the last sentence to either the character or the author. Was Flaubert identifying with Emma's fantasy or merely reporting it? His style did not seem to permit a firm answer.[41]

For Lorck, indirect free style was a means of one person re-experiencing the experiences of another (what Dilthey had called *nacherleben*),[42] but not of communicating it to a third. Thus, it is not something actually said in normal conversation, but only exists as a literary convention, only, that is, in written prose. If spoken aloud, it would sound more like a hallucination than a communicative speech act. Lorck thus emphasized its function as an incitement to fantasy, an example of language's ability to transcend the intellect and create anew, as evidence of its status as living *energeia*, to use Humboldt's terms, rather than dead *ergon*.

Subsequent students of free indirect style have agreed with Lorck's claim that intersubjective, public communication is not the goal of language used in this peculiar way. They have further endorsed his belief that it is inherently a written rather than spoken form, showing that language development does not always come from innovations in verbal performance. And they have shared his sense that it provides evidence of a creative capacity in language that calls into question seemingly watertight distinctions like direct and indirect discourse.

But they have vigorously challenged Lorck's Vosslerite assumption that "*erlebte Rede*" is the re-experiencing of an irrational *Erlebnis*. Instead, as Pascal has argued, the subjective function of the style is combined with a narratorial one, which is "communicated through the vocabulary and idiom, through the composition of the sentences and the larger passages, and through the context."[43] That is, there is a subtle distinction preserved in the style between character and narrator, even if the interiorities of the two seem to be perfectly conflated. Similarly, Vološinov claims that we hear a conflict between the evaluative orientation of the character whose speech is reported, and the narrator whose smooth narration is disrupted by its representation. "We perceive the author's accents and intonations being interrupted by these value judgments of another person," he writes. "And that is the way, as we know, in which quasi-direct discourse differs from substituted discourse, where no new accents vis-à-vis the surrounding authorial context appear."[44] The result of all this, as Banfield makes clear, is that the self whose thoughts are reported in the indirect free style, is not equivalent to a single, coherent, egocentric subject at all, a subject whose *Erlebnis* could be *nacherlebt*. "Represented thought," she thus argues, "is an attempt to render thought as nonspeech through the medium of language. Language makes this attempt feasible because it is not synonymous with speech or communication, because speaker and self are distinct concepts, both required by linguistic theory and, hence, both posited as part of the speaker's internalized linguistic knowledge."[45]

In addition to the stylistic expression of this non-personalized notion of experience, there is a grammatical correlate that was most clearly identified by Emile Benveniste in his 1950 essay "Active and Middle Voice in the Verb."[46] Not evident in all languages or equally prominent throughout the history of those where it can be found, the so-called "middle voice" challenges the alternative between active and passive voices, just as the *style indirect libre* calls into question the opposition between direct and indirect discourse. Voice, or to use the technical term, diathesis, indicates the way the subject of a verb is affected by its action. According to Benveniste, whereas verbs in the active voice signify a process in which the subject is outside the action that it achieves, the middle voice signifies a subject *within* that process, even if it entails an object as well. The passive voice was only a late offshoot of the middle voice, produced only when the distinction between agent (subject) and patient (object) came to be regarded as strict.

But the middle voice did not entirely die. Familiar examples in French would be "*Je suis né,*" I was born, and "*il est mort,*" he died. Another from Sanskrit grammar concerns the ritual self-sacrifice of a person, who takes the knife in his own hands and plays the roles of executioner and victim (*yajate* rather than *yajati,* when the priest does the killing).

Benveniste's stress on the importance of the middle voice has had a powerful impact on recent French theory. In his influential 1968 essay on "Différance," Jacques Derrida invoked it to explain the meaning of that crucial deconstructionist neologism. Claiming that différance is an operation that also cannot be conceived either as a passion or an action of a subject, he argued that "the middle voice, a certain nontransitivity, may be what philosophy, at its outset, distributed into an active and a passive voice, thereby constituting itself by means of this repression."[47] Undoing—or at least deconstructing—this repression, he implied, would be an emancipatory gesture, allowing some more primordial operation to re-emerge.

Also extrapolating from Benveniste, Roland Barthes contended, in an essay originally written two years before Derrida's, that the middle voice had recovered its central place in modernist writing, writing in which the authorial function was incorporated into the text, which seemed to write itself. Such writing could thus be called intransitive rather than transitive in the sense of not having an object exterior to it. Whereas Romantic writing involved a subject *an*terior to the actions about which it wrote, modernist writing's subject was *in*terior to and simultaneous with the writing itself. According to Barthes, "in the modern verb of middle voice *to write,* the subject is constituted as immediately contemporary with the writing, being effected and affected by it: this is the exemplary case of the Proustian narrator, who exists only by writing, despite the reference to a pseudo-memory."[48]

Rather than accepting Benjamin's critique of Proust for providing a retrospective and subjective simulacrum of *Erfahrung* through involuntary memory, Barthes insisted that the writing itself contained what Benjamin was seeking. For here we have an example of a linguistic version of experience without the subject, of *écriture* without an *écrivain.*[49] Although Barthes identified intransitive writing with modernism, where techniques like interior monologue are often employed, it would be possible to see its antecedents in the realistic novel in which the *style indirect libre* also appeared—for example in Flaubert. Thus, both on the level of style and on the level of grammatical voice, there is evidence in the novel of those attributes Benjamin denied to it.

One might also note parenthetically that Benjamin's own vaunted style (or rather several styles, because he did not always write in the same manner) can usefully be described as a form of intransitive writing. Even in his most seemingly autobiographical texts, his own expressive subjectivity was ruthlessly suppressed. Nowhere was Benjamin's yearning to efface his authorial presence more evident than in his celebrated desire to write a work composed entirely of quotations.

Whether or not one reads Benjamin's own writing as an example of how experience without a subject can appear outside the novel, it is significant that several recent theorists have found it in non-literary phenomena as well. Ann Banfield, for example, has claimed that in certain modern recording instruments, such as the camera, the thermometer, and the tape recorder, non-sensed sensibilia can manifest themselves without an actual subject present when the event occurs.[50] These phenomena she compares to the *style indirect libre* in the novels of Virginia Woolf and the narratives of Maurice Blanchot, and employs them to criticize the claim that sensibilia always need a subject to do the sensing. "The novel," she writes, "contains sentences with deictics which can be said to represent the perspective of no one; not objective, centerless statements, but subjective yet subjectless, they render the appearances of things to no one, akin in this to the light-sensitive plate."[51] Although she does not draw on Benjamin's famous discussion of photography's revelation of an "optical unconscious," her remarks suggest a similar concern for realities that escape subjective apprehension.[52]

In another context, the philosopher Berel Lang and the intellectual historian Hayden White have suggested that intransitive writing in the middle voice may be a helpful way to present the historical narrative of events such as the Holocaust that defy traditional attempts to write about them as an objective story.[53] For White, following Roland Barthes, modernism is "nothing less than an order of experience beyond (or prior to) that expressible in the kind of *oppositions* we are forced to draw (between agency and patiency, subjectivity and objectivity, literalness and figurativeness, fact and fiction, history and myth and so forth) in any version of realism."[54] This modernist experience, White suggests, is somehow appropriate to that of the Holocaust, "a new form of historical reality, a reality that included, among its supposedly unimaginable, unthinkable and unspeakable aspects, the phenomena of Hitlerism, the Final Solution, total war."[55]

The claims of Lang and White that the unspeakable acts of twentieth-century totalitarianism are best represented in the unsayable sentences we have been calling instances of subjectless experience are, to be sure, controversial; indeed, I have myself vigorously challenged them elsewhere.[56] But they suggest how powerful the appeal of that notion of experience now is. Benjamin's early hope for an "absolute experience," an ontological experience expressed in non-communicative language prior to the privileging of subjectivity in irrational *Erlebnis* or scientific *Erfahrung*, has found an echo in unexpected quarters, where no explicit residue remains of his theological concerns. Although few commentators have noticed the continuities— Banfield is an exception, as she uses the celebrated lines from "The Task of the Translator," "No poem is intended for the reader, no picture for the beholder, no symphony for the listener" as an epigraph for one of her articles[57]—it is clear that shorn of its religious aura, Benjamin's early theory of experience has shown itself to be remarkably durable.

Can it also be said in conclusion to be persuasive as well? In a recent essay addressing many of the themes we have just been discussing, the literary critic Vincent Pecora has expressed alarm at the way in which Benveniste's work on the middle voice has functioned to short-circuit serious discussions of political agency.[58] Betraying a kind of ethnological nostalgia for an allegedly prior state of undifferentiated unity, its celebrants, he claims, fail to ask the hard questions about how we are to find our way back to such a utopian state. "Like the jargon of phenomenology," Pecora protests, "middle voice only superficially 'dissolves' older logical and ethical dilemmas of subject/object relations."[59] As a result, it may even prove an unwitting handmaiden of an authoritarian politics, as Heidegger's philosophy, itself based on a search for experience without a subject, unfortunately did.

A somewhat less sinister scenario is suggested, however, by a reading of the *style indirect libre* that emphasizes its still contestatory impulses as a "dual style." Vološinov, Pascal, and LaCapra all argue for a dialogical rather than empathetic interpretation of it. That is, they stress the ways in which character and narrator remain in tension rather than smoothly be absorbed one into the other, as the Vosslerite theories of *nacherleben* suggest. Vološinov was a member of Michael Bakhtin's circle in the Soviet Union—in fact, some critics have claimed they were actually the same person[60]—so it is not surprising to find the now familiar idea of carnival associated with that of the *style indirect libre*. According to LaCapra, writing about *Madame Bovary* in particular, "the effect here is a carnivalization of narrative voice and a dissemination of the narrator—at times the author—in the text."[61]

It would not be the first time, moreover, that Bakhtin's notion of carnival has been introduced to flesh out Benjamin's arcane ideas. Terry Eagleton did so in the early 1980s, even suggesting certain similarities between the theological premises of the two positions.[62] The implication of this reading of the *style indirect libre* is perhaps not quite as nostalgic and affirmative as the one Pecora attributes to those who have used the middle voice as a way to overcome subject/object dichotomies. For it suggests a less settled notion of a unity prior to the split into direct and indirect discourse, active and passive voice. Here experience without the subject turns out to be experience with more than one subject inhabiting the same space.

Although Benjamin's early notion of absolute experience might not at first glance appear congenial to this version, it does fit well with one of his most intriguing contentions: that the aura involves an unsublatable interaction of gazes. Jürgen Habermas notes, "The experience released from the ruptured shell of the aura was, however, already contained in the experience of the aura itself: the metamorphosis of the object into a counterpart. Thereby a whole field of surprising correspondences between animate and inanimate nature is opened up, wherein even *things* encounter us in the structures of frail intersubjectivity."[63] Habermas's version of that intersubjectivity is, to be sure, more harmonious and reciprocal than the dialogic heteroglossia of Bakhtin, but he insightfully recognizes the importance of multiple subjectivities (indeed, of objects metamorphosed into subjectivities) in Benjamin's concept of *Erfahrung*. If such a reading of absolute experience is allowed, and admittedly it is highly speculative, it might help rebut the charge of recent critics like Leo Bersani that Benjamin was hopelessly nostalgic for a putative lost wholeness, which came dangerously close to the fascist aestheticization of politics he decried.[64]

However one interprets the political implications of absolute experience, the *style indirect libre* or the middle voice, Benjamin's contention that experience is a multi-faceted and internally contested concept has thus been confirmed by the linguistic evidence of novels that Benjamin himself failed to appreciate. Whether we then conclude that absolute experience has virtually vanished from the world or that its utopian spark remains hidden in the pages of those novels, waiting somehow to be actualized by their readers in ways that are impossible to foretell, is a question that no one can confidently answer.

PART II

Aesthetic Politics and
Aesthetic Religion

DEBORA SILVERMAN

Weaving Paintings: Religious and Social Origins of Vincent van Gogh's Pictorial Labor

Introduction: Van Gogh's "Subjectivity": Self and Society in a Distinctively Dutch Historical Context

During this period following the centenary of his death, as Vincent van Gogh soars to new heights as an exceptional genius, reattaching the artist to the social foundations of his creative consciousness is an important and pressing task (Fig. 1). Yet as we begin to relocate van Gogh within the society that produced him, problems quickly emerge with our methodological assumptions, suggesting a cultural history too dependent on one model of modernism. The categories we apply to artists' formations and ideologies are largely generated by the national context that gave the avant-garde its name and its institutional practice in the nineteenth century: that of France. We approach our subjects primed for a history of extrusion, mapping the accelerating detachment of artists from a common value-centered society sundered by Romantic isolationism, the political disillusionment of 1848, and the economic disaggregation of an emerging capitalist market. Expecting to encounter artists who, in response to these historical conditions, embrace their own subjectivity as the ground of modern existence and creation, scholars have constructed their primary tasks to be those of demystification and resocialization. "Contextualist" historians and art historians have waged critical battles against the nineteenth-century myth of the defiant avant-garde, exposing how deeply class, gender, and political strategies were inscribed in an ethic of social and spiritual deracination, and how the practice of self-invention exhibited a strikingly close fit to the marketing tactics of an emerging capitalist economy of spectacle.

In situating van Gogh within the particular social and cultural world of the mid nineteenth-century Netherlands, these French-inspired categories

137

FIG. 1. Photograph of Vincent van Gogh at about eighteen years old. Rijksmuseum Vincent van Gogh, Amsterdam/Vincent van Gogh Foundation.

for interpreting the modernist avant-garde lose their hold and reliability. Indeed, scholars have consistently eluded the most obvious and urgent problems that van Gogh inherited from the distinctive features of his Dutch national environment—the role of religion and the impermissibility of the free individual. In the case of van Gogh, the project of demystification can go too far; our secular need to privilege the analysis of the artist's class-bound codes removes us from the primary religious core of his being. Throughout his life, van Gogh remained an admirer and emulator of Jesus Christ. And though he defied institutional religious practice, van Gogh always construed his art and his life as part of a larger, transcendent, and purposive order, what he called the infinite, mysterious "quelque-chose là-haut."[1]

Most importantly, assimilating van Gogh to a critique of avant-garde subjectivity fails to distinguish the radically different cultural resources available for self-formation in nineteenth-century France and Holland. In mid-century Holland, an intact theological and corporate culture erected powerful barriers to the development of free individualism; indeed, the very notion of a discrete, autonomous ego, detached from the web of kin, community, and divine dependence barely existed in the society in which van Gogh grew up. Acknowledging the very different forms, meanings, and resonances of self and society in France and Holland should then press us to reverse our analytic priorities. Rather than adopting a posture of chastening artists who, given French historical conditions, embraced and inflated their own egoism, I believe we need to begin by appreciating van Gogh's struggle to create a space for the self out of profoundly anti-individualist legacies. This struggle inhered with conflict, and the collision of van Gogh's inherited codes of self-denial and his adoption of an artistic career based on self-development would be expressed not only in the seemingly familiar form of psychological crisis but in his choice of artistic subjects and his repertoire of visual techniques.

In this essay, I want to defamiliarize van Gogh by engaging first in a brief overview of the special social, economic, and religious traditions shaping his development, with particular emphasis on the strength of nineteenth-century Dutch cultural forms of receptivity to the visual and resistance to free subjectivity. I will move on to analyze how van Gogh defined a craft ideal and practice of painting, which led him to develop visual forms emulating the labor processes of pre-industrial weavers. I will demonstrate that the elaboration of painting as woven cloth emerges early in van Gogh's career as a central and unifying key to his stylistic development, extending well beyond the actual depiction of the subjects of weavers in his Nuenen period, and structuring his choices and attitudes in the new environments of Paris, Arles, and Saint-Rémy. I will treat this visual style of weaving paintings as providing van Gogh with formal solutions to culturally-transmitted problems of subjectivity and the sacred. The development of a pictorial language of labor was one response by van Gogh to a cultural heritage fraught with tension over the meaning and justification of the self. By visually incorporating himself into a community of labor by becoming a weaver-painter, van Gogh discovered those forms of connection, production, and interdependence demanded by corporate theological culture that afforded few sanctions for a detached, internally-generated model of creativity.

By focussing on this case study of van Gogh's stylistic choices and culturally-transmitted conflicts I hope to raise two larger issues for reinterpreting modernism: first, that we need to restore historical specificity and tension to the emergence of the notion of free artistic individualism that we assume to reign triumphant among the modernist avant-gardes of Europe; and second, that we need to reconsider the role of religiosity in generating the form, structure, and content of varied types of modernist expressive art. Here I am interested less in charting the symbols and iconography of religious aspiration than in exploring the underlying resources and conflicts generated by varying religious traditions, and their varying conceptions of the status of the self, the value of the image, and the meaning of the visible world.

Culture and Society in the Mid-Nineteenth Century Netherlands: The Avant-Garde as "Dominocratie"

As we move into the cultural ground of the nineteenth-century Netherlands, the institutional structures positioning intellectuals and society in Holland are very different from those of other developing European avant-gardes. In France, the history of intellectuals proceeds as a series of contractions. The Enlightenment legacy of a critical intelligentsia yields, across the revolutionary divides of the nineteenth century, to a separate and autonomous avant-garde of cultural producers, whose creativity is made possible by a cycle of provocation and accommodation to the bourgeoisie from which they issued. This process of French cultural formation is defined by encounters with two centers of power and authority—the Catholic Church and state Academy—which afforded unavoidable targets of resistance or affirmation. But whether embattled or engaged, the French case is dominated by the development of the avant-garde as a separate, identifiable institution, activated by its experience and perception of three monoliths—desiccated bourgeois values, centralized state power, and absolutist clerical authority.

In nineteenth-century Netherlands, neither the rigidity of an official Academy nor the pressures of centralized state power offered such opportunities for cohesive cultural formation. Although during the period of French domination King Louis Napoleon had created a state Academy, the centralized system did not take root, and Dutch artistic production continued to flourish in multiple, decentralized areas marked by strong regional traditions of patronage. The pattern of political rule in the new Kingdom of the Netherlands, established in 1848, remained bound to the corporate and municipal traditions of the Estates General. And in a country where national borders had been in constant flux until 1848, the questions of national identity, regional difference, and religious affiliation all superseded class division as the primary political problems of the 1850s and 1860s. While class tensions surely existed, they remained, until very late in the nineteenth century, subordinated to the religious and regional divisions marking the new Dutch Kingdom.[2] Most importantly, the unifying, constitutive power of the category of "the bourgeois" for the French avant-garde, however disproportionate that category was to its economic reality, was unavailable in the Dutch context of the 1850s. Instead, in the mid-century Netherlands, artistic and cultural innovation was generated not by the power of artists' antibourgeois reaction but within the domain of a liberal church.

Long marked by an Erasmian legacy and a hospitality to the arts, the Dutch Reformed Church emerged in the nineteenth century as the center of cultural production. Cultural activity was indeed so dominated by the clergy that historians have labelled nineteenth century Dutch culture a "dominocratie"—a republic of letters directed by the ministry.[3] Segments of this dominocratie, like the heterodox Dutch Calvinist theology that formed its members, were remarkably receptive to innovation, and functioned in Holland as did the secular avant-garde elsewhere in Europe. The battle over the ancients and the moderns, for example, waged in France by splitting classicist and Romanticist camps within the Academy, had its analogue in the Dutch context in the domesticated Romanticism of Reverend Nicolaas Beets. Beginning in the 1830s, Beets transported a mixed Romantic compound to Holland, adapting the themes and styles of Lord Byron, Sir Walter Scott, and Victor Hugo to existing Dutch literary genres. Beets's resulting works of poetry and prose were extremely popular, and he always combined his literary modernism with his clerical duties, first as pastor at Heemstede

(1840–53), and then at Utrecht (1854–74).[4] This same dual identity as artist and clergyman characterized many other writers of the mid-century Netherlands. "The foremost poet-translator of his day" was the Amsterdam Reverend J. J. L. ten Kate, who composed epic poetry and translated the works, among others, of Alfred de Vigny and Hans Christian Andersen. Eliza Laurillard, another Amsterdam Reformed pastor, not only preached to his flock but gave poetry readings to local literary societies, which awarded him numerous prizes for his artistic endeavors.[5] And Minister Bernard ter Haar, a favorite poet of Vincent van Gogh's father, combined a career publishing scholarly works of ecclesiastical history with his life-long production of poetry, specializing in Romantic meditative works celebrating the heaths, pinewoods, and dunes marking the Dutch regional topographies.[6]

The artistic endeavors of the Dutch clerical elite encompassed not only literary creation but visual forms of expression. For this particular Calvinist intelligentsia approached both word and image with equal comfort. The minister-poets like ten Kate and Beets included their poetry and commentary in lavishly illustrated albums devoted to modern prints and paintings, and also contributed their verses to a new genre of picture postcards popular in the first half of the nineteenth century. Laurillard and ter Haar referred to particular paintings in their sermons. Clergymen, not professional art critics, were the main writers who explicated the works of contemporary painters and printmakers to the readers of Holland's most important art magazine, the *Kunstkronik*.[7] Reverend Nicolaas Beets even wrote a poem in 1841 devoted to a winter landscape by the contemporary painter Andreas Schelfhouts.[8]

An even more telling dimension of this clerical embrace of the visual was the way some of the Dutch minister-poets celebrated the image as the primary form of artistic expression, and aspired to emulate visual evocation in their literary forms. Beets conceived his enormously popular classic of 1839, the tales and sketches he called *Camera Obscura*, as a series of snapshots fixing multiple images of country lives viewed through the writer's moving lens. And Bernard ter Haar offered an extraordinary statement privileging the visual in an essay of 1843 entitled "The Influence of Christianity on Poetry." The title of the essay was misleading; more than a discussion of the relation between Christianity and poetry, it was an exploration of the stylistics of communication, which included a comparison of the language of painting and the language of poetry as vehicles of divine and emotional truth. Ter Haar selected painting unhesitatingly as superior to poetry—the word was limited to its learned associations, he acknowledged, while the evocative nature of the image could "illuminate the whole of eternity in a single blink of an eye."[9]

Thus it was the Dutch dominocratie, a Calvinist clerical elite practicing and promoting the arts, who operated in the mid nineteenth-century Netherlands as the equivalent to the European avant-gardes of Romantic and Realist Europe. Far from isolated groups of intellectuals, these Dutch artist-dominies were deeply rooted in local society and were the directors of a public theological culture. They disseminated to their congregations throughout the Dutch provinces an unusual mixture of Christian teaching and modernist art, alluding, as did ter Haar and others, to contemporary poems and prints in their sermons, and, correspondingly, pressing their art in the service of morality. Their English and French colleagues in the intelligentsia of the mid-century could indeed look longingly on the Dutch case. Responding to the shock of industrial change and the market economy, English writers like Coleridge, Carlyle, and Ruskin envisioned a new clerisy, a secular intellectual elite, to regenerate society through art. French artists of the 1830s attached their ideals of beauty and harmony to the social ground, defining the artist as the vessel of truth, both *"moraliste et politique."* As this bond of the ethical and the aesthetic was shattered on the barricades of 1848, French artists sought new forms of detachment while continuing to cultivate their role as secular seers. The Dutch artist-dominies embodied within a still-intact religious framework the ideals envisioned by the English and French intellectuals for a secular religion of art. The dominocratie approximated Coleridge's clerisy, though still contained within the institution of the church. And the ministers of Holland lived out Hugo's Romantic ideal, pre-1848, of the deep unity of morality and art. This continuum of art and religion was able to flourish in the Netherlands, as we shall see, partly because of the absence of the radical jolts of economic and political revolution that split them apart for the intellectuals on the Continent. This absence of radical change, and the pre-eminence of the clerical artist-intellectual, were not, however, without their own forms of disruption and pressure.

Anti-Egoism in Mid Nineteenth-Century Dutch Political Economy and Theological Culture

The social system dominated by the Dutch clerical elite converged, from multiple directions, in a deep commitment to anti-individualism. Mutually reinforcing patterns in the Dutch economy, society, and religiosity during the period of van Gogh's youth interacted in their shared demotion of the detached individual and their elevation of a larger totality, both secular and sacred.

Economic structures in the Netherlands at 1850 were barely affected by the industrializing patterns already consolidated in sections of England, France, and Belgium. At mid century, 53 percent of the Dutch population was engaged in agricultural activity, and the "heavy industrial" sector comprised a few sugar beet refineries and munitions factories with less than 50 workers. The largest non-agrarian labor force was concentrated in the textile industry of the southern area of Twente and Brabant, the latter of which had only been attached to the Dutch Kingdom in 1848. Very few steam-powered machines were introduced into these areas until after 1875; for the first three quarters of the nineteenth century, textile production continued to rely on the traditional putting-out system of dispersed home industry, though it did so under increasingly intense pressure from competition with the mechanized power of its Belgian neighbor. Railroads began to transform the Dutch landscape also much later than European counterparts. By 1850, for example, Belgium had laid 867 kilometers of the new transport lines; the Netherlands only 170 kilometers. Dutch investors preferred until well into the decade of the 1860s to utilize and adapt an older system of transport and communication—the waterway canals whose arterial connections had begun, already in the seventeenth century, to penetrate the countryside with broad linear axes that other Europeans would find so shocking when a similar pattern took shape in their nineteenth-century iron rail lines.[10]

To be sure, while the Netherlands in 1850 was relatively unmoved by the shock-waves of industrial and technological change affecting her neighbors, the Dutch economy was by no means stagnant. Despite the problems of French domination and the Belgian secession, Dutch national wealth continued to flow in the first half of the nineteenth century from farming and from the traditional source of Dutch economic power since the seventeenth century: commerce, trade, and finance. The new kingdom of 1848 emerged as a prosperous entity, with very high population density, and social groups dispersed almost evenly between urban centers and rural enclaves, while lacking the emphatic divisions of city and country that sharpened in industrializing Europe.

Sustained as it was by the traditional mixture of agriculture and commercial activity, the Netherlandish economy did not unleash the Dutch equivalents of the new captains of industry of nineteenth-century England, France, and Belgium—those mythic bourgeois, self-made men, uprooted, mobile, and dedicated to their own expansive self-interest. Rather, Dutch economic progress through the mid-nineteenth century unfolded with a corporate nexus of connected families, concordant with the system set in place during Holland's first leap forward into economic modernity in the seventeenth century. Capitalism and the "consumer revolution" emerged early in the Netherlands and persisted by defying the equation of economic innovation and individual energy and enterprise. Historians searching for a way to capture the specifically Dutch carriers of capitalism have edged their way to defining what they call an economy driven by a "corporate self" or a "corporate ego," as distinct from our expectation of discrete individual "bourgeois" goaded by competition and the insatiable devotion to the profit motive. This Dutch economy of corporate connection exhibited interesting mixtures of entrepreneurial adventurism and civic duty, financial advantage and religious imperative, and it continued to characterize the development of Dutch capitalism during the period of van Gogh's youth.[11]

If the few advanced sectors of mid-century Dutch capitalism adapted economic innovation to corporate traditions, the economy of Zundert, the Brabant village near the Belgian border where Vincent van Gogh was raised, remained completely lodged in communal patterns of archaic pre-industrialism. The primary production of the area was small-scale farming, which supported only precariously the needs of the local market. At 1850, 50 percent of the heath-land around Zundert remained uncultivated; many of the plots of land that were cultivated still relied on primitive techniques of ox-driven rather than horse-driven ploughs to ready the grain and potato crops. Peasants managing a minimal existence on these farms were nonetheless more fortunate than the many landless rural laborers of Zundert, who barely survived by combining seasonal harvest work with winter basket-weaving and making brooms from the heath brush. Local commerce consisted of small retailers and handicraft workshops, including five tanneries, six wooden shoe shops, five linen-weaving ateliers, three brickworks, and five blacksmiths.[12]

Religious solidarity mediated the economic activities of Zundert. The corrosive leveling of the "cash nexus" isolated by critics of bourgeois society elsewhere in Europe by 1850 had no resonance here; in Zundert, bonds of deference, convention, and piety referred market relations to a chain of connection linking stable social groups of common religious allegiance. Between 1850 and 1870, primitive farming techniques, poor soil conditions, and cycles of disease and crop failure meant that only a tiny minority of peasant families were self-sufficient; indeed, most were permanently dependent on church and civic authorities for subsistence.[13] Vincent van Gogh's father, Theodorus, the Dutch Reformed minister in Zundert, facilitated a variety of methods of exchange and distribution to offset economic hardship among his parishioners. Peasants unable to pay their tenant fees were regularly supported by church collections. Another time Theodorus van Gogh arranged with a carpet manufacturer in the nearby town of Breda to allow a number of Zundert widows to work as spinners of small amounts of yarn to be used in the carpet weaving, a form of poor relief offering little economic benefit to the factory owner.[14]

Like its economic activities, the social divisions of van Gogh's Zundert world broke along the lines of corporate deference and religious identity. The sociologist Johan Goudsblom has suggested that twentieth-century Dutch society is best characterized by the system of "verzuiling," or pillarization, which sets up organized blocks of cross-class connection up and down the social scale by religious denomination. Goudsblom's model identified the subordination of class hostility to religious grouping, and the primacy of social perception framed by an individual's location within the pillar unit, rather than as a discrete, circumscribed individual.[15] The pillarized model of social relations epitomized the society of mid-nineteenth-century Zundert. Reverend Theodorus van Gogh rested at the apex of the pillar, actively binding together distant parts of the social scale by their common religious commitment. This cross-class pillar was facilitated and indeed an imperative in Zundert, where a tiny minority of Reformed believers existed in an area dominated by a Catholic majority. Unitary categories of "bourgeois" or "working class," undifferentiated by village or denomination, were wholly unavailable in the Dutch context of van Gogh's youth. Like his father's before him, Vincent van Gogh's society identified him as a Brabantine, a Zundert Protestant, and a member of an important family, not as a bourgeois individual.

Two features marked the daily rhythm of the van Goghs' family life in Zundert, each of which situated the family unit in a social structure strikingly different from those forming other members of the urbanizing European avant-garde. The first was integral cross-class connection. Vincent van Gogh grew up in close and constant interaction with peasant laborers and craftsmen who formed the majority of the 54 believers in his father's tiny country parish. This interaction extended beyond the expected round of ministerial duties, for Theodorus van Gogh had a concrete knowledge of agriculture and the peasants relied on him for technical advice on drainage and soil projects, tree planting, and crop rotation.[16] Second, the boundaries dividing the family unit from the community, private from public, were not sharply delineated—the parsonage was a spatial and social extension of the village church, and the van Gogh children were raised in a condition of high visibility and permeability.[17] The saturation of the family by the social in the Zundert parish house was deepened by the presence of an extensive network of kin who regularly expanded the domestic group. This intimacy and ubiquity of the social in the van Goghs' Zundert life underlined the sense that one was never alone. Vincent's sister Elizabeth described in her memoir the unalterable presence of "the other" in the rituals and temper of family life, and the ambiguous sense of belonging and surveillance, the comfort of location and the pressure of expectation that she experienced as she imagined someone always watching her through the half-length lace curtains of the neighboring houses.[18]

The particular form of van Gogh's parents' theology reinforced these systemic features of nineteenth-century Dutch anti-egoism, while it also built into the family a heightened receptivity to the visual. Theodorus van Gogh was an adherent of a new reform movement within Dutch Calvinism called the Groningen School, which rejected religious rationalism and rediscovered Thomas à Kempis as the basis of a revitalized emotional piety. The Groningeners exchanged the Old Testament God of law for the New Testament evangel of love, and promoted a modern Imitation of Christ through humility, self-surrender, and service to the poor.[19] In celebrating a new religion of feeling, the Groningen theologians accorded a privileged place to a seeing God, and to sight as a vehicle for salvation. They relied on the definition of redemption offered in *The Imitation of Christ*—that of seeing Christ directly—a condition of fixed, clear, and utterly transparent beholding of the Redeemer. The Groningeners also invoked a newer visual theme, adapted from Schleiermacher, Lessing, and Herder, of Christ as a prefiguration of all humanity. This was a "resemblance" or "mirroring" theory of salvation; man's goal was to keep the image of Christ before him, and to emulate his actions and perfect love. The projection of inner images of Christ for emulation also extended to external artistic representations of Him in paintings and prints. Groningen theologian and founder Petrus Hofstede de Groot, for example, was an admirer of Ary Scheffer, a Dutch-born painter working in France who became renowned for his depictions of Christ as sufferer and agent of consolation. Hofstede de Groot wrote the first biography of Scheffer with an appraisal of his oeuvre, testifying to the centrality of a humanized and visualized Christ in Groningen School theology. [20]

The social gospel of the Groningen theology led Theodorus van Gogh to live out a life of service in small rural communities, and to invest lowly peasant labor with a special holiness. And the Groningen visual religion galvanized the van Goghs to construe their God not as a dispenser of the last judgement but as a source of light and love, an all-seeing surveyor whose dominion was expressed in receptive penetrating sight. Van Gogh's parents combined this new strain of Groningen visuality with their inherited legacies of hospitality to the image that persisted in the nineteenth-century Dutch Calvinist culture guided by the dominocratie. The modest country parish house in Zundert was hung with a variety of etchings, engravings, and mirrors, and mother Anna van Gogh embellished the tables with patterned rugs and simple wickerwork planters. [21] Thus the particular form of Vincent van Gogh's religious system comprised powerful resources of the visual, while it also generated profound dilemmas for independent identity.

Vincent van Gogh's Dutch world then formed a series of concentric circles of connection, a world both buffered and restrained by the primacy of group identity over individuation. This was a world where, as Vincent noted, "we do not quite belong to ourselves." [22] His parents' theology affirmed dissolution of the ego, submission to God, and the sanctification of lowly labor; the Zundert realities of corporate economy and society consolidated a cultural system of anti-individualism. Springing from this distinctive historical setting, becoming a self was a protracted and difficult project, bearing up against extraordinary cultural weights.

Salvation by Association: Art and Labor Identification

Before he finally decided to become a painter at the age of 27, van Gogh had indeed engaged in a ten-year struggle for self-definition and self-justification, which encompassed a deep religious crisis concerning the nature and value of his own work and worthiness. The central problem of van Gogh's early adulthood was precisely the conflicting claims of different definitions and functions of work, embodied in his attempts to choose what he called a "profession" or a "vocation" between 1869 and 1880. This struggle both expressed and pressed against the limits of van Gogh's inherited legacies of anti-egoism. After rejecting the security of corporate commercial success afforded by his apprenticeship in his uncles' art dealing enterprise, van Gogh turned to an impractical, but sacredly worthy religious vocation, first as a Methodist lay preacher in England, then as a popular evangelist among the destitute miners of the Belgian Borinage. During each of these stages, van Gogh expressed profound distrust of what he called "self-will" and idleness, while he considered his own choices and changes as temporary way stations en route to greater attachment, service, and association. As a religious worker in England and Belgium, van Gogh consistently tried to live like the lowly laborers he associated with sanctification; he planted and grew potatoes, and made his own shirts out of sacking in attempts to realize without compromise his father's Kempisian model of the social Imitation of Christ. When van Gogh decided in 1880 to become an artist, he attached his new calling to his ongoing struggle with the ambiguous Calvinist meanings of justification and with his culture's multiple inhibitors to individual subjectivity. He approached painting in terms of questions that set him very far apart from his French Impressionist contemporaries, questions like, "How can I be of use in the world?" "What is the relation between inner faith and outer action?" "Am I deserving in God's eyes by earning a living, or do I merit God's grace by enduring trials of faith and earthly adversity?" Questions like these, inflected with his readings of John Bunyan, Thomas Carlyle, and Jules Michelet, led van Gogh to place recurrent pressure on the image to be both a sign of regular, productive work—what he called "earning my bread"—and a conveyor of spiritual transcendence—what he called "deserving God's grace." This dual imperative that visual art act simultaneously as tangible craft product and immaterial sacred presence structured stylistic choices as it transposed religious conflict into image-making, and it illuminates some of the distinctive historical texture of van Gogh's psychological being.

The remainder of this essay highlights one important and unexplored element of van Gogh's technical procedures as an artist: his definition of art as a craft, and his attempt to develop pictorial forms to emulate the labor processes of pre-industrial weavers.[23] Van Gogh's consistent attempt to treat painting as woven cloth carried his long-term religious and social project of identification with labor into pictorial practice, enabling him to find, for a time, what I call "salvation by association"—a visible and emphatic connection to the humble workers he admired as both worthy of God and useful in the world.[24]

Art, Craft, and Labor in the Hague, 1881–83

While van Gogh considered, from the very first, that his art would extend the goals of service and consolation of his religious evangelism, he approached his new work as a painstaking and rigorous craft, what he called his "métier," a product of methodical and arduous exertion rather than a sudden release of exalted vision. First in Brussels and then in the Hague between 1881 and 1883, van Gogh developed a program of disciplined self-instruction toward mastery of the handicraft of drawing, which he posed explicitly against the conception of art as a spontaneous outpouring of native genius. Pursuing his art as a métier from 1881, van Gogh placed his hopes in forging his skills as an illustrator through dogged effort, submission to rules and relentless repetition, and a model of slow, steady and incremental progress.[25]

In accordance with this process, van Gogh spent three years teaching himself the rules of anatomy, perspective, and drawing from popular art manuals that he had frequently sold during his time as an art dealer at Goupil in Paris and London. Here he was not starting from scratch, as is usually assumed. In every phase of van Gogh's life before he turned from religion to art we find the reliance on drawing handbooks, patient copying, and a model of graduated visual skill. Throughout his childhood van Gogh and his siblings had learned and practiced drawing with their mother, using Dutch art manuals popular since the seventeenth century.[26] As a state high school student in Tilburg, van Gogh's course of study included four hours a week of drawing—as many hours as math and French—under the well-known artist and polemicist Cornelius Huysmans. Huysmans had been waging a national campaign to revitalize Dutch arts and crafts and industrial design since the 1840s and was responsible for new education laws for visual literacy and drawing skill set into the secondary school system in 1857.[27] During even the most intense periods of van Gogh's religious evangelism, which on their own terms are not aberrant but express broader and particular strains of Dutch Calvinism and English Methodism, van Gogh complemented his Bible study with drawing maps, charting with colored pencils, for example, the routes most likely to have been traveled by various apostles, and consulting his uncle's collection of historical atlases for reference.[28] And in the Borinage, when van Gogh preached among the miners, he also sketched and refined his drawing skills with visits to a fellow practitioner, the Reverend Mr. Pietersen of the Protestant evangelical mission in the next village.[29]

So van Gogh's turn to art as a métier in 1881 mobilized and transformed long-term visual practices, and his choice of a career of art does not emerge, as is often assumed, as a sharp break with his personal and religious history. In training himself with the course of study now provided by the French manuals, van Gogh immersed himself in the techniques of pencil and charcoal drawing, wood engraving, and lithography. He refused to engage in any medium of paint until he had mastered the art of drawing with a sufficient level of dexterity. The French manuals offered van Gogh an easily accessible course of what they called "drawing without a master," conveyed through an artisanal language and filled with advice on the essential tools and tricks of the trade. These were "how-to" books intended neither for the amateur Sunday artist, nor for the artist destined for academic training, but for the skilled draftsman preparing his craft for saleable prospects. From Charles Bargues's *Exercices au Fusain*, published by Goupil in 1871 and copied patiently by van Gogh in 1882, van Gogh learned to approach the human figure as a set of elemental planes and linear geometric blocks (Figs. 2,3,4).[30] He also relied on Karl Robert's *Charcoal Drawing Without a Master* of 1880. This book began by advocating the use of a type of charcoal from the spindle tree, whose wood was most commonly used for making distaffs for spinning and carding needles; this material was more durable than the delicate conté-crayon favored by academic art circles from the time of Ingres and revitalized in 1880 by Georges Seurat. Karl Robert's manual also exposed van Gogh to particularly artisanal and practical methods of shading and streaking. Robert recommended rolling lumps of partly-dried bread crumbs for exposing the nub of the paper, which he advised the draftsman should carry with him at all times in a tin snuffbox in his pocket. Robert also demonstrated a method for sliding worn linen and wool rags across the image to even out the grain of the drawing.[31]

These kinds of handbooks, the sole training ground for van Gogh in his first years as an artist outside of occasional and short-lived experience with teachers and art school, activated a long-term encounter with the visual world as a world of physical ground and emphatic tangibility. It was the how-to training of the early years that provides a framework for understanding how one of van Gogh's first experiments with color in 1883 was to streak the paper with coffee grounds from his mother's kitchen rather than to reach for a paintbrush and color box.

While van Gogh thus set himself in a rigorous course of artisanal artistic apprenticeship, he also continued in the Hague to express his religiously-inspired identification with labor, and to attach himself to a corporate com-

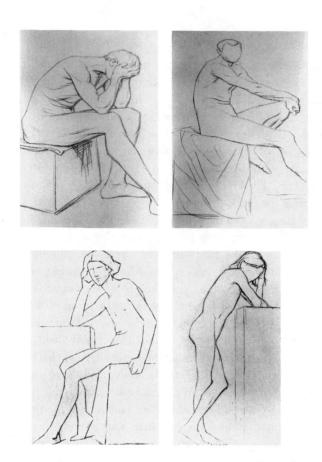

Top: FIG. 2. Lithograph sheets from Charles Bargues, *Exercices au Fusain* (Charcoal Exercises), *Seated and Standing Nude*, 1871.

Middle: FIG. 3. Van Gogh's copies after Bargues manual, *Seated and Standing Nude*. Charcoal on paper.

Bottom right: FIG. 4. Van Gogh, *The Sower*, 1881. Pen drawing. Rijksmuseum Vincent van Gogh, Amsterdam/Vincent van Gogh Foundation.

munal setting so powerfully structured by his social and Calvinist formation. As in the Borinage, he tried to live the life of a worker, frequenting
printers' shops to practice moving the lithographic stone to the press, and
assembling what he considered to be an authentic worker's household with
the former prostitute Sien Hartook and her children.[32] Laborers and the
under class also formed the primary subject matter of van Gogh's art in the
Hague, which he invested with the redemptive and sacred mission of his
former religious vocation. In preparing himself as an illustrator, van Gogh
defined his goal as developing what he called a body of graphic work "of
the people for the people," modeled on the English wood engravers he admired from the late 1860s and began systematically collecting in 1882.
Throughout his stay in the Hague, van Gogh sought out the sites of the
urban poor and labor types inspired by the earlier social realism of Fildes,
Herkhomer, Pinwell, and Walker, yielding a repertoire of images of the
soupkitchens, almshouses, and work sites of road-menders, carpenters, and
printers (Figs. 5-7).[33] Van Gogh considered his project of "prints for the
people" as both a commercial and a spiritual venture, linking his images to
what he called a "holy duty" and "noble calling" that would "touch people,"
spark sympathy and comfort, and provide messages of hope and consolation
for the poor and disinherited.[34] Van Gogh's continuing impulse to insert his
individual program of artistic progress into a corporate community of labor

FIG. 5. Auguste Lançon, *Snow-Shovelers*, 1881. Wood engraving.

FIG. 6. Van Gogh, *Peat-Cutters in the Dunes*, 1883. Charcoal, black chalk, ink.

FIG. 7. Van Gogh, *Digger*, 1882. Lithograph. Rijksmuseum Vincent van Gogh, Amsterdam/Vincent van Gogh Foundation.

emerged in his 1883 plan to establish a cooperative workshop joining drafts-men, wood engravers, lithographers, and printers in a common and profit-sharing enterprise.

Neither this collaborative craft workshop nor the holy brotherhood of artists that van Gogh envisioned working in it was realized in the Hague. And van Gogh's plan for a modern graphic art based on the model of the English magazines was, by 1882, already technically obsolete—the wood engraving medium of the 1860s had been superseded by a new mechanized lithographic process. But as the social and communitarian connection to craft work was obstructed, van Gogh turned to the art form itself to carry the weight of labor activity. Indeed, it is in the Hague period that van Gogh first consolidated visual techniques that reproduced the humble labor he associated with sanctification, developing pictorial forms to emulate the ac-tivities of those pre-industrial workers with whom he so deeply identified. The Hague period crystallized two modes of van Gogh's stylistic language of craft labor. The first is his insertion of visible signs of his own artisanal tools into the picture plane, offering the beholder palpable reminders of his own particular process of working the image to completion. As part of his program of self-instruction, van Gogh had built himself a perspec-tive frame in 1882 with the aid of a blacksmith and carpenter. The ob-long wooden frame, strung with lengths of thread into the pattern of a Union Jack, could be attached to adjustable notches on two wooden poles and staked into the ground for outdoor sightings (Figs. 8-9).[35] Looking through it like a window, the artist is trained to compare the proportions of objects nearby with those on a more distant plane, while the intersection of the threads pressed the eye to its point of convergence at the vanishing point. Van Gogh based his frame on similar perspective instruments he had studied in books by Albrecht Dürer and the nineteenth-century writer Armand Cassagne, though the diagonal threads and the wooden poles with adjustable notches were distinctly his own inventions.[36]

As in the case of the art manuals, van Gogh practiced repeatedly with the frame. He delighted in the way his instrument instantly organized the visual field into a manageable structure, and likened it to a small telescope that riveted his eye to a single point of focus. The practice with the frame yielded stylistic consequences, reinforced by van Gogh's abiding impulse for labor association. Many of the early drawings have a particular format of what I would call the framed landscape, leading the viewer into the dis-tance through emphatically-bounded wooden posts, reproducing the op-eration and even the component parts of the perspective frame (Fig. 10).

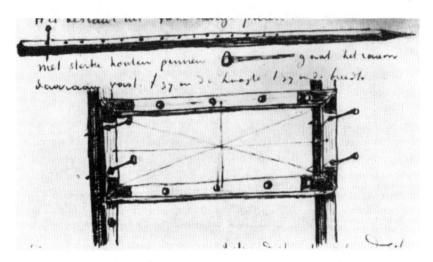

FIG. 8. Van Gogh's Perspective Frame, described and sketched in Letter #223 to Theo, 1882.

FIG. 9. Van Gogh illustrating his perspective frame in outdoor use, in Letter #222 to Theo, 1882.

PLATE 1. Van Gogh, *Loom with Weaver*, 1884, seen from the front. Oil.
Rijksmuseum Kröller-Müller, Otterlo.

PLATE 2. Van Gogh, *The Potato Eaters*, 1885. Oil. Rijksmuseum Vincent van Gogh, Amsterdam/Vincent van Gogh Foundation.

PLATE 3. Van Gogh, *Self-Portrait with a Straw Hat*, 1888. Oil. The Metropolitan Museum of Art, New York. Bequest of Miss Adelaide Milton de Groot.

Left: PLATE 4. Van Gogh, *Self-Portrait*, 1887. Oil. Rijksmuseum Vincent van Gogh, Amsterdam/Vincent van Gogh Foundation.

Below: PLATE 5. Théo van Rhysselberghe, *Portrait of Maria Sèthe*, 1891. Oil. Koninklijk Museum van Schone Kunsten, Antwerp.

Right: PLATE 6. Van Gogh,
Park Voyer d'Argenson, Asnières,
1887. Oil. Rijksmuseum, Vincent
van Gogh Amsterdam/Vincent
van Gogh Foundation.

PLATE 7. Van Gogh, *Outskirts of Montmartre,* 1887. Oil. Stedelijk Museum,
Amsterdam.

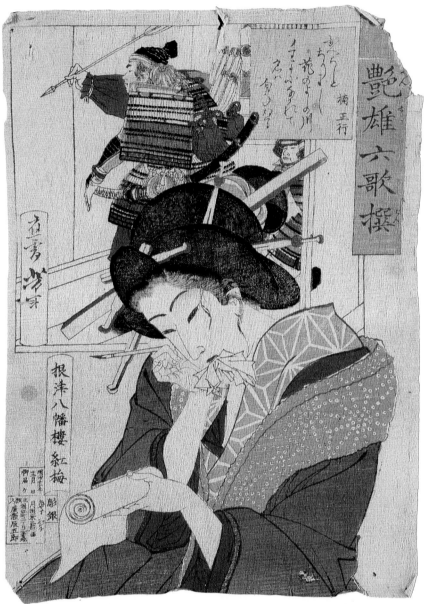

PLATE 8. Tsukioka Yoshitoshi, *The Courtesan Kobai Compared to Kusunoki Masatsura*, 1879. "Crépon" print in van Gogh's Japanese Color Woodblock Print Collection. Rijksmuseum Vincent van Gogh, Amsterdam/Vincent van Gogh Foundation.

Above: PLATE 9. Unsigned Japanese "Cré-pon" print sewn into book cover, from van Gogh's collection. Rijksmuseum Vincent van Gogh, Amsterdam/Vincent van Gogh Foundation.

Left: PLATE 10. Utagawa Hiroshige, *Famous Tie-Dye Fabrics at Narumi Drying.* Color woodblock print in van Gogh's collection. Rijksmuseum Vincent van Gogh, Amsterdam/Vincent van Gogh Foundation.

PLATE 11. Van Gogh, *Field with Poppies*, 1889. Oil. Kunsthalle, Bremen.

PLATE 12. Van Gogh, *Wheat Fields with Setting Sun*, 1889. Oil. Private collection.

PLATE 13. Van Gogh, *Self-Portrait*, 1887. Oil. Oeffentliche Kunstsammlung, Basel, Kunstmuseum.

PLATE 14. Jacques-Louis David, *Self-Portrait*, oil on canvas, 1794. Paris, Musée du Louvre.

PLATE 15. Annibale Carracci, *Self-Portrait with Other Figures,* oil on canvas, ca. 1584–90. Milan, Pinacoteca di Brera.

FIG. 10. Framed Looking: Van Gogh, *Vegetable Garden on the Schenkweg, 1882*. Pencil, India ink, and watercolor. Amsterdam, Rijksprentenkabinet (Rijksmuseum).

FIG. 11. Framed Looking II: Van Gogh, *Drawbridge at Nieuw-Amsterdam*, 1883. Watercolor, chalk, and pencil. Groningen, Groningener Museum.

The Drawbridge at Nieuw-Amsterdam of 1883 joins this type of structured looking-through with an oblong format that replicates exactly the shape of the frame (Fig. 11). In other images, van Gogh unexpectedly incorporates parts of his perspective frame directly into the image, arranging networks of tree branches into patterns that resemble the threads suspended on his oblong tool. One example can be seen in the difference between van Gogh's 1884 image of a lumber sale and a watercolor that he copied from his cousin, the Hague School artist Anton Mauve (Figs. 12-13). Van Gogh follows Mauve's grouping at the front, but he packs the back of the image with trees, where those at the upper right configure a frame positioned on two wooden stakes.

A second set of stylistic elements of a pictorial language of labor emerged in van Gogh's attempts to treat the picture surface as a piece of woven cloth. It is in the Hague period that van Gogh first explicitly associated the processes of weaving with his own work as a draftsman, when he compared the difficulty of drawing composition to the task of the weaver at his loom, who had to keep so many threads separate while interconnecting them.[37] During this first phase of his artistic apprenticeship, van Gogh is unusually atten-

FIG. 12. Anton Mauve, *Lumber Sale*, 1881. Watercolor. Rijksmuseum H. W. Mesdag, The Hague.

F I G. 13. Van Gogh, *Lumber Sale*, 1883–84. Black chalk and watercolor. Rijksmuseum Vincent van Gogh, Amsterdam/Vincent van Gogh Foundation.

tive to subjects such as fishnets, shawls, wicker baskets, and the activities of sewing and knitting (Fig. 14). He also sought visual techniques to maximize the coarseness and texturality of his own paper surfaces, which he hoped would appear as grainy, nubby, and abrasive as the objects he was representing. He comments on selecting paper with a quality of "unbleached linen or muslin," and intensifies these effects by using thick carpenter's pencils.[38] The equivalence between texturally-heightened techniques and the representation of woven clothes may be seen in the drawing of Sien Hartook's daughter in a shawl (Fig. 15). On the right side of the figure the woven shawl is visibly bumpy and creased in the paper surface, revealing the raised grain of the paper matching the woven quality of the material presented. This technique is used again in the top hat of the almshouse man (Fig. 16) and other drawings where the figures' clothes are marked by similar scraping and creasing, visibly emphasizing the link between the woven paper and the cloth depicted.

Top left: FIG. 14. Van Gogh, *Sien Sewing*, 1883. Pencil and chalk. Museum Boymans-van Beuningen, Rotterdam.

Top right: FIG. 15. Van Gogh, *Girl with Shawl*, 1882–83. Pencil and lithographic chalk. Rijksmuseum Vincent van Gogh, Amsterdam/Vincent van Gogh Foundation.

Right: FIG. 16. Van Gogh, *Almshouse Man with Top Hat*, 1882. Pencil, lithographic chalk and ink. Rijksmuseum Vincent van Gogh, Amsterdam/Vincent van Gogh Foundation.

Vincent van Gogh à Son Métier: The Frame of Art and the Frame of the Loom in Nuenen, 1884–85

The consistent pattern of labor identification and craft stylistic practices in van Gogh's early work, and the cultural and religious pressures that generated them, deepened as he developed a distinctive program for modern painting. When van Gogh left the Hague and settled in Nuenen, he set to work on his first major series, 34 images of the local hand-loom weavers living in his parents' Brabant village. In executing the weaver series, van Gogh articulated the equivalence between his artistic work, what he had called for three years his "métier," and the work of the weaver at his loom, "le canut à son métier." He expressed this equivalence by signing his own name on the wheel where the thread was released to the loom shuttle, and by presenting the weaver "drawing threads" in a position strikingly similar to that of an artist directing his pen across the surface of the paper. (Fig. 17) Van Gogh reinforced the identification between the two craft activities by comparing the artist's mechanical tool of his own construction, his perspective frame, to the rugged frame of the weaving loom. In the frontal *Weaver* of 1884 (Plate 1), van Gogh incorporates the component parts of his perspective frame onto the loom itself. The threads of the weaving loom are

FIG. 17. Van Gogh, *Weaver*, close-up, 1884. Pen and ink, bistre wash, heightened with white. Rijksmuseum Vincent van Gogh, Amsterdam/Vincent van Gogh Foundation.

suspended in the pattern echoing that of the perspective device, while the wooden stakes supporting the loom's oblong frame are marked by a series of notches. These notches replicate the functional holes on van Gogh's perspective tool, where they served as similar adjustable points where the wooden frame could be fixed to the two poles (Fig. 8). By highlighting the resemblance of the perspective frame and the frame of the loom, which he had already associated as he looked and drew through his frame in 1883, van Gogh visibly attached himself to the craft labor process depicted, uniting the distinctive feature of the frame of art with the frame of the weaver.[39]

Van Gogh's linkage of the skilled artisan situated at the métier and the artist engaged in his métier comprised more than visually-rendered analogies. In Nuenen, as he moved from the medium of drawing to tackling the problem of color, the months of daily observation of the weavers at work activated van Gogh's interest in applying paint as threads and color as fibers, to be placed on the canvas so as to intersect one another, like the woof and weft of weaving.[40] For van Gogh combined his close scrutiny of the production of colored cloth with reading books on color theory that highlighted the discoveries of the French chemist Michel Chevreul. Chevreul was the director of the Gobelins Tapestry works, and he had systematized laws to maximize the iridescence of color through their contrast, based on his experiments with dyeing threads and testing their luminosity when placed next to other color-dipped threads. Chevreul recommended not only that painters conform to these laws of color, but that his discoveries be adapted to raise the quality of many applied arts, especially the arts of weaving, tapestry-making, and rug-making under his direct supervision at the Gobelins.[41] Thus van Gogh witnessed the creation of multicolored cloth by the Nuenen weavers as he absorbed painting theories whose origin and impact were themselves based on the saturation of color dyes on fibers and fabrics. *The Potato Eaters* (Plate 2), executed in the period immediately after the 34 weaver images, is the first painting that van Gogh explicitly linked to the process of weaving, explaining that the composition came together as he wrestled with the right pattern and color effects:

But for the weaver, or rather the designer of the pattern or combination of colors, it is not always easy to determine the number of threads and their direction, nor more than it is easy to blend the strokes of the brush into a harmonious whole. . . . All winter long I have had the threads of this tissue in my hands, and have searched for the ultimate pattern, and though it has become a tissue of rough, coarse aspect, nevertheless the threads have been chosen carefully and according to certain rules.[42]

Long before van Gogh encountered Paris and the Impressionists, his color theory had been fundamentally shaped by his direct experience of the Nuenen weavers' use and disposition of colored threads, mediated by his study of texts on mixing colors and maximizing their iridescence which had systematized for painting laws that had originated in Chevreul's French weaving chemistry. And treating the canvas as woven cloth allowed van Gogh to re-enact the labor process of the subjects he was depicting, responding to persistent religious and cultural pressures for self-justification and corporate redemption.

Weaving Paintings in France, 1886–90

The interdependence of art and work continued to structure van Gogh's self-definition and stylistic development during the French period. Rather than a Post-Impressionist, an epileptic, or a proto-Expressionist, van Gogh remained a Dutch painter and a pastor's son, who, driven by Calvinist imperatives, came to define himself as a painter of work and as a worker-painter.

After a sojourn in Paris, van Gogh renounced urban existence for a pre-industrial oasis in Arles. There, as in Nuenen, he lived among and painted peasants, and he returned to the abiding concerns of his Dutch artistic apprenticeship. Van Gogh continued in Arles to depict the effort and strain of human labor and the integrity of humble people.[43] And he continued to seek out the company of individuals outside the world of avant-garde art. The closest van Gogh may have come to realizing his utopian vision of an artistic brotherhood was not the Yellow House with Paul Gauguin, but the mini-guilds he created first in Eindhoven in 1885 with a goldsmith, a tanner, and an art-supply store owner, and then in Arles in 1888, where he acted as a kind of master-craftsman, teaching painting to a grocer and a second lieutenant of the French zoave regiment, a man called Milliet. He gave Milliet lessons in the art of using the perspective frame, repeating his own training with the popular mechanical tool and reaffirming the accessibility of art to any practitioner of a patient, methodical métier.[44]

During the French period, van Gogh was again guided by the same deep identification with pre-industrial labor, and he validated workers' activities as the true salvation of the useful and honest. In Arles and later, van Gogh not only worked among and painted humble people, but he tried to become one of them, which we see in one of his self-portraits (Plate 3). As he explained to his mother:

You will see from my self-portrait that though I saw Paris and other big cities for many years, I keep looking more or less like a peasant . . . , and sometimes I imagine I also feel and think like them, only peasants are of more use in the world. . . . Well, I am plowing on my canvases as they do on their fields. [45]

Finally, van Gogh's identification with labor was again translated into the vocabulary of his pictorial style. There are multiple indicators, both visual and in his own statements, of van Gogh's continued efforts to emulate craft weaving in his later visual forms. I will highlight here just a few examples.

The Symbolist painter Emile Bernard, a close friend of van Gogh's during the Paris period, noted in a memoir that van Gogh collected balls of yarn in different interlacing tonalities, the very method used by Chevreul to test color contrasts at the Gobelins. [46] While Chevreul's work on the laws of color was well known to and adopted by many French Impressionists and Post-Impressionists, van Gogh alone actually operationalized Chevreul's discoveries with the fiber materials on which they were based. During the Nuenen period with the weavers, van Gogh had already absorbed Chevreul's theories as he witnessed the weavers' production of colored cloth. In Paris, van Gogh encountered new pictorial techniques, while he amplified the pre-existing lessons of paint as threads and color as fiber to be worked into the fabric of the picture surface. Consider two key elements of van Gogh's supposed shift to French modernist practices in Paris—his interactions with the Neo-Impressionists and with Japanese prints. When van Gogh painted alongside his new friend Paul Signac, he turned the techniques of divisionist painting into the structures of weaving painting. While Neo-Impressionist color theory did facilitate van Gogh's new brighter palette, he was unable to reproduce the shimmering micro-dots of the pointillist optical mixture. The figures and clothes painted by Signac and his circle offer a velvety smoothness of luminous immateriality; van Gogh's "Neo-Impressionist" canvases bristle with a brushwork of sticks, rickets, and fibrous blocks (Plates 4-5). The couple in a park at Asnières are linked by the interlocking pattern of their visibly woven clothes, each guided to a woof or weft direction (Plate 6). Another favored Neo-Impressionist site, the outskirts of Montmartre, is turned by van Gogh into a field of fabric surfaces, which draws his eye and hand in particular to the woven latticework covering the barrel in the center of the painting (Plate 7).

Van Gogh's interest in Japanese woodblock prints, which he collected and studied seriously in the Paris period, is also partly inspired by the interdependence of paper, image, and cloth. A. S. Hartrick, another friend and observer of van Gogh's working methods, described how van Gogh was fascinated by the textural surfaces of the Japanese crépons, or crêpe prints, in his collection, and tried, according to Hartrick, to emulate them in his brushwork.[47] The crépons have not been adequately distinguished from the flat colored woodblock prints in van Gogh's collection. The crêpe prints are pressed and stretched in a crinkling process to appear nubby and elasticized, akin to the feel and consistency of a washcloth (Plate 8). The color dyes seep through the crépon surface to the other side, and one in van Gogh's collection could be mistaken for a silk scarf, and another had indeed been sewn into a book cover (Plate 9). In seeking formal equivalents to the rough fabric surfaces of these crépons, van Gogh adapted the new lessons of Japan to his ongoing imperative to turn painting into work. Further evidence of this selective appropriation of Japan can also be traced in another unnoticed characteristic of his Japanese woodblock print collection—the number of prints that depict the activities of weaving, spinning, fulling, dyeing, cutting, and selling cloth (Figs. 18–19; Plate 10).[48] In Paris then, as in Nuenen and the Hague, weaving returned as a visual form of justification, facilitating van Gogh's abiding need to render the image to be as tangible, physically present, and textural as the canvas on which it was applied.

Throughout the later periods of van Gogh's career, he was consistently attracted to woven objects as subjects for composition—baskets of fruit with plaited bands carefully articulated and the rough strands of cane and wicker chairs are part of this repertoire of objects bearing woven materials. Van Gogh also engaged in the very unusual practice of painting on untreated surfaces like burlap, linen towels, and cotton bedsheets, all of which use the woven texture of the cloth as part of the composition.[49] Van Gogh relied on weaving techniques for his unique interlocking brushwork used in the backgrounds of later canvases, such as the woof and weft pattern of paint strokes applied on the left side of the 1890 *Vase with Rose-Mallows* (Fig. 20). Finally, weaving provides the compositional format for many of the last group of landscapes, which render broad, flat plains as fibrous checkerboard blocks of intersecting colors. Paintings such as *Wheatfield with Rising Sun* (1889), *Landscape with Carriage and Train in the Background* (1889), *Field with Poppies* (1889), and *Wheat Fields* (1890), share the legacy of weaving in van Gogh's visual language of work (Plates 11-12). The individual sections of the canvas display the regularity of the brushstrokes of warp and weft, deliberately interlocking. The strokes of paint appear as fibers of colored thread, woven together in iridescent patterning. The format of the paintings

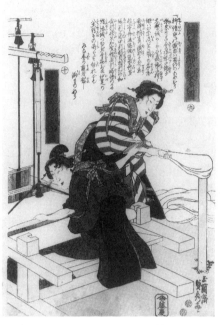

Top left: FIG. 18. Utagawa Kunisada, *The Gongen Shrine in Nezu*. Color woodblock print in van Gogh's collection. Rijksmuseum Vincent van Gogh, Amsterdam/Vincent van Gogh Foundation.

Top right: FIG. 19. Utagawa Sadahide, *Making Silk Floss and Weaving*. Color woodblock print in van Gogh's collection. Rijksmuseum Vincent van Gogh, Amsterdam/Vincent van Gogh Foundation.

Left: FIG. 20. Van Gogh, *Vase with Rose-Mallows*, 1890. Oil. Rijksmuseum Vincent van Gogh, Amsterdam/Vincent van Gogh Foundation.

embodies fields of woven cloth, in multicolored checkered planes of intersecting units.[50] The voices of the weavers, and of the artist-craftsman, converge in a late letter when van Gogh summarized his efforts:

Sometimes by erring one finds the right road. Go make up for it by painting your garden just as it is. . . . Being able to divide a canvas into great planes which intermingle, to find lines, forms which make contrasts, that is technique . . . it is a sign all the same that you are studying your handicraft more deeply, and that is a good thing.

However cumbersome . . . the times we are living in, if anyone who has chosen this handicraft pursues it zealously, he is a man of duty, sound and faithful.[51]

Conclusion: Modernist Religious Realism

During the last year of his life, van Gogh reacted politely but forcefully against the Parisian critic Albert Aurier's account of his art as the apotheosis of Symbolism. In an article entitled "Les Isolés, Vincent van Gogh," Aurier set the terms for a modernist canonization of the artist which has proven irresistible into our own time. Aurier glorified van Gogh as an isolated, mystic titan, a hyperaesthete, a visionary bound only by the lineaments of his inner dream.[52] The terms of van Gogh's response to Aurier exposed the distance between the world of French fin-de-siècle subjectivity to which he aspired and the world of mid-century Dutch theological culture that he had absorbed. I am uneasy, he tells Aurier, in being singled out as an isolated, creative initiator. My place is secondary, and my contributions are really only due to the work and insights of others, affirms van Gogh, yielding his singularity to an assertion of creative association and interdependence.[53] To Aurier's interpretations of his paintings as abstract, evocative forms of a transcendent, musical, and universal Soul, van Gogh countered "truth is so dear to me, and the search for being truthful too. I still prefer being a cobbler to being a musician who works in colors."[54] Like the cobbler's pride with his completed product, van Gogh offered Aurier a gift of what he called his own "sound and faithful handicraft" as a statement of gratitude for the article. The gift offered the most compelling antidote to Aurier's view of van Gogh's titanic anti-naturalism. He sent him a small painting of cypresses— rough work, he called it, the result of wrestling with clods of earth and hand-to-hand combat with nature. The solid piece of nature was rendered, he explained to Aurier, in color tones that reminded him of the combinations of "those pretty Scotch tartans"—green, blue, red yellow and black—again a woven canvas.[55]

FIG. 21. Van Gogh, Man dragging a harrow, sketch in Letter #336 to Theo, 1883.

Van Gogh's insistent naturalism, and the insistent physicality of his canvases (Plate 13), may, as Meyer Schapiro once noted, be the necessary counterweights to the terror of psychic disturbance—the reference to real objects, and the canvas's emphatic concreteness functioned as what Schapiro called "protective reactions" against inner disintegration.[56] Yet, for van Gogh, the flight to abstraction, and to the unfettered subjectivity that it formalized, were not only psychologically intolerable, but were also religiously, culturally, and socially impermissible (Fig. 21). How van Gogh came to define a modernist religious realism, and to resist modernist abstraction, have their roots deep in the theological cultures that spawned him. The discovery of weaving paintings configured at least one stylistic response to multiple and historically-specific pressures to refer the self to the larger totalities of corporate community and redemptive labor.

JAMES J. SHEEHAN

From Princely Collections
to Public Museums:
Toward a History of the
German Art Museum

Part One: Origins

Let us begin by looking at two pictures of *"Kunst Kenntnis,"* published
in 1780 by Daniel Chodowiecki as part of the second series of prints (with
text by Georg Christoph Lichtenberg) on the theme, "Natürliche und affec-
tirte Handlungen des Lebens" (illustration on p. 170). The pictures contrast
the responses of two men in front of a statue of Flora. In one, the pair stands
in quiet appreciation of the object. In the other, the observers seem more
interested in each other than in the statue; their gestures and expressions are
social and expressive rather than private and contemplative. In an interesting essay on Chodowiecki's *Bildbegriff,* Werner Busch uses these prints to
illustrate what he takes to be a fundamental shift in aesthetic attitudes during the closing decades of the eighteenth century: a shift from the "affected"
mode of courtly culture, with its highly articulated and conventional responses to the social experience of art, to the "natural" mode of *bürgerliche
Kultur,* with its internalized and individualized response to each particular
artistic event. Busch's reading of the pictures seems persuasive enough, but
the social implications of the contrast are less apparent. One can see at once
that the appearance of the men in the two pictures is almost identical; in
each, one of the figures wears a sword, which clearly marks him as an aris-
tocrat. From their external appearance, therefore, there is no reason to suppose that the two pairs are from different social groups. Given their costumes
and the setting in which they are placed, it is likely that they are both
courtiers.[1]

Chodowiecki's pictures point us towards two important elements in the
transition to the museum: first, that it involved a new way of seeing and thus
a new way of experiencing art; and second, that this mode of experience

Kunst Kenntnis
Connoissance des Arts

Kunst Kenntnis
Connoissance des Arts

"Art Appreciation" (*Kunst Kenntnis*), from Daniel Chodowiecki and Georg Christoph Lichtenberg, *Handlungen des Lebens* (1780)

first appeared in the world of the courts, when art objects began to be displayed and viewed in revolutionary new ways. The links between princely collection and museum are, therefore, not merely material: from the Old Regime, museums inherited not only a vast array of artworks, but also an essential set of new attitudes and assumptions about the nature and significance of art.

Perhaps the most fundamental of these innovations had to do with what we might call the accessibility of art. Of course, princely collections were rarely closed in the way a contemporary private collection might be, but they were not "public" either—concepts like *private* and *public* do not fit easily into the courtly world. In the course of the eighteenth century, the circle of those who could gain admittance to the collection steadily widened as a number of princes came to believe that their art, like their gardens, libraries, and theatres, should be more available to their subjects. Dresden, which Goethe visited in 1768, had been open to scholars and *Kunstfreunde* since the 1740s; in 1779, the Wittelsbach opened a gallery in the Munich Hofgarten for public use; anyone, Schiller wrote in 1785, could gain admittance to the Mannheim gallery—but this probably meant anyone who looked respectable, a condition generously defined by the keepers of the Vienna collections in 1792 as anyone wearing clean shoes.[2]

At the same time that more people could visit them, collections became accessible in other ways as well: through the production of catalogues, which made it easier to identify the objects; through modes of display, which made it easier to see them; and through various sorts of literary descriptions and graphic reproductions, which made them available even to those who could not directly view them. Wilhelm Heinse's "*Gemäldebriefe*," first published in the *Teutsche Merkur* in 1776–77, vividly described the collection in Düsseldorf and helped to popularize a new genre of art criticism. Journals devoted to artistic subjects also became increasingly popular in the late eighteenth century, further indicating the growth of an audience interested in art. In both the limited and the extended sense, therefore, the growing accessibility of art was part of that expanding public sphere that was so central to the cultural history of the eighteenth century.[3]

At the same time that the way in which art was displayed became more public, the way in which it was to be experienced became more private— this is, of course, the point Chodowiecki underscored in his pictures. Like reading (which became the model for cultural communication), experiencing art involved a direct and essentially individualized connection between viewer and object. Here too our story touches themes central to the century's culture: the emphasis on inward experience, on individual development, on that cluster of spiritual and social forms that the Germans call *Bildung*. No longer a backdrop for courtly ceremony or religious ritual, art came to be seen as a source of its own special sort of spiritual nourishment and moral enrichment. Slowly the arrangement of exhibitions began to reflect this new conception of art's significance: in more and more galleries, individual pieces of art were placed so that each was clearly visible; the setting itself was designed to encourage contemplative reverence. Goethe, for example, recalled his trip to the Elector's gallery in Dresden as being like visiting a shrine: "the space, which was used for viewing rather than for work, conveyed a unique feeling of solemnity that resembled the emotion one has upon entering a shrine."[4]

The creation of a separate environment for the appreciation of art expressed in spatial terms the growing belief in art's autonomy. This belief had two elements: first, *art* (now usually defined as painting, sculpture, and architecture) represented a separate category of things that should be distinguished from other products of skill or objects of value (which increasingly came to be thought of as crafts or curiosities); second, art objects had meaning and significance apart from their social, political, or religious functions. Art was of interest in itself, not as symbol of some higher value or as the expression of some greater power, but as a distinctive source of pleasure and edification. Art merited its own space, which should not contain other things and should not be used for other purposes—a space, as Goethe says, for *Schauende.*

A special branch of philosophy devoted to the study of artistic creation and experience, aesthetics, like the notion of artistic autonomy, was an eighteenth-century invention. From the start, aesthetics was concerned with the questions that necessarily arise when one comes to believe that art has no necessary connection with other political, social, or spiritual values and institutions. Beginning with Johann Joachim Winckelmann's great works in the 1750s and 1760s, the most influential German answers to these questions were historical: Winckelmann and his successors defined a vision of art's development that became the most important source of its meaning and purpose. For our purposes, two aspects of Winckelmann's historical vision are of particular importance. First, by helping to create a compelling account of art's history, he provided a new way of organizing collections, which could become what Christian Mechel, who redesigned the Habsburgs' gallery in 1781, called a "sichtbare Geschichte der Kunst." Second, by anchoring the chronology of art history in an idealization of the ancient world, Winckelmann and his successors created a canonical version of historical values that is still apparent in many art museums.[5]

By the 1770s, the emergence of the art museum in its modern form can clearly be perceived within the contours of the Old Regime. Nevertheless, most German collections remained spatially and spiritually tied to the life of the courts. We can see a good example of the distinctively transitional character of this period in the first independent museum building in Europe, the Fridericianum, constructed by Simon Louis du Ry for the Landgraf of Kassel between 1769 and 1779. Although the Fridericianum was built away from the court complex, its purpose was to house the Landgraf's collections and to provide him with the opportunity for joining with other scholars in their study and appreciation. And even though the building contained wax figures and old armor, its emphasis was on classical antiquities. To contemporaries, it seemed less to honor the prince than to serve as a "Tempel Apolls und der Musen," those ancient personifications of knowledge and beauty whose statues ornamented the structure.[6]

Part Two: The Monumental Musem

A new stage in the evolution of German aesthetic culture began in the 1790s. In culture, as in so many other aspects of German life, the pace of the innovations that had been building within the Old Regime quickened when Germans began to feel the impact of the French revolution. For the art museum, therefore, as for legal reform and social emancipation, political theory and administrative reorganization, the period from 1790 to 1820 was of critical importance.

The most obvious impact of the revolution on the German art world was brutally direct and immediate. To the occupying French armies, art was one more local resource to be exploited; under Napoleon, piecemeal looting was replaced by a policy of systematic confiscation which brought to Paris hundreds of masterpieces from throughout Europe. Equally important for the German situation were the effects of secularization, which divested abbeys, monastaries, and ecclesiastical principalities of their art—or, to put the matter more precisely, converted thousands of religious objects into commodities that could be bought and sold by collectors. A great many contemporaries shared the concern Goethe expressed in an essay of 1798, in which he considered what this "era of dispersion and loss" would mean for the development of art.[7] Like so much else, a nation's artistic heritage could no longer be taken for granted; in the revolutionary world, art would need to be defended, safeguarded, perhaps even restored. Because it was both historically valuable and historically at risk, art had to be shielded from the forces of history—an imperative that remains one of the essential elements in the spread of museums.

At the same time that the revolution revealed art's vulnerability, a new generation of aesthetic theorists began to insist on its unique spiritual value. The publication of Kant's *Kritik der Urteilskraft* in 1790 opened the great age of German aesthetics, in which the mature works of Schiller and Goethe, as well as the early writings of Hegel and Schelling, the Schlegels and Novalis, defined a conception of art that had European resonance and enduring influence. Two themes recur through most of these works. The first was a reaffirmation of art's special character, its necessary independence from political interference or social pressures. To flourish, art had to be free, authentic, able to reflect the artist's vision of his age. The second theme was often expressed as an extension of the first: in the modern era, art had a special role to play, both as a source of meaning for individuals and as a source of cohesion for society. Significantly, many (but by no means at all) of these writers spoke of the religious character of art, which could provide spiritual nourishment to an age in which traditional values seemed to be weakening. In its first monumental structures, the German art museum was a temple erected to celebrate this faith in art's spiritual power.[8]

The historical connection between these theories and the decision to build museums was provided by a group of architects, courtiers, and states-men who shared the theorists' belief that their age required new sources of meaning and cohesion. To a reformist bureaucrat like Karl von Altenstein, for instance, art was part of the state's cultural mission: "If it is the state's purpose to bring the highest good to humanity, then this can only be done through scholarship and the fine arts."[9] Wilhelm von Humboldt, who was close to Schiller while he was writing his most important aesthetic manifes-tos, shared this commitment to using state power as an instrument of cul-tural renewal. Men of affairs such as Altenstein and Humboldt found ready allies in architects like Karl Friedrich Schinkel, publicists like Alois Hirt, and *Kunstfreunde* like Carl Friedrich von Rumohr. Their views on the im-portance of art were shared by members of the ruling houses like the future kings of Bavaria and Prussia, Ludwig and Friedrich Wilhelm, who wanted to use their royal resources not only to patronize art but also to further the aesthetic education of their *Volk*.

We can observe the emergence of the museum with particular clarity in Berlin, where the quality of the protagonists—and of the source material— give the story a special exemplary power. In 1797, Alois Hirt, an art histo-rian at the Academy with strong connections to the court, delivered a lec-ture "Über den Kunstschatz des königlich-preussischen Hauses," which called for a unified collection of royal art that could give Berlin the same status as Dresden, Kassel, Düsseldorf, and Vienna. That same year Minister von Heinitz wrote the new king, Friedrich Wilhelm III, that "the collection of all the beautiful and masterful objects belonging to the fatherland in such a museum" would be desirable for artists, students of art, and *Kunstfreunde*. Heinitz's phrasing suggests the degree to which new assumptions about art had become absorbed into common usage: first, that there was a clear cate-gory of masterpieces; second, that these belonged to the fatherland; and finally, that they should benefit everyone with an interest in art. In the event, however, while Friedrich Wilhelm agreed in principle with both Hirt and Heinitz, economic pressures precluded any major investment in culture until after Napoleon's defeat in 1815.[10]

Plans for a museum in Berlin did not take final form until 1822, when the project came under the direction of the greatest architect of the age, Karl Friedrich Schinkel. Schinkel's building (now the so-called Altes Museum) captured a number of the prevailing hopes and aspirations about art's spiritual mission. In the first place, he positioned the museum to close a square formed by structures representing the foundations of the Prussian state—the royal palace, the cathedral, and the Zeughaus—a site that claimed a place for art equal to monarchy, church, and army. This claim was reinforced by the building's facade, whose powerful horizontality and weight emphasized its parallelism to the palace. Second, Schinkel designed the building to express both the autonomy and the spiritual significance of art: one entrance, into a rotunda, evoked the sacred quality of aesthetic experience; the other, an external staircase, re-established art's relevance to the everyday world. Finally, Schinkel wanted to decorate the walls of the museum with paintings (eventually completed on the basis of his sketches by Peter Cornelius) that juxtaposed the destructiveness in human history and the healing power of art. The contents of the museum, selected by a commission chaired by Wilhelm von Humboldt, emphasized classical sculptures and a set of historically-arranged paintings.[11]

The Munich Glyptothek, which opened a few weeks after Schinkel's Berlin Museum, was designed by Leo von Klenze to house the Wittelbachs' splendid collection of classical statues. Klenze, like Schinkel, produced a monumental structure, whose neoclassical lines and interior decorations proclaimed the enduring power of art. Even more than Schinkel, Klenze stressed the historical and canonical basis of artistic development: thus the organization of objects was chronological, so that "the viewer could clearly see the development of art, its rise and its decline." Before the Glyptothek was finished, work had begun on the Pinakothek, which Klenze designed for the royal paintings. Here, too, everything was done to produce the proper conditions under which art's power could be felt: both the interior and the exterior of the Pinakothek, Klenze wrote, were designed "to put the viewer's soul in an appropriate mood" to appreciate beauty. To do this, Klenze blended neoclassical elements into an essentially Renaissance structure, whose historical provenance recalled what was canonically accepted as the highpoint of European painting.[12]

Once the Bavarian and Prussian monarchies had invested in monumental buildings for their collections, the other German dynasties quickly followed. The grand dukes of Baden built the Kunsthalle in Karlsruhe (begun in 1837, opened in 1846), the king of Württemberg the Kunstgebäude in Stuttgart —1838, 1843), the king of Saxony the Gemäldegalerie in Dresden (1847, 1855). Before long, bürgerliche elites also built museums for their cities: the Kunsthalle in Bremen (1845, 1849), the Wallraf-Richartz Museum in Cologne (1856, 1861), the Kunsthalle in Kiel (1856, 1857), and the Kunsthalle in Hamburg (1863, 1869). Of course these various buildings differed from one another in design, contents, and organization, but all of them claimed a certain monumentality and all were devoted to what Gustav Waagen, an advisor to the Prussian court on artistic affairs, described as "the primary and most important purpose" of a museum: "the spiritual education of the nation through the appreciation of beautiful things."[13]

Because they were supposed to promote "die geistige Bildung der Nation," all of these museums were public, accessible to every citizen without limitation. In practice, however, this accessibility was not as equal or unlimited as it might seem. In most museums, the labelling of objects was minimal, catalogues were fairly expensive and designed for people with some artistic knowledge. Even the opening hours produced obvious restrictions: in the 1850s, for example, few German museums were open on Sundays, the only time most working people would be free to go. Many closed early (the Glyptothek at noon, the Pinakothek at 2 P.M.) and almost all refused to open in the evening. Writing in 1851, Friedrich Eggers urged museum administrators to open their doors as widely as possible, "so that everyone, at any time, could have access to these testimonies to genius and thus uplift his spirit with a bit of exhaltation." There was, Eggers pointed out, a long way to go before this could happen.[14]

In theory, museums were directed towards the nation; in practice they were part of a web of institutions that connected art and the bürgerliche public. Kunstvereine, which spread throughout central Europe in the 1820s and 1830s, were devoted to spreading interest in and knowledge about art among the middle strata. Exhibitions of various sorts provided artists a chance to sell their work to a broad public. Journals, such as the Kunstblatt, carried scholarly articles about art history and up-to-date information about contemporary work. Taken together, these institutions remind us that, far from being autonomous, nineteenth-century art was dependent on a complex, overlapping set of intermediaries, which provided what Arnold Gehlen once called "sekundäre Institutionalisierung." Through secondary institutionalization, artists developed alternative sources of meaning and support to replace the religious, political, and social structures that had once sustained and restricted them.[15]

For most of the nineteenth century, history provided the intellectual basis for these institutions. The emergence of art history as an academic discipline was marked by the appearance of scholarly journals, an increasingly large monographic literature, and a series of handbooks that established a canonical account of artistic development.[16] For the educated public, history was the most important source of ideas about what art was supposed to be, as well as of standards of taste and significance. People also drew from history evidence for their conviction that art was important, meaningful, essential for both individual *Bildung* and social cohesion. The great art of the past, especially the art of classical antiquity, pointed to periods of extraordinary energy and accomplishment, periods in which modern men and women could discover lessons and encouragement. And of course history was also important for artists, who learned their craft by copying the work of old masters, drew their subject matter from major historical events, and searched the past for models and inspiration. "Art depends on knowing," Friedrich Schlegel once remarked, "and art's knowledge is its history."[17]

In an aesthetic culture dominated by history, the museum had a special claim to significance. The museum contained the best of the past, displayed to emphasize its quality, organized to demonstrate its historical evolution. Artists went to museums in order to find masters they could emulate. The public went to acquire knowledge about the past, with which they might refine their taste and enrich their sensibility. In their architecture, interior design and decoration, collections and administration, museums were meant to further what the art critic Max Schasler defined in 1862 as "the noblest task of art": the "creation of monumental works, designed to make the greatest thoughts in artistic form the perpetual property of all people, to elevate the spirit, nourish the sense of beauty, and preserve the memory of great men and sublime historical experiences."[18]

In the middle decades of the nineteenth century, the museum's special role in this larger aesthetic project became identified with the validation, conservation, and "restoration" of historical authenticity. And this was, museum curators came to believe, a matter for specially-trained experts in the history of art. A particularly dramatic episode in the rise of the art historian within the museum world occurred in the early 1870s, when various experts engaged in a public dispute over the provenance of two paintings of the madonna, one in Darmstadt, the other in Dresden. Both had long been attributed to Holbein, an opinion that many art critics continued to defend, largely on aesthetic grounds. When historians successfully demonstrated that only one of the pictures could be by the master, they strengthened their claim to authority on questions of authenticity and to positions on museum staffs.[19] The strong ties between the emerging discipline of art history and museums were underscored at the first Internationale Kunstwissenschaftliche Congress, held in Vienna in 1873: among the four issues that dominated discussion, two—on the proper cataloguing of art works and on methods of conservation and restoration—were directly tied to museological practice.[20] This growing importance of scholarship for museums was part of a process anticipated by Hegel, who noted in his lectures on aesthetics that the modern response to art would have to be based on knowledge: "Knowledge about art is much more necessary now than in times when art offered full satisfaction in and of itself."[21] Just as art needed secondary institutions in order to establish its connections to society, so it needed specialized interpreters in order to establish its meaning.

The growing importance of scholars in the organization of museums was won at the expense of two groups, courtiers and artists. In the first phase of the museum's development, when the monarch was often personally involved in its construction and arrangement, it was essential that museum officials have direct access to court. The first director of the Berlin museum, for example, was Count Brühl, who was also director of the royal theatres. At the same time, the museum staff was characteristically composed of artists, who combined their curatorial functions with the teaching and practice of art. Thus the first curator of the classical antiquities in Berlin was Friedrich Tieck, a sculptor who had collaborated with Schinkel on a number of building projects. As long as the monarchy lasted, courtiers retained some influence over art policy, and some artists remained active in museum affairs; but almost everywhere art historians became increasingly important. In the museums, therefore, we can see the same processes of professionalization and specialization that were at work in so many other social, political, and cultural institutions.[22]

Part Three: Museums and Modernism

There was always a certain tension between the understanding of art as a historical phenomenon and the practice of art as a contemporary enterprise. Despite the fact that histories of modern art appeared very early in the century—the first volume of Athanasius Raczynski's *Geschichte der neueren deutschen Kunst* was published in 1836—historians were never quite sure how contemporary artists fit into the canon of artistic development. The only thing that most agreed upon was that modern art was inferior to the best products of the past: even those who did not share Hegel's often-quoted conviction that art "in its noblest manifestation is lost to us forever," doubted that modern artists would ever recapture the greatness of classical Greece or Renaissance Italy.[23] This assumption was built into the earliest museums: Schinkel's structure, for example, contained very little recent art (significantly, only some neoclassical sculpture that was displayed with the antiquities). Indeed, the whole idea of the museum presupposed a closed system of masterpieces in which new work would have no place. Even when museums devoted to contemporary art were built, the relationship of their contents and the treasures of the past was unclear.

By the 1870s, some artists and critics found the relationship between creative artists and the history of art increasingly problematic. The clearest expression of this was the growing disaffection with academic art, that is, with the art most firmly rooted in the study and emulation of historical models.[24] The sense that the past was a burden—given its most brilliant expression in Nietzsche's *On the Advantage and Disadvantage of History for Life*—spread among those who called for a new art, an art appropriate for the modern age. There were many different ideas of what this new art should be, but almost all of them involved a search for a new relationship to history.

As Foucault once pointed out in an interesting *aperçu* about Manet, the modernist approach to the past presupposed the museum, in which all art history seemed to be contained and neutralized.[25] At the same time, however, modernism represented three potential threats to the monumental museum. First, the attack on academic art could easily become an attack on the historical canon enshrined in most museums and on its relevance for artistic education. Such a split between the history and practice of art had to weaken the museum's claim to a privileged role in the aesthetic life of the nation. The second threat was closely connected to the first: as the attraction of academic art diminished, some artists began to look for alternative sources of inspiration, outside history (in genres usually regarded as of secondary value), outside the established canon (in so-called "primitive" objects housed in anthropological museums), and in forms of creative activity conventionally excluded from the "fine arts" (in the production of useful objects and other handicrafts). This trend called into question the definition of art on which the monumental museum had been based. Indeed, it raised the rather frightening possibility that almost anything could be thought of as "art." The third and by far the most dangerous of modernism's threats called into question the entire notion of the museum, not just its orientation and boundaries. In its most extreme form this total rejection of the museum was not common in Germany, but after the turn of the century, we do find a growing disenchantment with museums even among those who could not imagine a world without them. "The expression *museal*," Adorno once wrote, "has an unfriendly sound in German. . . . Museums and mausoleums have more than a phonetic association. Museums resemble graveyards of art."[26] The move from temple to tomb traced the ebbing of faith in art's spiritual power.

The museum establishment—that is, the institution's leadership, civil servants responsible for art policy, and influential figures at court—initially rejected all these attacks on historical traditions and the academic art they sustained. But as the influence of modernism over the cultural elite grew, simple rejection became insufficient. A more characteristic response, personified by the Berlin museum official Hugo von Tschudi and many others, was the attempt to revise the canon so that it could embrace some, if not all, of the modernist movements. The great Berlin exhibition of 1906 was one of the first examples of this kind of response. In it, Tschudi and his colleagues consciously sought to establish a historical pedigree for German modernism, a process that required a significant reordering of nineteenth-century art history.[27] This kind of compromise was never easy, however, in part because modernist movements continued to change, thereby pushing at the boundaries of what had to be embraced; in part because political pressure was often brought to bear in defense of conventional tastes and values. The history of twentieth-century German *Kunstpolitik* is filled with examples of this kind of political interference—Kaiser Wilhelm II, who tried to keep unwholesome, "foreign" elements from contaminating German art; Hitler, who much more ruthlessly imposed his own brand of fascist neoclassicism; and finally, the leaders of the former German Democratic Republic, who furthered a flexible but still clearly-delimited form of politically progressive realism.

Without political pressure, the resistance of most museums to the modernist challenge eventually collapsed. With varying degrees of enthusiasm, the museum world accepted modernism in all its forms. Whenever possible, this was done by opening the canon to include the new; more often, however, this had meant abandoning any clear connection between the historically oriented collections (which usually ran through the early twentieth century) and more contemporary works. At the same time, many museums abandoned the definition of art that had been institutionalized by their nineteenth-century predecessors. No longer were collections limited to classical and European objects, no longer was the separation between arts and crafts so clearly drawn. This porosity of boundaries within museums necessarily weakened the distinction between art museums and other kinds of museums. Of course, various institutions have their specialized function and professionalized staff, but their exhibitions all make the same kind of claim on the attention of the museum-going public. In that way, if in no other, many contemporary museums represent a return to those heterogeneous collections of curiosities and wonders assembled by early modern princes.

There is good reason to celebrate the museum's liberation from the politically imposed taste of individual monarchs and repressive regimes. Nor can we lament the collapse of the increasingly sterile conventions of nineteenth-century academicism. As the restraints of the old historicism have loosened, museums have become more open, flexible, and willing to respond to prevailing trends and enthusiasms. As a result museums have managed to preserve their place within, if not longer at the top of, a new set of secondary institutions connecting art and society. But the flexibility and openness of museums—their alleged if not always consistent universality—make them vulnerable to criticism from those who find them chaotic and formless. The error of the monumental museum had been to insist that it could define and delimit what was valuable in the history of art. By abandoning this claim, the contemporary museum risks admitting its own irrelevance. After all, if everything is potentially valuable enough to be there, then it may be that nothing is inherently valuable enough to merit the kind of permanent reverence a museum confers.

In a very influential critique of museums, Carol Duncan and Alan Wallach argue that "The museum's primary function is ideological. It is meant to impress upon those who use or pass through it society's most revered beliefs and values." [28] They provide no evidence to support this remarkable claim: one wonders how many of the millions of visitors who pass through art museums realize that they are in the presence of their society's "most revered beliefs and values." As far as I can tell, most museum goers do not suffer under the heavy ideological burdens that Duncan and Wallach suppose are being impressed upon them. In fact, the problem of contemporary museums comes less from their power to indoctrinate than from their inability to decide just what they are supposed to be about. Eugenio Donato, in a stimulating essay about museums, has suggested that this problem is best foreshadowed in Flaubert's *Bouvard et Pecuchet*, in which two clerks set out to collect all human knowledge. It is a project that swiftly overwhelms their feeble efforts at imparting order and meaning: "Sometimes they have real problems putting each thing in its proper place and suffer great anxieties about it—Onward! Enough speculation! Keep on copying! Every page must be filled: Everything is equal, the good and the evil. The farcical and the sublime—the beautiful and the ugly—the insignificant and the typical." Is this the museum's future? [29]

Compared to the monumental art museums of the nineteenth century, contemporary museums are heterogeneous and open: few have the kind of carefully articulated aesthetic program that Schinkel built into his Berlin museum. Nevertheless, these earlier conceptions of what a museum should be have not wholly disappeared, either in the architecture of museum buildings or in the way we think about them. In fact, among the things that museums conserve is their own past. Like a complex archaeological site, the modern museum is built on layers of historical experience which are often buried beneath the compelling activities of the present. In the architecture and decoration of some museums, for example, we can see traces of the institution's courtly origins. Almost every museum still preserves the solemn atmosphere of those aesthetic shrines so important to Schinkel and his contemporaries. The organization of the exhibits and, more important, the composition of the staff reflect the persistent power of art history as the museum's governing paradigm. And finally, closest to the surface, are the commercial considerations and democratic aspirations from our own culture. Treasure house, temple, scholarly resource, and source of popular spectacle—the museum seeks to be true to all of these facets of its heritage. We expect museums to be edifying without being pretentious, educational but not pedantic, scholarly but not elitist, democratic but not vulgar. In view of these competing missions, is it any wonder that the literature on museology is so full of doubts about the museum's legitimacy and disagreements about its purpose and organization? [30] These doubts and disagreements are themselves reflections of our culture's uncertainties about itself. Now, as was always the case in its history, the museum tells us at least as much about its own present as it does about the past it is supposed to contain.

Musical Historicism
and the Transcendental
Foundations of Community:
Mendelssohn's *Lobgesang* and
the "Christian-German" Cultural
Politics of Frederick William IV

The name of Felix Mendelssohn-Bartholdy seems out of place on the roster
of philosophers, scholars, and artists that Frederick William IV called to
Berlin after his accession to the Prussian throne in 1840 to provide the intellectual rationale, historical justification, aesthetic symbolization, and public
language for his vision of a "Christian-German" state, of a moral community of Prusso-Germans nurtured, disciplined, and bound together by its
rediscovered, revitalized relationship to the patriarchal God of the Apostolic
Christian Church. How was it possible that the grandson of Moses Mendelssohn and the child prodigy so carefully trained by teachers and family
to become the spiritual heir of the cosmopolitan humanism of classical
Weimar would be invited to join the company of Romantic historicists like
Friedrich W. J. Schelling, Ludwig Tieck, Friedrich Karl von Savigny, the
brothers Grimm, Leopold Ranke, Friedrich Julius Stahl, Friedrich Rückert,
and Peter Cornelius; and to participate in the project of Christian-German
cultural revival? What in Mendelssohn's achievements as a conductor and
composer attracted the attention of influential figures at the Prussian court?
And why would Mendelssohn, apparently so securely and happily established, both domestically as "philistine" *paterfamilias* and professionally as
director of Germany's finest orchestra in Germany's most musical city (the
Gewandhaus in Leipzig), accept this invitation, and thus, however hesi-
tantly and tentatively, attach his talent and reputation to the historical
dreams and projects of the Prussian king and his close advisors? Were there
recognizable, substantial affinities between Mendelssohn's musical intentions and achievements and the program for cultural reform proclaimed by
the new leadership in Berlin?

A paper of this length can hardly attempt to explore all of the dimensions of such questions about Mendelssohn's relationship to the Prussian regime between 1840 and 1845.[1] I will focus my analysis on one musical composition and one issue. The composition is Mendelssohn's choral symphony or "symphony-cantata" *Lobgesang* (Opus 52 in B-flat Major), first performed under the composer's direction at a concert celebrating the four hundredth anniversary of the Gutenberg printing press, in Leipzig on June 25, 1840. This extraordinary amalgam of the secular instrumental structure of the classical symphony and the vocal forms of a sacred cantata based on Biblical texts soon became one of Mendelssohn's best-loved, most-performed concert works, rivalled in popularity during the nineteenth century only by his oratorios *Saint Paul* and *Elijah*. It was a favorite of pious royalty (in England, Saxony, and Prussia) as well as of the evangelical protestant middle class in commercial and industrializing regions like the German Rhineland, the British midlands, and New England. In Birmingham the audience rose to attention for the climactic chorale of the Cantata movement, a response previously reserved for the Hallelujah Chorus.[2] At the Lower Rhenish Musical Festival in 1842 shouts of approval from the audience greeted the first notes of the opening brass hymn.[3] For many of Mendelssohn's contemporaries the *Lobgesang* gave exemplary expression to the distinctive musical voice and cultural message that had formed the basis for his international fame during the mid and late 1830s, combining the forms of traditional Protestant sacred music (epitomized by the revival of Bach) and classical symphony (epitomized by the cult of Beethoven) in a synthetic conception of ethical/cultural reform grounded in historical tradition and religious faith.

The problematic relations between musical form and ethical/cultural reform provide my thematic focus. The royal advisors who originally instigated the Prussian government's invitation to Mendelssohn in 1840, Alexander von Humboldt and Christian Bunsen, both envisioned the young composer in a dual public role. He would be composer and conductor of large-scale works whose public performance would express the musical dimension of officially-promoted cultural reform and the head of a state-supported system of musical education which would help actualize this reform. Humboldt's and Bunsen's proposals involved differing historical orientations and differing perceptions of the priority of secular and sacred orientations in the "moralizing" and "spiritualizing" process of musical education. Both, however, had been personally acquainted with Mendelssohn since his emergence as a child prodigy in the 1820s and their proposals spoke to, and reflected, a genuine ambiguity in Mendelssohn's own cultural experience and consciousness.

Humboldt's vision of reform in 1840 was historically oriented to the great period of Prussian bureaucratic reform during the Napoleonic Era. In musical terms his proposal recalled the proposals which Mendelssohn's teacher and mentor, Karl Friedrich Zelter, had prepared for the Prussian reform bureaucrats Wilhelm von Humboldt and Friedrich von Hardenberg and discussed with Goethe and Schiller in the first decade of the century.[4] Zelter had emphasized the need for music to be recognized, alongside the other fine arts, as "high and serious" art worthy of being represented in the Royal Prussian Academy of Arts and capable of fulfilling, perhaps better than the other arts because of its broad, emotive appeal, the pedagogical task of transforming sensual egotists into ethical, communal beings. Mendelssohn's loyalty to this reform tradition was still clearly evident in 1840, both in a general historical/political sense and in his specific, emphatic, and morally-focussed commitment to the "high art" of a "German" musical tradition. In Mendelssohn's idealized conception of this tradition sensuous materials and virtuosic techniques were subordinated as means for the representation of the musical "idea," and the effectiveness of musical composition and performance was judged by their ability to moralize or edify the audience, to elevate individual listeners into the unity and spirituality of the "idea."[5] For Mendelssohn the elder Bach was the founding father of this tradition of universalizing, spiritualizing music; a tradition sustained and developed by Handel, Gluck, Haydn, and Mozart, which reached its apogee in the work of Beethoven.

Christian Bunsen, a quarter century younger than Humboldt and a generational contemporary of the new king, oriented his reformist hopes most directly and immediately to the period of religious awakening after the Napoleonic wars and historically to the Protestant Reformation of the sixteenth century and the original Christian "reformation" instigated by the Apostolic Church. In his view, music functioned as a significant component of religious reform by recreating and revitalizing for public consumption the emotive core of traditional religious forms, both specifically liturgical and more broadly "national" or communal.[6] Mendelssohn had at times displayed a keen interest in this cultural trend as well. During the 1820s and 1830s he had occasionally composed music in the archaizing fashions of the "Palestrina" revival, emphasizing the pious subordination of the adoring subject to ritual order created by a transcendent father-God and the disciplining of subjective melody into the strict forms of contrapuntal order. However, he

had focussed especially on the revival and renewal of the more congrega-
tional, communal, or "fraternal" liturgical forms of the Protestant hymn
tunes or "chorales" and the more self-consciously "aesthetic" religious music of the Protestant baroque—that is, the great choral concert works of
Bach and Handel.[7] By 1840 Mendelssohn's European reputation was due as
much to his sacred music, especially his cantatas and his oratorios, as to the
secular, instrumental, "humanist" music in which he presented himself as
the heir of Haydn, Mozart, and Beethoven. The characteristic problem for
Mendelssohn in recreating and "reforming" the German Protestant tradition of sacred liturgical music, in remaking its "essence" in contemporary
musical idiom, might be described as the reconciliation of the authority of
the divine father and his revelation of moral and cosmic order with both the
individual subjective freedom of the believer and the immanent "fraternal"
order of human ethical community.

By 1840 Mendelssohn had already passed through one major phase in
his project of revisionist renewal and synthesis of the "German" traditions
of secular/classical and sacred/baroque musical composition. During his
first period of compositional creativity in his own distinctive voice, between
1825 and 1833, Mendelssohn's work focussed on the romantic subjectivi-
zation of the immanent structures of classical sonata forms and the ethical
universalization of liturgical genres. Inspired by what he perceived as a new
structural principle enunciated in Beethoven's late work, especially the string
quartets and piano sonatas, he experimented with cyclic forms in his instrumental works (most strikingly in a series of concert overtures and in the
string quartets, Opus 12 and Opus 13). In these, unity was provided not by
the dramatic structural synthesis of opposing tonal and thematic elements
but by the recognizable continuity of a pre-given musical subject through a
series of transformative variations or episodes.[8] In his revivals and modernizing reinterpretations of the sacred choral music of the Protestant Baroque,
on the other hand, the infusion of a lyrical romantic element was matched
by an equally powerful emphasis on the expansion of the liturgical Lutheran
chorale to the status of a musical representation of spirit-filled community
in a non-ecclesiastical, universally human sense. The series of chorale cantatas on traditional Lutheran hymn tunes composed in the late 1820s and
early 1830s marked his most concerted attempt to renew the collective, universally human meaning of Bach's sacred art for the modern world.[9]

The "Reformation Symphony" (in D Minor, posthumously published as
the Fifth), composed for the tercentenary celebration of the Augsburg Confession of Faith in 1829–30, can be viewed as an experimental attempt to

bring Mendelssohn's two projects together in a unified vision. The sonata forms of the classical symphony were adapted to the dominance of a unifying motif-like subject (the "spirit theme" of the introduction) and amalgamated with an "instrumental cantata" on Luther's Reformation hymn "*Ein feste Burg.*" An historical optimism fuelled this experiment in musical representation of the transformation of sacred ecclesiastical community into the immanent, universal forms of spirit-filled order. It was sustained at least in part by Mendelssohn's feeling of generational identity with a group of young artists and scholars in Berlin in the late 1820s.[10] As this optimism faded and solidarity dissipated after 1830, however, Mendelssohn perceived the synthesis of the Reformation Symphony as premature and forced. He rejected the piece as a failure and by 1833 had begun a general reconsideration of his compositional projects.

Mendelssohn's crisis of historical disillusionment, however, was subdued and limited; it led to a revision but not a transformation of his general vision of musical and cultural reform. In the mid 1830s the more radically emancipatory (emphasizing the claims of the individual romantic subject) and utopian, communal tendencies of Mendelssohn's compositions were subordinated to conservative tendencies which emphasized the discovered, "revealed" and "given" rather than constructed nature of subjective (and thematic) identity and the traditionalist, transcendental and "patriarchal" foundations of musical and ethical order. These shifts, first clearly and publicly articulated in the oratorio *Saint Paul* (1836), inaugurated a period of self-confident compositional maturity, cultural acceptance, and at least relative contentment. Mendelssohn's *Lobgesang* was a representative expression of this new phase in his development.

A number of changes in Mendelssohn's personal and professional circumstances contributed to the shift in his cultural perspective during the mid 1830s. In November 1835 his father died unexpectedly of a cerebral hemorrhage. The death came at a time when Mendelssohn had already made significant moves toward a reconciliation and identification with his father after the conflicts over musical reform and religious identity that had marked their relationship in the late 1820s. The psychological impact of the event was to seal and confirm this process. It marked, he wrote to his friend Karl Klingemann, the decisive end of his youth and thus also of his identification with the "fraternal" world of rebellious sons, and produced a conscious internalization of his father's role and perspective. As he finished *Saint Paul*, the composition of which his father had followed with great care, he felt himself driven by the wish to "become like his father" and fulfill all of his father's expectations.[11] This self-conscious internalization of his father's will or "spirit" was tied to an equally self-conscious desire to end his bachelor days and establish a family of his own, thus fulfilling his father's long-standing wish that he might emancipate himself from the subjective world of romantic fantasy and attain the solid ground of ethical responsibility. In the summer of 1836, during a visit to Frankfurt, he found an appropriate marriage partner in a somewhat conventional and pious young woman from a well known patrician, Huguenot clan. The first child (a son) arrived less than a year after his marriage in March 1837, and Mendelssohn soon found himself the patriarchal center of his own domestic world. In his letters to old friends he often alluded in an ironical, joking manner to the "philistine" happiness of his domestic life, but he also genuinely believed that he had attained a new level of inner equilibrium and that he felt more comfortable in his own skin than he had since leaving the protective parental nest in Berlin in the late 1820s.[12]

Mendelssohn's feelings of domestic tranquillity were clearly protected and re-enforced by two important changes in his professional life. In early 1835, in conformity with the expressed wishes of his father, he decided to leave the conflict-ridden post of City Musical Director in Duesseldorf and accept the directorship of the Leipzig Gewandhaus orchestra. The position proved a very comfortable fit for Mendelssohn's talents and proclivities. In the Gewandhaus he found one of Europe's most competent orchestral ensembles, which he was able to develop rapidly into an efficient instrument for his ambitious program of public education through systematically-organized, historically-oriented performances of great works in the "German" musical tradition. Moreover the local choral society and the musical institutions and traditions of the St. Thomas church (where Bach had been cantor) provided excellent opportunities for the modernizing development and public performance of works in the tradition of liturgical and sacred concert music. Finally in Leipzig he found a middle-class, evangelical culture which nurtured, and responded to, his own aesthetic tastes, moral concerns, and cultural perspectives; which affirmed his beliefs in the spiritualizing function of serious "art-music" and looked with concern on the tendencies toward egotistic virtuosity and amoral striving for novelty, shock-value, and surface brilliance that seemed to dominate the "new" music emanating from the French capital. Here was a "genuine German" society of solid *Bürger* equally removed from the sycophancy and theatricality of court society and the illiberal, conformist pressures of metropolitan "mass" society. It was a context in which ethical education toward spirit-filled community could proceed through individual inner reform and as a positive remaking of the essence of tradition and not fall into the schematic and "external" politics of revolutionary/reactionary confrontations.

The comfortable world, the "home," Mendelssohn found in Leipzig, however much he may have liked to set it against the disintegrative tendencies he perceived in larger urban centers, also extended far beyond the small-town old-German world of the Leipzig *Bürgertum*. The tremendous popular response to *Saint Paul*, not only among the professional and commercial/ capitalist Protestant middle classes in the Rhineland and Westphalia, but within similar social contexts throughout northern continental Europe and England, was the second decisive event in Mendelssohn's public career in the mid and late 1830s. He modestly played down his new celebrity status and interpreted his fame as a public recognition of, and useful educational instrument for, his general program of musical historicism and moral reform.[13] And in an important sense he was correct in perceiving his fame in the 1830s (in contrast to his celebrity as a child prodigy in the 1820s) as connected more to his cause or message than to his personal genius. The impact of *Saint Paul* revealed a powerful affinity between his personal musical vision and the moral and historical perspective of a significant segment of middle-class society in Protestant Europe.

Mendelssohn's bolstered self-assurance about the cultural relevance of his moral and aesthetic conceptions was articulated in his musical compositions between 1836 and 1840 in terms of progressive maturation and consolidation, of formal mastery, of his distinctive musical voice. In 1838 he wrote to a friend that he had never felt more comfortable within the recognized limitations of the German musical tradition and had reached a new level of self-confidence in his ability to find the appropriate musical form for his feelings and intentions.[14] The most striking examples of this new compositional assurance and self-confidence were in the genres of instrumental chamber music, and especially in that epitomy of classical sonata form, the string quartet.[15]

Mendelssohn's set of three string quartets, Opus 44 (1838), achieved a fully articulated expression of the transformative revisions of classical sonata form first adumbrated in his confrontation with Beethoven's late work in the late 1820s. The dramatic contrasts, conflicts, and discontinuities which impelled the classical sonata through the analytical work of "development" and the achieved mediations of the "recapitulation" were subdued to the point of vanishing altogether. They were replaced as an organizing and unifying principle by the evolution of a relatively simple subject toward full self-disclosure and articulation through a process of contextual enrichment and variation. Development within structural continuity (especially evident in Mendelssohn's cautiously conservative tonal and rhythmic relations), the evolving variation of a directing "idea" or musical subject, replaced the dialectical oppositions and heroic resolutions of the classical period. The striving for organic unity and continuity through a succession of musical episodes tended to displace the dramatic unification of opposites as the principle of aesthetic unity or closure. Mendelssohn's self-conscious, elaborate application of complex musical techniques to sustain the identity of the musical subject through a narrative sequence of transformative variations and enriching episodes produced for many later listeners (as well as some contemporary critics, like Richard Wagner) an impression of bland homogeneity, effortless simplicity, and "smoothness." Mendelssohn, however, worked laboriously to achieve this sense of a pre-given or "transcendent" identity, not a unity immanently constructed within the work or yearned for as an absent ideal or future possibility, but a unity "discovered" or "revealed" in an exegetical process. Two elements marked the distinctive character of Mendelssohn's musical narratives of the spiritual subject, or "idea," as stories of recognition and acceptance of a pre-given, revealed integration into absolute order. First was the belief that the musical subject entered into the world already formed as the child of a father or creation of a transcendent power. Even though Mendelssohn's musical subjects or motifs were relatively simple, so as to allow for flexibility in variation, adaptation, connection, and merger, they did have a figural identity that placed limitations on the process of self-making. Second, Mendelssohn conceived the evolution of these subjects within strictly defined boundaries, established not only transcendentally but also historically. The external frame of his compositions remained the classical sonata form, and however much he may have hollowed out its impelling internal dynamics, the ideal of working within an inherited set of rules that guaranteed closed structure and organic unity remained central to his aesthetic conceptions.

During the late 1830s Mendelssohn also worked on the application of his compositional techniques to the monumental public forms of the classical symphony. As conductor of the Gewandhaus orchestra, Mendelssohn played the role of authoritative performer and interpretor of the classical symphonic tradition from Haydn to Beethoven. The task of creatively assimilating this tradition, especially the gigantic Beethoven corpus, proved intimidating. This was especially true of the Ninth Symphony, which Mendelssohn had studied, puzzled over, and performed as both player and conductor on many occasions since its north German premiere in 1826. He conducted the Ninth in each of his first two seasons at the Gewandhaus,[16] as well as at the Lower Rhenish Musical Festival in the summer of 1836, but in December 1837 he still expressed his bafflement with the musical meaning of the final movement.[17] As a true believer in Beethoven's genius he was not willing to follow his sister Fanny in judging the Ninth a colossal "monstrosity,"[18] but he did find the ways in which Beethoven tried to express transcendence of the immanent structures of classical form in the last movement resistant to effective practical articulation—that is, virtually impossible to perform.

It would be misleading and unfair to Mendelssohn to judge the *Lobgesang* as a self-conscious attempt to remake or revise Beethoven's choral symphony in a manner which resolved its problematic relations between vocal and instrumental forms, and between immanent structures and transcendent yearnings. Although comparisons between the two works were immediately drawn by Mendelssohn's contemporaries, Mendelssohn himself claimed he had found the Beethoven model too daunting to emulate; his work approached similar issues from a different perspective. In fact the *Lobgesang* emerges from Mendelssohn's own development as an interesting attempt to merge his parallel "reforms" of sacred music (with Bach as model and mentor) and classical sonata form (with Beethoven as model and mentor) into a single musical conception of the relations between the sacred and secular, divine and human, transcendent and immanent; and to address the problem of the integration of the individual subject into an ethical community in terms of the historical and structural relations between these two dimensions. And all invidious comparisons aside, the *Lobgesang* does reveal how differently Mendelssohn viewed these sets of relations from the Beethoven of the Ninth Symphony.

In its general structure Mendelssohn's *Lobgesang* does parallel the Ninth Symphony in a number of ways and it is difficult to imagine that the Beethoven model was not in Mendelssohn's mind during the process of composition.[19] Three instrumental movements—an opening *sonata allegro*, a *scherzo/trio*, and an *adagio*—are completed with a choral finale. However, the balance of these movements within Mendelssohn's work diverges from Beethoven's in that the three instrumental movements are only half as long as the choral finale, and thus almost give the impression of a three part symphonic overture. The narrative of dramatic conflict, struggle, suffering, and yearning leading up to the vision of transcendent resolution is less intense and troubled in Mendelssohn's work and the resolution is much more self-assured, affirmative, and extended. But Mendelssohn did conceive the

instrumental movements as more than a mere introduction to a sacred cantata celebrating divine order, and he defined his genre as "Symphony with
chorus and orchestra" (the final title, *Symphony-Cantata*, was suggested by
his friend Klingemann).

Like Beethoven, Mendelssohn composed his choral symphony in relation to a specific written text. However, Mendelssohn's text was not a secular
poem about interhuman relations but an arrangement of sacred poetry (the
Psalms) concerning the relations between God and man, centered on a textual theme: "Alles was Odom hat Preise den Herrn" ("All that has Life and
Breath Praise the Lord"). Both instrumental and vocal segments, he informed Klingemann, were composed on this text, as an intensifying, elevat-
ing movement of praise, progressing from instruments to voices.[20] On the
title page of the published score Mendelssohn added another text, from
Martin Luther: "I would like to see all the arts and music in particular
function in the service of him who created them and gave them to us." The
joys celebrated in Mendelssohn's symphonic ode were not so much the joys
of Schiller's and Beethoven's odes to human freedom and brotherhood, as
the joys of filial piety, reverence for tradition, and enlightened reconciliation through subordination to the revealed will of the creator-father. The
historical memories aroused and transcended in Mendelssohn's musical narrative were not the memories of the revolutionary dawn of the late eighteenth century, but those of the sixteenth century Reformation and his own
hopes for moral/religious "reformation" in the 1820s. Mendelssohn's theme
was spiritual enlightenment through a receptiveness to divine revelation,
filial reconciliation through understanding of the essential meaning of the
father's word. As a celebration of Gutenberg's achievement in making the
word available to the many, Mendelssohn's symphony was also an ode to
enlightenment in a more general sense, to the awakening that comes from
grasping the word as it is presented through tradition and assimilated into
the consciousness of the present.

The first movement of the *Lobgesang* opens with a stately introduction
of 22 measures (*maestoso con moto*) in which the hymnic motif of the whole
work is intoned by the deep brass (trombones) playing in unison (Illus. 1).
Both the ascending and descending phrases of the motif are repeated in
antiphonal fashion in homophonic chords by the rest of the orchestra, and
then combined in a concluding phrase merging the brass into the full orchestra. Although this simple, memorable opening hymn is not a direct
citation from the liturgical tradition, Mendelssohn constructed its intervals
according to the requirements of a pre-modern modal scale connected to

ILLUS. 1. The Initial Proclamation of the Hymnic Motif (the "Idea").

liturgical music (the Eighth Psalm mode),[21] thus highlighting its sacred, and ancient, character. The fluttering open fifths of ambiguous tonality through which sound gradually emerges from silence in the opening of Beethoven's Ninth are thus replaced in Mendelssohn's work by a fully-developed, authoritative declaration, resonant with the authority of divine revelation and historical tradition. Beethoven's own striking use of archaic modal tonality in one of the choral variations of the "Ode to Joy" (the "Andante Maestoso") produces the effect of an ecstatic mystical yearning for spiritual transcendence. It is contrasted by Mendelssohn's affirmative revelation of the authoritative word of the divine creator as the starting point of the human spiritual quest.

After the introductory statement, Mendelssohn's first movement switches quickly into the rapid tempo of what appears to be the opening *allegro* movement of standard sonata form. The first theme, a lively, driving phrase with violins taking the leading voice and echoing a theme from Beethoven's first *Leonora* Overture, seems to leave the solemn ancient tones of the sacred hymn far behind. But after 40 measures, in what might schematically be defined as a transition or "bridge" passage to the second theme, the hymn re-enters. It now is caught in the driving secular tempo of the *allegro* and engages in a brief dialogue with the first "Beethoven" theme before fading into the tentative opening measures of the second theme, a pastoral, lyrical song-like phrase that seems more like a lyrical *intermezzo* than a fully developed second theme in classical style, a premonitory statement of the claims of natural human subjectivity for self-expression and recognition. These claims are almost immediately silenced and displaced by what appears (again in contrast to conventional sonata form) as a "third" theme whose rhythms and intervals are more easily integrated into the dominant relational web between the hymnic motif and the first theme. Mendelssohn obviously recognized Beethoven's creative use of premonitions and reminiscences as a unifying thread in the Ninth, but the balance of premonition and reminiscence is entirely different in Mendelssohn. His emphasis is on the continuous undergirding presence of the opening hymnic revelation, which constantly reappears as the essence within the appearance, whereas the Ode to Joy melody in Beethoven is gradually and tortuously pieced together and then finally articulated as a resolution and construction of unity from previously isolated fragments. If the Ninth could be imagined in Mendelssohnian form, the Ode to Joy theme would have appeared in its lapidary instrumental totality as the introduction of the first movement. It would be the given "idea" or spiritual subject, which would then be subjected to interpretive exegesis through a process of contextualization and combination.

The "development" section of Mendelssohn's first movement (measures 145–260), the moment of analytic dissection in standard sonata form, is transformed into an evolutionary narrative of musical episodes in which the themes, tonalities, rhythmic structures of the opening exposition are set in relation to each other and subjected to variations. In the *Lobgesang* the development moves through four distinct episodes culminating in a "return" (the fifth episode) to the first theme (the "Beethoven" theme) on the dominant (F). The evolving pattern of these episodes is a gradual movement away from the dominance of the hymnic theme (which virtually controls the first three episodes) toward a restatement of the lyrical *intermezzo* (the second theme, which dominates the fourth episode). This song-like theme is strikingly framed by changes in tempo and dynamics, emerging from virtual silence and calm and then suddenly breaking off in a sudden return to the *allegro* tempo. Again the impression is one of the emergence of the individual natural subject alongside, somehow not integrated into, the sacred/secular relations between the hymn and the main "Beethoven" theme.

This procedure is emphatic and striking and may suggest the problematic of the whole first movement as the integration of individual subjectivity into the collective historical process of struggle, transformation, and "reformation" whereby the transcendent, sacred revelation achieves historical incarnation or "secularization," incorporation into the immanent structures of the sonata form. At least such an interpretation helps make sense of the conclusion of the first movement, in which the apparent progress toward merger of the hymnic and Beethoven themes suddenly falters and stalls. A unison restatement of the hymn by the brass is greeted by a hesitant and tentative response that unexpectedly shifts into a lyrical recitative by the solo clarinet, ushering in the transition (without pause) to the dance rhythms of the *scherzo* movement.

The thematic subject of the *scherzo* (*allegretto un poco agitato*) is a simple Romantic song with strong suggestions of a folk-like or rustic melody and rhythm. This *scherzo* is much less animated and driven than its Beethoven correlate. The second movement in Mendelssohn's symphony begins with the problem raised in the first movement—the status of the individual "natural" subject, still defined in idyllic pastoral tones, to both divine will and human community. The central "trio" section of the second movement breaks the blithe naiveté of the *scherzo* by juxtaposing it with the phrases of an artificially constructed religious anthem or chorale. The first and last lines of the chorale echo well-known Lutheran hymn tunes. The hymnic motif from the first movement reappears almost unnoticeably integrated into the chords of the chorale in the middle voice of the oboes (Illus. 2), perhaps a reminder that the liturgical community confronting the natural subject is a spiritual community incorporating the revealed will of the divine father. Each line of the chorale is interrupted by a lyrical *intermezzo* from the rustic dance theme of the *scherzo*, creating a musical dialogue between the natural, secular subjectivity and the united voice of the religious community. Throughout the trio the two voices appear to simply alternate and talk past each other, but when the *scherzo* returns in the third part of the movement, Mendelssohn's score suggests that the dialogue has marked a change in the natural subject. The repetition of the *scherzo* is not developed in full *da capo* form but is short, truncated, and troubled. It is as if the natural subject has been forced to recognize its finite limitations, its lack of

ILLUS. 2. The Father's proclamation (the oboes) integrated into the communal chorale and confronted by the romantic subject (strings).

self-sufficiency, and been pushed to a boundary at which it can begin to experience a longing for integration into the spiritual world of the community and for reconciliation with the transcendent power of the father's will. The hidden integration of the ancient proclamation (the hymnic motif) into the communal chorale may suggest that for Mendelssohn the relationship between the natural human subject and its moral or spiritual essence (a relation defined by the demand for ethical integration and spiritualizing cultivation) assumed a fusion of patriarchal will and community tradition. The achievement of the first movement might be represented as precisely this merger (that is, of the hymn and the "Beethoven" theme), although the identification of human moral essence and divine will still left the integration of the natural subject into the universal (in both senses) unresolved. The second movement breaks the naive self-sufficiency of the natural subject, instigating an ethical claim and a religious need, or at least a feeling of spiritual discontent and desire.

Mendelssohn's *scherzo/trio* clearly has functional analogies to Beethoven's second movement, in that its intention appears to be a critical examination of the idyllic illusion of self-sufficient natural subjectivity. But where Beethoven places an ironic frame around his idyll (in his case placed in the middle trio section) with the hectic rhythms and driving power of the *scherzo*, Mendelssohn uses the *scherzo* to represent the idyll and then places it into a self-questioning dialogue with the forces of communal ethos and divine will. The illusion of the idyll does not decompose under the driving energies of life in Mendelssohns's musical narrative but comes to recognize its own limitations in the face of the higher authority of the community and its divine creator. The disquietudes of Mendelssohn's subject are backward oriented, pointing toward the need for an awakening and comprehension of the hidden, essential meaning contained within historical tradition.

The third movement—*adagio religioso*—explores the new depths and complexities of a subjectivity that has been confronted with its own limitations and the hopelessness of its longings for a return to Arcadia. It does so in a series of variations of a sweeping expressive melody orchestrated with emphasis on the darker tones of the middle instrumental voices. Mendelssohn's conception of religious yearning was not dramatically anguished. Tonal leaps, chromatic complexities, and dissonances are avoided. Only the surging upward arc and soft fadings of the melodic phrases and the broken triads of the accompaniment indicate the pain and suffering of unrequited longing within what appears to be overwhelmingly a song of resignation and expectancy, of "waiting for the Lord." The ache for the infinite, the longing for transcendence are not pushed to the emotional extremes evident in Beethoven's *adagio* movement. Again an echo of Beethoven marks the difference. In the middle of the *adagio*, Mendelssohn, like Beethoven, used a fully orchestrated crescendo (including brass) to mark a climax. Whereas Beethoven's crescendo brings the aching to an anguished breaking point, Mendelssohn's issues in a fanfare-like phrase that points ahead to the introductory phrases which immediately precede the choral affirmation of the finale. Mendelssohn's climax is a consoling look backward and forward, to the original revelation and its ultimate recognition and appropriation. The intensifying beat that introduces the awakening choral version of the hymnic motif at the beginning of the finale is thus also much more subdued than the "terror-fanfare" that introduces the finale of Beethoven's Ninth. For Mendelssohn the awakening from the dream-like state of subjective longing and expectancy was more like a response to a long familiar voice, finally recognized.

The musical narrative of the instrumental movements of the *Lobgesang* culminates in the expression of a romantic subjective longing ready to grasp the meaning of revelation in tradition once it is presented in the self-conscious articulation of the "word." Mendelssohn's choral finale is thus, like Beethoven's, the culmination of the musical narrative, the end point of the quest inaugurated by the trombones' first declarations. The opening chorus of the Cantata movement, a majestic Handel-like chorus that provides the verbal text for the hymnic theme, could thus be seen as the climax of the work, bringing to full self-conscious clarity the opening revelation. Unlike Beethoven, Mendelssohn conceived this resolution as a "rediscovery" or human appropriation of revealed truth. But like Beethoven, Mendelssohn treats the first full articulation of the resolution as the beginning of a new process of subjective appropriation and contextual enrichment that in a sense duplicates or repeats the evolutionary progress of the symphony as a whole.

The Cantata of the *Lobgesang* is structured on the pattern of a journey of spiritual education. The extended opening choral declaration of praise is followed by a tenor recitative which demands that individual human subjects examine and give articulate speech to the experiential reality of their praise, bear witness to their redemption, or awakening, from the powers of darkness. The next four numbers expand this process of confession and self-conscious examination with increasing intensity. The popular soprano duet "Ich harrete des Herrn" ("I waited for the Lord") duplicates with verbal specificity the instrumental *adagio* in its lyrical sweep as well as its emotional indulgence in the blissful surrender to the embrace of an "inclining" heavenly father. The culmination of this section of the cantata, however, clearly arrives with the dramatic anguish of the tenor solo: "The Bonds of Death had closed around us" ("Stricke des Todes hatten uns umfangen").

With rising urgency the tenor voice repeats its cry: "Watchman will this night soon pass?" The cautious stepwise modulations and extremely subdued use of dissonance throughout the work are temporarily abandoned as

I L L U S . 3. Mendelssohn's musical narrative of crisis and conversion.

startling leaps in tonality and strikingly dissonant chords emphasize the crisis-like turning point of this yearning for redemption as a plea for light (Illus. 3). Finally, after the fourth repetition of this cry, a high soprano voice responds: "The Night is Departed, the day has dawned," an announcement which is immediately followed and re-enforced by a majestic full chorus greeting the dawn of enlightenment and raising a battle cry for a concerted assault by the enlightened on the powers of darkness.

This conversion or transformation scene, which has striking parallels to the conversion of Saul into Paul in *Saint Paul*, articulated Mendelssohn's particular conception of ethical/social reform. Reform came in the form of an internal illumination, and this enlightenment occurred through an intellectual recognition of, and moral surrender to, the spiritual power of a transcendent father speaking through the revelations of historical tradition. Mendelssohn's own piety, as he himself noted, was defined not as a desire to escape the conditions of finitude, to attain salvation from the "sin" of being merely human, but as a desire to live in enlightened recognition and conformity with his created nature, his divinely-given spiritual essence as a human being.[22] Unlike Beethoven, Mendelssohn seemed to harbor no doubts that the process of enlightenment was sustained by a divinely-created cosmic and moral order, or that this order was embodied and represented in the man-made order of the cultural tradition, which functioned as the letter of the divine spirit. Whereas Beethoven's Ninth can be seen as a search for the fundamental principles of its own order (for example, its tonal basis), the musical foundations of Mendelssohn's symphony were never in doubt. The symphony organizes itself firmly in a journey grounded on a definite key and its final chorus concludes with a repetition of the opening hymnic phrase unmistakably on the tonic chord.

The second half of the Cantata movement however also addresses the issue of the relationship between individual enlightenment (as reconciliation with the understood will of the father) and communal identity. The choral celebration of enlightenment is immediately followed by a well-known Lutheran chorale (*Nun danket alle Gott*), whose first stanza is given a full traditional exposition in the a capella, cantional style of the liturgy before the orchestra enters with an independent theme configured with an elaborated version of the third stanza. This typically Mendelssohnian modernization of a liturgical form is followed by a tenor/soprano duet in the style of a romantic *Lied*, assimilating the significance of the awakening experience into the processes of individual subjectivity. The concluding chorus then appears to move outward into the sphere of communal ethics and politics again, suggesting a desire to transform the specifically confessional, ecclesiastical/liturgical expression of communal solidarity into the more inclusive secular relations of princes and peoples.

But this suggestion of a collective appropriation of revelation in a secular ethical community is only tentative, presented as a demand on the future, and firmly articulated in traditional patriarchal forms. The cultural unity of nations or peoples is not presented as a self-constructed human fraternity but as a union of children who share a common recognition and assimilation of the father's revealed will. Mendelssohn's decision to complete his choral symphony with a religious cantata was in keeping with his historical belief that the resolution of the human process of moral education, both individual and collective, would occur as the attainment of a regenerated, reformed version of a universal truth contained in traditional religious forms. The immanent, organic relations of the symphonic structure itself, the rules of its order, were ultimately given and guaranteed from the outside, derived from and dependent on the revealed truths of historical tradition, the spirit in the letter of the father's voice.

It is thus not surprising that for all of Mendelssohn's individual discontents with the Prussian regime after 1840, he felt a strong affinity with Frederick William IV's vision of cultural order and moral education. Nor is it surprising that Frederick William and many of his closest advisors saw their own historical/cultural perceptions mirrored in the musical universes of Mendelssohn works like the *Lobgesang*. Mendelssohn shared their conviction that individual redemption and communal order were grounded in a transcendent power; that this divine power had a personal (not pantheistic), patriarchal form; that its voice was embodied in historical tradition; and that this tradition, although universally human, had been preserved most successfully within the history of a distinctively German religious and aesthetic culture. Mendelssohn had a peculiarly universalist conception of the "German" tradition and merged his Christian confessional loyalties into a broader conception of the Judeo-Christian tradition. At the same time, he affirmed that peculiar combination of cultural historicism, patriarchal politics, and belief in a transcendent ground of earthly order shared by Schelling, Ranke, Savigny, the Grimm brothers, and other celebrities working in the romantic historicist tradition, who briefly attached their careers to the new regime in Berlin in the early 1840s.

MICHAEL P. STEINBERG

Broken Vessels: Aestheticism and Modernity in Henry James and Walter Benjamin

The ray of light falls from above, and the Grail glows brightest. From the dome descends a white dove and hovers over Parsifal's head. Kundry, with her gaze uplifted to Parsifal, sinks slowly lifeless to the ground. Amfortas and Gurnemanz kneel in homage before Parsifal, who waves the Grail in blessing over the worshipping Knighthood.

> Richard Wagner, stage directions for the final curtain of *Parsifal* (1882)

"But do you remember," she asked, "apropos of great gold cups, the beautiful one, that I offered you so long ago and that you wouldn't have? Just before your marriage"—she brought it back to him: "the gilded crystal bowl in the little Bloomsbury shop."

"Oh yes!"—but it took, with a slight surprise on the Prince's part, some small recollecting. "The treacherous cracked thing you wanted to palm off on me, and the little swindling Jew who understood Italian and who backed you up!"

"Don't you think too much of 'cracks' and aren't you too afraid of them? I risk the cracks," said Charlotte, "and I've often recalled the bowl and the little swindling Jew, wondering if they've parted company. He made," she said, "a great impression on me."

> Henry James, *The Golden Bowl* (1904)

The Breaking of the Bowls, of which we find exhaustive descriptions in the literature of Kabbalism, is the decisive turning point in the cosmological process. Taken as a whole, it is the cause of that

inner deficiency which is inherent in everything
that exists and which persists as long as the damage is not mended. For when the bowls were broken the light either diffused or flowed back to its
source, or flowed downwards. The fiendish nether-
worlds of evil, the influence of which crept into all
stages of the cosmological process, emerged from
the fragments which still retained a few sparks of
the holy light—Luria speaks of just 288. In this
way the good elements of the divine order came to
be mixed with the vicious ones. Conversely the restoration of the ideal order, which forms the original aim of creation, is also the secret purpose of
existence. Salvation means actually nothing but
restitution, re-integration of the original whole, or
Tikkun, to use the Hebrew term.

> Gershom Scholem, "Isaac Luria and His
> School" (1941)

I

I want to argue in this essay that the confrontation with modernity characteristic of critical intellectuals from the end of the last century into our
own "post-modern" period proceeds from the recognition that *Parsifal* lies.
The lie resides in the promise of aestheticism that totality and authenticity
will be restored to a reconsecrated world, purged of the dissipating demons
of modernity. Aestheticism in this sense refers to a strong discourse, not to
the withdrawal into art but to its opposite: to the empowerment of aesthetic
categories of harmony, form, and authenticity to return to the world the
aura which religion had once provided. The end of *Parsifal* claims to deliver
on that claim, or at the very least to show how to do so. The governing
metaphor of the Grail reinforces the enormity of the cultural claim: the cup
that held the blood of Christ is resanctified along with the world it represents. The means of the restoration is the cleansing of culture of the element
which spilled the blood: the Jews. The Jew or the Jews form the cultural
category, group, or person which calls into question, jeopardizes, or even
prevents closure, completeness, and, potentially, health in the body cul-

tural. The power of the ideology of aestheticism in the European fin de siècle—with resonances in the American one as well—is thus demonstrated by the force of its resulting exclusionary discourses. Anti-Semitism is one of these, not the only one.

This essay will be in two parts. Both parts examine the shape of an effort to develop a moral position in regard to the conundrum of modernity, aestheticism, and the cultural place of the Jews. In the first part the figure of the Jew appears as a cultural object; in the second as a—or the—cultural subject. The first part will address Henry James as the writer of, and moral actor in, the novel *The Golden Bowl*. With the help of references to the work of George Eliot and Edith Wharton, I will try to define some principles in what I take to be a moral and aesthetic fin-de-siècle English-language discourse, in which the boundaries between the moral and aesthetic construction of modernity are drawn. On these boundaries strides the figure and the person of the Jew. In the second part, I will turn to the same topic, as seen from within the Jewish intellectual culture of Walter Benjamin and Gershom Scholem during and after the First World War, as the promise of Jewish assimilation faded.

The juxtaposition of James and Benjamin is motivated most immediately by their shared attention to the image of the broken vessel. Both thinkers make the metaphor itself into a vessel for the currents of modernity: the critique of an aestheticized culture, and the central position in this critique of Jews, Jewish figures and thinkers, and debates about Jewish identity and assimilation. But beyond the metaphor itself, James and Benjamin provide, I want to argue, a normative example, methodologically and morally, for the ongoing historical discussion of the place of the Jews in the making of modern culture. They share the conviction that, where modernity is addressed, the Jews are *in* question, but not *the* question.

The Golden Bowl, like *Parsifal* a final creative statement, confronts and painstakingly, and painfully, undoes much of the ideological work of *Parsifal*. The physical object which controls the novel's symbolic world is not golden but gilded, and it is cracked from the first. At the novel's climax—its cracking point—the bowl is shattered entirely. My question will proceed in two parts. How far was Henry James willing to go in his acceptance of the crack and its full symbolic resonance? How far, in other words, did he come finally to confront and accept a modernity defined in terms of fragmentation rather than totality and in terms of life as severed from categories of art and aestheticism? This line of questioning is not new, although the terms in which I am casting it are altered. Most recently, the question has been asked by Martha Nussbaum in what strikes me as a definitive argument for the novel as a moral philosophical investigation; I will draw much on her work below.[1]

My second question enters an underlying realm of the novel which, so far as I know, has not been addressed in the context of the overall discussion of the metaphor of the bowl. The cracked bowl comes from the hands of a Jew. What this fact seems to me to do to the life of the metaphor of the golden bowl is the following: the authorial, philosophical confrontation with the crack—ultimately, with modernity—involves an authorial confrontation with the question of the place of the Jews in modern culture, with anti-Semitic discourse, and—most personally for Henry James—with the moral necessity to work toward the inner nonacceptability of the kind of casual anti-Semitism that has, until this point, lived peacefully within elegant prose and accepted norms. In the preface to the New York edition of *The Golden Bowl*, James renounced authorial moral superiority and wrote of his wish to endure the same moral passages he designs for his characters. The book itself thus works toward a moral position about modernity and cultural fragmentation which doubles as the moral education of the main character, Maggie Verver.

In 1904, Edith Wharton published *The House of Mirth*, which included in its menagerie of fin-de-siècle New York *arrivistes* the casually anti-Semitic characterization of Simon Rosedale, who is attracted to Lily Bart but decides resolutely not to marry her when her reduced status can no longer serve his own social ambition. Wharton's introduction of Rosedale as a "plump rosy man of the blond Jewish type" is casual, but her narrative manipulates him into a position of evil that has nothing to do with his own intentions: it is Rosedale who spots Lily as she leaves the bachelor apartment of Laurence Selden, a meeting that throws Lily into the self-doubt which initiates the psychological predisposition to her social downfall.[2] Rosedale is the waiting serpent that kills innocence. As one might expect, he turns out to be the landlord of Selden's building (named "The Benedick").

I think it is fair to assert that James's novel of the same year—in contrast to Wharton's—argues for the impossibility of any casual moral position. To say that it "argues" at all is to recognize the kind of philosophical intentions which Martha Nussbaum has attributed to it. This ban on the morally casual postures inherent in the fin-de-siècle world the novel portrays must include the extirpation of anti-Semitism if the book's moral voice is to have credibility. To come away from *The Golden Bowl*, for example, with the judgment "Of course the narration exhibits a certain degree of anti-Semitism, but that was universal in James's world and one can't expect him to be an exception" contradicts and would entirely defeat the desire of every fiber of the book to identify and then inhabit a morally justifiable life. (This is not the same as a morally perfect life, as will be addressed below.)

Although their correspondence shows no communication on the issue, it seems clear that James and Wharton took divergent paths in the crucial year of 1904—crucial in their publication history, but also, if largely circumstantially, in their shared exposure to political questions of Jews and anti-Semitism. *The Golden Bowl* was completed in the spring of 1904. During the height of the Dreyfus Affair and the scandal of Zola's *J'accuse*, James had supported Zola and offered to shelter him in England. He described Zola as a hero and, upon his guilty sentence in February 1898, suggested that only the guilty verdict had spared Zola from being "torn limb from limb by the howling mob in the streets."[3] The Anglophile adopted a Burkean Francophobia, but the enemy was on the right. In 1903 he wrote the essay "Emile Zola."[4] James's pro-Dreyfus and pro-Zola position caused the break of the friendship with the novelist Paul Bourget, an anti-Dreyfusard and an anti-Semite.[5] Curiously, there is no mention of the issue in the recently published James-Wharton correspondence.[6] Bourget had completed the triangular friendship that connected James and Wharton. The shattering of the golden bowl into three pieces may include in its resonances the breaking of this triangle.

Martha Nussbaum describes the world of *The Golden Bowl* as "a fallen world—a world, that is, in which innocence cannot be and is not safely preserved, a world where values and loves are so pervasively in tension with one another that there is no safe human expectation of a perfect fidelity to all throughout a life."[7] The recognition of this condition and the emerging will to negotiate it constitute the moral education of Maggie Verver. The first half of the novel explores the artificial world of her preserved innocence: the Edenic world provided by her tycoon father Adam, who lives in the whitewalled purity of Eaton [Eden] Square. Maggie's initial retention of this paternal innocence across the thresholds of her marriage and motherhood heralds the emotional danger she falls into. Like Adam Verver, she is a collector. He is building a great museum; she aids in their shared practice of the "aestheticization of persons." The resulting portrait is of "the inveterate tendency of both father and daughter to assimilate people, in their imagination and deliberation, to fine *objets d'art*."[8]

Maggie Verver's moral education moves from the novel's first volume, named for her husband, "The Prince," to the second volume, "The Princess." James states in the preface to the New York edition that the "Prince, in the first half of the book, virtually sees and knows and makes out, virtually represents to himself everything that concerns us—very nearly (though he doesn't speak in the first person) after the fashion of other reporters and critics of other situations. . . . The function of the Princess, in the remainder, matches exactly with his."[9] The novel's opening pages portray the Prince, a Roman in London, bent on recovering a personal style reflective of the *Imperium*. In question are "capture" and "pursuit," and his prey are the American father and daughter, Adam and Maggie Verver. The Prince's first name is, after all, Amerigo. His experience is thus clearer and more confident than that of the American Ververs, for whom conquest and exile are strangely mixed. His initial reported conversion with Maggie Verver reveals his place in the shared cosmos of father and daughter:

". . . the collection, the Museum with which he wishes to endow it, and of which he thinks more, as you know, than of anything in the world. It's the work of his life and the motive of everything he does."

The young man, in his actual mood, could have smiled again—smiled delicately, as he had then smiled at her: "Has it been his motive in letting me have you?"

"Yes, my dear, positively—or in a manner. . . . You're a rarity, an object of beauty, an object of price. You're not perhaps absolutely unique, but you're so curious and eminent that there are very few others like you—you belong to a class about which everything is known. You're what they call a *morceau de musée*."[10]

The strategies of the *Imperium* and the Museum differ: the Prince defines his conquests in terms of the unknown and the living; the future Princess in terms of the (allegedly) known and objectified.

Two pages later, Maggie describes her faith in the Prince as "divided . . . into watertight compartments," and then adjusts her image into "Watertight—the biggest compartment of all? Why it's the best cabin and the main deck and the engine-room and the steward's pantry! It's the ship itself—it's the whole line."[11] The author comments here on Maggie's ability to make images, and her image of her faith and herself is first that of an unsinkable vessel and then, after the adjustment, of an unbreakable one. In the subsequent encounter between the Prince and Fanny Assingham (the observer of the novel's action whom, along with her husband, Bob Assingham, Martha

Nussbaum places in the role of the Greek chorus), the image of the vessel is relied on by both, with the topic of the Prince's marriage discussed in terms of a vessel entering a port.[12]

The golden bowl of the title is first seen in the Bloomsbury antique shop by the Prince and Charlotte Stant, in their ostensible search for a wedding present for himself and Maggie Verver. They see the dealer's inventory in terms of historical debris: "[a] few commemorative medals of neat outline but dull reference; a classic monument or two, things of the first years of the century; things consular, Napoleonic, temples, obelisks, arches, tinily re-embodied, completed the discreet cluster. . . . It was impossible they shouldn't, after a little while, tacitly agree as to the absurdity of carrying to Maggie a token from such a stock."[13] The dealer's inventory offers a pan-orama of history which can be described by us as Benjaminian: history as ruin, perceived in terms of dissipated and severed objects. This is the op-posite view of culture and history from that of the still-confident American collectors, the Ververs, for whom objects of history are gathered by the au-thority with the power to represent history anew as a totality.

As the Prince and Charlotte converse in Italian about the forbiddenness of their outing (ostensibly so that Maggie will not know of the wedding present they intend to choose), the antique dealer is revealed as conversant in Italian and as an eavesdropper. "With ceremony," he presents the couple with "My Golden Bowl." The dealer is truthful but mysterious: the bowl is gilded crystal, he says, but the work of "some very fine old worker and by some beautiful old process . . . [c]all it a lost art . . . say also of a lost time."[14] The price (five pounds) is low. Charlotte is "evidently taken"; but by this time the Prince "had lost patience." Outside the store, the Prince says he saw the crack in the bowl, which he regards not as evidence of its worthless-ness but as a bad omen for his happiness and his safety. Charlotte's reply: "Thank goodness then that if there *be* a crack we know it! But if we may perish by cracks in things that we don't know—! . . . We can never then give each other anything."[15]

Notwithstanding James's authorial remark about the book's first part be-longing to the Prince, the acquisitional impulses of Adam Verver and of Charlotte Stant—for things, and by way of the collecting of things, for each other—gain in the attention of author and reader. Adam Verver undertakes his own collecting expedition, in Brighton, with two objects in view: "It served him at present to satisfy himself about Charlotte Stant and an extraor-dinary set of oriental tiles of which he had lately got wind, to which a provoking legend was attached, and as to which he had made out contentedly that further news was to be obtained from a certain Mr Gutermann-Seuss of Brighton."[16] Another *objet d'art* of mysterious origins and Jewish provenance. By this point in the novel, everyone has gone collecting except Maggie, and Charlotte has been exposed to both of the book's Jewish antiquarians. Again we have a casually anti-Semitic introduction; Gutermann-Seuss is "a remarkably genial, a positively lustrous young man" who receives "the great American collector" in his home, in the company of "his progeny—eleven in all, as he confessed without a sigh, eleven little brown clear faces, yet with such impersonal old eyes astride of such impersonal old noses." The room is completed by "fat ear-ringed aunts and the glossy cockneyfied, familiar uncles, inimitable of accent and assumption, and of an attitude of cruder intention than that of the head of the firm."[17] On the one hand, the company duplicates, in the narrator's perspective, the Damascene tiles Verver has come to buy, as well as the parallel small objects in the Bloomsbury shop: the Jewish family as displaced historical detritus. On the other hand, however, as Martha Nussbaum has pointed out, the sprawling and cheerful Gutermann-Seuss family "contrasts, ultimately, with the sexual failure of Adam with Charlotte," as Charlotte seems to sense. When Adam and Charlotte are conducted to the room with the "treasure," "the rest of the tribe, unanimously faltering, dropped out of the scene." Unlike Bloomsbury, however, this is the real thing; and, unlike the Prince, Adam Verver knows how to buy. The tiles "lay there at last in their full harmony and their venerable splendor." Again Nussbaum: "This image of harmony and totality gives Adam the idea of marrying Charlotte, so as to complete the aesthetic harmony of his own life."[18] The intimacy of the witnessed transaction bonds Adam and Charlotte, as does her acceptance of the "mystic rite of old Jewry"—her description, we are told, of the "heavy cake and port wine" offered by Gutermann-Seuss in celebration of his sale.[19] On the subject of the Prince's betrothal we heard about vessels in port; here we are told that Adam is thinking of burning ships—a reference to the Brighton coast but also, perhaps, to the eventual failure of his new marriage to be consummated.

The recollection of the Bloomsbury antique shop, quoted in the epigraph above, occurs shortly after the consummation of the doubly adulterous union of Charlotte and the Prince. The process of Maggie Verver's negotiation first of the knowledge of the affair and then of her strategy for handling it "all depends on the bowl," which she had purchased for her father (completing the square!) but has since placed on the mantle so that it might confront the gaze of her husband.[20] Her knowledge of the bowl's connection

to the Prince and Charlotte came from "the so distinctly remarkable incident of her interview at home with the little Bloomsbury shopman."[21] The
dealer had felt contrite for not telling Maggie of the crack:

Left alone after the transaction with the knowledge that his visitor designed the
object bought of him as a birthday gift to her father—for Maggie confessed freely to
having chattered to him almost as to a friend—the vendor of the golden bowl had
acted on a scruple rare enough in vendors of any class and almost unprecedented in
the thrifty children of Israel. He hadn't liked what he had done and what he had
above all made such a "good thing" of having done; at the thought of his purchaser's
good faith and charming presence, opposed to that flaw in her acquisition which
would make it verily, as an offering to a loved parent, a thing of sinister meaning
and evil effect, he had known conscientious, he had known superstitious visitings,
he had given way to a whim all the more remarkable to his own commercial mind,
no doubt, from its never having troubled him in other connexions. . . . He had
wished ever so seriously to return her a part of her money, and she had wholly
declined to receive it. . . . His having led her to act in ignorance was what he should
have been ashamed of; and if she would pardon, gracious lady as she was, all the
liberties he had taken, she might make of the bowl any use in life but that one.[22]

The dealer had then spotted photographs of the Prince and Charlotte and
revealed to Maggie that they had been in his shop and had looked at the
bowl: "He himself, the little man had confessed, wouldn't have minded—
about *them*." I'll speculate below as to how the relationship between Maggie
and the dealer seems to be symbolically constituted.

When Maggie reveals all this to Fanny Assingham, the latter smashes the
bowl. Her motives are unclear, but she apparently fails to realize that Maggie has arrived at the point where she recognizes the bowl's truth—and lives
with it—as residing in the cracks, not in the aesthetic claim of the *objet
d'art*. When Maggie picks up the pieces, we are told that "she could carry
but two of the fragments at once."[23] If these fragments are people, then the
comment possibly refers to her strategy of reclaiming the Prince, re-exiling
her father back to America, and ignoring Charlotte entirely.

The Bloomsbury antique dealer is certainly burdened with heavier ste-
reotyping than Simon Rosedale. He speaks Italian and is able to eavesdrop
on his customers, presumably with the goal of adjusting whatever business
subterfuge may be necessary. To the Prince, he is a Jewish swindler attempting to sell faulty merchandise. To Charlotte, he is a "Jewish swindler": I
think we can infer the quotation marks in her tone, for two reasons. First,
she is quoting the Prince's characterization, just spoken. But she also has a
different vantage point on the crack. For Charlotte, the crack holds an element of the bowl's authenticity. But her sense of authenticity is invested in

moral wisdom rather than in aesthetic perfection. She thus can be said to stand at a crossroads in the moral structure of James's characterizations. The third and final discussion of the antique dealer is governed by Maggie Verver, who in this respect achieves the moral stance acceptable to James, and, presumably, to the reader. Maggie buys the bowl and learns from the dealer that Charlotte and the Prince had spent time looking at it. For Maggie, then, the dealer becomes literally the source of the truth and of knowledge about the adulterous relationship.

The dealer, in this configuration, is the other father, the other Adam, the other first man, the truthteller who confirms the falseness of the formal, aesthetic composite of the four people. His particular discomfort at the prospect of the cracked bowl being offered to Maggie's father shows a sympathy with fatherhood in general and with regard to Maggie as daughter in particular. His prior injunction to Charlotte Stant—"Call it a lost art"—resonates here as well. The mystical tone here may well be, on the surface, the tone of the salesman, but it emerges as much more than that in the light of the later episode with Maggie. The dealer's voice takes on a divine aspect, both in the assumption of the godly prerogative of naming, and in the naming of an art that is lost. In identifying the category of lost art, he also identifies the categories of aestheticism and of the fallen world of the novel. The claim of the restoration of the "lost art" is in reality the ideological claim of aestheticism.

For Maggie, more decisively than for Charlotte, the crack in the bowl has direct heuristic power; from it and its source—the dealer—she learns the truth—according to the realized moral authority of the novel itself—of the split between life and art, between the negotiations with persons and, in Nussbaum's phrase, the "aestheticization of persons." In a passage that Nussbaum highlights, Maggie defends the flawed *objet d'art* and the morality of making a present of it: "The infirmity of art was the candor of affection, the grossness of pedigree the refinement of sympathy; the ugliest objects in fact as a general thing were the bravest, the tenderest mementos, and, as such, figured in glass cases apart, worthy doubtless of the home, but not worthy of the temple—dedicated to the grimacing, not to the clear-faced, gods." [24]

But is the theme of the superiority of moral realism over aesthetic perfection duplicated in the formal structure of the novel itself? Put another way, does the moral education of the novel itself, of its authorial voice, share itself in the re-evaluation of the process of the aestheticization of persons? Contrary to Nussbaum's view, I do not believe that James faced the possibility of questioning the aesthetic perfection of the novel. We must therefore ask whether the novel remains essentially guilty of the aestheticism it criticizes, and whether this condition places limits on the reach of the moral inquiry itself. James's own comment on his novel's stance, referred to above, appears in the preface to the New York edition (1909): "It's not that the muffled majesty of authorship doesn't here *ostensibly* reign; but I catch myself again shaking it off and disavowing the pretense of it while I get down into the arena and do my best to live and breathe and rub shoulders and converse with the persons engaged in the struggle that provides for the others in the circling tiers the entertainment of the great game."[25]

Henry James the novelist seems to share, in the end, Maggie's vantage point. Life and art are severed, but the meaning of this is that life cannot be made into a work of art—the trap of aestheticism. Despite his professed participation in the moral struggle of his characters, a struggle defined by the necessity of overcoming aestheticism, James does not engage the inverse of this command, namely the modernist imperative of an art that imitates life through the abnegation of holism and the rules of perfect form. I would suggest that his avoidance of this option resulted less from its unavailability than precisely from its challenging availability in the work of his predecessor and nemesis, George Eliot. The novel in question is *Daniel Deronda* (1876), which has to do, not at all coincidentally, with the social question of the Jews.

George Eliot's work was of course crucial to James's development as a novelist, and most evidently so in the work of the middle period. Leon Edel writes that "[a] great deal has been made of the resemblance of *The Portrait of a Lady* to *Daniel Deronda*."[26] Although Edel follows this comparison with a justified assertion of the autonomy of James's novel, he confirms the solidarity of the two heroines Isabel Archer and Gwendolen Harleth, as well as of the two bad husbands, Osmond and Grandcourt. But Edel also reinforces the long tradition, perhaps initiated with James's own practice and perpetuated by formalist critics such as F. R. Leavis, of dividing Eliot's unwieldy novel in two, into the "Gwendolen Harleth" novel, the good novel, and the "Daniel Deronda" novel.[27] Indeed Edel goes so far as to call *The Portrait of a Lady* "a 'George Eliot novel' written by James in the way he believed she *should* have written."[28]

The characters of Deronda and Gwendolen Harleth are drawn together by creaky coincidences of plot, and Eliot's interest did not lie in their interaction, or indeed in the interaction of the two spheres of the novel. But in an important way, that is the point. The world Deronda is drawn into, the pariah world of Mirah and Mordecai and, ultimately, of his own ancestry, is a separate world, and Eliot makes it formally so. One might almost describe this novel—Eliot's last—as a work of functional modernism for the courage of its formal fragmentation.

The question becomes, then, how far did Eliot go in allowing—in insisting on—a degree of formal fragmentation that would correspond to the dual worlds she wanted to engage? Is *Daniel Deronda* itself a broken vessel, and how useful are aesthetic, formal criteria in considering the situation? For Henry James, and, I think, for Martha Nussbaum as his unsurpassed and devoted reader, aesthetic form has no essential limitations in the representation of reality. The artist has an obligation "to render reality, precisely and faithfully"; in this way Nussbaum summarizes James's combined aesthetic and ethic.[29] In the same spirit, Wayne Booth reads Nussbaum's appreciation of James in terms of the restoration of the category of beauty "to something like the breadth that it would have had in classical praise for narrative: it includes an awareness that forms are truly beautiful only when they are morally valuable."[30] If this position is not problematic—and I clearly think that it is—then Eliot's flawed novel is simply flawed. But for how long can form include the awareness of its own limitations before giving way to them, even just slightly?

Modernist practice in regard to this question tends to de-essentialize the aesthetic, the beautiful, the formal, so that no border must be defined before the point of the non-aesthetic, the non-beautiful, and the non-formal is called. This position does not imply that non-art cannot be defined in practice, on a case by case basis, but rather that its essential identity cannot be predetermined philosophically. The history of aesthetic innovation is full of anecdotes about the calling of this border, and fin-de-siècle modernism contributes the lion's share of attending examples. To invoke one: Richard Strauss was accused of writing noise, not music, for the character of Klytemnestra in *Elektra* (1909). His renowned answer: "I am placing onstage the murder of a mother by her son; what do they want, a violin concerto?" The received implication of a long-term history of an aesthetic form is the routinization of shocking innovations: the dissonances of Strauss grew comfortable, even pleasing, to the twentieth-century ears exposed to Schönberg, just as the dissonances of Mozart—who also placed violence ruthlessly on the operatic stage—had grown pleasing to the nineteenth-century ears that couldn't, in turn, assimilate Strauss.

But once this de-essentializing move has been made, there can be no accepted borders for the aesthetic as opposed to the non- or extra-aesthetic. The distinction between the modernist and post-modernist drops out entirely here. James retains an essentialist aesthetic. Eliot, at least in the book in question, does not. A Jamesian essentialism will consider *Daniel Deronda* flawed, period. A Jamesian aesthetic cannot, it seems to me, coincide with the possibility of the radical critique of the claims of form. For James, the precise and faithful rendering of reality is still encoded into perfect form. Here I differ with Nussbaum: the Jamesian cystal is flawed because it is too perfect. The Jamesian voice, I would argue, has to be considered vulnerable to entrapment within its own aestheticism, and thus, through all its intense and intransigent work, prone to retain an affinity to the Maggie Verver of the first half of *The Golden Bowl*, who "wants, this woman, to have a flawless life."[31]

II

Midpoint in his study *Kabbalah and Criticism*, Harold Bloom describes the desire of the Kabbalah—and, a fortiori, of acts of criticism as he sees and wants them to be—to reform and relegitimate aesthetic experience from a new vantage point, not the vantage point of the claims of Being but of the reality of exile:

Are not the *Sefirot* ["heavenly spheres and stages"] also, and all of Kabbalah, an incarnation of the desire for difference, and for an end to Exile? *To be different, to be elsewhere*, is a superb definition of the motive for metaphor, for the life-affirming deep motive of all poetry.[32]

For Gershom Scholem, the scholar who restored Kabbalah and mystical traditions to Jewish history and memory, the Lurianic Kabbalah is, as Bloom asserts, itself an elaborate myth of exile. Isaac Luria's sixteenth-century compilation of the interpretative tradition which originated in twelfth-century Provence emanates from Palestine in the aftermath of the Spanish expulsion. The vantage point of exile returns in Scholem's life's work on Jewish mysticism, as first conceived in Germany during the First World War and after, and realized throughout a long career in Palestine, later Israel.

At the crux of Scholem's essay "Isaac Luria and His School," first published in 1941, comes the passage, cited in the epigraph above, about the Lurianic myth of the breaking of the vessels. This is one of two founding Kabbalistic myths in which the creation of the world is described in terms of the exile of God. The deepest symbol of exile, deeper than the breaking of the vessels, is the doctrine of *Tsimtsum*: the creation of the physical space of the world in terms of the shrinkage and contraction of God. "According to Luria," Scholem writes, "God was compelled to make room for the world by, as it were, abandoning a region within Himself, a kind of mystical primordial space from which He withdrew in order to return to it in the act of creation and revelation."[33] *Tsimtsum* is thus a doctrine of inner exile, whereas the breaking of the vessels describes the external exile of God. Both are myths of the origins of evil as a realm separate from God. *Tsimtsum* describes the creation of an autonomous space for evil; the breaking of the vessels resulted from the "cathartic cause": the necessity of cleansing waste products and their demonic forces from the pure substance of *Din* or "sternness."[34]

The answer to these myths of exile and fragmentation is the myth of redemption, and the doctrine of *Tikkun*: "the restitution of cosmic harmony through the earthly medium of a mystically elevated Judaism."[35] This myth of restoration is thus the counterpart to the myth of the breaking of the vessels. It contains, according to Scholem, "a strictly utopian impulse," as the "harmony which it reconstitutes does not at all correspond to any condition of things that has ever existed even in Paradise"—in other words, before the breaking of the vessels.[36] Its resolution occurs through Messianic agency. The problem lies in the question of the "earthly medium" which connects exile and human thought to Messianic action and cosmic restoration. The historical consequent to Lurianic Kabbalism is the phenomenon of the false Messiah in the person of Sabbatai Sevi. In Scholem's *Main Trends in Jewish Mysticism*, the chapter on Luria is followed by the chapter "Sabbatianism and Mystical Heresy," and the work to which Scholem turned on the completion of this book became his largest and most celebrated: *Sabbatai Sevi: The Mystical Messiah, 1626–1676*.[37] It seems to me that this connection is crucial to the principle of moral philosophy inherent in Scholem's work, despite, or rather because of, his consistent and modest posture as historian or "mere" chronicler of tradition. The historical passage from mystical Messianism (the myth of *Tikkun*) to the phenomenon of false Messianism resonates in Scholem's writing with an implicit moral warning against the temptation of Messianic discourse.

One can surely speculate that this fear of Messianism intensified Scholem's mistrust of Marxist discourse and fueled his sense of betrayal as his childhood friend Walter Benjamin, with whom he had first discussed his budding interest in Jewish mysticism, began to think in terms of Marxian categories in the mid 1920s. The problem of the relation of Marxism to secular Messianism is complicated—more complicated than Scholem thought it was—and will not be addressed here, short of the assertion that it was Benjamin's recognition of the problems in that association, if anything, that made him a good Marxian. Inherent in Marxian discourse, in other words, is the anti-utopianism which prevents the intellectual from anticipating and representing the future, which must first be materially constituted. Marxism as a theoretical discourse is thus a separate phenomenon from Communism either as a theory of political practice or as a practice in itself. Throughout Benjamin's career, and inherent in his Marxian turn, the key element in the connection of Communism and Messianism remains their shared identities as forbidden discourses.

It was in 1921, several years before the Marxian turn, that Benjamin wrote the two essays which most explicitly engage the themes of Messianism which he had absorbed from his discussions with Scholem. These are the "Critique of Violence," written early in the year, and "The Task of the Translator," written between March and November. The earlier Kantian essay "On Language As Such and the Language of Man" (1916) and the "Theologico-political Fragment (ca. 1920–21) should be included as well in this context of critical thought. These five years represent the period of Benjamin's maturation and of the attendant, intransigent Kantian position of the unavailability of absolute language, knowledge, and hence of absolute moral or political action. In opposition to the neo-Kantianism characteristic of the discourse of late Jewish assimilation—as in the work of Hermann Cohen—Benjamin arrived at the rejection of all claims to philosophical and political resolution or synthesis.

I will start and later conclude this short discussion with references to "The Task of the Translator," and say a few things as well about the companion essays of the period. The essay on translation assimilates explicitly the Lurianic myth of the breaking of the vessels and fashions it into a Kantian metaphor for the limits of human knowledge of the world, and hence of the possibilities of linguistic and historical practice. It is a paradoxical essay. On one level, it was generated as a practical, introductory essay to Benjamin's own translations of Baudelaire's "Tableaux parisiens" from *Les Fleurs du Mal*. As such, it has several fundamental and austere things to say about the incommensurabilities of different languages and the limitations (and illusions) of the process of translating from one language into another. On another level, the very issue of translation and its necessity becomes a metaphor for the fragmentary character of the world, and Benjamin illustrates this point not with the expected image of Babel but with an allusion to the myth of the breaking of the vessels. A single language is like a shard from the broken vessel:

Just as shards of a vessel which are to be joined together ("um sich zusammenzufügen") must fit together one after another in the smallest details, although they need not be like one another, in the same way a translation, instead of resembling the meaning of the original, must lovingly and in detail incorporate the original's way of meaning, so that both the original and the translation are recognizable as the broken piece of a vessel, as the broken pieces of a greater language. For this reason translation must in large measure refrain from wanting to communicate something.[38]

We can trace the allusion to the broken vessels to discussions the young scholars Scholem and Benjamin had in Berlin from the summer of 1915, when they first met, to the year of Benjamin's essay, 1921. From the beginning, they discussed famous translations, especially Stefan George's Baudelaire (with which Benjamin competed), Hölderlin's Pindar, Regis's Rabelais; and Flaubert, who Benjamin declared utterly untranslatable. Scholem translated passages from Benjamin's essay on language (1916) into Hebrew, which he read out loud to Benjamin, who joked that he wanted to hear them in the "*Ursprache.*"[39]

Benjamin's joke carried a bitter irony, as the essay of 1916, written in the midst of war, was a pessimistic declaration of the loss of absolute language. As such, it is not altogether dissimilar from Hugo von Hofmannsthal's 1901 "Letter of Lord Chandos," which also addressed the dilemma of the writer's loss of faith in the integrity of language. Here, the governing image is the loss of Paradise—the state of language after the fall. He wrote: "The paradisic language of man must have been one of perfect knowledge, whereas later all knowledge is again infinitely differentiated in the multiplicity of language."[40]

Anson Rabinbach has reminded us that this imagery of the fall carries a political reference reflective of the despair over the war.[41] Yet this connection does not imply that Benjamin saw the war as the apocaplypse *tout court.* He and Scholem did not respect the war and the aims of Germany in it, and we certainly cannot equate their view of the status quo of 1914 with an image of the world before the fall. This attitude was crucial to their friendship, as it was to their mutual mistrust of Martin Buber (Hermann Cohen as well), who had come out in favor of the war. Indeed, their wartime dialogue took place in the atmosphere of draft-dodging.

In May 1919 Scholem decided to devote himself professionally to philosophy and Judaism (at the University of Munich) rather than to mathematics.[42] At the same time, Scholem and Benjamin both read and both disliked, for the same reasons, Ernst Bloch's *Geist der Utopie* (*Spirit of Utopia*), which proposed an explicitly Messianic conception of history in which Jewish and Christian cosmologies merged. In a letter to Benjamin, Scholem wrote that he was particularly offended by the sections "On the Jews" and

"On the Form of the Unconstructable Presence." They bore the "terrible stigma of Prague," which meant the mark of Martin Buber. For Scholem, Bloch had presented a sweeping historical totality according to the rules of the philosophy of history, and he exhibited a philological incompetence which resulted in the misrepresentation of Jewish particularities.[43] Benjamin answered and expressed his "full agreement with your critique of the chapter 'The Jews.'"[44]

As 1920 progressed, Scholem "thought that Benjamin's turn to an intensive occupation with Judaism was close at hand."[45] On 29 December, however, Benjamin wrote to Scholem that he could not devote himself to "Jewish matters" before his career had stabilized.[46] During a visit to Munich in the summer of 1921, Benjamin made the celebrated purchase of Paul Klee's watercolor "Angelus Novus," and this image led Scholem to tell him of the Kabbalistic writings on the hymns of angels, to which, Scholem writes, Benjamin was very receptive.[47] Scholem does not record explicitly any discussion about the Lurianic Kabbalah and the myth of the breaking of the vessels. Until evidence to the contrary emerges, however, we can assume that Benjamin heard about the myth from Scholem. (Benjamin was in fact in contact with other Berlin Kabbalists, most notably Oskar Goldberg and his circle. Scholem's contempt for this group was, and remained, intense enough for us to assume that the group produced little actual scholarship.)[48]

The Kantian identification of Messianism and of *Tikkun* as forbidden discourses, forbidden imperatives, was common to Benjamin and Scholem. The one difference between their views has much to do with the awkwardness in the friendship, which occurred long before Scholem was aware of it. For Scholem, this recalcitrance stood entirely apart from the political choice of Zionism. For Benjamin, it precluded that choice. Benjamin arrived at this position much earlier than Scholem ever came, apparently, to suspect; he states it in a letter to Ludwig Strauss of January 1913. The letter adopts a standard German romantic position which posits politics as the realm of the particular. Benjamin writes: "I cannot make Zionism into my political element because politics is the choice of the lesser evil, the idea never appears in it, only the party." Zionism is thus another form of nationalism.[49]

If the early, romantic Benjamin rejected political action for its limitations and particularity, the mature Benjamin—within the First World War and after—hesitated in front of the politics of the universal, in front of political Messianism. The language essay of 1916 and the one-page "Theologico-political Fragment" also reflect this logic. The latter contains the clear assertion: "Nothing historical can relate itself on its own account to anything

Messianic."[50] The 1921 "Critique of Violence" develops the position further through the distinction between mythical and divine violence.

The essay's German title, "Zur Kritik der Gewalt" illustrates the limitations of translatability. *Toward* a critique is implied by the first word: a formed critique would reflect a Kantian stance in relation to the object world which is as yet unachieved in the essay's relation to its object. "Gewalt" means violence but also force; in other words it speaks to both the legitimate and the illegitimate possession and exercise of power. "The meaning of the distinction between legitimate and illegitimate violence is not immediately obvious," he writes.[51] Benjamin offers two kinds of violence, and then provides a third: law-making, law-preserving, and, finally, law-destroying. "Law-making," he says later, "is power making, and, to that extent, an immediate manifestation of violence."[52] Law-preserving is the activity of the state, and the actions of the police constitute both law-making and law-preserving.[53] The claims to legitimation of these two first forms of violence entail the category of myth. "Mythical violence in its archetypical form is a mere manifestation of the gods," he writes.[54] Myth has no need to justify itself; unconcerned with justification, it is unconcerned with justice as well. The only presence which genuinely incorporates the end within the means, and therefore can justify itself with reference only to itself—the illusion of myth but not the truth—is the divine. "Justice is the principle of all divine end making, power the principle of all mythical lawmaking."[55] A longer quotation is warranted here:

Just as in all spheres God opposes myth, mythical violence is confronted by the divine. And the latter constitutes its antithesis in all respects. If mythical violence is law-making, divine violence is law-destroying; if the former sets boundaries, the latter boundlessly destroys them. If mythical violence brings at once guilt and retribution, divine power only expiates; if the former threatens, the latter strikes; if the former is bloody, the latter is lethal without spilling blood.[56]

And in the concluding paragraph:

Only mythical violence, not divine, will be recognizable as such with certainty, unless it be in incomparable effects, because the expiatory power of violence is not visible to men. Once again all the eternal forms are open to pure divine violence, which myth bastardized with law.[57]

That the divine is a new term for the forbidden Messianic is, I think, clear. The opposition between the ideologically sustained, totalizing, mythicizing power of human political agency and the just violence, at once creative and destructive, of the Messianic is clear as well. Benjamin goes further, however, in attributing a Greek archetype to the mythical and a Judaic one to the divine. This Graeco-Judaic distinction implies a commentary on contemporary German culture and ideology.

At stake is what E. M. Butler called, in 1936, "the tyranny of Greece over Germany," in particular the power of the German reception of Greek myths and cultural models to authenticate the desire for cultural totality—in short, the power of aestheticism.[58] The aesthetic culture heralded in Nietzsche's *Birth of Tragedy* is the model of such a reception of Greece and its attendant program for Germany. The Nietzscheans of the 1890s—including, for example, Stefan George on the Christian side and Martin Buber on the Jewish side—favored this aestheticist Nietzsche and ignored the later, post-Wagnerian, critical Nietzsche. George had gone especially far in aestheticizing the violence of the First World War, which he described in terms of a heroic purge. The tentacles of Stefan Georgean hocus-pocus reached close to Benjamin, and included Alfred and Julia Cohn, who were assuming at this time the roles of the architect and Ottilie in Benjamin's personal *Elective Affinities* saga. (His study of Goethe's novel, dedicated to Julia Cohn, was begun in 1921.)[59]

In returning for a moment to "The Task of the Translator," we can see the concerns of these companion critical essays refracted in its argument. All language and languages operate according to the principle of the hidden, forbidden referent, which is the language of God, of "God's remembrance."[60] A translation enters into a dialectic with the original text in common reference to that hidden absolute. The life of the original text and language attains through translation a higher stage of development ("*Entfaltung*"), which is "governed by a special, high purposiveness" (Kant's "*Zweckmässigkeit*").[61] He continues: "Thus translation is ultimately purposive with regard for the expression of the innermost relationship between languages. Impossible for it to reveal this hidden relationship, impossible to recover it; it can, however, represent it, insofar as it realizes it in embryonic or concentrated form."[62] The translation, and the translation process, is thus synecdochical to the forbidden totality of absolute language, as the worldly shard is synecdochical to the divine vessel.

A translation conscious of this ethic will shun accessibility (which amounts to a dissipation of the forbidden reference) and point inwardly to the original language and to the hidden absolute. This principle generated the opening paragraph of the essay and its assertion that no work of art is intended for the reader, viewer, or listener. (A reminder that the essay accompanied Benjamin's own translations of Baudelaire may be in order here.)

The success of a translation must be judged according to its incompleteness, and its expression of "longing for linguistic completeness."[63] The essay thus ends in paradox, as it holds that the successful translation must be fragmented, cracked, and therefore faulty as a carrier of meaning. The examples are Hölderlin's Sophocles translations. They expand the German language, but they do not communicate meaning. They reveal "the monstrous and original danger of all translation: that the gates of a language thus expanded and subverted (*durchwaltet*) slam shut and enclose the translator in silence. The Sophocles translations were Hölderlin's last work. Meaning reels in them from abyss to abyss, until it threatens to lose itself in the bottomless depth of language. But there is a stop. It is granted however to no text other than the holy one, in which meaning has ceased to be the watershed for the flow of language and the flow of revelation."[64] It is impossible to know how literally Benjamin wishes to identify holy scripture with the word of God. But this is a secondary point. The word of God represents language absolute and *simpliciter*; it is therefore "*übersetzbar schlechthin*": translatable absolutely. (The emphasis here is on the "absolutely": in this light, it was not contrived at all for Paul de Man to make his notorious remark that on a certain level it makes no difference whether this phrase of Benjamin's is itself translated as "absolutely translatable" or as "absolutely untranslatable"—the latter result appearing, by error, presumably, in the French translation of Maurice de Gandillac.) If perfect translatability occurs *only* in a situation of absoluteness, then the everyday process of translation remains in the realm of untranslatability.[65]

The constant absent presence of this hidden absolute makes living in language especially painful. The formula is identical in the case of politics and personal political action. The only strategy for bridging the personal— in the form of the linguistic or the political—with the universal involves the aestheticizing redefinition of the universal as a totality within human reach. This is the strategy, and, I would dare to say, the attraction, of Heidegger's restoration of authenticity and the house of Being. The point of mediation between the aestheticizing universal and the unrewarding particular is precisely the mode of thinking and living which Benjamin's intransigence prevented him from finding. On the one hand, the forms of his intellectual and political exile precluded the aestheticist militancy (and the political irresponsibility) of a Heidegger; on the other, they could not proffer the vantage point of the Master of Lamb House, who showed enough ingenuousness to reflect, in 1909: "What indeed could be more delightful than to enjoy a sense of the absolute in such easy conditions?"[66]

III

Through his lineage, security, and sensibility, Henry James was able to pursue a career and an art with all the distance from historical contingency that he needed. Walter Benjamin reeled from one contingency to the next, professionally, personally, politically. James honed his sensibility in his later years; Benjamin radicalized and politicized his. Yet they do not wind up as opposites, as authors of texts that have nothing to say to each other. Although I have argued here that the categories of aesthetic form and human language remain absolute for James in ways they cannot remain so for Benjamin, I have also argued that their moral dialogues with the broken vessel of modernity, with its cultural representations and its demands on critical and creative thought, form a solid point of intersection—perhaps of translation. Politics retains a place in James's moral imagination, as the plays of form do in Benjamin's.

The late James was particularly sensitive to the question of the legitimacy of his political voice. The theme of politics and art, their confrontation and their incommensurability, had been explored most explicitly in *The Princess Casamassima* (1886).[67] The title character stands for the world of wealth and aesthetic taste, as it is introduced to the novel's up-from-poverty protagonist, Hyacinth Robinson. Hyacinth's dilemma is the choice between aestheticism (in the passive sense) and revolutionary politics. He cannot resolve the two imperatives, and the novel culminates in his suicide. But what does the suicide represent: the dissipation of the aesthetic sensibility once political consciousness has revealed the truth about the world, or the victory of the ultimate aesthetic, theatrical gesture? Does Hyacinth resolve this distinction, and does James?

In the 1909 preface to the New York edition, James discussed, five years after *The Golden Bowl*, the development of his own political imagination. He recalled conceiving the novel while "walking the streets" of London with his "eyes greatly open," all the while experiencing "the assault directly made by the great city upon an imagination quick to react." The story of Hyacinth Robinson "sprang up for me out of the London pavement." For Hyacinth and for James at once, "the reward of a romantic curiosity would be the question of what the total assault, that of the world of his work-a-day life and the world of his divination and his envy together, would have made of him, and what in especial he would have made of them."[68] For both Hyacinth and James, politics remains a world perceived and observed, with the security felt by the urban walker who knows he will soon be home.

Walter Benjamin committed suicide at the Spanish border in September 1940. Undoubtedly, his death has encouraged subsequent readers to define his life and his significance as those of a paradigmatic twentieth-century intellectual and political martyr. Yet he died for no political cause, and his participation in political discourse had been theoretically serious but not participatory. Whereas the pathos of his death is obvious, its significance is less so, short of a means of heroicizing his life and thought. It is clear, however, and important that Benjamin lived and died outside the boundaries of aesthetic discourse. This is true despite the high degree of personal aestheticism (in the passive sense) and *amour-propre* which his biographers and critical readers have been loathe to admit, for fear of compromising his political and critical profile.

In his best known work, the 1936 essay on "The Work of Art in the Age of its Technical Reproducibility," Benjamin identified the critique of political ideology with the critique of aestheticism. The ideological power of the aesthetic, he argued, resided throughout human history in the phenomenon of the aura. In religious culture, the aesthetic icon projected an aura that originated in its contact with the divine. Such contact might be material and physical, as in the case of a relic, or associative, as in an image or idol. Romantic aestheticism replaced the divine aura with the aura of genius. In both cultural manifestations, Benjamin argued, auratic power accrued through a claim of authenticity. What he did not argue systematically was the connection between the physical authenticity of the work of art and the *cultural* authenticity which the work of art accorded the receptive community that participated in its auratic field. Benjamin's critical and political rejection of the aura is identical with his rejection of the principle of authenticity—aesthetic and cultural. He understood with great clarity the principle with which I began this essay: that the purpose of modern aesthetic ideology was the provision of cultural authenticity. The point is not so much that he had no choice about the matter, but that he made the right choice in seeing the matter as he did.

PETER JELAVICH

"Girls and Crisis": The Political Aesthetics of the Kickline in Weimar Berlin

In the *Frankfurter Zeitung* of May 26, 1931, Siegfried Kracauer, one of the premier observers of mass culture in the Weimar era, published an article entitled "Girls und Krise." The "Girls" to which he referred were the Alfred-Jackson-Girls, a troupe of high-kicking precision dancers who had performed in Berlin since the middle of the 1920s. By "crisis" he meant *Krise* in the specific sense of the day, namely, the Great Depression. In this essay, I will examine the Girl troupes more generally, as well as the revues in which they appeared. Both were central to Germany's urban mass culture in the 1920s: in Weimar Berlin, revues were the most popular form of live entertainment, and Girls were the highlight of the revues. An analysis of them leads to a more generalized perception of "crisis" as well. Despite all the surface glamour, revues and Girls signified fundamental processes of structuring and destructuring in the modern world. There was, quite literally, more to the Girls than met the eye.

Whereas Girl troupes did not appear in Berlin until the 1920s, revues dated back to the turn of the century. The revues of the Metropol Theater, updated annually between 1903 and 1913, were performed over three hundred times each season, and were invariably the most popular shows in the capital.[1] The Metropol's monopoly on the genre was broken after the war, when revue stages proliferated. The 1926–27 Berlin theater season saw no less than nine concurrent revues, playing to nightly audiences totalling 11,000 spectators.[2] The major revues of the 1920s were those of Herman Haller, staged in the Admiralspalast, and Erik Charell, performed in the Grosses Schauspielhaus. Like other forms of urban entertainment, such as variety shows and cabaret, revues offered a concatenation of different numbers: songs, dances, comic monologues and dialogues, skits, acrobatics, magic acts. The revues surpassed the other shows in their length and their lavishness: the Weimar revue might offer 60 different scenes over the course of four hours, and the highpoints were invariably the spectacular production numbers featuring kicklines.

The success of the revues attracted the notice of cultural critics and social theorists, who attributed their popularity to their metropolitan character. Already at the turn of the century, observers like Georg Simmel and Richard Hamann had contended that the hustle and bustle of urban life, with its constant barrage of new sights, sounds, and smells, fragmented human perception and consciousness. Consequently, big-city dwellers became attuned to rapid and fleeting impressions, and lost the ability to concentrate for extended periods of time. In order to reflect and accommodate this new mentality, artists and entertainers gravitated increasingly to shortened forms and fractured styles. The turn of the century witnessed a proliferation of aphoristic writing, short stories, one-act plays, cabarets, revues, and ultimately film, with its use of montage and rapid cuts. These developments were international, and were most pronounced in the capitals and great centers of industry, commerce, and consumerism: New York, London, Paris, Berlin.[3]

Such prewar observations were updated by Siegfried Kracauer and Ernst Bloch in the 1920s, after Berlin suffered the added shocks of revolution and hyperinflation. Both noted the congruence between Berlin and the formal aspects of revue. For Bloch, that metropolis appeared to be "a city that is perennially new, a city built around a hollow space, in which not even the mortar becomes or remains hard." The revue seemed to Bloch to be congruent with such a "hollow" and perpetually transmutable Berlin, since revues were "one of the most open and unintentionally honest forms of the present, a cast of that hollow space. . . . The appeal of the revues comes precisely from the sensual power and turbulence of loosely-strung scenes, from their ability to change and to transform themselves into one another." Likewise, Kracauer praised the ability of revues (as well as cinema) to convey "precisely and openly the *disorder* of society. . . . In the streets of Berlin one is, not infrequently, struck by the realization that all of a sudden everything might split apart one day. The amusements to which the public throngs also should have that effect." Therefore Kracauer believed that "the Berlin public behaves in a profoundly truthful manner when it increasingly shuns [conventional forms of high art] . . . and shows its preference for the superficial luster of stars, films, revues, and production numbers. Here, in pure externality, it finds itself; the dismembered succession of splendid sensory perceptions brings to light its own reality." Producers of revues concurred. The program booklet for the Charell revue of 1924 contended that "the life of the big-city dweller is a multifarious interlacing of surfaces. And every life demands the art in which it recognizes itself." Predictably, the promotional article concluded that the revue, along with film, was the art most adequate to the urbanite's condition.[4]

Just as the structure of the revue—diversity, rapid changes, fast pace— came to represent and reflect the hectic nature of urban life, those same qualities were given a dynamic visual form on stage. The primary icon of the modern became, in fact, the kickline of Girls. They usually consisted of some ten to twenty young women who performed fast, perfectly coordinated dance steps (as the Rockettes of Radio City Music Hall do to this day). In the twenties the most famous of such troupes was the Tiller Girls, who actually were English. John Tiller had been a textile manufacturer in Manchester until the 1880s, when his business failed. Seeking a new vocation, he began to drill young women in perfectly synchronized movements. This act soon drew international attention, and by the 1920s there were Tiller troupes performing in major cities of Europe and America.[5] Haller hired one of them—the so-called Empire Girls—away from New York's Ziegfeld Follies. This created some confusion about their nationality, and throughout the twenties many observers believed that they were an American troupe. The Empire Girls, renamed the Lawrence-Tiller-Girls (after the founder's son) in future seasons, were such a hit in the Haller revues that Charell saw himself compelled to hire his own troupe, the John-Tiller-Girls. Other troupes—the Hoffmann Girls, the Jackson Girls—soon appeared as well. To proclaim their originality and superiority, Haller's Tiller Girls adopted the slogan: "Often copied—never equalled!" ("*Oft kopiert—nie erreicht!*")

At their first performance in the Haller revue of 1924, the Empire Girls garnered rave reviews. Herbert Ihering, arguably the outstanding theater critic of the day, concluded that the Girls, like the revue form itself, were a perfect expression of Berlin: "The revue accords with the needs of the modern metropolis. . . . For the audience reacts to movement, to tempo. The applause for comedians is often weak, but for the Empire Girls it thunders right on into the intermissions. The rhythm, the lightness, the exactness are electrifying. The American [sic] Girls are a sight worth seeing and a standard to follow." Ihering concluded: "Beauty on stage not through nudity, but through motion."[6]

The latter dichotomy—in essence, between tableaux of naked women and kicklines—was fundamental to contemporary perceptions of the Girls. It is important to realize the novelty of the image of womanhood that they represented. The display of women on stage was of course nothing new: the prewar revues also had included line-ups of singing and dancing women, usually in fantastic or allegorical costumes. Moreover, immediately after the war, the abolition of censorship led to a flood of shows featuring women in total or near-total nudity. In 1922 the police and the courts began to move against these performances. Conservatives opposed such shows because they worried about the moral fiber of the nation, especially the loss of traditional values in the wake of military defeat. The authorities were concerned about the perceptions of foreigners as well. A police report on a strip show in March 1922 noted: "Americans also supposedly attended these nude dances, and are reported to have said that after having seen such things there and at other venues, they had to conclude that Germany was not as badly off as it was trying to claim." At a time when Germany was attempting to prove its inability to meet reparations payments, it was unwise to have foreigners believe that Germans were squandering their money in immoral pursuits. By 1924 the police developed guidelines that were spelled out in a letter of Berlin's chief of police to his counterpart in Dresden: "Women dancers must cover completely their posterior, private parts, and navel with opaque fabrics, so that during dance movements these body parts cannot be revealed in a naked state. Furthermore, the breasts also must be covered to the extent that the nipples cannot be seen during dance movements."[7]

Since these restrictions applied only to women in motion, it was permissible to display fully naked women as long as they remained immobile; a nude woman at rest in a tableau vivant was deemed legally acceptable. These guidelines, which determined the presentation of women in the Weimar revues, embodied a curious paradox. Although the authorities were supposed to restrain obscenity, they were simultaneously complicit in shaping and sustaining it along conventional lines. Coupling nudity with immobility reinforced a traditional pattern of objectification: the naked woman, the woman most open to the gaze of others, was compelled by law to remain totally passive. As soon as she moved, she was required to adopt a series of coverings which defined—again, by law—her erogenous zones (breasts and pelvic area). The uncovering and covering of these parts, according to the immobility or activity of the woman, equated female sexual exposure with a passive female stance.

The dichotomy of passivity and motion greatly influenced the perception of the Tiller Girls, inasmuch as the display of nude, immobile women remained an integral part of Weimar revues. Some revue directors, such as James Klein of the Komische Oper, were particularly notorious in that regard, as the titles of his revues attest: *Die Welt ohne Schleier* (The World without Veils), *Berlin ohne Hemd* (Berlin without a Shirt), *Alles nackt* (Everyone's Naked), *Donnerwetter—1000 nackte Frauen!* (Goddam—1000 Naked Women!). At Klein's theater and similar venues, naked women would be objectified in supposedly "artful" tableaux, which made them appear as flowers, jewels, feathered fans, or stage architecture. Not only critics, but also the spokesmen for Haller and Charell often made fun of the "meat show" (*Fleischschau*) at Klein's theater, but the supposedly more respectable revues were by no means innocent. Although nude tableaux were less frequent at Haller's Admiralspalast and Charell's Grosses Schauspielhaus, they still had a role to play. Indeed, one of the most egregious illustrations of the traditional voyeuristic gaze appeared in Charell's revue of 1925. In a scene entitled "Wovon Matrosen träumen" (What Sailors Dream Of), a number of nude women were suspended in hammocks directly above a chorus of men dressed as sailors (Fig. 1).

In the eyes of contemporaries, the Girl troupes provided a marked contrast to the pornographic displays of naked and passive women. The Girls

FIG. 1. Scene from the Charell revue "Für Dich." From *Querschnitt* 5 (1925). From the Resource Collections of the Getty Center for the History of Art and the Humanities.

F I G. 2. Tiller Girls. From Hans Fischer, *Körperschönheit und Körperkultur* (Berlin: Deutsche Buch-Gemeinschaft, 1928).

performed vigorous athletic motions. The Tiller Girls were known for their coordinated kicklines, often moving up and down stairs (Fig. 2). The Hoffmann Girls specialized in even more athletic stunts, such as synchronized climbing of ropes suspended from the stage ceiling. This radically new image of womanhood, full of strength and energy, negated the picture of passive sexual receptivity that had prevailed until then, and made the Girls seem asexual. Fritz Giese, a professor of "psychotechnics" at the University of Stuttgart and the author of a book entitled *Girlkultur*, referred to the Girls' "neutralization of the sexes, the exclusion of the feminine." Theater critics wrote of their "absolutely unerotic dance," which resided "beyond sexuality." Even Kracauer argued that they were not primarily sexual, but rather "a system of lines which no longer has an erotic meaning, but at best signifies the place where the erotic may be found." The sexual inapproachability of troupes like the Tiller Girls was underscored by publicity reports which stressed that they were constantly chaperoned, roomed in pairs, and even travelled with their own pastor.[8]

Naturally, one may question whether the Girls' appeal was as asexual as many contemporary observers claimed. Aside from the obvious fact that no men were integrated into the kicklines, the male-oriented appeal of the performance was guaranteed by the dancers' "youthful" figures and "healthy" physiques, which were, of course, plainly visible even with the stipulated minimum of clothing. Indeed, Alfred Polgar, an outstanding critic of the day, admitted that he did not understand "why *women* actually go to revue theaters. . . . In revues the primacy of the male [*Primat des Mannes*] reveals itself still unshaken. There is nothing there for women." Fred Hildenbrandt, a dance critic for the liberal *Berliner Tageblatt,* likewise wondered what the women in the audience must have thought about the fact that "it is always members of their sex that run around on stage with hardly anything on." They must have concluded the obvious: "that's the way the world is, one has to cater to men, since they pay for the whole racket."[9]

Nevertheless, the persistence of claims that the Girls were asexual suggests that they could not be appropriated easily by more traditional voyeurism. After all, the conventional male gaze continued to be fortified by tableaux featuring naked women. Paul Morgan, a comedian who often appeared both in cabarets and at the Haller revue, wrote a supposedly witty vignette that contrasted the two options offered by the stage: "Olive is an Original-Tiller-Girl, Gerti is a German 'Girl.' Please do not confuse the two. Both are parts of the '300 cast members' in the revue, but the one young woman is a little cog in the 'often copied—never equalled' precision-dance-machine, the other is only capable of displaying a well-shaped bosom. And as a 'living flower vase,' a bit of ass as well."[10] The same dichotomy appeared on the printed page, in the program booklets of the revues. Whereas the Tiller Girls were invariably photographed in costume, the second string of women performers, such as the "Haller Girls," would often be shot in the nude. The reproduction of such pictures turned the revues' program books into a form of soft-core pornography.

Given the Tiller Girls' active demonstration of skills, Fritz Giese as well as many commentators in the popular media believed they represented a more general *Girlkultur.* In this wider sense, a "Girl"—also called, with more respect, "the New Woman"—was paradigmatically young (late teens, early twenties) and employed, usually as a secretary, typist, or department store salesperson. These white-collar jobs had seen an influx of women, and the presence of female employees in what traditionally had been male preserves caused a flurry of speculation—some of it serious and informed, much of it not. On screen, in popular literature, and in advertisements the employed "Girl" was touted as being self-assured, "matter-of-fact" (*sachlich*), and possessing a large degree of "independence" in her professional and personal life. That image, however, was all too often belied by reality. Sociological inquiries at the time uncovered great discontent among white-collar women, who received low pay, worked long hours at repetitive tasks, had no chance for career advancement, and often were subjected to sexual harassment in the office. Many of them laughed bitterly at the media image of *Girlkultur*.[11]

As for the Girls on stage, it is impossible to know how they experienced their own work. To be sure, there were many "interviews" with the Tiller Girls in particular in the popular press, wherein they stressed the combination of dedicated work and glamour that their occupation entailed. However, such "interviews" regularly had the women claim that they became dancers mainly in order to attract a wealthy husband in the audience. Since the same cliché saturated the popular literature and films dealing with the "office girl" (who invariably ended up marrying her boss), one may surmise that many statements by the dancers were fictitious, or at least dictated according to a pre-arranged pattern.[12]

The fact that the stage Girls were rigorously choreographed, worked long hours, and lacked a true career—they usually were terminated in their early twenties—belies the notion of independence and individuality that Giese attributed to them. The same holds true for their visual impact. After all, the main impression was that of de-individualized performers submerged into a larger mass. Walter Benjamin contended that the trademark of the Girls was their quantity, which increased every season: "The revue caters to the bourgeois desire for diversity, more in terms of number than in the nature and arrangement of its presentations. It will soon exhaust its store of inspiration; ever since it undressed the female body to the point of total nudity, its only available mode of variation was quantity, and soon there will be more Girls than spectators." The continual lengthening of the kickline entailed a progressive diminution of the individual performer. Polgar contended that "Girls are a so-called *plurale tantum*. That means that the concept appears linguistically only in the plural." A row of women became a troupe of Girls only with "the smelting of each individual entity into a collectivity." What resulted was something new, a creation whose allure resided in its precise movements and formal configurations. Oscar Bie, a respected dance critic, spoke of the Tiller Girls' "uncanny appeal of absolute body-motion" (*unheimliche Reiz der absoluten Körperbewegung*). Kracauer too suggested that the meaning of such displays resided in their form: "The ornament is an *end in itself*" (*Selbstzweck*), and "the constellations have no meaning beyond themselves."[13]

Although the Girls' kickline did not refer directly to anything beyond its own abstract configurations, indirectly it seemed to reflect a modern aesthetic—one derived not from the individual body, but from the machine. Kracauer contended that if the Girls did have a metaphorical meaning after all, then it would be "the functioning of a flourishing economy": "When they formed a line that moved up and down, they radiantly represented the superiority of the conveyor belt; when they step-danced at a rapid pace, it sounded like 'business, business'; when they tossed their legs into the air with mathematical precision, they joyfully approved the progress of rationalization; and when they continually repeated the same motions, without breaking their line, one imagined an uninterrupted chain of automobiles streaming from the factories of the world." When describing the various Girl troupes, other observers likewise resorted to mechanistic metaphors: they spoke of them as a "precision machine" (*Präzisionsmaschine*), a "motion machine" (*Bewegungsmaschine*), or a "Girl machine" (*Girlmaschine*). One reviewer wrote approvingly: "The Girls function well" (*Die Girls funktionieren gut*).[14]

The precision of the Girls evoked images not only of machinery, but of the military as well. The word "revue" had, after all, originated in the martial sphere, as a designation of the inspection of parading soldiers. The Girls themselves evoked that association on those occasions when they shouldered arms onstage (Fig. 3). This aspect of their appeal was especially clear to Polgar: "Another magic besides that of the erotic emanates from the appearance and the actions of the Girls: the magic of the military. Drilled, parallel, in step, correctly executing handholds and maneuvers, obeying an unseen but inescapable command . . . it provides the same appeal that makes soldiers' play so palatable to the spectator; but of course only as a *spectator*." Another critic repeated the common, but erroneous, belief that John Tiller had been an officer before becoming a capitalist: "Everything clicks as on a barracks drill-ground. . . . Not for nothing was the old Tiller, who first trained the Girls, a sergeant in the English army. However, they no longer appear in the military parade march, but in the rhythm of modern work, to the beat of the machine age."[15]

In the eyes of contemporaries, the Girls performed a fantastic masquer-

FIG. 3. Tiller Girls. From Wintergarten program booklet, Jan. 1930.

ade: they were cheerful and dynamic signs that signified fundamental forces of order and control. The kickline represented both military precision and economic rationalization—the two keys to domination in the modern world. Moreover, the Girls' attenuated femininity—the "magic of the erotic"— obscured, indeed sweetened, the powerful forces of order that they embodied. The Girls were a form of sexual bait, with a hidden hook: whoever consumed their image also internalized an appreciation for mass production, replicability, and military discipline.

The Girls themselves, as individuals and performers, were subjected directly to these same forces. While they might have been freed from some of the cruder forms of voyeuristic eroticism, they were depersonalized in a more fundamental manner. Not only was the individual subsumed into the collective, but, simultaneously, she was dissolved into her constituent appendages. In the kicklines, the unit of composition was no longer the whole person, but the body part, according to Kracauer: "The Tiller Girls cannot be reassembled retrospectively into human beings; the mass gymnastics are never undertaken by total and complete bodies, whose contortions defy rational understanding. Arms, thighs, and other parts are the smallest components of the composition." Just as the structure of the revue replicated the fragmentation of sensation in the metropolis, the depersonalization of the dancer paralleled the reduction of the worker's body to economically useful attributes: "The legs of the Tiller Girls correspond to the hands in the factories." [16] To be sure, the most obvious fragmentation of the body took place among the tableaux of naked women, whose overtly sexual attributes were emphasized (breasts and pelvic area). Nevertheless, the Tiller Girls were equally dismembered, though the knife cut along different lines: arms and especially legs seemed to take on a mass life of their own.

Predictably, there were women performers who criticized the Girl troupes. The sisters Grit and Ina van Elben used visual parody: in 1931, at the left-liberal "Kabarett Tingel-Tangel," they employed a series of cut-out figures to mock the replicability of women in the kicklines (Fig. 4). The most effective criticism was, potentially, the provision of counter-models. A dancer like Valeska Gert stood diametrically opposed to the Girl troupes (Fig. 5). On the one hand, she appeared singly, and her dances often sought to express her own personality. As Hildenbrandt noted, she spoke "only of herself," and performed "autobiographical dances"—the opposite, in short, of the Girls, who subsumed their personalities into the kickline. On the other hand, Gert also parodied the various popular dance fads of the day, which people imitated unthinkingly. One appreciative critic noted that one

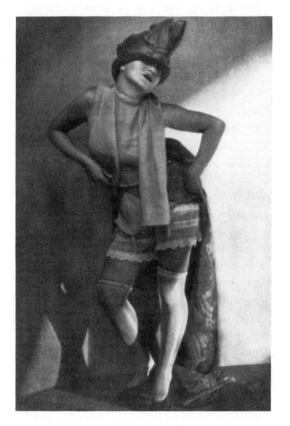

FIG. 4. Grit and Ina van Elben as the "Tingel-Tangel-Girls," at the Kabarett Tingel-Tangel in Berlin. From *Querschnitt* 11 (1931). From the Resource Collections of the Getty Center for the History of Art and the Humanities. Reproduction permission courtesy of Ullstein Bilderdienst.

FIG. 5. Valeska Gert. From Fred Hildenbrandt, *Die Tänzerin Valeska Gert* (Stuttgart: Hädecke Verlag, 1928).

might consider her dances obscene, inasmuch as they consisted of "uncovering": "Yet Valeska Gert does not uncover herself, but rather the sexuality of dance, and it is understandable that when she puts on the cloak of the tango, the Charleston, or the waltz, nothing but shreds remain in the end. It is not simply a parody or travesty of conventional dances, but rather a proof that bourgeois dance is not an expression of dance-like rhythm, but rhythmic nonsense." Predictably, Gert also performed a parody of the Girl troupes, which "annihilated the Tiller-nonsense" (*vernichtet die Tillerei*), according to Max Herrmann-Neisse, the premier cabaret critic of the Weimar era. But despite critical acclaim, parodies like those of the van Elben sisters or Valeska Gert appealed to, and were seen by, a limited number of spectators. Unfortunately, an "anti-revue" planned by dada artists Hannah Höch and Kurt Schwitters in 1925 never was realized. Significantly, it too had been inspired by a Berlin revue that was, in Höch's words, "one of the kitsch-presentations that is geared only to sexual impact by brutal means."[17]

The Great Depression marked the end of the great era of Weimar revues, but it did not spell the end of the Girls. To be sure, in his article on "Girls and Crisis," penned in May 1931, Kracauer questioned whether the Girls had anything more to say, now that the economic system that they represented lay in shambles. Speaking of the appearance of a troupe in the Scala variety theater, he exclaimed: "One doesn't believe them anymore, those rosy Jackson-Girls! . . . Their smiles are those of masks; their confidence, a leftover from better days; their accuracy, a mockery of the difficulties faced by the powers that they represent. As much as they snake and undulate, as if nothing had happened—the crisis, to which so many enterprises have fallen victim, has also silently liquidated these Girl machines."[18] In this case, at least, Kracauer's predictions proved false. Although the revues were gone, the Girls not only remained on variety show stages, but also migrated to other media. By 1927 Charell had ceased staging revues and mounted, instead, "revue-operettas." He ransacked and rewrote popular operettas from the past, and—most incongruously of all—interspersed kicklines throughout the plots. By the end of the Twenties, with the advent of sound film, Girl troupes likewise became staples in the cinematic versions of musicals.

The Girls were, of course, an international phenomenon, and in most contexts they failed to attract the attention of serious social critics. In Germany, however, where the strains of modernity were particularly severe, observers recognized the less savory forces that accounted for their appeal. Such discernment was prescient, since Germany ultimately became the site of the worst forms of dehumanization in modern times. Not surprisingly, the kicklines persisted there to the bitter end. Already in July 1931 Kurt Robitschek, the director of the most successful cabaret in the later Weimar Republic, wrote: "What Hitler does, what he trumpets and stages, is political Charell. An old political comedy is refurbished and equipped with Girls, which in this case are called storm troopers." Robitschek's facetious comment was not so funny after Hitler came to power, in the spring of 1933, and Robitschek, Charell, Haller, and numerous other Jewish entertainers fled the country. The storm troopers did not, however, replace the Girls, and kicklines persisted in the variety shows and musical films of the Nazi era. Adolf Hitler had been an admirer of the Tiller Girls in the twenties, since he approved of those types of "acrobatic dance" which required "a training that approaches the outermost limits of human capacity, up to the breaking point of the human body." Joseph Goebbels was a fan of Busby Berkeley musicals. With such taste among its rulers, the German film industry cranked out a seemingly endless number of musicals featuring Girl troupes.[19] Berlin's two major variety theaters in the thirties—the Scala and the Wintergarten—likewise had their kicklines. The most famous troupe was even named the "Hiller Girls," after the director, Kurt Hiller.

The outbreak of war did not halt such routines, but led to one significant modification: the army high command protested the numbers in which Girls imitated military maneuvers (Fig. 6). In May 1940 an internal report within the propaganda ministry verified the army's complaints: "The questionable numbers, supposedly found objectionable in military circles, are the military 'exercises' of the Hiller Girls. I am in fact of the opinion that these exercises may well be left out. The Girls present parade steps and shoulder arms to the strains of old Prussian military marches. To be sure, their exercises are precise, but the whole is nothing more than nationalistic kitsch and a superficial matter, which we could easily do without." Now that much of the male population was mobilized, the martial spirit embodied in the Girls was superfluous and could be dismissed as kitsch. That was not, however, the opinion of the audience, since the report proceeded to note: "There were no protests or complaints from the public, on the contrary, the spectators applauded loudly."[20] Needless to say, the Army High Command, rather than the audience, had its way. Girls no longer shouldered arms; nevertheless, they continued to entertain the German public until all theaters and cinemas were closed in August 1944.

The indispensability of Girls to entertainment was demonstrated by the fact that they appeared under the most impossible of conditions. With the

F I G. 6. Hiller Girls at the Scala Variety Theater. From Scala program booklet, Apr. 1940.

Nazis' coming to power in 1933, many Jewish performers fled abroad. Some of them opened cabarets in foreign cities, including Amsterdam. Caught by the Nazi invasion of Holland in 1940, Max Ehrlich and Willy Rosen, formerly stars of Berlin's cabaret and revue stages, were interned in the Westerbork camp. The Nazi commander there encouraged (or perhaps forced) them to mount revues to distract both the inmates and the German officers. Thus the programs in the fall of 1943 included numbers featuring the "Westerbork Girls" (Fig. 7). At a time when the first transports from Westerbork to the East were taking place—transports to Theresienstadt and ultimately

FIG. 7. Scene from the revue "Humor und Melodie" at the Westerbork camp, Sept. 1943. From the photoalbum of "Humor und Melodie," presented to Obersturmführer Gemmeker. Courtesy of Yad Vashem Archives, Jerusalem.

Auschwitz—the inmates were starved for distraction, and the revues were packed. Such distraction was not, however, uncontested. In a letter of July 9, 1943, written in Westerbork, Etty Hillesum noted:

It is a complete madhouse here. . . . Meetings, panics—it's all horrible. In the middle of this game with human lives, an order suddenly from the commandant: the *Dienstleiters* must present themselves that evening at the first night of a cabaret which is being put on here. They stared open-mouthed, but they had to go home and dress in their best clothes. And then in the evening they sit in the registration hall, where Max Ehrlich, Chaya Goldstein, Willy Rosen, and others give a performance. In the first row, the commandant with his guests. . . . The rest of the hall full. People laughing until they cried—oh yes, cried. . . . I wasn't there myself, but Kormann just told me about it, adding, "This whole business is slowly driving me to the edge of despair."

Another Westerbork inmate, Philip Mechanicus, did attend, and likewise expressed consternation. On August 31, 1943 he wrote in his diary: "There is something loathesome going on in the background when every transport leaves. This time, while the transport was being got ready and was moving off, people were dancing. Actually dancing. Rehearsals have been going on for some time for a revue." Two weeks later he reported: "Attended the première of the new revue yesterday evening. Absolutely packed out. Old numbers that had been refurbished, well acted. A great part of the programme consisted of dancing by revue girls with bare legs. The *Obersturmführer* present with Aus der Fünten. Went home with a feeling of disgust."[21]

This was, indeed, a terrible paradox: the presentation of kicklines in the context of Westerbork. By all accounts, the inmates who packed the shows did so to gain a couple of hours of distraction in a hopeless situation. Moreover, by attending a revue that featured Girls, the prisoners could pretend to relive the "normalcy" that they had enjoyed in the prewar era. Yet even in those better days of Weimar Berlin, the Girls never had personified a wholesome normality. If the camps were the absolutely worst results of certain political and economic processes operative in the modern world, the Girls were—indirectly and obliquely—signposts along the way. The Girls and the revues in which they appeared were products of human destructuring and dehumanized restructuring. The revue sacrificed dramatic unity in favor, as Kracauer said, of "the dismembered succession of splendid sensory perceptions." In turn, the kickline sacrificed bodily wholeness in favor of a dismembered succession of body parts. The human fragments were reordered into dynamic visual forms which, on the surface, appeared vital and progressive, a symbol of rational management and achievement. But more fundamentally, they revealed—or perhaps disguised?—an underlying sense of economic and military order that demanded the dissolution of all personality and the dismemberment of the person. The bodies of the Girls embodied a critique of the modernity that they ostensibly represented.

Constructing the Self

Gross David with the Swoln Cheek: An Essay on Self-Portraiture

Montaigne paints a good likeness of himself, but
in profile. Who knows if some scar on his cheek
or a lazy eye on the side of the face he has hidden
from us would not have totally changed his
physiognomy.

> Rousseau, preamble to the Neuchâtel manu-
> script of the Confessions, 1764.[1]

I am persuaded that one is always excellently
painted when one paints oneself, even when the
portrait is not a good likeness.

> Rousseau, letter to Dom Deschamps,
> 12 Sept. 1761.[2]

Five or six days after the downfall of Robespierre's government in July 1794
the painter Jacques-Louis David, who had been one of Robespierre's most
loyal and serviceable henchmen, was imprisoned in the Hôtel des Fermes.
He feared for his life, justifiably so. Robespierre and Saint-Just, with twenty
others of their party, had been guillotined the evening following their overthrow on Tenth Thermidor, and a further 71 Jacobins had been put to
death the next day; it was common knowledge that David had replied to
Robespierre's despairing last cry on the floor of the Convention—"Il ne
me reste plus qu'à boire la cigüe"—with the blurted promise, "Je la boirai
avec toi."[3]

Though the documents do not speak directly to the issue, it is safe to say
that David was kept alive in part because he was a painter, and seemingly
the one on whom the future of the French school still depended. It was not

long before his jailers allowed him the tools of his trade. One of the first things he did with them, after his pupil Delafontaine had brought him a mirror for the purpose, was to paint a portrait of himself (Plate 14, photo section following p. 156).[4] This essay treats David's self-portrait at length, and tries by fixing on it to bring into focus some of the problems that beset self-portraiture in general, considered as a genre, or at least as a long episode in Western painting with its own distinctive features. And here I have to confess myself torn. It is not that I doubt for a minute that the picture repays close study, or that the subject it opens onto—the conditions in which the self can be faced and made palpable for others *in extremis*, at a moment of defeat and fear—is one of more than academic interest. But whether I like it or not, I cannot entirely shake off the feeling that there may be something wrong, perhaps even something dangerous, in dealing with self-portraiture at all. This is partly, I think, a matter of class. The two great instructions having to do with self that come back to me from my lower-middle-class childhood are first, the whispered signal to stop "drawing attention to my-self"—it was the ultimate crime—and second, usually more loudly, the perplexing command to "Behave myself," something I never seem to have managed to do satisfactorily, or go on doing long enough. These two forms of words were the limit terms, I realize now looking back, of a specific and in its way quite strict regime of self, which it seems to me I still largely follow or at any rate feel uneasy disobeying. The hygiene has left its mark. You will find me, for instance, arguing at various points in what follows for a rough-and-ready version of behaviorism in the matter of self, at least in preference to the regime I think I detect in most self-portraiture—let me call it, for reasons I shall go on to explain, the regime of representation. And though the arguments I come up with strike me as cogent in their own right—they are, if I am pressed, what the essay is mainly about—I am aware that at bottom they are fueled by *ressentiment*. Representation, for me, does ultimately belong to someone else, my superiors, whose way with the self is too lordly by half.

These are the grounds, as far as I understand them, for my being uneasy at the prospect of writing about David's self-portrait. The genre is one that I come to a bit from the outside, or so I want to believe; and it is this degree of exteriority (real or imagined, it does not matter which) that I most want to preserve in the following pages; it is what I have to say on the subject. But how does one do that in writing? Perhaps what I am really afraid of in launching into self-portraiture at length is the discovery in the end that writing about the subject was just my way of writing myself into it, or coming to terms with the fact that I was never outside in the first place. Are there any outsides to this subject on offer? Is not the trouble with self-portraiture precisely that we are all too much at home with it, too eager with our answering scripts? Whom do I think I am fooling that my script will be any different?

None of this amounts to a reason to avoid the topic of self-portraiture altogether. On the contrary. The topic cries out to be taken seriously. The coming into being, mainly from the sixteenth century on and mainly in Europe, of a class of pictures in which the painter is shown eyeing him- or herself with a view to depiction and sometimes doing the depicting; the way these pictures take on a set of strong family resemblances, which persist through hundreds of years, as if there were one rather narrow or anyway exclusive way of conceiving the subject that was found adequate to the questions of painterly practice and self-consciousness it raised; even the flavor of doubt and duplicity hanging over the whole enterprise, which my epigraphs from Rousseau represent quite fairly, I think—features such as these emerge from the merest survey of the material, and look like they offer the key to mysteries. Here is that elusive, ubiquitous entity the self, actually shown—or do we mean caught?—in the act of intercepting its own gaze. Not even the genre of autobiography seems to promise such simple, immediate access to the moment of self-consciousness. Maybe what puts us off *is* the immediacy—David for one knows how to give it a hectic, overbearing character—but if what we want is to understand the powers and limits of that great fiction the "individual," then surely we ought to fasten on the opportunity of self-portraiture for dear life. We ought to thank our lucky stars for painting's matter-of-factness with the subject.

Justifications along these lines are all well and good—I do not mean to retreat from them—but in practice, when it gets to the pictures, they never quite disperse the previous misgivings. And there are others. For instance, a problem of mode. It turns out that writing at all on self-portraiture involves one, whether one likes it or not, in producing something a bit like philosophy. I have produced much the same thing, I warn you, in whole sections of the essay to come. The self is in question, and other important abstractions: spatiality, metaphor, agency, embodiment, interiority, representation—you will recognize the old codgers as they come up. Now it is not that I am in principle opposed to philosophical writing about the visual arts; no doubt we could do with more of it. It is just that I do not find myself particularly well qualified to *do* such writing; and in that I am in good company. My attempts will therefore tend to have a familiar odor to them: they will smell of literary theory in its lower (I did say lower) reaches, or, worse, of semiotic belles lettres. And most of them, I realize, would do about as well as their *semblables* if they were leaned on by, say, an averagely competent pupil of Quine or Davidson.

My excuse for this is twofold. First, as I say, I have not found a way to avoid the philosophizing when self-portraiture is the subject: it seems to come with the territory. Second, I think I can turn the very amateurishness of what follows, and maybe even its portentousness, to good account, or at least not have them turn utterly against me. What I shall produce is no doubt bad or naive philosophy, but in doing so I think I am reproducing—or shall I say elaborating—the bad philosophy of the self-portrait itself. The kind of thinking, that is, that seems to go with making this sort of picture and being its viewer; the discourse of the genre.

This is not meant, finally, as an excuse for local mistakes and sloppiness in whatever arguments I go on to present. Obviously I shall try to state them in logically defensible form, and if I do not manage it the false moves will bring the edifice down. The point I am making is slightly different: even if the edifice ends up just about standing, I still do not expect to be happy about the kind of edifice it has turned out to be. But whoever said—this has been my theme so far—that self-portraiture was an agreeable subject? Is it not necessarily bound up—here again Rousseau will be my touchstone—with self-regard and *amour propre*, with feints at profundity and feats of language to match?

I wish I thought there were a way out of all this onto firmer ground: towards, for example, some form of straightforward empirical enquiry into David's picture and its historical circumstances. I should enjoy that more. Could we not, for a start, set about reconstructing a plausible discursive context for a self-portrait done in 1794? Is it not possible to identify a pattern of late eighteenth-century questions about the self which would most likely have informed a painter's way of seeing things when he or she sat down in front of the mirror? Well yes, I think it might be. But new difficulties immediately loom, not the least of them being what we might call the prospect of infinite ramification. In a case like this, how are we supposed to decide where to put an *end* to inquiry? If what we are looking for is something as "deep" and all-encompassing as a culture's sense of self—something so thoroughly embedded, that is, in its ways of imagining just about everything—then what is going to count as irrelevant evidence? Is there anything that is not grist to the mill?

These are questions that occur in the heat of looking and writing, not just philosophical noises off. I have an idea that they are partly the reason self-portraits are written about so seldom, relatively speaking, and by and large so perfunctorily. (Readers wanting a sample of the kind of thing art-historical empiricism can manage on the subject could do worse than consult the entry on David's picture in the catalogue of the Louvre retrospective of 1989, coming as it does from a writer fiercely committed to the discipline of visual and documentary fact. The entry is not much of an advertisement for the method.[5]) The questions are embarrassing. None of the answers I can come up with satisfies me much, but I still intend to plunge on through the undergrowth. My way of proceeding will be rough and ready, and I dare say hit or miss, but at least it has the merits of simplicity: it consists of trying some obvious, distinctly audible voices from the eighteenth century on for size, and seeing how easy or hard it is to imagine them David's voice on this occasion. I suggest we take a look at certain kinds of question, doubt, and mode of presentation of the self that led a powerful life in the later 1700s— in a sense, the more hackneyed and familiar the sources the better—and see if they can be mapped onto David's picture of himself at all convincingly.

Here, for example, are two voices much attended to in the eighteenth century, in France as well as England, giving their answers to a question debated endlessly at the time, whether "the substance which thinks is distinct from the body." It is evidently a question with strong upshots for self-portraiture. The first voice is Ralph Cudworth's, in his *True Intellectual System of the Universe . . . Wherein All the Reason and Philosophy of Atheism is Confuted; and its Impossibility Demonstrated*. (The book appeared in London in 1678, and then again in 1743. It was given a Latin edition at Iena in 1733, and another at Leyden forty years later. Diderot read it and took some of its ideas seriously; it was certainly one of d'Holbach's negative points of reference in his *Système de la nature*.[6] More tantalizingly from our point of view, one finds that the long entry on MATÉRIALISTES (ATHÉES) in Naigeon's *Encyclopédie méthodique*, published in Paris in Year Two, amounts to not much more than a summary of Cudworth's best arguments—so much so that Naigeon, good friend and disciple of Diderot that he was, feels obliged to apologize for the article, "employé tel qu'il a été remis à l'éditeur."[7])

Cudworth, you will gather from his title, is in no doubt as to the distinction between mind and body, and spends much of his time raging against those "Sottish" or "Imprudent" enough to disagree with him. "The *Action* of an *Extended Thing* as such," he says,

is nothing but *Local Motion*, Change of Distance, or Translation from Place to Place, a meer Outside and Superficial thing; but it is certain, that *Cogitation* (*Phancy*, *Intellection*, and *Volition*) are no *Local* Motions; nor the meer *Fridging* up and down, of the Parts of an Extended Substance, changing their *Place* and *Distance*; but it is Unquestionably, an *Internal Energie*; that is, such an *Energie* as is *Within* the very *Substance* or Essence, of that which *Thinketh*; or in the Inside of it.[8]

The diction in a passage like this may strike us as quaint and outlandish (it was considerably toned down for Naigeon's readers in 1793), but the argument itself could hardly be more orthodox; and in a sense I take it to be irrefutable. Cudworth gives tongue to a set of assumptions about the self—about its being a substance of some sort, its being immaterial and inward, possessed of its own energies and presenting itself to us immediately and "unquestionably"—which are, or have proved so far, unshakeable. They are the assumptions, I take it, that animate self-portraiture as a genre: *our* assumptions, as presumably they were of most viewers and readers in Year Two; David's assumptions, however much the process of picturing himself may have put them under pressure.

Nonetheless this voice alone, of the self in full possession of its inwardness, will not do. Not everyone in the seventeenth and eighteenth centuries was content to let the matter rest where Cudworth left it; otherwise why was he so angry? Joseph Priestley, for instance, was in no doubt that natural philosophy after Newton had exploded the picture of matter on which the mind-body distinction had rested up till then. "I rather think," this is Priestley in the *Disquisitions relating to Matter and Spirit*, published to a great deal of hoohah in London in 1777, "that the whole man is of some *uniform composition*; and that the property of *perception*, as well as the other powers that are termed *mental*, is the result (whether necessary, or not) of such an organical structure as that of the brain."[9] We know now that "matter is not *impenetrable*, as before . . . it had been universally taken for granted; but that it consists of *physical points* only, endued with powers of attraction and repulsion."[10] It follows that

Since the only reason why the principle of thought, or sensation, has been imagined to be incompatible with matter, goes upon the supposition of impenetrability being the essential property of it, and consequently that *solid extent* is the foundation of all the properties that it can possibly sustain, the whole argument for an immaterial thinking principle in man, on this new supposition, falls to the ground; matter, destitute of what has hitherto been called *solidity*, being no more incompatible with sensation and thought, than that substance, which, without knowing any thing further about it, we have been used to call *immaterial*.[11]

This prose has none of Cudworth's quirky fire; but I wanted to quote it at the start of things precisely to establish the ordinariness, the ponderousness, of the materialist account of mind by 1777 or so. It is part of the point about Priestley that he is so stolid, so blandly confident of the world that scientists like Boerhaave and Boscovich have made.

And even if the cadences are unexciting, the ideas are not. People *were* excited by them in the eighteenth century, to an extent that sometimes makes the culture we are dealing with seem as foreign to ours as a culture could be. Gentlemen's magazines like *The London* or *The Monthly Review* devoted whole issues to synopses of Priestley's new work and replies from his critics. They received and printed pages of readers' letters on the subject. Nothing like this could happen so openly in France, for obvious reasons, but there is no doubt that the same ideas circulated and caught on. The Abbé Coyer, for example, took their fancied prevalence for granted in his *Lettre au R. P. Berthier sur le matérialisme* of 1782, and poked fun at them as old friends.[12] Likewise Denesle in 1765, in another *Examen du matérialisme* (hardly less trivial than Coyer's but considerably longer), who fastens on his opponents' notion of mind as no more than an arrangement or degree of organization of matter, and waxes sarcastic at a vocabulary he barely needs to italicize:

The Materialists have a clear idea of what *organization* it might be that invented the Arts and Crafts, that daily makes the most astonishing discoveries. . . . and that uses its skills to put nature—the very universal substance of which it is merely a point—at the service of its wishes and caprices. They know what *modification* it is that can reach logical conclusions about the nature that thinks through it. . . . They know finally what *arrangement* of parts it might be that so often murmurs against fate, that blind and inevitable necessity.[13]

"For in the end"—here is the same kind of tactic employed a hundred or so pages earlier, and again it is the vocabulary that Denesle thinks he can take as read which is interesting—

what do they understand by that final degree of subtlety, purity and activity in matter which they want to recognize as the substance that thinks? Can matter on its own, whatever we take the word to mean, be supposed to have knowledge of purity or impurity? Or subtlety and crudity, come to that? . . . Suppose we give it the most accurate combinations, the most exact and geometric distributions, the most varied and harmonious movements. . . . How much further have we got? Has it come to the point of knowing itself? [14]

All this, you will notice, is four years before Diderot's *Rêve de d'Alembert*, five before Baron d'Holbach's *Système de la nature*. The worst, in other words, was to come. "Don't you see what you're doing?"—here is Diderot in person, scribbling in the margins of a book much like Denesle's in 1773 or 1774:

So as to introduce properties that are essentially contradictory into the same substance, you make the soul indivisible, without extension, without attributes [*non figurée*]. . . . You talk of a being about which you don't have the least idea. You talk of a being that does and does not occupy space. You explain a phenomenon by a chimera. Is that philosophy? Who told you that matter as a whole was insensible? There are two sorts of sensibility, just as there are two sorts of force. A sensibility that is inert; a sensibility that is active. An active sensibility that can pass over into a state of inertia. An inert sensibility that can and does pass over into an active sensibility according to my will. This phenomenon happens under my very eyes; once it's admitted, and we add in memory and imagination, there are no difficulties to speak of. [15]

Or Diderot again, most probably from around the same moment—he is gathering material for a never-to-be-finished *Éléments de physiologie*— casting about for the means to make his account of self and sensibility more strictly a matter of bodily states, and coming up with just the vocabulary Denesle had pretended was old hat. (The butt of his criticism in this case is none other than David's beloved Marat, in his prerevolutionary incarnation as the temporizing author of a three-volume, two-substance *De l'Homme*.)

Why not regard sensibility, life and movement as so many properties of matter: since these qualities are to be found in every portion, every particle of flesh?

I defy anyone to explain how the passions are introduced into the soul without positing bodily movements, and starting from such movements.

Those who descend from the soul to the body are fools: it does not happen that way at all in man. Marat does not know what he's saying when he talks about the soul acting upon the body; if he had looked more closely, he'd have seen that the action of the soul upon the body is the action of one portion of the body on another, and the action of the body upon the soul is the action of yet another part of the body on another. . . .

The difference between a soul given over to sensibility and one given to reason is simply a matter of organization.

The animal is all *one* thing, and perhaps it's this unity which constitutes the soul, the self, the consciousness with the help of memory. [16]

"The more we come to think about it," writes d'Holbach in 1770—and here the tone veers back to Priestley's intimidating blandness—

the more we shall remain convinced that the soul, far from having to be distinguished from the body, is only the body itself considered from the point of view of certain of its functions, or of certain ways of being and acting which it is capable of as long as it lives. . . .

It is as a result of not having studied man that men have supposed there to be an agent inside themselves of a nature different from the body. . . . What produces the obscurity at this point is the fact that a man cannot see himself;

—this is the moment in d'Holbach when questions of self-portraiture seem to loom closest—

indeed, for that to happen he would need to be inside and outside himself at the same time. He could be compared to a kind of animate harp which produces sounds from itself, and then wonders what it is that makes the harp produce them; it does not see that just because it *is* animate it plucks its own strings, and is plucked and made to make music by everything that touches it. [17]

My hope is that this brief procession of quotations will conjure up at least the flavor of a vanished intellectual world. (It is the flavor as opposed to the force of the arguments that seems the thing to get hold of if what we are trying to do is visualize how David would have understood the issues; and especially we should pay attention to the way these writers' rhetoric see-saws between the histrionic and the ploddingly factual.) We have to imagine a culture, and it will be no mean feat, in which the mind-body problem was thought to be of general interest, and open to treatment in all kinds of ways—with a little help from the new physics, or from Haller on irritability, or Condillac's psychology, or the logic of accidents and attributes. No doubt there was an element of faddishness to a lot of this (Robert Darnton has unearthed clandestine booksellers' catalogues in which the *Système de la nature* is an item in between *Vénus dans le cloître* and *Margot la ravaudeuse*, all of them listed under the rubric "philosophie"[18]); maybe the interest I am pointing to was not deepseated or particularly widespread; certainly it did not last. But there does seem to have been a generation or two of the cultivated—one of them being David's—quite used to pondering the matter of self-consciousness in Diderot's and Priestley's terms.

The questions that came naturally were these. If there is such a thing as consciousness (and only La Mettrie was understood by some readers to have performed the ultimate reduction and disposed of the entity altogether) then what is it exactly? A substance? A property? An effect? A kind of motion or degree of rarefaction of matter? A level of bodily organization? A *sensibilité active* or an *inquiétude automate* (two typical stabs at the problems by Diderot)?[19] And however conceived, *where* is it? Are we sure it is helpful to think of it as having a location at all? (Some thought not; or granted it one only in the sense that a mathematical point has one; it did not, in other words, occupy space.) When I look at myself—and looking, of course, was held to be the form of knowledge where these things should be clearest—is the action of looking or even the attendant "Cogitation," adequately pictured as a physical transaction of some sort, a "mechanickal" one? Is what is going on an "acquaintance" of matters—the term has a whole world-picture built into it—to be explained "necessarily and physically"? Or has looking, especially when it is myself I am looking at, to be thought of as contact between two substances, the one material and the other not; the latter calling on stage a language of "dispositions," "motives," "free causes," "Self-Motive Powers"?[20] Is there anything these words can do that cannot be done as well by *tension, toucher, irritabilité, fibres, fils imperceptibles, le frémissement d'un corps élastique choqué?*[21]

The imagination, being infinitely superior to a Michael Angelo or a Raphael, delineates in the soul a faithful image of objects; and from divers representations which it composes, forms in the brain a cabinet of pictures, every part of which moves and is combined with an inexpressible variety and swiftness.

The brain of many, then, may be considered as so many mirrors, wherein different portions of the universe are painted in miniature. Some of these mirrors exhibit but a small number of objects; others comprehend a more extensive field; while others still represent almost the whole of nature. What is the relation between the mirror of the mole and that of a *Newton* or *Leibnitz!* What images were there in the brain of a *Homer*, a *Virgil*, or a *Milton!* What mechanism must that have been which could execute such wonderful decorations! That mind, which could read the brain of a *Homer*, would have there seen the Iliad represented by the various exercise of a million of fibres.[22]

Imagine a painter taking these questions seriously. Imagine him having been used to hearing Diderot in person on the subject, at the time he was preparing the *Éléments de physiologie* (it is clear that a lot more of that undertaking got treated conversationally in the 1770s, when David and Diderot were friends, than was ever put down on paper).[23] What would a painter be likely to look at differently as a result?

For a start, it might be that he would interest himself more than usual in the borderline between sentience and insentience in the world of things;

when he painted a portrait, he would be inclined to handle stuffs and flesh in ways which borrowed the characteristics of one for the other or set up analogies between the two. Further, he would be used to thinking of bodies and minds (even souls) as only contingently unities, made as they were out of plural and insubordinate parts—the *petits êtres sensibles* of d'Alembert's dream, the *frémissements, inerties, résonances, chocs* that haunt the *Pensées sur l'interprétation de la nature*. A particular notion of subjectivity would seem to follow from this: subjectivity thought of as an act or assertion of sheer will, a getting a grip or a fix on oneself most often against the odds; and that in turn would dictate not only a new treatment of the act of looking in self-portraiture but a new attitude to "handling" in general when the self is in question. What kind of fixing or finishing of one's own image would strike you as appropriate if this was your view of the issues at stake? (None of this, by the way, need necessarily lead to a staging or handling of self *in extremis*. Diderot's imagery is characteristically urbane: "The soul is in the midst of its sensations like a guest at a noisy dinnertable, who chats with his neighbor and does not hear anyone else."[24] It is David who turns the conversation into a shouting match.)

Imagine the painter trying to set aside even "the supposition of impenetrability" as it might apply to a face or a fist or a palette. The new metaphors of matter would seem to square with some parts of the world more readily than others: mirrors we already tend to think of as penetrable, and eyes and even hair. How does it go with fists and cheeks and chairbacks, or the bits and pieces of pigmented material left behind on a palette? How does it go with flesh? We know what we mean by calling flesh penetrable. "He gave it as a gift to père Fontaine"—this is Gigoux on David's self-portrait in his memoirs, by the look of it repeating what Delafontaine had told him—"and said to him, making a sign with his hand underneath his chin: 'They're going to cut my throat, dear chap!'"[25] The boundary lines between epistemology and affect—between self-knowledge and self-pity, say—are always hard to draw. Self-portraiture as a genre is partly about that difficulty. Why else is Rembrandt its presiding genius?

Deciding how far or how closely these questions apply in the case of David's picture is going to be difficult. But what I have been trying to do so far has in any case been more modest. I wanted to establish that questions such as these were commonplace, at least in the literate culture which David prided himself on belonging to. And that materialist answers to some of them were entertained quite seriously at the time—more seriously, I reckon, than ever before or since. It was not that materialism carried all before it in the later eighteenth century, or was even rampant in the way its enemies liked to imagine; but it existed, it ramified, it had its Old Testament and Book of Common Prayer. (The first book of *Leviathan* for the one and *Éléments de physiologie* for the other?) Maybe the net outcome of all this was temporary and slight. But any disturbance in the normal economy of reflection is rare, and for self-portraiture potentially scandalous (the game may be up). There was scandal in the air. The new men waxed sarcastic at their opponents' continued multiplication of essences and entities, and smiled at those writers for whom the Soul—this is Robinet quoted by an English reviewer in 1768—

is a little complicated body, made of finer stuff than ordinary, whose component parts answer to those of our grosser flesh; a kind of Jack in the box, whose wooden doublet fits him so nicely that everybody thinks it alive.[26]

I shall spare you the wisecracks about the Jack in this case being Jacques-Louis; but the painter, I have been arguing, was part of this odd world; these images and skepticisms may actually have inflected his way of looking at himself in the weeks after Thermidor. If they did, we should expect the picture that resulted to put some of the basic assumptions of self-portraiture under pressure.

So to Rousseau. If the first point on my rough map of discourses was occupied—that was partly what made it interesting—by a weird congery of voices, Diderot rounding on Marat or François Hemsterhuis, Denesle scoffing at Jean Baptiste Robinet, Anacharsis Cloots, no less, paying homage to the legendary Jean Meslier in the Convention on 27th Brumaire;[27] then the second is largely solitary, with no space for anyone but Jean-Jacques. It is the point of autobiography.

This is not to say that Rousseau's *Confessions* came upon the eighteenth century out of the blue, still less that they did not immediately have imitators. No doubt a great change in the culture's way of presenting the self was happening through the century as a whole, in a frame that exceeded any one language, let alone one man's will. The very word "autobiography" seems to enter French sometime in the 1790s, migrating to it from German. (French will have nothing to do, on the other hand, with the coinage *Selbstbildnis*, which English falls for in a big way. *Autoportrait* is a twentieth-century concession, and still seems not to trip off the tongue.) And yet these matters did center on Rousseau and his book; particularly for readers in the first years of the Revolution, who were still digesting the terrible *Seconde Partie des Confessions* brought out in Geneva and Paris in 1789.

Nobody, I dare say, would quarrel with the idea that Rousseau—the "Jean-Jacques, bon musicien" who crops up alongside Socrates and Poussin in one of David's reports to the Convention—was part of David's mental world. Of whose was he not in Year Two? The trouble begins when one tries to answer the more elusive question: What would it have meant, in 1794, to set oneself to paint a self-portrait under Rousseau's auspices? That is a more difficult question than it seemed ten or twenty years ago, because we have taken to reading Rousseau's books again ("ils redeviennent lisibles," to quote Philippe Lejeune[28]) and come to recognize them as a field of force in which everything about representation—self, text, signature, excuse, advocacy, inwardness, exteriority, the material resistance of writing or its sudden transparency to the movements of feeling—is pulled out of shape by an urgency it is hard to pin down. "Rousseau is the name of a problem," as more than one critic has put it lately, which for some reason has come back to haunt us.[29] Any attempt to sum up the problem briefly is bound to seem like an exorcism. Nor do I want to conjure up a "Rousseau" who is somehow conveniently quarantined from the arguments about materialism I have just been describing. Of course he is not. Where else did many eighteenth-century readers first come across the mind-body problem but in the first part of the *Profession de Foi*? Whom did Rousseau think he was speaking to if not Helvétius and Diderot?[30]

Nonetheless I think I can say this much. Doing a self-portrait under Rousseau's aegis, and particularly that of the *Confessions*—doing it in the Hôtel des Fermes, in face of the guillotine, in the wreckage of one's hopes—would have involved two things preeminently. First, a decision to stake everything on a *completeness* of self-exposure, even at the risk of abjection:

These long details about my early youth may well have seemed puerile, and I am sorry for that; although in certain respects I have been a man since birth, in many others I stayed a child for a long time, and still am one. I did not promise to offer the public a great personage; I promised to paint myself as I am. . . . I should like to be able somehow to make my soul transparent to the reader's eye, and in order to do that I am trying to show it from every point of view, to have it appear in all kinds of light, to make sure there is never a movement the reader does not see, so he may judge for himself from what principle those movements proceed. . . .

I have only one thing to fear in this enterprise; not that I may say too much or tell lies, but rather, that I may not say everything, and keep the truth from being spoken.[31]

Truth in self-portraiture would therefore depend, to use Rousseau's turn of phrase, on the painter moving—no, wrenching—his head from profile to full face, even if that meant revealing "quelque balafre à la joue." For "the features of a face only have the effect they do upon us because they are all there together; if one of them is missing, the face is disfigured."[32] Those words are taken from a sequence of manuscript fragments that Rousseau gathered together, maybe in the 1760s, and gave the title *Mon Portrait*. And of course they may seem to apply to David's particular case—to his literal disfigurement—almost too conveniently, in ways that are glamorous and hurtful; not that that shakes me from the conviction that David would have wanted them to apply, hurtful or otherwise, glamorous or not. But this is a topic I want to put aside for the moment, till more of my "Rousseau" is in place.

Taking Rousseau as one's master—this is my second point, and given the circumstances hardly easier to handle than the first—would have involved a willingness on the painter's part to adopt the paranoid tone. "Adopt" here immediately strikes me as too plodding a word, especially for the last half of the *Confessions*: it is part of the problem of Rousseau as autobiographer that the tone seems to adopt the writer rather than the other way round, and once adopted to invade every nook and cranny of the narrative and *become* the self's knowledge of itself. But supposing for a moment the tone could be managed pictorially; supposing one found a way, that is, to make a self-portrait explicitly against the portraits others had made; to make a likeness that had written on it, dictating its every move, the calumnies that had almost killed you. You would be Rousseau's child in this; and again, the qualities on which the whole operation would hinge would be completeness and distinctness, though now for reasons less philosophical than in the extract quoted previously.

In the enterprise I have undertaken to show myself to the public in my entirety, nothing about me must remain obscure or hidden; I must remain incessantly before the public's eyes, and be followed in all the wild wanderings of my heart, into the furthest recesses of my life; let the public not lose me from view for a single instant, for fear that, finding in my writing the least lacuna, the least gap, and asking themselves: What did he do during that time? they accuse me of not having wished to say everything. I leave myself open to the malignity of men enough by my writings, without adding to it by my silence.[33]

This is Rousseau in Book Two: it is the argument for his method that comes to predominate as the *Confessions* proceed. And could we not rewrite it word for word for David after Thermidor, putting "picture" for "writing" in the first place, and in the second the more capacious "deeds"; in particular those deeds—and they too were most dangerously writings, signatures the painter could not disown—that stood on the record from David's time as member of the *Comité du Sûreté Générale*?

"*L'on vous trompe, ce prétendu monstre est un homme.*"[34] Again, this desperate, culminant phrase from the First Dialogue of *Rousseau Juge de Jean Jaques* would presumably have been read by David in a special way. He would hardly have taken it for a figure of speech. His enemies never tired of reminding him that he *was* a monster, physically, *prima facie*. "I saw that David, so stupid, so wicked, and so veritably marked with the brand of reprobation. No one could be more hideous, more diabolically ugly. If he is not hung, there's no believing in physiognomies": this from the Royalist broadsheet *Journal à Deux Liards* in July 1792.[35]

But let me draw back. It may be that Rousseau's text and David's picture both issue from a wish to anticipate the worst that could be said about themselves. In both, to borrow a phrase from Thomas Kavanagh, "a consciousness [is] struggling to achieve the impossible exteriority to itself that would allow the subject to imagine how others might imagine him."[36] And in both the imagining is hectic. But that does not mean that with Rousseau, or even with David under Rousseau's aegis, we have entered an altogether different world from that of the *philosophes*. On the contrary:

There is another problem that has made me tiring to read; the difficulty, when one is obliged to speak of oneself incessantly, of speaking with justice and truth, without self-praise or self-blame. That is not difficult for a man to whom the public pays due homage: he is thereby spared the task of doing so himself. . . . But what about the man who considers himself worthy of honor and esteem and whom the public disfigures and defames at will? What tone will he adopt to do himself justice for once? . . . In such a case a proud and disdainful silence is suitable, and would have been more to my taste; but it would not have served my purpose, and to do so it was necessary for me to say with what eye, if I was someone else, I would see a man like me.[37]

What is most unnerving about a passage like this is its *tone*. Unnerving because so hard to put a finger on. Could we not imagine the passage— especially its clipped, almost antiseptic conclusion—spoken in something like Diderot's or d'Holbach's voice? Well, almost. Or to put it another way, is not the ultimate difficulty of Rousseau's writing precisely that the paranoia seems to be what generates its special brand of coolness—its equanimity, its determination to get things exactly right—as well as what threatens to overwhelm them. "I have resolved to take my readers one step further in the study of mankind. . . . I shall do my best so that in order to know oneself better, one should have at least one point of comparison; that everyone should know themselves and one other person, and that other will be me."[38] Nobody has ever bettered the dryness of that, the clinical quality. Nor has anyone shown us more vividly that when the subject is oneself, abasement is really at bottom the same thing as exaltation; for the movement of self-pity *is* the movement of lyric—lyric, as Paul de Man says, being "not a genre, but one name among several to designate the defensive motion of understanding."[39] No wonder Rousseau's writing still sticks in the reader's throat.

This discussion of Rousseau and David has been inching towards the central and intractable problem of Rousseau the writer—the problem of inwardness. Again it is an issue I should like to put off till later on. But this much had better be said by way of preliminary. No other author has ever so insisted on an inside-outside topology of consciousness as the founding structure of his or her work, and no one else has claimed so passionately, much to his first readers' delight, that it was the inside that counted:

I can make omissions or transmissions in the facts, or mistakes over dates; but I cannot be wrong about what I felt, and what my feelings made me do; and that is principally what is at stake. The proper object of my confessions is to make known exactly my interior, in all the situations of my life. It is the history of my soul that I have promised, and to write it faithfully I have no need of other memorials: it is enough for me, as I have done till now, once more to enter inside myself.[40]

A self-portraitist with a page like this in mind would have been strengthened in his conviction—it was anyway written deep in the genre he inherited—that his ultimate task was to enter (or re-enter) the space behind the eyes. But a page like this one was not exactly typical of Rousseau's writing: that was the problem for anyone wishing to learn from him. The vehemence of Rousseau's insistence on the outside-inside distinction, and the whole-heartedness with which he opted time and again for one side against the other, already seemed to readers in the eighteeenth century at odds with his writing's notorious public force. He had found a new language for solitude and disengagement from the world, but at the same time he was author of *Du Contrat Social*. "Il falloit necessairement que je disse de quel oeil, si j'étois un autre, je verrois un homme tel que je suis."

That is to say, there is a constant shuttling or flickering in Rousseau's work between the pure sense of one's existence, one's self-absorption and sufficiency, and their embodiment for other people. The self is a nothing, or almost nothing, and *therefore* the most treasured object of writing: "a more essential possession which, not having to do with the senses, with sex or age or appearance, is attached to everything that makes one a self, and which can be lost only when one ceases to be."[41] But the self is everything, and in writing it lays claim to—or discovers itself as—objective existence, a kind of being for others that it is writing's task to further, maybe to enforce. To the extent that the writing self, or the written self, "reestablishes an authentic relation to being, it extends itself to the entire human community, and its particular will becomes a general will": that is de Man's gloss on the issues as they occur in Hölderlin's reading of Rousseau.[42]

Here is the level at which "Rousseau," the problem, most resists solution and therefore over the years has had to be repressed or condescended to: that the very moment in these texts at which the turning away of self from world is finalized is also that of maximum instability for the terms that *do* the turning—the inside versus outside, the private versus political, the *mouvements* and *sentiments*, the self and the soul. Why this should be, and how this should be, and to what extent "Rousseau" was master of the shifting his words seem to induce: these are questions readers go on disagreeing about. Lately the disagreements have centered on one proposition, that right at the heart of this dance of the categories is language itself, and the part language is given by Rousseau in his opening onto inner light. "Consultons la lumiére intérieure": slogans like these are a constant in this body of work whatever the problem being tackled. And no picture of consciousness and understanding could give language more power; for it is precisely at the moment that a statement declares itself to have emanated from an "inside" that it makes its most coercive claim on us and our like minds. All the more strongly—and here Rousseau is taken to be exemplary above all—in that the inside here pointed to *is* language, its figures, effects, and powers of doing things. Rousseau is that moment when language comes into its dangerous own exactly by declaring itself pure transparency to a space within: this is the moment of linguistic activity we still inhabit, and for which Rousseau is the uncomfortable figure.

Painting one's portrait in the light of Rousseau turns out, then, not to be easy—not a matter, for instance, of just adding in some *sensibilité*. It seems to lead towards an area, or a kind of practice, in which most of the terms of the new self threaten to get out of hand, and language in particular—the bare procedures of representation—takes the language-user on a wild ride. This is not an esoteric reading of Rousseau; some or all of these issues must occur to any reader trying to follow Rousseau's drift; certainly to one with David's kinds of interest. The concern for completeness in self-representation, for example, and the mad wish to anticipate other people's

representations in one's own, are matters where claims to truth are inseparable from worries about technique. In them inwardness becomes a question of medium, or of the circumstances of enunciation. And the "or" in
that sentence precisely begs the Rousseauvian question. There seems not to
be an alternative in this writing between the positing of language as pure
immediacy, impressed with the least movements of an inner world, and its
deployment as a political weapon. That is the problem for self-portraiture
which Rousseau represents.

David was a reader of Rousseau in Year Two. He was not likely to have
thought of the author of the *Rêveries* as different in kind from that of *Du
Contrat Social*. The portrait he did of himself might just as well be looked
at with Saint-Just's collected speeches in mind, larded as they were with
quotations from the master, as with anything by Rousseau *tout court*. There
was a language of politics in 1794 which Jean-Jacques was taken to have
fathered, by readers who had no misgivings about the transition from inner
to outer truth—a discourse of virtue, authenticity, austerity, directness, of
heroism and naivety mixed. At this level, we know, David was unrepentant.
"Notwithstanding the fate of that unfortunate young man"—he means
Saint-Just—"and the prejudices entertained against him, he was 'véritablement à la hauteur de la Révolution.'"[43] The informant is Henry Redhead
Yorke (whoever he may be) writing home to England, and the date is 1794.
It is early, recklessly early, to be saying this kind of thing to strangers.

I am at the third point on my discursive map. Here is an eighteenth-
century voice—it will be the last I try to have David ventriloquize—
speaking again to the subject of self, and coming to a different conclusion
from any we have encountered so far. The voice is David Hume's, the book
his *Treatise of Human Nature*:

There are some philosophers, who imagine we are every moment intimately conscious of what we call our *self*; that we feel its existence and its continuance in
existence; and are certain, beyond the evidence of a demonstration, both of its perfect identity and simplicity. The strongest sensation, the most violent passion, say
they, instead of distracting us from this view, only fix it the more intensely, and make
us consider their influence on *self* either by their pain or pleasure. . . .

Unluckily all these positive assertions are contrary to that very experience which
is pleaded for them; nor have we any idea of *self*, after the manner it is here explained. For, from what impression could this idea be derived? . . . It must be some
one impression that gives rise to every real idea. But self or person is not any one
impression, but that to which our several impressions and ideas are supposed to have
a reference. If any impression gives rise to the idea of self, that impression must

continue invariably the same, through the whole course of our lives; since self is supposed to exist after that manner. But there is no impression constant and invariable. Pain and pleasure, grief and joy, passions and sensations succeed each other, and never all exist at the same time. It cannot therefore be from any of these impressions, or from any other, that the idea of self is derived; and consequently there is no such idea. . . .

For my part, when I enter most intimately into what I call *myself*, I always stumble on some particular perception or other, of heat or cold, light or shade, love or hatred, pain or pleasure. I never can capture *myself* at any time without a perception, and never can observe any thing but the perception. . . . If any one, upon serious and unprejudiced reflection, thinks he has a different notion of *himself*, I must confess I can reason no longer with him. . . . He may, perhaps, perceive something simple and continued, which he calls *himself*; though I am certain there is no such principle in me.[44]

These pages from the *Treatise* are justly celebrated, particularly in our own century. Indeed, that is when they *were* celebrated. The *Treatise*, as Hume told the story, fell deadborn from the presses in 1740 and never seems to have revived, for all the writer's general celebrity in his own time. It was the only book of Hume's not to have been translated into French while Hume was still alive.

Does this mean that the arguments simply ought not to figure on my map at all? I do not think so. Admittedly they represent a limit case of self-consciousness, one stated with a mixture of insolence and courtesy that seems to have made it inaudible to contemporaries. But the statement itself—the opinion or fear that the self was a delusion, that the more we attended to it the faster it volatilized—would not have been unfamiliar to the men and women of David's age.

They would have come across it, first, as a series of paradoxes that were held to follow from the materialist account of mind, and which therefore were seized on by enemies as evidence of the account's futility. For it must be, said reasonable men, that thoughts and perceptions belong to a single *Moi*—any other point of view is ridiculous—yet how can they do so if what the materialists say about the organism is true? Bonnet, for example, put the case this way in his *Essai de psychologie* of 1755:

If the Faculty of thought resides in a certain Part of our Brain, there are as many Selves in us as there are Points in that Part which are capable of becoming the seat of a Perception. Perception is inseparable from the feeling *of* Perceiving: a Perception which is not perceived to have happened is not a Perception. The feeling of Perceiving is no more nor less than the thinking Being in one of its modes of existence. Therefore there are as many thinking Beings in us as there are Points that perceive.

But we do not only perceive; we have wishes, and the Will is a movement that takes place at another Point in the thinking Substance. The Self that wills is thus not the same as the Self that perceives.

We can try our best, in order to take account of what we all feel, internally [Bonnet like others is in no doubt about what that feeling *is*], to bring the Perceptions and Volitions together in one Point: that Point will remain a composite of Parts; and those Parts are essentially distinct from one another.[45]

Or again, more crudely, in his *Essai analytique sur les facultés de l'âme*:

Any two objects that I see distinctly act upon two different Points of my *Senso-rium*. . . . A material [thinking] Substance is therefore not capable of comparisons; for the Point at which the Comparison would take place would always be quite distinct from those affected by the Objects to be compared. No singular Sentiment, no *Self*, could result from such a process.[46]

The reader, as I say, was supposed to recoil from these conclusions with a God-given sense of their absurdity; but the conclusions had been rehearsed, in terms that Hume if he had read them might not entirely have disowned.

And further, readers of David's generation would have been familiar with skepticism about the self transposed, so to speak, to the ethical and political register. They would have read the last pages of Rousseau's *Discours sur les origines de l'inégalité*:

There is a category of men who consider the regard of the rest of the universe to be worth something, and who can be happy and content with themselves on the basis of other people's judgments as opposed to their own. Such, indeed, is the true cause of all these differences [that is, the chaos and divisiveness of modern societies as Rousseau saw them]: the Savage lives inside himself; the sociable man, always out-side himself, knows how to live only in other people's opinion, and, if I can put it this way, it is only from their judgments of him that he gains a sense of his own existence.[47]

There is no need to press the similarity of this to the *Treatise* too far. Of course the argument is different. The self disperses in Rousseau under the play of other people's gazes as opposed to one's own. This is a theory of alienation, not a glimpse into the epistemological abyss. Nonetheless in both cases what is lost is the self. The fear that it might be, the thought that it could be, is an eighteenth-century thought. Hume's voice, in particular, is the one that may matter to an understanding of self-portraiture just be-cause it is the voice of *looking*—of looking inward and seeing nothing sin-gular there, of coming back to the surface and being of the opinion that surface (impression, "acquaintance") is all there is to it.

Could we not try to imagine at this point what the face of someone coming to Hume's conclusions would look like? The exercise, I promise you, will not be entirely whimsical—we could even take Rousseau as our guide. Writing to Hume from Wootton in July 1766, and trying to explain what had caused their horrible confrontation a few weeks before, Rousseau staged the scene in London as a meeting—a visual encounter—of two absolute contraries of self, the two the eighteenth century specialized in:

Very soon I am seized by violent remorse; I rage against myself. At last, in a transport that I still recall with delight, I throw myself on His neck, I Clasp him to my bosom [Hume is addressed in the third person here, but it is Hume who is meant]; Choking with Sobs, overflowing with tears, I cry out in a half-broken voice: *No, no, David Hume is not a traitor; If he were not the best of men, he would have to be the blackest of them all.* David Hume returns my embraces politely, and, patting me gently On the back, says quietly, over and over again, *What is it, my dear sir?* My dear sir! What can it be, my dear sir? That is all he has to say to me; I Feel my heart shrink back; we go to bed, and the next day I leave for the provinces.

And what was it that had touched off this debacle? The accident of Rousseau catching sight, after dinner, of how the good David *looked*:

After Supper, the two of us sitting in Silence by the fireside, I notice that he is staring at me, as he did very Often, and in a manner it is difficult to describe. This time His look was Dry, corrosive, mocking and prolonged, and it became more than disturbing. To make it stop I tried to stare back at him in turn; but once my eyes met His directly I Felt an inexplicable shudder, and soon I was forced to avert my gaze. The physiognomy and tone of the good David Are those of a good man, but where, for God's sake! does this good man borrow the eyes with which he fixes his friends?[48]

To which the answer might be: from the eyes with which he fixes himself.

Trying to get the measure of the self in the eighteenth century leads, you will see, to some pretty ferocious thought-experiments. What would a face be like, is the question, that precisely would not give in, or give expression, to those things called feelings because its owner had come to doubt that the feelings were *his*? What would the look be like of someone who had formed the opinion that his self was a convenient fiction, and therefore tried to have that fictitiousness be written into his conduct—into the way he met other people's eyes? Of course it would not be like the look of David in his self-portrait: that is not what I am saying. If we want to have David be a player at all in the ghastly scene in London, I guess we would put him in Rousseau's shoes more readily than Hume's: trembling, transported, choking on his tears: "Gross David, with the swoln cheek, has long painted, with genius

in a state of convulsion; and will now legislate."[49] But should we let ourselves be carried away by Carlyle's rhetoric? Is the face in David's picture
about to throw itself on anybody's neck? Is not one of the qualities that seems
most distinctive of the self-portrait, and grows on the viewer the longer the
look is engaged, the immense distance at which David has placed himself,
for all the picture's first display of intimacy and directness? It is not Hume's
distance exactly, but neither is it Rubens's or Sir Joshua's (Figs. 1–2). It is
not, so to speak, strictly technical. It is not just a matter of decorum. I want
to say—and in the end the claim can be left quite limited—that David's

F I G. 1. Peter Paul Rubens, *Self-Portrait*, oil on canvas, ca. 1636–38.
Vienna, Kunsthistorisches Museum.

F I G. 2. Sir Joshua Reynolds, *Self-Portrait*, oil on canvas, 1753–54. London, National Portrait Gallery.

look is at least touched by the Humean kind of scepticism, and in that too belongs to its time.

One last word here. I do not think we can come away from the point Hume occupies on the spectrum of discourse comforting ourselves with the thought that anyway it cannot be the one David occupied at the Hôtel des Fermes because, after all, what he chose to do there *was* self-portraiture, and from Hume's point no self-representation can emerge. If the self is lost, self-portraiture stops. Nothing could be further from the truth. The loss of self—the positing of self as a sliding or multiplying, an evaporating, a disillusion, a happening upon absence or emptiness—all this has been the fount of self-representation from the late eighteenth century on, not its drowning pool. De Man makes the point in his usual way:

Within the epistemological labyrinth . . . the recuperation of selfhood [is] accomplished by the rigor with which the discourse deconstructs the very notion of self.

The originator of this discourse is then no longer the dupe of his own wishes. . . . His consciousness is neither happy nor unhappy, nor does he possess any power. He remains however a center of authority to the extent that the very destructiveness of his ascetic reading

—this is not a commentary on the *Treatise of Human Nature*, by the way, but on Rousseau's preface to *Narcisse*—

testifies to the validity of his interpretation. The dialectical reversal that transfers the authority from experience into interpretation and transforms, by a hermeneutic process, the total insignificance, the nothingness of the self into a new center of meaning, is a very familiar gesture in contemporary thought, the ground of what is abusively called modernity. [50]

There is a line of self-portraiture these words fit well. The very fact of the painter being seated in front of a mirror tends to elicit a kind of dialectical to-and-fro in self-portraiture without undue effort on the dialectician's part; the mirror naturalizes the movement, so to speak, making it seem to take place in space, between a self here where I am and another out there in the glass; it is only an obvious gloss on this to have the two selves be strangers to one another. And sure enough, the face of loss stares out from scores of painters' pictures of themselves; of loss or doubt or distance or fascination with one's own unfamiliarity; the face being given back its unity—reappropriated as a totality—precisely *by* its look of having encountered the possibility that no such unity existed. Skepticism about the self, in other words, is one of self-portraiture's deepest and most ordinary conventions.

This is where my triangulation of discourses can come to an end. Except that it is immediately tempting to go through the whole process again, only this time visually. Does not each of us think we could produce, if pressed, quite plausible equivalents in paint for the kinds of address to the self so far described in words? Cannot we imagine David doing the same thing? Do we not think that in some sense he *did*, as part of the process of representing himself?

Was not his Diderot Chardin (Fig. 3)? And would not his Rousseau have been Rembrandt—Rembrandt, that is, as he was understood and idolized by a generation of readers of the *Confessions* (Figs. 4–5)? (I chose the two self-portraits I use as illustrations simply because they are ones that David could have known: the latter had been in the royal collection since the days of Le Brun, and the former was freshly confiscated by the Revolution from the Duc de Brissac. [51]) And Hume? What pictures would have stood in for

F I G. 3. Jean Siméon Chardin, *Self-Portrait with an Eyeshade*, pastel on paper, 1775. Paris, Musée du Louvre.

his tone of voice? Parmigianino's *Self-Portrait in a Convex Mirror* (Fig. 6)? Carracci's self-portrait in the Uffizi, the one with the painter's face marooned on an easel, adrift in an incomprehensible room (Fig. 7)? The Murillo in the Dundas collection—known to David presumably only through engravings[52]—where the artist's self-image suffers a similar though even more unnerving displacement, staring back at the viewer from a place that is not quite the surface of another picture but not quite anything else; with the instruments of painterly performance—the palette and brushes, the paper and chalk—given more of the look and feel of reality than the painter's cold hand only half transgressing its frame (Fig. 8)? (Which is more stony, Murillo's hand or the echoing cusps of foliage?) And whom do we take as painting's Saint-Just? Carel Fabritius? Salvator Rosa (Fig. 9)?

Of course by now we are far inside the field of interpretation, and the answers to some of my rhetorical questions may well be a firm, perhaps passionate, No. How dare I foist upon the reader a Rembrandt seen through Rousseau's eyes? Is not Rembrandt the real materialist? Would not Diderot have warmed to him in a way that Jean-Jacques never could? And do I expect anyone to stay satisfied long with the notion that just because Diderot wrote about him with such enthusiasm Chardin has much to do with the *Pensées sur l'interprétation de la nature*? The whole tone and intention of Chardin's self-portraits remain to be explored. Still more their development. If we are casting round for analogies to them, might not Hume in the *Treatise*—I mean the calm and punctiliousness with which the detail of perception is confronted there—strike us as closer to the mark than Diderot? And come to that, does not the implacable last pastel Chardin did of himself—it

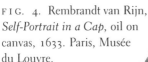

FIG. 4. Rembrandt van Rijn, *Self-Portrait in a Cap*, oil on canvas, 1633. Paris, Musée du Louvre.

F I G. 5. Rembrandt van Rijn, *Self-Portrait at the Easel*, oil on canvas, 1660. Paris, Musée du Louvre.

was one of two "têtes de vieillards" he showed in the Salon of 1779[53]—conjure up as much "ce prétendu monstre" as anything from the *Éléments de physiologie* (Fig. 10)?

The argument could go on indefinitely. In any case it seems to me there is a spurious vividness to the visualization being done here—as usual with such exercises, only more so. Painters do not operate with filecards of images in their minds' eye; least of all do they consult them, or walk round the corner to the Louvre, when they are painting in David's circumstances. Self-portraiture is a strange tradition: David certainly knew the tradition well and wanted to be part of it, but it came to him from a distance in 1794, recollected in its bare essentials. He was as likely to have brooded over Parmigianino's *Self-Portrait in a Convex Mirror* in Vasari's retelling of it as ever to have gone to see it in Vienna.

What we can say, I think, is that the field of self-portraiture would have been understood to possess this kind of discursive complexity, at least by a painter of David's cast of mind, brought up to eighteenth-century matters.

Socrates, skilful sculptor; Jean-Jacques, good musician; the immortal Poussin, tracing on his canvases the sublimest lessons in philosophy, are each of them witnesses, proving that the genius of the arts needs no other guide than the torch of reason.[54]

This is from David's report to the Convention in 1793 proposing a new *Jury National des Arts*. No doubt the basic proposition here turned out to be a poor guide to art policy; but it was one David believed in passionately, never more so than when the genius was his own.

What I have been trying to do so far is build a framework for interpretation; vivid enough, I hope, to suggest the form interpretation might take when it comes to aspects of the picture that clearly need deciphering—the

FIG. 6. Parmigianino, *Self-Portrait in a Convex Mirror*, oil on panel, 1524. Vienna, Kunsthistorisches Museum.

FIG. 7. Annibale Carracci, *Self-Portrait*, oil on panel, ca. 1595. Florence, Galleria degli Uffizi.

FIG. 8. Bartolomé Murillo, *Self-Portrait*, oil on canvas, 1670. London, National Gallery.

FIG. 9. Salvator Rosa, *Self-Portrait*, oil on canvas, ca. 1640.
London, National Gallery.

swoln cheek most notably, the painter's extraordinary way of looking at himself, his way of dressing, the handling of the palette he holds, and the question of some parts of the picture being aggressively "finished" and others as aggressively not. The best any framework can do, of course, is suggest readings, not provide them. There is always a gap between mapping and interpretation, though the two, I think, ought to contaminate one another as much as possible.

How then to proceed? Again, *ad hoc.* It will help if we try to build into our sense of the painting as much as we can of its immediate circumstances—and even these have been doubted. For a start, this does seem to be the picture David did under arrest in the Hôtel des Fermes. His pupil Delafontaine, who brought him the mirror, specifically says that the portrait was afterwards given to Isabey, and later writers who were close enough to

FIG. 10. Jean Siméon Chardin, *Self-Portrait at the Easel*, pastel on paper, ca. 1778. Paris, Musée du Louvre.

the chain of reminiscences to spot a weak link do not seem to have done so. That is notably true of the painter's grandson and biographer, Jules David.[55] What seems from time to time to have stood in the way of accepting this as Delafontaine's picture is the thought that if it is, its subject is forty-six years old. Writers do not reckon he looks his age. But this kind of art-historical empiricism will not, if we think about it, get us very far. As if self-depiction were not *always* a matter of transposition in time as well as space! What does it mean to represent oneself, after all, if not to elude the present, to put oneself in place of it, to posit oneself as one will be or might have been? Rousseau again is our best reminder of that fact, and this is the sense in which Rembrandt really is his painter.

In old age Delafontaine seems to have relived the moment in the Hôtel des Fermes as if it were yesterday, and was concerned to get it written into the record. It has pride of place in his manuscript memoirs, and evidently loomed large in his conversation. Perhaps Gigoux was forcing the note with his "Ils vont me couper le cou, mon cher!" but you would have had to be insensible not to strike the note at all. The picture must have been done with the thought of death in mind.

Let me begin then with David's terrible *look*. (And here straight away the problems of describing self-portraiture at all begin to press in on us. For any attempt to give an account of a particular feature in a self-portrait—even under the sign of circumstances as dreadful as this—finds itself pulled off course into generalities. What makes the generalities so hard to bear is not just that they seem ethically a betrayal, in the way they do here; but that in any case, however anodyne, they seem to fly in the face of the one great fact of self-portraiture—its simplicity, its directness. Self-portraiture of all things should not be an excuse for dialectical sophistries; but it is. The pull off course is irresistible: simplicity and generality are attributes of the subject that continually collapse back into one another. The best an interpreter can do is try to mimic the movement of resistance even as he or she provokes it—to put a naive stop to the argument in places and point impatiently at the *thing*.)

To begin with the look. If we take the basic fiction of this kind of self-portraiture seriously—the notion, I mean, that what we are looking at is what the painter saw in the mirror—then it follows that the look of self-portraiture must be a very specific one: the look, we could say, of someone looking at him- or herself looking. The trouble is that we can only decide where to put an end to that sentence by pure fiat. The sentence is designed to go on for ever. The look of someone looking at him- or herself looking at the look he or she has when it is a matter of looking not just at anything, at something else, but back to the place from which one is looking. . . . Would that do better? Is that what self-portraiture is about? Simple questions in this area, as I said, open conveniently onto infinite dialectical regress. And is not one of the things we admire in certain self-portraits the effort to represent just that dialectical vertigo? Is that what David is concentrating on?

Well, yes and no. The look in the picture does seem to be meant to be complicated, as if it issued from some process of inquiry, but it is also meant to be businesslike. There may be some epistemological anxiety about, but we are surely not supposed to take the subject as overwhelmed by it. His look is poised, cool, craftsmanlike: the look of a professional. (These last are class attributes as well as professional ones, and the look of self-portraiture is shot through with signs of class and gender. It is the look of mastery; of containment, detachment, distance, *sang froid*, self-possession. It comes out of an aristocratic matrix. The fact that the look seems to have come into being, or taken on a certain consistency, at the moment of Mannerism may not be beside the point.) Perhaps in the end, for all its coolness, this is a look that intends to break through the surface to some truth within; but we cannot be sure, and it is part of self-portraiture that we should not be; maybe the point or effect of the mirror is to let the look deal strictly with appearances. The look in self-portraiture never stops oscillating between these two possibilities, these two kinds of reading. The oscillation is what the look *is*. On the one hand Rembrandt, on the other Sir Joshua Reynolds. But are we so sure, on reflection, who is on the one hand and the other? Are not both of them on both? Is there not pathos even to Reynolds's professionalism?

The problems already have us by the throat. Let me try to restate them in less intractable form. For a start, we could ask if the painter of a self-portrait is normally taken to be a privileged witness to what he is looking at. (For reasons that will emerge in a moment, the masculine pronoun turns out to be the least offensive choice in this case.) If so, what kind of privilege is it? Presumably it would be stretching things to say that a self-portraitist does not have *some* special knowledge of—or access to—what he is like. But it does not follow that he is necessarily a good judge of what he *looks* like. And he may be exactly the wrong person to tell us or show us how his self—if we mean by that a certain continuity of character and attitude to things—is manifest on the outside, in the way he presents what is visible to others. This might be opaque to him, and in any case not open to inspection in a mirror; it might be something he (happily) took for granted and in a sense positively avoided observing in everyday life, whereas the rest of us had been doing the observing like mad, as part of our ordinary dealings with him. We would be better portraitists of him, if we had the skills, than he will ever be; there are plenty of pairs of portraits and self-portraits that seem to prove the point.

So what does a portraitist think he is doing looking in the mirror in the first place? Everyone knows the game is risky. Rousseau comes out with a platitude when he associates self-portraiture with Narcissus. English in general does much the same thing. Self-regard, for example, is not a neutral term in common usage, and shades off quickly into *amour propre*. Looking too hard at oneself is embarrassing. Even self-consciousness is an equivocal concept (more so in English than French): some contexts make it a high and difficult attainment, and others an unfortunate condition linked with adolescence and bad skin. Self-portraits are partly made, I think, against this

FIG. 11. Anthony van Dyck, *Self-Portrait*, oil on canvas,
ca. 1613. Vienna, Gemäldegalerie der Akademie der bildenden Künste.

background of suspicion, and the look in them has to signify before all else
that the painter cast a cold eye on his subject-matter as opposed to a warm
one. Hence there emerged a whole deeply conventional repertoire of poses
and expressions meant to prove the point: casual, momentary, disabused,
warts-and-all, professional, pessimistic, would-be Nietzschean—all of them
determined not to be self-absorbed or self-regarding, or not in ways viewers
could condescend to. (This is one of the reasons why the set-up in self-
portraiture which has the painter "looking back" at himself over his shoulder
becomes such a favorite (Figs. 11–12]. It looks so much like a pose struck
en passant, for no more than a moment, before the painter turned back to
what he was really interested in—in other words the canvas.)

FIG. 12. Pierre-Hubert Subleyras, *Self-Portrait*, oil on canvas, ca. 1746. Vienna, Gemäldegalerie der Akademie der bildenden Künste.

This kind of skepticism towards self-portraiture is not, I think, just something I have worked up for the occasion: it seems, as I say, to be built into the language and have had effects on practice. All the same, there is a sense in which it leaves our most deeply held prejudices untouched. Say what you will, nothing is ever quite going to budge us from the conviction that a self-portraitist *is* privileged and does look back at us from a special place. I can ironize about *amour propre* till I am blue in the face—put me back in front of a Rembrandt and the circuitry is largely intact. What is it then we cannot escape from?

First of all, there does not seem to be an exit from the situation *we* are put in as viewers of a self-portrait: we cannot entirely escape from *ourselves* and the invitation to double and project that entity—or location or condition: the game thrives on the ontology being so slippery—onto the image in front of us. This is a powerful constraint, a real generator of readings. The beholder of David's self-portrait, say, is put in that place—but is it a place at all, exactly?—from which or in which, it is imagined, the depicting got done; and that not metaphorically, but literally. Not that the "literally" here is at all to be trusted, or even meant to be; we are not physically in any such place, and on one level we know it. It is just that in order to get on any kind of terms with a self-portrait we have to accept that our eyes are roughly where the painter's once were, and not only eyes but mind. "We" (the word is always to be understood in quotation marks in this essay, but now it had better wear them with pride) are meant to assume—to *re*sume—the position of consciousness whose outside is there on the canvas. That outside is not just the evidence for the position, it is its product; and the cast of mind on show is not general—not an invitation to any and every projection on our part—but specific. What we are shown is consciousness directed to that exotic entity, its own outside, its "appearance." And is not that where and how *our* consciousness is directed? Cannot we duplicate as viewers those very movements of seeing or mind that are pictured and that led to the picturing? All viewing of paintings is a kind of complicity, no doubt. Not all of it involves haunting.

It does not really matter then if we are Humeans or not. We can take the movements of seeing and mind to add up to a unity or we can revel in their unraveling. We can have the self or its negation: intimacy can disperse into otherness, unity into multiplicity, soul into matter, what we meant into the "free play of the signifier." Any movement will do as long as it is we who do it (and anyone who thinks that the "we" in this sentence cannot possibly keep hold of that last movement, from meaning into the materiality of the sign, had better go back to the texts in which it is smugly proclaimed). They are all part of the same fiction, the same "figure of reading or of understanding." [56]

My imagery in the last page or so has been of coercion, as if I thought the game we had been inveigled into playing was one with actual costs and deficits, which it would be good not to run up. The reader may be wondering what I think the costs are. Is the account of self and self-knowledge I see in these pictures' set-ups strong enough to count as coercive? Have we been sold any very particular bill of goods?

I think we have; which is not to say I see any better bills on offer for the time being. The items are three. We have been sold a certain metaphysics of spatiality—a picture of the self as having insides and outsides, and being somewhere. We have acquiesced in an equation of seeing with knowing, one that is built deep into our accounts of the world: de Man calls it "the fundamental metaphor of understanding as seeing." [57] And we have given in to the great argument of self-portraiture, that a clear and fundamental distinction can be drawn between seeing and representing. I shall speak to the first two items straight away.

What does it mean, would be my question, to say that in the David we are looking at a self's outside, or at a body with a self inside it? We are looking at a body. A "self" is a way of describing it. Obviously we may want to specify all manner of things about that self, but why necessarily its *location*? And yet of course the movement to spatialize the self runs deep, and seems bound up, at least lately, with the effort to articulate what is special and irreducible in any one person's take on the world. Perhaps it is true, to quote a philosopher, that "the modern conception of a unified personality may not be possible" without a "space of disclosure . . . considered to be *inside*, in the mind." ("We may want to judge this in the end as fanciful a view as the ones which preceded it, but this doesn't dispense us from understanding the process of self-transformation which was partly constituted in this shift." [58])

Granted. And it may even be that the "movement of interiorization" Charles Taylor is talking about captures something about selfhood that is basic and ineradicable; it does not sound good to eradicate it; we all know the claptrap of collectivity when we hear it. Nonetheless I intend to stick to my guns. The movement in question seems impoverishing to me, and certainly it has come to stand in the way of capturing or even addressing various other dimensions to what it might mean to have or be a self. It may or may not be true, for example, that "the Dinka language . . . compels its speakers to integrate the moral and physical attributes of persons together within the physical matrix of the human body." [59] "Compels" is a difficult word here. Anthropologists disagree. But in any case, the point the anthropologist is making can stand *a contrario*: our language, in contrast to the Dinka, invites its speakers to think of persons and bodies separately. Likewise, it may or may not be useful to think of selfhood as a code of sorts, a kind of performance or negotiation, and therefore put our stress on the self's belonging to social practice. The language for this exists, of course; the language but not the *discourse*; no context of practice, that is—no proper language-games— of the kind that would mobilize the language and oblige it to draw on its full resources. So we simply do not know if the alternative models and metaphors of self could have purchase on new particulars or not, for what happens when they are tried is that the attempt to state them is infiltrated, not to say recaptured, by the very spacing and siding of self they see as the enemy. "We are never fully ourselves in our utterances. What we make or say is always somewhat alien to us, never wholly ours, as we ourselves are not wholly ours. . . . We are *outside* ourselves, and that 'outsidedness' . . . creates the tragedy of expression" (Morson on Bakhtin).[60] Either this, or bloodless abstraction. "A self is a repertoire of behavior appropriate to a different set of contingencies." "The self is the code that makes sense out of almost all the individual's activities and provides a basis for organising them" (Goffman).[61] The notion of code turns out in practice to be too thin to provoke much more than vague assent. Goffman's multiplication of particular social scenarios, which is where the real interest of his work is to be found, does not ultimately help. When it comes time to pin back the description of activities and contingencies to the concept of self—the word is in the title of Goffman's most famous book—the concept stays uninflected by its excursions.

Neither Goffman nor Morson is brought on here as an easy target—in a sense they are the least easy of the bunch. Morson in particular is working out of a rich tradition and puts it to good use. The quotes are here to show what it means to swim against the tide.

The model of inside and outside would not have the kind of hold on us it has if it were not bound up with the second item on my bill of goods, the equation of seeing and understanding. This takes me back to the painter's look. The type of self-portrait I am interested in, of which David's is a strong case, is out to show not just the likeness of a person who happens to be me—there are admittedly plenty of portraits with no higher ambition—but the activity of self-scrutiny. It wants to get down the physical "look" of looking at one's own face—in a mirror, most likely, though the mechanics of the transaction may be stressed or not—and the connection between this looking and that movement of totalization which is (what verb will do here?) possessing a self, or coming to consciousness of oneself as one.

Self-portraiture thrives on the further premise that *seeing*, in this connection, is uniquely privileged: we are being shown someone seeing the thing he or she understands best, or at least in a way nobody else could. And the understanding that the self has of itself *is too a kind of seeing*; or shall we say, it is a process that can only be properly imagined after the model of seeing: that is, as a discrete, continuous, immediate proceeding from a center; a movement out, as of some Will, but at the same time a stillness and receptivity, as of some Eye to which the world comes. Of course there is more to understanding the self than just seeing—self-portraits never tire of producing that piety—but the "more" is more of the same. Understanding is a seeing of the mind: a vector or trajectory of some kind, starting, so to speak (or do we mean really?), from an inch or two behind the eye, at the space or point which *is* our identity, and going out to the image in the mirror. And the fact that the model of seeing is thus generalized to mind reflects back prestige on seeing itself. People may say there is more to understanding the self than seeing, but they are not painters or epistemologists. Perhaps if they just looked hard enough.

This picture of the world is powerful. David's self-portrait shows us someone under its spell, I think, and part of the reason we respond to it so readily is that we know, as the saying goes, where the painter is coming from: we come from the same place. I have been arguing, and no doubt demonstrating, that it takes a lot of painful mental gymnastics to imagine even roughly what an alternative picture would be. It goes against the grain. What would it be like, for instance, to think of the self as a thing without sides? Sides as opposed to what? Moments? Deployments? Different kinds of outwardness with no inwardness to match? Places, aspects, modes, numbers, forms of ownership (one is not always self-possessed), kinds of texture or consistency? And even if a painter will not be inclined to do without the notion of the self as known *spatially*, then are there other conceivable relations in space besides those turning on "in" versus "out"? Do the various places of knowledge in the case of self have to be divided—by a partition which is all the more absolute for being at one and the same time so grossly, self-evidently material (in *here*, on the other side of *that*) and so entirely a matter of mind? "Il me suffit . . . de rentrer au dedans de moi." "Consultons la lumière intérieure." [62] "The soul, when it tries to remember ideas," writes Hemsterhuis, "sets in movement the last fibres of the organism which are turned towards its side [*de son côté*]." To which Diderot replies, underlining Hemsterhuis's last three words twice: "I don't know if you can say that the soul is in the body, or what side it is on [*de quel côté elle est*]." [63] Put "self" for "soul" in this exchange, and the doubts about topology still nag at something deep.

Suppose the stitching that normally holds seeing and understanding together in our view of things were to come undone. Where would that leave the look of self-portraiture? Nobody for the moment is out to deny that looking at one's face in a mirror *is* a form of self-knowledge. On the contrary, let us posit it as an ordinary and adequate one (with the emphasis on the ordinary): one among several or many, none of them distinct or immutable, none exactly trustworthy. We might choose to give up talking altogether about looking *in general* (or try to), and opt for ways of speaking in which looking is tied close to circumstances: *this* looking, constituted in any one case by a great pattern of contingencies: by mirrors and maulsticks and *abat-jours*, for certain, but also by the ways in which looking at a given moment is constituted by language—vaunted, doubted, distinguished from other mental operations, idealized, materialized, made subject to social constraints and permissions, and so on. It might be possible as a result to pose the question of identity in a new way, to rescue it from the one mode of cognition and have it be scattered among the modes of mask, place, sign, name, lineage, affiliation, performance, language-game. Under this rubric all forms of self-knowledge, looking included, would be "insufficient" (it is the dream of a sufficiency of self to self, with looking as the means to that sufficiency, that strikes me as self-portraiture's most deadly fiction). All of them would be external, in the sense of being always renegotiated in the public realm; maybe all of them would be open to description in materialist terms; and no doubt they would still be caught up in some version of Taylor's "movement of interiorization." Inside, outside; fragmentary, unitary; authentic or made up for the occasion; something acted out, something one has or is: the structures are not going to be dislodged merely by multiplying the materials they are called on to organize. That was Goffman's mistake. What might be thinkable, though—and here finally is my apology for pluralism—is a version of self-portraiture in which seeing would be pictured *as itself a form of representation*, not a proceeding somehow exempt from that circuit, or prior to it, or capable of breaking through it from one side to the other. That would lead to, and issue from, very different looks and poses from the ones we have.

The point of the exercise was not to indict a certain account of self and seeing but to find out what kind of account it was. The account is powerful. What I have to do now is try to pin down the ways David's picture capitalizes upon that power and puts it to good use. For the last thing I am saying is that David's self-portrait, to the extent that it shares the beliefs and procedures just laid out (or was it pilloried?), will be incapable of putting aspects of the self in a new light. The account is capacious: its assumptions do not dictate the detail of any and every description. Rousseau worked out of them to one set of conclusions, Diderot to another. Hume was able to subject at least some of the assumptions to a lot of pressure. So might David.

We are looking at a painter operating in the late eighteenth century. It is a moment when several opposing narratives of self are on offer, all of them sharing key features of the standard account, so to speak, but some giving those features an outlandish cast—one that struck people at the time as lunatic or whimsical, but which for some reason they could not put down. (Rousseau is the classic case.) The standard account was in trouble; perhaps as much trouble as it ever was. For the point is that Rousseau's and Diderot's stories of mind did not sit passively side by side in the culture: they were aimed at one another, and readers were expected to make up their minds between them or think of ways they could be reconciled. Lots of readers tried to. Whether this means David was given room for maneuver or confusion is what remains to be seen.

In any case the main constraints on self-portraiture had not evaporated. One of them, I have been arguing, is that the look of the painter in a self-portrait be given an "inside." The face that stares back at us has to be lent a quality of interiority somehow, ideally of a deeper sort than a mere portrait can manage. It is not enough to have the face just blankly be the information in the mirror: even Hume thought some kind of introspection was part of the game. (Not that there is any shortage of self-portraits that do not seem to have seen the point of self-scrutiny at all, and have painted their subject as if it were somebody else. But these are *portraits*. They have a different kind of ambition from the one I am describing. Self-portraiture is not so much a genre—not so much a finite set of objects labelled with their makers' names[64]—as a set of pretensions on the edge of a genre that normally has precious few.)

A large part of self-portraiture's best efforts therefore go to conjuring up a dimension in which the surface of the face, and particularly the eyes, can register as something to be looked through or behind. The face has to be robbed of its first self-evidence, and one way of doing that is to put it partly or wholly in shadow, with the shade maybe falling most deeply across the eyes (Fig. 13). The shadow is a metaphor for "inside." There is a problem of reading for a moment, and interiority thrives on problems of reading. Let there be just a moment of deferral—an averting of the eyes, an indirection, a slight movement away from full disclosure—and the viewer will turn the look into an "expression."

Which leads to the swoln cheek. The face in David's picture is seemingly pressed forward to meet its image in the mirror, glowering and intent, its

FIG. 13. Rembrandt van Rijn (or follower), *Self-Portrait*, oil
on canvas, after 1626. Kassel, Staatliche Gemäldegalerie.

features a trifle swollen, maybe choleric or even dropsical. The eyes look
almost as if they are imperfectly recessed. One pupil wanders slightly away
from the other. The effect is of staring to the point of exhaustion. There is
a great deal of mottled light and shade across the face, over the forehead and
under the lank wisps of hair, in the eyesockets, beneath the nose and the
bags under the eyes. (Some of the grey used to do this shading seems to have
been carried down without admixture to tie the knot in the cravat and outline its main flounces.) But the shadow is darkest on the painter's right
cheek. Dark enough for it to be hard to lay hold of the contour from jaw to
mouth visually, especially where the shadow seems to gather at the right
corner of the painter's mouth and the region next to it. The mouth is not
quite symmetrical; the lips on the shadowed side look to be pulled down

slightly, and the upper one thinned or flattened. There may even be a short straight line in the shadow area, ruled or incised across it in a deeper shade of black—it is visible only in the best Louvre daylight—leading up at an angle of 45 degrees from the corner of the mouth for an inch or so. If the line exists, it is not clear what it refers to: a scar perhaps? a crease of skin? an excrescence? Something appears to be the matter with the area where the shadow falls: we are not exactly shown what.

Let us immediately guard against the assumption that we know what was there. We know, I suppose, that *something* was there: a tumor of some sort, an "exostosis," which we are told was the result of an accident in the studio with the foils—horseplay or quarrelling, the tradition does not say. The accident happened in 1773 or 1774, when David was in his mid-twenties; the thing kept growing, and compounded a speech defect the painter had had since childhood.[65] As to what the side of David's face looked like, what we have are representations. They could be vicious: "S'il n'est pas pendu, il ne faut pas croire aux physionomies." Dates obviously matter: Rude's terrible likeness of his hero (Fig. 14) is of David at the end of his life—it was done from a death-mask[66]—and Rouget's Imperial portrait (Fig. 15) is also too late, and probably too tactful, to be a touchstone for 1794. The evidence is tainted; but even the most partisan of David's admirers in the Revolution—those who would have liked to look the other way—felt called on to speak to the thing on his face and the way it was taken for a sign. "The deformity of his features and a certain roughness in his manner did not dispose one in his favor; but if one got to know him, he had simplicity and *bonhomie*": this is from Thibaudeau in his memoirs, writing at the beginning of 1794.[67] Compare Delécluze in retrospect: "What's more, in spite of the swelling in one of his cheeks which disfigured him, and even though his look had something a bit hard about it . . ."[68] Farington in his diary for 1795 was a bit more clinical but to much the same effect: "One side of his face is much larger than the other and appears as if swelled";[69] and Montjoie the same year—like Farington a hostile witness—reports that David's nickname in the Year Two, even with his allies seemingly, was *grosse joue*.[70]

At the very least, then, we can assume that the decision what to do with the exostosis in a picture was charged. And not just for reasons of vanity or political rhetoric, but because there existed a whole ethic and aesthetic of disclosure in such matters to which, at one level, David was deeply committed. *Ce prétendu monstre, c'est un homme.* "They call me a cold and ferocious man. They do not know me as you do, to whom I speak with an

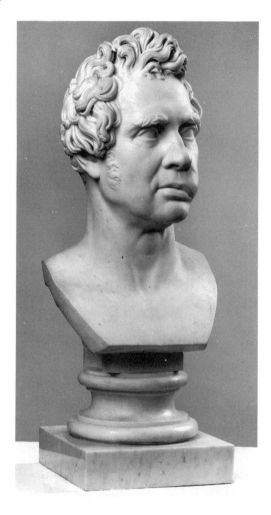

FIG. 14. François Rude,
Jacques-Louis David,
marble, 1829–30, from
model of 1826. Paris,
Musée du Louvre.

open heart. They will have mistaken the always pensive face of the artist for
the hideous mask of the conspirator": David to de Mainbourg, 8 November
1794, writing from his second prison in the Luxembourg.[71] "'Tis in vain
that you surround yourself with shadows; I shall shine my light into the
deepest hidden corners of your heart, I shall discover the secret springs of
your conduct, and I shall imprint on your brows the hideous character of
the passions that move you": David to his accusers, 3 May 1795.[72]

These last are political statements, of course, but the point is that the
language of portraiture came to hand so easily for political purposes. Shading—*ténèbres*—was an ethical question. Omission, of the kind that David

FIG. 15. Georges Rouget, *Jacques-Louis David*, oil on canvas, ca. 1815. Washington, D.C., National Gallery of Art, Chester Dale Collection.

appears to manage so skilfully in the picture he does of himself, is all the more serious and maybe vicious because the terms in which a portrait could be most tellingly criticized in the late eighteenth century—at any rate by one kind of viewer—had to do with what it deleted. The critic's voice had better be Rousseau's again, this time in *La Nouvelle Héloïse*.

When Saint-Preux in Book Two has recovered enough from the first shock of receiving Julie's picture to be able to say why it is not good enough, what he immediately seizes on in his letter is all the miniaturist has left out. Not just Julie's "modèle intérieur," which lovers are supposed to think cannot be painted, but her actual facial features; and here Saint-Preux is quite strictly a realist, at least by Rousseau's standards:

Let us forgive the Painter for having omitted several of your beauties; but he has done no less wrong to your visage in having omitted its faults. He did not put in that almost imperceptible scar which you have under the right eye, and which you got, they say, from a knife in your childhood, when you rushed to disarm a cousin of yours who was pretending to want to do himself harm; nor the blemish on your neck at the lefthand side. He did not put in . . . O God, was he a man of bronze, this artist? . . . He forgot the little *cicatrice* that remains beneath your lip. He made your hair and eyebrows the same color, which they are not: the eyebrows are more chestnut, and the hair is greyer. . . .

He made your jaw line exactly oval. He did not notice that slight change of direction which separates the chin from the cheeks, and makes their contour less regular and more graceful.[73]

Je ne veux pas qu'il t'ôte rien. Supposing a viewer of Saint-Preux's habits, who knew nothing about David's physical appearance and little or nothing about his reputation, lived for a while with David's picture. Would he be satisfied with it? I do not think so. On the one hand, he would presumably recognize and respond to the picture's overall idiom; he might think it specifically designed for him. Never was a painting so intent on clarity and distinctness, on dispensing with frills and furbeloes ("Jamais je n'avilirai mes pinceaux jusqu'à peindre une perruque"[74]) and showing the whole man. Everything seems to insist on an unsparingness of attention, a fixing, a gripping, a staring till it hurts. The eyes bulge with the effort. The hair could hardly be more dishevelled and greasy, more intent on saying "without a wig." Never did a button so signify "unbuttoned." A brush could not be held harder. The cold neutrality of the background serves to keep everything relentlessly in focus, forcing shapes forward, picking out their hard edges (no Rembrandt darkness here). And would it not further have occurred to Saint-Preux that this idiom of intentness was meant to have an ethical force, with the general clarity and distinctness offered as guarantee of other forms of rectitude, moral and perhaps political?

But then this viewer would have come across an unclarity at the center of things, an indistinctness; and surely this would register as an interruption in the picture's visual economy; or to put it another way, as something left outside the general circuit of fixing and illumination that gave the picture its force. "C'est en vain que vous vous enveloppez des ténèbres; je porterai la lumière." Was this the portrait's device or not?

We are not, in other words, bringing up an anecdotal fact when we focus attention on the swoln cheek: the passage of shadow is one that would strike any serious viewer as strange—certainly a viewer brought up on Rousseau and Diderot. Maybe the reasons for David's indeterminacy are obvious; or at least we think we could make them up fairly easily: reasons of vanity, of painterly decorum, etc. But the question that matters is not about motives but about meanings. What did it mean to set out in 1794 to paint oneself in full, and then end up devising such an extraordinary compromise formation for what it was marked you out for your enemies? The inquiry is into effects not causes, though even so we shall have to guard against teleology getting into our answers by the back door. ("Ah yes! interiority . . . let's put some in here.")

This last is not a retraction. Obviously there is a sense in which the shadow round the mouth does obey the rules of self-portraiture previously stated. What David manages to do by the shading, if I can put it this way, is convert a local and physical fact of deformity into an (unlocalized, psychological) quality of disturbance, one we attach to the face in general, and then to the face's center, the eyes. The *look* takes on the asymmetry and uncertainty of the mouth and jaw; which is to say, we end up seeing the distortion not as physical but mental—a quality of high anxiety, perhaps, or a hard edge to the painter's self-regard. There is plenty of interiority about.

To that extent we could say that the Saint-Preux-type viewer was just being inflexible and should have been able to see that the part that worried him did contribute to the picture's overall economy, maybe even tuning it up a notch. But Saint-Preux should be stubborn. There is an ellipsis at the heart of things, and one's eyes go back and back to the indeterminacy, wanting to make it out once and for all and not being able to. Something has been left out. The omission still has to be dealt with.

Presumably we would want to resist a swift Freudian reduction at this point, though it does not seem to me we can suppress the metaphor that the Freudian would bring on altogether. The swelling on David's cheek was perceived as somehow gross and scandalous at the time. Carlyle's (later) language reeks of sexuality; so does that of the *Journal à Deux Liards*—"si bête, si méchant . . . si véritablement marqué du sceau de la réprobation." Having to wear one's erection on one's face was a special kind of burden, where it is not clear whether what was hardest to bear was the suspicion of self-advertisement or of self-abasement. And when the erection gave rise to stammering, as it did in David's case, to a flow of imperfectly audible speech . . .

If we are still not willing to have the ellipsis simply be a castration—and the move does seem to me too easy—then what do we take it to mean? Our answer should not try to delete the possible equivalences the Freudian is pointing to, but ought to stay on the surface as much as possible and stick to the problems of self and identity that are self-portraiture's overt concern. It had better be general, speculative and brief.

Let us agree to take the swoln cheek to be a sign of some sort—of the body's contingency, of its excess, of its always already being marked by something exterior to itself; something other people do not have and which therefore the self (the integral self) *should not have.* Let the shadow stand for everything that gets in the way of the self's integrity, meaning closure, completeness, and self-sufficiency. "Montaigne se peint ressemblant mais de profil. Qui sait si quelque balafre à la joue . . . ?" "Les traits du visage ne font leur effet que parce qu'ils y sont tous; s'il en manque un, le visage est défiguré." But let us also accept that David's representation of himself—of his image in the mirror *as* a self—turns on its moment of obscurity; it is the interruption in the picture's language that generates the subject's particular, inimitable look, his "expression." For a body to become a self, or a set of physical features a face, it seems they must be given, in Neil Hertz's phrase, "the pathos of uncertain agency."[75] Pathos and uncertainty in this picture come out of the work of concealment done around the mouth. And we might want to say further that what happens thereabouts is the sign of David's gender, of how much and how little of that could be admitted into the world of sheer looking—the world of inside and out.

Not very much, apparently. But not *nothing*; gender is in the habit of getting in on the act somehow, spoiling the dream of transparency. Especially when what is transparent is a mirror. For "the elective embodiment of the pathos of uncertain agency"—here is Hertz's phrase completed—"is the specular structure, one that locates the subject in a vacillating relation to the flawed or dismembered or disfigured (but invariably gendered) object of its attention."

This is the way with self-portraiture in general: doing it under Rousseau's auspices only brings the problem up to the surface. What begins as a project of total disclosure, in which the uniqueness and universality of a mind will be put on show—a uniqueness the viewer will be able to enter into, it is hoped, and essentially duplicate—happens instead upon some evidence of the body's not being identical to others, and on that fact being bound up, indelibly it seems, with shame and anxiety. To disclose oneself completely therefore *is* shameful. And if shame is exactly not the affect in the light of which the self (in self-portraiture) should finally appear, then the sign of excess and contingency is bound to be painted out. Or rather, in this case, fixed so intently by a represented gaze that it migrates from a place to a mode of address: the excess becoming an aspect of the gaze itself, a matter not of body but of mind.

Had our picture of David's concerns as a painter been couched solely in Rousseau's terms then we could more or less stop here. But I meant from the start of this essay to argue that concerns of this kind must have been crossed by others in the late eighteenth century—by those I associated with Diderot—and that David would have been prepared to accept, in the process of painting, that picturing the self meant finding terms for physiology as much as mental life. If there were parts of his body he was unable to represent, others he gave free rein by means of metaphor. That is to say, he came to see that depicting the body—even aspects of it less unassimilable than a tumor on the cheek—always involves displacement, a putting of something in place of a brute fact. His metaphors of body were, as you would expect in the circumstances, in a dark register.

The most remarkable and difficult of them, I think, is the long red lapel and lining of the painter's *houppelande*, which cradles his body like a great serpent and which, especially in the section that falls from his left shoulder—the flat, frontal, half-twisted trapezoid I shall call the lapel for short—takes on such perturbing life. Four things at least contribute to its power. Its being so large: its going on and on across David's chest and lap till it ends abruptly in an edge drawn at right angles to one of the fingers holding the palette. Its being unfinished: that is, marked so openly with the painter's brush, whose traces are so broad and animate in places, notably halfway down, that they look like nothing so much as fingerprints. Its having such an evocative color, which most writers call crimson, but which might as well be that of dried or drying blood. (Crimson in the Shakespearian sense then, as in "Here thy hunters stand. . . . Crimsoned in thy Lethee," from *Julius Caesar*. In which case the dabbling of the fingers is darker still. Not that the color is uniformly dismal: at the upper tip of the lapel it turns almost as pink as the painter's lips or knuckles.) And above all, its having the look of being the *inside* of something, turned or folded out, exposed to view by a new Doctor Tulp.

A lot depends at this point on how hard and fast we take the analogy to be between the body and the clothes it wears. Some kind or degree of analogy there is. The lapel is simply too strange an object to stay safely inside the circuit of sensible reference: it is too long, too wide, too regular, too stiff with what seems to color it, too translucent or anyway too insubstantial (stiff with matter but also strangely impalpable). These qualities seem to be metaphorical. Could we not say that what we are looking at in the lapel is a kind of imagining of one's flesh as if it no longer belonged to you, as it would look if it were put on display? And is not David's imagining of his body all the more extraordinary—here is where the ghost of Diderot enters— because it turns on a kind of literalizing of the key metaphor of *mind* in the case, that of inside and out. As if the model of mind were parodied—this would be Diderot's tactic—by being given back its physicality. Of course this would fit in with David's circumstances.

Maybe too neatly. Even with the lapel it is possible, and I think necessary, to flip back from a metaphorical reading to one in terms of resemblance. The dabbling and paddling are surely in part directed to an idea of the lapel's surface texture, the feel of a kind of cloth with a soft nap to it, perhaps velvet. The lapel has not to be *too* fleshy; just as the skull-like palette has not to be too much like a skull and the kerchief not too much like a bond or a bandage. Reference had better be preserved (it was never really under threat) and one-to-one metaphorical equivalence be kept at bay, so that the body be evoked less by a set of equations than a pattern of qualities, attached quite firmly to an object-world. On the one hand, qualities of rigidity and tension: the clenched fingers, the strict angle of the brush handle stabbing the picture's bottom corner, the stiff neck, the staring eyes, the general up-rightness against the chairback. On the other, in the winding folds of the *houppelande,* qualities more or less opposite: slackness and heaviness, an absence of tension, a falling and crumpling as of something deeply inert. It is the visual counterpoint that carries the information here: the way some aspects of drawing and coloring speak to an object held inflexibly in place, seemingly under pressure, and others to an accidental, almost florid occupancy of space. The body is figured by putting its two possible states in proximity—the one wound inside the other, so to speak, so that they cannot be held imaginatively apart. (A lot depends on the sheer elaborateness of the greatcoat's outlines, playing more and more variations on the theme of asymmetry; and some of this elaboration seems to have come late in the day. The peculiar, slightly crude rectangle of the far collar, standing up stiffly against the light, has the look of a last-minute addition painted in thinly on top of the dry ground.)

The *houppelande* is the picture's main metaphor of body, and as is the way with metaphors it is what conjures away "the" body—that is to say, a singular, literal, physical entity that ought to be there beneath the clothes.

The more we look the less any such entity seems possible. Where, for example, is the line of the shoulder nearest to us, covered as it is—squared off, but also skewed and miniaturized—by the sagging flap of the greatcoat and the shadow on its underside? (The arc of the shadow is not helpful.) How much of the other shoulder is visible? How sharply does the body recede? (The last-minute wing of collar adds to the uncertainty here. Salvator Rosa, whose pose and garb are not dissimilar, makes a good point of comparison.) How frail is the body? Is it frail at all, for all its having the look of being bandaged—tied together somewhat loosely round the throat, as if in fear of hurting a wound? Is David bull-necked and stocky, his jaw set and his muscles in spasm, or is he a wisp of a man with his clothes falling off him?

These questions, just because they do not have answers, lead on to the more general one of "unfinish." The lining of the overcoat is by no means the only part of David's picture that is done in a freehand, thinly painted way; and from time to time in the literature the self-portrait has been characterized as something David left (at a bad moment) half completed.[76] Maybe so, but the terms of judgment hereabouts are notoriously slippery.

First of all, as we have been seeing all along in David's case, it is a question of familiar qualities put in unfamiliar juxtaposition, and in particular of finish and unfinish migrating to the wrong sides of the line between inside and out. "Unfinish" is a quality of outsides, backgrounds, and vacancies. It is what normally takes place in a painting where there is nothing (much) to be painted; there affect is allowed to take over, and shows of skill, and reflection on the physical qualities of oil paint. There painting is expected to talk to its status as "mere" representation, and the qualities of an artist's markmaking can be savored for their own sakes. The marks—their rhythm, size, energy, randomness or what have you—can be taken metaphorically. David was a master of just this kind of language, in the portrait of the Marquise de Pastoret, for instance, or the background to *Madame Trudaine* (Figs. 16–17). But the handling of the background in the self-portrait could not be more unlike what happens in these two works: it is bone-hard as well as bone-grey, and remarkably discreet about manufacture. There are one or two "accidental" dashes of a darker grey visible towards the left center, as if spun off from the work of shading where the lining intersects the palette, but they only go to emphasize the neutrality of the background in general, with its steady shift of light from left to right. Handling turns up instead on the insides of things—the lapel and the collar, the palette, the chairback, the upper part of the overcoat's sleeve. The qualities of David's pictorial

FIG. 16. Jacques-Louis David, *Madame de Pastoret and Her Son*, oil on canvas, 1791–92. Chicago, Art Institute.

FIG. 17. Jacques-Louis David, *Madame Trudaine*, oil on canvas, 1793. Paris, Musée du Louvre.

handling are ingested into the object-world, so to speak, and end up doing a lot of illusionistic work, if the viewer will let them. It really is *good*, the feel of the velvet; or the look of the overcoat's outside—thinner, harder, maybe a bit threadbare.

Metaphor in this picture, that is to say, is strongest where the object-world is most salient. The evidence of touch may open up the circuit of sensible reference a little and introduce fresh meanings into it, but these meanings do not disturb the work of resemblance; on the contrary, it seems to thrive on them. "Handling" itself is a metaphor that points two ways in the English language, towards competent management or free manipulation; and maybe we could see the painting as playing with these antinomies. One hand is intent on keeping hold of a palette and paints which look liable to slip out of the realm of reference altogether into that of nightmare. Perhaps the slippage has already happened: the bits and pieces of the hand seem as much extruded by the palette as getting a grip on it, and the configuration they become part of is only half legible (and wholly uncanny). The other hand is the opposite—clenched and close to us, coming out of its sleeve as abruptly as Jack in the box, a bit wooden like the knuckles on the chairarm, and hanging on to its brush like grim death. "Handling," by the looks of it, is a potentially insubordinate business; it tends to have a life of its own. The hand is to handling as eye is to finish—eye meaning gateway to mind, of course. Handling is the quality in a portrait that seems bound up with— maybe to generate—the most potent metaphors of body, and to pull the picture's whole metaphorical language in the direction of materialism. (The fact of the body's *being* material is normally so deeply hidden in representation as to need the most outlandish of metaphors to bring it to the surface.) Handling in the David goes with inertness, impalpability, a twisting and doubling as of some visceral Moebius strip, a falling and dispersing, a congealing into a substance—like that of the palette—from which digits and integers emerge like pseudopodia. We are in the territory of d'Alembert's dream.

Finish and unfinish, then, are terms with a difficult history in David's work, which this picture in a sense condenses. It cannot be, to return to our starting point, that the unfinish here is a matter of the artist not having got around to completing some finite set of entities that would have made up the whole picture. The picture is whole as it is, and the "unfinish" part of the wholeness. We are back to the question of the swoln cheek. If there is always an excess or extraneity to representation, something in painting that has to be left out, then there ought to be a sign of that fact in the picture itself; a sign, that is, of the body, of what it is like to be matter. "Handling" is one such sign, and potentially a strong one; especially if the sequence of marks is set up so as to make it impossible to decide whether they are arbitrary, or expressive, or just out to evoke material facts like the nap on the velvet.

The rhetoric of this essay has been edging me steadily closer to the question of representation—itself, in general—and the question, which I do not like the sound of, had better be faced head on. Much talk of leaving out and metaphor there may have been in the last few pages, but is not the main thing that self-portraiture leaves out, representation *per se*? I am not sure there is a *per se* in this case, but let us proceed as if there might be.

Could we not say that ultimately self-portraiture has a special claim on our interest because it puts on show, not one but two (both) terms—or categories, or entities, or figures of speech (it is part of the problem that we do not know what to call them)—that seem to us fundamental, perhaps constitutive? The terms are "self" and "representation." But constitutive of *what*? Again it seems to be part of the problem here—part of its seeming depth—that there is no answer to this question that does not immediately fall into tautology. Let us say, constitutive of "the world," or "a world," or the possibility of their *being* a world for human subjects; the possibility of world-making.

The self, and the something we want to call "representing." And of course it is the presence of the latter that marks self-portraiture off from portraiture in general: not just that the object of a self-portrait is supposedly the subject that made it, but that that making is part of what is portrayed. The self is to be shown representing itself; and there is the rub; for "shown" cannot possibly be meant literally here—or can it? What does it mean, after all, to "show" representation? (And do not pretend the puzzle in this question turns, for self-portraiture, on the literal, practical difficulty of painting the hand that is doing the painting—the one that reaches out of the mirror towards the painting itself. This kind of paradox sometimes crops up in commentary. And no doubt it is pointing to an aspect of the case: there is a circularity hereabouts that the painter has to negotiate, and it involves putting in parts of oneself where they did not really appear—that is, in the glass. Or not in the glass as one painted, only in the glass as one looked. But in any case the mirror is never the arbiter in self-portraiture, not even for Parmigianino; and this whole line of argument becomes the more absurd the harder its literalism is pressed. Just how much of the hand is it that simply cannot be included? And how about the wrist? And so on.) Representation by its very nature has to be signified, not shown. Something— some criss-cross of aspects taken from what is on offer to the eye—has to be made to stand for it. The picture as a whole has to be readable as a metaphor of representing.

And could it not be, further, that the metaphor of representing will ex- actly *be* the self: that is to say, the moment of immediacy and self-evidence which, so the picture tells us, comes to lack any such sufficiency the mo- ment representing starts (and therefore never had it in the first place)? Is it that the metaphor "self" comes to stand, in a kind of relay, for the metaphor "to represent"? And to lend the latter its tragic aspect, its flavor of loss and dispersal.

Maybe so. There are for sure self-portraits that seem to fit the previous description, portentousness and all—the late Rembrandt in the Louvre, for one. Others, I think, resist its dialectic with a vengeance. For one of self- portraiture's most basic forms of make-believe is that the entity we are being shown is caught *in between* representation—in between the acts of putting paint on canvas, at the moment of pure sight of itself. The lengths self- portraiture will go to preserve this fiction are sometimes inordinate.

We happen to know, for example, from photographic evidence, that the self-portrait by Ingres at Chantilly, first shown in the Salon of 1806, then had the painter turning back towards an easel with a canvas shown full-face on it, and rubbing out a chalk outline of a head and shoulders—those of a lawyer named Gilibert (Figs. 18–19).[77] The set-up was ingenious, and seemed to open in many different metaphorical directions. Perhaps too many. In the end Ingres painted out the image of Gilibert and turned the hand that had held the duster back towards his chest. There had to be, as I understand the alteration, an absolute identity established between the painter's look out at us and his half-turning back towards a picture—it is now implied not shown, or rather, shown end-on and partially—that is going to be, strictly and exactly, *what the look sees.* What has to be erased, it follows, is the act of erasing someone else's portrait as if to put one's own in its place; for one's *own* portrait precisely does not exist in this space of trials and errors, making and unmaking, good and bad likenesses. That is the space of representation. A self-portrait is not just another picture of someone who happens to be you; it does not occupy the space of alterity at all, or it can be called back from that space; it will be One, not Other; the likeness will be made at (or of) the very moment the self sees itself, *d'un seul jet.* (Perhaps if what Ingres had been erasing had been a representation of *himself* . . . but even in that there would have been too many mirrors.)

FIG. 18. Jean-Auguste-Dominique Ingres, *Self-Portrait at the age of 24*, oil on canvas, exhibited 1806, altered before 1851. Chantilly, Musée Condé.

I think the root premise of Ingres's alteration is the belief that the self can be seen—from a center, from a place nobody else can ever occupy—and can be represented *as it is seen*. The belief lies deep in the practice of self-portraiture; it is the genre's orthodoxy. That does not mean that all self-portraitists share it. The genre has room for doing things in ways quite contrary to Ingres's, and can happily accommodate the picture of self as trial and error, or even the understanding of it as something produced by, perhaps subordinate to, a further reality called painting. One could bring on the Carracci again at this point, or better still a picture as normal and sophisticated as the self-portrait with his brother and sister done by the court painter Heintz die Altere—again it comes from the moment of Mannerism

FIG. 19. Charles Marville, *Ingres's Self-Portrait in Its First State*, photograph, ca. 1845–50. Paris, Bibliothèque Nationale, Cabinet des Dessins, Collection Armand.

(Fig. 20).[78] Of course I want in the end to argue that David's self-portrait does not stay in Ingres's space of belief; but the point is that it starts in such a space, and does not ever decide to abandon it—certainly not knowingly. It is more Ingres's picture than Heintz die Altere's. There is seeing and there is painting; even if the priority of the first term cannot be maintained in practice, this exactly does *not* mean that practice gives priority to the second—that it ends up prioritizing itself. That would not be David's way.

The raw paint on David's palette, to point to the obvious claimant here, is no more set up as the Truth of this picture's world-making than the glassy stare of the eyes. Some care seems to me to have been taken to make the palette a poor candidate for the Truth of anything. It may not be a particu-

FIG. 20. Joseph Heintz die Altere, *Self-Portrait with Brother and Sister,* oil on canvas, 1596. Bern, Kunstmuseum.

larly good representation *of* a palette, but that does not mean (*pace* one current critical orthodoxy) that it can convincingly be seen as "paint itself." What is it we are looking at in this area? Even a basic inventory of features soon runs into trouble. A thumb there certainly is, and four fingers, with a segment of jet-black shadow underneath the last three—presumably the opening of the overcoat's other sleeve. There is a patch of yellow on the palette, a patch of red, some pink, some grey, and a dab of white towards the center which has been mixed with just a touch of pink as if to do the fingers. Further up the palette are two peculiar diagonal bands or seams in dark brown, like the join-lines of a skull. Between the index finger and the palette there seems to be a third substance, less rigid than either, done in fluid streaks of grey-green with a darker, wavering line dividing the substance in two. Just above is a cusp or comma of deep black, which it would be convenient to read as either another dab of paint on the palette or deep shadow underneath it—convenient but not really possible.

The area is strong in physiognomic suggestions. It has almost the look of an anamorphosis, or of a face discolored and turned on its side. There is something like a mouth in evidence, or a nostril, or an eye socket. Maybe the thing has more the look of a brain than a skull; the inside of a skull, again the interior literalized, this time ferociously; the substance pulpy and the color unwholesome, looking ready to liquefy at any moment or give off a bad smell. Priestley's "substance not unlike a brain" might do as a description, though of course David's imagining of mind could hardly be further from Priestley's bland impersonality. This is *his* brain, decomposing between his fingers. The thumb through the hole in the palette—this is Michael Fried's suitably grisly suggestion[79]—is his premonition of the guillotine.

Now we can get the measure of David's difference from Ingres or Heintz die Altere. No doubt at a certain level of generality the subject of David's picture can be said to be "representation." But we are exactly looking in the wrong place if we think we have found the root sign of that activity in the palette. Or rather, the palette will do only if we accept it as one more figure of inside versus outside, one more uncanny literalization of the figural. If we want to elect a root figure of representation at all in David's picture, it would not be the palette but the lining; that is to say, the process of endless metaphorizing of the body which is so powerfully, naively *there* in the unfinished velvet—the inside turned out, the elaborate and strangely self-sufficient *doublure*. (Ingres is the perfect opposite of David in this. One of the great things to be got rid of in the repainting of his self-portrait was any suggestion of the self's unsatisfactory or unfinished belonging to a body, of the kind associated with the half-discarded coat in version one, above all its weird empty sleeve. Ingres is the last painter to let us have even a hint of swoln cheek.) David, I have been arguing, was prepared to let the sleeve stay dangling. His picture's proposal is this: that the first (and last) figure of representation is that process—that formalization—*by which the body becomes a form for itself*; a form it can represent to itself and therefore take place in; give an inside and an outside and inhabit as something else: that location or substance or side or shifting we call the self. The self, we could say, is a way of being in the body without simply being it. It opens the space of representation. It lets us look back at what we are.

I want finally to extract myself from the signs of the self's dispersal and multiplication in David's picture and point again to the obvious—the forces that hold the self together. The eyes, above all, are still masters of the body they belong to, and in a sense they still provide us with a narrative that gives the oddities of body a rationale: maybe one's material existence is overlooked and elusive in the way it is here, clothes neglected, hands clenched, neck

stiff, palette peripheral, *because* they exist as part of a fierce effort of attention; they are there to be gathered and focused in one terrible, totalizing
look. The look can leave out as much as it likes; it can occlude and approxi-
mate and give free rein to metaphor just because in the end it will posit itself
as the self and depend on the viewer to reciprocate.

I have been trying to say two things about David's picture. First, that it is
a strong (maybe shrill) example of a certain regime of seeing and understanding, one that has the "self" as its key term. Second, that it was done in
circumstances—immediate personal circumstances, clearly, but also the
wider ones of discourse—that made it possible for other accounts of self-
possession to put in an appearance. Notions of honesty and completeness
in self-depiction, coming, I believe, from Rousseau, intersected with a willingness to conceive of the self in material terms, or at least to imagine what
the terms of such a self-conception would look like. There is a flavor of
skepticism in the picture as undertow to its vehemence. There is an admission of complexity, again of a specifically late-eighteenth century kind.
"The idea of *Self*," as Priestley put it, "or the feeling that corresponds to the
pronoun *I* (which is what some may mean by consciousness) is not essentially different from other *complex ideas*, that of our *country* for instance."[80]
Which is to put the idea back in the melting pot, of course, rather than give
it a neat linguistic solution.

One of the difficulties that occurs here is finding a form of words for the
kind of coexistence of accounts I think is there in the David. I wrote just
now that other, non-standard imaginings of self "put in an appearance."
Did I mean round the edges of one at the center? Or in its interstices? Or in
the spaces for elaboration it provides as part of its strength? Do the features
of other accounts in the David end up interfering with the overweening
stare, for example, or even contradicting it? Does the circuit of lining and
palette take on a life of its own? Was I right when I argued earlier that the
fact of deformity in the face is converted by David's treatment of it into a
quality of attention or expression? Does the conversion ever take place once
and for all?

I am not sure. One of the paradoxes of ideology, we should know by now,
is that often the most effective efforts at totalization are also the ones that
give us a sense of why the word "effort" is called for. It is the completeness
of the ordering that brings to the surface what the ordering is *of*. David's
self-portrait interests me above all because it puts certain assumptions about
the self under pressure and gives us a glimpse of contrary ones. But it is only

a glimpse: the swoln cheek never quite emerges from the shadows, the palette and lining are as effective as they are because they are only half done. We can take them or leave them.

In any case there is one founding assumption of self-portraiture that David's picture does not question even to this extent. It is that the self is *singular*, and that questions of self-knowledge and individuality are properly posed as concerning monads, or monads plus their reflections. This is by no means an immovable condition of self-portraiture, and some of the genre's most celebrated moments are those that put it in doubt: Subleyras, for example, in another of his self-portraits, sitting in the corner of his studio presenting his picture as one among many; Velasquez in Baltazar Carlos's apartment; the hands of friendship reaching out in Poussin's picture of himself; Rubens with Lipsius, Raphael with the man with the sword. The problem, in other words, is not that accounts of self as a social construction (or effect of practice à la Heintz die Altere) were lacking, but that the subject of the self *representing itself* came more and more to be conceived in the singular, as a matter of looking from inside out. And again what is interesting is not so much the general fact of that happening, or even the social explanation for it—we are back to Taylor's "movement of interiorization," I suppose—as the process in detail by which the self was singled out, and the kinds of resistance it met up with. This is a separate history which I do not pretend to understand. But I want to take one picture from towards the beginning of that history and have it be my last point of comparison with the David.

It is the painting by Annibale Carracci most often called *Self-Portrait with Other Figures*, variously dated between 1584 and 1590 (Plate 15).[81] Annibale would have been in his mid- to late-twenties when he did it. He shows himself at work in an interior, one hand holding a brush and reaching out with it towards the surface of a canvas whose nailed side is all we can see—roughly the format Ingres adopted. Perched on top of the painter's other hand, which is drawn receding abruptly into space, there is a rectangular palette, its front edge catching the light; patches of red and white paint are visible on the side towards the painter, and even Annibale's thumb, again in foreshortening. The painter looks out and slightly down towards the mirror. His look is intent but at the same time measured, with a practical air about it. He is close-cropped, moustachioed, and maybe has a hint of beard; his collar with its flounces and little tassels looks decidedly stylish as well as informal—it contrasts just enough with the small boy's ruff.

Of course there is something that goes against the grain in this dry catalogue of Annibale's features and belongings; the point is that in practice, in
the course of actual viewing, they cannot be separated from the strange
texture of half-figures and quarter-faces on either side. To the left, cut off
by the picture's framing edge, is a man with a greying beard, his face turned
back a little further into the picture space than Annibale's, seemingly intent
on what the other figures are doing or maybe on what Annibale is painting.
He wears a soft hat, whose shape and texture set off the plain prose of Annibale's haircut and are answered by a more peculiar piece of headgear on
the picture's right-hand side. That hat belongs to a character, presumably
male, most likely adult, who seems to be showing something to the small
boy. His hand emerges from behind the edge of Annibale's canvas, holding
a knife or a brush, with what one commentator understands as a dollop of
raw black paint on the end of it. Is the boy being given some studio lore?
We cannot be certain, and surely were never meant to be. Whatever is
taking place between the three actors in the background—the kind of space
they may be standing in, how they relate to Annibale's doings, whether their
faces are meant to bear a family resemblance to his—all this is tuned to the
point of deliberate uncertainty. The painter and his canvas intersect and
interrupt some other possible sequence of figures, some narrative we are
invited to try to reconstruct—and find we cannot.

In a series of fine discussions of this picture Roberto Zapperi has refused
to admit defeat.[82] He wants to see Annibale's self-portrait as poised at the
crossroads of two other sixteenth-century painting types: the family portrait,
with its wish to establish the hierarchy and continuity of generations and
make a solid memorial of them; and those allegorical pictures which show
the Stages of Life. He agrees with the old assumption about this picture that
the other figures in it must be Annibale's next of kin: the greybeard must be
his father Antonio, the other man his brother Agostino, the boy his nephew
Antonio, Agostino's natural son. Dating, he thinks, makes this just possible.
Other scholars doubt it.[83] Zapperi is well aware, of course, that the power
of the picture turns on the way these lines of affiliation and identity are put
out of joint by the painter in the foreground, who is and is not (at) one Stage
on Life's Way, and does and does not belong to the family matrix. He may
think the picture refers specifically to other versions of the Stages of Life by
Giorgione—it is a part of his argument where a lot has to be taken on
faith—but he knows it scrambles Giorgione's codes. He admits there was
never a family portrait like this. Nonetheless he thinks he can reconstruct
from the documents the meanings the picture would have had for Annibale

and his immediate circle. It is, he believes, a kind of portrait of the artist as a young man, indeed with a trace of the Joycean to it; admitting the young man's social and familial uncertainties but also wanting to take a decisive distance from them. It puts the painter in a space between his father's persisting artisan identity—Antonio was a tailor, and in the picture, according to Zapperi, he is still wearing an artisan's hat—and his brother's wish to carry on the male line and complete the family's social ascent.

Perhaps. I cannot help thinking that Zapperi wants the documents, rich as they are, to do a little too much work for him; and in particular wants to use them to have the picture tell a story—one of discontinuity, maybe even antagonism[84]—where the point may be that "story" is no longer the right mode. The sign of discontinuity here is precisely that "story" is displaced by something called "representation." I think we should hang on to Zapperi's insight that Annibale has set up that new fiction at a sort of crossroads, in a space made out of previous ways of picturing the individual—as part of a family or at one Stage of Life. We could even extend the concept "family" to include other possible narratives of social place and affiliation. What these older narrations had in common was that in them any one particular person or personality—and of course it was often important to mark out a subject's unique humor—was phrased in terms of what the person had in common with others, first of all, how he or she was like them or belonged to them, and was passing through stages that others had passed through previously or would pass in due course. Something is happening to those terms in Annibale's picture. They are breaking up and becoming garbled, being overtaken by another kind of understanding.

So here *is* "representation." The opportunity Annibale's picture seems to offer—in a way that none of the other plural self-portraits I listed quite does—is to take a look at the activity called representation actually emerging, at the moment of first coming to consciousness of itself, still half-embedded in its matrix. What is it then that marks the activity off from its neighbors?

In the first place, representation seems to mean here pre-eminently *looking*—a kind of movement or trajectory that takes one out of the mere world, out of the space of exchanges and places that other people provide. It seems to be a matter of *framing*—of putting a set of edges around what one simply, strictly sees, and accepting the way that that framing may interrupt the figures and sequences which up till then had made a Life. The concept "Life" is displaced by the concept "Self." That is to say, a form of temporal imagining gives way to a sort of spacing. Personhood is no longer to be pictured as a series of sequences, inheritances, successful or failed impersonations—managing to behave oneself or not—but as an (immaterial) matter that takes place *now*, at the moment the self sees itself. Representation, so Annibale's picture has it, is picturing taking on the self's assumptions, maybe its very structure—borrowing the movement of interiorization and replacing a narrated (narratable) world by a space of cognition.

Of course the tone of Annibale's self-portrait is restrained, not to say austere. The red on his palette is not much in use. Ringing the changes on words like dissonance and displacement risks missing the point of the painting's attentiveness, its picture of practice going steadily on. All the same, steadiness is not the whole story. There is more than a whiff of oddity and arbitrariness in the air. This is as much a mirror picture as Parmigianino's, and in both cases the mirror is above all the figure of seeing's strangeness—its interception of the world in ways that are the opposite of what we know to be the case. Seeing, in Annibale, is still in the process of dispersing other patterns of understanding, pushing them out to the edge of a new frame. The self in the foreground is still provided with doubles, faces that seem versions of his own, himself as he would have been or might still become if he were content to figure in the family drama. (What we know of Annibale's miserable ending—he died in 1609 after years of melancholy inactivity—is bound to cloud our reading here, and representation thrives on such premonitions.) Annibale is in two places, or more than two; in a temporal as well as a spatial sequence; reproducing his father's features as much as representing his own.

This is, as I have said, a self-portrait done at some kind of crossroads, and to that extent it invites the viewer to speculate about origins—about the relations Annibale was trying to show in it, and why the "movement of interiorization" finally organized the world the way it did. Perhaps Zapperi is right. It may ultimately be that what encouraged the movement of interiorization was the fact that in complex societies lines of descent and affiliation become too tangled to be of much use, and that more and more people stand in Annibale's place—between idioms, loyalties, classes, identities. The move inside is a way out of incompatible, contradictory places in the world. It is a movement of defense. That would bring us back to David's situation in 1794, and the purpose he may have had, so early in his imprisonment, in getting Delafontaine to bring the mirror. It too was partly defensive; perhaps the practice of painting oneself is always partly a matter of setting up a space from which the world can be made to vanish. A self wants to be singular, wants not to look at anything else—maybe never more so than in David's case. But this is what makes it all the more remarkable that in practice, as the business of looking and matching proceeded, David's picture opened itself to such a plurality of worlds. Just as much as Annibale's it is full of other people: not just the others whose verdict David anticipated, but the others he was, the others he could imagine himself becoming, in some dreadful exteriority where representation stops.

THOMAS CROW

Facing the Patriarch in Early
Davidian Painting

Surely one of the best-known monuments to patriarchy in modern European culture is Jacques-Louis David's *Oath of the Horatii* of 1785 (Fig. 1). On the level of symbol, the oath-taking represents a passage of male authority from the older generation to the younger one. The triplet sons of the venerable Horatius swear that they will defend Rome to the death in battle with the champions of Alba, their cousins the Curiatii. This exclusively male exchange leaves the women of the family, bound to both sides by lines of kinship and certain to be bereft whatever the outcome, excluded and shunted to the side of the composition.

The imbalances within that arrangement, however, are not exclusively masculinist in their bias; they are also generational. The action of the oath itself preserves ultimate power in the hands of the non-combatant father at the expense of his sons. Their common gesture would make no sense if we did not understand the awarding of the role of champions to be provisional, at least to some degree, on their satisfactory demonstration of patriotic zeal. The brothers are summoned to heroism by their father; David creates a moment in which the weapons are still in his hands. In the next moment, the oath having been completed, the weapons will pass to the new generation, and only then will its identity with the patriotic cause of Rome be unshakable. That, at any rate, is the argument of the painting.

No oath-taking episode appears in any ancient account nor does it figure in the primary text behind the picture: Corneille's tragedy *Horace*.[1] In the ancient account as related by Dionysius of Halicarnassus, for example, authority has already passed to the sons. The father states forthrightly to the brothers,

It is time for you to show that you yourselves now have discretion in matters such as these. Assume, therefore, that my life is now over, and let me know what you yourselves would have chosen to do if you had deliberated without your father upon your own affairs.[2]

FIG. 1. Jacques-Louis David, *The Oath of the Horatii Between the Hands of Their Father*, 1785. Oil on canvas, 330 × 445 cm. Louvre, Paris.

The same is true in Corneille's play, the text that would have been most present to the minds of David's contemporaries.[3] There one cannot imagine that such a ceremony could possibly have been proposed by either father or son. To reflect on heroism in any degree before undertaking its duties is the role of the cousin, friend, and eventual victim, Curiace. The younger Horace's utterly unhesitating and unreflective response to his city's summons to battle is made clear by means of this opposition between the two characters. Though Curiace accepts his horrific responsibility without any failure of courage, his different makeup is defined by the temporal gap between horrified recognition of its implications and complete acceptance of its necessity. His heroism, though not in doubt, has to be summoned up and verbalized. No such gap exists in the thoughts and actions of his Roman cousin. One senses that any suggestion that an oath was required, or even appropriate, would strike the character as an insult, a slur upon his virtue.

The formal and iconographic source of David's oath has rightly been traced by art historians to Gavin Hamilton's *Oath of Brutus* and Jacques-Antoine Beaufort's subsequent treatment of the same subject (David had copied the latter work).[4] These paintings celebrate the resolve of the first Brutus, the legendary founder of the Roman republic. When the virtuous Lucretia is raped by the heir to the throne, Brutus swears with her husband and father to drive the royal family out of Rome and put an end to monarchy. The aftermath of that action would be the subject of David's next monumental painting, exhibited four years later, but the similarity between the two oaths indicates that he was already preoccupied with the story of Brutus at the time of his conception of the *Horatii*.

But the effect of inserting what is essentially the oath of Brutus into Corneille's narrative was to subvert the certainties of the latter and undercut its hero's exultant belief that the inevitably terrible cost of his valor distinguished it from mere bravery unto death. Brutus's devotion to the new law of the republic eventually compels him to order the execution of his own treasonous sons, and David's painting of Brutus and his family receiving their bodies is decidedly ambivalent about the costs of that heroic resolve (Fig. 2). The grieving women as a group (who alone catch the light), the unheard protest of Brutus's wife (whose outstretched hand anchors the entire composition), are treated with as much if not greater sympathy. The criminal violence that provoked the oath begets unspeakable violence within the family of the one who gave it.

The painting thus allows room for both halves of Plutarch's famous judgment on his action, that it was "open alike to the highest commendation and the strongest censure," that his character was "at one and the same time that of a god and that of beast."[5] The social body can come into being only by means of a temporary transgression of the condition of humanity itself, by the hero's achieving a state of existence simultaneously above and below the human. As the existence of society violates the continuum of nature, so nature will have its revenge. In the *Brutus* David belatedly found form for the troubling complexities he had evaded in the *Horatii*'s grand parsimony of incident. That resolution was achieved by means of an even greater imbalance between the generations, by making the father literally murderous and the sons already corpses. Every move by David within this thematic territory serves to overvalue the father's power and diminish the son's.

The mesmerizing force exerted by the elder Horatius on his offspring came to captivate David's closest and most favored pupil as well. Jean-Germain Drouais's extraordinary homage to his master's project, the *Marius*

F I G. 2. Jacques-Louis David, *The Lictors Returning to Brutus the Bodies of His Sons*, 1789. Oil on canvas, 323 × 422 cm. Louvre, Paris.

at Minturnae of 1786, restages the generational conflict in reversed terms (Fig. 3). The episode chosen by the young artist for his first major painting depicts its hero, once Rome's greatest general and long-serving consul, exerting the inner force that elevated him above other men. Having been proscribed by his political enemies in the Senate, the aged Marius, wandering alone and abandoned, has been captured near the town of Minturnae and placed under arrest. At first, in deference to Rome, the town votes his execution, but, as Plutarch relates,

And when none of their own citizens durst undertake the business, a certain soldier, a Gaulish or Cimbrian horseman (the story is told both ways), went in with his sword drawn to him. The room itself was not very light, that part especially where he then lay was dark, from whence Marius's eyes, they say, seemed to dart out flames to the fellow, and a loud voice to say, out of the dark, "Fellow, darest thou kill Caius Marius?" The barbarian hereupon immediately fled, and leaving his sword in the place, rushed out of doors, crying only this, "I cannot kill Caius Marius."[6]

311

FIG. 3. Jean-Germain Drouais, *Marius at Minturnae*. 1786. Oil on canvas, 271 × 365 cm. Louvre, Paris.

Having prevailed at this crucial moment, Marius wins the sympathy of the local people and is allowed his freedom.

The outcome of this display of inner character in the "hero," however, is that he raises an army, returns to Rome, and in retribution subjects the population to a reign of indiscriminate executions:

> When they had now butchered a great number . . . Marius's rage continued still fresh and unsatisfied, and he daily sought for all that were in any way suspected by him. Now was every road and every town filled with those that pursued and hunted those that fled and hid themselves.[7]

His revenge, however, brings him no relief from his constant fears and tortured instability of mind; increasingly anxiety-ridden and delusional, he drinks himself to death.

Caius Marius, as vividly characterized in Plutarch's biography, was a leader whose jealousy, intemperance, greed, and murderous ferocity helped precipitate the collapse of the Roman republic into bloody civil conflict. A poor candidate for any *exemplum virtutis*, Marius nevertheless assumes in

Drouais's treatment of the subject the position of the positive figures of male authority in David's previous paintings. Like the hero of the latter's *Belisarius Begging Alms* (Salon exhibition of 1781), he wanders alone and abandoned, an abject figure cast out by the society he had once protected in victorious campaigns against barbarian invaders (at one point he is recognized and given refuge by a farmer who had known him in his former greatness, as is Belisarius in the 1767 novel of that title by Jean-François Marmontel[8]). But these strong iconographic parallels only underscore the stark differences between the two Roman generals. Marius is even capable of exaggerating his poverty and dejection in order to deceive his enemies into underestimating his strength. The inflexible nobility of bearing and behavior associated with Belisarius is utterly foreign to his character.

Overlaying this strong but problematic link to David's *Belisarius Begging Alms* is its unmistakable formal derivation from the *Horatii*. Here the inversion, now on the symbolic level, is just as complete. The power and civic authority of the older male no longer passes to the youth who stands in the position of the champions of Rome. Instead, that force paralyzes the younger man and prevents him from performing a legal duty that would have prevented future atrocities and enormous suffering for the city of Rome. To reverse the significance of the *Horatii* in this way was no easy task for Drouais, and the development of the painting reveals a painful awareness of its inherent contradictions.

An earlier drawing of the complete composition depicts Marius as a well-favored, bearded elder, very like the old Horatius in appearance and expression. So does the sheet containing individual studies of both figures—presumably the culmination of a series of experiments—on which David wrote, "Change nothing. This is the good one."[9] But the oil sketch, as well as a compositional drawing squared for transfer, shows a strikingly different face, stripped of the beard with its connotations of paternal venerability, revealed as distorted and ugly to the point of bestiality. This face, in its extreme vehemence, comes close to caricature, but it is truer to the narrative than the stern but handsome countenance that, in a last reversal, Drouais restores on the canvas. That other face, it seems, could not coexist with the formal order of the *Horatii*.

The worried and difficult effort to adapt the story of Marius to his master's composition seems to represent an inevitably insufficient effort to claim a share in its achievement. But Drouais's painting, even today, seems greater than the work of an imitative and overly enthusiastic disciple. It has a power of its own that parallels an independent charisma possessed by its maker. He had a claim to the role of virtuous antagonist against entrenched mediocrity that almost antedated David's. And the thorny narrative of *Marius at Min-turnae* proved to be a vehicle for perpetuating that identity in the face of David's preemptive success.

In the years prior to 1785, Drouais, more than his master, had cast himself as the reincarnation of antique virtue in the arts. In this he was both exploiting and rejecting his privileged family background. His father was the successful and wealthy society portraitist François-Hubert Drouais. In that fashionable household, the son's precocious talent was noticed early and abundantly encouraged.[10] But his father's death in 1775 brought with it a precocious independence that propelled him far beyond his comfortable family milieu. With the cushion provided by an inherited fortune, he chose to fashion a life in which privilege counted as little as possible. Blessed, the accounts tell us, with wealth, good looks, musical talent, and social magnetism, he nevertheless rejected all their benefits for a ceaseless devotion to his art: "*Je veux être peintre, et je n'ai pas trop de toute ma vie pour le devenir,*" was his reported credo.[11] He neglected his health by working beyond normal endurance, painting all day and drawing into the night. To evade the intervention of his worried family, he hid in his studio, answering the door only at a pre-arranged knock to receive his frugal meals. Once, when prevailed upon by friends to go out in fashionable society, he is said to have dressed and reached the door only to catch sight of his image in a mirror and seize scissors to cut away the curls "which the wigmaker had fashioned with so much skill";[12] thus crippled socially, he could return to his work.

This mutilation of the social self to enforce dedication to painting is something one associates with Géricault, who was reported to have shaved his head in 1818 during his work on the *Raft of the Medusa* to make himself similarly unacceptable in society.[13] But Drouais's priority here indicates that there was nothing necessarily "Romantic" about that gesture. In the context of the particular ideological pressures faced by ambitious young artists in the 1780s, it made sense as a conspicuous refusal of privilege and favoritism. In his first *Grand Prix de Rome* competition in 1783, he exhibited the same kind of coldly destructive fury on behalf of an ideal; when his entry (on the subject of *The Resurrection of the Son of the Widow of Naim*) disappointed him, he sliced the canvas in half and brought the torn pieces to David as a confession of inadequacy.[14]

Drouais's formation occurred during a period when the example of Greece and Rome—most of all Greece—had become significantly more compelling than it had been for his master. There was a degree of intensity in the veneration of the ancients that had been unknown a decade before. David, as we know from his autobiographical statements, had yet to fall under the spell of the antique before his first sojourn in Rome.[15] There ought to be no surprise in this, in that during the early 1770s the spell was weaker than we sometimes imagine. The rigorous and chastened vision of antiquity advanced by Winckelmann had not immediately taken hold in France. It did not achieve real force until the 1780s when it ceased to be a matter of antiquarian or aesthetic interest alone.[16]

Winckelmann's sharpened distinction between Greece and Rome was deployed in this period to link social hierarchy and artistic decline. The decadence of Roman painting, the German antiquarian had argued, followed from the employment of liberated slaves as artists.[17] Servitude was the enemy of artistic achievement; once acquired, servile and ignoble habits could not be shed. In modern times, the despotic hierarchy of the official art system, along with the degenerate taste of private patrons, meant that the great majority of artists were blocked from the education and economic independence necessary to emulate the free-born ancients.[18] Imitation of the ancient Greeks came to be understood—in a way that is true to the spirit of Winckelmann's text—to mean emulation of a whole way of life, one in which the artist was a selfless representative of a democratic and egalitarian society. The object of imitation was not cold marble alone, it was the liberated imagination and social conscience deposited in the marble. The perfection of ancient sculpture was a small window left to us through which a lost, better form of community might be glimpsed.

The rise of this line of thinking led to two linked and self-cancelling conclusions: independence from patronage and favoritism was both an essential prerequisite to great artistic achievement and a nearly impossible goal in modern society. The artisan-class background of most recruits to the profession, their early apprenticeship and arrested formal education, left even the best-intentioned without the requisite inner resources to match the Greeks and provide stirring models of virtue for their fellow citizens.

This was the case, that is, until the Davidians changed the rules. And in terms of the newly-charged mythology of antique art, Drouais was the most fascinating figure among them. His image was mediated by French classicism far less than was David's, to the point that his very being began to seem at one with Raphael and the virtuous artists of ancient Greece.

That image and the challenge to established authority contained in Drouais's growing personal myth surfaced forcefully in the events surrounding the competition for the *Grand Prix de Rome* in 1784. The events of the exhibition and judgment of the entries were reported with unusual interest in the clandestine journal *Les Mémoires secrets*. In one report written prior to the announcement of the results, Drouais's painting *The Caananite Woman at the Feet of Christ* is singled out for extraordinary praise:

> Although all of the paintings are generally well done, one among them seemed to rise infinitely over the others and to be beyond all competition. . . . The artist responsible for this painting, so praised and so deserving of it, is M. Drouais. . . . He is only twenty years old; he already enjoys an income of 20,000 livres and so is motivated to work only out of passion for his talent and love of glory. With this noble spur and with the fortunate abilities with which nature has endowed him, he cannot fail to go very far indeed.[19]

The stress on Drouais's inherited wealth and social position indicates that more was at stake here than precocious technical competence. Because of his freedom from any need for official favor or private patronage, Drouais was free to work, as the ancient Greeks had done, for *la gloire* alone. This was the condition for his artistic superiority and a tense separation from the normal channels of encouragement. In the midst of this praise of Drouais, the reporter pauses to state that the director and *les anciens* were opposed to him. Whatever their inner feelings, his entry in fact carried the day without significant opposition.[20] The decision was greeted with extravagant, raucous acclamation by the Academy's students, who were awaiting the outcome in the courtyard. In anticipation of the choice, Drouais's peers had helped themselves to a battery of drums from the military stores in the Hôtel des Invalides, and they set up a din of martial celebration for the triumph.[21]

This outcome, however, seems only to have spurred the determination of Drouais's admirers that he be a martyr to official disfavor. It was widely reported in the press that his victory in the competition prompted the audacious proposal from the floor that he be made an *agréé* of the Academy (the first stage of membership) on the spot, in advance of his training in Rome and without the formal presentation of a *morceau d'agrément*.[22] Entirely predictably, the proposal was dismissed, giving the *Mémoires secrets*, along with the partisans of the young painter, the opportunity to lament: "They appealed to rules and customs; they failed, by a servile submission to these customs, to these rules, to provide a great example to artists and a great object of emulation to students."[23]

This outrage might seem misplaced when one considers that its beneficiary was just over twenty years old and probably had only two completed canvases to his credit—both set subjects from the Bible. A *Grand Prix* for a young artist normally affirmed the institutional framework that made his achievement possible; Drouais's was being constructed as a victory over the system. The exemplary qualities to be found in art were now seen to belong to the painter as much as (and in Drouais's case more than) to what he painted. Though the critic tries to make an indisputable case for the painting, the *émulation* that Drouais offered his contemporaries proceeded primarily from his person, from the gifts of fortune that underwrote his talent. And these gifts, the conditions of his virtue, meant that antagonism and misunderstanding would be his lot. He was marked as an exception in a state system that placed a premium on conformity and control.

Once in Rome, Drouais did his best to live up to the expectations of his admirers. And distance from Paris did not relax administrative control; it rather intensified and concentrated the application of discipline to be resisted. In the decade prior to his arrival, a new, more rigorous regime had been established for the prize winners housed in the Palazzo Mancini.[24] Every minute of the day was to be accounted for: students were to rise at five in the morning, attend prayer "with attention and modesty required," and descend at six for the day's two-hour session with the live model. After breakfast, there were courses in anatomy and perspective, with the possibility of copying elsewhere in Rome—though wandering far was curtailed by required attendance at the mid-day meal. The rest of the day was similarly parcelled out, with bed-check at ten in winter and eleven in summer. Along with this control over time and movement, extreme plainness of dress was ordained. Indeed the royal funds to which the students were officially limited would not permit much more. The great historian of the eighteenth-century Academy, Jean Locquin, has written of the guiding assumption behind these reforms: "Art is intimately aligned with virtue, and virtue cannot be acquired, so it is assumed, except under the rod."[25]

David had accompanied Drouais to Rome with the expressed intention of painting the *Horatii* in the inspiring surroundings of antiquity and equally out of desire to delay his separation from his beloved pupil.[26] Drouais's very large role in the work on David's painting suggests that he evaded much of this schedule during his first year in Rome.[27] In the latter part of 1785 the director of the Rome Academy, Lagrenée the elder, wrote to Paris in frustration that the young artist would not submit his work to academic supervision or account for his time.[28] When faced with the standard requirement that he complete an old-master copy for the king, Drouais balked. In September 1786, Lagrenée made the following report to his superior in Paris, le comte d'Angiviller:

Drouais asks if, in place of the copy that he is required to make for the King's collection, you wish that he do an original picture, which would belong to the King and which would represent all of the fruits of his studies in Rome, because he swears to me that he had never copied in his life and that it was a martyrdom for him to copy anything but nature. [29]

The Rome director passed the request along with guarded sympathy, noting that there was general discontent among the students over the requirements: "it is not always those who make the most beautiful academic studies," he observed in grudging agreement, "who afterwards make the most beautiful paintings." [30]

D'Angiviller, however, was having none of it; discipline would prevail:

We cannot observe without distress that the youth of today, more confident than ever, seems to announce that it is better informed about the means of acquiring talent than were the most celebrated men who have come before. . . . These gentlemen must persuade themselves that they are not masters, that, far from being fit to try their own wings, they still need to study, and that they can follow no better course, despite their repugnance, than to follow the rules which have been laid down with full understanding of their purpose. If some among them find it too exacting to conform, they can master leaving the Academy. I will find it easy to replace them. [31]

Drouais's bravado had been troubling these officials in other ways as well. He had stepped in, though unarmed, to rescue one of the Academy's servants from two attackers with knives. [32] The servant went away unharmed, and one of the attackers was arrested. Threats from the family of the arrested man, however, led to serious fears for Drouais's wellbeing, and the artist himself carried pistols for some weeks. This courting of physical danger was accompanied by a heedless abuse of his body through lack of rest and general neglect of his health—no light matter in as pestilential an environment as eighteenth-century Rome. The pursuit of perfection in painting was bound up with putting oneself at risk—from authority, from injury, and from disease.

On account of this tendency to extreme personal witnessing of virtue, Drouais came to represent, for his master as well as for the world, an exemplary integration of art and life. In this light, one senses more than ever the depth of David's famous lament after the death of his pupil from smallpox in 1788: "I have lost my emulation." [33] The older artist, during this time, was still playing a waiting game, enjoying a life in fashionable society and avoiding any insistence on the hard line in virtue. But Drouais had already began to construct an identity that would reproduce the zeal of the young Horatii. But virtue, however relentlessly pursued, was never going to be a substitute for tested experience, and David's triumph in 1785 with the *Horatii* would mean that an enlightened transformation of artistic practice no longer remained in the realm of abstract possibility. Drouais was left behind in Rome to ponder his future while David returned to Paris with his painting rolled and ready, and no one foresaw its impact more clearly than the bereft pupil. It was more a challenge to him than it was to the complacent history painters of Paris. Lest his identity collapse, he was virtually compelled to match it in practice—and at some level surpass it.

A young student in Rome had of course no business undertaking a narrative canvas like the *Marius at Minturnae*, the scale and ambition of which are clearly intended for the public arena in Paris. Drouais continued working in secret, neglecting his obligatory student work in order to throw himself into a project beyond his years and his station.[34] The painting, out of necessity, had to perpetuate Drouais's existing role as David's purer, uncompromised self. It extended the aesthetic of the *Horatii*—the dialectical sharpness, abrupt transitions, self-aggrandizing utterance, and singleminded stress on pride and inflexibility in the mores of ancient Rome—to a degree that eliminates David's small allowances for prevailing taste. As did his master's painting, it overrode questions of how the painting transformed its text. Yet the unattractive aspects of the Marius narrative, glossed over on the surface, remain in another kind of figuration, one that includes the relationship between the two artists. The latter's paralysis in the face of his master's example was something he was only too ready to admit. Writing later to David on his difficulty in finding a new subject, he stated poignantly:

I have found many fine ones, but they are all either ones you have planned or ones you have done. On the one hand, I should not and would not honorably take on a subject that you should do, and if I do one that is analogous to one of yours, I will be mocked. . . . Tell me what should I do? The finest subjects arouse me as much as they do you.[35]

The helpless Cimbrian assassin gets this fear and anxiety onto canvas, while the positive transformation of Marius's features allows Drouais to recognize and express a devotion that overcomes the fear and rivalry in their situation, the darker side of which had emerged in the rejected studies. But at the same time the fear and rivalry will not stay supressed. It is figured most of all in the cloak with which the young Cimbrian shields his face. That gesture was not present in the first study; it enters the compositional process as a barrier against the monstrous Marius, but remains when the face of the hero reverts to the canon of nobility. And Drouais uses it to turn his painting diametrically against its model in the *Horatii*. David's heroes are engaged in rapt attention to the tense point of contact between them. The vision of the spectator is vicariously engaged with the same intensity. But when that same spectator puts himself in the place of either protagonist in the *Marius*, the effect is blindness and isolation. Neither actor can see the other. Vision reveals nothing. The false face of Marius is one that Drouais refuses to contemplate; he will accept it, even love it, but at the same time puts an abyss, a cancellation of vision, between it and himself. The conflict between generations is affirmed and denied in the same moment.

For all of Drouais's agonized self-doubt, the *Marius* was a sweeping success in Rome, and the academic judges in Paris were likewise full of praise.[36] When it was put on display in the Drouais family home in the early spring of 1787, public response was even more enthusiastic.[37] The painting was capable of creating the excitement of a Salon triumph without the necessity of a Salon. Thomas Jefferson joined the stream of spectators and came away overwhelmed by the experience: "It fixed me like a statue a quarter of an hour, or half an hour [he wrote], I do not know which, for I lost all ideas of time, even the 'consciousness of my existence.'"[38]

The intensity of the painting, which is in large part a result of its unresolvable contradictions of meaning, thus temporarily banished rational reflection from at least one spectator otherwise eminently capable of it. As long as the painting was taken to be fundamentally about its creator, the impression it conveys of a bristling, barely contained energy could readily be understood as the sign of virtue condemned to perpetual struggle in an unjust society. This simultaneous affirmation and denial, vision and blindness, left unresolved at the heart of the painting, were visible signs of the strain involved in controlling the refractory materials that went into its making. They worked in the end to its advantage. On the level of ideological argument over the social role of the artist, the drawing, composition, and handling of Drouais's *Marius* exhibited a powerful coherence for its time that was a direct outcome of its deep conceptual and emotional contradictions.

Saying "I": Victor Cousin, Caroline Angebert, and the Politics of Selfhood in Nineteenth-Century France

Much current work in feminist studies and, more generally, in the study of groups relegated to marginal status focusses on the politics of selfhood: who assumes the right to be a speaking subject; who, in different settings structured by different relations of power, gets to say "I" and thus stands a chance of influencing the course of debate. In my research on competing theories of psychology in the half-century following the French Revolution, I have encountered an historical situation where this ubiquitous politics of selfhood takes on a peculiarly striking literalness. Because the primary arena for competition among these theories in France was the newly-established state educational system, the outcomes directly at stake included such matters as who learned the formal discourse of psychology, and what variety of it they learned; and who would very probably internalize a certain conception of the "I," or be exposed to no clear-cut conception at all. If contemporaries could imagine the late eighteenth-century hospital as a "healing machine,"[1] so too the nineteenth-century secondary school might justly be imagined as a machine for the production of selfhood. In this paper, I begin an exploration of the gendered nature of that production process.

A competition of psychologies arose in France in the wake of the French Revolution for two related reasons. First, guilds and other corporate bodies had served as a matrix of individual life under the Old Regime. As the Paris glovemakers succinctly formulated this traditional relationship in 1776, when the royal government momentarily threatened their collectivity with extinction, "Each individual has an existence only through the *corps* to which he is attached."[2] Hence, by outlawing and effectively destroying corporate bodies, the French Revolution problematized the nature of the self. Second, by ratifying the epistemological ideals of the Enlightenment, the Revolution tacitly mandated a response to the very problem it had helped

321

to create. It proposed the construction of a "science" of psychology, which would place understanding of the human mental apparatus on a firm, objective footing and thus rescue the newly detached individual from indeterminancy. In fact—and almost as an ironic commentary on the Enlightenment project—not one such definitive science but three emerged during the period 1790–1850: *ideologie*, which was the updated version of the sensationalist psychology of Locke and Condillac; "eclecticism," the name generally given to the rational spiritualist psychology of the philosopher Victor Cousin; and finally, phrenology. Each acquired a distinctive political affiliation, each participated in a protracted and highly charged debate over the unity of the self, and one eventually achieved an enduring victory over the others. I need to say a word about these themes before turning to the place of gender in this configuration.

In taking up the issue of political affiliations, I should stress that I regard these as historically contingent affiliations, that I am not arguing for any essential or timeless link between certain constructions of the psyche and certain political positions. Sensationalism, which depicted the mind as a blank slate inscribed by sensory experience, was the psychological doctrine associated with the Revolution itself: it was regularly invoked by the revolutionaries, and its insistence on human malleability was consonant with their call for radical social and political change. Thus a wide variety of new cultural practices inaugurated during the Revolutionary decade—the revolutionary festivals, the new calendar, the renaming of Paris streets—were publicly justified in the language of sensationalism. Their supporters cited the expected sensory impact of such practices on the "imaginations" of the individuals composing the national collectivity and the increase in civic spirit that would thereby accrue.[3] By the end of the eighteenth century, the French proponents of sensationalism had elaborated its byword "sensory experience" with new research into the physiology of the nervous system, thus enhancing the scientific character of the doctrine and accentuating its biological roots.

Its challenger, eclecticism, was the psychological doctrine of the *juste milieu*, the cautious and conservative form of liberalism that became political orthodoxy under the July Monarchy and that sought a middle way in politics between the abstract egalitarian ideals of the Revolution and the traditions of the Old Regime. Articulated by Victor Cousin, eclecticism represented an analogous middle way in psychology: it combined a limited reliance on sensationalism with—and this is the crucial point—an a priori belief in a self, or *moi*, a repository of self-initiated mental activity and free will, known through introspection and serving, as Cousin liked to say, as the "vestibule" to metaphysics.[4] Siding with traditional practice, eclectics opposed the conversion of psychology into a branch of biology, resolutely defending the linkage between speculative metaphysics and any investigation of the human mind. But they nonetheless evinced a characteristically modern attitude toward knowledge in their efforts, ultimately successful, to professionalize philosophy as an academic discipline in France and in their use of the language of science. Their philosophical psychology was, they maintained, a full-fledged scientific endeavor, grounded in observation and differing from physics only as a function of its more elusive subject matter.

Finally phrenology, brought to France by its Viennese founder Franz Joseph Gall, lodged all intellectual and affective traits in discrete brain organs whose relative size in any given individual was revealed in the contours, or bumps, of that individual's cranium. Entering the scientific mainstream under the July Monarchy, phrenology affiliated politically in two directions—either with a brand of liberalism to the left of the *juste milieu*, or with the nascent socialist movement.

Thus of the three psychologies, two had biological roots and situated themselves on the left of the political spectrum, the other self-consciously eschewed biological roots and just as self-consciously located itself at the political center. This non-biologistic, politically centrist psychology—Cousinian eclecticism—also seized the offensive in the struggle among the three.

Eclectics designated the unity of the self as the most important criterion in the construction of a psychological science. As Cousin observed, "character is unity!" Modern men, in contrast to the men of antiquity, were filled with "anxiety (*inquiétude*) because they have not made for themselves a self which persists. They are not themselves," but are rather dissipated in "everything that surrounds them."[5] Having indicated the primacy of the unitary self, eclectics went on to charge that neither of their competitors was able to provide theoretical grounding for it. The sensationalists could not because they built up mind from the raw material of atomistic sensations and provided no means for it to overcome its fragmentary origins; the phrenologists could not because they dispersed mental attributes among a series of discrete brain organs and likewise failed to account for a unifying force or locus of personal identity. Herein, said the eclectics, lay their own obvious superiority: by de-emphasizing the material (and thus fragmentable) substratum of mind, and taking instead the high road of metaphysics, they affirmed the unity of the self a priori, making it incontrovertible.

Whether as a result of its rhetorical strategy, its greater harmony with the dominant cultural values of the day, or Victor Cousin's genius as an academic entrepreneur, eclectic psychology defeated sensationalism and phrenology. Indeed, through the control that Cousin gained over the educational bureaucracy, his intellectual creation achieved something like hegemony over French academic philosophy and held it until the closing decades of the nineteenth century. A "philosophical regiment" trained by him at the Ecole normale and the Sorbonne obtained academic employment and carried his message ("our cause") throughout the provinces. At the insistence of Cousin, a subject called "psychology" was added to the standard lycée course in philosophy. No mere afterthought, this "psychology" was made the first substantive section of the philosophy program—a curricular innovation voted in 1832 by the Royal Council of Public Instruction, of which Cousin was a member.[6] Henceforth all the middle-class youth of France would be instructed about the *moi* and taught the meticulous introspective techniques required to explore it at first hand. A pedagogical manual published in 1838 by one of Cousin's disciples bears witness to the centrality in the philosophy classroom of this training in introspection, enumerating the difficulties the teacher might encounter in his efforts to lead his young charges to grasp the so-called "interior reality" (*fait intérieur*).[7] Certainly the Cousinian canon emphasized the ability to verbalize the psychological life: students, says the 1832 decree, should be able to "*describe* the phenomenon of the will and the conditions surrounding and affecting it."[8]

The students in question, those who attended the French lycées at this date, were all middle class and all male. Institutional arrangements thus reflected and actualized the belief that possession of a *moi*—a coherent self that could be known through interior observation and talked about, that was the source of will and willed activity in the world—was a prerogative of the bourgeois male. The class-bound nature of this inculcated selfhood does not concern us directly here. Suffice it to note that François Guizot, the main politician of the *juste milieu* and Cousin's close collaborator in matters of public education, championed the bourgeoisie shamelessly. He brought forth spontaneous applause at his Sorbonne history course when he evoked the heroic, wonder-working nature of the medieval bourgeoisie.[9] Later, obdurately defending high property qualifications for suffrage, he advised the politically disgruntled of the 1840s to get the vote by getting rich. In an earlier and less well-known pronouncement, Guizot also aligned instruction in selfhood with his rather narrow class politics: he named psychology as one of those "sciences" whose subtle and difficult subject matter precluded its popularization among the masses.[10] Clearly, the much-vaunted *moi* of Cousinian philosophy was tied to the ideologies of bourgeois individualism and bourgeois social supremacy. But if, from the eclectic standpoint, the working class was "unselfed," did women of all classes share this deficit? Was the Cousinian *moi* gendered in theory, as it was in institutional practice?

There was no logical reason why it should have been. When he severed in his own psychology the biological roots he found so distasteful in the sensationalists and the *Idéologues*, Cousin also denied himself a mode of argumentation which could readily construct an explicitly female—and inferior—mental apparatus. Out of his reach were those visceral "commotions" and nervous vibrations accompanying menstruation that, for an *Idéologue* like Cabanis in the first decade of the nineteenth century, interfered with the idea-generating mechanism in the adult female and inevitably beclouded female ideas.[11] The biologistic turn of Western thought at the beginning of the nineteenth century furnished powerful tools for the construction of gender inequality. But Cousin, committed to mind/body dualism and to the view that consciousness must be treated exclusively on its own terms, could not avail himself of such tools.

And yet female inferiority nonetheless managed to find its way into his Sorbonne lectures. I was first alerted to this, not by my reading of the lectures, where gender rarely appears, but by discovering the dozen or so letters addressed to Cousin between 1828 and 1832 by one Mme Caroline Angebert.[12] Written in the neat, regular hand of the bourgeois lady, these letters vacillate in tone between combativeness and adulation. Mme Angebert, a self-taught convert to Cousinianism, does not reveal much about the circumstances of her life[13]—she is in her mid-thirties, married to a naval official stationed in Dunkerque, and from time to time large numbers of house guests interfere with her reading of philosophy. (Other sources tell us that she was a small, thin, and elegant woman with large dark eyes, that her husband was more than two decades her senior, and that she tended to gravitate toward "great men," entering into a correspondence with the poet Alphonse de Lamartine several years later and providing financial support for his first political campaign.[14]) The absence from the letters of more detailed biographical information conveys Angebert's desire to commune with Cousin as one disembodied intellect to another. Indeed it could be said that the disembodiment of intellects is precisely her point, and her opening epistolary gambit with Cousin.

Angebert had been following Cousin's 1828 Sorbonne philosophy course. The latter was an intellectual event of such magnitude in France—Cousin had returned in triumph to his podium after eight years of silence imposed by the ultra-royalists of the Restoration government—that it inspired the adoption of a technology previously reserved only for political speeches: the lessons were recorded by stenographers and published in separate install-ments immediately after the delivery of each.[15] Cousin took overt pleasure in the excitement surrounding his activities, commenting to his fellow phi-losopher G. W. F. Hegel in August that his lessons were currently "roam[ing] the world" and that three thousand copies of the complete set had already been sold. He enclosed one for his Berlin colleague in case the text had not yet wended its way across the Rhine.[16]

In the lesson of June 12, which focussed on the laws governing the his-torical process, Cousin paused to commend his own brand of philosophy and, in passing, mentioned its enemies: not only the materialist "philosophy of sensation" but also a "sentimental and cowardly spiritualism, good for children and for women [but] fatal to science."[17] It was this passing com-ment, probably unnoticed by the vast majority of Cousin's auditors and readers, that prompted Caroline Angebert to write to the famous Sorbonne maître for the first time. She begins:

You do not have a more fervent disciple than I nor one, I daresay, who better un-derstands your sublime lessons. I seek, I adore the truth, and yet I am a woman. Judge the impression that had to be produced on me by the disdain that you express for my sex in assimilating it to childhood! . . . Filled with your enthusiasm for reason [the literal translation is "penetrated by you with enthusiasm for reason"], I followed you with the abandon of a woman and with all her confidence in the guide of her thoughts; but suddenly that so stirring and persuasive voice pronounces an anathema on my entire sex. I seem to hear you say to me, with an accent of contempt, "Woman, incomplete being condemned to an eternal childhood, you claim to be raising yourself to [the level of] philosophy?"

It is not merely that Cousin has wounded her pride. Angebert's accusation is more serious: he is guilty of logical inconsistency. There is nothing in the structure of his thought, she points out quite rightly, that justifies his "dis-inheritance of women from the intellectual patrimony of humanity." The Cousinian mind is ungendered, or as Angebert puts in nineteenth-century language, a man's mind is "composed of the same elements" as that of his wife, his mother, or his sister. And even if, she continues, these elements exist in inferior form in the female mind, "the distance between woman and man is surely much less than that between man and God." Now Cou-sin's philosophy holds that God has endowed man with sufficient intelli-gence to understand the divinity; how then could God have possibly refused women sufficient intelligence to understand the philosophical ideas of human males? Nor does Angebert's criticism stop there; she exposes Cousin's self-contradiction at yet another point in his thinking. She quotes him to the effect that human intelligence exists for its possessor not because there is a principle of intelligence in us but because that principle has been developed. Developmental vicissitude, then, not inborn constraint, is the secret of that intellectual inequality between the sexes that we observe all around us.[18]

Angebert is thus recalling Cousin to the authentic Cousinian position on the disembodiment of reason. He had adopted that position at the outset of his philosophical career, we know, because he believed it conducive to social stability and moral order—in a word, to the avoidance of renewed revolution. Angebert shares his opinion in this regard. Later in the correspondence, she will fearfully depict sensationalist psychology as having "taken refuge" among "the masses" and will describe with alarm "a new materialism" based on "physiology" that activists are propagating among "the crowd."[19] But if Cousin's "scientific spiritualism," as Angebert calls it,[20] served the national political agenda of both Cousin and his admirer from Dunkerque, it served Angebert's views on women far better than those of her mentor; and she felt duty-bound to bring that embarrassing fact to his attention.

Though potential antagonists, Cousin and Angebert found a modus vivendi—at least for the four years that their correspondence continued—by means of a slightly disingenuous compromise. He hastened to present her with a toned-down version of his position ("Do not, I beg of you, confuse a manner of speaking with the articulation of a principle"[21]). She agreed in her second letter that her characterization of his views of the female sex had been "a little exaggerated," that she "sometimes lets myself be swept away by my imagination," that despite her nearly constant preoccupation with "the destiny of women, their education, their social position," he had assuaged her doubts "in a satisfactory manner."[22] Cousin, who deliberately cultivated by post a huge network of (mostly male) disciples and admirers, must have been loath to let go a woman of such powerful intelligence—and one who was also so obviously infatuated with him. For her part, the autodidact Angebert desperately wanted a supervisor for her philosophy reading.

What is particularly interesting for our purposes is that Cousin inducted Angebert into his psychological method, which proved to be a revelation to her. In January 1830 she reported, "I have [now] done enough to convince myself that psychology is neither cold nor arid; on the contrary, I feel that I will be strongly attached to it and that it is very fruitful."[23] Several months later she told him that "my psychological ardor has . . . taken me into depths where I have trouble seeing clearly and can hardly recognize myself."[24] Eventually she came to describe her relationship to psychology in gender terms. Psychology is, she says, far less accessible to women than ontology:

> I am, and with good reason, much more fearful when I speak to you in the name of those great truths that we all carry within ourselves. It is far easier for me to follow you headlong into ontology, whose most sublime roads are now and then accessible even to the weakest woman, than to approach you on the thorny path of psychological science.

That women in general should feel more comfortable with the impersonal and imposing truths of pure being than with the intimacy of psychology may seem counterintuitive to us. But Angebert explains quite convincingly why Cousin's psychological method presents her sex with the stranger, more unaccustomed experience. In the case of ontology, she could, in her words, ascend "on [Cousin's] wings," thinking that the great principles she encountered were "made to be obeyed" and that "one would always work out a suitable accommodation to them." Never had she "dreamed" that the ground rules of psychology would be so different, that they would entail actively "coordinating" great principles and "verifying them in my own mind." Thus she concludes: "Almost everything in psychology was new for me."[25]

Angebert's comments testify to the efficacy of Cousinian psychology as instruction in selfhood, as a kind of intellectual exercise in which one not only learned the arcane truths arrived at by others but vividly experienced one's self as the source of truth, as the locus of validation. At first the techniques of introspection make Angebert feel like a "poor little thing," alone on "an immense sea of time and space"; later she learns to "steer my little boat myself."[26]

The letters suggest, interestingly, that Angebert's gender identity swung back and forth erratically during the course of her Cousinian psychological education. At times she accentuated her feminine nature and seemed to be deliberately attempting to feminize the discipline of psychology. For example, she criticized Cousin's purely logical derivation of the temporal priority of consciousness of an infinite God over consciousness of the finite *moi* by citing her own observations of an infant's first moments of life. "The child whose birth I witnessed [sixteen months ago], when he had barely entered the world, sought and seized with his mouth everything he encountered."[27] She called into question Cousin's comparable assertion about the priority of consciousness of the *moi* over that of the *non-moi* by invoking the image of a "child who gives himself over so passionately to the objects which entice him. . . . Isn't his mind more attached to the butterfly, to the bird he pursues than to the mental operation occurring within himself?"[28] Thus Angebert dissented in a distinctly feminine voice from Cousin's conclusions ("That, Gentlemen, is how things happen psychologically," he had confidently told his Sorbonne audience[29]) by giving weight to a kind of data that the *maître* had completely ignored: the everyday, domestic data about child development to which women were in the nineteenth century presumed to have privileged access.

At other times, by contrast, a masculine note predominated, implicitly or explicitly, in Angebert's ruminations. She experienced the newfound solidity and self-initiated activity of her *moi* as an internalization of the figure of Cousin. "It is you, who without your knowing it, enlightens and sustains me ceaselessly," she confided on one occasion.[30] Later she found herself addressing all her thoughts to him: "Sometimes I forget myself in dialogue with you, even when I am in the midst of society."[31] Still later she described him as "the sole link by which I hold on to a world in which I live mentally" and begged him to address her as if she were male, believing that only then would he offer a frank opinion of her intellectual accomplishments and potential.[32] But whatever the phenomenology of the production of self in Angebert's case, however much it entailed "piggybacking" on a male model, it is clear that Cousinian psychological pedagogy played a critical role.

The identity Angebert acquired during this period of apprenticeship persisted, leaving its mark on the prose fiction she wrote intermittently during the next decades. All three of her published stories have a first-person narrator, an educated and highly articulate woman indistinguishable from Angebert herself; all three have the same basic structure, culminating in the narrator's wresting an intimate disclosure from a reticent individual. Though it is the selfhood of the Other that these stories apparently emphasize, that of the narrator is in fact equally carefully delineated. She appears not primarily in the stereotypically female role of sympathetic listener but rather more in the stereotypically male role of authoritative interrogator whose questions (albeit gently posed in the "feminine" manner) cannot go unanswered. In her ability to elicit personal information, she bears some resemblance to those confessional-scientific experts who, in the first volume of Michel Foucault's *History of Sexuality*, abet the constitution of subjectivity.[33] And particularly in the first story, written in the late 1830s, the narrator is very much an independent, self-contained Self, undaunted by the main character, who is depicted as terrorizing almost everyone else in his vicinity ("Il soulevait autour de lui un *haro* général de la part des personnes sensibles, de celle des femmes surtout.").

It is this first story, chronologically closest to Angebert's epistolary involvement with Cousin, that also most explicitly casts the narrator as a Cousinian psychologist. We learn that she is attempting to solve a "psychological problem" (*problème psychologique*—the adjective was more unusual and had more explicitly technical philosophical connotations in the early nineteenth century than it has today). Indeed, it is "the most astonishing psychological problem I had ever encountered," a comment indicating that she habitually engages in this line of work; and it appears in the form of the main character, an exceedingly cold and haughty bureaucrat nonetheless given to occasional, out-of-character displays of tenderness. As her efforts to "read in his soul" become increasingly obvious to him, the bureaucrat calls her "Madame the Metaphysician"—a reference to the Cousinian linkage between perspicacity in psychology and mastery of metaphysics that Angebert evidently takes for granted among her readers and that supplies additional evidence of the Cousinian model that undergirds her thinking here.[34]

The impact of Cousinian pedagogy upon Angebert reveals the significance of the ordinarily gender-specific nature of that pedagogy. Cousin's training of Angebert was an extraordinary event and, we can surmise, one that he was not inclined to repeat. Although his psychological theory in no way necessitated it, Cousin held, as he was to state baldly in the preface to his 1845 work on Blaise Pascal's sister Jacqueline, that women are domestic creatures, men public personages. While both sexes had the same God-given intellectual faculties and the same divinely imposed obligation to cultivate them—up to this point his published views concurred with the egalitarian ones contained in his first, conciliatory letter to Angebert—the use to which intellect might legitimately be put was nonetheless radically different for men and women. According to Cousin, a woman should take no personal pride or pleasure in exercising her mind but should do so only for the sake of the man in her life. She should acquire the knowledge that "permits her to enter into spiritual rapport [with her partner], to understand his work . . . to feel his sufferings in order to soothe them." Cousin summed up his position in a laconic dictum: "I make a sharp distinction between the woman of wit and learning (*femme d'esprit*) and the woman author. I infinitely honor the one, and I have little taste for the other."[35] Women could, in other words, tastefully deploy intellect in the context of the married couple, where they played an ancillary, collaborative role; but they could not be the freestanding, self-possessed subjects of their own intellectual activity.

If the philosophy classroom of the nineteenth-century lycée routinely furnished training in selfhood to bourgeois male youths, would the French state bestow this same gift of selfhood on their female counterparts when, in the early years of the Third Republic, it founded a national system of lycées for girls? While it is highly unlikely that republican educators explicitly connected academic philosophy with selfhood, they were certainly aware of the incomparable prestige that philosophy enjoyed in the secondary school curriculum. The *classe de philosophie*, which the student took during his third year, was regularly described as the "summit" or "crown" of lycée education.[36] Its supremacy was variously glossed. Some educators believed that a certain kind of philosophical temperament was the hallmark of a quintessential Frenchness:

Philosophy . . . has a salient place in our classrooms, after all, because it responds to the clearest needs of the national genius. To be sure, the French do not have a head for metaphysics like the Germans do; on the other hand, our literature is permeated with philosophy, as are our politics. For the French are perhaps the only people in the world to have made a philosophical revolution—one based on principles and ideas rather than on interests—and it is that which constitutes the moral personality and the grandeur of our country. . . . Hence the necessity that all our education be philosophical and that it lead our pupils, by a natural preparation, to that special course in philosophy, the culmination and completion of the enterprise (*l'achèvement de l'oeuvre*).[37]

Others cited the unique interpersonal dynamics of the philosophy classroom. While most lycée professors faced a horde of indifferent pupils whose names they hardly knew, "the philosophy professor has his own class, his own pupils, with whom he passes an entire year in intimate and regular commerce, and over whom he consequently possesses all the influence that he knows how to exercise."[38] Given these elite and nation-defining connotations of the *classe de philosophie*, it is significant that educators of the early Third Republic took pains to keep that class beyond the reach of their newly invented creature, the female lycée student.

The parliamentary commission that prepared the 1880 legislation excluded philosophy from the curriculum of the new lycées on the grounds that "all the philosophic knowledge usefully taught to girls is already included in moral instruction, in history, or in literary history."[39] From the rather telegraphic minutes of their proceedings, we can infer that they meant by this pronouncement, first of all, that girls simply had less practical use for philosophic knowledge because their future vocation lay in being "mothers and housewives" (albeit intellectually cultivated ones) rather than *savantes*.[40] But the commissioners gave second meaning to the lack of "usefulness" of a philosophy course for girls, a meaning imbued with the anticlerical aims that shaped so many late nineteenth-century French government policies on women.

At the meeting in question, Paul Bert expressed the wish that the new curriculum feature "moral instruction"; this abbreviated version of the traditional rubric "moral and religious instruction" would, he argued, "indicate from the outset the spirit informing this new education." Camille Sée found Bert's formula inadequate and urged that the term "philosophy" be included as well, but Bert—whose viewpoint eventually ruled the day— warned against the employment of a term which had already given rise to "so many objections." If we attempt to decode this interchange, it appears that Bert believed that suppressing the phrase "religious instruction" would send to parents and clerics the entirely appropriate message that the Third Republic, committed to laicization, intended to remove religious training from the state schools and confine it to voluntary, extracurricular settings. But he also apparently believed that replacing "religious instruction" with "philosophy" would be going too far. Because the clergy and its sympathizers had long alleged philosophy to be a subject matter corrosive of religious faith, such a maneuver would identify the curriculum not merely as religiously neutral but as actively antireligious and would thus generate unnecessary hostility.

In other words, *lycéennes* were to be deprived of a philosophy class in part because a prudent anticlerical politics dictated that the state accord a measure of respect to the longstanding bond between the Church and the female sex and that it not appear to be embarking upon the aggressive dechristianization of women. The conflation of the commissioners' two meanings tempered the discriminatory nature of the policy: girls were to be taught only a smattering of philosophy not because they were incapable of absorbing more but because philosophy—and especially philosophy for girls—was a red flag to influential segments of the public. Bert and his colleagues have here presented a paradigmatic version of early Third Republican reasoning on women's questions, with anticlerical requirements entering the picture as a justification for antifeminist policy decisions. In much the same way, for example, many republicans later refused to support women's suffrage, not because of any intrinsic defect of women but because the female vote would, they contended, vastly expand the political power of the clergy.[41]

The decision to omit a fullfledged philosophy course from the new lycées translated in practice into a course in morals, beginning in the third year and meeting a mere hour a week; in the fifth and final year it was devoted to a consideration of "Elements of psychology applied to education." A pathetically watered down version of the psychology given pride of place in the Cousinian *programme*, this psychology course for girls contained a brief mention of "Voluntary activity: liberty and personality" under an unintentionally comic heading which included such other forms of "activity" as the "instinctive" and the "gymnastic." There was no mention of the *moi* or of introspective technique.[42]

The absence of the *moi* from female secondary education must, of course, be assessed in context, by comparison not with the original Cousinian *programme* but with the reformed philosophy *programme* for boys promulgated in 1880 in an effort to harmonize the lycée curriculum with the ideals of the new Republic. Given the positivist bent of the Republic, and given the traditional role of the Cousinian *moi* as a jumping-off point to metaphysics, one might have reasonably expected the *moi* to disappear at this date from the instruction for boys. Yet it retained its old curricular centrality.[43] Some contemporary commentators alleged that it had undergone an epistemological alteration. Because the scientific wisdom of the later nineteenth century prescribed that psychology be freed from its earlier metaphysical trappings,

[t]he idea of the *moi*, the idea of the external world and the idea of God are no longer [in the new curriculum] laid down a priori (*comme des données primitives*), but are set forth simply as the products of intellectual activity. One will no longer be spared the task of seeking to explain, if one can, how these ideas are formed, modified, corrected.[44]

But others persuasively argued that the new *programme* represented continuity far more than change, and they adduced in support of this assertion that its chief author was none other than Paul Janet, "former secretary of Monsieur Cousin, very attached to the traditions of the [Cousinian] spiritualist school though . . . open to new ideas."[45]

This debate over the precise import of the 1880 reforms is probably beside the point for us. Even if the *moi* presented to *lycéens* under the early Third Republic was in the process of subtle epistemological mutation and was no longer as fully anchored in the nature of things as its pure Cousinian precursor had been, the crucial fact for our purposes is that *lycéens* were still receiving serious instruction in the *moi*; indeed, the educational bureaucracy had reaffirmed the stipulation that they do so at just the moment when it deemed that same psychological entity off limits to *lycéennes*. According to the terms of the official state curriculum, selfhood remained an exclusively masculine affair.

Although I have not looked here at the gender content of the two "losing" psychologies—sensationalism and phrenology—this consideration of the "winner" makes a point that might best be called Foucauldian in that it highlights the symbiosis of power and knowledge. The new human science of psychology did not in nineteenth-century France merely describe the female mental apparatus and thus mirror and contribute to a climate of opinion about women. Instead, institutionalized in the national educational system, psychology actively produced gender by providing training in selfhood to males and denying it to females. An elaborate public mechanism helped to construct, along strict sex (and class) lines, those private, interior spaces where individuals encounter themselves.

Since this argument, which hinges on a claim about the constitutive nature of discourse, is readily susceptible to misunderstanding, I ought to clarify it. I am *not* arguing that Cousinian psychology was responsible for giving young bourgeois males a "sense of self" broadly and figuratively construed—that is, a sense of being persons of some note, esteemed in their society, mattering more than women or run-of-the-mill poor people. A variety of other factors and cultural practices obviously produced and continually reinforced that component of their identities. My argument is rather that Cousinian psychology supplied such youths with an *explicit* language of selfhood, a way of thinking and speaking about their "selves" per se that was qualitatively different from a "sense of self" and that the linguistically unmediated experience of having money or being an object of deference could not alone supply. Thus Cousinian psychology did not simply and superfluously reflect a prior economic or social reality that made someone a person to be reckoned with. Instead, functioning much like Freudian psychoanalytic discourse in twentieth-century America, it constituted the particular terms in which being a self was lived out by a particular population: in this case, the male bourgeoisie of nineteenth-century France.

In the story as I have told it, Caroline Angebert holds the place of the exception that proves the rule. Had I accentuated another plot line, her role might have been characterized primarily as that of the proto-feminist or the feminist *manqué*. After all, by drawing attention to the internal inconsistencies of Cousin's philosophical psychology as applied to women, Angebert adumbrated—in the entirely discreet forum of a private correspondence with the author himself—a basic intellectual strategy that modern feminists would make audible and public. One of her own contemporaries, a woman who espoused moderate feminist views in the 1830s, even mentioned Cousin when angrily describing in a lecture the different criteria typically brought to bear on male and female speakers. Charismatic male intellectuals like Cousin, said Louise Dauriat, routinely got away with logically flawed arguments; unnoticed when uttered by authoritative men, those same arguments would be subjected to merciless criticism if they emerged from the mouth of a woman.[46] In our own day, the French feminist philosopher Michèle Le Doeuff has in effect generalized Angebert's analysis of Cousin, observing that "every theoretician falls short of his own standards whenever he speaks of women." Standing publicly for the principles that obsessed Angebert in private, Le Doeuff has decried the dual sexism of French philosophy: the "debatable things" about women still being incorporated into the writings of late twentieth-century male philosophers; the virtual exclusion of women from the institutionalized enterprise of philosophy.[47]

But while Angebert has all the credentials of a feminist precursor, she is less historically significant when assigned that role than when cast as a woman who defied in exceptional fashion the prevailing regimen of power/ knowledge in nineteenth-century France. Poaching upon the masculine terrain of Cousinianism, she quietly appropriated the language of selfhood that it offered. And as the exception that proves the rule, she enables us to see plainly what that regimen of power/knowledge ordinarily withheld from members of her sex. When her husband retired from the navy in 1835 and the couple left Dunkerque, Angebert wrote a poem of farewell addressed to the town. Her choice of words assumes added meaning in light of the Cousinian psychological education she had received—or, more accurately, engineered—there: "In moving away from you, it is my past, *myself* (*moi-même*), alas! that I abandon."[48]

MICHAEL S. ROTH

Freud's Use and Abuse of the Past

The recovery from loss is, in Emerson, as in Freud
and in Wittgenstein, a finding of the world, a returning of it, to it. The price is necessarily to give
something up, to let go of something, to suffer
one's poverty.
>   Stanley Cavell, "Finding as Founding"

Some impression of the event must have been left
inside me. Where is it now?
>   Freud to Wilhelm Fliess, Oct. 15, 1897

I

Let us begin with two sentences from Freud. The first is from his early
work with Joseph Breuer, *Studies on Hysteria* (1895): "Hysteric patients suffer mainly from reminiscences." The second is from *Three Essays on Sexuality* (1905): "The finding of an object is in fact a refinding of it." The
difficulties in defining the psycho-analytic use of the past, and its relation to
history, can be grasped through an examination of the tension between these
two sentences. On the one hand, memory can be the core of neurotic pain,
and on the other hand, pleasure is always sought along routes that carry us
through our histories. From Freud's perspective, the past surges up in our
memories as the stuff of both pathology and desire. We may abuse the past
by turning it against our own lives, by using it as fuel for our suffering.
Psycho-analysis would allow us to acknowledge, to claim, a past with which
we can live, to grasp our desires in relation to our pasts. Or so I have argued
in relation to the key concepts in Freud's oeuvre: psycho-analysis is a form
of history.[1]

In *Studies on Hysteria*, Breuer and Freud are committed to the view
that the reminiscences that cause hysterical suffering are historical in the

sense that they are linked to actual traumas in the patient's life. The affect associated with the past trauma can not be acknowledged, and the amnesia which results means that the force of that affect becomes dammed up. "The injured person's reaction to the trauma only exercises a completely cathartic effect if it is an *adequate* reaction," they wrote.[2] The past which continues to wound is the past which originally found no outlet. Denied an "appropriate" response, the ghost of past experience continues to haunt the hysteric:

The ideas which have become pathological have persisted with such freshness and affective strength because they have been denied the normal wearing-away process by means of abreaction and reproduction in states of uninhibited association.[3]

Through the uninhibited (free) association of the talking cure, the ghost is laid aside.

Studies on Hysteria belongs to the pre-history of psycho-analysis. That is, the analysis of the case studies was still greatly beholden to the seduction theory which Freud abandoned in 1897. This theory held that a neurotic had passively undergone a sexual experience with an adult, and that this experience became "reactivated" with the onset of puberty. The memory is then charged with libido and confined to the unconscious.[4] Until 1897, Freud was committed to the idea that the traumatic memory referred to a real passive experience which was later sexualized. In other words, he believed that the memory which remained charged with affect contained "indications of reality."

As Freud began to emphasize the importance of the unconscious and of infantile sexuality, he abandoned the seduction theory in favor of a science of interpretation which made meaning out of memory in the service of the present.[5] But what of the notion that hysterics suffer from reminiscences? Interestingly enough, Freud holds to this notion, repeating it in his 1909 lectures at Clark University. The inability to cut oneself off from something in the past was for Freud an important sign of pathology. "*Our hysterical patients suffer from reminiscences*," he repeated. "Their symptoms are residues and mnemic symbols of particular (traumatic) experiences."[6] Thus, although Freud would change many of his ideas during the course of his life, his fundamental interest in the ways the past can cause pain in the present was a stable component of his psycho-analysis. Why do some of us remain stuck in a way of being that is inappropriate to our present? Why do some of us not use the past in the service of life, but instead turn it into a poison from which we persist in seeking nourishment?

In this same lecture at Clark, Freud illustrates neurotic reminiscence in the following way:

But what should we think of a Londoner who paused today in deep melancholy before the memorial of Queen Eleanor's funeral instead of going about his business in the hurry that modern working conditions demand or instead of feeling joy over the youthful queen of his own heart? Or again what should we think of a Londoner who shed tears before the Monument that commemorates the reduction of his beloved metropolis to ashes although it has long since risen again in far greater brilliance? Yet every single hysteric and neurotic behaves like these two unpractical Londoners. Not only do they remember painful experiences of the remote past, but they still cling to them emotionally; *they cannot get free of the past and for its sake they neglect* what is real and immediate.[7]

Here Freud points to the core of the psycho-analytic conception of neurosis: an unpractical bondage to the past. The emphasis on "practicality" was a deliberate attempt to play to the sympathies of his American auditors. Attention to real and immediate things is practical, and such attention may require the kind of freedom from the past that was at the heart of American culture (especially as seen by Europeans). Psycho-analysis, Freud wanted his New England auditors to know, was on the frontier of science aiming at freedom from the past.

Not all ties to the past are bondage, however; not all painful reminiscences are signs of neurosis. Immediately after this passage in his 1909 Clark Lectures, Freud mentions mourning as a normal fixation to the memory of a dead person. Unlike the example of his Londoners, Anna O.'s "traumas dated from the period when she was nursing her sick father and . . . her symptoms can only be regarded as mnemic signs of his illness and death. Thus they corresponded to a display of mourning," Freud continued, "and there is certainly nothing pathological in being fixated to the memory of a dead person so short a time after his decease; on the contrary, it is a normal emotional process."[8] Mourning is the process through which one disconnects from a painful loss in the recent past. Psycho-analysis is the process through which one disconnects from a painful desire in the distant past. But how are the two related?

II

Freud knew something about taking care of a sick parent, and his comments on Anna O.'s reaction to her father's death should be seen in light of his own experience as a son who witnessed his father's slow decline. In the summer of 1896, the extremely ill Jacob Freud was in the resort of Baden, just outside of Vienna. His son feared to leave him for any length of time, knowing that the aged father was near the end. Freud announced the news to his friend Fliess on October 26, 1896: "Yesterday we buried the old man, who died during the night of October 23. He bore himself bravely to the end, just like the altogether unusual man he had been. . . . All of it happened in my critical period, and I am really quite down because of it."[9]

Freud was surprised by the depth of his reaction to his father's death. He was "prepared" for the demise of the elderly patriarch for months: "I don't begrudge him the well-earned rest, as he himself wishes it," Freud wrote.[10] Nevertheless,

I find it so difficult to write just now that I have put off for a long time thanking you for the moving words in your letter. By one of those dark pathways behind the official consciousness the old man's death affected me deeply. . . . By the time he died, his life had long been over, but in my inner self the whole past has been reawakened by this event.

I now feel quite uprooted.[11]

After having revealed his feelings and his lack of control over them to his good friend, Freud immediately tries to find something else to discuss. "Otherwise," he begins to try to change the subject (as if there were something else worthy of inclusion in the letter), and he does say something about his research, about his practice, about his desire to talk with Fliess. But he speaks only his own feeling of isolation, of aloneness, and of being misunderstood. His father is dead. At the end of the letter, he returns to the only subject there can be for him at that moment, an absent subject:

I must tell you about a nice dream I had the night after the funeral. I found myself in a shop where there was a notice saying:

> You are requested
> to close the eyes.

I recognized the place as the barbershop I visit every day. On the day of the funeral I was kept waiting and therefore arrived a little late at the house of mourning. At that time my family was displeased with me because I had arranged for the funeral to be quiet and simple, which they later agreed was quite justified. They were also somewhat offended by my lateness. The sentence on the sign has a double meaning: one should do one's duty to the dead (an apology as though I had not done it and were in need of leniency), and the actual duty itself. The dream thus stems from the inclination to self-reproach that regularly sets in among the survivors.[12]

Freud reports the dream to Fliess on November 2, eight days after the funeral. Freud is a latecomer, someone who gets stuck in one of his ritual habits and fails to arrive on time. We can see here one of his obsessions from this period of his life: that he had failed to *arrive*, that his professional ambitions were coming to naught. This picture of himself is connected to an episode in his childhood involving his father which was to become a source for several dreams. Freud reports that as a child he had "disregarded the rules which modesty lays down and obeyed the calls of nature in [his] parents' bedroom. His father spoke the foreboding words, "The boy will come to nothing."[13] In 1896 these words find deep echoes in the forty-year-old neurologist who feels at best ignored by the world, and at worst persecuted as one who practices "gruesome, horrible, old wives' psychiatry."[14] Freud is responsible for the funeral arrangements; the final duty to the old man is his. But he is late (again?); the family must close its eyes to his performance, even as he manages to fulfill his obligations.

The same dream is reported in *The Interpretation of Dreams* as an example of an either/or dilemma in interpretation. I quote the report in full in order to show its differences from the earlier version:

During the night before my father's funeral I had a dream of a printed notice, placard or poster—rather like the notices forbidding one to smoke in railway waiting rooms—on which appeared either

"You are requested to close the eyes"

or, "You are requested to close an eye."

I usually write this in the form:

the
"You are requested to close   eye(s)."
an

Each of these two versions had a meaning of its own and led in a different direction when the dream was interpreted. I had chosen the simplest possible ritual for the funeral, for I knew my father's own views on such ceremonies. But some other members of the family were not sympathetic to such puritanical simplicity and thought we would be disgraced in the eyes of those who attended the funeral. Hence one of the versions: "You are requested to close an eye," i.e., to "wink at" or "overlook." Here it is particularly easy to see the meaning of the vagueness expressed by "either—or." The dream-work failed to establish a unified wording for the dream-thoughts which could at the same time be ambiguous, and the two main lines of thought consequently began to diverge even in the manifest content of the dream.[15]

In this report, the problem of being the latecomer drops out. It is perhaps for this reason that Freud now remembers having the dream *before* the funeral. He is anticipating the reaction of his family members, not provoking it by his failure to arrive (on time). And the dream is, as Freud now reports it, clearly expressing a wish: that his puritanical arrangements will be overlooked by those family members wanting to put on a show.

In his letter to Fliess, the dream begins with a notice in the very familiar barber shop, and ends in the funeral. In *The Interpretation of Dreams*, it begins and ends with the notice. We are no longer in a barber shop, however; we are in a place "like those railway waiting rooms." And the notice has the authority of a command: *Rauchen Verboten!* although it has the syntax of a request. Freud does not discuss this aspect of the dream; he stays at the level of "winking" and "overlooking." But what has *he* overlooked?

He has overlooked the filial piety expressed in his letter and in his dream as reported to Fliess. He has also closed an eye to the connection between that piety and the guilt of one who comes too late, of one who continues to live after the father. When first reporting the dream, Freud is expressing his pain, his isolation, and his frustration to his close friend. Despite these feelings, or perhaps because of them, he also recognizes the guilt of continuing to live (and to feel these things) after such an important loss. When Freud wrote his friend after the funeral, the past stirred within him, he was torn up by the roots. From whence did the new relationship to the past and to this dream emerge?

Freud began systematic self-analysis sometime in the late spring or early summer of 1897, that is, less than a year after the death of his father. The sustained self-analysis was not undertaken for theoretical purposes only; he was afflicted with neurotic conflicts resulting in painful symptoms. In the 1890s Freud suffered from important mood swings, migraines, anxiety attacks, and phobias.[16] Given the theory he was developing at the time, in order to alleviate these symptoms he had to discover their roots, their development, and hence their significance. But how much self-scrutiny is "appropriate," or "practical"? Feeling oneself "torn up by the roots" might be a normal facet of mourning, of disconnecting from the past that one feels stirring within. Why consider this in relation to other conflicts? How to know if intensive self-scrutiny is not merely a delay from real work, an obstacle sought out by perennial latecomers, or an addiction, like smoking, which can prove most intense just when it is forbidden?

The only way to answer these questions was to risk the analysis. There was no knowing before the work was through. Mourning became work for Freud, as his reactions to his father's death became the substance of his understanding of desire, guilt, and the use and abuse of the past generally. In a manuscript draft sent with a letter to Fliess on May 31, 1897 (a letter in which he describes, in an aside, a presentiment that he is about to discover the source of morality!), Freud writes as follows:

Hostile impulses against parents (a wish that they should die) are also an integrating constituent of neuroses. . . . These impulses are repressed at periods when compassion for the parents is aroused—at times of their illness or death. On such occasions it is a manifestation of mourning to reproach oneself for their death (so-called melancholia) or to punish oneself in a hysterical fashion, through the medium of the idea of retribution, with the same states [of illness] that they have had. The identification which occurs here is, as can be seen, nothing other than a mode of thinking and does not make the search for the motive superfluous.[17]

The discovery of these "hostile impulses" helped Freud decide to give up his seduction theory. He announces this to Fliess in the fall of 1897, after an extended summer vacation. It was following the summer of 1896 that his father had fallen ill for the last time. Now, at the end of the traditional year-long mourning period for Jews, Freud unveils not only his refusal to believe that fathers, including his own, sexually molested their children *as a rule*, but also his exploration of sexual fantasies and desires that children develop about their parents. About a week before the first anniversary of his father's death, Freud announced to Fliess the "single idea of general value" which had occurred to him: "I have found, in my own case, too, [the phenomenon of] being in love with my mother and jealousy of my father, and I now consider it a universal event in early childhood."[18]

The "motive" for the hostile impulses was now clear, even if it had been repressed in Freud's own period "in which compassion for the parents was aroused." This role of repression in disguising the expression of these impulses was also part of the unveiling. The master theory of seduction by fathers would not work. Fame, wealth, and travel would all have to wait now that the key to all of hysteria clearly would not fit.[19] Yet Freud did not feel shame, or depression at having to give up what he had seen as his great insight into psychopathology, but "more the feeling of a victory than a defeat."[20] The exploration of dreams had assumed crucial importance, and Freud remained confident that he was on to something. The dream book would make clear the shift away from an emphasis on a trauma's "adequate reaction," and to the psycho-analytic focus on desire as that which enables us to understand our connections with our past.

The Interpretation of Dreams is, as Freud himself noted in the preface to the 1908 edition of the book, a reaction to his father's death. He also noted that he only realized this once he had completed the book. That is, only once he had completed the work of mourning, was he able to disclose to himself what would count as a reaction to "the most important event, the most poignant loss, of a man's life." [21] The book bore the marks of his process of disconnecting from the past, and of his reconnection to the present via an acknowledgement of the past. The discovery of oedipal impulses and of the fundamental nature of ambivalence changed the way he viewed his own past, and the way he understood how we make meaning and direction from our histories or how we deny them. We are not only the victims of our pasts, nor are we simply their (guilty) survivors. We do not only undergo trauma, we are capable of making meaning and direction out of our past. As we acknowledge desires over time, we come to see how we make (and can remake) our histories; how we create the pain of guilt, and how we can work our way out from under it. An interpretation of the signs of the past still legible in the present helps us to achieve this. In its "final" form, the "Close the Eyes" dream no longer expressed guilt, nor a fear of being (yet again) a latecomer. In closing the father's eyes, Freud turned his own gaze inward. He (or was it only his train?) had arrived.

III

Anna O.'s persistent symptoms were "mnemic signs" of her father's illness and death. What made this display of mourning pathological was not the attachment to the dead man it expressed, but her inability to recognize the signs *as* part of her reaction to loss, and her inability to feel she was the author of these signs. This was not the case with the unpractical Londoners: they knew very well that they were in mourning; indeed, they worked to maintain their attachment to the past. Their sorrow had become their pleasure. For Freud, however, the work of mourning consisted in the progressive detachment from the past. He came to see *The Interpretation of Dreams* as just such a work. It helped him to close the eyes.

Freud discussed the connections between normal grief and neurosis in some of his earliest writings. In 1895 he describes melancholia as "consist[ing] in mourning over loss of libido." [22] We have seen how in his evaluation of his own feelings following the death of his father he came to examine the role of the repression of "hostile impulses" in grief and in neurosis. How does the process of mourning succeed in channeling these impulses into ways of loving and working without merely repressing them (and thus making them potentially pathogenic)? How to understand the psychological dynamics of mourning when it is unsuccessful, when it leads to a disabling self-punishment under the guise of grief and fidelity to the past?

These are some of the questions Freud had in mind when he wrote "Mourning and Melancholia." This is one of the surviving papers from his excursions into metapsychology in 1915–17, a time in which much of psycho-analytic theory was in flux, and in which Freud was moving death and aggression to the center of his understanding of desire. Of course, death and aggression were all around Freud and the rest of Europe at this time, and much of his writing in this period and through the publication of *Beyond the Pleasure Principle* (1920) should be understood in relation to the enormous destruction of the war, to Freud's fears about his own death and about the deaths of those close to him.[23]

The paper begins with the idea that just as dreams have aided in the understanding of narcissistic mental disorders, the "normal emotion of grief" and its expression in mourning might "throw some light on the nature of melancholia."[24] Melancholia has many of the same characteristics as grief, although it also involves a "loss of self esteem" or self-persecution not characteristic of the mourning process. [244] Freud considers mourning to be work, a process through which the libido "shall be withdrawn from its attachments to this [the loved] object." [244] This withdrawal requires labor because "people never willingly abandon a libidinal position, not even, indeed, when a substitute is already beckoning to them." [244] The beloved is sought for but is no more; in response to the longing of the survivor, reality is firm, its orders are clear: Your desire is for nothing here, turn away. The work of mourning reveals a plethora of forms of this turning away; this, too, I must learn to live without . . . and this, and this. The confrontation with and turning away from absence in mourning is a repetitive task, and thus "the existence of the lost object is prolonged." [245]

Each single one of the memories and expectations in which the libido is bound to the object is brought up and hypercathected, and detachment of the libido is accomplished in respect of it. Why this compromise by which the command of reality is carried out piecemeal should be so extraordinarily painful is not at all easy to explain in terms of economics. It is remarkable that this painful unpleasure is taken as a matter of course by us. The fact is, however, that when the work of mourning is completed the ego becomes free and uninhibited again. [245]

How is the work of melancholy different from mourning so described? Although there is a loss of some kind behind the grief, the loss is unconscious for the melancholic: he or she experiences the absence and the longing, but is not aware of what has been lost. The mourner looks at the present world and sees it as "poor and empty," like an abandoned house; the melancholic tells us instead that he or she is empty, worthless, and, often, abandoned.

Thus, the mourner has lost something in the world, we might even say that the world has become lost to the person. She or he then gives up the world as it had been known, and gives it up piece by piece, slowly and painfully, until a connection with the world as it can be known is established as the period of mourning ends. The person in melancholy is lost to himself or herself; the work of melancholy is to preserve oneself *as* lost, as not worthy of being found. How does this happen?

The "key to the clinical picture" is that the self-degradation of melancholics, the reproaches that they aim at themselves, are those which were aimed at a loved object and shifted to the person's own ego. [248] A mild, or at least temporary, state akin to this is found in the guilt feelings that often accompany mourning. Melancholics would like to rail against the world which deprives them of love, they would like to revolt against a present reality which "orders" them to give up hopes of satisfaction, of happiness. But through a process of identification with precisely those aspects of reality which deny satisfaction, which refuse to return love, the melancholic now finds the object of revolt within. The revolt against reality becomes a revolt against oneself in the "crushed state of melancholia." [248]

Freud had already confronted this revolt against oneself during his own period of grief following his father's death. In trying to understand the "obscure routes behind the official consciousness" through which this loss affected him, he was led to examine the "hostile impulses against parents (a wish that they should die)." As we saw above, in 1897 he wrote that "it is a manifestation of mourning to reproach oneself for their death . . . or to punish oneself in a hysterical fashion, through the medium of the idea of retribution, with the same states [of illness] that they have had." This is exactly the process of pathological identification which he details in "Mourning and Melancholia." "The shadow of the object fell on the ego," he wrote in 1917, with the result that in the now split ego one part persecuted the other. The lost object is "saved" through introjection, the past is retained but at great cost, because the past becomes that which enables the present to be seen as something which is never good enough, always missing that which is essential.

The complex of melancholia behaves like an open wound, drawing to itself cathectic energies . . . from all directions, and emptying the ego until it is totally impoverished. [253]

The lost object-saved-within makes the external world seem like an empty place, even as it provides the satisfaction of always being superior to the present in which one is condemned to live. But essentially melancholics are always already latecomers, and they have an internal schedule according to which they can always condemn themselves.[25]

IV

In 1973 Carl Schorske published an extremely influential article on Freud's *The Interpretation of Dreams*.[26] Schorske examined what he called "the counterpolitical ingredient in the origins of psychoanalysis."[27] Faced with the intractable Viennese establishment, Freud retreated from overt political activity into a world of subversive intellection. The famous epigraph to *The Interpretation of Dreams* puts it this way: "If I can not shake the higher powers, I will stir up the depths." Freud gave up on the dream of a political career, and through his psycho-analytic work made politics itself epiphenomenal. "Having exhumed his own political past through dream analysis, he had overcome it by identifying his political obligations and impulses with his father, explaining them away as attributes of his father's ghost."[28] This "explaining away" is Freud's letting go of his past and the public desires which had helped to define it. Psycho-analysis here is seen as part of a more general modernist retreat from history, as "Freud gave his fellow liberals an a-historical theory of man and society that could make bearable a political world spun out of orbit and beyond control."[29]

Psycho-analysis in this view is compensation for political impotence. In its displacement of more concrete political problems, the science of the depths is conformist in relation to the status quo. Moreover, there is a political wish at the beginnings of psycho-analysis, but that wish is given up in the face of reality. How to find this originating desire? Schorske employs the tools of psycho-analysis itself to find the wish concealed in Freud's own dreams. Nothing is lost to the unconscious, and the traces of political wishes remain in Freud's accounts of his own dreams. Even when one abandons a quest, the longing remains. But how does one give up on something? What is the process through which a person lets go of an ambition, a desire, a goal?

We are perhaps now in a better position to understand the centrality of these questions for Freud. Throughout his corpus, the process of mourning—its work—figures for him as an extraordinary, but not a morbid, means available to us of letting go of the past without denying it. Anna O.'s symptoms, the signs (for us, but not for her) of her father's death, were her way of retaining a past which was dead. The cost of this retention was self-persecution, conflict, and pain which became a misery that was its own reward. The Londoners who stopped each day before The Monument were not only unpractical; from Freud's perspective in "Mourning and Melancholia" they were cultivating their pain as a vehicle for deprecating the present.

Is psycho-analysis itself, however, only an elaborate mnemic sign of the death of Freud's and his fellow liberals' political ambitions? Is the decision to ignore the "higher powers" in favor of the depths an extraordinary deprecation of the human and a failure to confront the loss of political, moral, and aesthetic values in modernity? How close are the dynamics of psychoanalysis and melancholia?

The relationship between melancholia and mourning is one of the crucial figures for Freud's thinking about the ways we can turn the past into fuel for our self-abuse, or use the past for our love and work. How to transform painful reminiscence into memory and desire that can be put in the service of the pursuit of satisfaction? In his own period of mourning for the death of his father, he discovered how difficult it was even to tell the difference between these two modes of relating to the past. This difficulty was the core of his self-analysis, which led him to an acknowledgement of the fundamental ambivalence—the contradiction of desires—in all important human relationships. This ambivalence, when unconscious, can lead to strategies of repetitious denial and self-denigration like those found in melancholia. Confined to those "obscure pathways behind the official consciousness," conflicts of desire which keep us lost to the world remain split off from us, and we remain alien to ourselves. When unveiled, the ambivalence does not disappear; it becomes that out of which we can make our histories so as to create the possibilities for change. Recognition of the ambivalence at the heart of Freud's relation to the "old man" was decisive for the creation of *The Interpretation of Dreams*, as he was able to acknowledge only retrospectively. That is, he turned the process of mourning and the work that came out of it (or was a large part of it) into a history—meaningful memory—with which he could live.

The possibility remains that "the history with which Freud could live" was a liberal lullaby meant to console those whose political dreams ended in disaster or desperation. But lullabies, like dreams, have more than one meaning, and they can, like history, be used or abused. Psycho-analytic acknowledging and freedom can help us apprehend the connections and conflicts between personal history and the demands of the groups to which we belong or which claim us. To grasp these connections and conflicts provides only some preconditions for change for some people with particular resources; not more than that. But it can facilitate transforming melancholic abuse of the past and thus of our present, into grief, and then into work and love. There is much to mourn, and psycho-analysis unveils the pain of a past unconsciously bound up in the present. Perhaps when the depths of this pain can be grasped and not merely suffered, we will not find it necessary to turn away from acknowledgement, negation, and freedom.

As Freud noted, the "Close the Eyes" dream had more than one meaning. In this dream which expressed his mourning and was used to overcome it, he closed his father's eyes, not his own. In so doing, he began to make history, not only to retreat from it.

The Subjectivity of Structure: Individuality and Its Contradictions in Lévi-Strauss

Although I am going to talk about what I have written, my books and papers and so on, unfortunately I forget what I have written practically as soon as it is finished. There is probably going to be some trouble about that. But nevertheless I think there is also something significant about it, in that I don't have the feeling that I write my books. I have the feeling that my books get written through me and that once they have got across me I feel empty and nothing is left.

You may remember that I have written that myths get thought in man unbeknownst to him. This has been much discussed and even criticized by my English-speaking colleagues, because their feeling is that, from an empirical point of view, it is an utterly meaningless sentence. But for me it describes a lived experience, because it says exactly how I perceive my own relationship to my work. That is, my work gets thought in me unbeknownst to me.

I never had, and still do not have, the perception of feeling my personal identity. I appear to myself as the place where something is going on, but there is no "I," no "me." Each of us is a kind of crossroads where things happen. The crossroads is purely passive; something happens there. A different thing, equally valid, happens elsewhere. There is no choice, just a matter of chance.

I don't pretend at all that, because I think that way, I am entitled to conclude that mankind thinks that way too. But I believe that, for each scholar and each writer, the particular way he or she thinks and writes opens a new outlook on mankind. And the fact that I personally have this idiosyncrasy perhaps entitles me to point to something which is valid, while the way in which my colleagues think opens different outlooks, all of which are equally valid.

Claude Lévi-Strauss, "An Introduction" to *Myth and Meaning* (1977)

It is vintage Lévi-Strauss, charming and exasperating, self-revelatory and mystifying, provoking thought together with the nagging suspicion that the reader's leg is being gently and deftly pulled. At stake is structuralism's great challenge to traditional humanism, embodied in the claim that "myths think themselves through men," that the mind is an empty place where "things happen." Where does this image of the mind's passivity and emptiness take rise? Here the answer lies not in linguistic theory or neural science, but in Lévi-Strauss's experience of his own self; the mind that possesses no power over its operations gives birth to a theory about the essential nature of human thought and culture. To give an extra turn to the screw, what begins as a plea for the nonexistence of the self ends in a relativism that makes the coexistence of "equally valid" selves the last word in the shaky domain of human knowledge.

What should we make of a writer who simultaneously places himself at the center of his thought and denies that he possesses a self to put there? In what follows I want to suggest that this question underlies much of Lévi-Strauss's work. The usual view that identifies structuralist method with a consistent marginalization of the individual self or subject does not describe the more complex and tortuous, but much richer, set of meditations about the moral and epistemological status of individuality Lévi-Strauss pursued. The anthropologist's "I," far from being empty or undiscoverable, was powerfully present in his writings, taking precisely the form of this conflict about individuality. If such a view contests what he said in passages like the one quoted above, it accords well with some of his late essays, where the self—especially the creative self—appears as far from passive, actively developing new meaning through a determined engagement with its social and cultural surroundings. These texts give strong, if rather veiled, hints that he had come to see his own creativity as the expression of a particular kind of personality, one so imprinted with the experience of division and fragmentation that he ended by comparing it with the psychopathology of schizophrenia. Here the vexed relationship between structuralism and subjectivity suggests that some of its roots need to be looked for in the experience of a particular sort of subject.

It is easy to be struck by Lévi-Strauss's repeated rejection of the status often attributed to human individuals in Western thinking. The conclusion of *Tristes Tropiques* went all the way to denying its author's existence "as an individual," on the grounds that a person's individuality was merely "a continually renewed stake in the struggle" between the nerve cells lodged in the brain and the body which served as its robot. "Not only is the first person singular detestable [the echo of Pascal's *le moi est haissable* was evident to many French readers], there is no room for it between 'ourselves' and 'nothing.'" [1] The philosophical currents that would flower in existentialism were objectionable because of their "indulgent attitude toward the illusions of subjectivity. To promote private preoccupations to the rank of philosophical problems is dangerous, and may end in a kind of shop-girl's philosophy," a renunciation of philosophy's real mission, which was "to understand being in relation to itself, and not in its relation to me." [2] The anti-individual stance asserted in *Tristes Tropiques* (published in 1955) reappeared regularly in its author's later works. *The Savage Mind* (1962) warned that knowledge of man (if not of men) was closed to those who "allow themselves to be caught up in the snare of personal identity." It was not any unity of the subject which gave continuity and wholeness to experience, but the linguistic structures that were necessarily presupposed by any individual as "a subject who speaks," structures that formed "a dialectical and totalizing entity but one outside (or beneath) consciousness and will." What some people (Sartre, for instance) supposed to be a "totalizing continuity of the self" had to be understood as "an illusion sustained by the demands of social life." [3] At the end of his massive, four-volume study of mythology, Lévi-Strauss declared that "if there is one conviction that has been intimately born in upon the author" through his work it was "that the solidity of the self, the major preoccupation of Western philosophy, does not withstand persistent application to the same object, which comes to pervade it through and through"; in reality an individual self was but the point of intersection of events whose solidity lent it a false stability, events

351

which "originate from countless other sources, for the most part unknown." Philosophers who sought to give a higher degree of unity to the individual were "chiefly concerned to construct a refuge for the pathetic treasure of personal identity." The subject was "an unbearably spoiled child" who had claimed our attention for too long.[4]

And yet, as the Introduction to *Myth and Meaning* would lead us to expect, this empty self occupied a much more substantial place in Lévi-Strauss's intellectual project than such assertions imply. As Clifford Geertz has observed, "No anthropologist has been more insistent on the fact that the practice of his profession has consisted of a personal quest."[5] *Tristes Tropiques* was at once a public and an intimate book, full of autobiographical descriptions and reflections on its author's motives and feelings. Anthropology attracted him because of an unconscious "structural affinity between the civilizations which it studies and my own thinking. I lack the ability to keep a single field under cultivation year after year: I have a neolithic intelligence." The intellectual satisfaction of anthropology lay in its joining together "at its two extremes the history of the world and my own history," revealing "at a single stroke their common basis."[6]

Lévi-Strauss affirmed the value of the individual human self from several points of view. As early as 1945, in an essay written for a collection published in America, he acknowledged that sociological theory—notably in its French variety—created possible confusions by its insistence that the individual not be accorded a central place. The problem was especially clear in Durkheim, for whom the methodological primacy of society over the individual harmonized all too well with a desire to exalt social existence as the source of a higher moral and spiritual life. Durkheim had judged societies according to the strength of collective feelings they developed, seeing greater health and virtue where social life was stronger and more stable. Such a view could too easily be used to "crush individual thought and spontaneity," or even be appropriated to justify regimes Durkheim had not imagined, as the 1930s had shown. Lévi-Strauss thought that Durkheim had provided essential methodological starting points, but his moral position was much more problematic: "Every moral, social, or intellectual progress made its first appearance as a revolt of the individual against the group."[7]

Sometimes Lévi-Strauss even found the origin of social institutions in the different qualities individuals carried with them into social life. In one of the societies studied in *Tristes Tropiques*, the Nambikwara, individual differences were so important in the choice of chiefs that the anthropologist had to conclude: "If there are chiefs, it is because there are, in every group of human beings, men who, unlike their companions, love importance for its own sake, take a delight in its responsibilities," and seek to take up burdens from which others shrink. Certainly different cultures gave varying scope to individual differences: "But the fact that they exist in a society so largely uncompetitive as that of the Nambikwara would suggest that their origin is not entirely social. Rather they are part of that raw material of psychology in which every society somewhere finds its foundations." So important was the chief's binding personal force, that he "is rather the cause of the group's wish to constitute itself as a group, than the effect of the need, felt by an already-existing group, for a central authority."[8]

Certain individuals, moreover, had irreplaceable significance because they provided a unique synthesis of experience. Against the above-cited warnings about "the snare of personal identity" stand evocations like the following one from *The Savage Mind*:

What disappears with the death of a personality is a synthesis of ideas and modes of behavior as exclusive and irreplaceable as the one a floral species develops out of the simple chemical substances common to all species. When the loss of someone dear to us or of some public personage such as a politician or writer or artist moves us, we suffer much the same sense of irreparable privation that we should experience were *Rosa centifolia* to become extinct and its scent to disappear for ever.[9]

The museums dedicated to great artists in the West provided an equivalent to other societies' temples. Were the works of Rembrandt or Michelangelo to be lost, "we would feel—quite rightly of course—that something irreplaceable had gone." To be sure, these human syntheses were of equal, but not greater, value with those represented by living species in nature. All the same, the special qualities and properties of humanity were evident in the circumstance that "humanity alone has achieved the realization of those unique and irreplaceable syntheses, which nature creates in the form of living species, in the form of individual persons," those who bore such names as "Poussin, Rembrandt, Rousseau, or Kant."[10]

Next to the moral rehabilitation of individuality these ideas implied, we also find in Lévi-Strauss's work a recognition that certain individual qualities could provide starting points for anthropological knowledge; these features were positive characteristics, not the absence of identity he claimed for himself in the introduction to *Myth and Meaning*. In his study *Totemism*— where totemic systems were denied any special existence, separate from the general impulse to use natural objects as a way of signifying social distinctions, the logic of classification found throughout primitive thought—the author discussed what his thinking owed to certain predecessors. Among these were anthropologists and sociologists, notably Radcliffe-Brown and Durkheim. But the earliest and clearest of these forerunners was no seeker of impersonal science but the philosopher Henri Bergson, the explorer of the inner life of intuition and the continuity of personal existence he called duration, *la durée.*

Twenty years before Radcliffe-Brown, Bergson came to recognize that the point of totemic classifications was not the identification between one group of men and a plant or animal species, but the distinctions established between and among groups through their associations with a series of symbols or signifiers. This understanding (in his last book, *The Two Sources of Morality and Religion*) drew on Durkheim's writings, but Bergson grasped what Durkheim could not: that the source of totemic thinking was in the intellect, which used outside counters to think with, not in what Durkheim presented as an interplay of socially determined consciousness and instinctual attachment to symbols. Precisely because Bergson did not share Durkheim's belief in "the primacy of the social over the intellect," he was able to locate totemic thinking properly "in the field of oppositions and ideas."

What allowed Bergson to achieve this result was not just his capacity for philosophical insight, but "because his own thought, unbeknownst to him, was in sympathy with that of totemic peoples." He shared with them a common vision of reality as a continuous stream of creative energy, ever-flowing but constantly broken up by its embodiment in separate, particular forms of existence—species, individuals, groups, as well as discrete events and experiences. Bergson called this energy *elan vital*, making it the source of "creative evolution"; totemic peoples—Lévi-Strauss cited American Indian myths—figured it in stories where "everything, as it moves, now and then, here and there makes stops." It was this similarity that accounted for Bergson's insight. "If he was able to understand certain aspects of totemism better than the anthropologists, or before them, is this not because his own thought presents curious analogies with that of many so-called primitive peoples who experience or have experienced totemism from within?"

Bergson's example showed how certain thinkers—Rousseau was another—were able to seize the essential truth about exotic institutions "by a process of internalization, that is, by trying on themselves modes of thought taken from elsewhere or simply imagined. They thus demonstrate that every human mind is a locus of virtual experience where what goes on in the minds of men, however remote they may be, can be investigated."[11] To generalize Bergson's experience in this way was to recall what Lévi-Strauss had written in 1950, in his introduction to the work of Marcel Mauss. Any observation of social life—whether of other societies or one's own—depended on "the subject's capacity for indefinite self-objectification," the human being's ability to recognize fragments of the self even in customs and forms of life that seem to embody the furthest extremes of otherness. The very foreignness of other cultures aids the individual in the project of self-understanding by bringing to view fragments which, otherwise, "the individual subject would have to pull painfully away from himself." What the social observer learns in the end is "that all those objects proceed from him, and that the most objectively conducted analysis of them could not fail to reintegrate them inside the analyst's subjectivity."[12] Here knowledge of human nature and culture has just the relationship to personal existence that many of Lévi-Strauss's other pronouncements deny it. To understand being "in relation to itself" was not, after all, different from understanding it "in relation to me."

What lay behind this pattern of contradictory denials and affirmations about the value of individuality? If there is an answer that penetrates to the deep layers of Lévi-Strauss's psyche, we cannot provide it here: too little is known about his early experience and his personal life. But at a more manifest level, his writings are rich in hints and glimmers of what was at stake. In various ways he tells us that he was someone who sought power beneath a façade of impotence, of self-renunciation; that his way of seeking an exalted place in the world was through the apparent abandonment of any personal claim to one. For such a person, self-denial and self-assertion are the warp and woof of a texture that requires both.

Such interwoven identities are common among intellectuals, and perhaps especially fitting for anthropologists. Lévi-Strauss suggested as much in *Tristes Tropiques*, when he presented the uprooted and unstable life anthropology demanded as the distilled essence of all those vocations which attract individuals who resist integration into the ordinary adult world, preferring the university as a kind of perpetual childhood. Such professions provided at once a refuge from society and a mission to it.[13] In this, the life Lévi-Strauss chose echoed the experience of youth in American Indian tribes, who sought to gain prestige by submitting themselves to an ordeal in adolescence.

He must travel to the frontiers where law and order give out, to the limits of physiological resistance and of the physically and morally bearable. For it is at this unstable border that one is opened up either to falling outside, never to return, or to capturing, from the immense ocean of unexploited forces which surrounds humanity in its well-regulated state, some personal provision of power, thanks to which an otherwise immovable social order may be cancelled in favor of the one who risks everything.[14]

In *Tristes Tropiques*, Lévi-Strauss made clear that he had been aware of this pattern's presence in his life at least from the 1930s, and that he associated it with renounced political ambition. While studying native tribes in South America, the young anthropologist had written a play. Reworked from Corneille, the drama told of the relations between the Roman Emperor Augustus and his childhood friend Cinna, who returns to Rome after ten years of adventurous travels among savages, just at the moment when Augustus is about to be declared a god. The details of the plot can be passed over here; the point is Cinna's attempt to seek outside society "a greater Empire" than Augustus achieved within it, through undergoing trials and forging "a new bond between myself and the universe." The attempt fails, however, and Cinna ends up losing everything.[15]

If the point of telling about this play in *Tristes Tropiques* was to claim some sort of finality for its author's renunciation of the attempt to gain power by abandoning any direct claim to it, then we should react with a certain skepticism: this book was one of the important elements in building up Lévi-Strauss's commanding position within French intellectual life. But the play's correspondence to the events of his own biography seems clear enough. During his twenties the future anthropologist was deeply involved in socialist politics, even presenting himself as a candidate in local elections during 1932. He wrote an academic essay on Marx, and many years later recalled that at the time "I saw myself very well becoming the philosopher of the socialist party."[16] His departure for Brazil in 1935 ended this phase in his life just as French socialism was about to face the great trial of the Popular Front. I do not know what turned Lévi-Strauss away from politics, but the play about Augustus and Cinna recalled in *Tristes Tropiques* suggests that giving up his vision of a political future left him split between his yearning for power and his flight from the forms of life and action where it could be exercised, the division that made him compare young Indians with European anthropologists. To claim that he possessed no stable self, no program to impose on the objects he studied, so that the mind or nature simply spoke through him, shifted the pattern of gaining power through renouncing any claim to it from the plane of politics to that of methodology.

For the person who experienced the world in this way, structuralist method had a special attraction. Lévi-Strauss first encountered structuralism when he met Roman Jakobson during their common wartime exile in New York. Drawing on the earlier work of Baudoin de Courtenay and Saussure, Jakobson analyzed language as a system of internal relations, within which elements—sounds and signs—that had no intrinsic meaning could acquire it solely through their relation to other parts of the system. Language carried meaning because it was a system of reciprocal oppositions. Extending this perspective to culture, Lévi-Strauss found the same underlying structure of relations in every form of meaningful human interaction: meaning always arose, and had to be comprehended, within a system of rule-governed oppositions between terms, constructed from materials which were purely material, hence meaningless, in themselves.

The most basic such rule, found in some form in all human societies, was the incest prohibition—making some individuals eligible as marriage partners and others not, organizing natural reproduction on the basis of structured exchanges. The incest prohibition turned human beings from natural objects into bearers of meaning; it thus accomplished on one level what language did on another, making communication, and hence group life, possible. *The Elementary Structures of Kinship* analyzed kinship systems on this basis, finding beneath all the relationships that composed them a binary logic that structured social relations as a system of meaningful exchanges. Individual understandings and projects could enter social life only within the frame of this universal logic.[17]

To analyze human cultures in a structuralist mode was therefore to prepare the ground for the many denials that human subjectivity was the source of cultural meaning we noted at the start. Interpreters of cultures were no more the source of the meanings found within them than were the individuals who inhabited them; both in their ways functioned as the "empty spaces" within which structural relationships became manifest. And yet, Lévi-Strauss's adaptation of structuralist method did not resolve his ambivalence about the moral and intellectual status of individuals; had it done so we would not have been able to assemble the catalogue of opposing views culled from his writings with which we began. Like the transactions with political and social eminence dramatized in his play about Cinna and Augustus, Lévi-Strauss's structuralism was a way of claiming power over culture through the renunciation of any special place for himself inside it. And, just as Cinna returned to the world he had claimed to abandon, Lévi-Strauss had to readmit his own person to the world of cultural interpretation from which he had sought to exclude it. That dialectic was especially visible in his great study of myth.

What myths did for those who employed them was to impart a sense of meaning to an incoherent and contradictory world.

A myth proposes a grid, definable only by its rules of construction. For the participants in the culture to which the myth belongs, this grid confers a meaning not on the myth itself but on everything else: that is, on the images of the world, of the society, and of its history, of which the members of the group are more or less aware, as well as on the images of the questions with which these various objects confront the participants. In general, these scattered givens fail to link up and usually collide with one another. The matrix of intelligibility supplied by the myth allows us to articulate the givens in a coherent system.[18]

Myths provided structures within which fundamental human dilemmas could be contained (in both senses) and lived with. The oppositions they brought together were large in scope: heaven and earth, nature and culture, life and death, "the most profoundly meaningful oppositions that it is given to the mind of man to conceive."[19] By setting these contrasts in relation with other, more manageable ones—fire and water; raw, cooked, and rotten; man and woman; particular plants and animals—myths linked the most universal and least stable oppositions to ones that were smaller and less distant, and which could be more easily defined and controlled.

To the student of human cultures and the nature of the mind that brought them forth, myth was an exemplary subject because there the mind appeared in its pure state, free of any distortions imposed by its commerce with external objects. In myth the mind was free to abandon itself to its own creative spontaneity, to engage in "a tête-à-tête with itself." In order to listen in on that discussion the analyst had to find within myths the elements that were analogous to the building blocks of language analyzed by Saussure and Jakobson; identifying these components would reveal myth to be, like language, a structure composed of elements able to bear meaning because they all stood to the others in a binary relationship of reciprocal opposition. These elements Lévi-Strauss dubbed "mythemes," in analogy to linguistic phonemes; by identifying and classifying them the mythographer arrived at "an inventory of mental patterns," capable of being "reduced to a meaningful system." Since this system had to take on the structure of binary oppositions that allowed material elements—whether sounds or things observed in the environment—to become bearers of meaning, the effect of making it visible was that "a kind of necessity becomes apparent, underlying the illusion of liberty." Thus the study of myth revealed the mind "itself to be of the nature of a thing among things," locating its products in the world of necessity and thinghood.[20]

This was one reason why the structures myths provided never genuinely resolved the dilemmas that lay behind them. A second was that all the contradictions and oppositions myths set out to reconcile had their deepest roots in Hamlet's question, itself a "still over-optimistic" way of seeing that "Man is not free to choose whether to be or not to be." Out of the clash between the necessities of an existence we have not chosen, and our attempt to impose a meaning on it, there arose "an unlimited series of other binary distinctions which, while never resolving the primary contradiction, echo and perpetuate it on an ever-smaller scale." The science of mythology showed how this fundamental opposition repeated itself on every level; such an understanding reminded mankind of its limits, and pointed toward the eventual disappearance of human meaning. [21]

A study of human culture could hardly make a stronger claim to objectivity and universal significance. But Lévi-Strauss had too much self-awareness to deny that what he had in fact produced was only one particular, deeply personal interpretation. To begin with, his work could not escape being a kind of myth itself. His analysis had to be embedded in the structure of mythic thought out of which it arose, since the architecture of myth reflected the deep structure of the mind, the ubiquitously present binary contrasts that underlay all its operations. Hence what he produced would have to be "as it were, the myth of mythology." At the end of his four volumes, coming to the demonstration that all the myths studied added up to one, he repeated that "I myself have been evolving a myth on the basis of myths." [22]

Everything in Lévi-Strauss's methodological orientation was calculated to deny that this result was somehow the author's personal myth, the emanation of his own personality. The experience of working on myths had confirmed his determination, stated in *The Savage Mind*, to reduce the individual subject to its proper proportions as "the insubstantial place or space where anonymous thought can develop"; this was the point of his claim, made at the start and the end, that "myths speak through men."

Yet this absence of the self could only persist up to a certain point. Having used the impersonal French plural "nous" throughout his work on mythology, even claiming it as a sign that his individual subjectivity had been absent from the work, Lévi-Strauss in his last chapter came back to the more personal "je," the emblem of his own singularity. [23] He justified this recourse to the personal self on the grounds that once the work was complete its author was no longer inside it, thus he could stand outside and view the project as a whole. But what the no longer anonymous author occupied himself with for the concluding chapter was a series of replies to critics and justifications of the procedures he had adopted while employing the impersonal "nous." The chapter ended with personal reflections and recollections, making clear that the author acknowledged his differences from other students of myth, and the presence in his work of a particular, highly personal point of view from the start.

The contradictions of this stance were precisely the ones Lévi-Strauss would confirm in his Introduction to *Myth and Meaning*. His own condition was first described as one of pure transparency, the absence of stable identity, which allowed myths to speak through him; and yet, this was but one of many possible and "equally valid" points of view, each provided by the personal condition of individual scholars. The claim to be a spokesman for the universal structures of the mind, implied by the use of "nous," as by the image of himself as transparent and empty of any particular purpose, collapsed once he had to acknowledge that his was but one of many different interpretations, each corresponding to a different form of personal existence.

At this point the image of an empty and passive self, on which the claim to be able to speak in the name of universal myth rested, no longer fit the person who now had completed four volumes on the meaning of myth. It needed to be replaced with a different view of the self, one that recognized its substantiality, along with its ability to give birth to new meanings and new points of view within existing cultures.

Two observations help to locate the places where we find this second view in Lévi-Strauss's work. First, none of them is in his major writings (although some notions that do appear there, such as the respect paid to great individuals who provide irreplaceable syntheses of experience, fit well with them). Second, they make their appearance at a particular moment: the immediate aftermath of the disturbances of 1968. If his later recollections are to be trusted, Lévi-Strauss found himself disgusted by the moral and intellectual disorder of the student rebellion; its trashing of public places and willingness to cover walls with graffiti testified to a decline in the level of university life that had been going on for a long time. [24]

In some way the radical culture of the late 1960s, with its rejection of traditional intellectual values, seems to have made Lévi-Strauss reconsider his own position in regard to the European civilization which his works had often seemed to call into question. That his fascination for the non-European world existed alongside a deep attachment to the values and traditions of Western culture was a point he made at many points during his career. In *Tristes Tropiques* he told how, to confront the trials of life in the wilds, he sought comfort in memories of his own civilization, sometimes inexplicably hearing in his mind the music of Chopin. When, in 1954, Roger Caillois tried to trace Lévi-Strauss's interest in primitive societies back to the rejection of European values expressed by avant-garde movements like Surrealism after World War I, the anthropologist rejected the suggestion, admitting the tensions in his stance, but insisting on his deep attachment to Western forms and traditions.[25] His writings often testified to a deep admiration for traditional Western art, especially that of the eighteenth century, and for Western music, notably that of Wagner. The tribute he paid to Bergson in *Totemism* linked his own thinking to the very idealist philosophy from which he had fled into anthropology as a student, returning himself to his own origins.

These underlying loyalties received expression in a way to surprise some of his admirers when, in 1971, UNESCO invited him to give a lecture to inaugurate a year of action against racism. Twenty years earlier he had written "Race and History" for the same body; speaking out against imperialism in that essay, and on behalf of the equal value of all human cultures, Lévi-Strauss had minimized the importance of cultural differences, attributing them to chance and circumstance, and calling fortunate those cultures which had been lucky enough to be enriched by interchanges with others. The anthropologist of 1971 still saw himself as an enemy of racism and imperialism, and as a supporter of global understanding. But he cautioned that the worldwide civilization coming into existence was "the destroyer of those old particularisms which had the honor of creating the aesthetic and spiritual values that make life worthwhile and that we carefully safeguard in libraries and museums because we feel ever less capable of producing them ourselves." Humanity, if it were not to become merely the sterile consumer of values inherited from the past, must learn once again that all true creation implies a certain deafness to the appeal of other values, even going so far as to reject or deny them. "For one cannot fully enjoy the other, identify with him, and yet at the same time remain different." The great creative eras were those in which communication had become adequate for mutual stimulation by remote partners, yet was not so frequent or so rapid as to eliminate the indispensable obstacles that protected individuals and groups from overly facile exchanges, ones that might nullify their diversity.[26] In this perspective, the universal structures underlying all production of meaning mattered less than what distinguished cultures from each other.

The values Lévi-Strauss was here concerned to defend included specifically Western and individual ones. These values appeared in an essay written a few years later, in which the same view of creativity and its relationship to separation was applied to education and culture. The occasion was a round table held to mark the centennial of a celebrated Parisian school, the Ecole Alsacienne. What Lévi-Strauss found problematic about the occasion, as well as how fully it breathed the cultural atmosphere of its time, appears in his comment that "some of the panelists and certain members of the audience [believed that] . . . wanting a child to learn is both a useless wish and an assault on his freedom; and as if a child's native spontaneity and intellectual resources were enough in themselves, excluded any constraint, and left the school with the sole function of not fettering their free development." What this view forgot was that all human life—and especially the creative possibilities it contains—begins from social constraints, against which individuals must test themselves. Lévi-Strauss was particularly bothered by the claim made by one conference participant, that Racine could be cited in defense of the idea that creativity begins from the poet's pure, unconstrained self.

Invention, says Racine, consists of making something out of nothing—not, in any way, of making something by starting from nothing. Racine himself would never have written *Bérénice* or any of his other works had he not, on a school bench, memorized Sophocles and Euripides, and had long intimacy with the Greek tragedies and with the Roman poets and playwrights not taught him, as he himself emphasizes, to deal with a slight subject by giving it dramatic force. One creates only by starting from something one knows thoroughly—if for no other reason than to oppose and surpass it.

The creative person transforms the material imposed on him by his social milieu, imposing a new shape on it. A masterpiece was "made up both of what it is and of what it denies, the ground it conquers and the resistance it meets. It is the result of fierce antagonisms which it reconciles, yet whose thrusts and counterthrusts create the vibration and the tension that we wonder at." [27]

Between this view of mental activity and the one that describes the mind as an empty and passive place where "something happens" there are no points of contact. Intellectual work is just that: work, the product of effort, tension, and determination. The person who accomplishes it is neither wholly enclosed within a culture nor tempted by desperate strategies in order to break free of it. The individual develops his creativity through an encounter with his own society from inside it, enriching his self and his culture at the same time, by merging the resources of the one with the different powers lodged in the other. Here the structuralist presupposition that both individual thought and collective cultural systems express the necessities of a single underlying set of binary relationships collapses in the face of that form of intellectual effort that begins from deep within the experiences and practices of a given culture, struggles to make them yield a sense they had not born before, and produces original work that leaves the culture enriched with new meanings and legacies.

The strong sense of personal identification with which Lévi-Strauss expressed this vision of creativity leads us to ask whether it does not describe his own practice better than the alternative he offered in the introduction to *Myth and Meaning*. Clearly his work bore the marks of effort and determination. In an interview published in 1988 he told how, at the time he was working on the study of myth, he would arise between five and six every morning, never taking a weekend off. "I really worked."[28] That he remembered to add that once the work was finished he felt empty and drained could not cancel out the admission that, on some level, the effort was his own.

Looking at Lévi-Strauss's particular readings of the myths he studied, it is very difficult to describe them as passive or directed from outside himself; their relationship to his own aims and intentions is too clear for that. For example, his first structuralist study of myths was a reading of the Oedipus story. Here certain events of the tale were separated out and put into relation with each other, according to whether they involved an "overrating of blood relations"—as in Oedipus's marriage to his mother Jocasta—or an "underrating" of the same relations—as in his murder of his father, Laios.[29] No amount of sympathy with Lévi-Strauss's project can hide the degree of arbitrariness in such a classification—both actions could just as easily be seen, for instance, as expressions of a single characteristic, self-assertion. Lévi-Strauss's way of reading the Oedipus myth depended on shifting Oedipus's search for the truth about his own self away from the myth's center, marginalizing the problem of self-discovery and dissolving it in a more general binary logic. Here, at the start of his project to analyze mythology we find the clearest denial of his own conclusion about myths: he speaks through them rather than they through him.

His own awareness of how arbitrary his readings could be emerges in a number of contexts. In a late work, *The Jealous Potter* (1985), he offered an extended analysis of the structural similarities between the Oedipus story and the popular novel *The Italian Straw Hat*. The similarities he found between them were of the order of his other readings, for instance of one in *Myth and Meaning* that linked hares, harelips, and twins, in order to show how certain myths were variations on each other. But the comparison between Oedipus and *The Italian Straw Hat*, it turned out, was a joke, offered to show how our minds can be drawn to purely formal resemblances.[30] The impulse to make the joke might be cited as evidence for Lévi-Strauss's passivity in the face of structural relationships imposed on him by the stories themselves; but the ability to recognize it as one, and to distinguish it from his other readings, establishes the presence of an active consciousness, able to reflect on itself and to judge the validity of its own readings, independently of any external "something" operating through it.[31]

Lévi-Strauss's understanding that the mind which gave birth to his views about human culture was neither passive nor empty, but the specific product of a particular set of experiences, which it organized in a definite way, received clear and yet veiled expression in an article published in 1976. Called "Cosmopolitanism and Schizophrenia," the essay discussed the similarities between features of schizophrenia, as presented by a Swedish psychiatrist, and elements found in certain myths. The myths came from the Chinook Indians of North America, whose stories—accounts of bodily organs missing, exchanged, or displaced—suggested experiences like those of schizophrenic patients, whose bodies similarly enacted the splits and dissociations, the irreconcilable oppositions of a fragmented world. The reasons for the similarities were not to be found in any collective psychological disorder among the Chinook, however: first because the myths were stories of ingenuity and defense against dangers, not of weakness or debility; and second because all the elements of the myth could be found among other peoples, the Chinook role having been only to combine and synthesize them.

What made their particular myths such a good counterpart to the psychiatric description of schizophrenia was this tribe's penchant for syncretism and eclecticism. Their mythology was "less like an original corpus than an ensemble of secondary elaborations—systematic at first in this sense—to adapt the ones to the others and reconcile, by transforming them, miscellaneous mythical materials." What made the phenomenon of binary opposition so prominent in Chinook mythology that it approached the description of a schizophrenic condition was that their mythology—surely the parallel with Lévi-Strauss's own does not need to be belabored—was a synthetic elaboration of other people's. Moreover, it was a "very special position" that made this role devolve on them. Shrewd businessmen, exploiting a favorable geographic situation, they "devoted themselves to commercial activities and operated as traders and intermediaries between near and distant tribes." Their language became the basis of a jargon that "served as a lingua franca" along the whole Pacific coast from California to Alaska. This Chinook ability to draw together and unify the world around them presupposed that without them it possessed no unity: "Chinook ideology thus echoes the political, economic, and social experience of a world in a dissociated condition." The Chinook were the Europeans—or was it the Jews?—of North America.[32]

Not only did Lévi-Strauss recall his own situation in the description of the cosmopolitan Chinook; with equal clarity he made the description of schizophrenia—shorn of its ultimate and most debilitating consequences—refer to himself as well. The schizophrenic experiences an oscillation "between two extreme feelings: the insignificance of one's own ego in relation to the world, and the overweening importance of oneself in relation to society." So did Lévi-Strauss move back and forth between the denial of his own subjectivity and the implication that it represented a privileged point from which to comprehend human culture. "The schizophrenic will never achieve the normal experience of living in the world. For him, the part will be equal to the whole." So was the Lévi-Straussian anthropologist—as he pointed out twenty years before—forever "dead to his world," the victim of a "chronic uprootedness," even "psychologically mutilated" by his constant experiences of separation, his attempt to discover humanity in its particular expressions and "the brutality of the changes to which he is subjected."[33] The schizophrenic was subject to the polar "feelings of being completely controlled by some entity perceived as the world or of being able to exercise over that entity a magical and sovereign power." So was Lévi-Strauss divided between seeing himself now as simply the empty space through which mythic and linguistic powers operated, now as the creator of one of those grand syntheses that made individuals as irreplaceable as natural species. The schizophrenic's world was forever afflicted by an intrinsic dualism that made reality appear to him divided between irreconcilable polarities of high-low, front-back, left-right. This was just the mode of thinking Lévi-Strauss had imposed on mythology, bringing it into a synthetic unity by virtue of seeing everywhere the same ever-returning and all-invading contradictions.[34]

That Lévi-Strauss himself believed the condition he attributed to the Chinook as a group could also characterize an individual—one with whom he identified closely—is clear in his comments about the person he regarded as his greatest predecessor in the synthesis of human mythology, Richard Wagner. It was the anthropologist's admiration for the composer of mythological operas that inspired the link between myth and music developed throughout his work, and which made the chapters of *The Raw and the Cooked* take on the names of overture, theme and variations, sonata, inventions, fugue, and chorus. Lévi-Strauss saw "that god, Richard Wagner" (the appellation came from Mallarmé) as "the undeniable originator of the structural analysis of myths." In his book Lévi-Strauss explained that Wagner had shown how myths, like music, transcend "articulate expression," and that both operate simultaneously on two levels, one of exterior events (sounds or narrative elements) and one of deep internal reality—physical in the case of music, social in that of myth. [35]

Although Wagner's famous *Ring* cycle figured important dilemmas of social life, his stature as a synthesizer of myth was clearest in *Parsifal*. That opera—as Lévi-Strauss explained in some notes written for the Bayreuth festival, a year before "Cosmopolitanism and Schizophrenia"—was not simply a retelling of the tale of Perceval and the holy grail, but a combination of that story with one that was its counterpart in many ways, the history of Oedipus. Wagner did this by inserting into Perceval's world the figure of Klingsor, a magician associated, like Oedipus, with sexual desire (in Wolfram von Eschenbach's stories he imprisons women in an enchanted castle) and special knowledge (a mirror in his observatory reflects everything that happens in the neighborhood). Out of Klingsor's world Wagner drew the figure of Kundry, through whose presence in *Parsifal* the Oedipal intimations of the Klingsor figure become explicit: she hopes to seduce Parsifal by identifying herself with his mother.

By integrating the two myths, Wagner brought together their opposite manners of figuring universal and irresolvable questions about communication, sexuality, and nature. Hence, "Wagner's genius anticipated by a good century the synthesis of universal myths that no one had ever before dreamed of connecting." He indicated that the synthesizer of myth would be, like Parsifal, caught between two worlds (of Oedipus and the grail), and able to respond to the contradictions of his position only through abandoning the search for an intellectual solution and accepting the way of "knowing through compassion" (*durch Mitleid wissen*) that allowed him to "go into and come out of the one world and be excluded from and re-enter the other world." [36] So did Lévi-Strauss renounce any claim to intellectual consistency in his work, making himself the vessel of passive sympathy that allowed him to move between his own world of the West and that of the peoples he studied.

To complete this self-portrait in the Wagnerian mirror, one needs to recall certain features of Wagner's career and character that Lévi-Strauss did not make explicit. Wagner began as a Romantic artist determined to assert the rights of human life in its earthly and sensual forms against inherited restrictions, and the subjects he chose to dramatize, from *Das Liebesverbot* ("The Denial of Love") to Siegfried, often focussed on the heroism of individuals in search of personal satisfaction. But beginning in the 1850s he was increasingly drawn to the pessimism of Schopenhauer, with its dark vision of a world of cosmic will that used human passions for its own purposes; in *Tristan and Isolde* Wagner told a story of people deluded by the daylight world of individual consciousness, and drawn into the night where fulfillment and personal annihilation, love and death, merged as *Liebestod*. The *Ring* cycle brought together elements and residues of both these positions. Wagner's mythical universe, in other words, expressed the contradictions that arose when personal self-assertion (Wagner's own egocentricity is a legend in itself) was raised to a level where the individual claimed universal significance; such a claim exploded the boundaries of the single human person, showing how the affirmation of individuality, carried to its highest point, turned into its opposite, dissolving the individual in the universality whose vessel he or she claims to be.

The myth that Lévi-Strauss acknowledged he had been constructing in his study of mythology was the myth of such an individual. By placing himself at the center of the project whereby world mythologies all revealed their common underlying structure, he enacted the contradictory vision of the individual as centrally significant and ultimately meaningless that he shared with Wagner, and that had long been an element of his personal mythology. In 1988 Lévi-Strauss came close to presenting his work in this light, comparing himself to the Surrealists he met in New York during the War.

Max Ernst constructed personal myths by means of images borrowed from another culture: that of old nineteenth-century books, and he made those images say more than they signified when looked at with an innocent eye. In *Mythologiques*, I too cut up a mythic material and recomposed its fragments in order to bring out more meaning.[37]

Max Ernst, Wagner, the Chinook—all three entered into Lévi-Strauss's understanding of what it meant to study myth because all three were mirrors of himself.

Lévi-Strauss was not alone in making "the death of the subject" a central theme in social and cultural theory; like his contemporaries Lacan and Sartre, and such later figures as Barthes, Foucault, and Derrida, his social and cultural theory proposed a deeply personal view in the name of denying selfhood; all made the displacement of Western values an occasion for as-serting one particular option within Western culture, the one that would have the self be all or nothing, wholly free or wholly bound, wholly saved or wholly damned.[38] The alternative Lévi-Strauss supported at some mo-ments is the recognition that those individuals and cultures that provide a legacy of meaning for themselves and those who come after are the ones that discover how difficult it can be, but how satisfying, just to be something.

PART IV

Narrative, History, Temporality

A Reflecting Story

When Miss Emily Grierson died, our whole town went to her funeral: the men through a sort of respectful affection for a fallen monument, the women mostly out of curiosity to see the inside of her house, which no one save an old manservant—a combined gardener and cook—had seen in at least ten years.[1]

William Faulkner's "A Rose for Emily" begins like any novel or short story. As the rules of the genre require, it presents the reader with the central character, Miss Emily Grierson, who is designated as an eminent individual; some associates, who are divided by sex and characterized in accordance with the stereotype of male conformism and female curiosity; a narrator, who is discreetly identified with the group (*"we* found," *"we* said," "our town"). There are also a whole set of cues, especially chronological ones ("in at least ten years"), which introduce a sense of something strange.

To present Emily, a "fallen monument," a splendid relic of a vanished past, Faulkner piles up details that are seemingly insignificant but likely to trigger the presuppositions of common sense—the very ones that ordinary novelists ordinarily use, without always being aware of it, to produce their "reality effect." He draws, for example, on the idea of aristocracy—and all it implies, such as the famous *noblesse oblige,* which is explicitly invoked in the text—to evoke the image of a venerable old lady, the last survivor of a ruined noble family, a symbol of past traditions, and to arouse all the anticipations and expectations that are contained in such a "social essence." The idea of nobility, a socially instituted favorable prejudice, which is consequently endowed with all the force of the social, functions as a principle of construction of social reality that is tacitly accepted both by the narrator and his characters and by the reader. It also functions as a principle of anticipations that are ordinarily grounded in facts, since nobility, as an essence that precedes and produces existence, opens or excludes by definition a whole range of possibles. The power of presupposition is so great, and the hypotheses of the practical induction of the habitus so robust, that they resist even what is self-evident:

"I want arsenic."

The druggist looked down at her. She looked back at him, erect, her face like a strained flag. "Why, of course," the druggist said. "If that's what you want."

The meaning of words and actions is predetermined by the social image of the person who produces them, and, in the case of a person "above all suspicion," the very idea of murder is excluded; the anticipations of common sense are stronger than the self-evidence of facts; the official truth ("Like when she bought the *rat poison*, the arsenic"; "there was written on the box . . . 'For rats'") is more credible than an ostentatious, wild, or cynical confession ("'I want some poison,' she said to the druggist"). And the same goes for all the suspicious signs that the narrator amasses—"the smell," Emily's madness in saying "that her father was not dead"—which are systematically ignored, or repressed, by Emily's fellow citizens and by the reader:

We did not say she was crazy then. We believed she had to do that. We remembered all the young men her father had driven away, and we knew that with nothing left, she would have to cling to that which had robbed her, as people will.

And just as it is only after Emily's death, that is to say 40 years "after the event," as the phrase goes, that the inhabitants of Jefferson discover that Emily has poisoned her lover and hidden his body in her house for all those years, so it is only on the last page of the story that the reader discovers his mistake.

But all this would be no more than the well-crafted plot of a realist narrative, if it did not appear retrospectively that, through his skillful manipulation of chronology, Faulkner has constructed his story as a trap in which the deepest assumptions of ordinary social existence and the conventions or presuppositions of the genre are exploited to encourage, right through the narrative, anticipation of the *plausible meaning* that will be abruptly belied at the end. Faulkner in fact stages a double deception. First, there is the deception that Emily performs when she plays on the more or less imaginary representation of the aristocracy ("We had long thought of them as a tableau") and the consensus on the meaning of the world that arises from the tacit agreement of habitus. She thereby deceives the druggist and all her fellow citizens, especially the men, who are particularly inclined to grant a favorable prejudice to the official, public truth (as opposed to women's gossip). Then there is Faulkner's own deception of the reader. He uses everything that is tacitly granted in the "reading contract" to direct the naive reader's attention towards misleading clues and false trails and to turn him

away from the indications, particularly as regards chronology, that he sur-
reptitiously plants in the story. Only a methodical reading, like Menakhem
Perry's,[2] can pick up and organize such clues (thus, in the opening pages:
"dating from that day in 1884 when Colonel Sartoris," "dating from the
death of her father," "the next generation," "on the first of the year"—but
we do not know which year, "eight or ten years earlier," "Colonel Sartoris
had been dead almost ten years," "thirty years before," "two years after her
father's death and a short time after her sweetheart . . . had abandoned
her").

In fact, Faulkner covertly breaks the "reading contract" that implicitly
exists between the novelist and his reader. (But then, is "contract" the right
word—even when we realize that, as Durkheim pointed out, not everything
in a contract is contractual—to describe the naive trust that the reader puts
into his reading, and the abandon with which he casts his whole self into
it, taking with him all the commonsense assumptions that orient his ordinary experience of the social world?) Despite the similarities in the procedures used—the scattering of clues designed to pass unnoticed—Faulkner's
method has nothing in common with the narrative convention of the detective story, which continues to rely on all the assumptions of common sense
to frustrate and disconcert the expectations apparently aroused by all the
foreground and background clues offered by the narrative. People do not,
generally, re-read detective stories, and for most ordinary readers (as opposed
to those extra-ordinary readers, the professional readers, *lectores* predisposed
to practice re-reading) a novel the end of which is known has lost all its
interest, which depends on suspense and surprise.

The reader that "A Rose for Emily" tacitly asks for is precisely this extraordinary reader, the "archreader" as some have called him—without really
thinking through the social conditions of possibility of this curious character. More accurate would be the "meta-reader," who reads not only the
narrative but the ordinary reading of the narrative, the presuppositions that
the reader puts into both his ordinary experience of time and action and his
experience of reading a "realist" or mimetic fiction, which purports to express the reality of the ordinary world and the ordinary experience of that
world.

"A Rose for Emily" is a reflexive story, a reflecting story, designed like a
mirror. It contains in its very structure (and not in its discursive utterances)
a reflection on the novel and on naively "novelistic" reading. It is, as it
were, a complex device which calls for a twofold reading. The impressions
of the first reading are to be combined with all the revelations that the sec-

ond reading provides, thanks to the retrospective light that knowledge of the dénouement, acquired at the end of the first reading, casts on the text itself and more especially *on the first reading*, and therefore on the presuppositions of the naively "novelistic" reading. By in a sense tricking the reader, by covertly breaking the standard "reading contract," Faulkner gives the possibility of seeing all that the ordinary reader unwittingly grants to authors who, moreover, do not know what they are demanding of him. But this possibility is only offered to a meta-reader capable of seeing objectively the illusions that his apparatus forces out into the open.

Bringing into play the whole range of presuppositions in ordinary experience of the world and in ordinary experience of writing or reading, Faulkner presents a whole set of apparent features. As in an ambiguous *Gestalt*, these hide the real structure, especially as regards its temporal dimension. By blurring the chronological order, he pushes the reader into anticipations of meaning which will eventually be belied. He gives him, in a carefully organized disorder, and generally out of phase, the chronological markers that might enable him to lift the narrative out of pure discontinuity and so to grasp, through the real order of successions, the significances and the links of cause and intention that will appear only retrospectively, through the final revelation. To do so, he plays on the assumptions and devices of conventional narrative writing and reading. Like a novelist who pretends to believe what he writes and who asks the reader to read his narrative while pretending to forget it is a fiction, Faulkner accredits his apparent narrative by presenting himself (through constant use of "we" or of impersonal, unanimous, anonymous phrases like "we all thought" or "the ladies said") as the spokesman of the group, whose members grant each other what each unconsciously grants him or herself, the non-thetic theses which constitute the common world view.

Thus, for example, although he duly points out the oddities of Emily's behavior, he relies on the common representation of aristocracy to suggest that they can be imputed not to madness but to a commitment to aristocratic grandeur and pride. By asking the reader to read his narrative conventionally, as a fictitious true story, Faulkner authorizes and encourages him to put into his reading the assumptions he brings into his ordinary perception. These include the prejudice which gives more authority to the male view, the official view which respects conventions and proprieties, than to the view of the women, who are sociologically inclined to question the official, that is, male verities and who will finally be proved right.

In short, he brings into the very writing of the narrative a practical mastery of the presuppositions of ordinary writing and reading, of everything that goes without saying in each of them and therefore goes unnoticed— such as the fact that one reads a book from the front to the back. And he also brings in a mastery of the gap between the naive reading, which is hurried and inattentive and does not take the time to reassemble the overall structure of times and places, and the scholastic reading, which can double back and, by re-establishing the true chronology of events, blows apart the whole construction insidiously suggested to the naive reader. The visible proof of this dual mastery is provided by all the phrases like "she looked," "her eyes looked," which recall the narrator's point of view and which can be seen retrospectively as underlining the ignorance of Emily's fellow citizens as to the real nature of the person and her actions.

This reflexive writing therefore calls for a reflexive reading which brings to light not only a set of misleading clues but the self-deception into which the overconfident reader has been led. Also revealed are the devices and effects, especially those relating to the chronological structure of the narrative and its reading, through which the novelist has been able to reawaken the social assumptions underlying the naive experience of the world and time.

If I restrict myself to this short story, I am not sure that one can say of "temporality in Faulkner" what Sartre says of it in a famous article.[3] No doubt because his work as a novelist led (or forced) him to attend closely to the relationship between the time of practice and narrative time, Faulkner opted to make a visible break with the traditional conception of the novel and with the naively chronological representation of the experience of time. As Sartre writes:

When you read *The Sound and the Fury*, you are first struck by the oddities of the technique. Why has Faulkner broken up the time of his story and jumbled up the pieces? Why is the first window that opens onto this narrative world the mind of an idiot? The reader is tempted to look for landmarks and to reconstruct the chronology for himself.[4]

But perhaps that is exactly what the author wants to make the reader do—take on the work of identification and reconstruction that has to be done in order to "find his way," and in doing so to discover how much he loses when he finds his way too easily, as in novels that are conventionally organized, especially as regards the temporal structure of the narrative.

Like kinetic art, which needs help from the onlooker in order to come into existence, Faulkner's novels are also "time machines" which—far from offering a ready-made theory of time, which only needs to be made explicit, as Sartre seems to have thought—force the spectator to make this theory him or *herself*, from the material supplied by the narrative and, more importantly, from everything that is brought to the surface by the reflexive return imposed by the disconcerting effect of reading the narrative of the events, i.e. the reader's temporal experience as an agent acting in ordinary existence and as a reader. Indeed, like the experimental breaks that ethnomethodologists sometimes induce—suggesting, for example, to a student that when his mother asks him to fetch milk from the kitchen, he should reply "But where's the kitchen?"—Faulkner's narratives denounce the tacit agreements on which common sense is based—for example, the one between the traditional novelist and his or her reader. They call into question the shared doxa which is the basis of doxic experience of the world and the novel's representation of that world.

In consciously taking on the task, a quite extraordinary one in its apparent banality, of *telling a story*, that is of placing himself in the distanced, neutralized relation to practice and its specific logic that is implied in the social act of narration, Faulkner found himself led to write into the very structure of his stories a very profound inquiry into the experience we have of time both in our lives and in the narration of our lives and of the lives of other peoples. This inquiry, and the beginnings of an answer that he brings to it, in accordance with the logic and with the specific means of his practice as a writer, invite and help us to *produce* a theory of temporality which is not, strictly, Faulkner's theory. Nor is it the theory Sartre attributes to Faulkner: I do not think it is true to say that "the time of Faulknerian man," a "creature deprived of possibles," is "without a future."

This theory—which can only be constructed on the condition that one repudiates and overcomes the spontaneous philosophy of time of which the novelistic representation, especially in its biographical variant, is the most typical manifestation—cannot be sketched in a few sentences, as I shall do here, without paying a somewhat perverse homage to the peremptory tone that Sartre so readily adopted in his article on time in Faulkner. The spontaneous theory of action, and of the narration of action, that the "pre-Faulknerian" novelist, and often also the historian, depend on in the writing of history—a theory which finds its natural extension in the philosophy of temporal consciousness (Husserl's or Sartre's)—forbids access to genuine knowledge of the structure of practice. The production of time that occurs in and through practice has nothing in common with an experience (*Erlebnis*) of time, even if it presupposes an experience (*Erfahrung*), or, as Searle puts it,[5] a set of "background assumptions." Examples in Faulkner include those which underlie the hypothesis of Emily's fellow citizens as to the meaning of her relationship with Homer Barron or its prospects, and those which underlie their unanimous, instant judgments:

So the next day *we all* said, "She will kill herself"; and we said it would be the best thing. When she had first begun to be seen with Homer Barron, *we* had said, "She will marry him." Then *we* said. . . .

The agent temporalizes himself in the very act through which he transcends the immediate present towards the future implied in the past of which his habitus is the product. He produces time in the practical anticipation of an immediate future which is at the same time the practical actualization of the past. Thus one can reject the metaphysical representation of time as a reality in itself, exterior and anterior to practice, without having to accept the philosophy of mind which, in Husserl's philosophy, is associated with the (central) idea of *temporalization*. Temporalization is neither the constitutive activity of a transcendental consciousness detached from the world, as Husserl would have it, nor even that of a *Dasein* engaged in the world (Heidegger), but that of a habitus orchestrated with other habitus (in opposition to Husserl's conception of transcendental intersubjectivity).

This practical relation to the world and to time, which is common to a set of agents bringing the same assumptions into the construction of the meaning of the world in which they move, is the basis of their experience of that world as a commonsense world. The habitus, a "practical sense" which is the product of internalization of the structures of the social world—and, in particular, of its immanent tendencies and its temporal rhythms—gives rise to assumptions and anticipations which are generally confirmed by the course of events. They therefore consolidate a relationship of immediate familiarity or ontological complicity with the familiar world that cannot in any way be reduced to a subject-object relationship. In short, the habitus is the principle of the social structuring of temporal existence, of all the anticipations and presuppositions through which we practically construct the "sense" of the world—both its meaning and its orientation towards the future. That is what Faulkner forces us to discover by methodically disconcerting the sense of the social game that we apply both in our experience of the world and in reading the narrative of that experience.

—Translated by Richard Nice

Fiction as Historical Evidence:
A Dialogue in Paris, 1646

Some years ago Marcel Detienne, the well-known author of many works on Greek mythology, mentioned with some irony the attempt made by Moses Finley in his *The World of Odysseus* to circumscribe some historical elements within Homer's poems.[1] Apparently, Finley's assumption that it was possible to trace a boundary between a mythical and an historical level within the same text implied a referential fallacy, smacking of positivistic naiveté. Behind Finley's attitude—Detienne wrote—there is a long story which would be interesting to reconstruct.[2] I will analyze an early chapter of it, in a perspective quite different from Detienne's.

I

The text I will deal with is a dialogue, written either at the end of 1646 or at the very beginning of 1647, but printed only eighty years later: *De la lecture des vieux romans (On reading old romances).*[3] Jean Chapelain, its author, spent twenty years writing and revising an ambitious poem—*La Pucelle or la France délivrée* (Leyden, 1656)—which, after an initial success, turned out to be a total disaster. Today, after Voltaire's parody (*La Pucelle d'Orléans*), nobody—not even critics—reads it.[4] Chapelain's fame rests either on his essays or on his letters.[5] *De la lecture des vieux romans*, published for the first time in 1728, was reprinted in 1870, in 1936, and in 1971. The text is, therefore, far from being unknown, at least to specialists; its implications, however, deserve (as I will try to demonstrate) further attention.[6]

The dialogue is addressed to Paul de Gondi, then vicar of the archbishop of Paris, later on to become cardinal of Retz. The other participants are Chapelain himself; Gilles Ménage, the philologist; and Jean François Sarasin, the historian (and poet as well) who, some time later, wrote a dialogue, *S'il faut qu'un jeune homme soit amoureux*, based on a similar situation and including more or less the same participants.[7] The Retz academy, meeting place of poets, critics, and antiquarians, was one of the best known literary circles in mid-seventeenth-century Paris.[8] Chapelain explains how he had been surprised by Ménage and Sarasin in the act of reading *Lancelot du Lac*, a romance (he owned two editions of it, as we learn from the catalogue of his library).[9] The reaction of the two friends was very different. Sarasin said that *Lancelot* was "the source of all those romances which, in the last four or five centuries, have had such a great success in all European courts." Ménage, being a partisan of antiquity, expressed his surprise that a man full of taste like Chapelain praised a book which had been scorned even by the partisans of modernity. Chapelain replied that he had started reading *Lancelot* in order to collect evidence for a book, projected by Ménage some years earlier, on the origins of French language.[10] In *Lancelot* Chapelain had found words and idioms showing how French developed from a crude stage to its present refinement.

Ménage did not object to this linguistic approach: but when Chapelain admitted that, in reading *Lancelot*, he had begun to appreciate the text itself, Ménage became furious. "How dare you to appreciate," he said, "such a dreadful corpse, scorned even by ignorant and vulgar people? Are you going to discover in such a barbarous writer [the author of *Lancelot*] a man comparable to Homer or to Livius?" This was, of course, a rhetorical question; but Chapelain's answer to this double, paradoxical comparison was far from being obvious. On a formal level, he explained, Homer and the author of *Lancelot* are very different, one being noble and sublime, the other vulgar and low. But the subject of their works can be easily compared. Both have written "fables," that is fictional narratives. Aristotle's judgement of *Lancelot* would have been as favorable as the judgment he gave of Homer's poems: the use of magic in the former is not so different from the gods' intervention in the latter.

All this would give to Chapelain a relevant place among those seventeenth-century erudites and critics who paved the way to Mabillon and Montfaucon, creating the premises for the discovery of the Middle Ages— or, as we read in *De la lecture des vieux romans*, of modern antiquity, "*l'antiquité moderne.*"[11] According to Chapelain, the author of *Lancelot* was a "barbarian, who has been praised by barbarians"—"although," he went on, "a complete barbarian, he was not." In this milder note, as well as in the acknowledgment that a romance like *Lancelot* fitted in with Aristotle's principles, we can see, retrospectively, the very beginnings of a deep change in taste. In the case of Chapelain, however, the discovery of the Middle Ages was related more to history than to literature, as the most original passages of his dialogue will demonstrate.

II

Chapelain's answer to Ménage's ironical question, whether the author of *Lancelot* should be compared to Livius, must be quoted in full: "To compare *Lancelot* and Livius would be as absurd as to compare Vergil and Livius, that is falsity and truth. I dare say, however, that even if *Lancelot*, being based only on fictional events, cannot be compared to Livius as an example of a true narrative (*par la vérité de l'histoire*), a comparison should be made on a different level, as a true account of customs and manners (*par la vérité des moeurs et des coutumes*). From this point of view both authors give us perfect accounts: either of the age on which one [that is Livius] has written, or of the age in which the other [that is, the author of *Lancelot*] has written."[12] Ménage looks puzzled. Chapelain, therefore, tries to justify his attitude from a theoretical point of view. A writer who creates a story, a fictional narrative based on human beings, must depict his characters according to the customs and manners of his own age—otherwise they would not be believable.[13]

Behind this sentence we can detect an implicit allusion to the famous passage of *Poetics* (1451 a), in which Aristotle makes clear that "a poet's object is not to tell what actually happened but what could and would happen either probably or inevitably." Chapelain, however, makes a truly original step by identifying an historical, not purely logical or psychological, element in what he calls "*le vraisemblable*"—that is, poetic plausibility.[14] *Lancelot*, he says, having been written "in the dark ages of our modern antiquity, under the sole inspiration of the book of nature, gives a faithful account, if not of what really happened among the kings and knights of that age, at least of what was supposed to have happened, on the basis either of still surviving practices, or of evidence showing that similar practices had been alive in the past."[15] Chapelain, therefore, concluded that *Lancelot* provided "a direct representation (*une représentation naïve*) as well as, in a sense (*pour ainsi dire*), a precise and accurate history of the customs then prevailing in the courts (*une histoire certaine et exacte des moeurs qui régnaient dans les cours d'alors*)."

To deal with literary works as stocks of historical information was not an absolute novelty in itself. Examples of this attitude can be found in classical historiography. Thucydides, for instance, in a famous passage at the very beginning of his work (1,10), tried to reconstruct the size of ancient Greek vessels on the basis of Homer's *Catalogue of Ship*. However, in suggesting that *Lancelot* should be regarded more as a document than as a monument, Chapelain had been certainly inspired by some recent examples provided by the antiquarians.[16] In his *Recherches de la France*, first published in 1560, and reprinted several times with notable additions, Etienne Pasquier devoted a whole section to the medieval origins of French poetry. Following the same track, Claude Fauchet wrote a *Recueil de l'origine de la langue et poesie françoise, ryme et romans*, in which he listed names and works of 127 French poets living before the year 1300.[17] More specifically, in his *Origine des dignitez et magistrats de France*, Fauchet used passages taken either from *Le Roman de la Rose* or from other medieval romances by Chretien de Troyes, and so on, in order to clarify which tasks had been attached to institutions like *maire du Palais, sénéschal, grand maistre*. "Any writer, including the most wretched," he wrote, "can be occasionally useful, at least as a witness of his own age (*au moins pour le temoignage de son temps*)."[18]

In the same spirit, Chapelain, at the end of his dialogue, mentioned a still unpublished treatise by Chantereau Le Fèvre, in which "the great antiquarian," he said, used to mention Lancelot as a real authority on customs and manners. In fact, in reading the *Traité des fiefs et de leur origine* published by Chantereau Le Fèvre's son seventeen years later, I found only one quotation from *Lancelot*, albeit a significant one. In order to explain the exact meaning of *meffaire*—the action by which a feudal lord broke the bond between a vassal and himself—Chantereau Le Fèvre quoted a passage of *Lancelot*. It provides, he said, the best illustration of such a term, in so far as the author—obviously a monk—had meant to describe, behind an invented plot and some fictitious names, "the manners and the way of living (*les moeurs et la manière de vivre*) of the knights living in that age."[19] The comparison suggested by Sarasin, another participant to the dialogue, has also an antiquarian flavor: "old tapestries, old painting, old sculptures," he said, "bequeathed to us by our forefathers, are like those old novels which (as Chapelain said) give an exact painting of customs and manners of those ages."[20]

But the most original implications of Chapelain's words are elsewhere, in a passage in which he suggests that some less accessible (and therefore more valuable) historical evidence can be drawn from fictional narratives *in so far they have a fictional character*: "Physicians analyze their patients' corrupted humours on the basis of their dreams: in the same way, we can analyze the customs and manners of the past on the basis of the phantasies described in their writings." In suggesting that history could be inferred from poetry, truth from imagination, reality from possibility, Chapelain was implicitly rephrasing the venerable distinctions traced by Aristotle in his *Poetics*. To label the anonymous author of *Lancelot* as "the historian of his age's manners," Ménage said, summing up Chapelain's attitude, is not that the highest possible praise? Especially because (he went on) you claim that his work "is a supplement of the extant chronicles. They tell us only that a prince was born, that a prince died; they mention the most important events of their kingdoms, and that's all. From a book like *Lancelot*, on the contrary, we become intimate friends of those people: we catch the very essence of their souls." [21]

III

We should resist the rather silly temptation of presenting Chapelain as a forerunner of some contemporary historiographical tendency, such as the so-called history of mentalities. However, the sheer originality of what I have quoted is not in question. [22] In another passage Chapelain says that *Lancelot* can be compared, from the point of view of truthfulness, to the most celebrated medieval chronicles—those by Saxo Grammaticus, Froissart, Monstrelets, and so on. However, he goes even further, comparing the cognitive potentialities of what he calls *histoire des moeurs*, history of manners, on one hand, and the chronicles' laconic attitude. Although he prudently says that they supplement each other, the implicit superiority of the former looks obvious. It must be emphasized that this attitude would have become widespread only one century later. Around 1650, a man like La Popelinière had been totally forgotten, as had been his lonely effort to write history in a transcontinental perspective, using concepts like *civilisation*. [23] Only jurists, antiquarians, and travellers were collecting evidence on customs and manners. To regard this kind of intellectual activity, as Chapelain was suggesting, as a more sophisticated kind of history was a sheer paradox—a double paradox, in fact, insofar as it was based on a romance like *Lancelot*. The reaction of Ménage was significant: to compare a romance and an historical work meant "to present as truthful a writer who, as you have been compelled to admit, is absolutely fabulous." In a mildly skeptical work published the same year (*Préface à un ouvrage historique*, 1646) La Mothe Le Vayer had remarked that the basic truth of an historical work is not destroyed by occasional mistakes. Chapelain's attitude was bolder, as the aforementioned words ascribed to Ménage show. [24]

In order to put Chapelain's dialogue in its context, we should start from these words. They implied two apparently obvious statements: first, that *vérité* and *fable*, truth and fable, were contradictory concepts; second, that history was intrinsically related to the former. Both statements were exhibited, so to speak, in the frontispiece of a book by Desmarets de Saint-Sorlin, printed in Paris in 1648: a diffuse allegorical interpretation of pagan religion. The title's puzzling oxymoron—*La vérité des fables* (*The truth of fables*)—was clarified by the subtitle: *ou l'histoire des dieux de l'antiquité* (*or the history of ancient gods*). Other contemporary examples could be easily quoted.

IV

Fable, the *Dictionnaire de l'Académie* said, means "a fictional narrative, invented in order either to teach or to amuse. . . . Fable means also subject, for instance the subject of an epic or dramatic poem, the subject of a novel."[25] In seventeenth-century France, therefore, *fable* had the same double meaning attributed to the Latin word *fabula* or the Greek word *mythos*. However, the contradiction between *fable* and *histoire* implies a conceptual framework which cannot be found in Aristotle's *Poetics*. The reason is obvious: *fable* is a perfect translation of *mythos*, but a comparison between *histoire* and *historía* shows that the former had a wider meaning (and one more contradictory as well).[26] As Furetière remarked in his *Dictionary*, "Histoire can be referred also to romances, to narratives centered on fictional but not intrinsically impossible events, either imagined by a writer, or presented in a disguised form."[27] The English language makes a distinction between *history* and *story*; but in contemporary French or Italian, words like *histoire* or *storia* can be referred either to a true (or pretending to be true) narrative, or to a fictional, even mendacious one, as in sentences like "Non raccontarmi delle storie," "Tu me contes des histoires."

A situation like this would have been literally unthinkable for a contemporary of Aristotle. In the late sixteenth century (and possibly even earlier) people began to express some uneasiness about it. La Popelinière, for instance, wrote in his book *L'histoire des histoires, avec l'idée de l'histoire accomplie* that a definition of history on purely etymological grounds would have been absurd, "because this word has such a general meaning that it can be referred to every kind of discourse, besides the historical one. As a synonym of narrative—from *historein*, to collect informations, to know, to narrate—history could be linked not only to every science, but also to every discourse, human, natural, or supernatural. Even fables, therefore, could be labelled 'histories.'"[28] More than fifty years later, Charles Sorel, in his treatise *Des histoires et des romans, On Histories and Romances,* which is included in a volume called *De la connoissance des bons livres, On the Knowledge of Good Books,* printed in Paris in 1671, emphasized that in praising history he meant only "History which is true and useful, not that fictitious one, which is invented only in order to amuse."[29] Scholars and learned people (he went on) are not familiar with this distinction. They ignore the fact that some people not only praise romances by labelling them "histories," but say that fictional narratives should be preferred to narratives based on truth.

V

Charles Sorel's intervention on a subject like the relationship between *histoire* and *roman* was particularly fitting. Before being appointed "first historiographer of France" (a charge inherited from his uncle), Sorel, born in Picardy from a family of *robins,* had written several novels. The most successful, *L'Histoire comique de Francion (The Comic History of Francion),*[30] was published in 1623 under a pseudonym ("N. de Moulinet, sieur du Parc, Gentilhomme Lorrain"). It was reprinted in an enlarged version three years later, with a slightly different title: *La vraye histoire comique de Francion (The True Comic History of Francion).* The emphasis on "true history" in the late writings of Sorel could be interpreted as a conscious rejection of the "true history" published when he was a young man. In other words, the historian should be regarded, at least in this case, as a repentant novelist.[31] However, a section on different varieties of novel included in Sorel's *Bibliothèque Françoise* (1664) seems to imply a more complex attitude. Romances, and more specifically *romans de chevalrie,* being written in an obsolete language, are nowadays out of fashion, Sorel says.

Many readers, he goes on to say, therefore have begun to look for "novels based on plausible circumstances, which would provide a representation of history." Unbelievable adventures centered on emperors, kings, princes, and knights are unfashionable: people are now looking for the opposite, for pastoral loves. Many people, however, rejected this literary genre as utterly implausible: those shepherds and shepherdesses looked in fact extremely polite, more similar to refined courtiers than to clumsy and vulgar peasants. "Readers asked for invented stories which would represent people's characters as they are, depicting their manners and their condition in a direct way."

Even heroic novels, in order to attain perfection, should be believable: "Many readers, however, like better the style of modern adventures, as it has been used in those narratives [but Sorel says *histoires*] which are presented as true, not only as plausible." The climax of this process, according to Sorel, is provided by "those fine novels, either comic or satiric, [which] more than anything else, seem to provide a representation of history (*des images de l'histoire*): their subject being provided by the most usual facts of life, it's much easier to find the truth in them." [32]

Again, we must refrain from anachronistic temptations. Sorel is a baroque novelist, not a late-nineteenth-century naturalistic writer. [33] In a crucial section of his *Bibliothèque Françoise*, centered on comic and satiric novels, we can find, besides a small group of Spanish titles (*Lazarillo, Don Quijote*, Quevedo's *Buscón*), a list of authors and texts which includes Rabelais, *Kepler's Dream*, Cyrano's novels, as well as, of course, Sorel's writings: *Francion*, defended notwithstanding its alleged obscenity, *Polyandre, Le Berger extravagant*. [34] Sorel's self-apologetic purpose does not affect the remarkable perceptiveness of his description. For some decades, as it has been shown by Erich Auerbach in his famous essay *La cour et la ville*, the relationship between French writers and their readers had been changing. [35] A growing audience, largely composed by women, was partly responsible for this revolution in taste. They were hungry for novels. [36] Some novelists were responding to this pressure by representing middle- or lower-class characters, involved in everyday life events, as well as by substituting fanciful stories with plausible plots, which could be regarded as "representations of history." Plausibility, therefore, had gone closer and closer to truth. [37] Twenty years earlier, Chapelain, in his unpublished dialogue, had compared a romance like *Lancelot* to an historical work, emphasizing its "truth" as well as the "perfect representations" embedded in it.

VI

In the Baroque age, in a culture obsessed by the elusive relationship between reality and illusion, the ambiguous meaning of a word like *histoire* seemed to express a feeling of contiguity and distance as well. Should we assume, therefore, that in seventeenth-century France there was a convergence between history and novel? Literary hybrids, such as the insertion of passages or even full pages taken from Livy or from Amyot's translation of Plutarch into narrative texts, would suggest a positive answer to this question. [38] From a general point of view, however, there was a clear-cut divergence between the two genres. In seventeenth-century French (let's even say European) historiography, those elements of historical truth, which had been praised by Sorel and Chapelain either in modern novels or in romances written in "modern antiquity," were conspicuously, as well as inevitably, absent. The same Sorel who was, as an historian, a follower of a severe classical taste, wrote in his *Advertissement sur l'histoire de la monarchie française* (1628) that in the past "l'on ne savait ce que c'estait parmy eux de fiefs, d'arrière fiefs ny de franc alleu, ou bien si on le scavait, les historiens ne s'amusaient pas à en faire de longues définitions."[39] An historical work was meant to deal with political and military events, in a noble style, derived from classical models. Customs and manners were subjects pertaining to antiquarians like Chantereau Le Febvre, not to history. Moreover, the stylistic filter worked as a social filter as well, insofar as it prevented dealing with characters or events which would have been unfitting to the lofty style required by historical works. Only biography (even in this case, since antiquity) could imply a partial transgression of history's stylistic and social boundaries. Collections of artists' lives, Sorel remarked, include sometimes even lower-middle-class people; but their presence is justified, he said, because they paint portraits of illustrious people.[40]

If we compare the so-called comic or satiric novel with seventeenth-century historiography, we can see that they were absolutely different, not to say, opposite, both in form and in content. The former, as we have seen, dealt with everyday life's events, acted by middle- or lower-class people, described in a mixed-up style. Elements related to a higher style, such as mythological metaphors, used to be debased by inserting them in a trivial or obscene context.[41] In his introduction to *Polyandre, histoire comique*, Sorel remarked that romance and novel appealed to different audiences: "There are people," he wrote, "who are fond of reading books about kings and emperors, princes and princesses, and their respective deeds. Other people, on the contrary, like better to read books about small events, such as a trip to Paris, a stroll—events which could happen to themselves or to their friends—because they regard them as more plausible and more believable."[42] As you can see, Sorel was implicitly addressing himself to a specific audience—a provincial, middle-class group.[43]

These sociological connotations are not surprising. In his essay *La cour et la ville* (which I mentioned before) Erich Auerbach lists both Sorel and Chapelain as members of a large group of writers who before 1650 built up the dominant criteria of French literary taste. Many of them (including both Sorel and Chapelain) came either from bourgeois or from *robins* families.[44]

The relationship between these writers and their audience, which was probably becoming larger and larger, as well as socially mixed, was presumably rather close. However, literary ideals such as *spontaneity* and *plausibility* could be used also by different writers for very different purposes. Between 1620 and 1630 Jean-Pierre Camus, bishop of Belley, wrote (having been inspired, apparently, by François de Sales) a long series of edifying novels, sometimes in a contemporary setting.[45] Camus criticized some novelists for choosing as main characters only kings and queens—a small minority among human beings. His argument was related to morality and plausibility as well: God, he said, "who cares only of humble people, usually chooses to manifest his power through feeble individuals."[46] He labelled his novels "historic booklets"; his own style, "historiographical style"; his own attitude comparable to "historians' attitude."[47] By these emphatic statements he meant to emphasize the truthfulness of his narratives. In a literal sense, however, either the history referred to by Camus or the *history of manners* mentioned by Chapelain did not exist.

VII

To be more precise: they did not exist yet. Voltaire's *Essai sur les moeurs*—the first example of a new kind of history, centered on customs and manners—was published only in 1758, that is one hundred years after Chapelain's unpublished dialogue. In the meantime, however, the reference to history had become more and more important, insofar as a new kind of fictional narrative had emerged. "The story," Daniel Defoe wrote, introducing *Robinson Crusoe*, "is told with modesty, with seriousness. . . . The Editor believes the thing to be a just history of facts; neither is there any appearance of fiction in it." Fielding explained that he had chosen for the title of his masterwork—*The History of Tom Jones, a Foundling*—the word "history" instead of "life" or "an apology of a life" because he had taken his inspiration from the historian's work. In our novel, he declared, "we intend . . . rather to pursue the method of those writers, who profess to disclose the revolutions of countries, than to imitate the painful and voluminous historian, who, to preserve the regularity of his series, thinks himself obliged to fill up as much paper with the detail of months and years in which nothing remarkable happened, as he employs upon those notable areas when the greatest scenes have been transacted on the human stage."

The allusion to "those writers, who profess to disclose the revolutions of countries" is clarified by another well-known passage, in which Clarendon's

History of the Rebellion is labelled by Fielding "so solemn a work." The passage is half ironical; there is no doubt, however, that Fielding learned from Clarendon to change the pace of his narrative according to the importance of the events. One year, half a year, three weeks, three days, two days, twelve hours, nearly twelve hours: the sequence of titles of *Tom Jones'* central books emphasizes the frantic acceleration of the plot. This disjunction between physical and narrative time will run to an extreme, as you know, with the works of two Irish writers—Sterne and Joyce. In a sense, it would be possible to say that the narrative revolution started by a novel based on the description of a single day in Dublin, had behind it, as a very indirect model, an historical narrative based on the first early modern political revolution.[48]

What am I talking about: fiction as historical evidence, or historiography as a fictional model? Inevitably, both. In recent years it has become fashionable to blur the distinction between novels and history by emphasizing the fictional element in both of them. This seems to me a very unilateral approach. It certainly prevents us from understanding why the relationship between the two narratives has always been so complex—sometimes apparently inexistent, sometimes overtly competitive. Both novels and historical works imply a reference to reality, insofar as every narrative, including the most fictitious, has cognitive implications.[49] This is why, as I have tried to show, in the last three centuries novelists have been, in many subterranean ways, a challenge for historians—and vice versa.

The Ephemeral and the Eternal: Reflections on History

Lucien Febvre: History in the Present Tense

When Baudelaire characterized beauty in his essay *Le Peintre de la vie moderne*, he thought that it was composed of two indissoluble elements: the ephemeral and the eternal.[1] In this attempt to reject the rigidity of the classical, academic vision of beauty founded on the rules of ancient Greek art, the poet of modern life introduced a category—the ephemeral—that claimed at the same time the right of history, of historical change, and the right of the present. Even if beauty gives us the sense of something lasting, or eternal, a large portion of it is contingent, transitory, because beauty is not fixed forever by permanent definitions. Beauty changes, corresponds to different values and different expectations, according to the place and the moment. Every epoch and culture has its visions of beauty; when we look at them we feel the touch of history, of time upon things and people. This means that the past should not dictate our taste, because the present determines needs, desires, and values. The classical rules of the Greeks were made by their very present, the ideas and actions still warm with life, sparkling with the ephemeral light of what happens in the moment it happens.

Like beauty, history is composed by two elements: past and present; history is the recording or the reconstruction of the past, and also the making of events, the present surrounding us. Historians are caught within two chronologies: the past that they want to recapture and the present, the time from which they are writing. And because that present changes, moving into another present, the past is not eternal. A prejudice frames narrative sentences, giving the impression that the past is determined, fixed, eternally settled, while the future is open, not decided.[2] But the past is open.

In Lucien Febvre's effort to renew historical studies, he had already in the 1940s launched his attack against a congealed conception of the past:

The Past does not exist, the Past is not a given datum. The Past is not a collection of cadavers nor should the historian's function be to find all these cadavers, giving them a number, taking pictures of each one of them, and finally identifying them. The Past does not produce the historian. It is the historian who gives birth to history. . . . History, like poetry, is the child of the century and of mankind. History does not exist. Only historians do exist.[3]

Febvre writes in a militant tone: sharp negative sentences and short statements that announce the contrast between an old vision of history and a new one. More than a contrast: a battle. Febvre perceives a dramatic change in historical studies and protests against the positivist method of writing history: positivist historians, the historians of the Sorbonne, such as Charles Seignobos, write history as if the past existed as a given substance, without realizing that, in order to have history, historians have to write it. Febvre's militant tone marks a fight against the previous generation of historians: the new historians define themselves against the immediately preceding ones who have institutional power.

As Carl Schorske suggests in his reading of the Ringstrasse, political and intellectual movements often take the shape of generational battles: the rebellion against the fathers, their beliefs, and their values structures the Oedipal struggle that regulates individual as well as collective phenomena. Febvre forcefully expressed his position: he could not accept "the history of the 1870s generation, their flickering prudence, their renunciation of all synthesis, their laborious but lazy cult of facts, and their almost exclusive taste for diplomatic history."[4] The historian who, together with Marc Bloch, founded *Les Annales* wanted to get rid of the meek scientific, positivist vision of the historian as a sort of doctor or policeman patiently dealing with past facts. Febvre's criticism of positivist intellectual laziness is not far from Walter Benjamin's characterization of historicism (or positivist history as opposed to historical materialism): "To historians who wish to relive an era, Fustel de Coulanges recommends that they blot out everything they know about the later course of history. There is no better way of characterizing the method with which historical materialism has broken. It is a process of empathy whose origin is the indolence of the heart [*intellectuellement paresseux*, intellectually lazy, said Febvre], *acedia*, which despairs of grasping and holding the genuine historical image as it flares up briefly."[5]

Febvre's style is nevertheless very different from Benjamin's aphoristic one.[6] It does not consist of the concentration and fragmentation which is typical of Benjamin. Febvre's style echoes Michelet's. Michelet is one of the great discoveries of the *Annales*' historians, mainly because of what we would today call his interdisciplinary orientation. Michelet's history did not privilege politics, but ventured into social and cultural analysis, history of medicine, of magic, of beliefs, of symbolic representations. In his inaugural lecture at Strasbourg, Febvre announced that his history was idealist in its spirit and would continue as such even if all analysis would prove the primacy of the economical sphere: "Economical facts are, as all other social facts, facts of belief and opinion: even richness, work, money, are not 'things' but ideas, representations, human judgements on 'things.'"[7] Febvre constantly fought against all those historians who make history "as their old grandmothers weaved and stitched canvas (*au petit point*)."[8] For him, the minute detail was not crucial: what was most important was an understanding capable of reconstructing a situation, a whole *mentalité*. Michelet, too, aimed at this understanding.

The first way by which the historian can give up his intellectual sluggishness—or sadness, to use Benjamin's word—is to be engaged in the work of a team. The first issue of the *Annales* (1929) stressed the desire of taking historians out of their strict disciplinary circle, shaking them from the reassuring practice of "their old good methods" applied to the documents of the past. The founders of the *Annales* wanted historians to work together with "the all the more numerous researchers who, often feverishly, dedicate their activity to the study of contemporary economies and societies."[9] Past and present are interwoven, and the present casts light into the past through the historical being who lives in his century and writes history. The historian is the measure of the past, the creator of history. Moreover the historian is not alone, buried in the dust of the archives, but works and should work with other people, dealing with other disciplines. Historical research, like scientific research in the twentieth century, should be collective.[10]

An indispensable tool for joining past and present in a constant dialogue is the book review. The book review has the value of a continuous up-to-date vision of long-term research; it carries the freshness of information, confronts the work of a researcher with the judgement of another. The *Annales*' historians have displayed an intense interest in commenting on contemporary studies about the most various historical periods, and from diverse disciplines, especially sociology, anthropology, and psychology. The book review represents the activity of the historian as a journalist who seizes other researchers at the moment they are writing, "creating" today the history of the past. The book review represents for historians the possibility to work not only with the archives of the past, but also with some present representations of it. In review articles historians do not just collect data from the past; they become critics, take positions in relation to the fabrication and circulation of knowledge, and express a value judgement about the way in which a project is composed, its material selected, and its argument articulated. In other words critics realize that history or any other field of knowledge has been written.

Febvre wanted the historians to think about the way in which they make history, the tools they use, the aspects of the present they bring together with any archival work. In "Examen de conscience," Febvre quoted an ironical remark by Péguy suggesting that historians do not have the time to investigate the foundations of history since they have to gather facts. Febvre believed that the historians in fact should ask themselves not only the question of *what* they write, but also the one of *how* they write history: that means to consider how history has been written and how one should write it today. The best way to do this is not to produce theoretical essays—abstract conceptualizations—which do nothing but re-establish the traditional division between philosophy and history, between the abstract and the concrete. The best way is to suggest concepts within the course of practices. The book review constitutes a concrete way of dealing with abstract problems.

For example, one of the most important contributions of the *Annales* group was introducing the concept of mentalities into the historian's language. To be aware of mentalities means to bring into the historical account the role of collective and unconscious forces that move history slowly but inevitably, in the same way as hidden geological forces move deep down in the earth. Instead of writing a whole theory about mentalities, congealing it in a list of concepts and programmatic rules, it seemed to Febvre more effective to seize the mentality in action, either taking a case, like Rabelais in the sixteenth century, or commenting on the work of another historian. Thus, Febvre admired Johan Huizinga's *Herbst vor Mittelalter*: a splendid work full of flashes on the medieval period that illuminate the history of mentalities. A new image of the late Middle Ages emerged from this book: the overwhelming power of passions, the need for revenge mixed with the sense of justice. Huizinga is showing the men and women of the Middle Ages to us, men and women of the twentieth century who try to manage our suffering with lucidity and precaution, to administer our sorrows slowly and moderately—I would say with a dropper. He is showing us the men and women of the end of the Middle Ages, who knew nothing but one brutal and categoric alternative: either death or grace. And grace often appears sudden, absolute, total, even undeserved, if grace could ever be undeserved. Huizinga concludes that life "was so dramatic and violent that it gave off the smell of blood and roses."[11]

In Huizinga's book, history is no longer "a sleeping necropolis where only disembodied, bloodless shadows go by."[12] Far from being the dry and sad account of dates, events, and persons, history is capable of speaking the past to the men of the present. It emerges with its smells, colors, images: "Every epoch symbolically constructs its own universe."[13] Febvre cannot accept Ranke's "naive realism,"[14] his view that the historian tries to discover the past "the way it really was." It is the symbolic construction that sparkles into the present.

A new journal or trend or discipline or approach cannot be conceived without a gesture of rebellion against the previous generation, their ideals, their methods. Chronos and Saturnus: that is the eternal myth. Lucien Febvre rejected the elementary, passionless determinism of Charles Seignobos and Charles-Victor Langlois, who were satisfied with the following statement: "All history of events is an evident and incontestable sequence of events, each one being the determining cause of the other." Their orderly chain of events, dates, people smoothly following each other was just an accumulation of details for a dull textbook; it was not history for the new generation. Febvre could not share the principles of the *école méthodique*, and its leader, Gabriel Monod, who had been the director of his dissertation *Philippe II et la Franche Comté.* How different was Febvre's fever from the respect for the past that Gabriel Monod suggested in his 1876 manifesto introducing his journal *La Revue historique*:

Our *Revue* will be a journal of positive science and free debate, but it will be confined to the domain of facts and will be closed to political and philosophical theories. . . . Historians cannot understand the past without certain feelings and ideas in order to identify for a moment with those of past men and women. . . . Historians will at the same time approach that past with a sense of respect, because they feel more than anybody else the many ties that link us to our forefathers.[15]

Respect was too mild for the new historian who did not want to count cadavers and thought that "the past does not exist." The historian living in the present should handle the past roughly, as Roland Barthes said that the critic should do with the text. In his foreword to *Le Problème de l'incroyance au XVIe siècle*, Febvre wrote that he does not want to copy his predecessors who studied the Renaissance: "Not because of a paradoxical and gratuitous taste for the new: but because I am simply a historian, and the historian is not the one who knows. He is the one who researches. Therefore he challenges already acquired solutions."[16] Being a historian means to conceive hypotheses and to choose facts.

History, *The Return of Martin Guerre*, and *The Spider's Stratagem*

Collective work and attachments to the contemporary world: nothing could be closer to the conditions Febvre wished for the new historian than film-making. History through films: it is a way to give life to the past, to endow it with light and color using the techniques of the present. I would like to discuss two very different films, *The Return of Martin Guerre* by Daniel Vigne (1982) and *The Spider's Stratagem* by Bernardo Bertolucci (1970), because they both represent powerful reflections on history. Of course, one could have chosen many other historical films, like Rossellini's *La Prise du pouvoir par Louis XVI* or Renoir's *La Marseillaise*; but I think that the advantage of the two films on which I will focus is that they do not deal with great historical events belonging to parliamentary or political history. Because of their subjects they respond to the demands of the new history proposed by the fathers of the *Annales* school. It is well known that Natalie Zemon Davis was an active collaborator of Vigne's. Davis is the historian who announced in *Society and Culture in Early Modern France* that she studied *le peuple menu*, their everyday life and its effects upon religion and social structures.[17] Bertolucci's film stages the problem of generations, the fight between fathers and sons that is an essential component of any intellectual history.

The two films allow a meditation on the notion of historical facts, because they pose the fundamental problem about them: authenticity. *Martin Guerre* deals with a famous trial in the sixteenth century. Martin Guerre left his village a few years after his marriage with Bertrande de Rols. Ten years later a man arrived in the village and claimed to be Martin Guerre. Bertrande seemed convinced that the man was her husband, and they returned to a life in common. But after Martin and his uncle started fighting about the revenues of Martin's land during his absence, the uncle accused Martin of being an imposter. There is a trial which is moved from the village to Toulouse, and finally the man is found guilty. Stephen Bann wrote in *The Clothing of Clio* that the film consists in a sort of *mise en abîme* of the question of authenticity, since the actor and the film must convince us as much as Martin Guerre has to convince the village about his identity.[18]

The issue is complicated by the fact that Gérard Depardieu is playing Martin, therefore there is a continuous overlapping between the character and the star. Bann points out that the audience is continuously recognizing Depardieu as an actor, as the famous French actor. The actor is the person whose identity consists of taking other identities: authenticity and fiction are then doubly staged, since Martin Guerre is the enigmatic story of the making up of an identity.

In other words, Vigne's film is going back and forth between *res factae* and *res fictae*, spectacularly presenting the conditions of both historical research and film-making, since both fluctuate between fiction and reality, objective vision and subjective glimpse. Davis says that the historian must often reconstruct an historical truth from incomplete documentation; therefore the historian must complete what is missing with his or her imagination.[19] Pure realist historians, like Ranke or Fustel de Coulanges, would have said that history had nothing to do with literature or art, that it was a science founded on documents, on facts, and that the historian must be completely objective. They would be suspicious of the blurred line between subjectivity and objectivity. For this reason, Michelet has been perceived by the positivists as a dangerous historian because he confused facts with his imagination, as was suggested by one of the founding fathers of French positivism in the second half of the nineteenth century, Hippolyte Taine. Taine attacked Michelet because of his "lyrical history."[20] But according to Davis, one of the major practitioners of *Annales* School history, there is no clear border between the realm of reality and the realm of fiction in historical representation; it oscillates between *res factae* and *res fictae*, between document and literary creation.[21]

Davis's book *Fiction in the Archives: Pardon Tales and their Tellers in Sixteenth Century France* is the product of the undecided separation between literature and history. Her interest in *Martin Guerre* was, indeed, justified by the spectacular character of the specific case centering on the question of the fake and the authentic, and by the subject, which corresponds to the suggestions of Febvre and Bloch—the history of a small rural community. In the introduction to her book on *Martin Guerre*, she remarks that the film lacked the complexity necessary to explain some important aspects of this cultural history, such as the role of religion. But in her writings we detect Davis's enthusiasm for an artistic form or technique which is actually not so distant from the montage work of the historian. In her article responding to Robert Finlay's criticism, she explains that her whole reading of the Martin Guerre story is "an exploration of the problem of truth and doubt," while she wanted "to develop an expository style for the first part of the book that could provide the equivalent of cinematic movements, with flash-forwards, rather than flash-backs."[22]

The Spider's Stratagem is the story of Athos Magnani, who comes back to his village in Emilia-Romagna in order to discover the truth about his father, also named Athos Magnani. The father was publicly considered a hero of the Italian Resistance to fascism. But since Athos Magnani (son) received a letter from a woman who had been his father's lover claiming that he had actually been a traitor, he is haunted by a terrible doubt about his father and wants to discover the truth. Hence he travels to his father's village and plans to meet with the people who knew him. The spectator will learn together with the son how Athos Magnani intended to betray his anti-fascist comrades but was unmasked by them. He was therefore executed by them during a performance of *Rigoletto*. Athos Magnani (father) agreed to die without destroying the popular myth of his heroism. The popular myth was politically necessary, as in the case of the Irish traitor Fergus Kilpatrick in "The Theme of the Traitor and the Hero," the short story from Borges's *Fictions* that inspired Bertolucci. Athos Magnani (son) discovers the truth, but he is himself taken into the spider's web: he will not be able to destroy his father's heroic image. This is the point where history and psychoanalysis meet. For Athos Magnani (son) there is no escape—as suggested by his name repeating his father's: his search for the truth will not allow him to break away from the destiny that stubbornly links fathers and sons.

The two films form a chiasma. *Martin Guerre* was conceived thanks to real historical documents and debates around the story of Martin Guerre, and it ends up with the question of fiction as a necessity for the historian in order to reconstruct the past. The historian-film maker starts from some archival material, reconstitutes a milieu, and composes a narrative structure. *The Spider's Stratagem* was, on the contrary, inspired by a literary text. The film leads to the question of the ambiguity of history, an ambiguity that is particularly puzzling because it deals with a recent epoch whose historical effects are still working upon us (and were even more when the film came out in the late 1960s).

Martin Guerre attempts to establish an historical experience, to make the past close to us, to reconstruct a social milieu. Paradoxically enough, I would say that *Martin Guerre* is a positivist film, even if it derives from the *Annaliste* tendency that rejected the positivism of the end of the century. It is positivist in its realistic naiveté, its taste for detail, its folklorist accuracy and color. *Martin Guerre* confronts historical difficulties in an academic way, even if the film is a commercial one—and a splendid one—because of the dutifulness of the execution, *"au petit point,"* Febvre would have said, as when he complained about his predecessors' way of making history. In other terms, the film takes into account the most visible lessons of an historical school and popularizes them, as a textbook, according to Febvre, popularizes diplomatic history. *The Spider's Stratagem* on the contrary explores the problem of historical representation, dramatizing the tension between the collective and the individual; it is an intellectual, avant-garde film in the vein of the Italian *nouvelle vague*. Bertolucci's film is apparently less historical than Vigne's: it has been defined as mythical or psychological because of the tension between a father and a son.[23] Its temporality is blurred: the flash-back technique; the use of the same actor, Giulio Brogi, playing both father and son, showing always the same age; Draìfa, the father's ex-lover—played by Alida Valli—whom we see old and young, following a cyclical or better a concentric conception of time, like the threads of the spider's web.[24] As in Borges's short story, the hero of Bertolucci's film discovers "a secret form of time, a design whose lines repeat themselves."[25] History is part of the inextricable network of time's circular labyrinths.

Bertolucci's film is more complex than *Martin Guerre* in its philosophy of history. Both films pose the question of what is the truth, but *The Spider's Stratagem* touches more deeply the problem of historical facts as reality and as symbolic representations. That problem is a crucial issue in any reflection on history, and both films avoid the two extreme positions of flat realism and anti-realism. The traditional positivist position is that reality speaks directly in history: Adolphe Thiers believed that history was nothing but things themselves; Hippolyte Taine praised François Guizot because he would give up any temptation of literary embellishment and let events speak by themselves. Taine admired the way Guizot wrote history, not like an orator who talks but like a statesman who does things.[26] But historians cannot simply juxtapose documents, even if they follow a strict chronology, because, as Davis herself pointed out, documents are never complete; because they are written by people, they are always colored by human subjectivity. Historians must continuously make choices, construct a system of causality, and give explanations that can convince their readers. All this breaks down any factual purity, while showing the interplay of past and present, of the ephemeral and the eternal.

The non-positivistic position, that I call anti-realist, anti-referential, was a fashionable critical perspective in the 1970s and 1980s, following—and I would say exaggerating—the Nietzschean mistrust of any positivism: facts are above all words, discourses, rhetorical practices. Roland Barthes, for example, insisted on the imaginary construction of historical discourse:

As we see, by its very structure and without there being any need to appeal to the substance of the content, historical discourse is essentially an ideological elaboration or, to be more specific, an *imaginary* elaboration, if it is true that the image-repertoire is the language by which the speaker (or "writer") of a discourse (a purely linguistic entity) "fills" the subject of the speech act (a psychological or ideological entity). Hence we understand why the notion of historical fact has so often given rise to a certain mistrust. Nietzsche has written: "There are no facts *as such*. We must always begin by introducing a meaning in order for there to be a fact." Once language intervenes (and when does not it intervene?), a fact can only be defined tautologically.[27]

If for nineteenth-century positivism reality was triumphant, for many critics associated with structuralism and post-structuralism language was the omnipotent structure webbing all human practices. The structuralist turn has had an impact on historical research. As Davis pointed out in "Du conte et de l'Histoire," questions on the writing of history such as those posed by Barthes and Hayden White "made historians realize again the literary aspects of their production."[28] Lucien Febvre also wanted to introduce the study of language into history, but as another object of investigation with which to decipher the past, to offer phenomenological evidence of beliefs and symbolic activity. The anti-referential attitude, on the other hand, focusses exclusively on language, on its untrustworthy rhetorical texture that molds beings and things. This attitude produces a thorough criticism of the foundations of historical research, and not simply the rejection of the positivistic approach. The anti-referential stand produces the deconstruction of history as the discourse that legitimizes itself with the real, as if the real were obvious, natural.

These meta-historical analyses have pushed historians to realize that they are writers, that they make use of language, and that history is something written. The historian is caught in the spider's web of language. This consciousness is more than desirable for the historian; nevertheless, there is the danger of leading the critic/historian to an endless nihilism, to a bottomless deconstructionist position for which there is never any escape from the ideological implications of language itself, from its eternal conspiracy. As Barthes wrote, facts can only be defined tautologically. Neither historical narration nor explanation seems possible. Such a critical and impotent position is, I would say, temperamentally very different from the position of the historian as indefatigable researcher who must have faith to resurrect glimmers of the past, to explain events and behaviors. When Davis underlines the importance of the study of literature for the historian, she does not find the cruel law of tautology, but the possibility "to penetrate the mental structure" of a past period and a concrete place.[29]

Truth is the question of *Martin Guerre*. Suspended between two options—the Martin Guerre who came back is or is not the authentic Martin Guerre—the film inevitably suggests the solution which was taken by the judges. Even if the spectator is pushed to believe in the return of Martin Guerre because of the intense desire with which Bertrande welcomes him, the Martin Guerre who came back is faking. All doubts are dissolved by the final evidence, *the* fact par excellence: the true Martin Guerre reappearing to claim his own identity. Bertrande was the accomplice of the imposter.[30] Legal, historical, and fictional truth are but one. Only the interpreter who stubbornly wants to make a scandal can object to the whole story and construct a Pirandellian vertigo that jeopardizes all certainties. But the temptation to scandal persists, as in all stories that we would continue or change.

Truth is also the question of *The Spider's Stratagem*. Athos Magnani's search is useless, because he cannot change anything. His effort to destroy a myth ends up in reinforcing the myth itself. Bertolucci's message is that we are taken into the web of history and cannot get out of the labyrinth of its ambiguities; nevertheless the film is not fully an exercise in meta-history. Words do not have primacy over things and neither do things have primacy over words, but there is a continuous interaction: some facts create discourses that function as historical realities. The film's pessimistic vision of an inescapable fate also suggests that no historical solution can emerge from the efforts of an individual.

Bertolucci's film is thus suspended between a bourgeois tragedy and a 1968 hope. The bourgeois tragedy consists in the impotence of the single individual when faced with history, in the Oedipal struggle with no escape. Athos Magnani is an anti-Ulysses: his voyage does not end up in a dangerous and successful adventure, like Odysseus's. If Theodor Adorno rightly saw the Homeric character of Ulysses as the symbol of bourgeois entrepreneurial power, Bertolucci proposes a modern, Joycean, negative vision of the bourgeois symbol: any search fails; no will, no adventure can redeem one from the weight of the past; no rationality can triumph over the lies ensnaring society. Not unlike the modern man of the Viennese Secession Schorske relentlessly studies, Athos Magnani tries "to strike through the masks of historicity that concealed modern man"[31] and, like Klimt in his famous drawing for the first issue of the Secession journal *Ver Sacrum*, he questions and shows the empty mirror of *Nuda Veritas*. The final scene shows Athos Magnani waiting for a train; he now knows the truth about his father, but he cannot make it public: his father will remain a hero of Italian resistance. The son is leaving the station of the Emilia-Romagna town, called *Tara*, which means *Flaw*.

Bertolucci's film was produced in the late 1960s, exactly in those years that gave rise to so many cultural changes in Western Europe. The film hints at the illusions of 1968: the rebellion against the fathers might lead to nothing, to the empty mirror of *Nuda Veritas*, to the persistent "flaw" of which we can never be rid. We are doomed to the same fate as the previous generation: that is the terrible "flaw" of our lives. Here, too, we can hear echoes of the generational conflicts in fin-de-siècle Vienna. Schorske identifies the tension between the liberals who built the Ringstrasse in Vienna in the 1850s and the following generation which could not believe in the same values but nevertheless could never completely break with them.

If one were to understand Bertolucci's film as an extension of the Marxist investigation that had been the center of his 1964 movie, *Prima della rivoluzione (Before the Revolution)*, one might see *The Spider's Stratagem* as announcing that one must leave *Tara* and try to start all over again. One must get rid of the darkness of the past, go away, find new things, search for a more fulfilling relationship between the past and the present. One must be completely aware of the "flaw" in order to begin to be liberated from it. In this regard, Bertolucci would have been close to some of Lucien Goldmann's questions. Goldmann wrote in *Sciences humaines et philosophie*: "History poses a preliminary problem. Why is man interested in some facts that are unique and localized in time? Why is man interested in the past?"[32] But Goldmann's position, unlike Bertolucci's, is that the foundation of history is "the relationship of man with other men, the very fact that the individual exists only on the background of the community."[33] Thanks to history, we learn to know "human beings who in very *different* conditions, with very *different* means, and most often not applicable to our time, fought for values analogous to our own. This gives the awareness that we belong to a whole transcending ourselves, we continue in the present, and men to come will continue into the future." But, perhaps (especiallyin light of the recent events in Eastern Europe) one can see how even the early Marxist commitment of Bertolucci stumbled onto the impossibility of avoiding the fatal circularity of history, the eternal recurrence of the ephemeral.

Let us imagine that history is like a big city: immense, infinite. Different epochs pile up; various people live in it, cram into it; stones heap up, old streets and buildings persist through changes; some landmarks disappear, lost forever; new ones come up; the eternal and the ephemeral collapse one into the other, past and present are ineluctably intertwined. The great city can be grasped as the crow flies: we can see its monumental structure, large boulevards, big buildings. But one has to walk through the city, to concentrate on some areas, in order to grasp its most colorful details, its most lively aspects, its most secret corners which are nevertheless its distinctive traits.

There are also two ways of representing the city. One consists of description with precise details; it is what has been called the realist mode of representation and corresponds to a concept of realism as an artistic school. Such is the style of Balzac, his *peinture des moeurs*: in his novels Paris is described meticulously—its streets, faubourgs, buildings, colors, walls; the different floors of a house; the furniture of an apartment and the shades of tapestries. The physical aspect and the personality of many characters stand up in front of us as if we were watching them. The other way of representing the city is the one adopted by Baudelaire: in his works Paris is never described in its physical aspects but it is undoubtedly represented. The representation is carried through the effects of the metropolis upon the soul. Baudelaire showed that the experience of the great city has changed the conditions of experience, perception, consciousness, mental life. Not an accurate documentation, but a brief, condensed allegorical shortcut characterizes Baudelaire's style. In the same way as the ephemeral and the eternal are inseparable, reality and allegory are but one in the poems of *The Flowers of Evil* or in the prose of *Paris Spleen*. It would be enough to quote from the famous poem "Le cygne," to see the power of what one can call Baudelaire's larger and deeper understanding of realism (allegorical realism):

> Paris change! Mais rien dans ma mélancolie
> N'a bougé! Palais neufs, échafaudages, blocs,
> Vieux faubourgs, tout pour moi devient allégorie,
> Et mes chers souvenirs sont plus lourds que des rocs.

(Paris changes! But nothing of my melancholy
Gives away. New buildings, scaffoldings, blocks
And the old suburbs, for me, they all become allegory,
While my dear memories are heavier than rocks.)[34]

Inspired by the *Annales* school, and by Natalie Davis's interpretation of Bertrande's role in the whole story, *Martin Guerre* is a film which describes, like Balzac's novels. We see a sixteenth-century *peinture de moeurs*; we enjoy the objects, the dresses, the details of another era—everything we can call external realism. Davis is conscious of the limits of such realism: she asks questions about the way people felt in the sixteenth century, something that the movie could not actually reconstitute: "Our film was an exciting suspense story that kept the audience as unsure of the outcome as the original villagers and judges had been. But where was the room to reflect upon the significance of identity in the sixteenth century?"[35] Even if *Martin Guerre* is faithful to some of Lucien Febvre's motifs, Vigne's film ultimately proposes the past as nature in diachronic movement, and tries to be the true reproduction of the empirical essence of things and people.

The Spider's Stratagem is an allegorical film, but nevertheless it reaches a broader conception of realism. Bertolucci does not try to reconstitute in detail an historical milieu. He does not describe particular events of Italian fascism but he interiorizes the problem of fascism, linking the uncertainty of the past with the complexity of the present. The Italian film points out some of the deep effects of fascism on the present, up to the ambiguity of a political position. One of Athos Magnani's father's friends and executioners comments while tasting some ham produced in the area—the most communist region of Italy: "Fascism is now in the minds of people."

Bertolucci, who decided to deal with the recent past, does not describe this history as Baudelaire does not describe Paris. He blends past and present, the ephemeral and the eternal, in the same way Baudelaire blends the classical French language with the tough language of his contemporary world; in the words of Walter Benjamin, Baudelaire's style is Racine plus the journalistic language of the 1850s.[36] Bertolucci questions what we can call the tragic fragility of history confronted by a mythical-anthropological relationship between one generation and the following, their complicity in spite of the opposition. Athos Magnani's story—fiction constructed upon a fiction—ends up in the genre of Baudelairean realism. Following his master Pier Paolo Pasolini, Bertolucci said that the language of film was the language of reality, but he also felt that he wanted to go beyond Pasolini's realistic vision.[37] The past is not a collection of cadavers that the historian or the film director has to make up in order to give the illusion of life; the past mysteriously persists in the changes of the present: it is still blood in our veins.

The Spider's Stratagem proposes a serious reflection on history, on the interplay of the past and the present, and seems to respond to Nietzsche's meditation on history, on its uses and disadvantages for life: "A historiography could be imagined which had in it not a drop of empirical truth and yet could claim to the highest degree of objectivity."[38]

LIONEL GOSSMAN

Cultural History and Crisis: Burckhardt's *Civilization of the Renaissance in Italy*

J'espère avoir écrit le présent livre sans préjugé,
mais je ne prétends pas l'avoir écrit sans passion. . . . En étudiant notre ancienne société dans
chacune de ses parties, je n'ai jamais perdu de vue
la nouvelle.

> Tocqueville, *L'Ancien Régime et
> la Révolution*, Foreword.

From its beginnings, cultural history has been written chiefly by and for those who are excluded from power. Jacob Burckhardt's *Civilization of the Renaissance in Italy* (1860) did not by any means inaugurate the genre. Following Pierre Bayle, nearly all the writers of the age of Enlightenment denounced traditional history: not only was it largely determined by rhetorical and narrative patterns, and often quite fabulous, but it concerned itself with only part of the story of the past and not the most important part. Its subject matter, it was alleged, was the superficial gesta of the princes and states it was designed to celebrate, while it told nothing of the uneventful, industrious lives of the humble and powerless, the merchants, artisans, writers, and philosophers who—the men of the Enlightenment claimed— produce the culture that is the enduring part of human history. In his *Essai sur les moeurs* Voltaire contrasted the busy, violent, and pointless history of "eagles and vultures tearing each other apart" with the peaceful, purposeful, but invisible history of "ants that silently dig out dwelling places for themselves" beneath the surface of things.[1] Similar negative judgements of political historiography were pronounced throughout the eighteenth century by d'Alembert, Rousseau, Turgot, Adam Ferguson, Adam Smith, Malthus, and many others, and again in the nineteenth by Macaulay, Carlyle, and Emerson.[2]

Because the quiet underground activities of the "ants" had been ignored by traditional historiography, they had to be discovered before they could be related. In addition, many nineteenth century historians wanted not simply to record these activities, but—in the spirit of Romanticism—to restore them to life in the reader's imagination, to "resurrect life in its totality," as Michelet was to put it later, and thus redeem the humble forgotten millions on whose labors the triumphs of the present rested. By "giving a voice to history's silences" (in Michelet's words again), the French Romantic historians in particular hoped to repair the troubling rift between the pre-Revolutionary past and the post-Revolutionary present and bring the dead into the Great Community they saw as the dream of the French Revolution.[3] As the only way to re-present the past, however, was in the form of historical narratives or stories, and as narratives of humble life were hard to come by in traditional historiography, it was necessary at first to invent these. In the age of Scott and Manzoni, the historical novel, the fictional story of the private life of the past, was an authentic form of cultural history. Augustin Thierry held that the true history of Scotland was to be found not in the pages of Robertson's History of Scotland, but in the novels of Scott.[4] In the astonishing first part of one of his most successful works, The Witch, Michelet himself resorted to myth or fable in order to tell the earliest, undocumented history of woman.

There was always a tendency, of course, to revert to political history, partly because it is the easiest kind of history to construct in the form demanded of historians since the Renaissance, namely that of a narrative with recognizable agents, well defined actions, and a dramatic story line, but also because, in France at least, the Revolution had transformed a considerable colony of ancien régime ants into vultures and eagles. As lawmakers, administrators, military heroes, moulders of opinion, and captains of commerce and industry, the French bourgeoisie, in the years after 1789, a fortiori after 1830, was at the helm of the ship of state. The nation, theoretically, had become the state. The established history of France was no longer tellable as the res gestae of kings and noblemen, but it was still eminently tellable as the story of the glorious actions of the now sovereign people and of the progress of this new hero from obscurity to success, from serfdom to freedom. The familiar history-of-France, as Henri Martin declared, was now meaningful as the story of the construction of the nation-state.[5] If the novel was pre-eminently historical in the early nineteenth century, in sum, history was pre-eminently narrative. In France, the first histories on a different model were probably Tocqueville's *Ancien Régime* and Fustel's *Cité antique*, both dating from after the 1848 Revolution.

A non-narrative cultural history, a history without heroes, *was* developed in the early nineteenth century, principally in Germany, where the bourgeoisie remained rigorously excluded from power and the nation was distinct from the state. It took several forms. Sometimes it was a compilation of facts, about population, agriculture, industry, trade, religion, the arts, folklore, and so on, partly in the spirit of the so-called statistical works of the eighteenth century (surveys of different societies for the use of statesmen and diplomats), partly in the spirit of a generally progressive account of the evolution of civilization. Sometimes it reflected the Romantic interest in the folk or people, in society as opposed to the state, as the ground of all social life and as more fundamental and enduring than the ephemeral political and religious institutions built on it or emerging out of it.

The work of Wilhelm Riehl, a contemporary of Burckhardt's and a pioneer sociologist, was of this type. Riehl released cultural history, the history of society and the private sphere, completely from the history of the state and the public sphere and brought it close to what we might call ethnography or folklore studies. According to Riehl, cultural history should be concerned with the nation, or the people, that is to say, the permanent ground or soil on which, in his view, the ever changing forms of the state are constructed and which outlives them all. Writing in the aftermath of the disastrous failure of the Revolution of 1848 (while 1848 deeply shook the optimism of the ruling bourgeoisie in France, in Germany it signified the collapse of the last effort of the bourgeoisie to achieve political power), Riehl demoted political history to secondary status. He devoted himself entirely to studying the life, manners, and beliefs of peasants and artisans, seen as the most important elements of the nation or people. Ironically, this popular emphasis led him to take up an extremely conservative political position, in that he accepted the division of society into orders (peasants, townsfolk, gentry) as a permanent or "natural" feature of social life, analogous in his own terms to the difference between male and female, and advocated a politics that took that division as its starting point. Thus Riehl's chief works, "The Society of the Town" (*Die bürgerliche Gesellschaft*, 1851), "The People of the Land" (*Land und Leute*, 1853), "The Family" (*Die Familie*, 1855), were designed as contributions to what he called "The Natural History of the People as the Foundation of a German Social Politics" (*Natur-*

geschichte des Volkes als Grundlage einer deutschen Socialpolitik)—and one should remember that in the expression "natural history" the term "history" still meant something closer to "description" than to what we understand by history. Burckhardt's fellow-citizen Johann Jacob Bachofen—author of the pioneering *Mother-Right* (1861)—was also drawn to this type of cultural history. Bachofen, who, like Burckhardt, belonged to the ruling elite of Basle, did not claim, however, that there was a history separate from the history of power, from political history. The pure sphere of society, for Bachofen, corresponded to pre-history, the world of the Mothers; history, in contrast, the world of violence, repression, and paternal law, was eminently the sphere of the state.

In general, the idea of culture underlying Romantic cultural history in Germany was different from that of the eighteenth-century historians of civilization, such as Voltaire, or of so-called "statisticians" such as Süssmilch. Culture was understood neither as a particular achievement of refined civilization, which occurs from time to time in favorable circumstances; nor as the sum total of the discrete elements making up civil society; but as an autonomous system, a deeply-rooted, self-contained and enduring organism, all of whose parts reflect and contribute to the life of the whole. In Germany it was widely held that the two most completely developed and harmonious cultures in this sense were the culture of ancient Greece and the culture of the so-called "Germanic" Middle Ages. Only these two were original, autonomous, whole and undivided, free of self-conscious imitation or innovation. All other European cultures were derivative, heteronomous, made up of borrowings from and adaptations of previous cultures. Accordingly, the Parthenon and Cologne Cathedral were held to be the two most beautiful buildings in the world, each of them perfectly embodying its own culture.[6] (The idea that the Greeks and the Germans are the true spontaneously creative peoples—in contrast, clearly, with the French, and with the Latins generally—runs through the writings of the German neohumanists and remains alive in Wagner and in the Nietzsche of *The Birth of Tragedy*.)

As a citizen of one of the last surviving city-states of Europe (the others included Frankfurt, Hamburg, Bremen, the Lübeck so beautifully evoked later by Thomas Mann, and intermittently Danzig [Gdansk], the birthplace of Schopenhauer), Burckhardt was naturally drawn to cultural history rather than political history. All the city-states were commercial republics, to borrow the term they used to describe themselves. All were run by their merchant elites and were better known for their wealth and industry than for their roles as actors on the stage of European history. It seems not fortuitous that when he tried to describe to a Basle correspondent the perspective from which the modern historian-*philosophe* should write his histories, Voltaire picked that of a city-state: working on his *Siècle de Louis XIV*, he told Johann Bernoulli, "je me mets à la place d'un hambourgeois" ("I put myself in the position of a citizen of Hamburg").[7] Burckhardt's Basle was certainly no great power. On the contrary, the lilliputian city-state with its narrow band of surrounding countryside had always had to fear the far larger powers between which it was wedged and on which, as trading partners, its prosperity depended. It does not seem surprising therefore that aside from a couple of short pieces on the so-called "epic age" of Swiss history (the fifteenth century), written very early in his career, Burckhardt devoted himself entirely to cultural history and the history of art. The political history of his "hole-in-the-corner fatherland," as he called it (by which he meant Basle, not Switzerland), was hardly of universal significance.[8]

On the other hand, Burckhardt could not be expected to view the histories of the great powers with the interest and sympathy of Frenchmen, Englishmen, Prussians, and Russians, whose patriotism had been galvanized by the Napoleonic invasions and the era of Great Patriotic Wars and Wars of Liberation; or of those Germans whose hearts were set on turning Germany too into a Great Power. On the contrary, as a citizen of a virtually defenseless, anachronistic city-state, he was deeply apprehensive of modern nationalism and of the development of state power all over Europe. By the time Burckhardt was growing to manhood, it had become apparent to him that the Restoration had not restored anything, and that, between them, the French Revolution and the Napoleonic adventure had radically altered the mentality as well as the political, social, and economic life of Europe. Mass political movements, the rapid spread of democracy, demagoguery, and nationalism, the substitution of industrial production in factories for artisanal production, the development of a literary market, and the commercialization of culture on a scale hitherto unknown filled him with dismay and apprehension. Even little Switzerland, until 1848 a weak federation of small, autonomous city-states and rural republics, of which Burckhardt's Basle had been a half-hearted member since the early sixteenth century, had been affected by the movement toward national identity and centralized state power. In 1848, at the end of a twenty-six-day civil war between the liberal (predominantly Protestant and increasingly industrial) cantons, which supported greater centralization, and the conservative (predominantly Catholic and rural) cantons, which, being weaker, clung to the old autonomies, a new federal constitution established a Swiss national assembly and gave unheard-of power to a central government permanently located in Bern. (Before 1848 Switzerland had no fixed capital.)

From Protestant, enterprising, but politically conservative Basle these developments were viewed with deep misgiving. The merchant oligarchy of the city, seeing its interests in international trade and finding no advantage for itself in the development of a single national market, was unsympathetic to the centralizing policies of the liberal regimes of Zürich and Bern and unenthusiastic about the Swiss nationalism of which Zürich and Bern were the champions. In 1833, it had given the measure of its determination to hold on to its power and preserve the character of the old city-state: after three years of armed conflict between the citizens of Basle and their rural subjects, the city government agreed to the secession of the rural territories, which were reconstituted as a separate canton, rather than yield to their demand for adequate political representation and thereby relinquish control of the city's destiny. The Basle oligarchy was thus the only one in any of the more important Swiss cantons to remain in power after the liberal revolutions of 1830. Burckhardt foresaw, however, that the end was not far off for the last surviving European city-states, including his own, for the class of educated and patrician merchant-governors to which he belonged, and for the form of culture he associated with that class. For him, writing cultural history rather than political history, construing history as a synchronic section rather than a diachronic political narrative was almost certainly a way of repudiating the optimistic success-story political histories of the national historians and the liberal view of history as the story of the appropriation of state power by the people—the "great optimist-rationalist-utilitarian victory" and the "prejudices of our democratic age" in the bitter words of Nietzsche, his future colleague at the University of Basle.[9] By the mid-1840s, there is little doubt that Burckhardt was far less inclined than his teacher Ranke and others in the German historical school to elevate the state to the position of a "higher," autonomous power capable of reconciling ideologically the opposing claims of popular sovereignty and traditional princely authority.

At the same time, no member of the Basle elite—least of all a Burckhardt—could entertain as naively and radically negative a view of political power as some of the German Romantics. Unlike the German bourgeoisie, the bourgeois of Basle had been a ruling class for centuries. Wealthy, enterprising, and provided with modern industrial and commercial know-how, the elite families, a fair number of which had come to the city as refugees from the religious wars in France and Germany or from the Inquisition in Italy and the Spanish Netherlands, had quickly won control of the all-powerful guilds or corporations of artisans that ran their host city. In the years between 1630 and the drastic constitutional reforms of 1874–75, which finally transformed Basle from a city-state into a mere municipality, the Burckhardts alone supplied the city with eleven of its thirty-seven Bürgermeisters, or heads of state. Their influence was such that Isaac Iselin, the leading figure of the Basle Enlightenment and himself a scion of a powerful and even older family than the Burckhardts, once confided to his diary the wish that "Heaven would deliver us from these Medicis!"[10]

Though Jacob Burckhardt—who stemmed, incidentally, from a less well-to-do, professional branch of the Burckhardt clan—was strongly influenced for a while by German Romanticism (his youthful conviction that Cologne Cathedral was the most beautiful building in the world is one sign of that influence), it was unlikely that he would subscribe for long to the Romantic idea of culture as an enduring substratum on which the political floats "like beads of fat on the top of the soup," to borrow an image used by Werner Sombart. His entire experience of life in his native city ran counter to such an idea. If Basle was virtually powerless on the international scene, like a middle-class merchant among warrior knights, on the domestic scene the Burckhardts and others of their class were accustomed to wielding power and were striving mightily, as already noted, to hold on to it. Not unexpectedly, therefore, though Burckhardt did share to some extent an understanding of culture as a self-contained system, he saw it as something far more dynamic, unstable, and shifting, and far less easily isolated from the play of power, than Riehl, for instance.[11]

In addition, Burckhardt also retained a view of culture as the highest achievement of individual talent and imagination, as *Bildung* or self-cultivation. No friend of the "loud-mouthed masses called the people," as he once wrote, the Basle patrician looked on the rise of popular democracy as a threat to culture as he understood it, that is to say to the creative activity of gifted and educated individuals. Even his fellow-citizen Bachofen, though more sympathetic to Romantic notions of culture, insisted that while the people prepares the ground for the highest conceptions of man, it is the individual citizen, artist, thinker, or entrepreneur, who shapes the products of its immemorial labors.[12] To these sons of two of the leading families of Basle the idea of a purely artisanal or popular culture had to be thoroughly alien. As their families had played and continued to play a leading part in the ribbon industry, which was the foundation of the prosperity and culture of their native city, both were fully aware of the role of enterprising individuals in reorganizing and transforming traditional artisanal labor.[13] It is hard to imagine that either of them could have considered the higher culture as anything other than one in which outstanding individuals produce work that is appreciated and enjoyed by a considerable body of their fellow citizens.

To sum up: Burckhardt's experience as a citizen of Basle and a member of one of the city's leading families led him to develop a distinctive view of cultural history. Cultural history for him was not separable from political history. Instead, he saw culture, political power, and religion as constitutive elements of any society and as standing in any society in a dynamic and changing relation to each other, which might be more or less favorable to each. The power of the state or of religion might be so oppressive and pervasive that the space of culture (which Burckhardt defines as "the sum total of those mental developments which take place spontaneously and lay no claim to universal or compulsive authority"[14]) is drastically reduced. Conversely, culture is capable of undermining the respect for authority, sense of community, and religious belief that are the foundations of the state. Its action on state and religion, he writes, is "one of perpetual modification and disintegration and is limited only by the extent to which they have pressed it into their service and included it within their aims."[15] Societies are defined, according to Burckhardt, not by their place on a supposed line of development—cyclical, spiral, or simply vertical—but by the hierarchy of values, the relationship realized in each among the three forces of culture, religion, and the state.

No citizen of Basle could have failed to be aware that culture in Burckhardt's sense had flourished in the city intermittently—most brilliantly perhaps in the period that corresponded to the one Burckhardt was to celebrate in his *The Civilization of the Renaissance in Italy*. At that time, when Basle had been the residence of Erasmus and Reuchlin and Holbein, a member of a merchant family, such as the handsome Bonifacius Amerbach, whose portrait by Holbein inspired Lucien Febvre to a remarkable meditation on the special qualities of the free cities strung along the Rhine, could become a notable humanist and connoisseur.[16] In fact, it is almost impossible not to recognize in the magnificent account of Florence in Burckhardt's book the ideal model not only of humanist Basle but, to a lesser extent, of the Basle of Burckhardt's own youth. That early nineteenth century Basle, reanimated by the *neo*humanism of Winckelmann, Wolf, and Wilhelm von Humboldt, was remembered with nostalgia by the mature scholar, at a point in his life when he could overlook the suffocating narrowness and bigotry he had once bitterly complained of.

Equally, however, no one in Basle could have been unaware that the state, including the city-state, could be repressive and unfavorable to cultural development. If humanist and neohumanist Basle lies behind the brilliant description of Renaissance Florence, as I believe it does, it is another Basle—the narrowly orthodox and Pietist Basle from which Burckhardt suffered grief enough as a young professor and from which he escaped as often as he could—that is evoked by the rather grim picture of the early Greek city-states in the posthumously published *Greek Cultural History*. Neither Burckhardt's idea of culture nor his practice of cultural history can be divorced, in short, from political considerations. As many commentators have pointed out, the opening section of *The Civilization of the Renaissance* is primarily political—an account of the breakdown of feudal power in Italy, resulting in the creation of the political conditions that permitted the astonishing release of individual energies in the course of the fourteenth, fifteenth, and sixteenth centuries.

Cultural history, for Burckhardt, could not, in other words, be the antiquarian recovery of the past that still informs much of Riehl's work and that flourished in hundreds of local learned societies throughout Europe,[17] nor could it be the basis of a populist anti-political ideology. To both Burckhardt and Bachofen the study of past culture had a moral and social function: it was intended to instruct and fortify the current generation, faced as it was with the prospect of drastic decline and catastrophic revolutions. It was addressed neither to "the people" or the nation nor to professional specialists, but to independent-minded (and that meant socially and economically independent) laymen of culture throughout Europe. This was the class of people referred to in Burckhardt's own city as the *Nichtstudirende*, that is to say, well-to-do citizens destined to pursue a career in business while also participating in government and public life. These were the people, together with their spouses, to whom Burckhardt lectured on the history of art in his public lectures of the 1840s and to whom he again addressed his popular lectures on art, literature, and history after he returned to Basle in 1858 and deliberately gave up publishing his work. Through his family and friends, he knew many such people personally. His own brother, Lucas Gottlieb, was typical of Burckhardt's desired readers. Upon finishing his schooling in Basle, Lucas Gottlieb entered his uncle's import-export business in Russia. He returned to Basle a year or two later, married into the Alioth family, which was prominent in the silk-spinning industry in the villages around Basle, took over the technical direction of his father-in-law's firm, and retired in his fifties to seek election as a *Ratsherr*, or senator, with a special interest in education.

Basle owed its economic prosperity to the manufacture of silk ribbon and the forwarding of goods between Northern and Southern Europe. Connections with Italy had for that reason always been close. In Burckhardt's own time, it was not unusual for the sons of prominent Basle merchants to spend a year or so apprenticed to a Northern Italian firm with which their fathers did business. Italian was quite widely spoken among the elite and was the first modern foreign language, along with French, to be introduced into the curriculum at the city-state's institutions of higher education. *The Civilization of the Renaissance in Italy* is dedicated to Burckhardt's old Italian teacher at the Basle *Pädagogium*,[18] the "eternally young" Luigi Picchione, a one-time *carbonaro*. By the early nineteenth century, moreover, thanks to Winckelmann, Goethe, and many others, a journey to Italy had become a highly desirable part of the general education of well-to-do German-speaking youth. Having promised to assist his former art history teacher at the University of Berlin, Franz Kugler, on his *Handbook to the History of Art* and having contracted to write a number of entries on art and artists for a new edition of the Brockhaus *Encyclopaedia*, Burckhardt had additional, quite precise and practical, reasons for making an extended trip to Italy in 1846–47.

Nevertheless, Burckhardt's departure for Italy in 1846 was by no means casual. It occurred in the immediate aftermath of the first attempts by bands of radical vigilantes, *Freischaren* as they were called, recruited chiefly in the Protestant cantons of Zürich, St. Gallen, Bern, and to some extent Basle itself, to overthrow the conservative Catholic government of the canton of Lucerne. The Basle elite was horrified by these outbursts of populist violence—the prelude to the Swiss civil war, or *Sonderbundkrieg*, of 1847. The effect on Burckhardt, Bachofen, and other products of the neohumanist education of the 1820s and 1830s at Basle, who until that time had considered themselves liberals in revolt against their conservative elders, was immediate, profound, and lasting. Before 1845–46, Burckhardt had participated in the general optimism of *juste milieu* liberals about the course of history. The close friendship he formed while a student at Bonn in the spring of 1841 with Gottfried Kinkel, the future revolutionary socialist, was not an aberration. As a member of Ranke's medieval history seminar at the University of Berlin, he appears to have shared his teacher's confident belief in the continuity of European history since the Middle Ages and in the evolution of a basic European order which had emerged tested and strengthened from the trials of the Revolution and the Napoleonic upheaval. "When I see the present lying quite clearly in the past, I feel moved by a shudder of profound respect," he declared in 1842.[19] By 1845, all that had changed. "Conditions in Switzerland—disgusting and barbarous—have spoilt everything for me. The word freedom sounds rich and beautiful, but no one should talk about it who has not seen and experienced slavery under the loudmouthed masses called the people."

Burckhardt now warns his liberal friends in Bonn, whose populist sympathies and enthusiasm for the German Middle Ages he had shared when he was a student there, that they are political simpletons in their failure to grasp the reality around them and their blindness to the coming "despotism of the masses."[20] Some years later he referred bitterly to what he called the "illusions of the spirit of 1830." "At that time books appeared," he wrote, with a malicious allusion to Ranke, "which . . . aimed to provide in a spirit of moderation and calm persuasion a general view of the years from 1789 to 1816 as if that period had come to a close. Now we know, however, that we too are swept up in the very same storm that carried men away after 1789."[21] Ranke's conviction that the revolutionary episode had been integrated into the continuity of European history and that the modern age, therefore, was the latest point in an unbroken evolution was now judged utterly mistaken. The unprecedented release and mobilization of popular demands and desires brought about by the French Revolution and the Revolutionary and Napoleonic wars, Burckhardt was now convinced, had inaugurated a radically new era of history; far from having been restored and strengthened, Europe was perceived as advancing inexorably toward the abyss.

The cooling of Burckhardt's enthusiasm for the Middle Ages and his turn to Italy thus coincided directly with a retreat from Ranke's serene confidence in the continuities of European history and in the crucial role of Germany as a powerful, uncorrupted, conservative force capable of ensuring these continuities and mediating between tradition and change, and with a new and intense vision of discontinuity and crisis as facts of historical existence. Correspondingly, this vision led to a complete revaluation of the Renaissance, of which the first signs appeared in 1854 in the celebrated *Cicerone* or *Guide to the Enjoyment of the Art Works of Italy*.[22] The 1789 Revolution was now seen as having ushered in a crisis that signalled the end of one period of culture and a painful time of transition to another. The Italian Renaissance, equally, was now seen not as a stage in the evolving history of Christian, "Germanic-Romanic" Europe (in Ranke's terms), but as an almost demonic outburst of individual energies, and the model of an original and distinctively individualist and modern culture. The Renaissance "would be conceivable without [the revival of antiquity]," Burckhardt maintains in *The Civilization of the Renaissance*. "We must insist upon it, as one of the chief propositions of this book, that it was not the revival of antiquity alone, but its union with the genius of the Italian people, which achieved the conquest of the western world."[23] Those who dream nostalgically of the Middle Ages, he now observes rudely, would have an unpleasant awakening if ever their dreams were realized for they would quickly find themselves out of their element, gasping for the free air of their own modern culture.[24]

Burckhardt's re-evaluation of the Italian Renaissance, his discovery of historical discontinuity, and his sense of an imminent crisis of what he called "the old culture of Europe" led him to reconsider and revise his understanding of historical study itself. The historian, he now declared, again no doubt directing a barb at his old teacher Ranke, can no longer devote himself to showing reverentially how everything contributes to a supposed grand historical design. "It is high time for me to free myself from the generally accepted bogus-objective recognition of the value of everything, whatever it may be, and to become thoroughly intolerant."[25] As the pieties of liberal and idealist historiography are rejected and the close connections between the highest achievements of culture and the concrete and earthly desires and energies of individuals are unmasked (as we are made, in other words, to acknowledge what in modern terms would no doubt be described as the *body* of culture), the object of historical study ceases to be the progressive disclosure of a providential spiritual order in which everything has its place and from which everything derives its value and justification. At the heart of the practice of history Burckhardt now puts not some putative historical science (*Wissenschaft*) but the education (*Bildung*) of the free individual; not the judgement *of* history—that is to say, the determination of the rightness or wrongness of historical acts and events by their success or, in other words, their conformity with the supposed providential course of history, which it is the object of historical *Wissenschaft* to reveal—but the reflections and judgements *on* history made by free and thoughtful individuals who know that men "are not privy to the purposes of eternal wisdom" and that these must remain forever "beyond our ken."[26] The historian's task, as Burckhardt now saw it, was to liberate and stimulate the mind, not to distract it with more or less relevant information or subordinate it to a cosmic plan; history should have as its goal not to disclose a grand design but to reveal the possibilities and limits of individual decisions and actions. In other words, the ideal reader of history, in Burckhardt's sense, was not an obedient subject, but a free citizen. Even where he accepts an event or a situation as inevitable, he must still weigh its value and freely assess its benefits and disadvantages.

As a student of Droysen's in Berlin in 1839–40, Burckhardt had dutifully noted down his teacher's condemnation of Demosthenes for failing to un-

derstand that the triumph of Philip of Macedon was necessary for the salvation of Greece. The mature Burckhardt, however, passionately rejected
the point of view of Droysen.

Droysen says: "History knows few figures more pathetic than the great Athenian
orator. He misunderstood his time, his people, his opponents, and himself. With
the obstinacy of impotence and habit, even after the complete victory of Macedonia
and the beginning of a new era that was to reshape the world, he did not give up his
old hopes and plans, which had outlived their time, along with him." But here no
one cuts a more pathetic figure than the *vir eruditissimus* Johann Gustav Droysen
himself. Whether Demosthenes knew or did not know that his judgment of Philip
was false is irrelevant. There are desperate moments in the lives of nations when it
is a crime against patriotism to speak the truth. Had Demosthenes appeared before
the people and said, "*Andres Athinaioi* [You men of Athens], behold, you have been
judged politically and morally. Your Republic is a *liros* [a trumpery]; today it is the
monarchical principle that is being born along by the Zeitgeist. Submit to it like
reasonable men and bow deeply before the great king," he would stand branded in
the eyes of posterity like Aeschines, Philocrates and their entire condemned society.
Whether it triumphs or dies, the minority is always what makes world history. For
what fills the hearts of men with enthusiasm and pride is to see a noble personality,
a great character stand firm like the Titans against the unalterable decree of historical
development and go under rather than give up what it believes in." [27]

Burckhardt summed up his repudiation of the historical optimism of his
Berlin teachers in a letter to Nietzsche in 1874. "I never taught history for
the sake of the thing which goes by the high-falutin name of World History,"
he wrote, "but essentially as a general subject. My task was to put people in
possession of that solid foundation which is indispensable to their future
work if it is not to become worthless. I wanted them to be capable of pluck-
ing the fruits for themselves, nor have I ever had in mind to train scholars
or disciples in the narrower sense." [28]

The apparently modest disclaimer of authority in the opening paragraph
of *The Civilization of the Renaissance* (1860), the designation of the work as
an "essay" (*Versuch*), the sparing use of scholarly notes and references, and
the ease and frequency of authorial commentary and judgement, as well as
the acknowledgment that "to each eye . . . the outlines of a given civilization present a different picture" make it clear that Burckhardt did not intend
his work to be a contribution to historical "*Wissenschaft*," a term he almost
always seems to use ironically. "Our dear father in heaven will have his little
joke from time to time," he wrote to Kinkel in 1847. "So he created phil-
ologists and historical scholars of a certain kind who imagine themselves
vastly superior to the rest of humanity because they have made it a matter

of scientific knowledge [*wissenschaftlich ermittelt haben*] that on May 7, in the year 1030, Emperor Conrad II went to the toilet in Goslar, and other items of similar universal interest."[29]

As a Swiss, Burckhardt took special pleasure in professing his indebtedness to the French Romantic historians, notably Thierry, Michelet, and Guizot, knowing well that this would irritate his Teutonic colleagues.[30] What he had learned from the French, he insisted, was to write for a general public rather than a professional one. He constantly repeated that he intended to be *"lesbar"* (readable); he even urged that no history book should be longer than a single volume.[31] In the preface to his first major work, *The Age of Constantine the Great* (1853), he announced provocatively that he wrote "not primarily for scholars but for thoughtful readers of all ranks of society." In the *Reflections on History* he reiterated that position: "Our aim is not to train historians."[32] As a professor of art history, he took exactly the same stand: "I do not lecture for art historians."[33] In every way possible, in other words, Burckhardt let it be known that as a scholar he was not interested in writing for professional scholars—virtually all of whom, in Continental Europe, were paid servants of the state, bureaucrats—or, for that matter, to glorify any political orientation or any nation. Rather, he wanted to reach an audience of free individuals and citizens. Burckhardt's ideal readers, in sum, bear a strikingly strong resemblance to the classic figure of the bourgeois, especially in the form taken by that type in the merchant city cultures of sixteenth-, seventeenth-, and eighteenth-century Europe.

Not surprisingly, his somewhat aristocratic disdain for routinized professional scholarship (one of the things the term "science" or "*Wissenschaft*" was intended to designate) corresponds closely to the humanist tradition of his native city and in particular to the ideal of education that had inspired the Basle elite of the Restoration, when it undertook a major overhaul of the city-state's educational organization, institutions, and programs in 1817–18. One of the chief concerns of the reformers had been a group referred to in the literature as the *Nichtstudirende*—the non-scholars or non-professionals—that is to say those students in the high school or *Gymnasium* who planned not to go on to further study in one of the professional faculties of the University but to enter and ultimately assume the direction of the family business. These *Nichtstudirende*, in a predominantly commercial city like Basle, were the cream of society and came from the best families (in stark contrast with Germany). As they were expected, once they had done their stint in the business, to contribute without remuneration, simply in fulfillment of their obligation as citizens, to the government and administration of the state, the reforms of 1817–18 aimed to provide them with the best possible all-round education and with the humanist culture considered desirable in an elite governing class. A special school, unique to Basle, was established between the *Gymnasium* and the University, at which the *Nichtstudirende* and those headed for the University were to pursue their education together in classes taught by the professors at the University. Burckhardt himself was a product of the *Pädagogium*, as the school was called, and he also taught at it from 1858, when he returned to Basle to take up a chair at the University, until his retirement in 1893.[34]

It was necessary to insist on the political context in which Burckhardt elaborated his view of historical study, on the educative or formative function he attributed to it, and on the public for which, in the first instance, he intended it, since some of his own pronouncements appear to lend support to the view that he practiced history simply as a form of escape. In 1846, for instance, he announced to his friends that he was leaving for Italy out of disgust with events in Switzerland and with the direction in which modern Europe was moving generally. "You weather-wise fellows vie with each other in getting deeper and deeper into this wretched age—I on the other hand have secretly fallen out with it entirely, and for that reason am escaping from it to the beautiful, lazy south, where history is dead."[35] There is certainly an escapist element in Burckhardt's passion for Italy. His letters often express the typical Northern tourist's interest in good places to eat and to stay; his delight at being able to get excellent coffee and seats at the opera at half the price he would have to pay at home; his disgust with those changes to the Italian scene (newspapers, socialist parties, nationalism) that were bringing Italy into line with the rest of Europe and making it harder to indulge escapist fantasies; his irritation with other tourists, especially the hordes of *nouveaux-riches* Germans, the beneficiaries of Bismarck's new Reich, who were now to be found everywhere, gaping solemnly at monuments and paintings in their determination to acquire "culture" as expeditiously as possible. Nevertheless, escape is far too simple a term to describe Burckhardt's objective in his journeys through the Italian peninsula or in the works inspired or informed by these journeys.

The historian's aim in *The Civilization of the Renaissance in Italy* was more than the painting of a "living picture," as some have claimed.[36] It was, as Burckhardt several times clearly stated, to lead himself and his readers toward a better understanding of their own culture and of the crisis into which, in his view, it had entered—just as the civilization of the Italian cities had entered its crisis in the sixteenth century. "We may all perish," he wrote, "but at least I want to know the interest for which I am to perish, namely the old culture of Europe."[37]

To the modern European reading Burckhardt's account of the Italian Renaissance in the second half of the nineteenth century, and in particular to the citizens of a city that still thought of itself as an independent polity, the political lessons to be learned from considering the fortunes of the Italian Renaissance city-states must have been obvious. Florence, they were told, "deserves the name of the first modern state in the world." It is "the workshop of the Italian and indeed of the modern European spirit."[38] At the same time, if "the Florentines are the pattern and the earliest type of Italians and modern Europeans generally, they are so also in many of their defects."[39] The qualities that most brilliantly exemplify the culture of the greatest city of the Italian Renaissance, it turns out, also contributed to its political decline. In the Florentines' constant tampering with their constitution, in particular, Burckhardt's nineteenth-century readers could not have failed to recognize an allusion to one of the salient political circumstances of their own time. Revolutionary France, of course, had led the way in the fabrication of constitutions. But even conservative Basle had in the end not escaped the universal trend. Like his fellow-citizen Bachofen, Burckhardt was convinced that the repeated revisions made to the Basle constitution in response to pressure from the local radicals had eroded that reverence for the law that they both saw as the foundation of social order and stability.

The problem, in Burckhardt's words, was not the interruption of tradition in itself; it was "the total lack of respect shown by the radicals not simply for old, conservative political forms (toward these one can expect no piety) but for the laws and institutions they themselves have created";[40] it was, as he put it elsewhere, "the spirit of endless revision" ("der Geist der ewigen Revision").[41] Dante, Burckhardt claimed, being still attached to a Christian-medieval vision of political order, had long ago made the point about Florence that he and others were currently making about nineteenth-century Basle. While "that wondrous Florentine spirit, at once keenly critical and artistically creative, was incessantly transforming the social and political condition of the State," Burckhardt writes, Dante deplored "the incessant changes and experiments in the constitution of his native city" and compared a city "which was always changing its constitution with the sick man who is continually changing his posture to escape from pain."[42] Those *Nichtstudirende* who were the present or future governing class of Basle and whom Burckhardt saw as his immediate audience were thus invited to reflect that the first manifestations of "the great modern fallacy that a constitution can be made, can be manufactured by a combination of existing forces and tendencies" were already "cropping up in stormy times" in the Italian cities of the Renaissance.[43] The state as a work of art—the memorable title of the first section of *The Civilization of the Renaissance*—that is to say, the secularization of politics and its emancipation from religion and tradition, was not, Burckhardt implies, an unmixed blessing, especially, no doubt, when law loses its mystery and is exposed as a human creation before the eyes of the *demos*. In Paul Valéry's words, "Could any society endure if it eliminated all that is vague and irrational, relying only on what is measurable and verifiable? . . . Order is always a burden to the individual. Disorder makes him wish for the police or death."[44] Burckhardt's disturbing message is that the flowering of culture, the order of the state, and moral or civic virtue are no more necessarily connected, despite the best efforts of post-Enlightenment idealism and of sentimental liberalism to convince us otherwise, than are the good, the beautiful, and the true.

To those in his own community and class who might still harbor illusions about the distinctiveness of the city of Erasmus and Holbein and its ability to resist the tide of modern life, Burckhardt offered some sobering reflections. In the portrait he drew of the merchant and statesman of Renaissance Florence in its heyday, many of the historian's compatriots would no doubt have liked to recognize their own image. "The Florentine merchant and statesman," Burckhardt wrote,

was often learned in both the classical languages; the most famous humanists read the Ethics and Politics of Aristotle to him and his sons; even the daughters of the house were highly educated. . . . The humanist, on his side, was compelled to the most varied attainments, since his philological learning was not limited, as it is now, to the theoretical knowledge of classical antiquity, but had to serve the practical needs of daily life.[45]

Products, like Burckhardt himself, of the *Pädagogium*, the merchant-statesmen of the city of Erasmus and Holbein were known for the pride they took in their humanistic education and in their knowledge of the classical languages and literatures, which they appear to have thought of in part as a legitimation of their authority, a title to rule. Calmly but surely, however, Burckhardt exposed the historical eccentricity of humanist culture even in its last bastions, such as Basle. Classical literature, he made clear, is no longer a source of practical knowledge in the modern world. For that reason neither humanistic study nor any other form of culture can any longer play the central role in the life of the modern merchant that they played in Renaissance Florence, where philology and art contributed to industry and to daily life.

The features of the Florentine merchant stand in sharp contrast to those Burckhardt saw as increasingly characteristic of the businessmen who were his friends and relatives in Basle. Harried by the intensity of modern commercial competition, virtually chained to their offices, obliged to be ready at all times to respond to the latest telegraphic communication about changing market conditions, the businessmen of late-nineteenth-century Basle enjoyed virtually no leisure. While they often expressed regret that they no longer had time to read, with the loss of the habit of reading, Burckhardt noted, they had also lost most of the inclination.[46] The economic forces they themselves, as independent and enterprising individuals, had helped to unleash were in the end proving inimical to the cultural development and independence of the individual. The future would be characterized by a degree of rationalization and organization in every sphere—business, government, and education, as well as the military—that would make all previous activity seem positively amateurish.[47] In other words, humanity is entering the age of Weber's "iron cage" and the individualism essential to early merchant capitalism has been doomed by the "corporate culture" of the new joint-stock companies and the welfare state.

The very effort to stand back and take stock, to reach a realistic and independent judgement of things, was characteristic, according to Burckhardt, of the modern individual who created and was created by the culture of the Italian Renaissance. The pleasures of mountain climbing and panoramic landscape views, he claimed, were a discovery of the Italians of the fourteenth century. The modern practice of historiography was itself an invention of the Florentines.[48] Above all, the Italian Renaissance discovered the value of exile. Whereas exile from the ancient *polis*, as Burckhardt takes care to remind the readers of his *Greek Cultural History*, meant absolute loss of identity and of all human rights, often literally death (the individual having no existence, no protection, and no identity distinct from his *polis*), the modern individual grows and develops in the experience of exile. Exiled from Florence, Dante

finds a new home in the language and culture of Italy, but goes beyond even this in the words, "My country is the whole world." And when his recall to Florence was offered him on unworthy conditions, he wrote back: "Can I not everywhere behold the light of the sun and the stars; everywhere meditate on the noblest truths." . . . The artists exult no less defiantly in their freedom from the constraints of fixed residence. "Only he who has learned everything," says Ghiberti, "is nowhere a stranger . . . and can fearlessly despise the changes of fortune." In the same strain an exiled humanist writes: "Wherever a learned man fixes his seat, there is home."[49]

Burckhardt even suggests, as did Bachofen, that the individual's self-cultivation, his *Bildung*, may be linked to estrangement from the public sphere.[50] Self-realization, as Burckhardt saw it, was not necessarily incompatible with certain forms of political despotism, with exclusion from the political arena;[51] and conversely it was probably incompatible with most forms of democracy—or at best developed in reaction to the rise of democracy, as in the case of the later Greek philosophers.[52] The relations of culture and politics, in other words, especially democratic politics, are complex and by no means as straightforward as optimistic liberalism would have us believe. Just as the development of the state does not necessarily promote culture, the development of culture does not necessarily promote the state. Between culture and religion, Burckhardt suggests, the relation may be no more harmonious. The modern individual invented by the Renaissance is not necessarily identical, in short, either with the citizen or with the Christian.

Such notions challenged the pieties of traditional civic humanism and of Romantic republicanism in the manner of Michelet or of Hugo. They were not more favorable to the nationalist ideologies of the new age of blood and iron. And they revealed disturbing tensions in the Winckelmannian and Humboldtian neohumanism in which Burckhardt himself had been raised, along with most Baslers of his generation and class. No doubt they reflected the collapse of the moderate liberalism of the historian's own youth, to which we referred earlier; his ever deepening disenchantment with politics, not least in his native city; his resentment of the growing power of the lower orders; and his growing apprehension of mass society and its accompanying "demi-culture." "I mean to be a good private individual, an affectionate friend, a good spirit," he had written in 1846 at the time of the *Freischaren*. "I can do nothing more with society as a whole."[53]

Burckhardt's own life, as is well known, was lived in constantly renewed exile from the community, to the historical memory of which he nevertheless always remained sentimentally attached. He was not as free-floating an intellectual as his younger colleagues at the University of Basle, Nietzsche and Franz Overbeck, both exiles from the Germany of the *Gründerzeit*. Through all the years he spent fleeing the oppressiveness and narrowness of Basle—in Berlin, in Bonn, in Munich, in frequent journeys to Paris or London, in a stint as Professor of Art History at the newly founded Federal

Polytechnic in Zurich, above all in wanderings up and down the Italian peninsula—he never for a moment lost sight of himself as a product of his family, his class, and his native city, with its peculiar accommodation of commerce and culture, provincialism and cosmopolitanism, Protestant piety and opportunism. (He was a master of the Basle dialect, for instance, and many of his best witticisms, it is said, were spoken in it.) This attachment to his "hole-in-the-wall fatherland," as he called it with characteristic irony,[54] together with a residual, ironical respect for its down-to-earth realism and its conciliatory, Erasmian pursuit of compromise imparts to Burckhardt's entire account of Renaissance Italy a tinge of skepticism, a canny guardedness, that sets his work apart from that of more radical contemporaries. Notoriously, he always kept his distance from Nietzsche, who craved his friendship; and he seems not to have been surprised by the madness that finally overtook him. What Burckhardt admired in the end was the art of the Italian Renaissance, not its politics or morality, Raphael, not the *condottieri*.[55] "I have never been an admirer of *Gewaltmenschen* and *Outlaws* in history," he wrote toward the end of his life, "and have, on the contrary, held them to be *flagella Dei* [scourges of God]. I really interested myself in the creative aspect of things, that which makes men happy."[56] Burckhardt's irony and reserve should not obscure, however, the depth of his estrangement from the world of nineteenth-century liberalism and progressivism. And in that estrangement Italy played a crucial role.

Throughout Burckhardt's mature life Italy, *a fortiori* Renaissance Italy, served both as the historian's mountain peak, the vantage point from which he surveyed and tried to understand his own situation, and as his exile or refuge. In an obvious sense, Basle (the *polis*) was home, and Italy (the land of *culture*) was exile and refuge; but Burckhardt turned that relation on its head. Basle—*terra aspera et horrida*, as Bachofen, borrowing from Tacitus, had described it[57]—became a place of exile and refuge from the *terra aspera et horrida* of modern culture, an observation post on the edge of modernity. By leaving "purse-proud" Basle[58] for Italy in 1846, Burckhardt had deliberately taken his distance from his own time and its pursuit of political and material "progress" and exiled himself to the realm of culture, where history is not "progressive" and the modern has no automatic superiority over the ancient. (Around the same time Bachofen began to bury himself in the timeless pre-historical world of "the Mothers.") Twelve years later, that move was repeated when he gave up his position in liberal, go-ahead, and rapidly expanding Zürich, the nerve center of the new centralized post-1848 Switzerland (the Berlin of Switzerland, one might say), and went "home" to politically conservative and anachronistic Basle, the "sulking-corner" of Europe, as Treitschke called it.[59] He still needed to escape from time to time from the little city where he knew everyone and everyone knew him. In 1860, for instance, he spent "14 days in London and 11 in Paris, torturing the English language and chattering in French among utter strangers, primarily to take a great bath of neutrality," as he put it in a letter to his friend the poet Paul Heyse, and "bring home a bit of objectivity."[60] There is no doubt, however, that Burckhardt now saw Basle as a place where he was less likely to have to participate in the demi-culture he considered characteristic of modern societies than anywhere else and where he would therefore enjoy greater freedom to pursue his cultural interests and pleasures unimpeded. This concern for his freedom is almost certainly the motive behind his turning down an invitation to fill the most prestigious chair of history in Europe, Ranke's chair at Berlin. "In my youth," he told a friend in 1877, "my imagination was always turned toward distant . . . places, and only in recent years do I feel properly at home here."[61]

Basle had changed drastically in political, social, and economic terms since Burckhardt's youth, and the Biedermeier city in which he had once naively hoped to have a political influence had been made over into a modern industrial town with a large immigrant population of factory workers. Though Burckhardt complained of the soullessness of this increasingly unfamiliar Basle of factories and railway lines,[62] he also knew that because of its greater openness to the world outside and his own reputation in that world, he enjoyed far more personal freedom in the new Basle than he could ever have known in the *polis* of his youth, where he had repeatedly fallen foul of political and religious pressure groups. Sustained morally by historical and familial attachments and materially in modest but adequate circumstances, he was largely left alone to cultivate his interests as he saw fit and to create within the historical city a modest utopia of culture, consisting of the University, the *Pädagogium*, and the audiences of citizens who attended his popular public lectures. It was to this community of culture in the ruins of the *polis* where he was both citizen and stranger, that he dedicated the rest of his life. "I have long since simplified my outlook by relating every question to the University of Basle," he declared, "and asking whether this or that is good or not good for it."[63]

Burckhardt maintained his freedom of judgement even with respect to what he saw as the decay of the culture in which he himself had grown up and of which the Italian Renaissance had been the harbinger. Such a time of decay has its advantages, he acknowledged, ambiguous as they may be.

The culture of the nineteenth century, he declared, is "in possession of the traditions of all times, peoples and cultures, while the literature of our age is a world literature. In this, it is the beholder who profits most. . . . Even in straitened circumstances, a man of finer culture now enjoys his few classics and the scenes of nature much more profoundly, and the happiness life offers much more consciously than in bygone times. State and Church now impose little restraint on such endeavors, and gradually adjust their outlook to very manifold points of view. They have neither the power nor the desire to suppress them. They believe their existence less menaced by an apparently limitless development of culture than by its repression."[64] Similarly, in the introductory lecture to the course on art history that he taught at Basle from 1874 until 1890, while recognizing that the culture of his own age was fragmented, incapable of the "cohesion" he admired in the art of the Renaissance, Burckhardt also observed, in almost Hegelian terms, that "only our century has an inner and outer sense for everything and is capable of assimilating cultural values of every variety," so that "the good side" of the present age is "that . . . the observer can develop a correspondingly wide-ranging understanding of all the arts." Art history itself belongs to this late moment of culture. "In the midst of our hurried age it is a domain of general contemplation, of which past centuries had little or no experience; a second dream existence, in which quite special spiritual organs are brought to life and consciousness."[65]

From the viewpoint of Burckhardt's ironical understanding of history— on the other side of crisis and death, there is the possibility of new birth; beyond the coming collapse of old Europe, perhaps only after a considerable period during which culture is overwhelmed again by the state, as in the ancient *polis*, or by religion, as in the Middle Ages, there will almost certainly arise a new age of culture, some other Renaissance[66]—*The Civilization of the Renaissance in Italy* appears as a traditional epideictic discourse, distributing praise and blame, and serving at once as lament and consolation. The historian's intention is to salvage what he can of the culture of which he feels he is one of the last representatives—"I want to save things as far as my humble station allows," he wrote in 1846[67]—so that in a future time of restoration, a later generation might build on it, as the Renaissance Italians had been able to use the culture of antiquity to guide them in the construction of their own original, modern culture. "Out of the storm," Burckhardt declared, "a new existence will arise, formed, that is, upon old and new foundations. Our destiny is to help build anew when the crisis is past."[68] His own task was therefore to "debauch" himself, as he put it, "with a real eyeful of aristocratic culture, so that when the social revolution has exhausted itself, I shall be able to take an active part in the inevitable restoration."[69]

Political activity was futile and probably counterproductive,[70] the force of social change irresistible. In these circumstances, writing, recording, was the humanist's chief obligation. "I must strike up new relations with life and poetry, if I am to become anything in the future." That was what he had to do and that was his place, "not in the forefront of irresponsible action."[71] The historiography of culture, in other words, was to help maintain a continuity or permanence of culture beyond the historical experience of discontinuity and crisis—beyond the coming rule of the "loud-mouthed," half-educated masses. His own role, *mutatis mutandis*, was similar to that of a fifth-century abbot whose example he evokes frequently in his writings and in his letters from the 1840s until the 1890s. As the Roman Empire disintegrated around him, St. Severin calmly continued to carry out his ministry to the Germans from the monasteries he had set up along the valleys of the Inn and the Danube, thus ensuring that something would be transmitted from the world that was dying to the world not yet born. "If you would like to read something consoling," Burckhardt advised his best patron in Basle, Andreas Heusler, after the latter's political career was shipwrecked in 1848, "have a look at the Life of St. Severin. . . . There you will see a man who held out amid the collapse of everything."[72]

While writing about "a culture which is the mother of our own and whose influence is still at work among us,"[73] as he put it, Burckhardt aimed to salvage for the benefit and enjoyment (*Genuss*, as he stated in the subtitle of his *Cicerone*) of all men and women of culture, not only Florence and Venice but his native Basle, not only the artists, poets, and historians of the Italian Renaissance but himself as a modern individual and a modern historian, not only the civilization of the Renaissance in Italy but the essence of "the old culture of Europe." Both the historian and his native city are woven into the description of Renaissance Italy. Fourteenth-century Florence with its cultivated merchants and practical humanists, its acid tongues,[74] its combination of criticism and creativity, its repeated constitutional revisions, is a heightened image of Burckhardt's Basle. The historian himself slides in and out of the figures he drew of the great Florentine historians and, above all, of Dante, "matured alike by home and exile,"[75] as later in the *Greek Cultural History* he insinuated himself into his portraits of the ancient philosophers, notably Socrates, Epicurus, and Diogenes. In the image of the humanist who sees the true value and proper combination of private happiness and public obligation,[76] and who, while a decent member of his community, is first and foremost a free individual, a citizen of the entire world and of all ages, Burckhardt inscribed himself and his ideal readers in the monument he raised to the Italian Renaissance. It was no doubt the historian's hope that his book would help to furnish that imaginary museum in which was preserved, for him, the true unity of Europe and which substituted, in his eyes, both for his youthful neohumanist ideal of the *polis* and for the ruined Rankean vision of an underlying and progressively unfolding unity of history.

Some years later, in the midst of the Franco-Prussian War, Burckhardt expressed his foreboding that the future would be quite unlike the world with which he and his friends were familiar: *Es wird Anders als es gewesen ist*. Much of modern literature would simply die off. Novels and plays that had won wide applause would become unreadable and unperformable; authors who had pleased publishers and won the hearts of the public with their eager modernity, their talent for adapting to the tone of the decade, the year, even the month, would be forgotten. "Only what contains a fair portion of eternity will survive. And new works that are to have a chance of enduring will result only from the most arduous efforts of genuine poetic imagination." It is a time, therefore, to "'Put one's house in order' etc." There is no doubt that Burckhardt had had such ideas in mind for many years. The war simply gave them greater urgency. Nor can there be any doubt that he had arranged his life and designed his own work with a view to the coming crisis. "As a history teacher," he noted, the war and the crisis it signals have "made one phenomenon unmistakably clear: the sudden devaluation of all mere 'events' of the past. From now on, my courses will emphasize only cultural history and will retain only what is indispensable of the external scaffolding."[77] Cultural history, in short, was a survival kit for hard times, the repository of what is essentially human and humanly essential about the "old culture of Europe."

Publications of Carl E. Schorske

Publications of Carl E. Schorske

A. Books

(with Hoyt Price) *The Problem of Germany*, Council of Foreign Relations, Harper, 1947.

German Social Democracy, 1905–1917, Harvard University Press, 1955; Russell and Russell, reprint, 1976; paper edition, John Wiley and Sons, 1966; Harper Torchbook, 1972; Harvard paperback, 1983; German translation, *Die grosse Spaltung*, Olle and Wolters, 1981.

Editor (with Elizabeth Schorske), W. L. Langer, *Explorations in Crisis*, Harvard University Press, 1979.

Fin-de-siècle Vienna: Politics and Culture, Alfred A. Knopf, 1980; paper edition, Vintage, 1981; translations in Italian, Spanish, German, French, and Japanese.

Editor (with Thomas Bender), *Budapest and New York: Studies in Metropolitan Transformation, 1870–1930*, Russell Sage Foundation, 1994.

B. Articles and Chapters in Books

1. *International and Political History*

"The Dilemma in Germany," *Virginia Quarterly Review*, Winter, 1947, 29–42.

"Two German Ambassadors: Dirksen and Schulenburg," in Gordon Craig and Felix Gilbert, eds., *The Diplomats* (Princeton, 1953), 477–511.

(with Franklin Ford) "The Voice in the Wilderness: Robert Coulondre," in Craig and Gilbert, *The Diplomats*, 555–78.

"A New Look at the Nazi Movement," *World Politics* 9, 1 (Oct. 1956), 88–97.

2. *Cultural and Intellectual History*

"The Idea of the City in European Thought: Voltaire to Spengler," in Oscar Handlin and John Burchard, eds., *The Historian and the City* (Cambridge, MA, 1963), 95–114.

"Die Geburt des Moeglichkeitsmenschen," in Special Supplement on Sarajevo, *Die Presse* (Vienna, June 1964).

"The Quest for the Grail: Wagner and Morris," in Kurt Wolff and Barrington Moore, Jr., eds., *The Critical Spirit: Essays in Honor of Herbert Marcuse* (Boston, 1967), 216–32.

"Professional Ethos and Public Crisis," *PMLA* 83 (1968), 979–84.

"Weimar and the Intellectuals," *New York Review of Books* 14, nos. 9 and 10 (May 7, 21, 1971).

"'Ver Sacrum' im Wien der Jahrhundertwende," *Die Presse*, July 1, 1973.

"Observations on Style and Society in the Arts and Crafts Movement," *Record of the Art Museum*, Princeton University, 34, 2 (1975).

"Cultural Hothouse," *New York Review of Books*, Dec. 11, 1975.

"Generational Tension and Cultural Change: Reflections on the Case of Vienna," *Daedalus*, Fall 1978, 111–22. (French translation in *Actes de la recherche en sciences sociales*, Apr. 1979).

"Freud: The Psycho-archeology of Civilizations," *Massachusetts Historical Society Proceedings* 92 (1980), 52–67. Reprinted in *The Cambridge Companion to Freud*, ed. Jerome Neu (New York, 1991), 8–24.

"Mahler and Klimt: Social Experience and Artistic Evolution," *Daedalus*, Summer 1982, 29–50.

"Otto Wagner," in *Macmillan Encyclopedia of Architects*, ed. Adolf K. Placzek, 4 vols. (New York, 1982), 4:357–61.

"Foreword," *Kandinsky in Munich 1891*, Guggenheim Museum (New York, 1982).

"Mahler et Ives: archaïsme populiste et innovation musicale," in *Colloque internationale Gustave Mahler*, 1985 (Paris, 1986), 87–97.

"Oesterreichs ästhetische Kultur, 1870–1914: Betrachtungen eines Historikers," in *Traum und Wirklichkeit Wien 1870–1930* (exhibition catalog, Vienna, 1985),

12–25. (English translation: "Grace and the Word: Austria's Two Cultures and Their Modern Fate," *Austrian History Yearbook* 22 [1991], 21–34.)

"Abschied von der Öffentlichkeit: Kulturkritik und Modernismus in der Wiener Architektur," in *Ornament und Askese*, ed. Alfred Pfabigan (Vienna, 1985), 47–56. Translations: "De la scène publique à l'espace privé," in *Vienna 1880–1938* (exhibition catalog, Musée de l'art moderne, Paris, 1986), 72–81; "Revolt in Vienna," *New York Review of Books*, May 29, 1986, 24–29; "Revolta en Viena," *Saber* (Barcelona), no. 11 (1986), 47–53.

"Vienna 1900: An Exhibition at the Museum of Modern Art," *New York Review of Books*, Sept. 25, 1986, 19–24.

"A Life of Learning," American Council of Learned Societies, *Occasional Papers* no. 1 (New York, 1987). Abridged version in *Recasting America: Culture and Politics in the Age of Cold War*, ed. Lary May (Chicago, 1989), 93–103.

"Wagner and Germany's Cultures in the Nineteenth Century," in *The Mirror of History: Essays in Honor of Fritz Fellner*, ed. Solomon Wank et al. (Santa Barbara and Oxford, 1988), 171–80.

"Science as Vocation in Burckhardt's Basel," in *The University and the City*, ed. Thomas Bender (New York and Oxford, 1988), 198–209.

"History and the Study of Culture," *New Literary History* 21 (1989/1990), 407–20.

"Medieval Revival and Its Modern Content: Coleridge, Pugin and Disraeli," in *Modern Age—Modern Historian: In Memorium György Ránki*, ed. Ferenc Glatz (Budapest, 1990), 179–92.

"The Refugee Scholar as Intellectual Educator: A Student's Recollection," in Hartmut Lehmann and James J. Sheehan, eds., *An Interrupted Past: The German-Speaking Refugee Historians in the United States After 1933* (Washington, D.C./ Cambridge, Eng., 1991).

"Gustav Mahler: Formation and Transformation," *Leo Baeck Memorial Lecture*, 35 (New York, 1992).

"Museum in umkämptem Raum. Schwert, Szepter und Ring," in Wolfgang Hardturig and Harm-Hinrich Brandt, eds., *Deutschlands Weg in die Moderne: Politik, Gesellschaft un Kultur im 19. Jahrhundert* (Munich, 1993), 222–42.

"Freud's Egyptian Dig," *New York Review of Books*, May 27, 1993, 35–40.

"Introduction," *Geneva, Zurich, Basel: History, Culture and National Identity* (Princeton, 1994).

Notes

Notes

ROTH: Introduction

1. Carl E. Schorske, "A Life of Learning," American Council of Learned Societies, *Occasional Papers* 1 (1987), 10.

2. Michael S. Roth, "History and . . . : Introduction," *New Literary History* 21, 2 (1990), 250. This issue of *New Literary History* is the basis for a volume I am co-editing with Ralph Cohen, *History And . . .* (Charlottesville, 1994).

3. Schorske, "A Life of Learning," 13.

4. Carl E. Schorske, *Fin-de-siècle Vienna: Politics and Culture* (New York, 1980), xvii.

5. Ibid., 19.

6. Carl E. Schorske, "History and the Study of Culture," *New Literary History* 21, 2 (1990), 407–20. See Michael S. Roth, "Performing History: Modernist Contextualism in Carl Schorske's *Fin-de-siècle Vienna*," *American Historical Review* (1994), forthcoming.

7. Schorske, "A Life of Learning," 15.

8. We might call this the "historical unconscious." See my introduction to the "History and . . ." issue of *New Literary History* 21, 2 (1990), 248–51, and Robert Dawidoff's "History . . . but" in the same issue, 395–406.

9. For example, see Hayden White, *Metahistory: The Historical Imagination in Nineteenth Century Europe* (Baltimore, 1973), *Tropics of Discourse: Essays in Cultural Criticism* (Baltimore, 1978), and *The Content of the Form: Narrative Discourse and Historical Representation* (Baltimore, 1987); Dominick LaCapra and Steven L. Kaplan, eds., *Modern European Intellectual History: Reappraisals and New Perspectives* (Ithaca, NY, 1982); Dominick LaCapra, *Rethinking Intellectual History: Texts, Contexts, Language* (Ithaca, NY, 1983); John Toews, "Intellectual History after the Linguistic Turn: The Autonomy of Meaning and the Irreducibility of Experience," *American Historical Review* 92, 4 (1987), 879–907; Donald R. Kelley, "Horizons of Intellectual History: Retrospect, Circumspect, Prospect," *The Journal of the History of Ideas* 48, 1 (1987), 143–69; David Harlan, "Intellectual History and the Return of Literature," David Hollinger, "The Return of the Prodigal: The Persistence of Historical Knowing," and Harlan, "Response to David Hollinger," all in *American Historical Review* 94, 3 (1989), 581–626; Michael S. Roth, "Cultural Criticism and Political Theory: Hayden White's Rhetorics of History," *Political Theory* 16, 4

(1988), 636–46; Lynn Hunt, ed., *The New Cultural History* (Berkeley, 1989); Michael S. Roth, "Narrative as Enclosure: The Contextual Histories of H. Stuart Hughes," *The Journal of the History of Ideas* 51, 3 (1990), 505–15.

VIDLER: Psychopathologies of Modern Space

1. See Robert A. Nye, *The Origin of Crowd Psychology in Gustave Le Bon and the Crisis of Modern Democracy in the Third Republic* (London: Sage, 1975).

2. See Debora L. Silverman, *Art Nouveau in Fin-de-Siècle France: Politics, Psychology, and Style* (Berkeley: University of California Press, 1989), 79ff.

3. Camillo Sitte, *City Planning According to Artistic Principles*, trans. George Collins and Christiane Crasemann Collins (New York, 1965), 45. First published as *Der Städte-Bau nach seinen künstlerischen Grundsätzen: Ein Beitrag zur lösung modernister Fragen des Architektur und monumentalen Plastik unter besonderer Beziehung auf Wien* (Vienna: Carl Graeser, 1889).

4. Ibid., 53.

5. Ibid., 107. Sitte would no doubt have been happy to read the report of a lifelong sufferer of this modern disorder some twenty years later, who, while managing to outgrow his fear of crowds, nevertheless continued to be adversely affected by spaces and their surrounding buildings: "an immense building or a high rocky bluff fills me with dread. However the architecture of the building has much to do with the sort of sensation produced. Ugly architecture greatly intensifies the fear." The anonymous author of this account had evidently incorporated the lessons of the Viennese planner into his own self-analysis: "I would remark that I have come to wonder," he noted, "if there is real art in many of the so-called 'improvements' in some of our cities, for, judging from the effect they produce on me, they constitute bad art." "Vincent," "Confessions of an Agoraphobic Victim," *American Journal of Psychology* 30 (1919), 297.

6. Sitte, *City Planning*, 53.

7. Wilhelm Worringer, *Abstraction and Empathy: A Contribution to the Psychology of Style*, trans. Michael Bullock (New York: International Universities Press, 1953), 15. First published as *Abstraktion und Einfühlung: Ein Beitrag zur Stilpsychologie* (Munich: R. Piper, 1908).

8. Worringer, *Abstraction and Empathy*, 15.

9. Ibid., 129, from the appendix, "Transcendence and Immanence in Art." Worringer's diagnosis was to prove enduring in art history: the Viennese architectural historian Emil Kaufmann found it useful in order to distinguish between traditional pre-baroque and post-baroque forms of planning. In 1933, he wrote of the fear that inspired the medieval city-builders to, so to speak, crouch low to the ground like frightened animals. *Von Ledoux bis Le Corbusier: Ursprung und Entwicklung der Autonomen Architektur* (Vienna: Rolf Passer, 1933), 17.

10. Carl Friedrich Otto Westphal, "Die Agoraphobie, ein neuropathische Erscheinung," *Archiv für Psychiatrie und Nervenkrankheiten* 3 (1871): 138–61. This

essay has recently been translated, with an introduction, in Westphal's "Die Agoraphobie", with commentary, "The Beginnings of Agoraphobia," by Terry J. Knapp and Michael T. Schumacher (Lanham, MD: University Press of America, 1988). Westphal followed this article with three shorter notes: "Nachtrag zu dem Aufsatze 'Ueber Agoraphobie,'" Archiv für Psychiatrie und Nervenkrankheiten 3 (1872), 219–21; "Ueber Platzfurcht. Briefliche Mittheilungen," Archiv für Psychiatrie und Nervenkrankheiten 7 (1877), 377; and "Agoraphobie (1885)," in Carl Westphal's Gesammelte Abhandlungen, 2 vols. (Berlin: August Hirschwald, 1892), 1:374–87. Dr. E. Cordes replied at length to Westphal's first article in "Die Platzangst (Agoraphobie), Symptom einer Erschöpfungsparese," Archiv für Psychiatrie und Nervenkrankheiten 3 (1872), 521–74.

11. Emile Littré and Robin, Dictionnaire de médecine (Paris: Baillière, 1865), 30.

12. Westphal, "Die Agoraphobie," 139–51.

13. E. Gélineau, De la Kénophobie ou peur des espaces (Agoraphobie des allemands) (Paris, 1880), 24.

14. Legrand du Saulle, Etude clinique sur la peur des espaces (agoraphobie, des allemands) Névrose émotive (Paris: V. Adrien Dalahaye, 1878), 6. The first part of this mémoire appeared in Gazette des hôpitaux of Oct., Nov., and Dec., 1877. Du Saule practiced at the hospital of Bicêtre and was doctor-in-chief at the Dépôt de la Prefecture.

15. Legrand du Saulle, Etude clinique, 6–7.

16. Ibid. The "poetics" of agoraphobia reached a high point in the protophenomenological study of Claude-Etienne Bourdin, Horreur du vide (Paris: Charles de Lamotte, 1878), who concluded that the primary cause of "peur des espaces" was moral rather than physical.

17. Legrand du Saulle, Etude clinique, 7–8.

18. Ibid., 9.

19. Ibid., 10.

20. Ibid., 11. Unlike the other cases cited, this patient was equally unable to support large open spaces in the countryside, experiencing agoraphobic fear when asked to draw maps of the territory for maneuvers. "Il est effrayé à la vue d'une plaine sans fin" (11).

21. Ibid., 13.

22. Emile Littré, Dictionnaire de la langue française, 4 vols. and supplement (Paris: Hachette, 1883), Supplément, 355.

23. Legrand du Saulle, Etude clinique, 31, noted that his agoraphobic patient, a consumer of large amounts of coffee and a heavy smoker, was terrified in the face of a wide bridge, always feeling as if he were in front of a void. Suppression of coffee and stimulants helped diminish the symptoms.

24. Ibid., 32–33.

25. Benjamin Ball, De la claustrophobie. Mémoire lu à la Société Médicopsychologique dans la séance du 28 Juillet, 1879 (Paris: E. Donnand, 1879).

26. Ibid., 5.

27. Ibid., 6.

28. Gilles de la Tourette, *Les états neurasthéniques* (Paris: J.-B. Baillière, 1898), 15–16.

29. Ibid., 16.

30. Ibid., 45–46.

31. Ibid., 90.

32. Jean Martin Charcot, *Leçons du mardi à la Salpêtrière*, Notes de cours de MM. Blin, Charcot, et Colin (Paris: Centre d'étude et de promotion de la lecture, Les classiques de la psychologie, 1974), 104.

33. Ibid., 103.

34. Sigmund Freud, *Standard Edition* 1:139, from J. M. Charcot, *Poliklinische Vorträge* 1 (1887–88), trans. Sigmund Freud (Leipzig and Vienna: Deuticke, 1892–94), 224.

35. Fernand Levillain, *La Neurasthénie, maladie de Beard* (Paris: A. Maloine, 1891), 30.

36. David Frisby, *Fragments of Modernity* (Cambridge, MA: MIT Press, 1989).

37. Georg Simmel, *Philosophie des Gelds*, ed. David Frisby and Klaus Christian Köhnke (Frankfurt: Suhrkamp, 1989), 661. "Berührungsangst" is translated as "agoraphobia" in the English edition *The Philosophy of Money*, trans. T. Bottomore and D. Frisby (London: Routledge, 1978), 474.

38. Georg Simmel, "Soziologie des Raumes," *Jahrbuch für Gesetzgebung, Verwaltung und Volkswirtschaft* 27 (1903), 27–71, cited in Frisby, *Fragments of Modernity*, 77.

39. Georg Simmel, *Soziologie. Untersuchungen über die Formen der Vergesellschaftlung* (Munich and Leipzig: Duncker and Humblot, 1923), 460–526.

40. Simmel, *Soziologie*, as summarized in N. J. Spykman, *The Social Theory of Georg Simmel* (New York: Russell and Russell, 1964), 144–62.

41. Simmel elaborated this notion by examining the interdependency of spatial exclusivity and spatial non-exclusivity. Some social forms—the state, for example— manifested themselves in a unique and localized space, that excluded the possibility of other forms inhabiting the same space; other institutions, like the church, for instance, were not so dependent on locational fixity, allowing for the possibility of other churches operating on the same territory. Social elements might then be characterized on a scale from the spatially exclusive to the supra-spatial.

42. Georg Simmel, "Metropolis and Mental Life," trans. from "Die Grossstadt und das Geistesleben," *Die Grossstadt. Jahrbuch der Gehe-Stiftung* 9 (1903), 325.

43. Ibid., 337–38.

44. Simmel, "Exkurs über die Soziologie der Sinne," in *Soziologie*, 486.

45. Simmel, *The Philosophy of Money*, 477.

46. Simmel, "Exkurs über den Fremden," *Soziologie*, 509–12.

47. Siegfried Kracauer, *Ginster. Von ihm selbst geschrieben* (Berlin: S. Fischer, 1928) in Kracauer, *Ginster. Georg* (Frankfurt: Suhrkamp, 1979).

48. Kracauer, *Ginster. Georg*, 106.
49. Ibid.
50. Ibid., 199.
51. Siegfried Kracauer, *Jacques Offenbach und das Paris seiner Zeit* (Amsterdam: A. de Lange, 1937).
52. Siegfried Kracauer, "Hotelhalle," in *Der Detektiv-Roman. Ein Philosophischer Traktat, Schriften I: Soziologie als Wissenschaft, Der Detektiv-Roman, Die Angestellten* (Frankfurt: Suhrkamp, 1971), 128–37.
53. Ibid., 129.   54. Ibid., 134.
55. Ibid., 135.   56. Ibid., 136.
57. Ibid., 137.
58. Walter Benjamin, *Gesammelte Schriften* 3 (Frankfurt: Suhrkamp Verlag, 1982), 196.
59. Ibid., 1, 527.
60. Ibid., 645.
61. Ibid., 646.
62. Jean Martin Charcot, *Leçons sur l'hystérie virile*, intro. Michèle Ouerd (Paris, 1984), 214.
63. Ibid., 237.
64. Jean-Martin Charcot, *Charcot the Clinician: The Tuesday Lessons*, trans. with commentary by Christopher G. Goetz (New York: Raven Press, 1987), 31.
65. Ibid., 41.
66. Ibid., 647.
67. Benjamin, *Passagen-Werk* 5, II: 1054.
68. Benjamin, *Passagen-Werk* 5, 1:135.
69. Benjamin, *Gesammelte Schriften* 3: 197.
70. Benjamin, *Gessammelte Schriften* 5:679.
71. Sigfried Giedion, *Bauen in Frankreich* (Berlin, 1928), 85; in Benjamin, *Gesammelte Schriften* 5:533.
72. Ibid., 514.

LIEBERSOHN: Selective Affinities

1. See James A. Boon, *The Anthropological Romance of Bali, 1597–1972: Dynamic Perspectives in Marriage and Caste, Politics and Religion* (Cambridge, 1977); idem, *Affinities and Extremes: Crisscrossing the Bittersweet Ethnology of East Indies History, Hindu-Balinese Culture, and Indo-European Allure* (Chicago and London, 1990); and Clifford Geertz, "Person, Time, and Conduct in Bali," in Geertz, *The Interpretation of Cultures* (New York, 1973), 360–411. On nineteenth-century Europeans' interest in religion and kinship, see George W. Stocking, Jr., *Victorian Anthropology* (New York, 1987), chap. 6.
2. Cf. Friedrich Meinecke's periodization of three generations of German academic politics in "Drei Generationen deutscher Gelehrtenpolitik," *Historische Zeit-*

schrift 125 (3d series, vol. 29) (1922), 248–83. My title in part echoes Meinecke's, in part reasserts a cosmopolitanism played down in his essay. On the concept of "generation," cf. Carl E. Schorske, "Generational Tension and Cultural Change: Reflections on the Case of Vienna," *Daedalus*, Fall 1978, 111–22, esp. 121.

3. See Friedrich Schlegel to August Wilhelm Schlegel, 21 July 1791, on German national character, and Friedrich to August Wilhelm, 24 Nov. 1793, on France, in *Friedrich Schlegels Briefe an seinen Bruder August Wilhelm*, ed. Oskar F. Walzel (Berlin, 1890), 26 and 146.

4. For an introduction to Schlegel, see Hans Eichner, *Friedrich Schlegel* (New York, 1970). *Friedrich Schlegel's "Lucinde" and the Fragments*, trans. and ed. Peter Firchow (Minneapolis, 1971), is an excellent compendium in English of some of the most important early writings. See also the penetrating interpretation in Walter Benjamin's dissertation, "Der Begriff der Kunstkritik in der deutschen Romantik," in Benjamin, *Gesammelte Schriften* 1, 1 (Frankfurt, 1974). For the appreciation of Forster as a model for German *Bildung*, see Friedrich Schlegel, "Georg Forster. Fragment einer Charakteristik der deutschen Klassiker," in Schlegel, *Charakteristiken und Kritiken* 1 (1796–1801), ed. Hans Eichner (Munich-Paderborn-Vienna, 1967), esp. 78ff, 82. On the Berlin salons, see Deborah Hertz, *Jewish High Society in Old Regime Berlin* (New Haven and London, 1988).

5. Friedrich Schlegel, *Vermischte Kritische Schriften. Dabei: Über die Sprache und Weisheit der Indier: Ein Beitrag zur Begründung der Alterthumskunde (Sämtliche Werke* 8) (Bonn, 1877), 278. My translation.

6. Schlegel was cosmopolitan but not universal in his cultural sympathies. He had no difficulty defending Arabic, Persian, and Old Testament poetry to his contemporaries and attacking stereotypes of the luxuriant "Oriental style," a phrase which could apply just as well, he pointed out, to poetry in modern Western literatures, and which did not apply to Indian or Chinese poetry. But it was always *educated* peoples whom he regarded as one big family. See ibid., 380–81.

7. "Die physische Verschiedenheit der Menschenstämme ist, wenigstens so weit sie bis jetzt entwickelt worden, von nicht so grosser historischer Wichtigkeit." Ibid., 356–57. Schlegel speculated that physical characteristics were changeable and that migration would give birth to new nations though they might then retain their character virtually unchanged for thousands of years. Ibid., 357.

8. Ibid., 359–64.

9. Ibid., 370, 378.

10. On Treitschke see Andreas Dorpalen, *Heinrich von Treitschke* (New Haven, 1957), and Walter Bussmann, *Treitschke: Sein Welt- und Geschichtsbild* (Göttingen, 1952).

11. See *Der Berliner Antisemitismusstreit*, ed. Walter Boehlich (Frankfurt am Main, 1965), which contains the initial essay, contemporary responses, and Treitschke's replies to his critics, as well as a valuable interpretive essay by the editor.

12. Ibid., 10. My translation.

13. Ibid., 14.

14. Ibid., 13.

15. Heinrich von Treitschke, *Deutsche Geschichte im 19. Jahrhundert, 2. Teil: Bis zu den Karlsbader Beschlüssen* (Leipzig, 1917), 67. My translation.

16. Ibid., 68, 72.

17. See Treitschke's general critique of early Romanticism in ibid., 12ff. On Schlegel, see the reference to *Weisheit*, ibid., 72; the unfriendly reference to Schlegel's novel *Lucinde* (which conventional nineteenth-century opinion considered pornographic) ibid., 1, 206; and the attack on the conversion to Catholicism as evidence of spiritual decay, ibid., 2, 95.

18. The rapprochement of bourgeoisie and nobility was not restricted to Germany or the late nineteenth century alone. It took place in France as well beginning in the society of orders of the *ancien régime* and continuing in the class society of the nineteenth century. See the trenchant analysis in C. B. A. Behrens, *Society, Government and the Enlightenment: The Experiences of Eighteenth-Century France and Prussia* (New York, 1985), especially the concluding remarks, p. 205.

19. Treitschke was a visitor to the home of Weber's father, a city politician in Berlin whose house was a meeting-place for the intellectual elite of the capital. During the 1880s Weber watched the bitter conflict that arose when his uncle, Hermann Baumgarten, criticized the Prussian chauvinism of volume two of Treitschke's *Deutsche Geschichte*. Baumgarten played an important role as Weber's political educator and helped him gain distance from Treitschke's adulation of Bismarck and his works. Nonetheless Weber was not immune to the voice of the political prophet. "Hinter allen politischen Einseitigkeiten spürte er (Weber, HL) das echte Pathos und den Ernst einer grossen Persönlichkeit." Wolfgang J. Mommsen, *Max Weber und die deutsche Politik 1890–1920*, 2d ed. (Tübingen, 1974), 9; see also, 1, 7, 9–10.

20. Weber's terminology wavers slightly; sometimes he speaks of *Verwandtschaft*, sometimes of *innere Verwandtschaft*, without distinguishing between them. See the uses of *Verwandtschaft* and *innere Verwandtschaft* in Max Weber, "Die protestantische Ethik und der 'Geist' des Kapitalismus," in *Die Protestantische Ethik. I. Eine Aufsatzsammlung*, ed. Johannes Winckelmann (Gütersloh, 1981), 35, 38, 68, 87, 88, 98, 116, 197, 259.

On Weber's nationalism and *The Protestant Ethic*, see also Harry Liebersohn, "Weber's Historical Concept of National Identity," in *Farewell to the Protestant Ethic: Origins, Evidence, Contexts*, ed. Hartmut Lehman and Guenther Roth (Cambridge; 1993), 123–31; and Liebersohn, *Fate and Utopia in German Sociology, 1870–1923* (Cambridge, MA, and London, 1988), chap. 4.

21. The most important comparisons are the following: in the first edition Weber notes the attraction of the Puritans to the Old Testament, but argues that they made a highly selective choice of texts to legitimate their own, distinctive experience, while omitting texts such as the Song of Songs and the Psalms which contained an alien "Oriental eroticism" and "Oriental quietism" respectively. Weber,

Protestantische Ethik 1, 138–39, 172–74. In the second edition he speaks of Puritans' feeling of "inner affinity" (*innere Verwandtschaft*) with Judaism. Ibid., 259. More important, he introduces the category of disenchantment of the world, a recurring process which begins with Old Testament prophecy, joins with Hellenic systematic (*wissenschaftlich*) thinking, and reaches its conclusion in the Puritans. Ibid., 123. See also the addition distinguishing Jewish and Puritan disenchantment of the world from sacramental Catholic religiosity, ibid., 133.

22. Ibid., 170, 253.

23. In the aftermath of the Nazi era, when the temptation was especially strong for Americans to think otherwise, Carl Schorske was able to state with special clarity that German nationalism depended on particular historical conditions: "Scholars have striven in vain for an agreed view concerning the roots of German nationalism. For the purposes of this study it is of little consequence whether they be found in the ancient Teutoburg forest or in the Lutheran Reformation. Our concern is with the evolution of German nationalism during the nineteenth century, when it became associated with political authoritarianism. . . . Authoritarian nationalism in Germany is not the result of a different human development in that country, but the product of a peculiar historical evolution." Carl E. Schorske, "Social and Cultural Aspects of the German Problem," in Hoyt Price and Carl E. Schorske, *The Problem of Germany* (*Studies in American Foreign Relations* 5) (New York, 1947), 93, 99.

ROSE: The First Viennese Psychoanalysts

1. *Minutes of the Vienna Psychoanalytic Society*, ed. Herman Nunberg and Ernst Federn, 4 vols. (New York: International Universities Press, 1962–75), 1, Apr. 1, 1908, 359.

2. Ibid. 2, Oct. 28, 1908, 31–32.

3. See Hermann Broch, *Hugo von Hofmannsthal and His Time: The European Imagination, 1860–1920*, ed. and trans. Michael P. Steinberg (Chicago: University of Chicago Press, 1984).

4. The official membership in 1906–7, when minutes, attendance, and yearly enrollment were first recorded, numbered 17; grew to 37 in 1910–11, the year of the schism between Freud and Alfred Adler; reached 32 in 1912–13; and fell to 22 by the beginning of the First World War. The attendance at meetings was far lower, averaging 10 in 1906–7, 19 in 1910–11, and finally 14 from 1912 to 1914. These figures were compiled from the attendance and enrollment lists in the *Minutes*, and exclude individuals who were guests of the society or visiting members of psychoanalytic societies from other cities.

5. Sixteen members will come under consideration in this essay. Freud and four physicians—Wilhelm Stekel, Alfred Adler, Max Kahane, and Rudolf Reitler—founded the Psychological Wednesday Evenings in 1902. Paul Federn, also a general practitioner, joined the group a year later. Music critic David Bach came to the society during the first three years of its existence. By the end of 1905, Eduard

Hitschmann, a physician, and Max Graf, a music critic, had also become members. Graf became well known to later psychoanalysts as the father who compiled the case history of the animal phobia of his son, "little Hans." In 1906, Otto Rank, an aspiring writer, entered the circle and took on the task of recording the minutes of its meetings. Two of the first practicing analysts, Maxim Steiner and Isador Sadger, began to attend the meetings in 1907. A few months after Sadger joined the society, he proposed for membership his nephew, the journalist Fritz Wittels. In 1908, Victor Tausk, a former lawyer and writer, introduced himself to Freud, and in the following year entered his circle. In 1910, Hanns Sachs, a lawyer with literary ambitions, became a member. Finally, Alfred von Winterstein, president of the Vienna Society after the Second World War, joined the group in 1910, and Theodor Reik, a student of psychology and literature, entered in 1911. Not only were these members' occupations equally divided between the medical and non-medical, but several physicians pursued second careers as writers and cultural critics.

6. Adler's opposition to psychoanalysis began at least as early as 1909, although he did not withdraw from the Vienna Society until 1911. The essay will focus on the views of members who remained within the movement after Adler's schism as the views most representative of a Freudian vanguard.

7. Carl Schorske, "Politics and the Psyche: Schnitzler and Hofmannsthal," in Schorske, *Fin-de-siècle Vienna: Politics and Culture* (New York: Knopf, 1980), 8.

8. The psychoanalysts' registration and graduation forms at the University of Vienna recorded the professions of fourteen fathers: three businessmen, two civil servants, two journalists, a bank executive, a railroad executive, a lawyer, a physician, a railroad inspector, a produce merchant, and an accountant for a wholesale firm. See Universitätsarchiv, Universität Wien, *Matrikel* and *Rigorosenprotokollen*. Another source reveals that David Bach's father, who died the year Bach entered the university, first worked as a bookkeeper and later owned a small hat business. [Henriette Kotlan-Werner, *Kunst und Volk: David Josef Bach, 1874–1947* (Vienna: Materialen zur Arbeiter Bewegung, 1978), 9–10.] Isador Sadger's father died before Sadger enrolled at the university. His profession is unknown. For further information, see Louis Rose, "The Psychoanalytic Movement in Vienna: Toward a Science of Culture," Ph.D. diss., Princeton University, 1986, app. 1.

9. Hanns Sachs, *Freud, Master and Friend* (Cambridge: Harvard University Press, 1944), 158.

10. Ernst Federn, with Annie Urbach, Heinrich Meng, and Edoardo Weiss, "Thirty-five Years with Freud," *Journal of the History of Behavioral Sciences* 8, Jan. 1972, 13.

11. Philip L. Becker, "Eduard Hitschmann," *Psychoanalytic Pioneers*, ed. Franz Alexander, Samuel Eisenstein, and Martin Grotjahn (New York: Basic Books, 1966), 160. Of the six fathers in business professions, we know the occupation not only of Mathias Hitschmann, but also of Leopold Adler, a produce merchant, and of Eduard Bach, owner of a hat business. In contrast, David Bach's mother labored for a "textile business" after her husband's death. Kotlan-Werner, *Kunst und Volk*, 10.

12. See Theodor Reik, *Fragment of a Great Confession: A Psychoanalytic Biography* (New York: Farrar, Straus, 1949), 230.

13. Universität Wien, *Matrikel, Philosophie,* Summer 1909. In Rank's early youth, his father had worked as a jeweller. See Dennis Klein, *Jewish Origins of the Psychoanalytic Movement* (New York: Praeger, 1981), 108, and E. James Lieberman, *Acts of Will: The Life and Work of Otto Rank* (New York: The Free Press, 1985), 1.

14. Paul Roazen, *Brother Animal: The Story of Freud and Tausk* (New York: Knopf, 1969), 8–9.

15. Four psychoanalysts—Reitler, Federn, Hitschmann, and Graf—graduated from the *Akademisches Gymnasium,* the institution turned by the liberal middle class into a stronghold of secular education, in conscious opposition to the aristocratic *Theresianum* and religious *Schottengymnasium.*

16. Stekel described his artistic ambitions and career decision in his *Autobiography* (New York: Liveright Publishing Corp., 1950), 43–57 and 99–100.

17. In their registration forms, Reitler and Winterstein recorded their religion as Catholic. According to Ernst Federn, Reitler's family had converted from Judaism. (Interview with Ernst Federn, 1979.)

18. Sachs, *Freud, Master and Friend,* 22.

19. Federn et al., "Thirty-five Years with Freud," 13.

20. One of Alfred Adler's biographers states that Adler officially converted to Protestantism. Phyllis Bottome, *Alfred Adler: A Biography* (New York: G. P. Putnam's Sons, 1939), 4. Adler's university registration forms, however, show that at least throughout his education he recorded his religion as Jewish. Although her father was Jewish, Victor Tausk's wife adhered to Christianity. Tausk chose to be baptized a Protestant before their wedding. He never ceased, however, to identify himself as Jewish, and few were aware of his official conversion. See Roazen, *Brother Animal,* 11, and Freud, *The Psychopathology of Everyday Life, Standard Edition of the Complete Psychological Works of Sigmund Freud,* trans. and ed. by J. Strachey, 24 vols. (London: Hogarth Press, 1953–74), 6:92–93. Although born Jewish, Otto Rank described himself on the university registration form in 1908 as "non-confessional" (*Konfessionslos*). In the same year, he formally converted to Catholicism so as to justify to the government changing his name from Rosenfeld to Rank, thereby dissociating himself from his father. In 1922, he returned to Judaism. See Klein, *Jewish Origins of the Psychoanalytic Movement,* 110 n.28.

21. Max Graf, *Wagner-Probleme und andere Studien* (Vienna: Wiener Verlag, 1900), 148. Translations are my own unless indicated otherwise.

22. Ibid., 150.

23. Max Graf, *Legend of a Musical City* (New York: Philosophical Library, 1945), 79–80.

24. Ibid., 174 and 181.

25. Sachs, *Freud, Master and Friend,* 25–27.

26. Ibid., 27–28.

27. Ibid., 28.

28. Fritz Wittels, *Der Taufjude* (Vienna: M. Breitenstein, 1904), 12.

29. Ibid., 29.   30. Ibid., 23 and 30.

31. Ibid., 30.   32. Ibid., 19.

33. Ibid., 35. I have used the Bayard Taylor translation (New York: Collier Books, 1962 ed.) for Wittels's quotation from Goethe's *Faust*, pt. 1.

34. Otto Weininger, *Sex and Character*, 6th ed. (London: William Heinemann, 1906), 54.

35. Ibid., 130–31.   36. Ibid., 83.

37. Ibid., 162.

38. Ibid., 161.   39. Ibid., 346.

40. Otto Rank, *Tagebücher* 2, Feb. 24, 1904, Box 1a, Otto Rank Collection, Rare Book and Manuscript Library, Columbia University.

41. See Klein, *Jewish Origins of the Psychoanalytic Movement*, 116–29 and app. B for information on Rank's father, family life, schooling, and employment.

42. Rank, *Tagebücher* 2, May 3, 1904.

43. Ibid., Apr. 3, 1904.

44. Ibid., Feb. 22, 1904. For Rank's early ideas on cultural renewal, see Klein, *Jewish Origins of the Psychoanalytic Movement*, 116–121.

45. Wilhelm Stekel, "Der Fall Otto Weininger," *Die Wage* 44 (Oct. 29, 1904), and 45 (Nov. 5, 1904), 1031.

46. Eduard Hitschmann, "Schopenhauer. Von P.J. Möbius," *Wiener klinische Rundschau* 19, 18 (May 7, 1905), 317.

47. Ibid.

48. Ibid., 318.

49. Carl Schorske, "Explosion in the Garden: Kokoschka and Schoenberg," in Schorske, *Fin-de-siècle Vienna*, 363.

50. Walter Benjamin, "Karl Kraus," in Benjamin, *Reflections*, ed. Peter Demetz, trans. Edmund Jephcott (New York: Harcourt, Brace, Jovanovich, 1978), 271.

51. Karl Kraus, "Die demolirte Literatur," in Kraus, *Frühe Schriften, 1892–1900* 2, ed. Johannes J. Braakenburg (Munich: Kosel Verlag, 1979), 278.

52. Ibid., 281.

53. Hanns Sachs, [Introduction], *Soldaten-Lieder und andere Gedichte, von Rudyard Kipling* (Leipzig: Julius Zeitler, 1910), 1.

54. Ibid., 1.

55. Theodor Reik, *Richard Beer-Hofmann* (Leipzig: Sphinx Verlag, 1911), 3.

56. Ibid., 39.

57. Sachs, *Freud, Master and Friend*, 39–40.

58. Karl Kraus, "Die Kinderfreunde," *Die Fackel* 7, 187 (Nov. 8, 1905), 19.

59. Karl Kraus, "Der Prozess Riehl," *Die Fackel* 8, 211 (Nov. 13, 1906), 9.

60. Ibid., 10.

61. Ibid., 25.

62. *Minutes* 2, Jan. 12, 1910, 388.

63. Fritz Wittels, *Die sexuelle Not* (Vienna: W. Stern, 1909), ix–xiii.

64. Edward Timms, *Karl Kraus, Apocalyptic Satirist. Culture and Catastrophe in Habsburg Vienna* (New Haven: Yale University Press, 1986), 99–100.

65. Kraus, *Die Fackel* 10, 266 (Nov. 30, 1908), 20.

66. *Minutes* 2, Dec. 16, 1908, 89.

67. *Minutes* 2, Jan. 12, 1910, 391.

68. On the Freud-Kraus correspondence in its context, see Timms, *Karl Kraus, Apocalyptic Satirist*, 64–67 and 94–97.

69. Freud to Kraus, Nov. 11, 1906, trans. Thomas Szasz, in Szasz, *Karl Kraus and the Soul Doctors* (Baton Rouge: Louisiana State University Press, 1976), 21–22.

70. For an excellent exploration of the personal break between Kraus and Freud, and the later conflicts between *Die Fackel* and Freud's followers, see Timms, *Karl Kraus, Apocalyptic Satirist*, 97–114.

71. Freud to Jung, Feb. 13, 1910, *The Freud/Jung Letters: The Correspondence between Sigmund Freud and C. G. Jung*, ed. William McGuire (Princeton: Princeton University Press, 1974), 295.

72. Max Graf, "Reminiscences of Professor Sigmund Freud," *Psychoanalytic Quarterly* 11, 4 (1942), 470.

73. See William McGrath, *Dionysian Art and Populist Politics in Austria* (New Haven: Yale University, 1974).

74. Graf, *Wagner-Probleme*, [p. 7].

75. Ibid., 21–22.

76. Ibid., [p. 8].

77. Ibid., [p. 5]. While a student at the University of Vienna, Graf had supported the rebellion of *Jung Wien*. He now rejected it: "The old criticism was rigid, dogmatic, narrow-minded; the new flexible, without convictions, indulgent. . . . It made no value judgments, that was its chief weapon." Ibid., [p. 10].

78. Ibid., [p. 6].

79. Ibid., 78.

80. Ibid., 83–84.

LOEWENBERG: The Clinical Situation

I wish to acknowledge valued critiques of earlier drafts of this paper by the deeply mourned Robert J. Stoller and by John Kafka, Fritz Stern, Nancy Chodorow, Jessica Benjamin, Leonard Shengold, Blema Steinberg, Herbert and Marjorie Morris, Arthur Rosett, Norman Abrams, Kenneth Graham, Jr., Daniel J. Bussel, Barbara Rosecrance, Harry and Edith Swerdlow, Martin Levine, Helen Eisenstein, and Samuel Loewenberg. I thank David Lee and Sonja Fritzsche for their diligent research assistance.

1. June 5, 1910, Sigmund Freud-Oskar Pfister, *Briefe 1909–1939* (Frankfurt am Main: S. Fischer Verlag, 1963), 36.

2. Handbill of the Psychoanalytic Center of California, Los Angeles, July 17, 1990. Cf. Douglas Kirsner, "Is There a Future for American Psychoanalysis?" *Psychoanalytic Review* 77:2 (Summer 1990), 175–200.

3. Herbert Marcuse, "Obsolescence of Psychoanalysis," address to the American Political Science Association, New York City, Sept. 4–7, 1963, p. 1. See also Russell Jacoby, *The Repression of Psychoanalysis: Otto Fenichel and the Political Freudians* (New York: Basic Books, 1983), and Herbert Marcuse's classic "Critique of Neo-Freudian Revisionism," in Marcuse, *Eros and Civilization: A Philosophical Inquiry into Freud* (Boston: Beacon Press, 1955; New York: Alfred Knopf, 1962), 217–51.

4. By "Counter-Enlightenment," I refer to Walter Benjamin's critique of Kant: "The reality with which, and with the knowledge of which, Kant wanted to base knowledge on certainty and truth is a reality of a low, perhaps the lowest, order [*eine Wirklichkeit niedern, vielleicht niedersten Ranges*]. . . . It is obviously a matter of that same state of affairs that has often been mentioned as the religious and historical blindness of the Enlightenment [*religiöse und historische Blindheit der Aufklärung*]. . . . Experience, as it is conceived in reference to the individual human and his consciousness, instead of as a systematic specification of knowledge, is again in all of its types the mere *object* of this real knowledge, specifically of its psychological branch. . . . The source of existence lies in the totality of experience (*Die Quelle des Daseins liegt nun aber in der Totalität der Erfahrung*)." From "Über das Programm der kommenden Philosophie," *Gesammelte Schriften*, Rolf Tiedemann and Hermann Schweppenhäuser, eds. (Frankfurt am Main: Suhrkamp Verlag, 1988), 2, 1:157–71. The quotations are from 158, 159, 162, 170, *passim*. Translated by Mark Ritter as "Program of the Coming Philosophy," in *The Philosophical Forum* 15, 1–2 (Fall–Winter 1983–84), 41–51.

5. Friedrich Nietzsche, "Aus dem Nachlass der Achtzigerjahre," in *Werke in drei Bänden*, ed. Karl Schlechta (Munich: Carl Hanser Verlag, 1956), 3:486.

6. Ibid., 903.

7. Nietzsche, "Jenseits von Gut und Böse," in Schlechta, ed., *Werke* 2:730.

8. Donald P. Spence, *Narrative Truth and Historical Truth: Meaning and Interpretation in Psychoanalysis* (New York: W. W. Norton & Co., 1982), and *The Freudian Metaphor: Toward Paradigm Change in Psychoanalysis* (New York: W. W. Norton & Co., 1987).

9. Sigmund Freud, "Die 'kulturelle' Sexualmoral und die Moderne Nervosität" (1908), *Studienausgabe*, ed. by A. Mitscherlich, A. Richards, J. Strachey, 11 vols. (Frankfurt am Main: S. Fischer Verlag, 1969–79), 9:27; idem, "'Civilized' Sexual Morality and Modern Nervous Illness," in *The Standard Edition of the Complete Psychological Works of Sigmund Freud*, trans. and ed. by James Strachey, 24 vols. (London: Hogarth Press, 1953–74), 9:198.

10. Freud, *Studienausgabe* 9:22; *Standard Edition* 9:192.

11. Sigmund Freud, "Das Unbehagen in der Kultur" (1929), *Studienausgabe* 9:234; "Civilization and its Discontents," *Standard Edition* 21:105.

12. Apr. 1, 1908, *Minutes of the Vienna Psychoanalytic Society*, ed. Herman Nunberg and Ernst Federn (New York: International Universities Press, 1962), 1:358–59.

13. Oct. 28, 1908, Ibid. 2:31–32.

14. Sigmund Freud, "Massenpsychologie und Ich-Analyse" (1921), *Studienausgabe* 9:130–31; "Group Psychology and the Analysis of the Ego," *Standard Edition* 18:140.

15. Sigmund Freud, "Fragment of an Analysis of a Case of Hysteria" (1905), *Standard Edition* 7:50; "Bruchstück einer Hysterie-Analyse," *Studienausgabe* 6:124–25.

16. Sigmund Freud, "Three Essays on the Theory of Sexuality" (1905), *Standard Edition* 7:139; "Drei Abhandlungen zur Sexualtheorie," *Studienausgabe* 5:51.

17. Ibid., *Standard Edition* 7:139, n. 2; *Studienausgabe* 5:51, n. 1.

18. Freud to anonymous, Apr. 9, 1935 (written in English), in Ernst Freud, ed., *Letters of Sigmund Freud* (New York: Basic Books, 1960), no. 277, p. 423.

19. Jacob Arlow, "Psychoanalysis and the Quest for Morality," in H. P. Blum, E. M. Weinshel, F. R. Rodman, eds., *The Psychoanalytic Core* (Madison, CT: International Universities Press, 1989), 148.

20. John S. Kafka, "On Reality: An Examination of Object Constancy, Ambiguity, Paradox, and Time," in Joseph H. Smith, ed., *Psychiatry and the Humanities*, vol. 2, *Thought, Consciousness, and Reality* (New Haven: Yale University Press, 1977), 133, 147.

21. John S. Kafka, "Technical Applications of a Concept of Multiple Reality," *International Journal of Psycho-Analysis* 45, 4 (1964), 576–77. See also *Multiple Realities in Clinical Practice* (New Haven, CT: Yale University Press, 1989).

22. Kafka, "On Reality," 156.

23. Sigmund Freud, "Zur Dynamik der Übertragung" (1912), *Studienausgabe*, Ergänzungsband, 167; "The Dynamics of Transference," *Standard Edition* 12:107.

24. Sigmund Freud, "Zur Einleitung der Behandlung" (1913), *Studienausgabe*, Ergänzungsband, 195, n.1; "On Beginning the Treatment," *Standard Edition* 12:135–36, n.1.

25. Ibid.

26. *California Evidence Code*, Art. 7, Secs. 1010–12 and 1024. See also Abraham S. Goldstein and Jay Katz, "Psychiatrist-Patient Privilege: The GAP Proposal and the Connecticut Statute," *Connecticut Bar Journal* 36, 2 (June 1962), 175–89.

27. *California Civil Code*, Sec. 43.92.

28. *Tarasoff v. Regents of University of California*, 17 C. 3d 425, quotation from p. 439; 131 California Reporter 14, 551 P.2d 334 (1976).

29. *Tarasoff v. Regents*, 17 Cal. 3d at 442.

30. Kim Oppenheimer and Greg Swanson, "Duty to Warn: When Should Confidentiality Be Breached?," *Journal of Family Practice* 30, 2 (1990), 181.

31. *Tarasoff v. Regents*, 17 Cal. 3d 451, 452 (Mosk, J. dissenting).

32. Ibid., at 457 (Clark, J. dissenting).

33. Ibid., 460 (Clark, J. dissenting).

34. Ibid., 462–63, n.6 (Clark, J. dissenting).

35. Roxanne Parrott et al., "Privacy Between Physicians and Patients: More Than a Matter of Confidentiality," *Social Science and Medicine* 29, 12 (1989), 1385.

36. Daniel O. Taube and Amiram Elwork, "Researching the Effects of Confidentiality Law on Patients' Self-Disclosures," *Professional Psychology: Research and Practice* 21, 1 (1990), 74.

37. *Schuster v. Altenberg* (1988), 144 Wis. 2d 223, 424 N.W. 2d 159.

38. "Psychiatry is not an exact science, and psychiatrists disagree widely and frequently on what constitutes mental illness, on the appropriate diagnosis to be attached to given behavior and symptoms, on cure and treatment, and on likelihood of future dangerousness." *Ake v. Oklahoma*, 470 U.S. 68, 81 (1985). See also John Monahan, *Predicting Violent Behavior: An Assessment of Clinical Techniques* (Beverly Hills, CA: Sage Publications, 1981), and *The Clinical Prediction of Violent Behavior* (Rockville, MD.: U.S. Department of Health and Human Services Publication No. [ADM] 81-921, 1981).

39. Steven C. Bednar, "The Psychotherapist's Calamity: Emerging Trends in the Tarasoff Doctrine," *Brigham Young Law Review* 1, 261–81 (1989). The quotation is from 277, 281.

40. John Stuart Mill, *On Liberty* (1859) (Indianapolis: Bobbs-Merrill, 1956), 92.

41. For an exhaustive consideration of reasons other than "harm" for criminalization, critiqued from a liberal point of view, see Joel Feinberg, *The Moral Limits of the Criminal Law*, 4 vols. (New York: Oxford University Press, 1984–88).

42. Richard Green, *Social Science and the Law* (Cambridge, MA: Harvard University Press, 1992), 144–55, at 153.

43. *California Evidence Code*, Secs. 1030–34. This and subsequent statements of case or statute law will, unless otherwise noted, apply to California law only. However, all 51 jurisdictions in the United States require physicians and other professionals to report suspected child abuse.

44. Leonard Shengold, *Soul Murder: The Effects of Childhood Abuse and Deprivation* (New Haven: Yale University Press, 1989). Lenore Terr, *Too Scared to Cry: Psychic Trauma in Childhood* (New York: Harper & Row, 1990).

45. I am indebted to Lisa Friedman for drawing this to my attention.

46. Virginia Woolf, "A Sketch of the Past," in Jeanne Schulkind, ed., *Moments of Being*, 2d ed. (New York: Harcourt Brace Jovanovich, 1985), 68–69.

47. Quentin Bell, *Virginia Woolf: A Biography* (New York: Harcourt Brace Jovanovich, 1972), 2:6. See also: Leon Edel, *Bloomsbury: A House of Lions* (Philadelphia: J. P. Lippincott Co., 1979), 86, 89–90; Alma Halbert Bond, *Who Killed Virginia Woolf?* (New York: Insight Books/Human Sciences Press, 1989); Louise De Salvo, *Virginia Woolf: The Impact of Childhood Sexual Abuse on Her Life and Work* (Boston: Beacon Press, 1989).

48. *California Penal Code*, Sec. 11165.8.

49. *California Penal Code*, Sec. 11166 (b).

50. *California Penal Code*, Sec. 11166 (a).

51. Cf., for example, Seth C. Kalichman: "I am not aware of any legal options other than reporting. . . . Failure to report is not a viable option under current state statutes." Kalichman, "Reporting Laws, Confidentiality, and Clinical Judgement: Reply to Ansell and Ross," *American Psychologist* 45 (Nov. 1990), 1273.

52. "As citizens we not only enjoy the right but also bear the obligation to evaluate existing laws and their flawed systems of enforcement from a higher moral perspective. . . . Consequently, we may sometimes choose private or public disobedience of current laws. . . . Following the letter of a current reporting law may sometimes subject a child to numerous harmful consequences and, under those conditions, may be unconscionable." Thomas Greening, "Individual Conscience and Psychologist's Responsibility." I am indebted to Dr. Greening for sharing with me this unpublished manuscript.

53. "Instead of . . . thoughtful considerations, a handful of psychologists rushed to spread alarm among psychologists by equating the demand for obedience to reporting laws with ethical practice. Clearly, that kind of thinking subordinates the clinical function to a policing function." Charles Ansell and Harvey L. Ross, "Reply to Pope and Bajt," *American Psychologist* 45 (Mar. 1990), 399.

54. Sharon D. Herzberger, "Cultural Obstacles to the Labeling of Abuse by Professionals," in Ann Maney and Susan Wells, eds., *Professional Responsibilities in Protecting Children: A Public Health Approach to Child Sexual Abuse* (New York: Praeger, 1988), 33–44. See also the focus on the differences in conceptions of child abuse, diagnostic behavior, and labeling between nurses and physicians in Richard O'Toole, Patrick Turbett, and Claire Nalepka, "Theories, Professional Knowledge, and Diagnosis of Child Abuse," in David Finkelhor et al., eds., *The Dark Side of Families: Current Family Violence Research* (Beverly Hills: Sage Publications, 1983), 349–62.

55. John Eckenrode et al., "Substantiation of Child Abuse and Neglect Reports," *Journal of Consulting and Clinical Psychology* 56, 1 (1988), 9–16.

56. Alayne Yates and Tim Musty, "Preschool Children's Erroneous Allegations of Sexual Molestation," *American Journal of Psychiatry* 145, 8 (Aug. 1988), 989–92.

57. J. Martin Kaplan, "Pseudoabuse—The Misdiagnosis of Child Abuse," *Journal of Forensic Sciences* 31, 4 (Oct. 1986), 1420–28. The quotations are from 1420 and 1425.

58. Fred S. Berlin, H. Martin Malin, and Sharon Dean, "Effects of Statutes Requiring Psychiatrists to Report Suspected Sexual Abuse of Children," *American Journal of Psychiatry* 148, 4 (Apr. 1991), 449–53, *passim*.

59. Jerrold Pollak and Sheldon Levy, "Countertransference and Failure to Report Child Abuse and Neglect," *Child Abuse and Neglect* 13 (1989), 515–22. The quotation is from 518.

60. Robert Weinstock and Diana Weinstock, "Child Abuse Reporting Trends: An Unprecedented Threat to Confidentiality," *Journal of Forensic Sciences* 33, 2 (Mar. 1988), 418–31. The quotation is from 421, 422, *passim*.

61. Harold P. Blum, "Punitive Parenthood and Childhood Trauma," in Blum, Weinshel, and Rodman, eds., *Psychoanalytic Core*, 174–75.

62. Ibid., 176.

63. Ibid., 183.

64. Ibid., 183.

65. Robert D. Miller and Robert Weinstock, "Conflict of Interest Between Therapist-Patient Confidentiality and the Duty to Report Sexual Abuse of Children," *Behavioral Sciences & the Law* 5, 2 (1987), 161–74.

66. Donald N. Duquette, "The Expert Witness in Child Abuse and Neglect: An Interdisciplinary Process," *Child Abuse and Neglect* 5 (1981), 325–34.

67. Jon R. Conte, "Structural Reconciliation of Therapeutic and Criminal Justice Cultures," in Maney and Wells, *Professional Responsibilities in Protecting Children*, 139–49.

68. *Los Angeles Times*, July 17, 1991, p. A5.

69. Daniel W. Shuman and Myron F. Weiner, "The Privilege Study: An Empirical Examination of the Psychotherapist-Patient Privilege," *North Carolina Law Review* 60, 5 (1982), 893–942. The data is from 920.

70. Samuel D. Warren and Louis D. Brandeis, "The Right to Privacy," 4 *Harvard Law Review* 5, 193–220 (1890). The quotation is from 205–7, *passim*. See also Robert Weisberg and Michael Wald, "Confidentiality Laws and State Efforts to Protect Abused or Neglected Children: The Need for Statutory Reform," *Family Law Quarterly* 18, 2 (Summer 1984), 143–212.

71. Gail L. Zellman and Robert M. Bell, *The Role of Professional Background, Case Characteristics, and Protective Agency Response in Mandated Child Abuse Reporting* (Santa Monica, CA: RAND R-3825-HHS, Jan. 1990), 94, 96, 97, *passim*. I am indebted to Rick A. Eden, Army Research Division of the RAND Corporation, for making this report available to me.

72. *California Penal Code*, sec. 11166 (a).

73. *Tarasoff v. Regents*, 17 Cal. 3d, at 451.

74. I am not opposed in principle to reporting the sexual molestation of children. I have, with due ambivalence and deliberation, reported the ongoing abuse of adolescent boys by an adult man in a position of trust and stewardship. My governing consideration was the individual interests of a group of boys whose emotional development was at risk and the social consequences of permitting the molestation to continue unimpaired. I have also had patients blackmailed and reported. This paper is the partial working through of those experiences.

75. Cf. the well thought out recommendations for legal modifications by Weinstock and Weinstock, "Child Abuse Reporting Trends," 428–30.

76. The author experienced this political education in lobbying the passage of

the "Research Psychoanalysts Law" (1977), now *California Business and Professions Code*, Division 2, chap. 5.1, secs. 2529–30, which authorizes the graduates of named institutes "who have completed clinical training in psychoanalysis" to "engage in psychoanalysis as an adjunct to teaching, training, or research."

77. See Michael S. Roth, *Psycho-Analysis as History: Negation and Freedom in Freud* (Ithaca, NY: Cornell University Press, 1987), 99–133 ("Sublimation and Transference").

78. D. W. Winnicott, "Delinquency as a Sign of Hope," in *Home is Where We Start From: Essays by a Psychoanalyst*, ed. C. Winnicott, R. Shepherd, and M. Davis (New York: W. W. Norton, 1986), 96–97.

COHEN : Ideals and Reality

1. On the Berlin reforms, see Charles E. McClelland, *State, Society, and University in Germany 1700–1914* (Cambridge: Cambridge Univ. Press, 1980), 101–45.

2. Quoted in Konrad H. Jarausch, *Students, Society and Politics in Imperial Germany* (Princeton, NJ: Princeton Univ. Press, 1982), 23–24.

3. Letter of Jakob Burckhardt to Friedrich von Preen, 13 Apr. 1882, quoted in "Die Studierenden an schweizerischen Hochschulen. Erhebung 1946," *Beiträge zur schweizerischen Statistik*, Heft 17 (Bern, 1947), 36.

4. Theodor Billroth, *Über das Lehren und Lernen der medicinischen Wissenschaften an den Universitäten der Deutschen Nation nebst allgemeinen Bemerkungen über Universitäten* (Vienna: C. Gerold, 1876), 148–50; idem, "Wünsche und Hoffnungen für unsere medicinische Facultät," *Wiener klinische Wochenschrift* 1. Jahrgang, no. 36 (6 Dec. 1888), 733–36.

5. Ministerial-Erlaß, 20 Aug. 1880, no. 12050; published in the *Wiener Zeitung*, 28 Aug. 1880.

6. Gustav Kolmer, *Parlament und Verfassung in Österreich* (Vienna and Leipzig: Carl Fromme, 1902–14), 4:6–7.

7. See Helmut Engelbrecht, *Geschichte des österreichischen Bildungswesens*, Band 4: *Von 1848 bis zum Ende der Monarchie* (Vienna: Österreichischer Bundesverlag, 1986), 222–34; Gustav Strakosch-Grassmann, *Geschichte des österreichischen Unterrichtswesens* (Vienna: A. Pichler, 1905), 188–209; Friedrich Freiherr von Schweikhardt, ed., *Sammlung der für die österreichischen Universitäten giltigen Gesetze und Verordnungen*, 2d ed., 2 vols. (Vienna: K. K. Schulbücherverlag, 1885), passim; and Leo Ritter Beck von Mannagetta and Carl von Kelle, eds., *Die österreichischen Universitätsgesetze* (Vienna: Manz, 1906), passim.

8. See Wilhelm von Hartel, *Bonitz und sein Wirken in Österreich* [Vortrag gehalten in der Sitzung der 'Mittelschule' vom 15. December 1888] (Linz: Selbstverlag des Verfassers, 1889), 4–6; and Helmut Engelbrecht, "Zur österreichischen Bildungspolitik im Sekundarschulbereich in der zweiten Hälfte des 19. Jahrhunderts,"

Jahresbericht des Bundesgymnasiums Krems am Schlusse des Schuljahres 1974/75 (Krems a. D., 1975), 16–17.

9. On secondary and higher education for women in Austria, see Engelbrecht, *Geschichte des öster. Bildungswesens* 4:278–94; Martha Forkl and Elisabeth Koffmann, eds., *Frauenstudium und akademische Frauenarbeit in Österreich* (Vienna and Stuttgart: W. Braumüller, 1968); and Anna Lind, "Das Frauenstudium im Österreich, Deutschland und in der Schweiz" (Vienna Univ., Diss. der Rechts- und Staatswiss. Fak., 1961).

10. Fritz K. Ringer, *Education and Society in Modern Europe* (Bloomington, IN: Indiana Univ. Press, 1979), 291–300.

11. G. A. Schimmer, "Frequenz der Lehranstalten Österreichs von 1841 bis 1876 im Vergleich mit der Bevölkerung," *Statistische Monatschrift der öster. Statistischen Central-Commission* 3 (1877), 65; *Österreichische Statistik*, N.F., 7 (1913), 3. Heft, 2. Schimmer does not indicate whether his statistics derive from the winter or summer semesters. The 1909–10 statistics derive from the winter semester.

12. The Austrian enrollment statistics and age stratification of the population derive from *Österreichische Statistik* 2 (1882), 1. Heft, 530–65; 3 (1884), 2. Heft, III; 32 (1892), 1. Heft, 178–83; 38 (1895), 4. Heft, 2; 63 (1903), 3. Heft, 14–33; 68 (1903), 3. Heft, 2; N.F., 1 (1914), 3. Heft, 2–39; N.F., 7 (1913), 3. Heft, 2. The German statistics derive from F. Ringer, *Education and Society*, 291. Twenty-to-23-year-olds are treated as the prime age group for students in the German universities, but the 19-to-22-year-old group is used for Austria because the course of studies in Austrian *Gymnasien* was one year shorter than in Germany. The Austrian enrollments all derive from the winter semesters of the years cited; the German from the summer semesters. This inflates the Austrian enrollments marginally compared to the German in each year. The raw registration totals used here may also be skewed somewhat by differences in the length of time that students in particular groupings took to complete their university education compared to students in other groupings, but no statistics are readily available for Austria on the total numbers of individuals who matriculated in any particular period of years as opposed to the total registered in individual semesters.

13. *Öster. Statistik* 3, 2. & 4. Hefte; 28, 4. Heft; 68, 3. Heft; N.F., 7, 3. Heft; Peter Urbanitsch, "Die Deutschen in Österreich. Statistisch-deskriptiver Überblick," in Adam Wandruszka and P. Urbanitsch, eds., *Die Habsburgermonarchie 3: Die Völker des Reiches*, 2 pts. (Vienna, 1980), pt. 1, p. 38, table 1. Statistics are not available on the total school-aged population for each language and religious group in Austria during the second half of the nineteenth century.

14. See sources in n. 13. For further discussion of Jewish overrepresentation in Austrian education, see G. B. Cohen, "Education, Social Mobility, and the Austrian Jews 1860–1910," in Victor Karady and Wolfgang Mitter, eds., *Bildungswesen und Sozialstruktur in Mitteleuropa im 19. und 20. Jahrhundert* [*Studien und Doku-*

mentation zur vergleichenden Bildungsforschung, Band 42] (Cologne and Vienna: Böhlau Verlag, 1990), 141–61.

15. Konrad H. Jarausch, "The Social Transformation of the University: The Case of Prussia 1865–1914," *The Journal of Social History* 12 (1979), 619–20.

16. See sources in nn. 11 and 12 above.

17. On Germany, see Jarausch, *Students, Society*, 146–54. On the origins of the first generation of women students in the Vienna University, see G. B. Cohen, "Die Studenten der Wiener Universität von 1860 bis 1900: Ein soziales und geographisches Profil," in Richard G. Plaschka and K. Mack, eds., *Wegenetz europäischen Geistes* 2: *Universitäten und Studenten* (Vienna: Verlag für Geschichte und Politik, 1987), 312–13.

18. See Engelbrecht, *Geschichte des öster. Bildungswesens* 4: 252–55; František Jílek, Václav Lomič, and Pavla Horská, *Dějiny českého vysokého učení technického* [History of the Bohemian Technical College] 1 (in 2 pts., Prague, 1973–78), pt. 2, 269–74; and Jarausch, *Students, Society*, 32, 44, 48, 74.

19. On Germany, see Ringer, *Education and Society*, 51–53, 291.

20. See sources in nn. 11 and 12.

21. The samples of the registration records for the Vienna and Prague universities were drawn systematically from the whole alphabetic runs of the *Katalogen der Hörer* or *Nationalen*, found in the Archiv der Universität Wien, Vienna, and the Archiv Univerzity Karlovy, Prague, respectively, with the nonmatriculated (*ausserordentlich/mimořádný*) students excluded. The number of students in each sample for whom the father's or guardian's occupation was indicated is given as the "n" in Tables 3 and 4. The various occupations are grouped here in broader social categories following those used by Jarausch in *Students, Society*. Registration records for four discrete semesters taken at ten- or twenty-year intervals were selected to make possible time-series analyses rather than making one sample of registrations for each institution from a longer period of years as Jarausch did. Within their respective eras, the years 1879–80, 1899–1900, and 1909–10 do not appear to have been atypical for Austrian demography or the educational system. Austrian university enrollments in the 1850s were erratic overall, and 1859–60 may show some of the aftereffects of the "hungry 'forties," the economic difficulties of 1857–58, and the war in northern Italy during the spring of 1859.

22. On Austrian students' economic conditions, see Karl Engliš, "Eine Erhebung über die Lebensverhältnisse der Wiener Studenten," *Statistische Monatsschrift*, N.F., 20 (Brno, 1915), 273–354; and Wilhelm Winkler, *Die soziale Lage der deutschen Hochschulstudentenschaft Prags* (Vienna: F. Tempsky, and Leipzig: G. Freytag, 1912), passim.

23. On the German universities, see Jarausch, *Students, Society*, 120–21. See n. 21 for sources on the social composition of the student bodies in the Vienna and Prague universities. For further discussion of enrollment by the nobility in the Vienna University, see Cohen, "Die Studenten der Wiener Universität," 299.

24. Billroth, *Über das Lehren und Lernen*, 150–51.

25. Statistics derive from Jarausch, *Students, Society*, 125; and *Preußische Statistik* 223 (Berlin, 1910), 182–91; 236 (Berlin, 1913), 140–41.

26. See Jarausch, "Social Transformation," 627; and idem, *Students, Society*, 123–130.

27. Jarausch, "Social Transformation," 625.

28. See sources cited in n. 21 above. On the social composition of the Czech students in Prague, see G. B. Cohen, "Education and Czech Social Structure in the Late Nineteenth Century," in Hans Lemberg, K. Litsch, R. G. Plaschka, and G. Ránki, eds., *Bildungsgeschichte, Bevölkerungsgeschichte, Gesellschaftsgeschichte in den Böhmischen Ländern und in Europa: Festschrift für Jan Havránek zum 60. Geburtstag* (Vienna: Verlag für Geschichte und Politik, und Munich: Oldenbourg, 1988), 32–45.

29. Wolfdieter Bihl, "Die Juden," in Adam Wandruszka and P. Urbanitsch, eds., *Die Habsburgermonarchie 1848–1918*, 3: *Die Völker des Reiches* (Vienna: Öster. Akademie der Wissenschaften, 1980), pt. 2, 915–16.

30. For statistics on the enrollment of Jewish students, matriculated and non-matriculated, in all Austrian universities for winter 1899–1900, see *Öster. Statistik* 68, 3. Heft (Vienna, 1903), 5. On the social origins of matriculated Jewish students in the Vienna University, see Cohen, "Education, Social Mobility, and the Austrian Jews 1860–1910," 161.

31. *Öster. Statistik* 68, 3. Heft, 5; and Cohen, "Die Studenten der Wiener Universität," 296–97.

32. McClelland, *State, Society, and University*, 119–40.

33. See, for example, the discussion of the Czech philosophical faculty in Prague in Josef Petráň, *Nástin dějin filozofické fakulty Univerzity Karlovy* [Outline of the History of the Philosophical Faculty of the Charles University] (Prague: Univerzita Karlova, 1983), 220; and the listing of dissertations actually completed in Prague's Czech and German philosophical faculties between 1882 and 1913–14 in Jan Havránek and Karel Kučera, eds., *Disertace pražské university* [Dissertations of the Prague University] [*Sbírka pramenů a příruček k dějinám University Karlovy 2*], 2 vols. (Prague: Universita Karlova, 1965).

34. Billroth, *Über das Lehren und Lernen*, 440; passage translated in Erna Lesky, *The Vienna Medical School of the 19th Century* (Baltimore: The Johns Hopkins Univ. Press, 1976), 269.

35. Billroth, "Wünsche und Hoffnungen," 733–36.

36. *Gutachten und Anträge zur Reform der medicinischen Studien und Rigorosenordnung. Erstattet von den medicinischen Facultäten der österreichischen Universitäten* (Wien: K. Gorischek, 1894), 63–64.

37. Allgemeines Verwaltungsarchiv [hereafter, AVA], Vienna, Ministerium für Kultus und Unterricht [hereafter, KUM], Praesidium 1895, no. 740, "Protokollen über die Sitzungen der im Ministerium für Cultus und Unterricht veranstalteten

457

Enquête betreffend die Reform der medicinischen Studien und Prüfungsordnung" (Dec. 1895).

38. Engelbrecht, *Geschichte des öster. Bildungswesens* 4:230.

39. AVA Vienna KUM 1870 P. Nr. 2370; KUM 1880 in gen., 12050/1880; KUM 1895 in gen., Z1 30011/1895, 16 Dez. 1895. See the discussions in Engelbrecht, *Geschichte des öster. Bildungswesens* 4:159, 166, 178; and Berthold Windt, *Stand und Frequenz der österreichischen Gymnasien im Decennium 1873–1882* (Vienna: C. Gerold, 1883), 5.

40. See Engelbrecht, *Geschichte des öster. Bildungswesens* 4:232–34. Due to acute overcrowding, the Ministry did invoke limitations on enrollments in most of the technical colleges at various times between 1902 and 1914. See Wilhelm Jähnl, ed., *Vorschriften für die Technischen Hochschulen Österreichs* (Vienna: K. K. Schulbücherverlag, 1916), 433–37.

MCGRATH: Freedom and Death

1. Flodoard Frhr. von Biedermann, ed., *Goethes Gespräche* (hereafter Biedermann) (Leipzig: F. W. v. Biedermann, 1910), 3:408. All translations from the German are mine unless otherwise indicated.

2. Wilhelm Mommsen, *Die politischen Anschauungen Goethes* (Stuttgart: Deutsche Verlags-Anstalt, 1948), 167–68.

3. Biedermann, *Gespräche* 3:213 (June 29, 1825).

4. Ibid., 163.

5. Colonel Leicester Stanhope, *Greece in 1823 and 1824; Being a Series of Letters and Other Documents on the Greek Revolution Written During a Visit to that Country* (London: Sherwood, Gilbert, and Piper, 1825).

6. William Parry, *The Last Days of Lord Byron: with his Lordship's Opinions on Various Subjects, Particularly on the State and Prospects of Greece* (London: Knight and Lacey, 1825).

7. Johann Wolfgang von Goethe, *Goethes Briefe* (hereafter *Briefe*) ed. Karl Robert Mandelkow (Hamburg: Christian Wegner Verlag, 1967), 4:146.

8. Biedermann, *Gespräche* 4:254 (Mar. 28, 1830).

9. Parry, *Last Days*, 189.

10. Stanhope, *Greece*, 89–90.

11. Parry, *Last Days*, 173.

12. Stanhope, *Greece*, 31–32.

13. Biedermann, *Gespräche* 4:203, 244, 271.

14. Ibid., 271.

15. Ibid., 2:205.

16. Ibid., 3:327.

17. Ibid., 328.

18. Ibid., 327.

19. Leonard Krieger, *The German Idea of Freedom* (Chicago: University of Chicago Press, 1957), 18.

20. Ibid., 19.

21. Biedermann, *Gespräche* 3:328.

22. Ibid.

23. Johann Wolfgang von Goethe, *Faust Part Two*, (hereafter *Faust Two*) trans. Philip Wayne (Baltimore: Penguin Books, 1959), 104, ll. 6956–57, 6962–63.

24. Ibid., 106–7, ll. 7012–21.   25. Ibid., 159, 8459.

26. Ibid., 163, l. 8678.   27. Ibid., 167, ll. 8784–86.

28. Ibid., 169, ll. 8826–29.

29. My translation, ll. 8915–16. Hereafter when translating from the German original I will include line numbers in the text.

30. *Faust Two*, 172, l. 8918.

31. Ibid., 186, l. 9256.

32. Ibid., 187, ll. 9281–82, 9289–92.

33. Ibid., 190, ll. 9372–84.   34. Ibid., 192–93, ll. 9462–65.

35. Ibid., 193, ll. 9474–75.   36. Ibid., 193, ll. 9478–82.

37. Ibid., 202, ll. 9711–14.   38. Ibid., 205–6, ll. 9821–25.

39. Ibid., 206, ll. 9843–50.   40. Ibid., 208, ll. 9893–94.

41. Biedermann, *Gespräche* 3:163, Feb. 24, 1825.

42. Ibid., 407, July 5, 1827.   43. *Faust Two*, 207, ll. 9863–64.

44. Ibid., 221, ll. 10215–21.   45. Ibid., 267, ll. 11499–501.

46. Ibid., 258, l. 11246.

47. Ibid., 269, ll. 11563–64, 11569–70, 11574–76, 11579–80.

48. Ibid., 250, ll. 11035–36. Goethe had originally intended to include a scene involving Faust's formal investiture with the fief. See Dierdre Vincent, "'*Die Tat ist alles*': A Reconsideration of the Significance of Faust II, Act Four," *Seminar: Journal of Germanic Studies* 18, 2 (May 1982), 127, 133.

49. Ibid., 140.

50. Biedermann, *Gespräche* 3:313.

51. Alexander R. Hohlfeld, "Die Entstehung des Faust-Manuscript von 1825–26 (VH2)," *Euphorion Zeitschrift für Literaturgeschichte*, Dritte Folge 49 (1955), 291.

52. *Faust Two*, 269; Hohlfeld, "Die Entstehung," 284–86; the manuscript fragments are given and described in *Goethes Werke* (hereafter Weimar Edition), ed. im Auftrage der Grossherzogin Sophie von Sachsen, (Weimar: Hermann Böhlau, 1888), 15, 2:147, 157.

53. There are three fragments bearing on this line, and in this case, where the evidence happens to reveal the order of composition, only the last one contains the freedom reference. Weimar Edition, vol. 15, pt. 2, pp. 147, 154. How much earlier the early fragments are remains an open question, but Hohlfeld ("Die Entstehung," 297) shows that the revisions must have been made after 1825.

54. Weimar Edition, 15, 2:65.

55. Karl August Meissinger, *Helena, Schillers Anteil am Faust* (Frankfurt am Main: Verlag Gerhard Schulte-Bulmke, 1935), 74–75.

56. Ibid., 53.   57. Ibid., 79.

58. Stanhope, *Greece*, 6–7.   59. Ibid., 12–13.

60. Jeremy Bentham, *The Works of Jeremy Benthem*, ed. John Bowring (New York, Russell & Russell, 1962), 10:538–39.

61. See Bentham, *Works* 4:535–93, which contains the *Codification Proposal addressed by Jeremy Bentham to All Nations Professing Liberal Opinions; or Idea of a Proposed All-Comprehensive Body of Law*. This proposal also includes a section of "testimonials" which contains some of Bentham's correspondence with these liberal groups.

62. Biedermann, *Gespräche* 5:244.

63. Ibid. 4:80–81.

64. John Stuart Mill, *Autobiography* (Indianapolis: Bobbs-Merrill, 1957), chap. 5, particularly 99–100, 104–5, 109; John Stuart Mill, *Essays on Politics and Culture*, ed. Gertrude Himmelfarb (Garden City, New York, Doubleday, 1963), 124–33, 146.

65. Sigmund Freud, "Dissection of the Personality," *New Introductory Lectures*, *The Standard Edition of the Complete Works of Sigmund Freud*, ed. and trans. James Strachey et al. (London: Hogarth, 1953–74), 22:80.

JAY: Experience Without a Subject

1. Hans-Georg Gadamer, *Truth and Method* (New York, 1986), 310.

2. Michael Oakeshott, *Experience and Its Modes* (Cambridge, 1933), 9.

3. Philip Rahv, "The Cult of Experience in American Writing," in Rahv, *Literature and the Sixth Sense* (New York, 1969), and Joan W. Scott, "The Evidence of Experience," *Critical Inquiry* 17, 4 (Summer 1991).

4. Gary Smith, "Thinking Through Benjamin: An Introductory Essay," in Smith, ed., *Benjamin: Philosophy, Aesthetics, History* (Chicago, 1989), xii.

5. Richard Wolin, *Walter Benjamin: An Aesthetic of Redemption* (New York, 1982); Marleen Stoessel, *Aura: Das vergessene Menschliche* (Munich, 1983); Torsten Meiffert, *Die enteignete Erfahrung: Zu Walter Benjamins Konzept einer "Dialektik im Stillstand"* (Bielefeld, 1986); Michael Jennings, *Dialectical Images: Walter Benjamin's Theory of Literary Criticism* (Ithaca, 1987); Miriam Hansen, "Benjamin, Cinema and Experience: 'The Blue Flower in the Land of Technology,'" *New German Critique* 40 (Winter 1987); Michael Makropolous, *Modernität als ontologischer Ausnahmezustand? Walter Benjamins Theorie der Moderne* (Munich, 1989).

6. Walter Benjamin, *One-Way Street and Other Writings*, trans. Edmund Jephcott and Kingsley Shorter (London, 1979); "Erfahrung und Armut," in Benjamin, *Gesammelte Schriften* 2, 1, ed. Rolf Tiedemann and Hermann Schweppenhäuser (Frankfurt, 1977); "The Storyteller" and "On Some Motifs in Baudelaire," in Benjamin, *Illuminations*, ed. Hannah Arendt, trans. Harry Zohn (New York, 1968).

7. See Wilhelm Dilthey, *Das Erlebnis und Dichtung: Lessing, Goethe, Novalis, Hölderlin*, 13th ed. (Göttingen, 1957). For a discussion of Dilthey's usage, see Michael Ermarth, *Wilhelm Dilthey: The Critique of Historical Reason* (Chicago, 1978), 97f.

8. Edmund Husserl, *Experience and Judgment*, ed. Ludwig Landgrebe, trans. J. S. Churchill and K. Ameriko (Evanston, 1973).

9. Ernst Jünger, *Der Kampf als innere Erlebnis* [1922], *Werke* 5 (Stuttgart, n.d.).

10. Gadamer, *Truth and Method*, 317, where he credits Hegel for a dialectical concept of experience as "skepticism in action."

11. Yosef Hayim Yerushalmi, *Zakhor: Jewish History and Jewish Memory* (New York, 1989). Curiously, Benjamin is never mentioned in this remarkable book. For a discussion of the relevance of Yerushalmi to Benjamin, see Susan A. Handelman, *Fragments of Redemption: Jewish Thought and Literary Theory in Benjamin, Scholem, and Levinas* (Bloomington, IN, 1991), 164. It would be fruitful to compare Benjamin's distinction between two types of memory, *Gedächtnis* (the memory of the many) and *Erinnerung* (the interiorization of the past) or *Eingedenken* (the memory of the one) with Yerushalmi's distinction between memory and history. For a helpful account of Benjamin's ideas on this issue, see Irving Wohlfarth, "On the Messianic Structure of Walter Benjamin's Last Reflections," *Glyph* 3 (1978).

12. A similar argument is suggested by Reinhart Koselleck in "'Space of Experience' and 'Horizon of Expectation': Two Historical Categories," in Koselleck, *Futures Past: On the Semantics of Historical Time*, trans. Keith Tribe (Cambridge, MA, 1985). Koselleck argues that modernity is defined by the growing gap between experience, which he defines as "present past, whose events have been incorporated and can be remembered," (272) and an expectational horizon which distances itself radically from the status quo. He links this transformation with the notions of "history in general" and "progress," both of which were anathema to Benjamin.

13. For a discussion of the implications of this word, see Makropoulos, *Modernität als ontologischer Ausnahmezustand*, chap. 3.

14. Benjamin, "On Some Motifs in Baudelaire," 165. Benjamin's ambivalence about the ability of the masses to recover *Erfahrung* is discussed in Hansen, "Benjamin, Cinema and Experience." She stresses the links between his concept of aura and experience, and argues that "with the denigration of the auratic image in favor of reproduction, Benjamin implicitly denies the masses the possibility of aesthetic experience" (186).

15. For an analysis of it in these terms, see Wolin, *Walter Benjamin*, chap. 7; and "Experience and Materialism in Benjamin's *Passagenwerk*," in Smith, *Benjamin: Philosophy, Aesthetics, History*.

16. Gershom Scholem, *Walter Benjamin: The Story of a Friendship*, trans. Harry Zohn (New York, 1981), 60. Here Scholem describes the lengthy discussions he had with Benjamin in Muri, Switzerland, in 1918 over the issue of experience in the work of Hermann Cohen.

17. Walter Benjamin, "On the Program of the Coming Philosophy," in Smith, ed., *Benjamin: Philosophy, Aesthetics, History*. For discussions of the importance of this essay, see Smith's introduction and Jennings, *Dialectical Images*, chap. 3. Prior to this piece, when he was in the Youth Movement, Benjamin published a short

essay in 1912 entitled *"Erfahrung,"* in which he attacked the concept as an excuse for adults to lord it over the young. See Benjamin, *Gesammelte Schriften* 2, 1.

18. Benjamin, "On the Program of the Coming Philosophy," 10.

19. Ibid., 11.

20. Ibid., 5.

21. For an example, see Peter Bürger, "Art and Rationality: On the Dialectic of Symbolic and Allegorical Form," in Axel Honneth et al., eds., *Philosophical Interventions in the Unfinished Project of Enlightenment*, trans. William Rehg (Cambridge, MA, 1992), where an *Erfahrung* "deserving of the name" is defined as something that "does not happen to us but rather is *made* by us." (234)

22. Ibid., 9.

23. Winfried Menninghaus, "Walter Benjamin's Theory of Myth," in Gary Smith, ed., *On Walter Benjamin: Critical Essays and Reflections* (Cambridge, MA, 1988), 321–22. Benjamin, to be sure, was skeptical of certain types of mythic thinking, even attacking *Lebensphilosophie* as proto-fascist for its interest in myth. See "On Some Motifs in Baudelaire," 158. But Menninghaus shows the extent to which he distrusted the simple myth/enlightenment dichotomy.

24. Theodor W. Adorno, *Prisms*, trans. Samuel and Shierry Weber (London, 1967), 235.

25. See, for example, Heidegger's critique of *Erlebnis* as too dependent on the Cartesianism it purports to transcend in *Grundfragen der Philosophie: Ausgewählte "Probleme" der "Logik"*, *Gesamtausgabe* 45, ed. Friedrich-Wilhelm von Herrmann (Frankfurt, 1984), 149.

26. For an attempt to do so, see Rainer Nägele, "Benjamin's Ground," in Nägele, ed., *Benjamin's Ground: New Readings of Walter Benjamin* (Detroit, 1988).

27. Walter Benjamin, "Surrealism: The Last Snapshot of the European Intelligentsia," in Benjamin, *Reflections: Essays, Aphorisms, Autobiographical Writings*, ed. Peter Demetz, trans. Edmond Jephcott (New York, 1978), 179.

28. Georg Lukács, *The Theory of the Novel*, trans. Anna Bostock (Cambridge, MA, 1971), 41, cited by Benjamin, "The Storyteller," 99.

29. Benjamin, "The Storyteller," 87.

30. According to Benjamin, "the important thing for the remembering author is not what he experienced, but the weaving of his memory, the Penelope work of recollection." "The Image of Proust," in *Illuminations*, ed. Arendt, 205.

31. Roland Barthes, "To Write: An Intransitive Verb?," in Barthes, *The Rustle of Language*, trans. Richard Howard (Berkeley, 1989).

32. Walter Benjamin, "Theses on the Philosophy of History," in *Illuminations*, ed. Arendt, 257. In a letter to the author of Aug. 23, 1992, Richard Wolin contends that Benjamin would not have accepted the formalist distrust of plenitudinous meaning evident in critics like Barthes; for him, the stylistic moments of absolute experience demanded an experiential fulfillment that such critics thought impossible.

33. Charles Bally, "Le style indirect libre en français moderne I et II," *Germanisch-Romanische Monatsschrift* (Heidelberg, 1912). There were some prior discus-

sions in the work of the linguists A. Tobler and Th. Kaplevsky, but it was not until Bally, who was one of the two students of Saussure who published the notes of the *Cours de linguistique générale* in 1916, that a sustained analysis was made. "Libre" means syntactically independent.

34. Marcel Proust, "About Flaubert's Style," in *Marcel Proust: A Selection from his Miscellaneous Writings*, trans. Gerard Hopkins (London, 1948).

35. Étienne Lorck, *Die "Erlebte Rede": Ein sprachliche Untersuchung* (Heidelberg, 1921); Otto Jespersen, *The Philosophy of Grammar* (London, 1924).

36. V. S. Vološinov, *Marxism and the Philosophy of Language* [1930] trans. Ladislav Metejka and I. R. Titunik (New York, 1973); Stephen Ullmann, *Style in the French Novel* (New York, 1964); Dorrit Cohn, *Transparent Minds: Narrative Modes for Presenting Consciousness in Fiction* (Princeton, 1978); Roy Pascal, *The Dual Voice: Free Indirect Speech and its Functioning in the Nineteenth-Century European Novel* (Manchester, 1977); Hans Robert Jauss, "Literary History as a Challenge to Literary Theory," in Jauss, *Toward an Aesthetic of Reception*, trans. Timothy Bahti (Minneapolis, 1982); and Ann Banfield, *Unspeakable Sentences* (Boston, 1982).

37. Dominick LaCapra, *"Madame Bovary" on Trial* (Ithaca, 1982).

38. For an account of Vossler and the Vosslerites, see Vološinov, *Marxism*, 32.

39. LaCapra, *"Madame Bovary,"* 138.

40. Cited ibid., 57–58.

41. It also might be conjectured that anxiety about another confusion was also reinforced by the *style indirect libre*, that between character and reader. In the eighteenth century, the moral implications of the novel were contested precisely because of the dangerously fluid boundaries between amoral characters and sympathetic (often female) readers. *Madame Bovary* itself, of course, draws on the fear that impressionable readers will confuse their lives with those of romantic heroines.

42. Interestingly, one of the other Vosslerites who worked on *erlebte Rede*, Gertraud Lerch, used the Diltheyan notion of *Einfühlung* (empathy) as the key to the style. See the discussion in Vološinov, *Marxism*, 150.

43. Pascal, *Dual Voice*, 25.

44. Vološinov, *Marxism*, 155.

45. Ann Banfield, "Where Epistemology, Style, and Grammar Meet Literary History: The Development of Represented Speech and Thought," *New Literary History* 9, 3 (1978), 449.

46. Emile Benveniste, *Problems in General Linguistics*, trans. Mary Elizabeth Meek (Coral Gables, FL, 1971), chap. 14.

47. Jacques Derrida, "Différance," in Derrida, *Margins of Philosophy*, trans. Alan Bass (Chicago, 1982), 9.

48. Barthes, "To Write," 19.

49. For an analysis of *écriture* in terms of intransitive writing, the middle voice, and the *style indirect libre*, see Ann Banfield, "Écriture, Narration and the Grammar of French," in Jeremy Hawthorn, ed., *Narrative: From Malory to Motion*

Pictures (London, 1985). She makes the point that the impersonal grammatical function of writing was lost in America when the pragmatists substituted "The Experience Curriculum" in the 1930s (pp. 17–18). In the Benjaminian terms we have been using, the "absolute experience" of *écriture* was replaced by mere *Erlebnis*.

50. Ann Banfield, "Describing the Unobserved: Events Grouped Around an Empty Center," in Nigel Fabb et al., eds. *The Linguistics of Writing: Arguments Between Language and Literature* (Manchester, 1987); and "L'Imparfait de l'Objectif: The Imperfect of the Object Glass," *Camera Obscura* 24 (Fall 1991).

51. Banfield, "L'Imparfait de l'Objectif," 77.

52. Walter Benjamin, "A Short History of Photography," *Screen* 13, 1 (Spring 1972). For a discussion of the links between Benjamin's visual concerns and the issue of experience, see Hansen, "Benjamin, Cinema and Experience."

53. Berel Lang, *Act and Idea in the Nazi Genocide* (Chicago, 1990) and Hayden White, "Historical Emplotment and the Problem of Truth," in Saul Friedländer, ed., *Probing the Limits of Representation: Nazism and the "Final Solution"* (Cambridge, MA, 1992). White has explored these issues in an unpublished paper entitled "Writing in the Middle Voice," which he has kindly allowed me to read.

54. White, "Historical Emplotment," 49.

55. Ibid., 52.

56. Martin Jay, "Of Plots, Witnesses and Judgments," in Friedländer, *Probing the Limits of Representation*. The distinction between active agent and passive victim seems to be nowhere as important to maintain as in accounts of the Holocaust; otherwise, we risk the travesty of evenhanded remembrance evident at Bitburg and in the work of certain historians during the *Historikerstreit*.

57. Banfield, "Epistemology, Style, and Grammar," 415.

58. Vincent Pecora, "Ethics, Politics and the Middle Voice," *Yale French Studies* 79 (1991), 203–30.

59. Ibid., 212.

60. See the discussion in Katerina Clark and Michael Holquist, *Mikhail Bakhtin* (Cambridge, MA, 1984), chap. 6; and the translators' introduction to Vološinov, *Marxism*.

61. LaCapra, "*Madame Bovary*," 149.

62. Terry Eagleton, *Walter Benjamin: Or Towards a Revolutionary Criticism* (London, 1981), where he claimed that in Bakhtin exists a "Judeo-Christian mysticism in some ways akin to Benjamin's—that *Marxism and the Philosophy of Language* [which he takes to be written by Bakhtin] contains as its secret code a theological devotion to the incarnational unity of word and being similar to that which marks Benjamin's own meditations" (pp. 153–54).

63. Jürgen Habermas, "Consciousness-Raising or Redemptive Criticism: The Contemporaneity of Walter Benjamin," *New German Critique* 17 (Spring, 1979), 45–46.

64. Leo Bersani, *The Culture of Redemption* (Cambridge, MA, 1990), 60. Ber-

sani's own anti-redemptive concept of experience derives in large measure from Georges Bataille, *Inner Experience*, trans. Leslie Anne Boldt (Albany, NY, 1988).

SILVERMAN: Weaving Paintings

This article is part of a forthcoming book, an interpretive biography of Vincent van Gogh highlighting weaving as a key to van Gogh's visual style, and the religious and cultural conflicts that generated its development. Both the article and the book draw on a core of research and interpretation originally presented in my 1980 master's essay for Professor Carl E. Schorske, "Loom with a View: Weaving and Vincent van Gogh's Métier." In redeveloping the project in its present form, I have benefited from the hospitality and resources of the Rijksmuseum Vincent van Gogh in Amsterdam, and would like to thank Museum Director Ronald de Leeuw, Curators Louis van Tilborgh and Hans van Crimpen, and Documentary Specialist Fieke Pabst. My thanks as well to Joyce Appleby, Edward Berenson, Ruth Bloch, Albert Boime, Natalie Zemon Davis, Carlo Ginzburg, Cor van der Heijden, Lynn Hunt, Margaret Jacobs, Rachel Klein, Sarah Maza, Jeffrey Prager, Peter Reill, Gerard Roo'jakkers, Simon Schama, Gary and Loekie Schwartz, Jerrold Seigel, Paul van Seters, Marjolijn Sorbi, Norton and Elaine Wise, and Carol Zemel. Carl Schorske's consistent mixture of support and constructive skepticism contributed immeasurably to this project both in its past and present form. Research for this article was supported by the UCLA Academic Senate, the National Endowment for the Humanities, and the University of California President's Fellowship in the Humanities. I am also grateful for the research assistance of N. Gregory Kendrick, Francis de Blauwe, and Aaron Segal.

1. A recent corrective to the exclusion of religion from the accounts of van Gogh's career is provided by Tsukasa Kōdera, *Vincent van Gogh, Christianity Versus Nature* (Amsterdam: John Benjamins, 1990), who emphasizes iconographic substitutions of religious for natural symbols in van Gogh's art.

2. At mid-century, for example, a political crisis erupted in 1853 following the announcement of the Papal restoration of the Catholic bishopry in the Netherlands, provoking riots between Protestants and Catholics and forcing the resignation of the Liberal Thorbecke government, which had come to power only a few years earlier as the champion of religious freedom. And between 1848 and 1887, the "schools question" dominated the government agenda, pitting Catholics and their new allies, the orthodox Calvinist Anti-Revolutionary Party, against the Liberals over state subsidies for religious education. See Max Schuchart, *The Netherlands* (London: Thames and Hudson, 1972), 34–37; 79–83; Albert Réville, "Les écoles et les controverses religieuses en Hollande," *Revue des deux-mondes* ser. 8, vol. 27, (May–June 1860), 935–52; P. M. Hough, *Dutch Life in Town and Country* (New York: Putnam, 1901); and Kenneth Scott Latourette, *Christianity in a Revolutionary Age, The Nineteenth Century in Europe, The Protestant and Eastern Churches* (New York:

Harper and Row, 1959), 237–51. Johan Goudsblom, in his *Dutch Society* (New York: Random House, 1967), states that even "today *stand* and class are unpopular subjects in the Netherlands," and that "religious diversity has remained a pervasive determinant" of political power blocs, cross-cutting social levels. He also notes that in contrast to other European movements, organized labor "had a rather late and timid start in the Netherlands," and was permanently split into segments by religious affiliation. See 63, 73, 105–7.

3. The term was coined by the Dutch literary scholar Gerard Brom and rediscovered by art historian Tsukasa Kōdera as a context for van Gogh's development in his *Vincent van Gogh*, 14–26. I am indebted to Kōdera's account for the discussion that follows.

4. See P. C. Molhuysen and P. J. Blok, *Nieuw Niederlandsch Biografisch Woordenboek* 3 (Leiden: Sijthoff, 1914), 82–86; and Beets's own *Navolgingen van Lord Byron* (Amsterdam: G. L. Funkl, 1873); and his *Dichtwerken, 1830–1873* (Amsterdam: W. H. Kirberger, 1876), 1:63–70, "Naar Walter Scott" and "Naar Lord Byron."

5. Kōdera, *Vincent van Gogh*, 15–21; see also J. P. De Bie, J. Lindeboom, G. P. van Iherzon, eds., *Biografish Woordenboek van Protestantische Godgeleerden in Nederland* ('sGravenhage: Nijhoff, 1943), 5:631–44.

6. See Molhuysen and Blok, *Biografisch Woordenboek* 2 (Leiden: Sijthoff, 1912), 536–37; and Frank Kools, *Vincent van Gogh en zijn geboorteplaats, Als een boer van Zundert* (Zutphen: De Walberg Pers, 1990), 14, for van Gogh's father's admiration for ter Haar.

7. Kōdera, *Vincent van Gogh*, 15–17. Ter Haar wrote books such as *Photogrammen: Schetsen en verhalen* (Nijmegen: Blomhert, 1869), while Nicolaas Beets' *Paulus in den wichtigsten augenblicken seines lebens und wirkens. Biblische schilderungen.* (Gotha: F. A. Perthes, 1857) offered an illustrated biography of the Apostle and he collaborated with painter Josef Israëls in a volume of poems and prints entitled *De kinderen der zee: Schetsen anar het leven aan onze Hollandsche Stranden door Jozef Israëls. Gedichten van Nicolaas Beets* (Annhem: D. A. Thieme, 1872).

8. See Nicolaas Beets, "Schelfhout's Winterstukken" (1841), in *Dichtwerken 1830–1873* 2:398.

9. Ter Haar's statements are cited in Kools, *Van Gogh en zijn geboorteplaats*, 113.

10. Carlo Cippola, *The Fontana Economic History of Europe: The Industrial Revolutions* (London: Collins, 1973), 28–30, 47, 62, 165–69, 460–68, 593; Carlo Cippola, ed., *The Emergence of Industrial Societies* (London: Collins, 1973), 329–66; J. A. De Jonge, *De industrialisatie in Nederland tussen 1850 en 1914* (Amsterdam: Scheltema & Holkema, 1968), 20–245; C. C. Huysmans, "De Kunstbeschaving van den nijverheids-stand en de middelen om haar te behourduren," *De Gids*, May 1853, 583–88; A. P. Smaal, *Looking at Historic Buildings in Holland* (Zeist: Rijksdienst voor de Monumentenzorg, 1982), 134–35.

11. My conception of the corporate ego as distinct from the detached autonomous individual as a characterizing feature of the modern Dutch bourgeoisie is derived from J. H. Huizinga, *Dutch Civilization in the 17th Century and Other Essays* (London: Wm. Collins Sons, 1968); Simon Schama, *The Embarrassment of Riches, An Interpretation of Dutch Culture in the Seventeenth Century* (New York: Knopf, 1987); Svetlana Alpers, *The Art of Describing: Dutch Art in the Seventeenth Century* (Chicago: The University of Chicago Press, 1983); and Johan Goudsblom, *Dutch Society* (New York: Random House, 1967).

12. Kools, *Vincent van Gogh en zijn geboorteplaats*, 76−81. Kools has provided the first detailed archival study of van Gogh's first sixteen years in Zundert, offering essential information on the social, political, religious, and economic contexts of the village.

13. Ibid., 5−6, 43−55, 74−81.

14. Ibid., 48−49. For other examples of how piety subordinated individual profit among Theodorus van Gogh's parishoners and his own contributions, see also 50−80.

15. Goudsblom, *Dutch Society*, 32−33, 50−55, 63, 73, 88, 94, 102−6, 118−27, 142−51.

16. Theodorus van Gogh's agricultural work derived in part from his involvement with the Brabant Protestant Rural Welfare Society, an organization committed to replenishing the dwindling ranks of Reformed communities by buying plots of land and leasing them to Protestant farmers, whom the Society relocated in Brabant from other parts of Holland. The ideal of the project, begun in 1825, was to revitalize Reformed Calvinism in the South by creating a prosperous and expanding peasantry; the reality, which set in quickly, was that the combination of poor skills and unfavorable land conditions meant that at best the program maintained a small number of homesteads at minimal levels of return. In the Zundert area, conditions were especially difficult; nonetheless, Theodorus van Gogh devoted himself with uninterrupted energy and resolution to the farming projects in his domain. It was he who located and assessed the vacant land plots to be purchased by the Welfare Society; and he worked very closely with the individual families once they arrived. It was indeed the Welfare Society-sponsored farmers, such as M. Prins, Artsen, Honcoop, Peaux, and Strake, who bolstered the thinning ranks of the small Zundert parish, supplying the community with a choirmaster, church warden, and church elders. The range of Theodorus van Gogh's agricultural activities and his involvement with the Brabant Protestant Welfare Society and with the Zundert peasant families have been reconstructed in Kools, *Van Gogh en zijn geboorteplaats*, esp. chaps. 4 and 6, and pp. 38−56, 69−71, 118−20, 131, 140, 153.

17. Visiting parties and religious meetings placed the family in constant social interactions. Traffic flowed into the spacious front room of the parish house for diverse kinds of activities, such as evening church council meetings, catechism lessons, Bible readings, and coffee hour receptions after Sunday services. In addition,

the facade of the parish house, situated on the main road in the heart of the village square, offered a view of the busiest areas of Zundert life—the market, the local hall, and the postmaster's office—while also affording the neighbors direct access to the family's activities. See Kools, *Van Gogh en zijn geboorteplaats*, 16, 56–58.

18. Elizabeth Duquesne-van Gogh, *Personal Recollections of Vincent van Gogh* (London: Constable, 1913), 6.

19. Unlike another contemporary anti-rational religious movement—the orthodox Netherlandish Réveil—the Groningeners remained bound to Dutch humanist legacies while celebrating Kempis, and rejecting John Calvin, as the basis for a revitalized national Reformed religion. And, unlike the Réveil challengers, Groningen theologians (also known as the "Evangelicals") were not anti-modernists, adapting their revival of Kempis to new strains of Platonism and to the Christocentric teachings of the contemporary German theologian Friedrich Schleiermacher. On the Groningen School see Albert Réville, "Les Controverses et les écoles religieuses du Hollande," *Revue des deux-mondes*, ser. 8, vol. 27 (May–June 1860), 935–52; Eldred C. Vanderlaan, *Religious Thought in Holland* (London: Oxford University Press, 1911), 14–19; and D. Chantepie de la Saussaye, *La crise religieuse en Hollande* (Leyden, De Breuk & Smits, 1860), 70–73. For Theodorus van Gogh and the Groningen School see M. E. Tralbaut, *Vincent van Gogh* (London: Chartwell Books, 1969), 12; and Kools, *Van Gogh en zijn geboorteplaats*, 9–14.

20. For the approach to redemption through the clarity of sight, enveloping light, and direct beholding, see Thomas à Kempis, *The Imitation of Christ*, trans. Aloysius Croft and Harry F. Bolton (Milwaukee: The Bruce Publishing Company, 1962), 92–93, 99–101, 111–13, 174–76, 251–52. For Hofstede de Groot and primacy of the visual in religious experience see P. Hofstede de Groot, *Ary Scheffer, Met Vijf Platen* (Groningen: P. Noordhoff, 1872); and his *De Wereldtentoonstelling te Parijs, uit een Christelijk Oogpunt Beschowd* (Groningen: P. Noordhoff, n.d.).

21. Mrs. van Gogh was an accomplished watercolorist, crocheter, and embroiderer. She even embellished the family Bible with a special bookmark of intricate micro-patterns framing her husband's name. (This paper and ribbon design is preserved in the collection of the Amsterdam Rijksmuseum Vincent van Gogh). Newly available archival descriptions of the interiors of the van Gogh Zundert house offer evidence of the patterns and textures created by carpeted tables, prints, mirrors, paint, and wallpaper that enlivened the family residence. An inventory of the van Gogh household compiled after Theodorus's death indicates the presence of prints and paintings in many rooms of the house. Parson Theodorus's comfort with the visual world was also evident in the instances recorded by Vincent van Gogh when the two visited museums together and discussed particular paintings and collections. And the exchange of gifts in the form of images was a favored practice in the van Gogh family. See the room by room description of the Zundert house in Kools, *Van Gogh en zijn geboorteplaats*, 16–22 and 75; and the 1885 inventory of the household republished in Hans van Crimpen, "The Van Gogh Family in Brabant," in Noord-

brabants Museum, s'Hertogenbosch, *Van Gogh in Brabant, Paintings and Drawings from Etten and Nuenen* (Zwolle: Waanders, 1987), 86–89.

22. Vincent van Gogh, *The Complete Letters of Vincent van Gogh* (Boston: New York Graphic Society, 2d ed., 1978), 1:120.

23. Other discussions of van Gogh and the weavers have explored the topic in terms of subject matter confined to the early Nuenen Dutch period, rather than as a constitutive mode of van Gogh's self-definition and pictorial practice. These are Linda Nochlin's "Van Gogh, Renouard, and the Weaver's Crisis in Lyon: The Status of a Social Issue in the Art of the Late Nineteenth Century," in Moshe Barasch and Lucy Freeman Sandler, eds., *Art and the Ape of Nature: Studies in Honor of Horst Woldermar Janson* (New York: H. Abrams, 1981), pp. 669–88; and Carol Zemel's "The 'Spook in the Machine': Van Gogh's Pictures of Weavers in Brabant," *Art Bulletin* 47, 1 (Mar. 1985), 123–37. My analysis reconstructs the centrality of weavers and weaving in van Gogh's pre-Nuenen and post-Nuenen periods, emphasizing (1) that van Gogh's approach to the Nuenen weaver series in 1883 was itself prepared by, and the culmination of, long-term religious needs, literary structures, and social experiences of his pre-painting biography; and (2) that the identification of painting and weaving provided an enduring mental framework and stylistic preference long after the actual depiction of weavers, structuring van Gogh's transformation of the lessons he absorbed in France after 1886.

24. Scholarly assessments of van Gogh's relation to labor fall into two groups. Social art historians have emphasized van Gogh's visual and ideological detachment from workers, while scholars privileging the issue of religion have highlighted the continuity of religious symbols in van Gogh's depictions of labor. In contrast to these two lines of inquiry, this analysis rediscovers van Gogh's lifelong project of identification with laborers, the early religious conflicts that necessitated it, and the stylistic consequences that issued from it, which extend beyond the inclusion of religious symbols to the search for formal equivalents to particular labor activities. For the critical social art history accounts of van Gogh's relation to workers see especially Griselda Pollock, *Vincent van Gogh in zijn Hollandse jaren* (Amsterdam: Rijksmuseum Vincent van Gogh, 1980), and her "Stark Encounters: Modern Life and Urban Work in van Gogh's Drawings of the Hague, 1881–1883," *Art History*, Sept. 1983, 330–58; and Carol Zemel, "The 'Spook in the Machine'." For the role of religious symbology see Kōdera, *Vincent van Gogh*, esp. chap. 5; Lauren Soth, "Van Gogh's Agony," *Art Bulletin* 68 (June 1986), 301–13; and Judy Sund, "The Sower and the Sheaf: Biblical Metaphors in the Art of Vincent van Gogh," *Art Bulletin* 70 (Dec. 1988), 660–76.

25. See, for example, the discussions of perfection through practice, work, and rules rather than through "inborn" revelation, and of the skill of a job as illustrator and of "handicraft" in Van Gogh, *Letters* 1:217–18, 324–32, 368, 416–17, 438–39, 477–78; and 2:176, 198, 297.

26. Among the earliest surviving drawings of Vincent van Gogh were copies that

he made after his mother's illustrations of a bouquet of flowers and a thistle plant. See Jan van Gelder, "Juvenilia," in J. B. de La Faille, *The Works of Vincent van Gogh, His Paintings and Drawings* (Amsterdam: Meulenhoff, 1970), 600–6; Anne Stiles Wylie, "Vincent's Childhood and Adolescence," in *Vincent, Bulletin of the Rijksmuseum Vincent van Gogh* 4, 2 (1975), 10.

27. See H. F. J. M. van den Eerenbeemt, "The Unknown Vincent: The State Secondary School at Tilburg," *Vincent* 2, 1 (1972), 2–12; and "The Drawing Master Huysmans," *Vincent* 2, 2 (1973), 2–10.

28. Van Gogh, *Letters*, 1:148–51.

29. Ibid., 190.

30. Van Gogh's former employer at the Hague Goupil and Co. originally sent him drawing manuals when he was still in the Borinage in early 1880. On his study of the Bargue books in Brussels and at the Hague see van Gogh's comments in *Letters* 1:153–239, 504; Charles Scott Chetham, *The Role of Vincent van Gogh's Copies in the Development of His Work* (New York: Garland Press, 1976), 12–77; Anne Stiles Wylie, "An Investigation of the Vocabulary of Line in Vincent van Gogh's Expression of Space," *Oud Holland* 85, 4 (1970), 210–22; and Albert Boime, "The Teaching of Fine Arts and the Avant-Garde in France During the Second Half of the Nineteenth Century," *Arts Magazine* 60 (Dec. 1985), 53–54.

31. Karl Robert, *Charcoal Drawing Without a Master, A Complete Practical Treatise on Landscape Drawing in Charcoal Followed by Lessons on Studies After Allongé*, trans. E. Appleton (Cincinnati: R. Clarke, 1880), esp. 35–62. My thanks to Albert Boime for sharing his copies of the Robert books with me.

32. On the experiments with lithography and the printing process, see van Gogh, *Letters* 1:488–515. For a perceptive analysis of the liaison with Sien Hartook, see Carol Zemel, "Sorrowing Women, Rescuing Men: Van Gogh's Images of Women and the Family," *Art History* 10, 3 (Sept. 1987), 351–68.

33. On van Gogh's collection of the English prints and his conception of a popular graphic art highlighting urban work and poverty see *Letters* 1, esp. 384–512; Ronald Pickvance, *English Influences on Vincent van Gogh* (London: Arts Council of Great Britain, 1974–75); and Julien Treuhez, *Hard Times, Social Realism in Victorian Art, With Contributions by Susan P. Casteras, Lee M. Edwards, Peter Keating, and Louis van Tilborgh* (London: Lund Humphries, in Association with Manchester City Art Galleries, 1987).

34. Van Gogh, *Letters* 1:416–17, 476–77, 506–9.

35. Van Gogh describes the construction and operation of the frame in *Letters* 1:383, 430, 432–33.

36. See the discussion by van Gogh himself and also A. S. Wylie, "An Investigation of the Vocabulary of Line in Vincent van Gogh's Expression of Space," *Oud-Holland* 85, 4 (1970), 210–22, and Ann H. Murray, "'Strange and Subtle Perspective . . .' Van Gogh, the Hague School and the Dutch Landscape Tradition," *Art History* 3, 4 (Dec. 1980), 410–24.

37. Van Gogh, *Letters* 1:467; 2:5 and 7.

38. Selections from the early drawings which demonstrate the appeal of woven subjects and sewing figures may be seen in the reproductions in the 1990 Kröller-Müller exhibition, *Vincent van Gogh's Drawings* (Milan, Arnoldo Mondadori Arte srl, 1990), esp. 62–118, though these choices and their meaning are not addressed; the full complement of these types of subjects is traceable in the reproductions in J. B. de la Faille, *The Works of Vincent van Gogh. His Paintings and Drawings*, 336–401, 565–69. Van Gogh's search for rough and textural paper recurs in the Hague letters; see some examples in *Letters* 1:350, 360–61, 417, 423, 432.

39. There are many other ways that van Gogh visualizes the equivalence between his artistic work and the work of the craft weaver in the 34 images the weaver series comprises. These include his depiction of the weavers with brushes and pipes— the accoutrements of his own work—and van Gogh's tendency to alter the appearance of the weaver or the loom to more closely fit his own work process. One example of this alteration is evident in Fig. 17, where the pattern of the threads drawn down by the weaver are inaccurate, but match exactly the intersecting diagonal pattern of the threads suspended on van Gogh's own perspective frame (Fig. 8).

40. For van Gogh's concentration on the problem of color in Nuenen see the *Letters* 2:249–441 (to Theo) and 3:303–423 (to van Rappard). The discussion that follows on the critical role of weaving in van Gogh's early developing technique expands the analysis first presented in my "Loom with a View," esp. 51–60.

41. Chevreul's color studies, first published in 1838 and extensively republished through the 1880s, were rapidly assimilated by artists beginning with Eugene Delacroix. Van Gogh was exposed to Chevreul's theories through the writing of Charles Blanc, one of the primary popularizers of Chevreul's discoveries. Van Gogh studied Blanc's chapter on Delacroix in his *Les Artistes de mon temps* (Paris: Firmin-Didot, 1876), 23–88, and his larger treatise, the *Grammaire des arts de dessin* (Paris: Laurens, 1880), both of which featured Chevreul's experiments and highlighted their application to painting on canvas and to color saturation on draperies, cushions, and other fabric stuffs.

42. Van Gogh, *Letters* 2:369–70.

43. For example the Arles depictions of sowers, reapers, and harvesters, and the portraits of peasants, soldiers, and the postman Roulin and his family. These latter portraits hark back in content and format to van Gogh's vision of popularizing a print series of "heads of the people," which he conceived in Nuenen as "Brabant labor types."

44. On the Eindhoven amateur painting group see Van Gogh, *Letters* 2:436–51 and 298–352. The Arles lessons to Milliet are mentioned in *Letters* 3:493.

45. Van Gogh, *Letters* 3:226. In another self-portrait, *The Painter on the Road to Tarascon*, also of 1888, van Gogh again realizes visually the equivalence of the artist's and peasant's labor. He shows himself en route, in peasant clothes and broad-rimmed hat, his tools and frame strapped to his back. The positioning of the artist

replicated exactly the mirror image of the *Sower* in the fields. Both were depicted in the active pose of arms swinging and legs astraddle, the sun casting their respective shadows in front of them. As van Gogh looked into the mirror and found himself "looking more or less like a peasant," this self-portrait mirrored the pose and appearance of the rural laborer he admired as the agent of nature's productivity. (My thanks to Miriam Wimpfheimer-Blech for first suggesting the link between these two paintings.)

46. Bernard, quoted in Bogomila Welsh-Ovcharov, ed., *Van Gogh in Perspective* (Englewood Cliffs, NJ: Prentice-Hall, 1974), "Emile Bernard on Vincent," 38 (originally published by Bernard in his memorial article "Vincent van Gogh" in *Les Hommes d'aujourd'hui* 8, 390 [1891]). I discussed the balls of yarn as evidence of the continuity of the lessons of the Nuenen weavers in "Loom With a View," 65–69 and 87. Van Gogh stored these balls of yarn in a Japanese lacquer box which is preserved at the Rijksmuseum Vincent van Gogh in Amsterdam and has recently been the subject of study by the art historian and restoration expert at the Museum, Cornelia Peres. Van Gogh's balls of yarn are very similar to those still used today at tapestry looms, such as the ones that can be seen in process at the Netherlands Tilburg Textile Museum and Factory. My thanks to this Tilburg Textile Museum's technical director, Piet Arendse, for allowing me to study these looms.

47. A. S. Hartrick, *A Painter's Pilgrimage Through Fifty Years* (Cambridge: Cambridge University Press, 1939), 46. The full range of van Gogh's Japanese collection, including the "crépons," can be found in Rijksmuseum Vincent van Gogh, *Japanese Prints Collected by Vincent van Gogh* (Amsterdam, 1978); and *Catalogue of the Van Gogh Museum's Collection of Japanese Prints* (Zwolle: Waanders, 1991).

48. The Kunisada print of the *Gongen Shrine in Nezu* (Fig. 18) resembles one of the weaver images van Gogh had already completed in Nuenen a number of years earlier. The girl sits at a weaving loom with a view of the shrine behind her in an inset. In van Gogh's *Weaver* of 1884, (Munich: Neue Pinakothek collection), the male weaver sits at his loom with a view out to the local church.

The depiction of activities related to textile production and consumption proliferated in ukiyoe prints due to the expansion of the clothing trade and the democratization of luxury from the late eighteenth century. Between 1765 and 1865, an unusually close association flourished among the creators of the varied arts of painting, printmaking, and textile decoration in Japan, with artists crossing over regularly from one medium to another and sharing innovations in color dyes and pigments applied to both paper and cloth. Part of this interchange was signalled by the origins of the colored woodblock prints such as those collected by van Gogh—from their emergence in 1765, these prints were known as "nishiki-e,"—the "brocade print," which built up a comprehensive design from multiple individual color blocks, similar to the additive integration of color layered for brocade cloth. This and other examples of the particularly Japanese interchangeability of paper, cloth, paint, ink, dye, and thread in the late eighteenth and nineteenth centuries are keys to understanding van Gogh's receptivity to and selection of types of Japanese art in the Paris period.

49. *Wild Flowers and Thistles* (1890), for example, was painted on a red-striped linen hand towel, whose border was similar to the striped towels made by the Nuenen weavers; *Enclosed Field in the Rain* (1889) was painted on an untreated cotton sheet. The *Rain* canvas, now in the Philadelphia Museum of Art collection, shows particularly clearly how the flimsy, gauzy cloth surface catches the paint on the nap, and how van Gogh left the canvas weave open in many areas adjacent to his own interlocking woven brushstrokes. My thanks to Philadelphia Museum restoration specialist Mark Tucker for discussing these special qualities of the painting with me.

50. Indeed it is during this late period that van Gogh explicitly compares his color effects and dispositions to those of textiles, such as when he described a canvas reminding him of "a piece of Scotch plaid," in *Letters* 3:188.

51. Ibid., 525.

52. Portions of Aurier's article are reprinted in Linda Nochlin, ed., *Impressionism and Post-Impressionism, Sources and Documents. 1874–1904* (Englewood Cliffs: Prentice-Hall, 1966), 135–39. The complete text is included in Ronald Pickvance, *Van Gogh in Saint Rémy and Auvers* (New York: Metropolitan Museum of Art, 1986), 310–15.

53. Van Gogh mentions Monticelli, Delacroix, Gaugin, Jeannin, Father Quost, and Gauguin as his co-equals in painting; he also notes that "a good picture" is equivalent to "a good deed," further de-emphasizing Aurier's theme of detachment. See van Gogh's response to Aurier, in *Letters* 3:256–57.

54. Quoted in Nochlin, *Impressionism*, 152; originally in van Gogh's discussion of Aurier in his letter to Theo, *Letters* 3:254.

55. Ibid., 257.

56. Meyer Schapiro, *Vincent van Gogh* (New York: Abrams, 1950), 11–34.

SHEEHAN: From Princely Collections to Public Museums

A slightly different version of this essay will be published in German in *Macrocosmos in Microcosmo: Die Welt in der Stube*, ed. by Andreas Grote.

1. W. Busch, "Chodowieckis Darstellung der Gefühle und der Wandel des Bildbegriffes nach der Mitte des 18. Jahrhunderts," in W. Barner, ed., *Tradition, Norm, Innovation—Soziales und literarisches Traditionsverhalten in der Frühzeit der deutschen Aufklärung* (Munich, 1989). See also the remarks in W. Kemp, "Die Kunst des Schweigens," in T. Koebner, ed., *Laokoon und kein Ende: der Wettstreit der Künste* (Munich, 1989), 96–119.

2. N. von Holst, *Creators, Collectors, and Connoisseurs: The Anatomy of Artistic Taste from Antiquity to the Present Day* (New York, 1967), 204ff, and N. Pevsner, *A History of Building Types* (Princeton, 1976), 117ff.

3. W. Heinse, *Briefe aus der Düsseldorfer Gemäldegalerie*, ed. A. Winkler (Leipzig and Vienna, 1912). On eighteenth-century journals, see E. Lehmann, *Die Anfänge der Kunstzeitschrift in Deutschland* (Leipzig, 1932).

4. J. W. Goethe, *Dichtung und Wahrheit: Werke* (Hamburger Ausgabe Munich, 1981), 9:320.

5. Mechel quoted in L. H. Wüthrich, *Christian von Mechel* (Basel, 1956), 162. The classic work on Winckelmann remains C. Justi, *Winckelmann und seine Zeitgenossen* (Leipzig, 1898); on Winckelmann and art history, see W. Waetzoldt, *Deutsche Kunsthistoriker* (Leipzig, 1921–24), vol. 1.

6. *Aufklärung und Klassizismus in Hessen-Kassel unter Landgraf Friedrich II (1760–1785)* (Kassel, 1979), 79. See also F. Drier, "The *Kunstkammer* of the Hessian Landgraves in Kassel," in O. Impey and A. MacGregor, eds., *The Origins of Museums* (Oxford, 1985).

7. J. W. Goethe, "Einleitung in die *Propyläen*," *Werke* 12:38ff.

8. On these developments, see B. Steinwachs, *Epochenbewusstsein und Kunsterfahrung: Studien zur Geschichtsphilosophischen Ästhetik an der Wende vom 18. zum 19. Jahrhundert in Frankreich und Deutschland* (Munich, 1986), and Peter Szondi, "Antike und Moderne in der Ästhetik der Goethezeit," *Poetik und Geschichtsphilosophie* 1 (Frankfurt, 1974).

9. E. Müsebeck, *Das preussische Kultusministerium vor hundert Jahren* (Stuttgart and Berlin, 1918), 241.

10. Paul Seidel, "Zur Vorgeschichte der Berliner Museen: Der erste Plan von 1797," *Jahrbuch der Preussichen Kunstsammlungen* 49, Beiheft (1928), 55–64; Friedrich Stock, "Zur Vorgeschichte der Berliner Museen: Urkunden von 1786–1807," ibid., 65–174; "Urkunden zur Vorgeschichte des Berliner Museums," ibid. 51 (1930), 205–22; "Urkunden zur Einrichtung des Berliner Museums," ibid. 58, Beiheft (1937), 11–31.

11. Paul O. Rave, *Karl Friedrich Schinkel: Berlin I. Teil. Bauten für die Kunst Kirchen und Denkmalpflege* (Berlin, 1941); Sabine Spiero, "Schinkels Altes Museum in Berlin. Seine Baugeschichte von den Anfängen bis zur Eröffnung" (Diss. Marburg, 1933).

12. V. Plagemann, *Das deutsche Kunstmuseum, 1790–1870: Lage, Baukörper, Raumorganisation, Bildprogramm* (Munich, 1967), 58 and 83. On the Glyptothek, see Britta Schwann, *Die Glyptothek in München* (Munich, 1983) and K. Vierneisel and G. Leinz, eds., *Glyptothek München, 1830–1980* (Munich, 1980).

13. Gustav Waagen, *Kleine Schriften* (Stuttgart, 1875), 8.

14. F. Eggers, "Die Zugänglichkeit der Museen," *Deutsches Kunstblatt* 2, 4 (27.I.1851), 25.

15. A. Gehlen, *Zeit-Bilder. Zur Soziologie und Ästhetik der modernen Malerei* (Frankfurt and Bonn, 1960), 207.

16. Heinrich Dilly, *Kunstgeschichte als Institution. Studien zur Geschichte einer Disziplin* (Frankfurt, 1979); Wilhelm Waetzoldt, *Deutsche Kunsthistoriker*, 2 vols. (Leipzig, 1921–24).

17. Quoted in Werner Hofmann, *Das irdische Paradies. Motive und Ideen des 19. Jahrhunderts* (Munich, 1974), 61.

18. Quoted in Helmut Börsch-Supan, *Die Deutsche Malerei von Anton Graf bis Hans von Marees, 1760–1870* (Munich, 1988), 269.

19. Adolf Bayersdorfer, "Der Holbein-Streit," in Bayersdorfer, *Leben und Schriften aus seinem Nachlass* (Munich, 1908).

20. Rudolf Eitelberger von Edelberg, *Die Resultate des ersten internationalen kunstwissenschaftlichen Congresses in Wien* (Vienna, 1874). See also Dilly, *Kunstgeschichte*, 173ff.

21. G. W. F. Hegel, *Vorlesungen über die Ästhetik: Werke* 13 (Frankfurt, 1970), 25–26.

22. On the changing character of museum administrators, see the memoirs of Wilhelm von Bode, *Mein Leben*, 2 vols. (Berlin, 1930) and Ludwig Pallat, *Richard Schöne. Generaldirektor der königlichen Museen zu Berlin* (Berlin, 1959).

23. Hegel, *Ästhetik*, 25. On the problematic relationship of art and art history, see my essay, "Vergangenheit und Gegenwart in der Geschichte der Kunst," in *Deutschlands Weg in die Moderne. Politik, Gesellschaft und Kultur im 19. Jahrhundert*, ed. W. Hardtwig and H.-H. Brandt (Munich, 1993).

24. See, for example, Adolf Bayersdorfer's critique of the German art shown in Vienna in 1873: *Leben*, 211–12; another example is Richard Muther, *Geschichte der Malerei im 19. Jahrhundert*, 3 vols. (Munich, 1893–94).

25. Michel Foucault, "Fantasia of the Library," in *Language, Counter-Memory, Practice*. D. F. Bonchard, ed. (Ithaca, 1977), 92–93.

26. T. Adorno, "Valery Proust Museum," *Gesammelte Schriften* 10, 1 (Frankfurt, 1977), 181.

27. *Ausstellung deutscher Kunst aus der Zeit von 1775–1875 in der Königlichen Nationalgalerie Berlin 1906*, 2 vols. (Munich, 1906). On these matters, see Peter Paret, *The Berlin Secession, Modernism and its Enemies in Imperial Germany* (Cambridge, MA, 1980).

28. Carol Duncan and Alan Wallach, "The Universal Survey Museum," *Art History* 3, 4 (1980), 449.

29. Eugenio Donato, "The Museum's Furnace: Notes towards a Contextual Reading of *Bouvard and Pecuchet*," in *Textual Strategies: Perspectives in Poststructuralist Criticism*, ed. J. Harari (Ithaca, 1979), 214.

30. See, for example, Douglas Crimp, "On the Museum's Ruins," in *The Anti-Aesthetic: Notes on Postmodern Culture*, ed. H. Foster (Port Townsend, WA, 1983); Nelson Goodman, "The End of the Museum," in Goodman, *Of Mind and other Matters* (Cambridge, MA, 1984), 174–87; K. Hudson, *Museums for the 1980s* (London, 1977); R. Lumley, ed., *The Museum Time Machine* (London, 1988); B. O'Doherty, ed., *Museums in Crisis* (New York, 1972); E. Spickernagel and B. Walbe, eds., *Das Museum. Lernort contra Musentempel* (Giessen, 1976); Stephen Weil, *Rethinking the Museum and other Reflections* (Washington and London, 1990).

TOEWS: Musical Historicism

1. This relationship has received relatively little attention in the vast Mendelssohn literature. For the best surveys of the 1840–45 period in Mendelssohn's career see the relevant chapters in two standard modern synthetic works: Eric Werner, *Mendelssohn: A New Image of the Composer and His Age* (London, 1963; rev. German ed. Freiburg, 1980); Wulf Konold, *Felix Mendelssohn-Bartholdy und seine Zeit* (Regensburg, 1984).

2. Georg Feder, "Zu Felix Mendelssohn-Bartholdy's geistlicher Musik," in *Religiöse Musik in nicht-liturgischen Werken von Beethoven bis Reger*, ed. Walter Wiora (Regenburg, 1968), 113.

3. Susanna Grossmann-Vendrey, *Felix Mendelssohn-Bartholdy und die Musik der Vergangenheit* (Regensburg, 1969), 112.

4. The nature of Humboldt's proposal and his discussions with the king can be indirectly gleaned from Bunsen's letter to Humboldt on Nov. 1, 1840, reprinted in Friedrich Nippold, ed., *Christian Karl Josias von Bunsen*, 3 vols. (Leipzig, 1868–71), 2:143–44. Zelter's negotiations with the Prussian Reformers are recounted with full citation of documents in Cornelia Schroeder, *Carl Friedrich Zelter und die Akademie der Künste* (Berlin, 1959).

5. Various expressions of these positions are scattered throughout Mendelssohn's correspondence, but they are most systematically presented in two memoranda he wrote in 1840 and 1841 for the establishment of musical academies in Prussia and Saxony. These are reprinted in Felix Mendelssohn-Bartholdy, *Briefe aus den Jahren 1830 bis 1847*, 2 vols. (Leipzig, 1875), 2:150–54, 191–93.

6. See Bunsen's letters to the king (Oct. 30, 1840) and to Humboldt (Nov. 1, 1840), in Nippold, ed., *Bunsen* 2:142–43.

7. A general overview of Mendelssohn's early liturgical compositions is available in Rudolf Werner, *Felix Mendelssohn Bartholdy als Kirchenmusiker* (Phil. diss., Frankfurt a.M., 1930).

8. A systematic analysis of the formal consequences of Mendelssohn's confrontation with the works of the late Beethoven can be found in Friedhelm Krummacher, *Mendelssohn der Komponist: Studien zur Kammermusik für Streicher* (Munich, 1978), esp. 70–73, and in Konold, *Mendelssohn Bartholdy*, 111–38.

9. Brian Pritchard, "Mendelssohn's Chorale Cantatas: An Appraisal," *The Musical Quarterly* 62 (1976), 1–24; Larry Todd, "A Passion Cantata by Mendelssohn," *American Choral Review*, Jan. 1983, 2–17.

10. The core members of this group, active in both the Beethoven cult and the Bach revival, were Fanny Mendelssohn, the historian Gustav Droysen, the music critic Adolf Marx, and the opera singer Eduard Devrient.

11. Letter to Karl Klingemann, Dec. 14, 1835, Karl Klingemann, ed., *Felix Mendelssohn Bartholdy's Briefwechsel mit Legationsrat Karl Klingemann in London* (Essen, 1909), 195.

12. Mendelssohn, *Briefe* 2:100, 116, 122.

13. Letter to Paul Mendelssohn, Oct. 1837, ibid., 98–99.

14. Letter to F. David, July 30, 1838, ibid., 110.

15. Friedhelm Krummacher has summarized his detailed analysis of Mendelssohn's compositional maturation in terms of self-conscious formal shifts away from the conventions of classical sonata forms in "Zur Kompositionsart Mendelssohns: Thesen am Biespiel der Streichquartette," in Carl Dahlhaus, *Das Problem Mendelssohn* (Regensburg, 1974), 169–84. My analysis of the *Lobgesang* attempts to apply the general principles of his analysis beyond the genres of chamber music and place them in historical/cultural context.

16. The programs of Mendelssohn's Gewandhaus concerts are described in Alfred Doerffel, *Geschichte der Gewandhausconcerte zu Leipzig vom 25. November, 1781 bis 25. November, 1881* (Leipzig, 1884, repr. 1980), 83ff.

17. Letter to Droysen, Dec. 14, 1838, in Rudolf Huebner, ed. *Johann Gustav Droysens Briefwechsel, Vol. I: 1829–1851* (Osnabrueck, 1967, repr. of 1929 ed.), 128.

18. Fanny's response to an 1836 performance conducted by Felix is cited in Werner, *Mendelssohn* (German ed. 1980), 314.

19. My comparative analysis has been most influenced on the Beethoven side by the interpretations in Maynard Solomon, *Beethoven Essays* (Cambridge, MA, 1988) and Leo Treitler, *Music and the Historical Imagination* (Cambridge, MA, 1989). As far as I know there exists no systematic musical analysis of the *Lobgesang*. I have found brief commentaries in the following studies useful: Thomas Ehrle, *Die Instrumentation in den Symphonien und Overtüren von Felix Mendelssohn-Bartholdy* (Wiesbaden, 1983); Mathias Thomas, *Das Instrumentalwerk Felix Mendelssohn Bartholdys: Ein Systematisch-theoretische Untersuchung mit besonderer Berücksichtigung der zeitgenössischen Musiktheorie* (Goettingen, 1972).

20. July 21, 1840, Klingemann, ed., *Briefwechsel*, 200.

21. Thomas, *Instrumentalwerk*, 235; Werner, *Mendelssohn*, 92.

22. Letter to Schirmer, Nov. 21, 1838, Mendelssohn, *Briefe* 2:115–16.

STEINBERG: Broken Vessels

1. Martha Nussbaum contributed directly to this essay by way of a generous and enormously helpful reading of an early draft, for which I am very much in her debt.

2. Edith Wharton, *The House of Mirth* (1904), in *Wharton: Novels* (Library of America Edition: New York, 1985), 5.

3. See Daniel H. Borus, *Writing Realism: Howells, James, and Norris in the Mass Market* (Chapel Hill, 1989), 154, and Leon Edel, *Henry James*, 5 vols. (New York, 1972), 4:274.

4. *Atlantic Monthly*, Aug. 1903.

5. Edel, *James* 5:167.

6. Lyall Powers, ed. *Henry James and Edith Wharton, Letters: 1900–1915* (New York: 1990).

7. Martha C. Nussbaum, "Flawed Crystals: James's *The Golden Bowl* and Literature as Moral Philosophy," in Nussbaum, *Love's Knowledge: Essays on Philosophy and Literature* (Oxford, 1990), 133.

8. Nussbaum, "Flawed Crystals," 131.

9. Henry James, *The Golden Bowl* (1904), 20–21. Citations will refer to the Penguin Classics ed. (Harmondsworth, 1987).

10. Ibid., 49.

11. Ibid., 51.

12. See Nussbaum, "'Finely Aware and Richly Responsible': Literature and the Moral Imagination," in Nussbaum, *Love's Knowledge*, 157.

13. James, *The Golden Bowl*, 115.　　14. Ibid., 119.

15. Ibid., 123.　　16. Ibid., 179.

17. Ibid., 190.

18. Martha Nussbaum, letter to me of Mar. 21, 1991.

19. James, *The Golden Bowl*, 192.　　20. Ibid., 440, 437.

21. Ibid., 479.　　22. Ibid., 479–80.

23. Ibid., 451.

24. See Nussbaum, "Flawed Crystals," 137.

25. James, *The Golden Bowl*, 20.

26. Edel, *James* 2:432.

27. See Barbara Hardy, Introduction to George Eliot, *Daniel Deronda* (Harmondsworth, 1967), 17–18.

28. Edel, *James* 2:371.

29. Nussbaum, "'Finely Aware,'" 155.

30. Wayne Booth, *The Company We Keep* (Berkeley, 1988), 288.

31. Nussbaum, "Flawed Crystals," 125.

32. Harold Bloom, *Kabbalah and Criticism* (New York, 1975), 52. The translation of the term *Sefirot* is from Gershom Scholem, *Major Trends in Jewish Mysticism* (New York, 1946), 13.

33. Gershom Scholem, "Isaac Luria and His School," in Ibid., 261.

34. Ibid., 267.

35. Ibid., 287.

36. The quotation is from Gershom Scholem, "Toward an Understanding of the Messianic Idea," in Scholem, *The Messianic Idea in Judaism* (New York, 1971), 13.

37. Gershom Scholem, *Sabbatai Sevi*, trans. R. J. Zwi Werblowsky (Princeton, 1957).

38. Walter Benjamin, *Gesammelte Schriften*, ed. Rolf Tiedemann and Hermann Schweppenhauser (Frankfurt, 1977), 4:1:18. Translations will be mine unless otherwise indicated.

39. Gershom Scholem, *The Story of a Friendship*, trans. H. Zohn (New York, 1981), 14, 28, 43, 32, 38.

40. Walter Benjamin, "On Language as Such and on the Language of Man," in Benjamin, *Reflections*, trans. E. Jephcott (New York, 1979), 326–27.

41. Anson Rabinbach, "Between Enlightenment and Apocalypse: Benjamin, Bloch and Modern German Jewish Messianism," *New German Critique* 34 (Winter 1985), 105n.

42. Scholem, *The Story of a Friendship*, 83.

43. Ibid., 88–89.

44. Walter Benjamin, *Briefe*, ed. G. Scholem and T. Adorno (Frankfurt, 1966), 1:234. This chapter dated from 1912. It was included in the 1918 edition of Ernst Bloch, *Geist der Utopie* but deleted in the edition of 1923. See Rabinbach, "Between Enlightenment," 89n.

45. Scholem, *The Story of a Friendship*, 91.

46. Benjamin, *Briefe* 1:248.

47. Scholem, *The Story of a Friendship*, 100–1.

48. Ibid., 95–98.

49. See Rabinbach, "Between Enlightenment," 98.

50. See Benjamin, *Reflections*, 312.

51. See Walter Benjamin, "Critique of Violence," in Benjamin, *Reflections*, 279.

52. Ibid., 295.

53. Ibid., 286–87.

54. Ibid., 294.

55. Ibid., 295.

56. Ibid., 297.

57. Ibid., 300.

58. See E. M. Butler, *The Tyranny of Greece Over Germany* (Cambridge, 1936).

59. The path of Greek-inspired German aestheticism ends in Heidegger (and his use of Hölderlin), specifically in Martin Heidegger, "The Origin of the Work of Art" of 1936. Translated in Heidegger, *Basic Writings*, ed. D. F. Krell (New York, 1967), 149–87.

60. Walter Benjamin, "The Task of the Translator," in Benjamin, *Illuminations*, trans. Harry Zohn (New York, 1968), 70.

61. Ibid., 72; translation altered.

62. My translation of "So ist die Übersetzung zuletzt zweckmässig für des innersten Verhältnisses der Sprachen zueinander. Sie kann diese verborgene Verhältnis selbst unmöglich offenbaren, unmöglich herstellen; aber darstellen, indem sie es keimhaft oder intensiv verwirklicht, kann sie es." Benjamin, *Gesammelte Schriften* 4, 1:12.

63. In German: "Sehnsucht nach Sprachergänzung," in ibid., 18.

64. Ibid., 21.

65. See Paul de Man, "Conclusions: Walter Benjamin's 'The Task of the Translator,'" in de Man, *The Resistance to Theory* (Minneapolis, 1986), 80. At the same time I want to add that de Man's discussion of Benjamin's invocation of the broken vessels—de Man, 89–91—is faulty. In insisting, correctly, that Benjamin resists the implication that the lost totality can be restored, de Man insists, incorrectly, that Benjamin is not discussing a synecdochical relationship of fragments to a vessel. Of course he is discussing such a relationship, but insisting at the same that it cannot be restored by human agency.

66. James, *The Golden Bowl*, 27.

67. See Martha Nussbaum, "Perception and Revolution: *The Princess Casamassima* and the Political Imagination," in *Love's Knowledge*, 195–219.

68. Henry James, Preface (1909) to *The Princess Casamassima* (Penguin ed.), 33, 34, 35.

JELAVICH: "Girls and Crisis"

1. On the Metropol revues, see Walter Freund, "Aus der Frühzeit des Berliner Metropoltheaters," in *Kleine Schriften der Gesellschaft für Theatergeschichte*, no. 19 (Berlin, 1962), 45–66; Otto Schneidereit, *Berlin wie es lacht und weint: Spaziergänge durch Berlins Operettengeschichte* (Berlin: Lied der Zeit, 1976), 110–39; and Peter Jelavich, *Berlin Cabaret* (Cambridge: Harvard University Press, 1993), 104–17.

2. "Rekord der Revue: Neun Berliner Theater wollen Revue spielen!" in *Berliner Tageblatt*, July 7, 1926. For a general history of the Weimar revues, see Wolfgang Jansen, *Glanzrevuen der Zwanziger Jahre* (Berlin: Edition Hentrich, 1987). See also Franz-Peter Kothes, *Die theatralische Revue in Berlin und Wien, 1900–1938: Typen, Inhalte, Funktionen* (Wilhelmshaven: Heinrichshofen, 1977).

3. For example, see Georg Simmel, *Philosophie des Geldes* (Leipzig: Duncker & Humblot, 1900), and "Die Grossstädte und das Geistesleben," *Jahrbuch der Gehe-Stiftung zu Dresden* 9 (1903): 187–206; and Richard Hamann, *Der Impressionismus in Leben und Kunst* (Cologne: Dumont, 1907).

4. Ernst Bloch, "Berlin, Funktionen im Hohlraum," 212, and "Revueform in der Philosophie" (1928), 368–69, both reprinted in Bloch, *Erbschaft dieser Zeit* (Frankfurt: Suhrkamp, 1962); Siegfried Kracauer, "Kult der Zerstreuung" (1926), in Kracauer, *Das Ornament der Masse: Essays* (Frankfurt: Suhrkamp, 1977), 314–15; Maximilian Sladek, "Unsere Schau," in program book, *An Alle . . !* *Die grosse Schau im Grossen Schauspielhaus* (1924), reproduced in Jansen, *Glanzrevuen*, 146.

5. On the origin of the Tiller Girls, see Derek and Julia Parker, *The Natural History of the Chorus Girl* (Indianapolis: Bobbs-Merrill, 1975), 102–6.

6. Herbert Ihering in *Berliner Börsen-Courier*, Aug. 28, 1924.

7. Report of Mar. 16, 1922, in Brandenburgisches Landeshauptarchiv, Pr. Br. Rep. 30 Berlin C, Pol. Präs. Tit. 74, Th 1508, f. 3; and Polizei-Präsident Berlin to Polizeipräsidium Dresden, Nov. 4, 1924, in Th 1504, f. 102.

8. Fritz Giese, *Girlkultur: Vergleiche zwischen amerikanischem und europäischem Rhythmus und Lebensgefühl* (Munich: Delphin-Verlag, 1925), 122; Theodor Lücke, "Gedanken der Revue," in *Scene* 16 (1926): 114; Adam Kuckhoff, "Grösse und Niedergang der Revue," in *Die Volksbühne* 3, 1 (Apr. 1928), 4; Siegfried Kracauer, "Das Ornament der Masse" (1927), in Kracauer, *Das Ornament der Masse*, 52.

9. Alfred Polgar, "Girls" (1926), in *Auswahl: Prosa aus vier Jahrzenten* (Reinbek: Rowohlt, 1968), 187; Fred Hildenbrandt in *Berliner Tageblatt*, Sept. 9, 1925.

10. Paul Morgan, "Kleine Tragödie," *Querschnitt* 8 (1928): 655.

11. See Giese, *Girlkultur*, passim; and compare with the accounts of Weimar Germany's white-collar women in Ute Frevert, *Women in German History: From Bourgeois Emancipation to Sexual Liberation* (New York: Berg, 1989), 176–85; and Atina Grossmann, "*Girlkultur* or Thoroughly Rationalized Female: A New Woman in Weimar Germany?" in Judith Friedlander et al., eds., *Women in Culture and Politics: A Century of Change* (Bloomington: Indiana University Press, 1986), 62–80. The Girl image in the workplace, in the media, and on stage is compared in Günter Berghaus, "*Girlkultur*–Feminism, Americanism, and Popular Entertainment in Weimar Germany," *Journal of Design History* 1 (1988), 193–219.

12. For examples of questionable interviews, see Berghaus, "*Girlkultur*," 203–4. It is interesting to note that the myth of the Tiller Girls' marriages to rich men was parodied in a program book of the Haller revue: see E. Breitner, "Das Tiller-Girl und die Liebe," in program book, *Wann und Wo* (1927), 26.

13. Walter Benjamin and Bernhard Reich, "Revue oder Theater," in Benjamin, *Gesammelte Schriften* (Frankfurt: Suhrkamp, 1972), 4:802; Polgar, "Girls," 186; Oscar Bie in *Berliner Börsen-Courier*, Sept. 3, 1927; Kracauer, "Das Ornament der Masse," 52.

14. Siegfried Kracauer, "Girls und Krise," *Frankfurter Zeitung*, May 26, 1931. The machine imagery appeared in *Vossische Zeitung*, Aug. 19, 1926; Giese, *Girlkultur*, 15, 111; and *Vossische Zeitung*, Mar. 19, 1927.

15. Polgar, "Girls," 186–87; Paul Landau, "Girlkultur: Von der Amerikanisierung Europas," *Westermanns Monatshefte*, no. 845 (Jan. 1927), 566–67.

16. Kracauer, "Das Ornament der Masse," 53, 54.

17. Fred Hildenbrandt, "Tanzabend Valeska Gert," *Berliner Tageblatt*, Oct. 27, 1927, evening edition; "L." in *Kritiker*, Nov. 1926, 169; Max Herrmann-Neisse, "Endlich eine Revueparodie," *Kritiker*, Apr. 1926, 61; Götz Adriani, *Hannah Höch* (Cologne: DuMont, 1980), 39.

18. Kracauer, "Girls und Krise."

19. Kurt Robitschek, "Sieg des Theaters über die Weltgeschichte," *Die Frechheit*, July 1931, 1. Hitler's quote refers directly to Marion Daniels; the Tiller Girls are mentioned immediately thereafter, in Henry Picker, ed., *Hitlers Tischgespräche im Führerhauptquartier 1941–1942*, 2d ed. (Stuttgart: Seewald, 1965), 209; cf. 359–60. For a discussion of revue films in the Nazi era, see Helga Belach, ed., *Wir tanzen um die Welt: Deutsche Revuefilme 1933–1945* (Munich: Hanser, 1979).

20. Report of Oberregierungsrat Scherler, May 8, 1940, in Bundesarchiv, Abteilungen Potsdam, Reichsministerium für Volksaufklärung und Propaganda Nr. 474, f. 127; see also ff. 128–29.

21. Etty Hillesum, *Letters from Westerbork*, trans. Arnold J. Pomerans (New York: Random House, 1986), 89; Philip Mechanicus, *Year of Fear*, trans. Irene S. Gibbons (New York: Hawthorn, 1969), 144–45, 176. The women are referred to as the "Westerbork Girls" in the typed program of the revue "Bravo! Da Capo!" (Bühne

Lager Westerbork, premiere Oct. 16, 1943); see the copy in the Rijksinstituut voor Oorlogsdocumentatie in Amsterdam. For a treatment of a similar theme by a modern Israeli playwright, see the dramatization of variety shows in the Vilna ghetto: Joshua Sobol, *Ghetto: Schauspiel in drei Akten: Mit Dokumenten und Beiträgen zur zeitgeschichtlichen Auseinandersetzung*, ed. Harro Schweizer (Berlin: Quadriga, 1984).

CLARK: Gross David with the Swoln Cheek

1. Jean-Jacques Rousseau, *Oeuvres complètes* (Paris: Gallimard [Bibliothèque de la Pléiade], 1959–), 1:1150: "Montaigne se peint ressemblant mais de profil. Qui sait si quelque balafre à la joue ou un oeil crevé du côté qu'il nous a caché, n'eut pas totalement changé sa physionomie."

2. Ralph Leigh, ed., *Correspondance complète de Jean-Jacques Rousseau* (Geneva: Institut Voltaire, 1965–), 9:120, quoted in Jean Starobinski, *Jean-Jacques Rousseau: La transparence et l'obstacle* (Paris: Gallimard, 1971, first published 1957), 237: "Je suis persuadé qu'on est toujours très bien peint lorsqu'on s'est peint soi-même, quand même le portrait ne ressemblerait point."

3. See Daniel and Guy Wildenstein, *Documents complémentaires au Catalogue de l'oeuvre de Louis David* (Paris: Wildenstein, 1973), 112–13, docs. 1117, 1118, 1122.

4. See Wildenstein, *Documents*, 114, doc. 1131, Delafontaine's manuscript memoirs.

5. See Musée du Louvre, *Jacques-Louis David 1748–1825* (Paris: Réunion des Musées Nationaux, 1989), 304. Entry by Antoine Schnapper.

6. On Diderot and Cudworth, see "Appendice" to the *Pensées sur l'interprétation de la Nature* in Herbert Dieckmann and Jean Varloot, eds., *Oeuvres Complètes de Denis Diderot* (Paris: Hermann, 1975–), 9: 109–10, n. 162.

7. See *Encyclopédie méthodique, philosophie ancienne et moderne par le citoyen Naigeon* (Paris, L'An Deux), 3:215. Compare 351–65 and 415–27, likewise paraphrases of Cudworth.

8. Ralph Cudworth, *The True Intellectual System of the Universe* (London: R. Royston, 1678), 831, cited in John Yolton, *Thinking Matter, Materialism in Eighteenth-Century Britain* (Minneapolis: University of Minnesota Press, 1983), 8–9. I have leaned heavily on Yolton's book in what follows, partly because the British material, not being subject to the same kind of censorship as the French, allows us more direct access to the phenomenon that interests me most—the entry of materialist arguments into the public realm, and the degree to which they became common currency with the educated for a while. (In any case a glance at the publishing histories of the items I quote from in this essay will be enough to suggest that the argument we are looking at is conducted with scant regard to national boundaries.) The writer Cudworth attacks as "Sottish," etc. on 761 is Hobbes, who goes on being a target in the eighteenth century.

9. Joseph Priestley, *Disquisitions relating to Matter and Spirit* (London: J. Johnson, 1777; repr. New York: Arno Press, 1975), xiii–xiv, quoted in part in Yolton, *Thinking Matter*, 111. Priestley's work was known, admired, and widely translated in France, though his overtly "materialist" books stayed in English.

10. Priestley, *Disquisitions*, 19, quoted in Yolton, *Thinking Matter*, 113.

11. Priestley, *Disquisitions*, 18, quoted in Yolton, *Thinking Matter*, 113. Yolton's whole discussion of the reception of Priestley's ideas, on 115–25, is an excellent window onto this cultural world.

12. See Abbé G.-F. Coyer, *Oeuvres complètes de Coyer* (Paris, 1782). There does not seem to be much work on the filtering down of materialist arguments to this common level of controversy in France, but plenty of scattered clues exist. The word "matérialiste" is first recorded in French in 1702; it appears in the 1762 edition of the *Dictionnaire de l'Académie* as "Opinion de ceux qui n'admettent pas d'autre substance que la matière."

13. Denesle, *Les Préjugés des anciens et nouveaux philosophes sur la nature de l'âme humaine, ou examen du matérialisme* (Paris, 1765), 1:326: "Les Matérialistes concoivent nettement ce que c'est qu'*une organisation* qui a inventé les Arts, les Métiers, qui fait chaque jour les découvertes les plus surprenantes . . . qui, par son adresse asservit la nature, cette même substance universelle dont elle n'est qu'un point, à ses volontés comme à ses caprices. Ils sçavent ce que c'est qu'une *modification* qui fait des raisonnemens conséquens sur la nature de ce qui pense en elle. . . . Ils sçavent enfin ce que c'est qu'*un arrangement* de parties qui murmure souvent contre le sort, cette nécessité aveugle et inévitable."

14. Ibid., 210–11: "Car enfin qu'entendent-ils par ce dernier degré de subtilité, de pureté et d'activité dans la matière qu'ils veulent reconnoitre pour la substance pensante? La matière en quel sens qu'on la prenne, peut-elle seulement être supposée connoitre la pureté ou l'impureté? Connoitra-t-elle davantage la subtilité ou la grossiereté? . . . Donnons-lui ensuite les combinaisons les plus justes, les distributions les plus exactes & les plus géométriques, les mouvemens les plus variés et les plus harmonieux. . . . En quoi sommes-nous plus avancés? Est-elle parvenue à se connoitre elle-même?" It is not easy to say whom precisely Denesle is aiming at. Parts of Robinet's *De la nature*, perhaps, published in Amsterdam in 1761? Aspects of early Diderot? The fact is that targets abounded, and the vocabulary would not go away. There are passages in d'Holbach's *Système de la nature*, above all, where the language of dilation, rarefaction, interpenetration, etc. is deployed with a brio Denesle might have dreamed up to prove his point; see e.g. chap. 2 of pt. 1.

15. See François Hemsterhuis, *Lettre sur l'homme et ses rapports, avec le commentaire inédit de Diderot* [Georges May, ed.] (New Haven and Paris: Yale University Press and P.U.F., 1964), 151, quoted in part in Roland Desné, *Les Matérialistes Français de 1750 à 1800* (Paris: Éditions Sociales, 1965), 147–48: "Mais voyez-vous ce que vous faites? Pour introduire des propriétés essentielles contradictoires dans une même substance, vous rendez l'âme inétendue, indivisible, non figurée. . . .

Vous parlez d'un être dont vous n'avez pas la moindre idée. Vous parlez d'un être qui est, et qui n'est pas dans l'espace. Vous expliquez un phénomène par une chimère. Est-ce là de la philosophie? Qui est-ce qui vous a dit que toute la matière n'était pas sensible? Il y aura deux sortes de sensibilité, comme il y a deux sortes de forces. Une sensibilité inerte; une sensibilité active. Une sensibilité active qui peut passer à l'état d'inertie. Une sensibilité inerte qui peut passer et qui passe à ma volonté à une sensibilité active. Ce phénomène, qui s'exécute sous mes yeux, une fois admis, avec la mémoire et l'imagination, plus de difficultés." It is perhaps unfair to Hemsterhuis to put him on Denesle's level. Certainly his book provoked some of Diderot's most brilliant marginalia. On Diderot's materialism, I would single out Jean Varloot, "Genèse et Signification du 'Rêve de d'Alembert,'" in Denis Diderot, *Le Rêve de d'Alembert* (Paris: Éditions Sociales, 1971); the notes and introductions by Dieckmann, Varloot, and Jean Mayer to the volumes of the *Oeuvres complètes* containing the *Pensées sur l'interprétation de la nature*, the *Rêve* and the *Éléments de physiologie*; and Wilda Anderson, *Diderot's Dream* (Baltimore and London: Johns Hopkins University Press, 1990) especially pt. 1, "Diderot's Materialism: Vibrant Organization." Anderson's is the only text really to explore the upshots of Diderot's materialism for his practice as a writer, in ways I found particularly suggestive.

16. Jean Mayer, ed., *Oeuvres complètes de Denis Diderot* 17:333–35: "Pourquoi ne pas regarder la sensibilité, la vie, le mouvement comme autant de propriétés de la matière: puisqu'on trouve ces qualités dans chaque portion, chaque particule de chair? . . . Qu'on cherche à s'expliquer comment les passions s'introduisent dans l'âme sans mouvements corporels, et sans commencer par ces mouvements, je le défie. C'est sottise à ceux qui descendent de l'âme au corps: il ne se fait rien ainsi dans l'homme. Marat ne sait ce qu'il dit, quand il parle de l'action de l'âme sur le corps, s'il y avait regardé de plus près, il aurait vu que l'action de l'âme sur le corps est l'action d'une portion du corps sur une autre, et l'action du corps sur l'âme, l'action d'une autre partie du corps sur une autre. . . . La différence d'une âme sensitive à une âme raisonnable n'est qu'une affaire d'organisation. L'animal est un tout *un*, et c'est peut-être cette unité qui constitue l'âme, le soi, la conscience à l'aide de la mémoire."

Marat's book, a distinctly cautious and middle-of-the-road production, was published in French in Amsterdam in 1775; there had been an English version, *A Philosophical Essay on Man*, brought out in London two years earlier. In his first draft of this part of *Éléments de physiologie* Diderot had begun by addressing poor Marat directly: "J'ai pensé fermer le livre, Eh ridicule Écrivain" (see Mayer, *Oeuvres complètes* 17:331).

17. Paul Thiry, Baron d'Holbach, *Système de la nature* (London, 1770), 99–100: "Plus nous réfléchirons, plus nous demeurerons convaincus que l'âme, bien loin de devoir être distinguée du corps, n'est que ce corps lui-même envisagé relativement à quelques-unes de ses fonctions, ou à quelques façons d'être et d'agir dont il est susceptible, tant qu'il jouit de la vie. . . . C'est pour n'avoir point étudié

l'homme, que l'on a supposé dans lui un agent d'une nature différente de son corps. . . . Ce qui met de l'obscurité dans cette question, c'est que l'homme ne peut se voir lui-même; en effet il faudroit pour cela qu'il fût à la fois en lui et hors de lui. Il peut être comparé à une harpe sensible qui rend des sons d'elle-même, et qui se demande qu'est-ce qui les lui fait rendre; elle ne voit pas qu'en sa qualité d'être sensible, elle se pince elle-même, et qu'elle est pincée et rendue sonore par tout ce qui la touche."

18. Robert Darnton, "Reading, Writing and Publishing" in Darnton, *The Literary Underground of the Old Regime* (Cambridge, MA: Harvard University Press, 1982), 199–200.

19. The second phrase is from the notes on Maupertuis's *Essai sur la formation des corps organisés*, in Dieckmann and Varloot, *Oeuvres complètes* 9:84 and note. Aram Vartanian in *Diderot and Descartes: A Study of Scientific Naturalism in the Enlightenment* (Princeton: Princeton University Press, 1953) translates it nicely as "automatic unrest" (268).

20. The quoted words are those that figure largest in Yolton's discussion of the debates between Samuel Clarke, Anthony Collins, Samuel Colliber, Samuel Strutt and co., see Yolton, *Thinking Matter*, especially 64–89 and 127–52. On "acquaintance" see John Yolton, *Perceptual Acquaintance: from Descartes to Reid* (Minneapolis: University of Minnesota Press, 1984).

21. The vocabulary of the *Pensées sur l'interprétation de la nature* in general, and particularly of its "Cinquièmes conjectures." See Dieckmann and Varloot, *Oeuvres complètes* 9, and the discussion in chap. 1, "The Philosopher's Task," of Anderson, *Diderot's Dream*.

22. Charles Bonnet, *The Contemplation of Nature* (London, 1766), 1:84. (The English publication seems to be the first, maybe the only, available form of this work.) Bonnet, a pioneering experimental biologist, is officially agnostic on the great question of how "two such different substances as the soul & body act reciprocally on each other" (78), but in practice he is interested in seeing how good an account of memory and imagination he can give in terms of brain-fibers alone. The passage I quote is the climax of his effort. Compare what I take to be the essentially more conservative positions of his earlier *Essai de psychologie* (London, 1755) and *Essai analytique sur les facultés de l'âme* (Copenhagen, 1760), discussed below.

23. See Michael Fried, *Absorption and Theatricality: Painting and Beholder in the Age of Diderot* (Berkeley, Los Angeles, London: University of California Press, 1980), 138 and 232–33, for a discussion of the evidence of close contact between the two men.

24. *Éléments de physiologie*, in Mayer, *Oeuvres complètes* 17:467: "L'âme est au milieu de ses sensations comme un convive à une table tumultueuse, qui cause avec son voisin, il n'entend pas les autres."

25. Jean Gigoux, *Causeries sur les artistes de mon temps* (Paris, 1885), quoted in the dossier on David's self-portrait in the Louvre, Département des Peintures: "Il en

fit cadeau au père Fontaine, et il lui dit avec un geste significatif de la main sous le menton: 'Ils vont me couper le cou, mon cher!'"

26. The remark is cited in a review of Bonnet's *Essai analytique* in the *Monthly Review*, quoted in Yolton, *Thinking Matter*, 116. I have not found its source in Robinet's works.

27. See Jean Meslier, *Oeuvres de Jean Meslier* (Paris, 1971), 3:500–510 for the rediscovery of Meslier in the Revolution. Naigeon wrote an article on Meslier in the *Encyclopédie méthodique*. Materialists of all stripes fared well for a while in the 1790s: La Mettrie's works were re-edited in three volumes in 1796; the manuscript of *Éléments de physiologie* was presented to the *Comité d'instruction publique* in Germinal, Year Two (the committee had no time to do anything with it).

28. Philippe Lejeune, *Le pacte autobiographique* (Paris: Editions du Seuil, 1975), 243, quoted in Georges May, *L'Autobiographie* (Paris: Presses Universitaires de France, 1979), 93; the essay in question is now translated as "The Order of Narrative in Sartre's *Les Mots*" in Philippe Lejeune, *On Autobiography* (Minneapolis: University of Minnesota Press, 1989).

29. My quote is from Peggy Kamuf, *Signature Pieces: On the Institution of Authorship* (Ithaca and London: Cornell University Press, 1988), 23: "Rousseau is the name of a problem, the problem of the idealist exclusion of writing—of materiality, of exteriority—in the name of the subject's presence to itself." Behind that statement of the case, of course, lie Starobinski, *Rousseau*; pt. 2 of Jacques Derrida, *De la Grammatologie* (Paris: Éditions de Minuit, 1967); and pt. 2 of Paul de Man, *Allegories of Reading: Figural Language in Rousseau, Nietzsche, Rilke, and Proust* (New Haven and London: Yale University Press, 1979). Starobinski's chap. 7, on Rousseau as autobiographer, and de Man's chap. 8, "Self (Pygmalion)," are basic to the discussion that follows.

30. See the discussion of his points of reference in Rousseau, *Oeuvres complètes* 4:1509–67.

31. Ibid. 1:174–75. The passage is central to Starobinski, *Rousseau*, see 219ff: "Ces longs détails de ma prémiére jeunesse auront paru bien puériles et j'en suis fâché; quoique né homme à certains égards, j'ai été longtems enfant et je le suis encore à beaucoup d'autres. Je n'ai pas promis d'offrir au public un grand personage; j'ai promis de me peindre tel que je suis. . . . Je voudrois pouvoir en quelque façon rendre mon ame transparente aux yeux du lecteur, et pour cela je cherche à la lui montrer sous tous les points de vue, à l'éclairer par tous les jours, à faire en sorte qu'il ne s'y passe pas un mouvement qu'il n'apperçoive, afin qu'il puisse juger par lui-même du principe qui les produit. . . . Je n'ai qu'une chose à craindre dans cette entreprise; ce n'est pas de trop dire ou de dire des mensonges; mais c'est de ne pas tout dire, et de taire des vérités."

32. Rousseau, *Oeuvres complètes* 1:1122, quoted by Starobinski, *Rousseau*, 228: "les traits du visage ne font leur effet que parce qu'ils y sont tous; s'il en manque un, le visage est défiguré."

33. Rousseau, *Oeuvres complètes* 1:59–60, quoted by Starobinski, *Rousseau*, 228: "Dans l'entreprise que j'ai faite de me montrer tout entier au public, il faut que rien de moi ne lui reste obscur ou caché; il faut que je me tienne incessamment sous ses yeux, qu'il me suive dans tous les égaremens de mon coeur, dans tous les recoins de ma vie; qu'il ne me perde pas de vue un seul instant, de peur que, trouvant dans mon recit la moindre lacune, le moindre vide, et se demandant, qu'a-t-il fait durant ce tems-là, il ne m'accuse de n'avoir pas voulu tout dire. Je donne assés de prise à la malignité des hommes par mes récits sans lui en donner encore par mon silence."

34. Rousseau, *Oeuvres Complètes* 1:768, Rousseau's italics.

35. See Wildenstein, *Documents*, 41, doc. 352: "J'ai vu ce David si bête, si méchant, et si véritablement marqué du sceau de la réprobation. On n'est pas plus hideux et plus diaboliquement laid. S'il n'est pas pendu, il ne faut pas croire aux physionomies."

36. Thomas M. Kavanagh, *Writing the Truth: Authority and Desire in Rousseau* (Berkeley, Los Angeles, London: University of California Press, 1987), 24. See the whole of Kavanagh's chap. 2, "Writing from Afar." Compare the discussion of the Dialogues in Philippe Lejeune, "Autobiography in the Third Person," in Lejeune, *On Autobiography*, 48–51.

37. Rousseau, "Rousseau Juge de Jean Jaques," *Oeuvres complètes* 1:664–65: "Une autre difficulté me l'a rendu fatigant; c'étoit, forcé de parler de moi sans cesse, d'en parler avec justice et vérité, sans louange et sans dépression. Cela n'est pas difficile à un homme à qui le public rend l'honneur qui lui est dû: il est par là dispensé d'en prendre le soin lui-même. . . . Mais celui qui se sent digne d'honneur et d'estime et que le public défigure et diffame à plaisir, de quel ton se rendra-t-il seul la justice qui lui est due? . . . Un silence fier et dédaigneux est en pareil cas plus à sa place, et eut été bien plus de mon goût; mais il n'auroit pas rempli mon objet, et pour le remplir il falloit necessairement que je disse de quel oeil, si j'étois un autre, je verrois un homme tel que je suis." Compare the discussion of the concluding phrase in Kamuf, chap. 4, "Seeing through Rousseau," in Kamuf, *Signature Pieces*, esp. 100–102.

38. Rousseau, preamble to the Neuchâtel manuscript, *Oeuvres complètes* 1:1149: "J'ai résolu de faire faire à mes lecteurs un pas de plus dans la connoissance des hommes. . . . Je veux tâcher que pour apprendre à s'apprecier, on puisse avoir du moins une piéce de comparaison; que chacun puisse connoitre soi et un autre, et cet autre ce sera moi."

39. Paul de Man, "Anthropomorphism and Trope in the Lyric," in de Man, *The Rhetoric of Romanticism* (New York: Columbia University Press, 1984), 261.

40. Rousseau, Book Seven of the *Confessions*, *Oeuvres complètes* 1:278: "Je puis faire des omissions dans les faits, des transpositions, des erreurs de dates; mais je ne puis me tromper sur ce que j'ai senti, ni sur ce que mes sentimens m'ont fait faire; et voila de quoi principalement il s'agit. L'objet propre de mes confessions est de faire connoitre exactement mon interieur dans toutes les situations de ma vie. C'est

l'histoire de mon ame que j'ai promise, et pour l'écrire fidellement je n'ai pas besoin d'autres mémoires: il me suffit, comme j'ai fait jusqu'ici, de rentrer au dedans
de moi."

41. Rousseau, Book Five of the *Confessions*, *Oeuvres complètes* 1:222: "une
possession plus essencielle qui, sans tenir aux sens, au sexe, à l'âge, à la figure tenoit
à tout ce par quoi l'on est soi, et qu'on ne peut perdre qu'en cessant d'être." I am
aware of pushing at the literal sense here—the "essential possession" is on the face
of it Rousseau's love for Madame de Warens—towards the strange sense of the self's
lack of attributes which seems to me to haunt the *Confessions* as a whole. This opens
onto another and deeply unsettling aspect of Rousseau's version of autobiography:
the way it is designed, especially in the first six books, to keep the reader in suspense
as to the ultimate question: whether the self being narrated is "worth reading about,"
what it might be that makes a life presentable to others, whether what ultimately has
to be told about the self is its ordinariness, its featurelessness, its constant slide towards a state of next to nothing. This again is an aspect of Rousseau's writing that
has been massively repressed by most of his readers.

42. Paul de Man, "The Image of Rousseau in the Poetry of Hölderlin," in de
Man, *The Rhetoric of Romanticism*, 41. The whole essay is splendid. My next paragraph obviously depends on de Man at every point, and tries (a bit simple-mindedly)
to construe the implications of *Allegories of Reading* in the light of the Hölderlin
essay, the account of Rousseau in "Shelley Disfigured," *The Rhetoric of Romanticism*, 95ff, the disagreement with Derrida in "The Rhetoric of Blindness: Jacques
Derrida's Reading of Rousseau," in de Man, *Blindness and Insight: Essays in the
Rhetoric of Contemporary Criticism* (Minneapolis: University of Minnesota Press, 2d
edition, 1983), esp. 131ff, the remarks on allegory in *La Nouvelle Héloïse* in "The
Rhetoric of Temporality," *Blindness and Insight*, 200ff, and even the ending to the
earlier "Madame de Staël and Jean-Jacques Rousseau," in de Man, *Critical Writings, 1953–1978* (Minneapolis: University of Minnesota Press, 1989), esp. 178: "As
is indicated only too well by the critical history of *La Nouvelle Héloïse*, Rousseau's
apparent positivity risks masking the depth of negativity and renunciation from
which his oeuvre derives and at the price of which it could develop."

43. Henry Redhead Yorke, *France in eighteen hundred and two* (London, 1906),
123, quoted in Wildenstein, *Documents*, 119, doc. 1161.

44. David Hume, *A Treatise of Human Nature* (Oxford: Oxford University Press,
1978, first published 1739–40), 251–52.

45. Bonnet, *Essai de psychologie*, 115: "Si la Faculté de penser réside dans une
certaine Partie de notre Cerveau, il y a en nous autant de Moi qu'il y a de Points
dans cette Partie, qui peuvent devenir la siége d'une Perception. La Perception est
inséparable du sentiment de la Perception: une Perception qui n'est point apperçuë,
n'est point une Perception. Le sentiment d'une Perception n'est que l'Etre pensant
existant d'une certaine manière. Il y a donc en nous autant des Etres pensants qu'il
y a de Points qui apperçoivent. Mais nous n'appercevons pas seulement; nous vou-
lons, et le Vouloir est un mouvement qui s'excite dans un autre Point de l'Etenduë

pensante. Le Moi qui veut, n'est donc pas le Moi qui apperçoit. En vain, pour satisfaire à ce que nous sentons intérieurement, entreprendrons-nous de réunir les Perceptions et les Volitions en un Point: ce Point est un composé de Parties; et ces Parties sont essentiellement distinctes les unes des autres."

46. Bonnet, *Essai analytique*, xix: "Ces deux Objets que je vois distinctement agissent sur deux Points différens de mon *Sensorium*. . . . L'Etenduë matérielle ne compare donc pas; car le Point où tomberoit la comparaison seroit toûjours très distinct de ceux que les Objets comparés affecteroient. Il ne pourroit donc en résulter un Sentiment unique, un *Moi*." Bonnet even mounts in passing (p. 113), a kind of ordinary-language critique of what he takes to be the implication of the materialists' arguments, viz. that a thought must have speed, mass, and direction. "L'extrême dissonance de ces expressions n'est cependant pas ce qui fait ici la principale difficulté."

47. Rousseau, *Oeuvres complètes* 3 : 193: "Il y a une sort d'hommes qui comptent pour quelque chose les regards du reste de l'univers, qui savent être heureux et contens d'eux mêmes sur le témoignage d'autrui plûtôt que sur le leur propre. Telle est, en effet, la véritable cause de toutes ces différences: le Sauvage vit en lui-même; l'homme sociable toûjours hors de lui ne sait vivre que dans l'opinion des autres, et c'est, pour ainsi dire, de leur seul jugement qu'il tire le sentiment de sa propre existence."

48. Letter of 10 July 1766, in Ralph Leigh, ed., *Correspondance complète* 30 : 35–36. "Bientôt un violent remords me gagne; je m'indigne de moi-même. Enfin, dans un transport que je me rappelle encore avec délices, je m'élance à Son cou, je le Serre étroitcment; Suffoqué de Sanglots, inondé de larmes je m'écrie d'une voix entrecoupée: *Non non, David Hume n'est pas un traître; S'il n'etoit le meilleur des hommes, il faudroit qu'il en fut le plus noir*. David Hume me rend poliment mes embrassemens, et, tout en me frappant de petits coups Sur le dos me répete plusieurs fois d'un ton tranquille *Quoi, mon cher monsieur? Eh mon cher monsieur! Quoi donc, mon cher monsieur?* Il ne me dit rien de plus; je Sens que mon coeur se resserre; nous allons nous coucher, et je pars le lendemain pour la province." "Après le Soupé, gardant tous deux le Silence au coin de Son feu je m'aperçois qu'il me fixe, comme il lui arrivoit très Souvent, et d'une manière dont l'idée est difficile à rendre. Pour cette fois Son regard Sec ardent, moqueur et prolongé devint plus qu'inquiétant. Pour m'en débarrasser j'essaiai de le fixer à mon tour: mais en arrêtant mes yeux Sur les Siens je Sens un frémissement inexplicable, et bientot je Suis forcé de les baisser. La physionomie et le ton du bon David Sont d'un bon homme, mais où, grand Dieu, ce bon homme emprunte-t-il les yeux dont il fixe ses amis?" See the discussion in Starobinski, *Rousseau*, chap. 6, esp. 162–63.

49. Thomas Carlyle, *The French Revolution, A History* (London: Methuen and Co., 1902, first pub. 1837), 2 : 328.

50. De Man, *Allegories of Reading*, 173–74. Compare, among many other passages, 111–12 on Nietzsche.

51. See Arnauld Brejon de Lavergnée, Jacques Foucart, and Nicole Reynaud,

eds., *Catalogue Sommaire Illustré des Peintures du Musée du Louvre* 1, Inv. 1745. Exact dates for the Revolutionary confiscations are hard to come by. The Revolutionary armies later brought back several Rembrandt self-portraits as part of their loot from the Hague and Kassel: see Christopher Wright, *Rembrandt: Self-Portraits* (London: Gordon Fraser, 1982), 130.

52. The picture was in the Dundas sale of 1794. It had been engraved by Richard Collin in Brussels in 1682, and on several later occasions. See N. Maclaren, *National Gallery Catalogues: The Spanish School* (London, 2d ed. revised by Allan Braham, 1970), 71–74.

53. See Yseult Séverac, "Catalogue," 132, in Jacques Derrida, *Mémoires d'aveugle: L'autoportrait et autres ruines* (Paris: Réunion des musées nationaux, 1990).

54. Wildenstein, *Documents*, 72, doc. 677: "Socrate, habile sculpteur; Jean-Jacques, bon musicien; l'immortel Poussin, traçant sur la toile les plus sublimes leçons de la philosophie, sont autant de témoins qui prouvent que le génie des arts ne doit d'autre guide que le flambeau de la raison."

55. See J. L. Jules David, *Le Peintre Louis David* (Paris, 1880), 640. The picture was given to the Louvre by Isabey's son Eugène, whose letter of 3 Dec. 1852 is, along with Delafontaine, the basis of later identifications. See the dossier on the picture in the Louvre, Département des Peintures.

56. De Man, "Autobiography As De-Facement," in *The Rhetoric of Romanticism*, 70: "Autobiography, then, is not a genre or a mode, but a figure of reading or of understanding that occurs, to some degree, in all texts. The autobiographical moment happens as an alignment between the two subjects involved in the process of reading in which they determine each other by mutual reflexive substitution. . . . This specular structure is interiorized in a text in which the author declares himself the subject of his own understanding, but this merely makes explicit the wider claim to authorship that takes place whenever a text is stated to be *by* someone and assumed to be understandable to the extent that this is the case." One way of putting my question about David's picture would be to say that I am interested in whether it ends up being *by* someone—and understandable to the extent that this is the case.

57. De Man, *Allegories of Reading*, 60, n. 5.

58. Charles Taylor, "The person," in Michael Carrithers, Steven Collins, and Steven Lukes, eds., *The Category of the Person: Anthropology, philosophy, history* (Cambridge: Cambridge University Press, 1985), 277. Compare now Charles Taylor, *Sources of the Self: The Making of the Modern Identity* (Cambridge, MA: Harvard University Press, 1989).

59. Godfrey Lienhardt, "Self: public, private. Some African representations," in Carrithers, Collins, and Lukes, *The Category of the Person*, 150.

60. Gary Morson, "Who speaks for Bakhtin? A dialogic introduction," *Critical Inquiry* 10, 2 (Dec. 1983), 242. Morson is fully aware of the pitfalls here: this statement of Bakhtin's case is put in the mouth of one of two speakers, and is immediately

disputed by the other, who "sees no tragedy" and wants a Bakhtin of Vygotsky's "empirical and scientific" frame of mind.

61. Erving Goffman, *The Presentation of Self in Everyday Life* (New York: Doubleday, 1959), quoted in Martin Hollis, "Of Masks and Men," in Carrithers, Collins, and Lukes, *The Category of the Person*, 227.

62. Rousseau, "Profession de foi," *Oeuvres complètes* 4:569. One main purpose of de Man's chapter on the *Profession* is to demonstrate how the text in practice cannot (or anyway does not) sustain the opposition of inner and outer on which its epistemology ostensibly depends.

63. Hemsterhuis, *Lettre sur l'homme*, 254–55: "L'âme, pour se rappeler les idées, met en mouvement les dernières fibres de l'organe qui sont tournées de son côté. . . . Je ne sais si vous pouvez dire que l'âme soit dans le corps, ni de quel côté elle est."

64. It strikes me that Philippe Lejeune's genial essay, "Looking at the Self-Portrait," in Lejeune, *On Autobiography*, gets a little bogged down in this question of criteria for classification.

65. See Jules David, *Le Peintre Louis David*, 8.

66. See Louis de Fourcaud, *François Rude* (Paris: Librairie Georges Baranger, 1904), 449–50 and 456–57.

67. See Wildenstein, *Documents*, 85, doc. 796: "La difformité de ses traits et une certaine rudesse de manières ne prévenaient pas en sa faveur; mais, dans l'intimité, il avait de la simplicité et de la bonhomie."

68. E. J. Delécluze, *Louis David, son école et son temps* (Paris: Éditions Macula, 1983, first published 1855), 29: "Bien plus, maigré le gonflement d'une de ses joues qui le défigurait, et quoique son regard eût quelque chose d'un peu dur."

69. Wildenstein, *Documents*, 136, doc. 1232.

70. Ibid., 112, doc. 1119: Montjoie's booklet was entitled *Histoire de la Conjuration de Maximilien Robespierre*.

71. Wildenstein, *Documents*, 116, doc. 1143: "On m'appelle un homme dur et féroce. Ils ne me connaissent pas comme vous, à qui je parlais à coeur ouvert. On aura confondu la figure toujours pensive de l'artiste avec le masque hideux du conspirateur."

72. Ibid., 123, doc. 1190: "C'est en vain que vous vous enveloppez des ténèbres; je porterai la lumière dans les replis les plus cachés de votre coeur, je découvrirai les ressorts secrets qui vous font mouvoir, et j'imprimerai sur vos fronts le caractère hideux des passions qui vous agitent." This document is a public refutation of the charges against him, addressed to the Section du Muséum. The one quoted previously is a private letter sent from prison.

73. Rousseau, *Oeuvres complètes* 2:291–92: "Passons au Peintre d'avoir omis quelques beautés; mais en quoi il n'a pas fait moins de tort à ton visage, c'est d'avoir omis les défauts. Il n'a point fait cette tache presque imperceptible que tu as sous l'oeil droit, [et que tu fis dit-on d'un canif dans ton enfance en désarmant étourdi-

ment ton cousin qui feignait de s'en vouloir blesser,] ni celle qui est au cou du côté gauche. Il n'a point mis . . . ô Dieux, cet homme étoit-il de bronze? . . . Il a oublié la petite cicatrice qui t'est restée sous la levre. Il t'a fait les cheveux et les sourcils de la même couleur, ce qui n'est pas: les sourcis sont plus châtains, et les cheveux plus cendrés. . . . Il a fait le bas du visage exactement ovale. Il n'a pas remarqué cette légere sinuosité qui séparant le menton des joues, rend leur contour moins régulier et plus gracieux." The phrase in parentheses comes from Rousseau's *Brouillons*. It was the note on the "portrait" in Rousseau on p. 164 of de Man's *Allegories of Reading* that first sent me in the direction of Saint-Preux's letters.

74. David on Cardinal Caprara in the *Sacre*; see Wildenstein, *Documents*, 174, doc. 1501.

75. Neil Hertz, "Lurid Figures," in Lindsay Waters and Wlad Godzich, eds., *Reading de Man Reading* (Minneapolis: University of Minnesota Press, 1989), 102.

76. This goes back to Isabey: "Ce portrait n'est qu'une ébauche, mais il donne une idée exacte de la facilité que David avait à peindre." See dossier, Louvre, Département des Peintures.

77. See Georges Wildenstein, *Ingres* (London: Phaidon Press, 1954), 162–63. There is a discussion of the two states of the picture, reaching very different conclusions, in Pascal Bonafoux, *Les peintres et l'autoportrait* (Geneva: Albert Skira, 1984), 96–97.

78. See the entry on the picture in *Prag um 1600: Kunst und Kultur am Hofe Kaiser Rudolfs II* (Vienna: Kunsthistorische Museum, 1988), 1:236–37.

79. In response to a version of this essay given at Johns Hopkins. (I could not see any one place in my text—though no doubt some readers will see many—where I was sure my argument specifically intersected with Michael Fried's on Courbet as self-portraitist, now available in Fried, *Courbet's Realism* [Chicago and London: University of Chicago Press, 1990], but I am certain Fried's treatment of the subject—his sense of the issues at stake in self-portraiture at this moment in French painting—influenced mine in all kinds of ways. At least I hope so.)

80. Priestley, *Disquisitions on Matter and Spirit*, 88.

81. See *The Age of Correggio and the Carracci: Emilian Painting of the Sixteenth and Seventeenth Centuries* (Washington, D.C.: National Gallery of Art, 1986), 275, catalogue entry by Donald Posner.

82. Roberto Zapperi, "Selbstbildnis und Autobiographie. Über ein Gemälde von Annibale Carracci," *Idea. Jahrbuch der Hamburger Kunsthalle*, no. 5 (1986); Roberto Zapperi, "I Ritratti di Antonio Carracci," *Paragone Arte*, no. 449 (July 1987), esp. 15–17; Roberto Zapperi, *Annibale Carracci: Ritratto di artista da giovane* (Turin: Giulio Einaudi, 1989), esp. chap. 5 [French translation, *Annibale Carracci: Portrait de l'Artiste en Jeune Homme* (Aix-en-Provence: Éditions Alinea, 1990)].

83. For instance Posner, *The Age of Correggio*, 275. Zapperi, being an historian,

wins the battle of the documents, and the connoisseurs do not speak with any unanimity against his dating. But any conclusion is touch and go.

84. Zapperi, "Selbstbildnis," 27: "Die antagonistische Haltung, die eine jede der vier Figuren den anderen drei Figuren gegenüber einnimmt, unterbricht die Dauer und bringt eine irreparable Diskontinuität ins Spiel." This reading is expanded in the later book, and connected more closely to Zapperi's reconstruction of the Carracci family history.

CROW: The Patriarch in Davidian Painting

1. The point was demonstrated first in E. Wind, "The Sources of David's Horaces," *Journal of the Warburg and Courtauld Institutes* 4 (1940), 124–38.

2. Dionysius of Halicarnassus, *The Roman Antiquities*, trans. E. Cary and E. Spelman (Cambridge, Mass.: Loeb Classical Library, 1961), 2:66–67.

3. Corneille, *Horace*, Act 2, Scene 3. The relationship of David's *Horatii* to Corneille, taken as fundamental in the nineteenth century, has long since been relegated to secondary importance in the modern literature. But we underestimate the literary culture of the artist and a significant part of his audience if we ignore it. By no means every viewer in the 1780s was thoroughly versed in Corneille and the ancient historians of early Rome, but many of the educated members of his audience would have been, and that group included the politically dissenting publicists of the 1780s—and future Revolutionary leaders—who came to see the Davidian project as at one with their own. It is against the ground provided by Corneille most of all that his iconographic choices would have been read as deliberate and distinct. On the currency of Corneille's drama in the period and the ideological resonance of his style, see T. Crow, "The Construction of Patriotism in Pre-Revolutionary French Art," *French Politics and Society* (summer 1989), 14–29.

4. See R. Rosenblum, "Gavin Hamilton's *Brutus* and its Aftermath," *Burlington Magazine* 103 (Jan. 1961), 8–16.

5. Plutarch, *The Lives of the Noble Grecians and Romans*, trans. John Dryden and rev. Arthur Hugh Clough (New York: Modern Library, n.d.), 120.

6. Ibid., 519.

7. Ibid., 522.

8. Ibid., 142; J.-F. Marmontel, *Oeuvres complètes* (Geneva, 1968), 3:221–25.

9. Lille, Musée des Beaux-Arts, pl. 1323: "Ne changez rien. Voila le bon."

10. For an early compendium of recollections of the younger Drouais's life, see J.-B.-A. Suard, "Eloge de M. Drouais, élève de l'Académie royale de peinture," *Mélanges de la littérature* (Paris: 1806), 3:273–84.

11. Ibid., 280.

12. See P. Chaussard, "Notice historique sur M. Drouais, Elève de l'Académie Royale de Peinture," *Le Pausanias Français, Etat des arts du dessin en France, à l'ouverture du XIXᵉ siècle, Salon de 1806*, (Paris, 1806), 337–53.

13. The story is most probably apocryphal: see the remarks of Bruno Chenique in "Géricault: Une Vie," his admirably complete and judicious chronology included in Régis Michel and Sylvain Laveissière, *Géricault* (Paris: Réunion des Musées Nationaux, 1991), 1:281–82. The attachment of the story to Géricault's myth is most likely a reappearance of a topos originally associated with Drouais and a feature of the continuing cult surrounding the latter during the first decades of the nineteenth century.

14. The restored canvas is in Le Mans, Musée de Tessé; on the mutilation of the canvas, see David, manuscript autobiography, in D. and G. Wildenstein, eds., *Documents complementaires au catalogue de l'oeuvre de Louis David* (Paris, 1973), 157.

15. Ibid.

16. For an excellent discussion of the cult of Winckelmann in France, see Edouard Pommier, "Winckelmann et la vision de l'antiquité dans la France des Lumières et de la Révolution," *Revue de l'Art* 83 (1989), 9–20.

17. Johann-Joachim Winckelmann, *L'histoire de l'art dans l'Antiquité*, trans. M. Huber (Leipzig, 1781), 2:342.

18. See, for example, *L'Ami des Artistes au Salon par M. L'A.R.*, (Paris, 1787), 10–11, 16; *Sur la Peinture. Ouvrage succinct qui peut éclairer les artistes sur la fin originelle de l'art et aider les citoyens dans l'idée qu'ils doivent se faire de son état actuel en France*, (The Hague, 1782), 66–67.

19. *Mémoires secrets* 26 (27 Aug. 1784): "Quoique tous ces tableaux soient en général bien fait, un d'eux a paru l'emporter infiniment sur les autres et être au-dessus de toute concurrence. . . . L'auteur de ce tâbleau si vanté et si digne d'être est M. Drouais. . . . Il n'a que vingt ans, il jouit déjà de 20 mille livres de rentes et ce n'est que par une passion pour son talent et par l'amour de la gloire qu'il travaille. Il ne peut qu'aller très loin avec ce noble aiguillon et les heureuses dispositions dont la nature l'a doué."

20. See J.-G. Wille, *Mémoires et journal*, ed. G. Duplessis (Paris, 1957), 2:103.

21. "Lettre aux auteurs du Journal de Paris au sujet de cette distribution," n.d. [1784], manuscript copy in Collection Deloynes, Bibliothèque Nationale, Paris, no. 319, pp. 6–7.

22. For a summary of press accounts of the prize-giving and discussion of the *agrément*, see R. Michel, "Jean-Germain Drouais et Rome," in Académie de France à Rome, *David et Rome* (Rome, 1981), 201; also Musée des Beaux-Arts de Rennes, *Jean-Germain Drouais* (Rennes, 1985), 42.

23. *Mémoires secrets* 26 (31 Aug. 1784): "On réclame les règles et les usages; on manqua, par une soumission servile à ces usages, à ces règles, à donner un grand exemple aux Artistes, et un grand sujet d'émulation aux Elèves."

24. See "Règlements qui doivent être observés par les pensionnaires de l'Académie de France à Rome d'après les ordres de Monsieur le Directeur général," *Corre-*

spondance des directeurs de l'Académie de France à Rome, A. de Montaiglon and J. Guiffey, eds. (Paris, 1904), 13:158.

25. Jean Locquin, *La peinture d'histoire en France de 1747 à 1785* (Paris, 1912), 113: "L'art est intimement lié à la vertu, et la vertu ne s'acquiert, pense-t-on, que sous la férule."

26. See the lesser known of David's two manuscript autobiographies, reproduced in Philippe Bordes, *Le Serment de Jeu de Paume de Jacques-Louis David: Le peintre, son milieu et son temps de 1789 à 1792* (Paris: Réunion des musées nationaux, 1983), 174.

27. See A. Péron's resumé of the recollections of David's pupil J. B. Debret, who accompanied his master to Rome, *Examen du Tableau du Serment des Horaces peint par David, suivi d'une Notice historique du tableau, lus à la Société des Beaux-Arts* (Paris, 1838), 33ff.

28. *Correspondance des directeurs,* xv (24 Oct. 1785), p. 50.

29. Ibid. 15 (6 Sept. 1786), 101: "Le s^r Drouais demande si, en place de la copie qu'il est obligé de faire pour le Roi, vous voulez qu'il fasse un tableau original, qui apartiendra au Roi et qui serait le fruit de toutes ses études de Rome, car il m'a avoué qu'il n'avait jamais copié de sa vie et que c'etait pour lui une martire que copier toute autre chose que la nature."

30. Ibid: "Ce n'a pas toujours été ceux qui ont fait les plus belles académies qui, ensuite, ont fait les plus belles tableaux."

31. Ibid. (26 Sept. 1785), 105–6: "On ne peut voir sans peine aujourd'hui que la jeunesse, plus confiante que jamais, semble annoncer qu'elle en sait davantage sur les moyens d'acquérir les talents qu'en savaient les hommes les plus célèbres qui l'ont précédée. . . . Ces Messieurs doivent se persuader qu'ils ne sont pas les maîtres, que, loin d'être en état de voler de leurs propres ailes, ils ont encore besoin d'étudier et qu'ils ne peuvent mieux faire, malgré leur répugnance, que de suivre les règles qui ont été établies avec pleine connaissance de cause. Si, parmi eux, quelques-uns trouvent trop dur de s'y conformer, ils sont les maîtres de quitter l'Académie. Je trouverai facilement moyen de les remplacer."

32. Ibid. (26 July, 21 Sept., 11 and 30 Oct. 1786), 95, 104, 110–11, 115; see also Drouais's letter to David in J.-L.-J. David, *Le peintre Louis David, 1748–1825: souvenirs et documents inédits* (Paris, 1880), 38–40.

33. See *Mercure de France,* 7 June 1788, 40: "J'ai perdu mon émulation."

34. *Correspondance des directeurs* 15 (12 Apr. 1786), 84.

35. David, *Le peintre Louis David,* 44–45: "J'en ai trouvé beaucoup de beaux, mais les uns sont des sujets que vous avez faits. D'un côté, je ne dois pas et n'aurais garde pour mon honneur de faire un sujet que vous devez faire, et si j'en fais un qui ait de l'analogie avec ce que vous avez fait, on se moquera de moi . . . Dites-moi, que dois-je faire? Les plus beaux sujets, quoique difficiles, me chatouillent autant de vous."

36. *Procès-Verbaux de l'Academie Royale de peintre et de sculpture (1648–1792)*, A. de Montaiglon, ed. (Paris, 1875–1892), 9: 334 (28 Jan. 1787), "d'une composition simple et noble, d'un bon style, d'un pinceau ferme, et de l'expression dans la tête de Marius et du Soldat qui veut assassiner." Though the proviso was added, "Enfin le Sʳ Drouais, Drouais, marquent les talents non équivoques, doit être invité de voler de ses propres ailes." On the last point, see Pierre's comment noted below.

37. The success of the painting on its return to the Paris Academy prompted a waspish observation by the First Painter Pierre in a letter to d'Angiviller: "David . . . a déjà mandé à son élève de se faire une manière plus éloigné de la sienne, et il a raison, car si M. Drouais mont toujours en suivant le faire, il dépassera dans ce même faire son instituteur; et puis la guerre allumé! M. Furcy-Raynaud, "Correspondance de M. d'Angiviller avec Pierre," *Nouvelles Archives de l'art Français* (1906), 194–95. On the crowds at its exhibition, see also David's recollection in his unfinished autobiography (Wildenstein, *Documents*, 158).

38. *The Papers of Thomas Jefferson*, ed. J. P. Boyd (Princeton, 1955), 11:187.

GOLDSTEIN: Saying "I"

1. The phrase was coined in the 1780s by the surgeon and formulator of enlightened health policy Jacques Tenon. See Michel Foucault et al., *Les machines à guérir (aux origines de l'hôpital moderne)* (Paris: Institut de l'environnement, 1976), first page of preface (n.p.) and 55 n.1.

2. "Observations des maîtres-gantiers," Bibliothèque Nationale, Paris: MS collection Joly de Fleury 596, fol. 114. The original reads, "chaque particulier n'a d'existence que celle du corps, auquel il est attaché."

3. For examples of the rhetoric of sensationalist psychology employed in the revolutionary festivals, see Mona Ozouf, *La fête révolutionnaire* (Paris: Gallimard, 1976), 241–45. For similar rhetoric in the justification of the revolutionary calendar, see the report of Philippe Fabre d'Eglantine to the Convention on 24 Oct. 1794, in J. Guillaume, ed., *Procès-verbaux du Comité d'instruction publique de la Convention nationale*, 7 vols. (Paris: Imprimerie Nationale, 1891–1959), 2:697–706, esp. 699. For its use in the renaming of Paris streets, see the report of the Abbé Henri Grégoire, *Système de dénominations topographiques pour les places, rues, quais, etc. de toutes les communes de la République* (Paris, 1794), 10.

4. For the vestibule metaphor, see Victor Cousin, *Introduction à l'histoire de la philosophie* (Paris: Pichon & Didier, 1828), Lesson 13, p. 14.

5. Sorbonne MS 1907, p. 5; the manuscript is a bound notebook of notes taken on Cousin's course of 11 Dec. 1819–18 Mar. 1820 by the student Louis de Raynal. The material on p. 5 is apparently not part of the course but is presented by Raynal as a quotation from Cousin.

6. See Archives Nationales, Paris: F17*1795, "Procès-verbaux des délibérations

du Conseil royal de l'instruction publique" (July–Sept. 1832), Session of 28 Sept., fols. 434–36.

7. See Gatien Arnoult, *Cours de lectures philosophiques, ou dissertations et fragmens sur les principales questions de philosophie élémentaire* (Paris and Toulouse: J.-B. Paya, 1838), 81 n. 1, where the author reproduces some personal notes written down upon leaving his class one day in 1828.

8. Ibid., my italics.

9. François Guizot, *Historical Essays and Lectures*, ed. Stanley Mellon (Chicago: University of Chicago Press, 1972), 210, editor's note.

10. François Guizot, article "Abrégé," in *Encyclopédie progressive* (Paris, 1826), 311–13.

11. See Pierre-Jean-Georges Cabanis, *Rapports du physique et du moral de l'homme* (1802), Memoir 5, "De l'influence des sexes sur le caractère des idées et des affections morales," in *Oeuvres philosophiques de Cabanis*, ed. Claude Lehec and Jean Cazeneuve, 2 vols. (Paris: Presses universitaires de France, 1956), 1:272–315.

12. The manuscript letters are located at the Bibliothèque Victor Cousin in Paris; see vol. 214 of the Cousin correspondence.

13. She is quite self-conscious about this reticence. As she tells Cousin in her letter of 30 Sept. 1828, she finds it fitting (*convenable*) to "speak to you not at all about myself," but she nonetheless feels a need to assure him that her impulse to write to him comes from herself alone.

14. Léon Séché, *Les amitiés de Lamartine*, 1st ser., 2d ed. (Paris: Mercure de France, 1911), 177–78, 237–40. Séché learned of the existence of Mme Angebert in the course of his research on Lamartine; see 174–75.

15. See Cousin, *Introduction à l'histoire de la philosophie*. The volume, which includes *Cours de philosophie* on the title page, is a compendium of the lessons published individually by the Paris printer Rignoux and lacks consecutive pagination. On the earlier exclusive use of the stenographic technique for political purposes, see Anne Martin-Fugier, *La vie élégante, ou la formation du Tout-Paris, 1815–1848* (Paris: Fayard, 1990), 244. Martin-Fugier notes that the technique was also employed in 1828 for the Sorbonne courses of Guizot and Villemain who, like Cousin, were leaders of the liberal opposition prevented from teaching during the earlier part of the decade.

16. Cousin to Hegel, 15 Aug. 1828, in G. W. F. Hegel, *Correspondance*, trans. from the German by Jean Carrère, vol. 3 (Paris: Gallimard, 1967), 203. The letter was written just after the conclusion of the lecture series.

17. Cousin, *Introduction à l'histoire de la philosophie*, Lesson 8, 12 June 1828, p. 19.

18. Caroline Angebert, Letter of 30 Sept. 1828, Cousin correspondence, vol. 214.

19. Ibid., Letter of 8 Apr. 1829.

20. Ibid., Letter of 22 Aug. 1830.

21. See the undated letter quoted in Séché, *Amitiés de Lamartine*, 187–88. In fact, Cousin would seem in this letter to have granted all the contested points to Angebert. "Gallantry apart, how would I have refused to women the power to know, I who assert that every being endowed with consciousness knows at one and the same time himself, God, and the world; and that each instance of consciousness already contains within it the most sublime conceptions to which reflection will later be able to rise by the means appropriate to it? Woman, like man, is endowed with consciousness; like him she has an intelligence capable of attaining all truths and a free will capable of enacting all virtues."

22. Caroline Angebert, Letter of 12 Oct. 1828, Cousin correspondence, vol. 214.

23. Ibid., Letter of 21 Jan. 1830.   24. Ibid., Letter of 26 Apr. 1830.

25. Ibid., Letter of 22 Aug. 1830.   26. Ibid.

27. Ibid. Angebert indicates that the argument she is disputing is the one put forth by Cousin in Lesson 7 (5 June) of his 1828 *Introduction à l'histoire de la philosophie*; see pp. 31–32 of that text for the passages to which she is referring.

28. Caroline Angebert, Letter of 22 Aug. 1830, in Cousin correspondence, vol. 214.

29. Cousin, *Introduction à l'histoire de la philosophie*, Lesson 7, p. 32.

30. Caroline Angebert, Letter of 12 Nov. 1829, in Cousin correspondence, vol. 214.

31. Ibid., Letter of 21 Jan. 1830. In the same letter she thanks him for "having called me back to the plan [of study] that I must follow," observing that "one needs, *a woman especially*, to be approved and sustained in one's resolutions or else one doubts oneself and the reed bends in every wind." My italics.

32. Ibid., Letter of 22 Aug. 1830. This portion of the letter reads: "Where science and profound ideas are concerned, women are, you know, treated a little like children; and you also know that I do not mean this as a joke. Treat me then as a male pupil (*en écolier*) rather than as a female pupil (*en écolière*)." She goes on to use language with unmistakably masochistic connotations: "I want to be beaten (*battue*); I want it, all the while fearing it, if I deserve it because I need the truth. I also need to learn from you where I am and what I am capable of."

33. Michel Foucault, *The History of Sexuality, Volume I: An Introduction*, trans. Robert Hurley (New York: Vintage, 1980), pt. 3, esp. p. 60.

34. The three stories are "Le vieil égoiste" (1838), "Un legs" (1842), and "Soeur Louise" (1858); all can be found in *Oeuvres dunkerquoises*, ed. Benjamin Kien, 4 vols. (Dunkerque: C. Drouillard, 1853–59), the first two in vol. 1, 97–118, 260–80, the last in vol. 4, 113–32. My direct quotations from "Le vieil égoiste" are from 97, 103, 106, 108–9.

35. V. Cousin, "Les femmes illustres du dix-septième siècle," *Revue des deux mondes*, 15 Jan. 1844, 193–203, esp. 194–95. This article was reprinted as the opening of Cousin's *Jacqueline Pascal* (Paris: Didier, 1845).

36. For this assessment of the nineteenth-century *classe de philosophie*, see Jean-Louis Fabiani, *Les philosophes de la république* (Paris: Minuit, 1988), 10.

37. A. Blanchet, "De l'enseignement de la philosophie dans les lycées," *Revue internationale de l'enseignement* 2 (July–Dec. 1881), 436–50, esp. 438.

38. Henri Marion, "Le nouveau programme de philosophie," *Revue philosophique* 10 (1880), 414–28, esp. 416.

39. Commission relative à l'enseignement secondaire des jeunes filles, Archives Nationales, Paris: C3279, dossier 1379 (a small unpaginated notebook), Meeting of 19 Feb. [1879]. I learned of the existence of this source in Françoise Mayeur, *L'enseignement secondaire des jeunes filles sous la Troisième République* (Paris: Presses de la Fondation nationale des sciences politiques, 1977).

40. Ibid. This generally-accepted point about the purpose of the lycées for girls was made in the present context by Sée and Duvaux, who also suggested that courses in "hygiene" and "domestic economy" would underscore the educators' intentions.

41. See Steven C. Hause with Anne R. Kenney, *Women's Suffrage and Social Politics in the French Third Republic* (Princeton, NJ: Princeton University Press, 1984), 13–14, 16, 60.

42. For the text of this 1882 *programme*, see Camille Sée, ed., *Lycées et collèges de jeunes filles: Documents, rapports et discours* (Paris: L. Cerf, 1884), 488–89.

43. The new psychology program figures as an appendix in Marion, "Nouveau programme"; see esp. 427.

44. Ibid., 422–23, 423 for the quotation. That the new *programme* freed the discipline of psychology from metaphysics is also the contention of Blanchet, "Enseignement de la philosophie," 440–41.

45. Emile Beaussire, "L'Enseignement de la philosophie avant les nouveaux programmes," *Revue internationale de l'enseignement* 3 (Jan.–June 1882): 59–65, quotation on 65.

46. Mme Louise Dauriat, "Discours d'ouverture du cours de droit social des femmes prononcé au Ranelagh, en séance publique, le 29 mai 1836" (Imprimerie de Beaulé & Jubin, n.d.), 8. Dauriat's main target is the literary critic and Sorbonne professor Saint-Marc Girardin, whom she allusively likens to Cousin.

47. Michèle Le Doeuff, "Ants and Women, or Philosophy without Borders," in A. Phillips Griffiths, ed., *Contemporary French Philosophy* (New York: Cambridge University Press, 1987), 41–54, esp. 41–42, 46.

48. The entire poem, "A Dunkerque: Adieu," is printed in Séché, *Amitiés de Lamartine*, 228–30; the quotation comes from 228; my italics.

ROTH: Freud's Use and Abuse of the Past

1. Michael S. Roth, *Psycho-Analysis as History: Negation and Freedom in Freud* (Ithaca, NY, 1987).

2. Sigmund Freud and Josef Breuer, *Studies on Hysteria*, in *The Standard Edi-*

tion of the Complete Psychological Works of Sigmund Freud, trans. and ed. James Strachey, 24 vols. (London 1953–74), 2:8.

3. Ibid., 11. The passage appears in italics in the *Standard Edition.*

4. Ibid., 133–34, 173.

5. For a detailed account of Freud's complex motivations for abandoning the seduction theory, see William McGrath, *Freud's Discovery of Psychoanalysis: The Politics of Hysteria* (Ithaca, NY, 1986), chaps. 4–6.

6. *Five Lectures on Psycho-Analysis, Standard Edition* 11:16.

7. Ibid., 16–17.

8. Ibid., 17. Freud had briefly discussed Anna O.'s case in this first lecture at Clark. See also *Studies on Hysteria, Standard Edition* 2:21–47.

9. *The Complete Letters of Sigmund Freud to Wilhelm Fliess, 1887–1904,* trans. and ed. Jeffrey Moussaieff Masson (Cambridge, MA, 1985), 201. Originals are published in *Sigmund Freud Briefe an Wilhelm Fliess 1887–1904: Ungekürzte Ausgabe,* ed. J. M. Masson (Frankfurt: S. Fischer Verlag, 1985).

10. Ibid., 195. See also Peter Gay, *Freud: A Life for Our Time* (New York, 1988), 88.

11. Masson, *Freud to Fliess,* 202. The last sentence in the original reads: "Ich habe nun ein recht entwurzeltes Gefühl."

12. Ibid., 202.

13. Freud, *The Interpretation of Dreams, Standard Edition* 4:216.

14. These were, Freud reported to Fliess, "some of the things that were said" about his early "incursion" into psychiatry. Masson, *Freud to Fliess,* Nov. 2, 1896, 202.

15. Freud, *Interpretation of Dreams,* 317–18.

16. The letters to Fliess are full of references to Freud's physical and mental problems. See also Max Schur, *Freud: Living and Dying* (New York, 1972), 71–73, 97–110.

17. Freud, "Draft N," May 31, 1897, Masson, *Freud to Fliess,* 250.

18. Ibid., 272 (Oct. 15, 1897).

19. Ibid., 265–66 (Sept. 21, 1897).

20. Ibid.

21. Freud, *Interpretation of Dreams,* xxvi.

22. Masson, *Freud to Fliess,* 99. On the same page he writes the following: "The affect corresponding to melancholia is that of mourning or—that is, longing for something lost."

23. On Freud's suspicions about his own approaching death, see Ernest Jones, *The Life and Work of Sigmund Freud* (New York, 1955), 194; Schur, *Freud: Living and Dying,* 185–89, 231–33. These sources also discuss his anxiety about his two soldier sons. Both would survive the fighting, but his youngest daughter Sophie fell to influenza in January 1920. The death of her younger son, Heinele, in 1923 completely stunned Freud: "I am taking this loss so badly, I believe that I have never

experienced anything harder." See Gay, *Freud*, 421–22. On World War I, see "Thoughts for the Time on War and Death" (1915), *Standard Edition* 14:275–300, and Introductory Lectures on Psycho-Analysis, *Standard Edition* 15:146. On the war and mourning, see the brief "On Transience," *Standard Edition* 15:305–7.

24. Freud, "Mourning and Melancholia," *Standard Edition* 14:243. Subsequent references to the essay will be given in brackets in the text.

25. See Julia Kristeva, *Soleil Noir: Dépression et Mélancolie* (Paris, 1988), especially 13–41; and Eric L. Santner, *Stranded Objects: Mourning, Memory and Film in Postwar Germany* (Ithaca, NY, 1990), especially 1–13.

26. The essay first appeared in the *American Historical Review* 78:328–47. The page references in the text refer to the republication in Carl E. Schorske, *Fin-de-siècle Vienna: Politics and Culture* (New York, 1980), 181–207.

27. Ibid., 183.

28. Ibid., 202.

29. Ibid., 203.

SEIGEL: The Subjectivity of Structure

1. Claude Lévi-Strauss, *Tristes tropiques* (Paris, 1955), 496–97; English ed., trans. John Russel, sometimes published with the French title and sometimes as *A World on the Wane* (London and New York, 1961), 397–98. (Below I cite this work as *TT*, referring to the original French text except where the English version is specifically indicated.)

2. *TT*, 50; Eng. ed. 62.

3. Claude Lévi-Strauss, *The Savage Mind*, trans. of Lévi-Strauss, *La pensée sauvage* (Chicago, 1966), 249, 252, 256.

4. Claude Lévi-Strauss, *The Naked Man: Introduction to a Science of Mythology: iv*, trans. John and Doreen Weightman (London 1981; orig. Fr. ed. 1971), 625–26, 687.

5. Clifford Geertz, "The Cerebral Savage: On the Work of Claude Lévi-Strauss," in *The Interpretation of Cultures* (New York, 1973), 346.

6. *TT*, 44, 51.

7. Claude Lévi-Strauss, "French Sociology," in *Twentieth-Century Sociology*, ed. Georges Gurvitch and Wilbert E. Moore (New York, 1945), 530. Lévi-Strauss did not share Lucien Lévy-Bruhl's rejection of Durkheim, but recognized that Durkheim's own position laid the ground for Lévy-Bruhl's equally one-sided inversion of it.

8. *TT*, 339, 331; Eng. ed. 310, 303.

9. Lévi-Strauss, *The Savage Mind*, 214.

10. "Claude Lévi-Strauss Reconsiders," interview with Jean-Marie Benoist, *Encounter*, 1979, 26.

11. Claude Lévi-Strauss, *Totemism*, trans. Rodney Needham (London, 1969;

orig. ed. 1962). Quotes in regard to Bergson are on 170–71, and in regard to Rousseau, 176 of the Penguin edition.

12. Claude Lévi-Strauss, *Introduction to the Work of Marcel Mauss*, trans. Felicity Baker (London, 1987), 28–33.

13. *TT*, Eng. ed., 58.

14. *TT*, 29–30.

15. *TT*, 453–57; Eng. ed., 376–80.

16. Claude Lévi-Strauss and Didier Eribon, *De près et de loin* (Paris, 1988), 24, 26.

17. Claude Lévi-Strauss, *Les structures elementaires de la parenté* (Paris, 1949). Translated into English as *The Elementary Structures of Kinship* (from the revised edition, 1967) by James Harle Bell, John Richard von Sturmer, and Rodney Needham (Boston, 1969).

18. Ibid., 145–46.

19. Lévi-Strauss, *Naked Man*, 624; *The Raw and the Cooked: Introduction to a Science of Mythology: I*, trans. John and Doreen Weightman (New York, 1969), 63.

20. Lévi-Strauss, *The Raw and the Cooked*, 1, 10.

21. Lévi-Strauss, *Naked Man*, 693.

22. Lévi-Strauss, *The Raw and the Cooked*, 6, 12; *Naked Man*, 563.

23. For the personal pronouns, English readers are referred to the translators' notes in *Naked Man*, 625 and 630.

24. For his negative views of 1968, especially in terms of the attitudes toward education and culture represented by the radicals, see Lévi-Strauss and Eribon, *De près et de loin*, 116.

25. See Roger Caillois, "Illusions à rebours," *La nouvelle nouvelle revue française* 2 (Dec. 1954), and 3 (Jan. 1955), and Lévi-Strauss, "Diogène couché," in *Les temps modernes*, 1955. For a restatement of Caillois's thesis, with much interesting material, see Sergio Moravia, *La ragione nascosta* (Florence, 1969), esp. chap. 1.

26. Claude Lévi-Strauss, "Race and Culture," in Lévi-Strauss, *The View from Afar*, trans. Joachim Neugroschel and Phoebe Hess (New York, 1985), 23–24. For Lévi-Strauss's account of the surprise and opposition provoked by his talk, see his preface to the same volume, xii–xv.

27. Claude Lévi-Strauss, "A Belated Word About the Creative Child," in Lévi-Strauss, *View*, 271–74.

28. Lévi-Strauss and Eribon, *De près et de loin*, 129.

29. Claude Lévi-Strauss, "The Structural Study of Myth," in Lévi-Strauss, *Structural Anthropology* I, trans. C. Jacobson and B. C. Schoepf (New York, 1963), 214–16.

30. Claude Lévi-Strauss, *La potière jalouse* (Paris, 1985), 259–63; *Myth and Meaning* (New York, 1979), 24ff.

31. Lévi-Strauss was particularly aware of this dilemma in regard to the structuralist analysis of literary works. In a 1965 article originally published in the Italian

journal *Paragone*, he declared that a structuralist analysis of literature will always run the danger of seeming to be a play of mirrors, "wherein it becomes impossible to distinguish the object from its symbolic reverberation in the consciousness of the subject. The work studied and the analyzer's thoughts reflect themselves in each other, and we are denied any means of discerning what is simply received from the former and what the latter puts there." Quoted by James A. Boon in *From Symbolism to Structuralism: Levi-Strauss in a Literary Tradition* (New York, 1972), 55. For Boon's awareness also of the general problem of seriousness in Lévi-Strauss's work, see 36.

32. Lévi-Strauss, *View*, 184.

33. *TT*, Eng. ed., 58, and Lévi-Strauss, "Diogène couché," 1217.

34. Lévi-Strauss, *View*, 177–78; cf. the table of "binary operators," in Lévi-Strauss, *Naked Man*, 559.

35. Lévi-Strauss, *The Raw and the Cooked*, 14ff.

36. Ibid., 233–34.

37. Lévi-Strauss and Eribon, *De près et de loin*, 54.

38. For some further meditations on this theme, see my discussion of "La mort du sujet: origines d'un thème," *Le débat* 58 (Jan.–Feb. 1990), 160–69.

BOURDIEU: A Reflecting Story

1. W. Faulkner, "A Rose for Emily," in Faulkner, *The Collected Stories* (Harmondsworth: Penguin Books, 1985), 119.

2. M. Perry, *Literary Dynamics: How the Order of a Text Creates Its Meanings* (Poetics and Comparative Literature) (Tel Aviv: Tel Aviv University, 1976).

3. J.-P. Sartre, "A propos de 'Le bruit et la fureur,' la temporalité chez Faulkner," *Situations* 1 (Paris: Gallimard, 1947), 65–75.

4. Ibid., 65.

5. Cf. J. R. Searle, *Intentionality: An Essay in the Philosophy of Mind* (Cambridge: Cambridge University Press, 1983).

GINZBURG: Fiction as Historical Evidence

1. Cf. M. Detienne, *The Creation of Mythology*, trans. M. Cook (Chicago, 1986), 23–26, 141n.19, 142n.32. According to Detienne, Vidal-Naquet's introduction to the *Iliad* (1975) "outstrips Finley's interpretation based on history" (142n.29). In fact, Vidal-Naquet's position is much more nuanced, as the following sentence, criticizing a remark by J. Chadwick, shows: "Les tablettes [mycéniennes] sont un document pour l'histoire, s'ensuit-il que les poèmes ne le soient pas? Le dire serait avoir une conception bien étroite et bien mesquine du travail historique." P. Vidal-Naquet, "L'Iliade' sans travesti," in Vidal-Naquet, *La démocratie grecque vue d'ailleurs* (Paris, 1990), 38–39. See also "Economie et société dans la Grèce ancienne: l'oeuvre de Moses I. Finley," ibid., 55–94, esp. 59ff. Having stressed a cautious

note regarding Finley's approach to Homer, Vidal-Naquet writes: "Il reste que, sous cette réserve, une sociologie du monde homérique est possible et que M. I. Finley en a dressé plusieurs pans de main de maître" (62). On Detienne's *The Creation of Mythology*, see A. Momigliano, *Rivista storica italiana* 94 (1982), 784–87, esp. 784–85.

2. Cf. Detienne, *The Creation*, 150 n. 75.

3. On its date cf. F. Gégou, *Lettre-traité de Pierre-Daniel Huet sur l'origine des romans suivie de la lecture des vieux romans par Jean Chapelain* (Paris, 1971), 152 n. 1. This edition has a useful commentary.

4. See *Lettres de Jean Chapelain*, 2 vols., ed. Ph. Tamizey de Larroque (Paris, 1880–93), 1:54 n. 3.

5. See for instance J. Chapelain, *Soixante-dix-sept lettres inédites à Nicolas Heinsius (1649–1658)*, ed. B. Bray (La Haye, 1966).

6. I used (except for a minor correction) the text edited by A. C. Hunter, based on the only surviving manuscript: a seventeenth-century copy which is preserved in Bibliothèque de l'Arsenal (Recueil Conrart, t. VIII; cf. J. Chapelain, *Opuscules critiques*, ed. A. C. Hunter [Paris, 1936], 205–41). On this dialogue, see J. de Beer, "Literary Circles in Paris, 1610–1660," *PMLA* 53 (1938), 730–80, esp. 757–58; J. Frappier, "Voiture amateur de vieux romans" (1951), in Frappier, *Amour courtois et Table Ronde* (Geneva, 1973), 283ff; Ch. Delhez-Sarlet, "Le Lancelot 'fabuleux et historique': vraisemblance et crédibilité d'un récit au XVIIe siècle," in *Mélanges offerts à Rita Lejeune* (Gembloux, 1969), 2:1535ff.

7. At that time Paul de Gondi was the patron of Ménage. In 1652, their relationship having become rather tense, Ménage left. He rejected an offer, immediately transmitted to him by Sarasin, to enter the court of Monseigneur de Conti: see the undated letter (written probably in the August of the same year) sent by Ménage to Sarasin, and published by G.G., "Ménage et le cardinal de Retz," in *Revue d'histoire littéraire de la France* 38 (1931), 283–85 (on its date see B. Bray, intro. to J. Chapelain, *Soixante-dix-sept lettres*, 168–69 n. 2). The friendship between Ménage and Sarasin went on; Chapelain, on the contrary, broke with both of them (ibid., 112, 285). Sarasin's works, edited by Ménage, include a dialogue named *S'il faut qu'un jeune homme soit amoureux* (J.-F. Sarasin, *Oeuvres* [Paris, 1694], 139–235, which clearly had been inspired by Chapelain's dialogue, written a few months before (208). The characters involved in the dialogue, besides M. de Pille and Louis Aubry, sieur de Trilleport, are the same; even the situation is similar (the discussion's starting point is the *Roman de Perceforest* instead of *Lancelot*).

8. For a general overview see J. de Beer, "Literary Circles." On libertins, cf. R. Pintard, *Le libertinage érudit dans la première moitié du XVIIeme siecle* (Paris, 1943; repr. with a new introduction, Geneva-Paris, 1983); for the above-mentioned names, see the index.

9. Cf. *Catalogue de tous les livres de feu M. Chapelain*, ed. C. Searles (Stanford, 1912), 70 nn. 2328, 2329 (*Histoire de Lancelot* [Paris, 1520, 1591]; *Le premier volume de Lancelot du Lac nouvellement imprimé* [Paris, 1633]).

10. Some echoes of the conversations with Chapelain can be found in the epistle, addressed to du Puy, written by Ménage as an introduction to *Les origines de la langue françoise* (Paris, 1650). "Et pour remonter jusques à la source . . . il faudroit avoir leu tous nos vieux Poëtes, tous nos vieux Romans, tous nos vieux Coustumiers, et tous nos autres vieux Escrivains, pour suivre comme à la piste et découvrir les alterations que nos mots ont souffertes de temps en temps. Et je n'ay qu'une légère connoissance de la moindre partie de ces choses." This is the last item of a quite extraordinary list which includes "l'Hébreu et le Chaldée." "la langue qui se parle en Basse-Bretagne, et l'Alleman avec tous ses dialectes," "les divers idiomes de nos Provinces, et la langue des paysans, parmi lesquels les langues se conservent plus longuement."

11. Cf. J. Chapelain, *Opuscules* 219. On this and similar related expressions, cf. N. Edelman, *Attitudes of Seventeenth Century France toward the Middle Ages* (New York, 1946), 1–23 (still a fundamental book).

12. See J. Chapelain, *Opuscules*, 209.

13. Ibid., 217.

14. See Aristotle, *Poetics*, 1451 a–b. This point has been missed by M. Magendie, *Le roman français au XVIIᵉ siècle* (Paris, 1932), 131. Detienne's polemical reaction to Finley, who stressed the verisimilitude of Homer's poems as a condition requested by their audience, is much more pertinent: "But what can it mean for an auditor to demand verisimilitude, probability? What does verisimilitude mean? Surely something other than what Aristotle meant" (*The Creation* 142 n. 33).

15. On this passage see [Desmolets], *Continuation des mémoires de littérature et d'histoire* 6, 2 (Paris, 1728), 304, on the basis of which I corrected a slip in Hunter's edition. A. Feillet, being unaware of the 1728 edition, printed Chapelain's *Dialogue* as if it were unpublished (Paris, 1870; reprint, Geneva, 1968). For an early response to the first publication of Chapelain's *Dialogue*, see La Curne de Sainte-Palaye, *Mémoires sur l'ancienne chevalerie* 1 (1759), ed. Ch. Nodier (Paris, 1829), 431–52. See on this L. Gossman, *Medievalism and the Ideologies of the Enlightenment. The World and Work of La Curne de Sainte-Palaye* (Baltimore, 1968), 153.

16. On antiquarianism in general see A. Momigliano, "Ancient History and the Antiquarian," in Momigliano, *Contributo alla storia degli studi classici* (Rome, 1955), 67–106.

17. Cf. C. Fauchet, *Les oeuvres . . . revues et corrigées* (Paris, 1610), 482 v ff. See on him J. G. Espiner-Scott, *Claude Fauchet* (Paris, 1938); on 372 the absence of Fauchet in Chapelain's *Dialogue* is mentioned. See also L. Gossman, *Medievalism*, 153.

18. Cf. C. Fauchet, *Les oeuvres*, 591 v.

19. Cf. L. Chantereau Le Febvre, *Traité des fiefs et de leur origine avec les preuves tirées de divers autheurs anciens et modernes, de capitulaires de Charlemagne, de Louis le Debonnaire, de Charles le Chauve, et des ordonnances de S. Louis, et de quantité d'autres actes mss. extraicts de plusieurs cartulaires authentiques* (Paris, 1662), 87–89. *Meffaire* (but the corresponding passage of *Lancelot* has

a synonym, *mesprendre*) designates the feudal lord's breaking of the pact with the vassal, who is therefore exempt from the obligations implied in the homage. The comprehensive survey by G. Baer Fundenburg, *Feudal France in the French Epic. A Study of Feudal French Institutions in History and Poetry* (Princeton, 1918), does not mention the existence of the seventeenth-century antiquarian tradition. For a much more sophisticated approach (which takes into account the narrative dimension) see D. Maddox, "Lancelot et les sens de la coutume," *Cahiers de civilisation médiévale* 29 (1986), 339–53; "Yvain et les sens de la coutume," *Romania* 109 (1988), 1–17.

20. Cf. J. Chapelain, *Opuscules*, 219. See also a later remark by B. de Montfaucon: "Ce différent goût de sculpture et de peinture en divers siècles peut même être compté parmi les faits historiques" in Montfaucon, *Les monumens de la monarchie françoise* (Paris, 1729–1733), 1:11, quoted by G. Previtali, *La fortuna dei primitivi dal Vasari ai neoclassici* (Torino, 1964), 70.

21. Cf. J. Chapelain, *Opuscules*, 222.

22. It reveals, according to M. Magendie, a "sens du relatif rare au XVIIᵉ siècle." *Le roman* 121.

23. In his *Idée de l'histoire*, 362–64, La Popelinière says that "poets were the first historians" (quoted by D. Kelley, "History as a Calling: The Case of La Popelinière," in *Renaissance Studies in Honor of Hans Baron*, ed. A. Molho and J. A. Tedeschi [Florence, 1971], 773–89, esp. 785, who speaks of an "interesting anticipation of romantic theories of the origins of history"). In the same essay Kelley remarks (776): "It is perhaps not surprising that La Popelinière should have been neglected in the 17th century, when historical knowledge was going out of fashion." La Popelinière's work is mentioned by Ch. Sorel in *La Science de l'Histoire* (Paris, 1665), 91; and for *La Bibliothèque Françoise* (2d ed. Paris, 1667), 165, 333–34. On La Popelinière see C. Vivanti, "Alle origini dell'idea di civiltà: le scoperte geografiche e gli scritti di Henri La Popelinière," *Rivista storica italiana* 74 (1962), 225–49; M. Yardeni, "La conception de l'histoire dans l'ocuvre de La Popelinière," *Revue d'histoire moderne et contemporaine* 11 (1964), 109–26.

24. Cf. J. Chapelain, *Opuscules*, 217. F. de La Mothe le Vayer, *Oeuvres* (Dresden, 1756, t. iv, II), Slatkine Reprints, Geneva, 1970, II, pp. 82–89, especially p. 84. I am very grateful to Peter Burke, who pointed out to me the connection between this text and Chapelain's dialogue. On La Mothe Le Vayer's later (and much more skeptical) views about history, see C. Borghero, *La certezza e la storia* (Milan, 1983), 57–83.

25. See Ch. Sorel, *De la connoissance des bons livres*, ed. L. Moretti Cenerini (Rome, 1974), 84 n. 23.

26. A similar remark, concerning Fontenelle, has been made by F. Graf, *Il mito in Grecia*, Italian trans. (Bari, 1987), 11–12.

27. Quoted by Ch. Sorel, *De la connoissance* 84 n. 22. On this see the (rather predictable) remarks made, on some later evidence, by F. Furet, "L'ensemble 'his-

toire,'" in *Livre et société dans la France du XVIIIe siècle* 2 (Paris-La Haye, 1970), 101–20.

28. Cf. La Popelinière, *L'histoire des histoires, avec l'idée de l'Histoire accomplie* (Paris, 1599), 23ff.

29. Cf. Ch. Sorel, *De la connaissance*, 83–84.

30. There has been much interest in Sorel's work in the last two decades, after publication of the article by Jean-Pierre Faye, "Surprise pour l'anti-roman" (1965), in Faye, *Le récit hunique* (Paris, 1967), 36–55. Among recent monographs see A. G. Suozzo, Jr., *The Comic novels of Charles Sorel. A Study of Structure, Characterization and Disguise* (Lexington, KY, 1982) (with an useful bibliography); G. Verdier, *Charles Sorel* (Boston, 1984).

31. Cf. E. Roy, *La vie et les oeuvres de Charles Sorel sieur de Souvigny (1602–1674)* (Paris, 1891), who on 344–45 lists the historiographer's tasks: to look over archives, to deal with ceremonial problems, to reconstruct genealogies, to participate in ambassadors' meetings, and so on. In 1663 Sorel lost the pension connected to his appointment, but Colbert left him his title (349). Cf. O. Ranum, *Artisans of Glory. Writers and Historical Thought in Seventeenth Century France* (Chapel Hill, NC, 1980), esp. 128–47: but see the review by G. Huppert in *History and Theory*, 1980, 140–44.

32. Cf. Ch. Sorel, *La Bibliothèque* 174ff.

33. Cf. J. Serroy, *Roman et réalité. Les histoires comiques au xviie siècle* (Paris, 1981), 160ff.

34. Ibid., 194ff. On French translations of *Lazarillo de Tormes* and *Buscón*, cf. R. Chartier, *Figure letterarie: la letteratura della furfanteria*, in *Figure della furfanteria*, Italian trans. (Rome, 1984), 77ff, esp. 81, 108ff. The vogue of picaresque novels in France was related to their vivid representation of humble people by Desfontaines, *Observations sur les écrits modernes* (1735–43), quoted by G. Natoli, "Lineamenti di una teoria del romanzo dal secolo classico a quello dei Lumi," in Natoli, *Figure e problemi della cultura francese* (Messina-Florence, 1956), 153.

35. Cf. E. Auerbach, *Scenes from the Drama of European Literature* (New York, 1959), 133–79 (translated from the German).

36. More than ten thousand of them had been published since the end of sixteenth century, Sorel wrote in a rather inflated tone, *Polyandre. Histoire comique* (Paris, 1648 [repr. Genève, 1972]), intro.

37. Cf. M. Magendie, *Le roman*, 130–35 (who mentions Le Vayer de Boutigny, intro. to vol. 3 of *Mithridate* [Paris, 1648]); on Sorel, ibid., 150ff. See also Auerbach, *Scenes*, 159.

38. Cf. ibid., 30ff.

39. Quoted by P. Ariès, *Le temps de l'histoire* (Paris, 1986 [1st ed., 1954]), 140.

40. Cf. Ch. Sorel, *La Bibliothèque*, 155; *La Science de l'Histoire*, 182–83, on the history of professions.

41. The beginning of *Francion* is typical: "Les voiles de la nuict avoient couvert

tout l'Orison, lorsqu'un certain vieillard qui s'appelloit Valentin, sortit d'un Chasteau de Bourgogne avec une robbe de chambre, un bonnet rouge en teste et un gros pacquet sous son bras, encore ne sçay je pourquoy il n'avoit point ses lunettes, car c'estoit sa coustume de les porter tousjours a son nez ou à sa ceinture." Ch. Sorel, *Histoire comique de Francion* 1, ed. E. Roy (Paris, 1924), 1.

42. Ch. Sorel, *Polyandre. histoire comique,* intro.; italics are mine.

43. This point is missed by A. Viala, "Pragmatique littéraire et rhétorique du lecteur: le cas Sorel," *Cahiers de Littérature du XVIIe siècle* 8 (1986), 107–24.

44. Cf. E. Auerbach, *Scenes,* 133–79. Chapelain was son of a notary (cf. G. Collas, *Jean Chapelain* [Paris 1912], 1–2); Sorel of a procurator, although later on he pretended to come from a noble family (cf. Verdier, *Charles Sorel,* 4–5). On *vraisemblance,* see 158.

45. See J. Descrains, *Bibliographie des oeuvres de Jean-Pierre Camus évêque de Belley (1584–1652)* (Paris 1971), who lists 285 titles (not including translations and posthumous reprints). On Camus see V. Gastaldi, *Jean-Pierre Camus, romanziere barocco e vescovo di Francia* (Catania, 1964); A. Garreau, *Jean-Pierre Camus* (Paris, 1968) (who ignores Gastaldi); J. Descrains, *Jean-Pierre Camus (1584–1652) et ses Diversités (1609–1618) ou la culture d'un évêque humaniste,* 2 vols. (Paris, 1985). See also the introductions to the abridged edition of *Agathonphile* (Geneva, 1951) by P. Sage, and to *Homélies des Etats Généraux (1614–1615)* (Geneva, 1970) by J. Descrains.

46. Cf. J.-P. Camus, *Marianne ou l'innocente victime, événement tragicque arrivé à Paris au faux-bourg Saint-Germain* (Paris, 1629), quoted by Magendie, *Le roman,* 141. On Camus cf. ibid., 140–49, 383ff. and *passim.*

47. Cf. J.-P. Camus, *La Pieuse Julie, histoire parisienne* (Paris, 1625), 504, 507, 523 (quoted by Magendie, *Le roman,* 142 n. 5).

48. In this paragraph I have freely used some passages taken from a previous essay: "Proofs and Possibilities: In the Margins of Natalie Zemon Davis' *The Return of Martin Guerre,*" *Yearbook of Comparative and General Literature* 37 (1988), 114–27.

49. Such an hypothesis explains the presence of Tacitus, Ammianus Marcellinus and Gregory of Tours and Saint-Simon in E. Auerbach's great book, *Mimesis. Dargestellte Wirchlichkeit in der abendländischen Literatur* (Bern, 1946) (*Mimesis: the Representation of Reality in Western Literature* [New York, 1957]).

LOMBARDO: The Ephemeral and the Eternal

1. See Charles Baudelaire, *Le Peintre de la vie moderne, Oeuvres complètes* 2 (Paris: Gallimard, Bibliothèque de la Pléiade, 1976), 695–96.

2. See Arthur C. Danto, *Analytic Philosophy of History* (Cambridge: Cambridge University Press, 1965).

3. Lucien Febvre, "Avant-propos," in Charles Morazé, *Trois Essais sur histoire*

et culture (Paris: Cahiers des Annales, 1948), vii. My translation. It will always be my translation unless otherwise noted.

4. Febvre, "Avant-propos," in Febvre, *Combats pour l'histoire* (Paris: Armand Colin, 1965), vii.

5. Walter Benjamin, "Theses on the Philosophy of History," in Benjamin, *Illuminations*, ed. H. Arendt (New York: Schocken Books, 1989 [1969]), 256.

6. Febvre would not subscribe to Benjamin's concept of materialistic history, even if he substituted the economical man agitated by interests and passions for the political man agitated by events.

7. Febvre, *Revue de synthèse historique* 30 (1920), 15.

8. Febvre, "Face au vent," in Febvre, *Combats pour l'histoire*, 41.

9. *Annales d'histoire économique et sociale* 1 (1929), 1–2.

10. Febvre, "Pour une histoire dirigée. Les recherches collectives et l'avenir de l'histoire," *Revue de Synthèse* 11 (1936).

11. Cited in Febvre, "Comment reconstituer la vie affective d'autrefois? La sensibilité et l'histoire," in Febvre, *Combats pour l'histoire*, 226–27 (*Annales d'Histoire Économique et Sociale* 3 [1931]).

12. Febvre, "Vivre l'histoire," in Febvre, *Combats pour l'histoire*, 32 (Lecture to the students of the École Normale Supérieure, 1941).

13. Febvre, *Le Problème de l'incroyance au XVIe siècle* (Paris: Albin Michel, 1942, 1947), 2.

14. Febvre, "Les recherches collectives," in Febvre, *Combats pour l'histoire*, 58.

15. Gabriel Monod, "Du progrès des études historiques en France," *La Revue historique* 1 (1876).

16. Febvre, *Le Problème de l'incroyance au XVIe siècle*, 1–2.

17. See Natalie Zemon Davis, "Introduction," *Society and Culture in Early Modern France* (Stanford: Stanford University Press, 1975), xv–xviii.

18. Stephen Bann, *The Clothing of Clio* (Cambridge: Cambridge University Press), 1984, 172.

19. See Natalie Davis, "Du conte et de l'histoire," *Le Débat* 54 (1989), 139.

20. Hippolyte Taine, "M. Michelet," in Taine, *Essais de critique et d'histoire* (Paris: Hachette, 1908), 95. But also today there is a tension between the historians who give a sovereign importance to sources and documents, and those who are conscious of the interaction of invention and documents. See the debate between Robert Finlay and Natalie Davis about *The Return of Martin Guerre*. "What Davis terms 'invention,' the employment of 'perhapses' and 'may-have-beens,' is, of course, the stock in trade of historians, who are often driven to speculation by inadequate and perplexing evidence. Depth, humanity and color in historical reconstruction are the product of imagination and do not flow from a vulgar reasoning upon data. But speculation, whether founded on intuition or on concepts drawn from anthropology and literary criticism, is supposed to give way before *the sover-*

eignty of the sources, the tribunal of the documents." (I underline.) Robert Finlay, "The Refashioning of Martin Guerre," *American Historical Review* 93 (June 1988), 571.

21. See Davis, "Du conte et de l'histoire," 139.

22. Natalie Davis, "On the Lame," *American Historical Review* 93, 572, and 575.

23. See Gianfranco Corbucci, "La Strategia del ragno," *Cinema nuovo* 20, n. 209 (Jan.–Feb. 1971).

24. See the very interesting essay by Barthélemy Amengual, "Portrait de l'artiste en jeune homme d'avant la trentaine," *Etudes cinématographiques* 122–26 (1979), 36.

25. J.-L. Borges, "The Theme of the Traitor and the Hero." The passage by Borges is cited in Amengual, "Portrait," 31.

26. See Hyppolite Taine, "M. Guizot," in Taine, *Essais de critique et d'histoire*, 135.

27. Roland Barthes, "The Discourse of History," in Barthes, *The Rustle of Language* (New York: Hill and Wang, 1986), 138. See also Hayden White, *Metahistory* (Baltimore: Johns Hopkins University Press, 1973).

28. Davis, "Du conte et de l'histoire," 138.

29. Ibid., 139. This is Natalie Davis's comment on the work of Emmanuel Le Roy Ladurie and his analysis of an occitan popular story "whose literary structure allows one to penetrate the mental world of Languedoc in the eighteenth century as much as the references to events and values."

30. This is the reading of Natalie Davis, contested by Robert Finlay's "The Refashioning of Martin Guerre," *American Historical Review* 93:553–71.

31. Carl Schorske, "Gustav Klimt: Painting and the Crisis of the Liberal Ego," in Schorske, *Fin-de-siècle Vienna* (New York: Alfred Knopf, 1980), 217.

32. Lucien Goldmann, "La pensée historique et son objet," in Goldmann, *Sciences humaines et philosophie* (Paris: Gonthier, 1966), 20.

33. Ibid., 25.

34. Charles Baudelaire, "Le cygne," in Baudelaire, *Les Fleurs du mal, Oeuvres complètes* 1 (Paris: Gallimard, Pléiade, 1974), 86.

35. Natalie Davis, "Preface," *The Return of Martin Guerre* (Cambridge: Cambridge University Press, 1983), viii.

36. Walter Benjamin, "On Some Motifs in Baudelaire," in Benjamin, *Illuminations*, 155–200.

37. Bernardo Bertolucci, "Entretien," in Aldo Tassane, *Parla il cinema italiano* (Paris: Edilig, 1982), 47.

38. Friedrich Nietzsche, "On the Uses and Disadvantages of History for Life," in Nietzsche, *Untimely Meditations*, trans. R. J. Hollingdale (Cambridge: Cambridge University Press, 1983), 110.

GOSSMAN: Cultural History and Crisis

1. "Je voudrais définir quelle était alors [13th and 14th centuries] la société des hommes, comment on vivait dans les familles, quels arts étaient cultivés, plutôt que répéter tant de malheurs et tant de combats, funestes objets de l'histoire, et lieux communs de la méchanceté des hommes. Les artisans et les marchands que leur obscurité dérobe à la fureur ambitieuse des grands, sont des fourmis qui se creusent des habitations en silence, tandis que les aigles et les vautours se déchirent." Voltaire, *Essai sur les moeurs*, chap. 81, in Voltaire, *Oeuvres complètes*, ed. Moland, 52 vols. (Paris, 1877–85), 12:53–54.

2. In his overview of traditional academic disciplines in the *Discourse on Method*, Descartes had already rejected history on the grounds that, in his own words, "même les histoires les plus fidèles, si elles ne changent ni n'augmentent la valeur des choses, pour les rendre plus dignes d'être lues, au moins en omettent-elles presque toujours les plus basses et moins illustres circonstances" ("even the most faithful histories, those that do not change or enhance the value of things to make them more worthy of being read, almost always leave out the most base and undistinguished circumstances"). Garnier-Flammarion ed. (Paris, 1966), 37.

3. Jules Michelet, *Journal*, ed. P. Viallaneix and C. Digeon (Paris, 1959–76), 1:378. See also, among many similar passages, *Le Peuple*, ed. L. Refort (Paris, 1946), 201: "Que pouvais-je donner à ce grand peuple muet? ce que j'avais: une voix"; and *Oeuvres complètes*, ed. P. Viallaneix (Paris, 1971–), 4:8.

4. Augustin Thierry, *Dix Ans d'études historiques* (Paris, 1867; orig. ed. 1834), 146–59. See also 138–46 and preface, 9.

5. Henri Martin, *Histoire de France* (Paris, 1865), 1:vii–viii.

6. Werner Kaegi, *Jacob Burckhardt: eine Biographie* (Basle, 1947–77), 3:60–61.

7. *Voltaire's Correspondence*, ed. T. Besterman, 107 vols. (Geneva, 1956–65), letter 1914 (8.5.1739). Cf. a letter to Shuvalov, the Russian general (letter 7090; 17.7.1758): "La grande difficulté de ce travail [the projected History of Peter the Great] consistera à le rendre intéressant pour toutes les nations. C'est là le grand point."

8. Burckhardt accepted the neoclassical view that the historian's first task is the selection of an appropriate topic. The "sujet," he wrote, should be an episode or situation capable of interesting large numbers of people. *Briefe*, ed. Max Burckhardt, 9 vols. (Basle 1949–80), 5:78ff; to Bernhard Kugler, 11.4.1870.

9. Friedrich Nietzsche, *The Birth of Tragedy. The Genealogy of Morals*, trans. Francis Golffing (New York, 1956), 9.

10. Tagebuch Isaak Iselin (MS), 27.8.1755, quoted by Werner Kaegi, *Burckhardt* 1:38.

11. Though Riehl was held in high regard as a historian of culture, Burckhardt

appears to have had little to do with him. Kaegi mentions only a couple of indirect and unimportant contacts. See Kaegi, *Burckhardt* 3:664 and 6:420–21.

12. See, for instance, J. J. Bachofen, *Griechische Reise*, ed. Georg Schmidt (Heidelberg, 1927), 111, 169.

13. Until the mid-nineteenth century, the Basle ribbon industry was organized on a putting-out basis: the merchant-manufacturers supplied the materials, designs, and sometimes the looms themselves to artisans in the town and then later to piece workers in the surrounding country districts. The merchant-manufacturers consistently sought to introduce new, more efficient looms and production techniques; the artisans, for obvious reasons, resisted innovation.

14. Jakob Burckhardt, *Reflections on History*, trans. M.D.H. (London, 1943), 55.

15. Ibid.

16. Albert Demangeon and Lucien Febvre, *Le Rhin: problémes d'histoire et d'économie* (Paris, 1935), 96–97.

17. Both Burckhardt and Bachofen were members of the Basle Antiquarian Society and of the Historical Society, as were many members of the city's prominent merchant families; but neither had any illusions about the quality or significance of most of the activities of these societies.

18. The Basle *Pädagogium*, set up in 1817 as part of a comprehensive new state education system, corresponded to the upper forms of a German *Gymnasium*. But it had some distinctive features which reflected the interests of the merchant oligarchy. It included, from its inception, a modern track with emphasis on the sciences and modern languages as well as a classical track.

19. *Letters of Jacob Burckhardt*, ed. and trans. Alexander Dru (London, 1955), 73 (19.6.1842).

20. Ibid., 93 (18.4.1845).

21. Jacob Burckhardt, *Historische Fragmente*, ed. Emil Dürr (Stuttgart, 1957), 270. Cf. Tocqueville: "Ce qui est clair pour moi, c'est qu'on s'est trompé depuis soixante ans en croyant voir le *bout* de la révolution. . . . Il est évident que le flot continue à marcher, que la mer monte. Ce n'est pas d'une modification, mais d'une transformation du corps social qu'il s'agit." Letter of 28.2.1850, quoted in Koenraad W. Swart, *The Sense of Decadence in Nineteenth Century France* (The Hague, 1964), 92.

22. Kaegi notes that Burckhardt was already altering his understanding of the Renaissance at the time of his public lecture series on the history of painting, given at Basle in 1845/46. See Werner Kaegi, *Burckhardt* 3:476–77. The revision of Franz Kugler's *Geschichte der Malerei*, on which Burckhardt worked from 1847 on, also indicates a shift in the interpretation of Renaissance art. Ibid., 83ff.

23. Jacob Burckhardt, *The Civilization of the Renaissance in Italy: An Essay*, trans. S. G. C. Middlemore (Oxford and London, 1945; 2d ed. rev.), 104. Hereafter CRI.

24. Ibid., 104.

25. Dru, *Letters of Jacob Burckhardt*, 111 (15.8.1852).

26. Burckhardt, *Reflections on History*, 16.

27. Burckhardt's notes on Droysen's lectures reported in Kaegi, *Burckhardt* 2:42. The text is from a public lecture given by Burckhardt in his later years, in Kaegi, *Burckhardt* 2:44–45, quoting from Heinrich Gelzer, "Jacob Burckhardt als Mensch und Lehrer," *Zeitschrift für Kulturgeschichte* (1899).

28. Quoted in Burckhardt, *Reflections on History*, introductory note, p. 7.

29. Letter of 17.4.1847. Burckhardt, *Briefe* 3:68.

30. See Kurt Breysig, *Aus meinen Tagen und Träumen: Memoiren, Aufzeichnungen, Briefe, Gespräche*, ed. Gertrud Breysig and Michael Landmann (Berlin, 1962), 79: "I tell him that I have come to think he occupies a quite special place in the history of historiography. He denies it. 'But what about the French,' he says, and names Guizot, The History of Civilization, and Thierry; he has read them, as well as other French historians." On Burckhardt's acknowledgments of his debt to the French, see Niklaus Rothlin, "Burckhardts Stellung in der Kulturgeschichtschreibung des 19. Jahrhunderts," *Archiv für Kulturgeschichte*, 1987, 69:399–403.

31. See Rothlin, "Burckhardts Stellung," 404. On Burckhardt's concern that he be *"lesbar"* ("readable"), ibid., 399, 401; and Kaegi, *Burckhardt* 3:137. The emphasis on brevity is directly related to the French historiographical tradition. Voltaire always advocated brevity and economy to achieve readability and bring out the essential significance of what is being described or narrated: "Je n'y ai fait qu'un petit volume sur l'histoire de Charles 12, feu Mr de Limiers, docteur en droit, en compila sept," he wrote to Johann Bernoulli. Besterman, *Voltaire's Correspondence*, letter 1914 (8.5.1739). See also letters to Henault of 8.1.1752 (letter 4163) and to the duc de Bellisle of 4.8.1752 (letter 4345).

32. Burckhardt, *Reflections on History*, 26.

33. Quoted by Kaegi, *Burckhardt* 2:505.

34. In the early 1850s Burckhardt had taught in the "scientific" or modern track at the *Pädagogium*. At the Federal Polytechnic he again taught future scientists, engineers, and architects. His aim as a teacher was at no time the production of future professional scholars.

35. Dru, *Letters of Jacob Burckhardt*, 96 (28.2.1846).

36. E.g. Hannelore Schlaffer and Heinz Schlaffer, *Studien zum ästhetischen Historismus* (Frankfurt am Main, 1975); Manfred Hinz, *Die Zukunft der Katastrophe: Mythische und rationalistische Geschichtstheorie im italienischen Futurismus* (Berlin and New York, 1985), 44–45.

37. Dru, *Letters of Jacob Burckhardt*, 97.

38. CRI, 48, 56.

39. CRI, 54.

40. Letter to Von Preen, 17.11.1876. Burckhardt, *Briefe* 6:113–16.

41. Burckhardt, *Historische Fragmente*, 274–75.

42. CRI, 48, 49, 54.

43. CRI, 54.

44. Introduction to *Persian Letters* of Montesquieu, in P. Valéry, *History and Politics*, trans. Denise Folliot and Jackson Matthews, *The Collected Works of Paul Valéry* 10 (New York, 1962), 219.

45. CRI, 85.

46. Burckhardt, *Briefe* 5:98 (to von Preen, 3.7.1870). See also Kaegi, *Burckhardt* 7:135.

47. Letter to von Preen, 26.4.1872. Burckhardt, *Briefe* 5:160–61.

48. CRI, 48, 52.

49. CRI, 83–84.

50. On Bachofen and *Selbstbildung*, see my article "Basle, Bachofen, and the Critique of Modernity in the Second Half of the Nineteenth Century," *Journal of the Warburg and Courtauld Institutes* 47 (1984), 136–85, at 167. On the German tradition of *Selbstbildung*, see the valuable study by W. H. Bruford, *The German Tradition of Self-Cultivation* (Cambridge, 1975).

51. See CRI, 82: "Even the subjects whom [the despots] ruled over were not free from the same impulse. Leaving out of account those who wasted their lives in secret opposition and conspiracies, we speak of the majority who were content with a strictly private station. . . . No doubt it was often hard for the subjects of a Visconti to maintain the dignity of their persons and families, and multitudes must have lost in moral character through the servitude they lived under. But this was not the case with regard to individuality; for political impotence does not hinder the different tendencies and manifestations of private life from thriving in the fullest vigor and variety. . . . The private man, indifferent to politics, and busied partly with serious pursuits, partly with the interests of a *dilettante*, seems to have been first fully formed in these despotisms of the fourteenth century." Cf. Burckhardt's comment in a letter of 28 Feb. 1846, announcing his departure for Italy: "Yes, I want to get away from them all, from the radicals, the communists, the industrialists, the intellectuals, the pretentious, the reasoners, the abstract, the absolute, the philosophers, the sophists, the fanatics of the State, the idealists, the 'ists' and 'isms' of every kind—I shall only meet the Jesuits on the other side, and among 'isms' only absolutism; and foreigners can usually avoid both." Dru, *Letters of Jacob Burckhardt*, 96.

52. See letter of 22 Mar. 1847 in Dru, *Letters of Jacob Burckhardt*, 105: "It is a long story . . . the spread of culture and the decrease of originality and individuality, of will and capacity; and the world will suffocate and decay one day in the dung of its own philistinism." On the Greek philosophers and their indifference to or contempt for politics and the state, see Jacob Burckhardt, *History of Greek Culture*, trans. Palmer Hilty (New York, 1963), 305–17.

53. Dru, *Letters of Jacob Burckhardt*, 96 (28.2.1846).

54. "O Krähewinkel, mein Vaterland!" Burckhardt, *Briefe* 2:86 (21.4.1844).

55. See Kaegi, *Jacob Burckhardt* 3:689. Cf. his answer to Albert Brenner, a Romantic young man who had written him for advice: "If you truly believe you are a daemonic being, I ask only one thing of you: that you never, not for a single instant, take pleasure in that thought. Whatever the cost, remain always kind, amiable and benevolent." Burckhardt, *Briefe* 3:247–49 (16.3.1856). Likewise his reflections on the suicide of a brilliant and gifted German friend from his youth, in 1846: "What a man! . . . He was of truly divine race. . . . I can't say that I really loved him; he was too violent for me from the beginning for that, too unrestrained by far. . . . Taking it all in all, I say—God forgive me—it is better not to be a genius and to have, instead, good strong nerves and a strong conscience, that, when one has sinned, is cured and refreshed in hearty benevolence to others. That, you see, would be *my* ideal." Quoted by James Hasting Nichols, pref. to Jacob Burckhardt, *Force and Freedom: Reflections on History* (New York: Pantheon Books, 1943), 29.

56. Letter to Ludwig Pastor, 23.1.1896, in Otto Markwart, *Jacob Burckhardt: Persönlichkeit und Jugendjahre* (Basle, 1920), 44.

57. Bachofen, *Gesammelte Werke* 10 (Correspondence), ed. Fritz Husner (Basle and Stuttgart, 1967), letter 69 (25.1.1851); cf. letter 162 (10.6.1863).

58. Dru, *Letters of Jacob Burckhardt*, 83 (20.8.1843).

59. Heinrich von Treitschke, *Briefe*, ed. Max Cornelius (Leipzig, 1914–20), 3:375 (to Overbeck, 28.10.1873).

60. To Paul Heyse, 16.11.1860. Burckhardt, *Briefe* 4:76.

61. Letter to Von Preen, 30.5.1877. Burckhardt, *Briefe* 6:133.

62. E.g. letter to von Preen, 17.3.1872, Burckhardt, *Briefe* 5:154.

63. Letter of 17.11.1876, in Dru, *Letters of Jacob Burckhardt*, 171–72.

64. Burckhardt, *Reflections on History*, 64.

65. Jacob Burckhardt, *Gesamtausgabe*, ed. Emil Dürr et al., 14 vols. (Stuttgart, Leipzig and Berlin, 1929–34), 13:23–28.

66. Cf. Burckhardt, *Reflections on History*, 63: "A peculiarity of higher cultures is their susceptibility to renaissances. Either one and the same people, or a later people partially adopts a past culture not its own by a kind of hereditary right or by right of admiration."

67. Dru, *Letters of Jacob Burckhardt*, 97.

68. Ibid.

69. Ibid.

70. See likewise Bachofen's comment that "the role of eternal opposition to the dominant opinions of the time simply embitters without doing any good." *Selbstbiographie*, ed. A. Baeumler (Halle/Saale, 1927), 35.

71. Dru, *Letters of Jacob Burckhardt*, 97.

72. Letter of 4.3.1848. Burckhardt, *Briefe* 3:103. The figure of Severin appears at various points in Burckhardt's writing. He had earlier suggested to his friend Willibald Beyschlag that he read the *Vita Sancti Severini*. (Beyschlag was inspired by

this reading to compose a ballad about Severin.) In the 1850s Burckhardt chose to give a public lecture at Basle on Severin, and at the very end of his life, in a letter to Otto Markwart of 15.11.1893 (quoted in Markwart, *Jacob Burckhardt*, 44–45), he again referred to St. Severin—"for me, one of the greatest of mortals."

73. CRI, 1.

74. Ibid., 98.

75. Ibid., 49; cf. 83.

76. Ibid., 83, 84.

77. To von Preen, Sylvester, 1870. Burckhardt, *Briefe* 5:119–20.

Index

In this index an "f" after a number indicates a separate reference on the next page, and an "ff" indicates separate references on the next two pages. A continuous discussion over two or more pages is indicated by a span of page numbers, e.g., "57–59." *Passim* is used for a cluster of references in close but not consecutive sequence. Entries are alphabetized letter by letter, ignoring word breaks, hyphens, and accents.

Index

Index

Index

Index

Index

Index

Index

Index

Index

Library of Congress Cataloging-in-Publication Data

Rediscovering history : culture, politics, and the psyche / edited by
    Michael S. Roth.
    p. cm.—(Cultural sitings)
Includes index.
ISBN 0-8047-2309-5—ISBN 0-8047-2313-3 (pbk.)
1. Europe—Civilization.   2. Politics and culture—Europe—History.
    I. Roth, Michael S., 1957– .   II.   Series.
CB203.R38   1994
940—dc20   93-33732
                                                            CIP

∞ This book is printed on acid-free paper. It was typeset by G & S
Typesetters in 10/13 Electra.

Designed by Kathleen Szawiola